Artificial Intelligence Applications for Improved Software Engineering Development:

New Prospects

Farid Meziane
University of Salford, UK

Sunil Vadera
University of Salford, UK

A volume in the Advances in
Computational Intelligence and Robotics
(ACIR) Book Series

Director of Editorial Content: Kristin Klinger
Senior Managing Editor: Jamie Snavely
Assistant Managing Editor: Michael Brehm
Publishing Assistant: Sean Woznicki
Typesetter: Sean Woznicki
Cover Design: Lisa Tosheff

Published in the United States of America by
    Information Science Reference (an imprint of IGI Global)
    701 E. Chocolate Avenue
    Hershey PA 17033
    Tel: 717-533-8845
    Fax: 717-533-8661
    E-mail: cust@igi-global.com
    Web site: http://www.igi-global.com

Library of Congress Cataloging-in-Publication Data

Artificial intelligence applications for improved software engineering development : new prospects / Farid Meziane and Sunil Vadera, editors.
    p. cm.
 Includes bibliographical references and index.
 Summary: "This book provides an overview of useful techniques in artificial intelligence for future software development along with critical assessment for further advancement"--Provided by publisher.
  ISBN 978-1-60566-758-4 (hardcover) -- ISBN 978-1-60566-759-1 (ebook) 1. Computer software--Development. 2. Artificial intelligence. I. Meziane, Farid. II. Vadera, Sunil.
  QA76.76.D47A82 2009
  006.3--dc22
                    2009018603

This book is published in the IGI Global book series Advances in Computational Intelligence and Robotics (ACIR) Book Series (ISSN: 2327-0411; eISSN: 2327-042X)

British Cataloguing in Publication Data
A Cataloguing in Publication record for this book is available from the British Library.

Advances in Computational Intelligence and Robotics (ACIR) Book Series

ISSN: 2327-0411
EISSN: 2327-042X

MISSION

While intelligence is traditionally a term applied to humans and human cognition, technology has progressed in such a way to allow for the development of intelligent systems able to simulate many human traits. With this new era of simulated and artificial intelligence, much research is needed in order to continue to advance the field and also to evaluate the ethical and societal concerns of the existence of artificial life and machine learning.

The **Advances in Computational Intelligence and Robotics (ACIR) Book Series** encourages scholarly discourse on all topics pertaining to evolutionary computing, artificial life, computational intelligence, machine learning, and robotics. ACIR presents the latest research being conducted on diverse topics in intelligence technologies with the goal of advancing knowledge and applications in this rapidly evolving field.

COVERAGE

- Adaptive & Complex Systems
- Agent Technologies
- Artificial Intelligence
- Cognitive Informatics
- Computational Intelligence
- Natural Language Processing
- Neural Networks
- Pattern Recognition
- Robotics
- Synthetic Emotions

IGI Global is currently accepting manuscripts for publication within this series. To submit a proposal for a volume in this series, please contact our Acquisition Editors at Acquisitions@igi-global.com or visit: http://www.igi-global.com/publish/.

Titles in this Series

For a list of additional titles in this series, please visit: www.igi-global.com

Intelligent Technologies and Techniques for Pervasive Computing
Kostas Kolomvatsos (University of Athens, Greece) Christos Anagnostopoulos (Ionian University, Greece) and Stathes Hadjiefthymiades (University of Athens, Greece)
Information Science Reference • copyright 2013 • 349pp • H/C (ISBN: 9781466640382) • US $195.00 (our price)

Mobile Ad Hoc Robots and Wireless Robotic Systems Design and Implementation
Raul Aquino Santos (University of Colima, Mexico) Omar Lengerke (Universidad Autónoma de Bucaramanga, Colombia) and Arthur Edwards-Block (University of Colima, Mexico)
Information Science Reference • copyright 2013 • 347pp • H/C (ISBN: 9781466626584) • US $190.00 (our price)

Intelligent Planning for Mobile Robotics Algorithmic Approaches
Ritu Tiwari (ABV – Indian Institute of Information, India) Anupam Shukla (ABV – Indian Institute of Information, India) and Rahul Kala (School of Systems Engineering, University of Reading, UK)
Information Science Reference • copyright 2013 • 320pp • H/C (ISBN: 9781466620742) • US $195.00 (our price)

Simultaneous Localization and Mapping for Mobile Robots Introduction and Methods
Juan-Antonio Fernández-Madrigal (Universidad de Málaga, Spain) and José Luis Blanco Claraco (Universidad de Málaga, Spain)
Information Science Reference • copyright 2013 • 497pp • H/C (ISBN: 9781466621046) • US $195.00 (our price)

Prototyping of Robotic Systems Applications of Design and Implementation
Tarek Sobh (University of Bridgeport, USA) and Xingguo Xiong (University of Bridgeport, USA)
Information Science Reference • copyright 2012 • 321pp • H/C (ISBN: 9781466601765) • US $195.00 (our price)

Cross-Disciplinary Applications of Artificial Intelligence and Pattern Recognition Advancing Technologies
Vijay Kumar Mago (Simon Fraser University, Canada) and Nitin Bhatia (DAV College, India)
Information Science Reference • copyright 2012 • 784pp • H/C (ISBN: 9781613504291) • US $195.00 (our price)

Handbook of Research on Ambient Intelligence and Smart Environments Trends and Perspectives
Nak-Young Chong (Japan Advanced Institute of Science and Technology, Japan) and Fulvio Mastrogiovanni (University of Genova, Italy)
Information Science Reference • copyright 2011 • 770pp • H/C (ISBN: 9781616928575) • US $265.00 (our price)

Particle Swarm Optimization and Intelligence Advances and Applications
Konstantinos E. Parsopoulos (University of Ioannina, Greece) and Michael N. Vrahatis (University of Patras, Greece)
Information Science Reference • copyright 2010 • 328pp • H/C (ISBN: 9781615206667) • US $180.00 (our price)

www.igi-global.com

701 E. Chocolate Ave., Hershey, PA 17033
Order online at www.igi-global.com or call 717-533-8845 x100
To place a standing order for titles released in this series, contact: cust@igi-global.com
Mon-Fri 8:00 am - 5:00 pm (est) or fax 24 hours a day 717-533-8661

Editorial Advisory Board

List of Reviewers

Table of Contents

Section 1
Project Management and Cost Estimation

Norman Fenton, Queen Mary, University of London, United Kingdom
Peter Hearty, Queen Mary, University of London, United Kingdom
Martin Neil, Queen Mary, University of London, United Kingdom
Łukasz Radliński, Queen Mary, University of London, United Kingdom, and
University of Szczecin, Poland

Emilia Mendes, The University of Auckland, New Zealand

Tad Gonsalves, Sophia University, Japan
Kei Yamagishi, Sophia University, Japan
Ryo Kawabata, Sophia University, Japan
Kiyoshi Itoh, Sophia University, Japan

Salvatore A. Sarcia, Università di Roma Tor Vergata, Italy
Giovanni Cantone, Università di Roma Tor Vergata, Italy
Victor R. Basili, University of Maryland, USA

Section 2
Requirements Engineering and Specification

Section 3
Software Design and Implementation

Section 4
Software Testing and Maintenance

Detailed Table of Contents

Section 1
Project Management and Cost Estimation

Chapter 1

Norman Fenton, Queen Mary, University of London, United Kingdom
Peter Hearty, Queen Mary, University of London, United Kingdom
Martin Neil, Queen Mary, University of London, United Kingdom
Łukasz Radliński, Queen Mary, University of London, United Kingdom, and
University of Szczecin, Poland

Chapter 1 provides an introduction to the use of Bayesian Network (BN) models in Software Engineering. A short overview of the theory of BNs is included, together with an explanation of why BNs are ideally suited to dealing with the characteristics and shortcomings of typical software development environments. This theory is supplemented and illustrated using real world models that illustrate the advantages of BNs in dealing with uncertainty, causal reasoning and learning in the presence of limited data.

Chapter 2

Emilia Mendes, The University of Auckland, New Zealand

Web effort models and techniques provide the means for Web companies to formalise the way they estimate effort for their projects, and help in obtaining more accurate estimates. Accurate estimates are fundamental to help project managers allocate resources more adequately, thus supporting projects to be finished on time and within budget. The aim of this chapter is to introduce the concepts related to Web effort estimation and effort forecasting techniques, and to discuss effort prediction when the estimation technique used is Bayesian Networks.

Chapter 3

    Tad Gonsalves, Sophia University, Japan
    Kei Yamagishi, Sophia University, Japan
    Ryo Kawabata, Sophia University, Japan
    Kiyoshi Itoh, Sophia University, Japan

Chapter 3 shows how the recently developed Computational Intelligence techniques can effectively improve the prediction power of existing models. In particular, the authors focus on the adaptation of the Multi-Objective Particle Swarm Optimization (MOPSO) algorithm in simultaneously minimizing two objective functions – prediction error rate and model complexity. This provides the project manager with an opportunity to choose from a set of optimal solutions represented in a trade-off relationship on the Pareto front. Traditional search algorithms use knowledge of the terrain and expert heuristics to guide the search; such uses make them problem-specific and domain-dependent. The MOPSO meta-heuristic approach relies neither on the knowledge of the problem nor on the experts' heuristics, making its application wide and extensive.

Chapter 4

    Salvatore A. Sarcia, Università di Roma Tor Vergata, Italy
    Giovanni Cantone, Università di Roma Tor Vergata, Italy
    Victor R. Basili, University of Maryland, USA

In Chapter 4, the authors focus on improving regression models by decreasing their redundancy and increasing their parsimony, i.e., they turn the model into a model with fewer variables than the former. They present an empirical auto-associative neural network-based strategy for model improvement, which implements a reduction technique called Curvilinear component analysis. The contribution of this chapter is to show how multi-layer feedforward neural networks can be a useful and practical mechanism for improving software engineering estimation models.

Section 2
Requirements Engineering and Specification

Chapter 5

    Leonid Kof, Technische Universität München, Germany

Chapter 5 presents an approach that analyzes textual scenarios with the means of computational linguistics, identifies where actors or whole actions are missing from the text, completes the missing information, and creates a message sequence chart (MSC) including the information missing from the textual scenario. Finally, this MSC is presented to the requirements analyst for validation. The book chapter presents also a case study where scenarios from a requirement document based on industrial specifications were translated to MSCs. The case study shows feasibility of the approach.

Chapter 6

José del Sagrado Martínez, University of Almería, Spain
Isabel María del Águila Cano, University of Almería, Spain

Chapter 6 focuses on the construction of "Requisites", a Bayesian network designed to be used as a predictor that tells us whether a requirements specification has enough quality to be considered as a baseline. Requisites have been defined using several information sources, such as standards and reports, and through interaction with experts, in order to structure and quantify the final model. This Bayesian network reflects the knowledge needed when assessing a requirements specification. The authors show how Requisites can be used through the study of some use cases. After the propagation over the network of information collected about the certainty of a subset of variables, the value predicted will determine if the requirements specification has to be revised.

Chapter 7

Muthu Ramachandran, Leeds Metropolitan University, UK

Chapter 7 provides insights into the application of knowledge based approaches to the development of agile software development, software product line, software components and architecture. In particular, it presents three research systems that demonstrate the potential benefits of utilising knowledge based approaches to support agile methods. The first system, called SoBA, supports the use of a story board for agile software development; the second system, called .NET designer, provides design rationale for choosing appropriate architectural solutions, and the third system, called RAIS, provides reuse assessment and improvement for designing reusable software components.

Chapter 8

Chad Coulin, University of Technology Sydney, Australia & LAAS CNRS, France
Didar Zowghi, University of Technology Sydney, Australia
Abd-El-Kader Sahraoui, LAAS CNRS, France

Chapter 8 presents a collaborative and situational tool called MUSTER, that has been specifically designed and developed for requirements elicitation workshops, and which utilizes, extends, and demonstrates a successful application of intelligent technologies for Computer Aided Software Engineering and Computer Aided Method Engineering. The primary objective of this tool is to improve the effectiveness and efficiency of the requirements elicitation process for software systems development, whilst addressing some of the common issues often encountered in practice through the integration of intelligent technologies. The tool also offers an example of how a group support system, coupled with artificial intelligence, can be applied to very practical activities and situations within the software development process.

Section 3
Software Design and Implementation

Chapter 9

Xiaoqing (Frank) Liu, Missouri University of Science and Technology, USA
Ekta Khudkhudia, Missouri University of Science and Technology, USA
Lei Wen, Missouri University of Science and Technology, USA
Vamshi Sajja, Missouri University of Science and Technology, USA
Ming C. Leu, Missouri University of Science and Technology, USA

In Chapter 9, the authors present a web-based intelligent computational argumentation method for supporting collaborative software development decision making. It provides tools for argumentation reduction, assessment of impact of indirect arguments on design alternatives, and detection of self-conflicting arguments using fuzzy logic for supporting decisions in software development processes. A software application case study is provided to demonstrate the effectiveness of the proposed method and system.

Chapter 10

Alvaro Soria, ISISTAN Research Institute and CONICET, Argentina
J. Andres Diaz-Pace, Software Engineering Institute, USA
Len Bass, Software Engineering Institute, USA
Felix Bachmann, Software Engineering Institute, USA
Marcelo Campo, ISISTAN Research Institute and CONICET, Argentina

It is argued that AI-based tools can assist developers to search the design space more effectively. In this chapter, the authors take a software design approach driven by quality attributes, and then present two tools that have been specifically developed to support that approach. The first tool is an assistant for exploring architectural models, while the second tool is an assistant for the refinement of architectural models into object-oriented models. Furthermore, they show an example of how these design assistants are combined in a tool chain, in order to ensure that the main quality attributes are preserved across the design process.

Section 4
Software Testing and Maintenance

Chapter 11

Nikolai Kosmatov, CEA LIST, Software Safety Laboratory, France

In Chapter 11, the authors discuss some innovative applications of artificial intelligence techniques to software engineering, in particular, to automatic test generation. Automatic testing tools translate the program under test, or its model, and the test criterion, or the test objective, into constraints. Constraint solving allows then to find a solution of the constraint solving problem and to obtain test data. They focus on two particular applications: model-based testing as an example of black-box testing, and all-paths test generation for C programs as a white-box testing strategy. Each application is illustrated by a running example showing how constraint-based methods allow to automatically generate test data for each strategy. They also give an overview of the main difficulties of constraint-based software testing and outline some directions for future research.

Software testing is primarily a technique for achieving some degree of software quality and to gain consumer confidence. It accounts for 50% -75% of development cost. Test case design supports effective testing but is still a human centered and labour-intensive task. The Unified Modelling language (UML) is the de-facto industrial standard for specifying software system and techniques for automatic test case generation from UML models are very much needed. While extensive research has explored the use of meta-heuristics in structural testing, few have involved its use in functional testing, particularly with respect to UML. This chapter details an approach that incorporates an anti-Ant Colony Optimisation algorithm for the automatic generation of test scenarios directly from UML Activity Diagrams, thus providing a seamless progression from design to generation of test scenarios. Owing to its anti-ant behaviour, the approach generates non-redundant test scenarios.

In Chapter 13, the authors describe an approach to mine significant rules of the above format occurring above a certain statistical thresholds from program execution traces. The approach start from a set of traces, each being a sequence of events (i.e., method invocations) and resulting in a set of significant rules obeying minimum thresholds of support and confidence. A rule compaction mechanism is employed to reduce the number of reported rules significantly. Experiments on traces of JBoss Application Server and Jeti instant messaging application shows the utility of our approach in inferring interesting past-time temporal rules.

Chapter 14 summarises current research on the use of artificial intelligence techniques to improve the software development process. The chapter looks particularly at the use of AI in requirements engineering, with a special emphasis on the attempts to translate natural language requirements into different specification languages, software design and implementation, software testing and software project management. The chapter concludes with a discussion on some of the issues related to AI applications for software engineering and the future developments in the field.

Foreword

The notion of supporting software development using artificial intelligence techniques has been around for more than 20 years. In the 1980s, work on the Programmer's Apprentice project led to an 'intelligent' program editor and this led to a number of other projects that aimed to build an intelligent programming environment.

Although some of the work in these projects was exploited under other headings, the notion of an intelligent environment was never realised in practice. Sadly, the whole area of AI and software engineering was oversold and this set back the whole area for many years.

One reason for this was that relevant AI techniques are often computationally expensive and scaling these to apply to large software systems was simply impractical. Now, the limit on computation is disappearing and new hardware and software architectures mean that there is now a real possibility of making AI work effectively in the development of large and complex software systems.

This is an important book because it reflects the re-emergence of AI and Software Engineering as a valid and potentially very valuable research field. The key areas addressed are project management, requirements engineering, software design and software testing. These are all areas where our conventional approaches to software engineering are running out of steam as system sizes increase and industry demands higher quality, shorter times to deployment and lower costs. We see themes emerging that cross-cut these different areas such as the use of Bayesian networks and the encoding and utilisation of domain knowledge in tools to support software engineering activities.

The papers in this book represent an excellent summary of the state of the art in AI and Software Engineering. Most of the work described here is still at an early stage of development and there are surely many engineering challenges to be overcome before these techniques can be routinely used to support large system construction. The challenges to be addressed are to scale the techniques to larger systems and to demonstrate that these are cost effective in reducing costs and schedules and improving the quality of real systems. I believe that the work described here is a sound foundation for this engineering work and that the book should be read by all researchers interested in AI and Software Engineering and by far-sighted practitioners who are interested in the future of the discipline.

Ian Sommerville
St Andrews, Scotland
March 2009

Ian Sommerville *is Professor of Software Engineering at St Andrews University, Scotland and was previously Professor of Computer Science at Lancaster University. He has been involved in software engineering research since the 1980s and his current research interests are in socio-technical systems and the dependability of large-scale enterprise systems. His textbook on software engineering was first published in 1982 and the 8th edition of this book was published in 2006. The text is used all over the world as a student text and has been translated into at least 10 different languages.*

Preface

Software Engineering is concerned with the planning, design, development, maintenance and documentation of software systems. It is well known that developing high quality software for real-world applications is complex. Such complexity manifests itself in the fact that software has a large number of parts that have many interactions and the involvement of many stakeholders with different and sometimes conflicting objectives. Furthermore, Software Engineering is knowledge intensive and often deals with imprecise, incomplete and ambiguous requirements on which analysis, design and implementations are based on.

Artificial intelligences (AI) techniques such as knowledge based systems, neural networks, fuzzy logic and data mining have been advocated by many researchers and developers as a way to improve many of the software development activities. As with many other disciplines, software development quality improves with the experience and knowledge of the developers, past projects and expert opinions. Software also evolves as it operates in changing and volatile environments. Hence, there is significant potential for using AI for improving all phases of the software development life cycle.

From the management point of view, during the course of a project, developers and managers need to make important decisions, plan and predict resources and time. Expert systems, neural networks, Bayesian networks and machine learning techniques have been found to be useful at this stage. Similarly, expert systems and ontologies have been proposed for organizing and eliciting user requirements. Natural language processing techniques can be used to understand requirements and research prototypes have been developed for automatic translation of requirements into Object Oriented and formal models as well as detecting ambiguities and incompleteness in requirements. Fuzzy logic can be used in modeling uncertainty due to linguistics in order to aid requirements engineering.

AI techniques have also been advocated for generating test data, devising optimal integration test orders and for fault detection. Data mining techniques have been proposed to help identify related components in the source code in order to aid software maintenance.

Thus, there is significant potential and research on utilizing AI for software development. This potential is being explored by a number of research groups but much of it is distributed in different sources such as international conferences like the World Congress on Computational Intelligence, Software Reliability Engineering, Genetic and Evolutionary Computation, and Neural Information Processing, that each has its own focus and community.

In creating this book, our aim has been to bring together some of the most advanced and innovative research on utilizing AI for software development in a single source. The book should be useful for researchers, SE practitioners and postgraduate students. Researchers and postgraduate students should find a wealth of interesting ideas and gain an appreciation of the state of the art and find useful pointers to related studies throughout the book. Practitioners and software development institutions undoubtedly have the most to gain from improvements to the software engineering process. The results and experiences contained in the chapters should provide valuable insight into how to improve current practices and where greater investment of resources is likely to reap rewards.

BOOK ORGANIZATION

The book is organized in four section, reflecting key phases of the software engineering process: (1) Project Management and Cost Estimation, (2) Requirements Engineering and Specification, (3) Software Design and Implementation (4) Software Testing and Maintenance. In editing the book, we've been conscious that readers will want to select and read chapters independently of other parts of the book and have therefore allowed some duplication of material.

Section 1: Project Management and Cost Estimation

Good project planning involves many aspects: staff need to be assigned to tasks in a way that takes account of their experience and ability, the dependencies between tasks need to be determined, times of tasks need to be estimated in a way that meets the project completion date and the project plan will inevitably need revision as the project progresses. AI has been proposed for most phases of planning software development projects, including assessing feasibility, estimation of cost and resource requirements, risk assessment and scheduling.

Models for estimating software development costs, such as the COCOMO have existed for some time now and indeed are taught as part of most undergraduate programmes in computer science and software engineering. So why attempt to use any other methods, let alone AI? There are several reasons. First, it still remains the case that the chances of completing a software project on time and within budget remains low, suggesting that the estimates using these models may be not be reliable. Second, the conventional models don't cope well with uncertain parameters and lack the kind of flexibility that is needed for modern approaches such as agile development. The first part of the book presents four studies that use AI for cost estimation and planning in software development.

Chapter 1, by Fenton, Hearty, Neil and Radliński, presents work that has been widely regarded and cited as the leading research on use of Bayesian networks for predicting the cost and effort of software development. The chapter begins with an introduction to Bayesian networks and some of their properties that make them appropriate for estimation and classification. One of the key properties includes the ability to use a network by providing required outcomes as evidence and deducing the parameters that need controlling to achieve the desired outcomes. The chapter includes a description of the MODIST model for predicting cost and a model for predicting the number of defects. Versions of both of these have been tested at Phillips and have achieved high accuracy. These models are then extended to a model, called PRODUCTION, that allows further customisation to allow inclusion of context, such as local productivity rates, to be taken into account. These models are illustrated with examples of how they can be used to carry out risk assessment and trade-offs, showing the benefits of using Bayesian networks. After describing these models, which are applicable to traditional software development methodologies, the chapter describes how Bayesian networks can be used for agile methods. In particular, it shows how the Project Velocity, as used in Extreme Programming, can be estimated using Temporal

Bayesian networks. This model is further adapted to show that it is possible to produce Burnout charts as utilised by the Scrum method. The predictions from the models for Project Velocity and Burnout are both compared with data from actual projects and show remarkable accuracy.

Chapter 2, by Emilia Mendes, continues the theme of using Bayesian networks for cost estimation covered in the first chapter of the book. The focus, however, is on a more specific subset of applications, namely the effort required to develop web sites. The chapter begins with the challenges of estimating the effort required for web applications, which have their own characteristics, including the range of technologies available, the more diverse user base, range of domains, the greater variability in specialist knowledge and experience, and indeed the greater number of small and medium enterprises engaged in the industry. The chapter argues that these characteristics have led to projects that have rarely completed on time and are in need of specific tools for estimating effort required. It then proceeds to study the task of estimating the effort required in detail. First, a general framework for estimating effort, that is based on the size of a project and cost drivers, is developed. The size is characterised by factors such as expected number of pages, features and functionality and the cost drivers include factors such as number of developers and their average experience. Second, the chapter presents an extensive review of related research on estimating effort for developing web sites that includes a summary of the main features of the different approaches. The chapter then presents how to develop a web effort prediction model using Bayesian networks and presents a real case study that has already been successfully utilised in four projects of varying size and complexity.

Unlike the first two chapters, which present alternatives to models such as COCOMO, Chapter 3, by Gonsalves, Yamagishi, Kawabata and Itoh, aims to improve the COCOMO model more directly by use of swarm optimization methods. The chapter begins by providing the motivation for improvements, citing studies that show that the error rates when the COCOMO model is used in practice have been high. The cost estimation problem is formulated as a multi-objective optimization problem, where one of the objectives is to minimise the error rate and a second objective is to minimise model complexity. Minimising the model complexity as well as the error has the advantage that data collection to estimate parameters is simplified, hopefully also leading to greater accuracy. The chapter provides a brief review of existing methods for cost estimation, including regression analysis, case-based reasoning, and data mining methods. It also provides appropriate background knowledge on multi-objective optimization using genetic algorithms, COCOMO models and Pareto fronts. Swarm optimisation, which is based on the social behaviour of ants, birds and fish, is introduced and a multi-objective swarm optimization algorithm is described. An empirical evaluation of the algorithm is carried out on benchmark data sets available from the PROMISE repository and includes the well known COCOMO 81 data and NASA projects. The empirical evaluation confirms that the model is capable of making accurate estimates and also provides a Pareto front that allows managers to trade-off cost and model complexity.

Chapter 4, by Sarcia, Cantone and Basili, presents a study of how multi-layer feed forward neural networks can be a used for improving effort estimation models. The chapter begins by an introduction to parametric models and regression functions. It argues that we should consider using non-linear-in-the-parameter models instead of the linear models that have been adopted more commonly because they have closed form solutions. The potential advantages of the non-linear models include greater flexibility, parsimony and accuracy. A significant aim of the proposed approach is to reduce the number of parameters utilized. The approach aims to achieve this by utilizing a refined version of Principal Component Analysis (PCA), known as Curvilinear Component Analysis (CCA), to reduce the number of input variables. The CCA is implemented using an auto-associative multi-layer feed forward network, consisting of coder and decoder sub-networks, and where the coder part provides the reduction or compression of input variables. The chapter concludes with an empirical evaluation based on the COCOMO 81 data set and shows that use of CCA can result in significant improvements to the accuracy of log-linear models for cost estimation.

Section 2: Requirements Engineering

Section 2 of the book is composed of four chapters that tackle different aspects of the Requirements Engineering (RE) phase. Chapter 5, by Leonid Kof, tackles the problem of incompleteness in natural language (NL) requirements, which is one of the fundamental problems in NL based requirements. This is often due to assumptions about the obviousness of some facts in the requirements and hence omitting to include them. The chapter presents a method that identifies the missing information and produces a message sequence chart (MSC) to reconstruct the missing information. Two Natural Language Processing (NLP) techniques, namely the Part-Of-Speech (POS) and parsing are used to translate NL scenarios into MSCs, where each MSC consists of an action, a sender and a receiver. POS associates a predefined POS category with each word and builds a parse tree. During the translation process, some NL deficiencies such as a missing sender, receiver or action are identified. A pre-processing phase of the system splits complex sentences into simpler ones that contain only one verb, making the identification of the sender, receiver and action easy. Some sentences are translated into messages, while others into conditions.

Chapter 6, by Martínez and Cano, shows how the use of Bayesian networks can improve requirements engineering. They state that there are two different ways of improving the requirements engineering phase. It can either be achieved by improving the RE process itself, or by improving the methods used in each activity or artifact used in the RE process. The chapter proposes a new method for dealing with the lack of certainty in individual requirements. RE is an iterative process and starts by building requirements, removing ambiguities, improving completeness and resolving conflicts and the whole process culminates in the contract. Here the problem lies in knowing when the requirements specification is good enough to stop the iterative process. So the Requirements Engineer has to take the uncertain decision about the stability of the requirements specification and decide on whether to stop the process or not. To deal with this situation, they use Bayesian networks, which are known to be good at modeling domains with uncertainty, and decide on the stability of the requirements. Their approach is composed of four steps: variables identification, structure identification, parameter elicitation, validation and testing. In the variables identification step, the domain expert and the Bayesian network builder must agree on the variables involved in the problem and their possible values or states. The purpose of the Bayesian network is to estimate certainties for unobservable or observable events. These events are called hypothesis events, and once they are detected, they are grouped into sets of mutually exclusive and exhaustive events to form hypothesis variables. The structure identification step is to set up the qualitative part of the model, with directed links connecting the variables in a directed acyclic graph. The parameter elicitation step aims to acquire the numbers necessary to estimate the conditional probabilities for the Bayesian network model. Finally, the purpose of the validation and testing step is to check the suitability of the Bayesian network model for the job it is designed to do, answering questions such as: Does the structure reflect the fundamental independence relationships of the problem? What is the level of predictive accuracy acquired? And, is the network sensitive to changes? The Bayesian network they develop forms the core of a system called Requisites, which is capable of assessing whether a requirements document needs further revision.

Chapter 7, by Muthu Ramachandran presents three research prototypes that demonstrate the potential benefits of utilizing knowledge based approaches to support agile methods. The first system, called SoBA, supports the use of a story board for agile software development. SoBA supports agile development by providing a tool that allows users to create story cards that capture functional and non-functional requirements. A novel aspect of the system is its use of a case based approach to retrieve similar past stories and suggest requirements, acceptance tests, and levels of risk. The second system, called .NET designer, provides design rationale for choosing appropriate architectural solutions. The system consists of a knowledge base of rules that represent best practice based on several years of experience and publicly available guidelines. A user of the .NET designer is guided through the architecture selection process, providing advice and recommendations based on the developed best practice knowledge base. The third system, called RAIS, explores the use of knowledge based systems to support reuse of component specifications. RAIS uses both language and domain knowledge to analyze reusability, assess reusability and suggest improvements for designing reusable software components. Together, the three systems show the kind of knowledge based software engineering tools that could be possible in the future.

Chapter 8, by Coulin, Zowghi and Sahraoui, presents the MUSTER CASE tool. MUSTER is a collaborative and situational tool that has been specifically designed and developed for requirements elicitation, and which utilizes, extends, and demonstrates a successful application of intelligent technologies for Computer Aided Software Engineering and Computer Aided Method Engineering. The overall objectives of the tool were identified as: 1) improve the process of requirements elicitation in terms of the time and effort required, and 2) directly address some of the common issues and challenges often encountered in practice, such as an incomplete understanding of needs and ill-defined system boundaries. In addition, the main functional areas required within the tool were established as 1) visualization, navigation, and administration through the elicitation process, 2) externalization, representation and organization of the elicited information, 3) process guidance, 4) cognitive support, 5) task automation, 6) interaction assistance for the participants, and 7) education of the users on requirements elicitation, primarily by osmosis. For the implementation of MUSTER, the authors have adopted a multi-agents plug-in architecture. The tool is an online browser-based application, and the sever-side components are based on the LAMP platform.

Section 3: Software Design and Implementation

Section 3 of the book consists of two chapters on software design and implementation. Chapter 9, by Liu, Khudkhudia, Wen, Sajja and Leu, develops a web-based system using an intelligent computational argumentation model for collaborative decision making in software development that facilitates selection of the most favoured development alternative. A major strength of the system is that it allows stakeholders to capture their development rationale from multiple perspectives and allows the assessment of arguments in an argumentation network using fuzzy logic based inference mechanisms.

Chapter 10, by Soria, Diaz-Pace, Bass, Bachmann, and Campo, describes two tools to support design decisions in the early stages of software development. The first tool, ArchE is an assistant for exploring architectural models, while the second tool, called SAME, is an assistant for the refinement of architectural models into object-oriented models. ArchE (**Arch**itecture **E**xpert) is a knowledge-based tool that helps the developer to explore architecture alternatives for quality-attribute scenarios while SAME (**S**oftware **A**rchitecture **M**aterialization **E**xplorer) is a case based reasoning tool for deriving object-oriented models based on previous materialization experiences. The outputs of ArchE serve as inputs for SAME. This integrated tool approach is beneficial as it augments the designer's capabilities for navigating the design space and evaluating quality-attribute tradeoffs. Preliminary results have shown that tools like ArchE and SAME can help enforce quality-attribute requirements across the design process.

Section 4: Software Testing and Maintenance

Despite the wealth of research in the last two decades, software testing remains an area where, as cases of reported failures and numerous releases of software suggest, we cannot claim to have mastered. The final part of the book includes three chapters on the use of constraint satisfaction methods, use of ant colony optimization and temporal data mining for software testing and maintenance.

Chapter 11, by Nikolai Kosmatov, describes the use of constraint-based techniques for white and black box testing. It begins by motivating the importance of the testing phase, pointing out that it can account for as much as fifty percent of the total project costs. A background section introduces test criteria, such as structural, control flow, and data coverage criteria. After introducing the idea of model based testing, which is based on modeling a system using specification languages like VDM-SL and Z, the chapter gives a detailed example illustrating how to carry out black-box testing using constraint-based techniques. The example involves generating test cases for a uniprocessor scheduler. First, the scheduler is specified using B notation. Then, the model is parsed and each operation is transformed to pre/post conditions. The coverage criteria together with the conditions provide the definition of the constraint satisfaction problem which is solved using available tools to generate tests. The tests may not be ready to execute since the system may need to be in a particular state, hence some additional work may be necessary to complete the test oracle. Having illustrated use of constraint-based techniques for black box testing, the chapter describes how it could be used for white box testing. The central idea is to carry out a search over the conditions in a program but use the capabilities of a constraint-satisfaction solver to instantiate the variables. The chapter describes the steps involved and gives a small example to illustrate the method in detail. The chapter concludes with an excellent review of current problems in using constraint-based techniques for software testing and the future directions of research.

As well as testing goals such as achieving coverage and boundary cases, one must aim to minimize the size of the test data since carrying out the tests can be time consuming and redundant test cases add little value to the testing process. Chapter 12, by C. Peng Lam, proposes a novel method that aims to generate effective test data by utilizing ant colony optimization over UML Activity Diagrams (ADs). Ant colony optimization, which is based on the pheromone trail left by ants following a path to some food, is introduced and the problems that need addressing to utilize it for software testing are discussed. These include formulating a search problem by defining a quality measure, devising a method for updating the level of pheromone and developing state transition rules. The technique takes an AD and produces a directed graph whose vertices consist of object nodes, fork nodes, join nodes, and initial nodes of an AD and whose edges represent the activities. An ant colony optimization algorithm is developed specifically for generating test thread trees and illustrated on AD for an ATM system. The chapter includes a critical appraisal of the developed algorithm, suggesting that further trials are needed on larger and more complex ADs. The chapter also includes a section on future research directions that will be of interest to anyone pursuing research on the use of ant colony optimization for testing.

Chapter 13, by Lo, Cheng, Khoo and Liu, argues that software maintenance activities can form a significant proportion of the cost of developing software. Software can change late in the development cycle and often, pressures to deliver it to a market on time make it difficult to revise a specification properly and generate tests systematically. Where this happens, which the chapter argues is more common than acknowledged, tools are needed that support re-engineering specifications from program behavior. One line of research that aims to re-engineer specifications is to adopt data mining methods to discover rules from execution traces. Once discovered, the rules can aid specification revision, program comprehension and test generation. Chapter 13 describes specific research on mining rules describing events that occur in the past. The chapter begins with a brief survey of existing work on specification mining, covering the Daikon tool, mining future temporal event rules, and research on extracting specifications from code. The chapter describes the format of the rules which are based on Linear Temporal Logic and develops a theory for temporal mining of traces that includes pruning of redundancy. The developed approach is tested on the JBoss Application Server and the Jeti instant messaging application using an adaptation of an existing sequential pattern miner.

The book concludes with a survey of AI methods in Software Engineering that we carried out specifically for the book. The book includes a number of chapters that describe seminal research and it is important to acknowledge that such a book cannot include all the useful research in the field. Hence, the survey aims to provide pointers to a number of other important studies and places this book in the context of the field.

We hope you enjoy reading the chapters of this book and find them as stimulating and interesting as we have done.

Farid Meziane and Sunil Vadera
University of Salford
April 2009

Acknowledgment

We are grateful to the authors for their contributions. This book would not have been possible without their willingness to share their knowledge, experience and expertise of this field. Our thanks go to the members of the Editorial Advisory Board and the reviewers.

Both editors would like to thank their families for their patience and understanding while they spent their weekends and a few evenings editing the book. Farid thanks his wife Nassiba, and his sons Amir, Yacine and Adam. Sunil thanks his wife Anila, daughter Angeli and son Sumith.

Section 1
Project Management and Cost Estimation

Chapter 1
Software Project and Quality Modelling Using Bayesian Networks

Norman Fenton
Queen Mary, University of London, United Kingdom

Peter Hearty
Queen Mary, University of London, United Kingdom

Martin Neil
Queen Mary, University of London, United Kingdom

Łukasz Radliński
Queen Mary, University of London, United Kingdom, and University of Szczecin, Poland

ABSTRACT

This chapter provides an introduction to the use of Bayesian Network (BN) models in Software Engineering. A short overview of the theory of BNs is included, together with an explanation of why BNs are ideally suited to dealing with the characteristics and shortcomings of typical software development environments. This theory is supplemented and illustrated using real world models that illustrate the advantages of BNs in dealing with uncertainty, causal reasoning and learning in the presence of limited data.

INTRODUCTION

Software project planning is notoriously unreliable. Attempts to predict the effort, cost and quality of software projects have foundered for many reasons. These include the amount of effort involved in collecting metrics, the lack of crucial data, the subjective nature of some of the variables involved and the complex interaction of the many variables which can affect a software project. In this chapter we introduce Bayesian Networks (BNs) and show how they can overcome these problems.

We cover sufficient BN theory to enable the reader to construct and use BN models using a suitable tool, such as AgenaRisk (Agena Ltd. 2008). From this readers will acquire an appreciation for the ease with which complex, yet intuitive, statistical models can be built. The statistical nature of BN models automatically enables them to deal with the

DOI: 10.4018/978-1-60566-758-4.ch001

uncertainty and risk that is inherent in all but the most trivial software projects.

Two distinctive types of model will be presented. The first group of models are primarily causal in nature. These take results from empirical software engineering, and using expert domain knowledge, construct a network of causal influences. Known evidence from a particular project is entered into these models in order to predict desired outcomes such as cost, effort or quality. Alternatively, desired outcomes can be entered and the models provide the range of inputs required to support those outcomes. In this way, the same models provide both decision support and trade off analysis.

The second group of models are primarily parameter learning models for use in iterative or agile environments. By parameter learning we mean that the model learns the uncertain values of the parameters as a project progresses and uses these to predict what might happen next. They take advantage of knowledge gained in one or more iterations of the software development process to inform predictions of later iterations. We will show how remarkably succinct such models can be and how quickly they can learn from their environment based on very little information.

BACKGROUND

Before we can describe BN software project models, it is worthwhile examining the problems that such models are trying to address and why it is that traditional approaches have proved so difficult. Then, by introducing the basics of BN theory, we will see how BN models address these shortcomings.

Cost and Quality Models

We can divide software process models into two broad categories: cost models and quality models. Cost models, as their name implies, aim to

predict the cost of a software project. Since effort is normally one of the largest costs involved in a software project, we also take "cost models" to include effort prediction models. Similarly, since the "size" of a software project often has a direct bearing on the effort and cost involved, we also include project size models in this category. Quality models are concerned with predicting quality attributes such as mean time between failures, or defect counts.

Estimating the cost of software projects is notoriously hard. Molokken and Jorgensen (2003) performed a review of surveys of software effort estimation and found that the average cost overrun was of the order 30-40%. One of the most famous such surveys, the Standish Report (Standish Group International 1995) puts the mean cost overrun even higher, at 89%, although this report is not without its critics (Glass 2006). Software quality prediction, and in particular software defect prediction, has been no more successful. Fenton and Neil (1999) have described the reasons for this failure. We briefly reproduce these here since they apply equally to both cost and quality models.

1. Typical cost and quality models, such as COCOMO (Boehm 1981) and COQUALMO (Chulani & Boehm 1999) take one or two parameters which are fed into a simple algebraic formula and predict a fixed value for some desired cost or quality metric. Such parametric models therefore take no account of the inaccuracy in the measurement of their parameters, or the uncertainty surrounding their coefficients. They are therefore unable to attach any measure of risk to their predictions. Changes in parameters and coefficients can be simulated in an ad-hoc fashion to try to address this, but this is not widely used and does not arise as a natural component of the base model.
2. Parametric models cannot easily deal with missing or uncertain data. This is a major problem when constructing software process

models. Data can be missing because it simply wasn't recorded. It can also be missing because the project is in a very early stage of its lifecycle. Some of the problems appear quite prosaic, for example ambiguity arises because of difficulties in defining what constitutes a line of code. Do comments, empty lines and declarative statements count? Similarly there is uncertainty about what counts as a defect. What is regarded as a defect in one project might be regarded as a user change request in another. Do only post production software failures count as defects, or do defects uncovered during testing count towards the total?

3. Traditional models have difficulty incorporating subjective judgements, yet software development is replete with such judgements. The cost and quality of a software project clearly depend to a significant extent on the quality of the development team, yet such a metric is rarely available form that is easily measured and is more usually the subject of opinion than of measurement.

4. Parametric models typically depend on a previous metrics measurement programme. A consistent and comprehensive metrics programme requires a level of discipline and management commitment which can often evaporate as deadlines approach and corners are cut. Failure to adjust the coefficients in a parametric model to match local conditions can result in predictions which are significantly (often several hundred percent) different from actual values (Briand et. al. 1999; Kemerer 1987).

5. Metrics programmes may uncover a simple relationship between an input and an output metric, but they tell us nothing about how this relationship arises, and crucially, they do not tell us what we must do to improve performance. For example, if we wish to reduce the number of defects, are we better off investing in better test technology,

in more training for the test team, or more experienced developers?

Many attempts have been made to find alternatives to simple parametric models. These include multivariate models (Neil 1992), classification and regression trees (Srinivasan & Fisher 1995), analogy based models (Shepperd & Schofield 1997; Briand et. al. 1999), artificial neural networks (Finnie & Wittig & Desharnais 1997) and systems dynamics models (Abdel-Hamid 1989). However no single one of these approaches addresses all of the problems outlined above. In the next section, we demonstrate how BNs can help overcome these disadvantages and add considerable value and insight to software process modelling.

Introduction to Bayesian Networks

A Bayesian Network (BN), (Jensen, 2001), is a directed acyclic graph (such as the example shown in Figure 1), where the nodes represent random variables and the directed arcs define causal influences or statistical or functional relationships. Nodes without parents (such as the "Probability of finding defects" and "Defects In" nodes in Figure 1) are defined through their prior probability distributions. Nodes with parents are defined through Conditional Probability Distributions (CPDs). For some nodes, the CPDs are defined through deterministic functions of their parents (such as the "Defects Out" node in Figure 1), others (such as the "Defects Found" node in Figure 1) are defined as standard probability distribution functions. Conditional independence (CI) relationships are implicit in the directed acyclic graph: all nodes are conditionally independent of their ancestors given their parents. This general rule makes it unnecessary to list CI relationships explicitly.

Trivial as this example may seem, it actually incorporates a great many of the features that make BNs so powerful. within comparison with regression based models there are a number of beneficial features and advantages:

1. One of the most obvious characteristics of BNs is that we are no longer dealing with simple point value models. Each of the random variables in Figure 1 defines a statistical distribution. The model simultaneously deals with a wide range of possible outcomes. In particular, its predictions, in this case limited to the "Defects out" node, is in the form of a marginal distribution which is typically unimodal, giving rise to a natural "most likely" median value and a quantitative measure of risk assessment in the form of the posterior marginal's variance.

2. We can run the model without entering any evidence. The model then uses the prior distributions which can be based on empirical studies of a wide range of software projects, such as those provided by Jones (1986; 1999; 2003), or by publicly available databases (ISBSG 2008). Nodes such as "Probability of finding defects" may be assigned priors in this way. The "Defects in" node can also be assigned a prior based on empirical studies. In more complex BNs it will often be assigned a distribution which is conditional on other causal factors, or on evidence gathered from the project.

3. The nodes in this model are all represented by numeric scales. BNs are not limited to this however. Any set of states which can be assigned a probability can be handled by a BN. We shall show shortly how ordinal measures can be used to include subjective judgments into BN models.

4. Unlike parametric models, where the underlying variation in software process measurement has been "averaged" out, this model contains all of the available information. It is therefore not limited to an "average" project, but can encompass the full range of values included in its priors. As we shall see later, this dramatically reduces the amount

Figure 1. A simple Bayesian Network illustrating defect detection in a software project

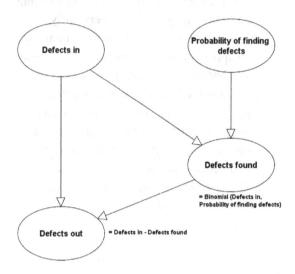

of information needed in order to adapt a BN model to local conditions and enables us to dispense with the metrics collection phase traditionally used to tune parametric models.

5. Unlike simple regression models the relationship between all the causal factors is explicitly stated. This means that, in addition to using the model to make predictions, we can set our desired outcome (for example to how many defects are acceptable in the released product) and the model will be able to tell us how many "Defects in" are the most likely explanation of this and what our probability of finding a defect must be. In larger models, where our initial conditions are defined by the available resources, such models can be used for management decision support as well as project management and planning.

When a variable is actually observed, this observation can be entered into the model. An observation reduces the marginal probability distribution for the observed variable to a unit probability for the observed state (or a small interval containing the value in the continuous) and zero otherwise. The presence of an observation updates the CPD of its children and, through Bayes theorem (Equation 1), the distributions of its parents. In this way observations are propagated recursively through the model. BN models can therefore update their beliefs about probable causes and so learn from the evidence entered into the model. More information on BNs and suitable propagation algorithms can be found in Jensen (2001) and Lauritzen & Spiegelhalter (1988).

$$P(A \mid B) = \frac{P(B \mid A)P(A)}{P(B)} \qquad (1)$$

Dynamic Bayesian Networks

Dynamic Bayesian Networks (DBN) extend BNs by adding a temporal dimension to the model. Formally, a DBN is a temporal model representing a dynamic system which changes state usually over time (Murphy 2002). A DBN consists of a sequence of identical Bayesian Networks, Z_t, $t = 1,2,...,T$ where each Z_t represents a snapshot of the process being modelled at time t. We refer to each Z_t as a *timeslice*. For iterative software development environments this is a particularly apt approach.

The models presented here are all first order Markov. Informally this means that the future is independent of the past given the present $P(Z_t \mid Z_{1:t-1}) = P(Z_t \mid Z_{t-1})$ and in practice it means that we do not need to recompute the model afresh each time a new prediction is needed. The first order Markov property reduces the number of dependencies, making it computationally feasible to construct models with a larger numbers of timeslices. Consistent propagation is achieved using standard junction tree algorithms (Lauritzen & Spiegelhalter 1988). These algorithms provide exact (as opposed to approximate) propagation in discrete BNs and are generally regarded as among the most efficient BN propagation algorithms

(Lepar & Shenoy 1998).

Indicator Nodes and Ranked Nodes

Two types of nodes deserve special mention - these are indicator nodes and ranked nodes. Indicator nodes are nodes with no children and a single parent. They are often used in circumstances where the parent is not directly observable but where some indicator of the parent's status can be measured easily (hence their name). When no evidence is entered into an indicator it has no effect on its parent. When evidence *is* entered into an indicator node it causes a change in the likely distribution of states in the parent.

Indicator nodes can also be used where a large number of causal factors all have a direct impact on a single child node. The number of entries in the CPD of the child grows exponentially with the number of parents. If there are more than a couple of such causal factors then the CPD of the child can become unmanageable. Thanks to Bayes Theorem (Equation 1) we can reverse the direction of the arrows and turn the causal factors into indicators. Since each indicator node only has a single parent, their CPDs become much easier to define.

Ranked nodes are nodes whose states are measured on an ordinal scale, often with either three or five states ranging from "Very Low" through to "Very High". They are used to elicit subjective opinions from experts so that they can be entered as observations into the model. In the tool used to build most of the models described here (Agena Ltd. 2008), the underlying ordinal scale is represented by an equi-partitioned continuous scale in the range [0, 1]. It is thus possible to easily combine ranked nodes and variables consisting of numeric states in the same distributions.

THE MODIST MODEL

Fenton and Neil's pioneering paper (Fenton & Neil 1999) inspired a number of research groups to apply BNs to software process modelling. Wooff, Goldstein, and Coolen (2002) have developed BNs modeling the software test process while Stamelos et al (2003) used COCOMO81 cost factors to build a BN model of software project productivity. Bibi and Stamelos (2004) have shown how BNs can be constructed to model IBM's Rational Unified Process. Fenton and Neil's own research group have also gone on to develop a series of BN models, culminating in the AID tool (Neil, Krause, & Fenton 2003), the MODIST models (Fenton et. al. 2004), and the trials of revised MODIST models at Philips (Neil & Fenton 2005; Fenton et. al 2007a; Fenton et. al 2007b). A similar model has been developed by Siemens (Wang et. al. 2006). Here we will discuss the MODIST models and its successor, the "Philips" model.

A greatly simplified version of the MODIST model, with many of the causal factors and indicator nodes removed, is shown in Figure 2. The model is most easily understood as a series of subnets, fragments of a whole BN, which capture specific aspects of the software development process. The subnets are:

- **Distributed communications and management**. Contains variables that capture the nature and scale of the distributed aspects of the project and the extent to which these are well managed.
- **Requirements and specification**. Contains variables relating to the extent to which the project is likely to produce accurate and clear requirements and specifications.
- **Process quality**. Contains variables relating to the quality of the development processes used in the project.
- **People quality**. Contains variables relating to the quality of people working on the project.

- **Functionality delivered**. Contains all relevant variables relating to the amount of new functionality delivered on the project, including the effort assigned to the project.
- **Quality delivered**. Contains all relevant variables relating to both the final quality of the system delivered and the extent to which it provides user satisfaction (note the clear distinction between the two).

The full BN model is too large to be fully described here but in the next section we discuss just one of the subnets, the "People quality" subnet and use it as an example to show subjective judgements can be entered into the model.

People Quality Subnet

Figure 3 shows the variables and causal connections in this subnet. A description of the main variables, including the model's rationale is given in Table 1. All of the variables shown in Figure 3 are ranked nodes, measured using a five point scale ranging from very low to very high. Observations are not normally entered directly on the variables described in Table 1. Instead we enter observation at primary causes (variables with no parents in the BN) and indicators.

In the 'people quality' subnet (Figure 3), indicator nodes are used to infer the staff quality. The default variables in our model for this are: staff turnover, staff experience, staff motivation, staff training and programming language experience. This can be varied to suit local process needs and is replicated in a similar way in the other subnets.

Although this approach is very flexible and does not insist on an organisation using specific metrics it does depend on some regularity in the way that development projects are estimated. This ensures that there are usable indicators for key attributes of quality and size, which our model can be adapted to use. It also makes it likely that the organisation's project managers will have

Figure 2. A simplified version of the MODIST model

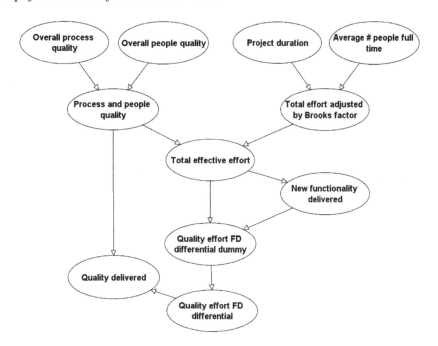

accumulated the experience to be able to make stable judgments about the strength of these indicators. Some organisations may also accumulate data from past projects; there is no difficulty in principle in using such data in adapting the model and we hope to provide this capability in future versions of the toolset.

Using the Bayesian Net for Decision Support

What makes the Bayesian resource model so powerful, when compared with traditional software cost models, is that we can enter observations anywhere to perform not just predictions but also many types of trade-off analysis and risk assessment. So we can enter requirements for quality and functionality and let the model show us the distributions for effort and time. Alternatively we can specify the effort and time we have available and let the model predict the distributions for quality and functionality delivered (measured in function points).

As an example of this, if we simply set "New functionality delivered" to 1000 function points, the model produces the predictions shown in Figure 4. This tells us that the most likely duration is 6 to 8 months (the modal value), although the mean and median values are considerably larger at 21 months and 17 months respectively. The standard deviation is very large, at 16 months, because we have not entered any of the other project attributes. The model similarly predicts that the number of people required will have a modal value of one or two, but large mean and median values of 21 and 16 respectively.

If we fix the number of people at 10 and set the "Process and people quality" to "Very High", we get a modal value for the duration of 2 to 4 months, and mean and median values of 10 and 5 months respectively with a standard deviation of 13 months, making the model far less uncertain in its predictions. These figures are consistent with typical parametric models. However, this ability to vary the project constraints in any desired way while producing consistent estimates of the risk,

Figure 3. The "People quality" subnet of the MODIST model

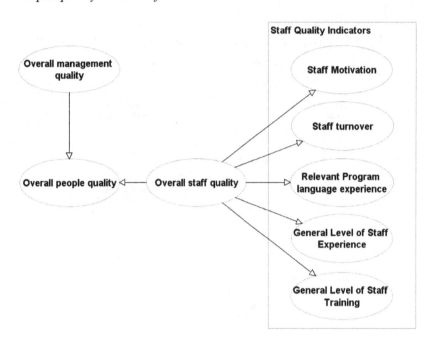

provides far greater insight into the interplay between variables and allows far greater flexibility than is possible with parametric models.

THE DEFECT MODEL

As with the MODIST model, the defect model (Neil & Fenton 2005) is too large to be shown here in full. The core of the model is shown in Figure 5.

Separate subnets governing: the scale of new functionality, specification and documentation quality, design and development quality, testing

and rework quality, and features of the existing code base, all feed into this core defect model. Unlike the MODIST model, the defects model does not require all of its subnets to be included. The defects model is designed to model multiple phases of software development where not all aspects of the full software development process are present in each development phase. So there could be phases which involve requirements and specification, but no development or test. These give rise to specification errors only. Alternatively there can be phases which have development stages but no new requirements, giving rise to new code defects. The model can link these different

Table 1. Details of subnet for people quality

Variable Name	Description
Overall management quality	This is a synthetic node that combines 'communications management adequacy', 'subcontract management adequacy' and 'interaction management adequacy'. If any of these three is poor then generally the value of 'overall management quality' will be poor.
Overall staff quality	This is the quality of non-management staff working on the project.
Overall people quality	This is a synthetic node that combines 'overall management quality' and 'overall staff quality'.

Figure 4. Probability distribution of "Project duration" for 1000 FPs

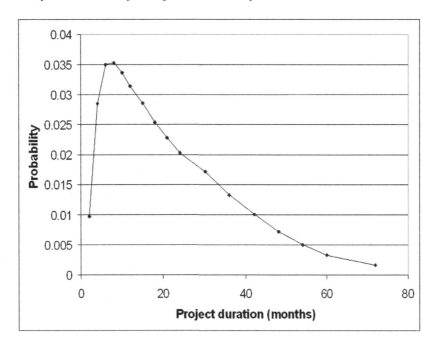

phases together so that the defects which arise, but aren't fixed, in one phase, to be carried over to the next. In this way, the model can handle a very large and diverse range of possible software development processes.

The model operates as follows. A piece of software of a given size, in this case measured in thousands of lines of code (KLOC) gives rise to a certain number of defects. Some of these defects will be the result of inaccuracies in the specification and requirements. A mature software process, combined with close customer contact and experienced management can help to mitigate this. This gives rise to the "Probability of avoiding specification defects" node. Similarly, a good development team can reduce the number of defects introduced during development, leading to the "Probability of avoiding defects in development" node. The effort and experience of the test team affects the probability of finding the remaining defects, and the quality of the rework phase affects the ability to fix them.

The model shown in Figure 5 actually comes from a model validated at Philips (Neil & Fenton 2005; Fenton et. al 2007a; Fenton et. al 2007b). This differed from the original defects model in several important respects.

Project size was measured in KLOC. The original defects model used function points (FPs) as its size measure. However, FPs were not widely used at Philips and it seemed unlikely that they could be introduced purely to validate this model. Initialling the model was simply modified to deduce the number of FPs from the KLOC. This led to problems because it introduced a level of uncertainty in the FP measure which was not originally present. FPs also include a measure of problem complexity which is absent from the KLOC measure. Eventually it became clear that the "scale of new functionality" subnet had to be re-written to accommodate the switch from FPs to KLOC.

The second big change from the defects model was that many of the original indicator nodes were converted to causal factors. This was because the development managers at Philips found it easier

Figure 5. The core of the defects model

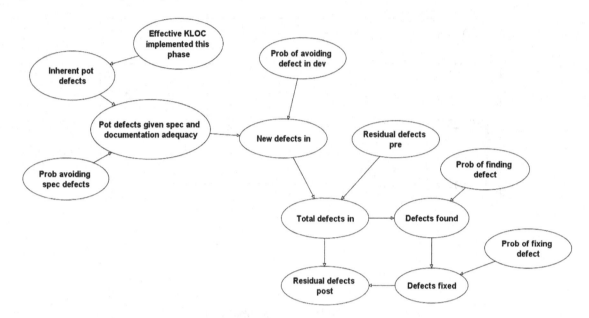

to understand the model when expressed in these terms. Managers frequently added evidence to both an indicator node *and* its parent, thus blocking the indicator evidence. However, turning indicator nodes into causal factors led to the classic problems that arise when nodes have multiple parents: how to construct CPDs involving large numbers of nodes, and how to provide tools so that such CPDs can be easily elicited from domain experts. These problems were solved by devising a comprehensive set of weighted mean functions (Fenton, Neil & Caballero 2007).

The model has been extensively trialed at Philips, with considerable success. The R^2 correlation between predicted and actual defect values is in excess of 93%. It is of course possible to construct regression models with similar, or even higher correlations, but only by including most of the data as training data, which implies an extensive metrics collection programme. The defects model's success was achieved using only empirical data from the literature, and observational data from the projects on which the model was being tested. Much of the raw data for these

trials has been published and is available for use with the model (Fenton et. al 2007b).

THE PRODUCTIVITY MODEL

While the MODIST and defects models were successful in practical applications they contain some limitations. Overcoming or reducing these limitations became the motivation for the Productivity Model. This model provides unique features which were not available in previous models:

1. This model permits custom prior productivity rates and custom prior defect rates. Companies typically gather some data from their past projects. Productivity and defect rates are among the easiest to extract from project databases. Even if a company does not collect effort data, which may happen, it is often quite easy to estimate post hoc. The ability to enter such prior rates arose from criticism of past models, which work well but only within their targeted domain. This

Productivity Model can accommodate local user data by explicitly capturing prior rates provided by users. In cases where providing such custom productivity and defect rates is not possible, these rates can be estimated by our PDR model discussed later.

2. This model enables trade-off analysis between key project variables on a numeric scale. All the key project variables, namely: functionality, software quality and effort are expressed as numbers, not on a ranked scale, as effort and quality were in some of the past models.

3. This model enables customised units of measurement. Previous models captured key variables expressed in fixed units of measurement. For example, effort was captured only in person-months. This model can express key numeric variables in various units. Users can use one of a set of predefined units provided by the model, and can even introduce their own units.

4. The impact of qualitative factors can be easily changed by changing weights in node expressions. We provide a questionnaire which can help determine users' opinions on the relationships between various model variables. These opinions can be different for different software companies and may depend on the type of software developed, the processes used and various other factors. Proper model calibration ensures that the model reflects reality more accurately.

5. This model allows target values for numeric variables to be defined as intervals, not just as point values. For example, this model can answer the question: how can we achieve a defect rate between 0.05 and 0.08 defects/FP for a project of a specific size and with other possible constraints.

6. Numeric variables in this model are dynamically discretised. This means that setting intervals for numeric variables occurs automatically during model calculation.

This not only frees us from spending time setting these intervals for each numeric variable, but as a main benefit, ensures that the discretisation is more accurate because it takes into account all observations entered into the model.

An early version of this model has been published in (Radliński et al. 2007). The structure of the most recent version of the model is illustrated on Figure 6. Ellipses represent key model variables while rounded rectangles are subnets containing detailed variables.

There are three steps which need to be followed before the Productivity Model can be used in performing analyses:

Step 1: Calibrate the model to the individual company. This step involves adding new detailed factors or removing those which are not relevant. This is achieved by setting new weights in weighted means: aggregated project, process and people factors. Regardless of whether the list of detailed factors has been changed or not, another task here is to define the impact of the aggregated factors on the adjusted defect and productivity rates. This is done by entering proper values for constants (multipliers) in expressions for the adjusted rates. The user has to answer questions like: if project factors change to the most/least desired state how would defect and productivity rates increase/decrease? We calibrated the model using the results of questionnaires obtained from employees working in software companies (mostly managers at different levels) and researchers with some commercial experience. We suggest recalibrating the model again with a similar questionnaire to ensure that the model reflects the terminology and development process used in a particular company.

Step 2: Nominate a typical past project from

Figure 6. The core of the Productivity Model

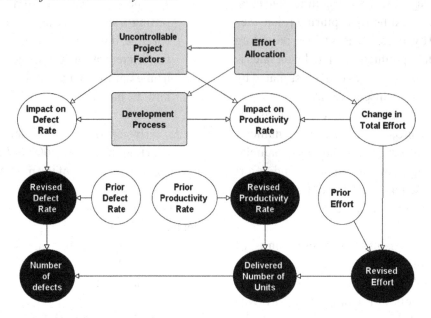

the past project database. The user nominates a past project developed by this company which is closest to the project to be modelled. The effort, defect and productivity rates achieved in these projects should be entered as observations to the model (*prior defect rate*, *prior productivity rate* and *prior effort*). If there are many relevant past projects which could be picked, their distributions should be entered to the model.

Step 3: Estimate the difference in the current project. This step involves assessing how the current project is different from the project(s) nominated in step 2. The differences in detailed variables should then be entered into the model in subnets: *uncontrollable project factors*, *development process* and *effort allocation*.

Using Productivity Model in Decision Support

Let us suppose that a software company has to deliver software consisting of 500 function points but constrained to 2500 person-hours of effort. Suppose that in similar projects in the past the defect rate was typically 0.15 defects per function point, productivity rate was 0.2 function points per person-hour and the effort was 2000 person-hours. For a fair comparison in these examples we assume that all other factors included in the model are the same in all scenarios. With this information passed to the model, it predicts the number of defects delivered will be around 79 defects (all predicted values discussed here are median values of the probability distribution unless stated otherwise). Managers decide that this number of defects is unacceptably high and they wish to know how they can improve it to, say, just 40 defects. The model predicts that to achieve this quality target a better development process and more productive people are required. Also, allocating more effort on specification and testing at the cost of effort on coding is required. The lower effort on coding is balanced by the better coding process and the ability of more productive people to deliver the assumed product size.

Now let us further assume that the company is not able to improve the process and people for this project. Thus we need to perform trade-off analysis between key project variables. We might remove a constraint for the product size. This would result in predicting lower product size containing lower total number of defects. But sacrificing product size would rarely be a good solution. We rather analyze how much more effort is required to achieve the target for the number of defects. The model now predicts that this company should spend around 7215 person-hours on this project to achieve the lower number of residual defects after release. The majority of the increased effort should be allocated to specification and testing activities.

As a second example of using the Productivity Model in decision support, let us assume that we analyze the impact of uncontrollable project factors on estimates provided by the model. Suppose that the size of the software to be developed is 1000 FPs. We leave the prior effort, productivity and defect rates at their default states. The model initially predicts *revised productivity rate* of 0.177 FP/person-hour and *revised defect rate* of 0.056 defects/FP. Now we further assume that *project complexity* is as high as possible – which means as high as has been observed by the company in its previous most complex projects. In this case the model predicts that we are likely to achieve a lower *revised productivity rate* (0.161 FP/person-hour) and that the developed software will be of lower quality (higher *revised defect rate* with median=0.062 defects/FP) compared to the scenario which assumes no change in *project complexity*.

In addition to the higher *project complexity*, suppose we also assume that there is the highest possible *deadline pressure*. In this case, increased *deadline pressure* causes the developers to work faster and thus become more productive (0.176 FP/person-hour). However, it also means they are less focused on delivering software of similar quality and thus their revised defect rate is expected to further increase (0.073 defects/FP).

Let us now assume that in addition to the

previously entered known project factors they anticipate receiving *input documentation* of higher quality. We assume that the exact improvement in *input documentation* quality is unknown. It is only certain that it is of higher quality. We enter such information as *soft evidence*. Entering observations in this way means that we believe that the first four states from 'extra lower' to 'the same' are impossible while the last three from 'higher' to 'extra higher' are equally probable according to our knowledge. The model predicts that with increased quality of input documentation we should expect to be more productive (0.180 FP/person-month) and deliver better software (0.067 defects/FP).

Modelling Prior Productivity and Defect Rates

The PDR model aims to estimate prior productivity and defect rates which are then passed as inputs to the Productivity Model. This model has a Naïve Bayesian Classifier structure (Figure 7). Observations are entered into qualitative factors describing the software to be developed (white ellipses). The model then estimates the log of productivity and defect rates. Finally, dependent variables (productivity and defect rates) are calculated on their original scale.

The links between these qualitative factors and dependant variables do not reflect any causal relationship. However, choosing this structure enables easier model creation since only pairwise relationships need to be analyzed (between each dependant variable and one predictor). As a result the model does not capture any relationships between predictors which need to be independent of each other in this type of model.

We identified the qualitative factors and their impact on productivity and defect rates by analysing the ISBSG dataset R9 release (2005). While fitting various distributions for these dependent variables we observed that LogNormal distribution fits the data best. We adjusted the

Figure 7. PDR Model

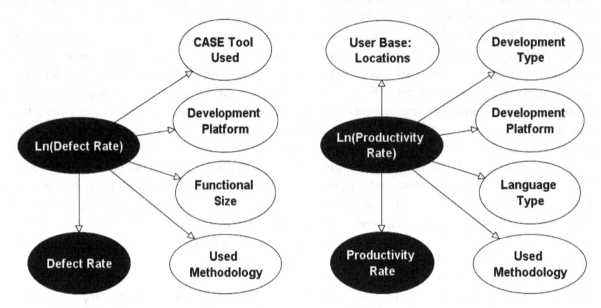

impact of qualitative factors on productivity and defect rate by other reported data, most notably (Jones, 2002 cited after Sassenburg 2006) and according to our expert-judgement. Details on the steps of empirical analysis, the structure of the model and various scenarios on model usage can be found in (Radliński et al., 2008a).

Here we demonstrate one example of the kind of analysis which this model can perform. We also pass the results obtained from the PDR model for productivity and defect rates to the Productivity Model. We analyze two scenarios for the same functional size (1000 FPs), the same target defect rate (0.1 defects/FP) and wish to get a prediction for development effort from the Productivity Model. In the first scenario we assume that the software project will be developed on a mainframe and with a 3GL programming language. The second scenario assumes that a project will be developed on multiple platforms using an application generator. We enter observations for the appropriate qualitative factors into variables in the PDR model. For fair comparison we further assume that in both scenarios the process and people quality and other factors from the Productivity Model have

'average' values.

After running both models we observe that the observations entered into the PDR model significantly change the predictions provided by the Productivity Model. Predicted revised effort is about 3.5 times higher in scenario 1 (10740 person-hours) than in scenario 2 (3074 person-hours). However, it would be wrong to conclude from this that we should only use application generators and multiple platforms, while avoiding 3GL languages and mainframe platforms. The predictors in the PDR model should be treated as uncontrollable factors which describe the inherent nature of the software project. This nature determines the best platform, language type to be used and other factors.

AGILE DEVELOPMENT ENVIRONMENTS

The models discussed so far mostly apply to large, traditional, waterfall style development environments. There has been a significant trend in recent years, especially in web based and other interactive applications, towards so-called "agile" development techniques (Agile Manifesto 2008). Agile methods eschew extensive specification and design phases in favour of rapid prototyping, iterative development, extensive customer feedback and a willingness to modify requirements in the face of changing business circumstances.

Agile development environments present two problems for traditional models. The first problem is that the lack of a formal requirements gathering phase makes it very difficult to quantify the size of the project. There is unlikely to be sufficient written documentation in an agile project to justify a rigorously determined function point count or any similar measure of problem size.

The second problem that traditional models face concerns data gathering and entry. The defects model described in an earlier section can require over 30 individual pieces of data in order to be fully specified. Although not all data is required in all phases of development, there will normally be a need to gather several separate numbers or subjective values. In the case of the subjective judgements, these must also be entered consistently across iterations. There is considerable redundancy here. If the node "Programmer capability" is set to "High" on the first iteration, then it is likely to remain high in subsequent iterations.

We can turn these problems into opportunities as follows. First, by restricting our models to whatever data is routinely collected by agile development processes. This means that we do not require agile projects to collect metrics, such as function points, which do not naturally arise in that environment. The looser definition of some of these metrics means that we somehow have to learn the exact interpretation of agile metrics on a given project. As we shall see, the iterative nature of agile projects makes this perfectly possible.

Second, instead of modelling all the causal factors which contribute to a project, we subsume their combined effect in our learning mechanism. We then model only *changes* in the development environment. This greatly reduces the amount of data which needs to be entered into models and completely eliminates the redundancy that would otherwise be present.

This combination of intelligent model adaptation, and learning using minimal data input, is only possible because of the empirically derived priors and the causal relationships elicited from domain experts. The BN models already represents a very wide range of possible development environments. Rather than "training" the model, data is needed to simply "nudge" the model towards a set of variable states that are consistent with the environment being modelled.

Here we present two models that take this approach. In the first we show how productivity, and consequently timescales, can be modelled in an Extreme Programming environment. In the second we present a learning defects model for use in iterative environments.

Extreme Programming Project Velocity Model

Extreme Programming (XP) is an agile development method that consists of a collection of values, principles and practices as outlined by Kent Beck, Ward Cunningham and Ron Jeffries (Beck 1999; Jeffries, Anderson & Hendrickson 2000). These include most notably: iterative development, pair programming, collective code ownership, frequent integration, onsite customer input, unit testing, and refactoring.

The basic unit of work in XP is the *User Story*. Developers assign the effort that they believe is required for them to design, code and test each user story. Once iteration i is complete, the estimates for the completed user stories are added together. This is the *Project Velocity V_i* for iteration i. Assuming that the next iteration, $i + 1$, is the same length, the customer selects the highest priority uncompleted user stories whose estimated efforts sum to V_i. These user stories are then scheduled for iteration $i + 1$. The project velocity can therefore be thought of as the estimated productive effort per iteration.

The BN used to model project velocity is shown in Figure 8. To model the relationship between total effort E_i and the actual productive effort A_i, there is a single controlling factor that we call Process Effectiveness, e_i. This is a real number in the range [0,1]. A Process Effectiveness of one means that all available effort becomes part of the actual productive effort. The actual productive effort is converted into the estimated productive effort (or project velocity) V_i, via a bias b_i, which represents any consistent bias in the team's estimations.

The Process Effectiveness is, in turn, controlled by two further parameters: Effectiveness Limit, l_i, and Process Improvement, r_i. The Process Improvement is the amount by which the Process Effectiveness increases from one XP iteration to the next. To allow for failing projects, the Process Improvement can take on negative values.

Only E_i and V_i are ever entered into the model.

The model shown in Figure 8 is what is known as a 1.5 TBN (for 1.5 timeslice temporal BN). It shows the interface nodes from the previous timeslice and their directed arcs into the current timeslice. This is essentially the full model, it is not a cut down core such as the ones presented for the MODIST and defect models. Notice the tiny size of this mode compared to the others. This is due to the fact that it is only trying to predict one thing, V_i, and that is does so, not by taking into account all possible causal factors, but by learning their cumulative effect on the process control parameters: l_i and r_i.

The model works as follows. Initial estimates for the amount of available effort E_i are entered into the model for each iteration. At this stage the number of iterations is unknown, so a suitably large number must be chosen to be sure of covering the entire project. Using empirically derived industry priors for l_0, r_0, e_0 and b_0 the model then makes generic predictions for the behaviour of V_i. This enables the project management to see how many user stories are likely to be delivered in each iteration. The model correctly reproduces rapidly rising values for V_i over the initial iterations - a phenomenon that has been observed in multiple studies (Ahmed, Fraz, & Zahid 2003; Abrahamsson & Koskela, 2004; Williams, Shukla, & Anton, 2004).

At each project iteration measured values for V_i become available and are entered into the model. This causes the learned parameters l_i, r_i and b_i to update, modifying future predictions. Using data from a real XP project (Williams, Shukla, & Anton, 2004), we were able to enter observations for V_1 and V_2, and verify the model's predictions of the remaining V_i. Initially this generates improved predictions for early iterations, but significantly worse predictions for later iterations. It turns out that there was a significant change in the environment half way through the project, when much better customer contact and feedback became available. This was added to the model by adding an "Onsite customer" indicator node to l_i. The effect of this indicator node had to be calibrated independently using a training model which was a slightly modified version of the project velocity model. Once the effect of the changed environment had been taken into account (Figure 9), the model was able to produce very good predictions for all future values of V_i (Hearty et. al. in press).

The model is not limited to productivity predictions. By adding a node which sums the V_i distributions, we can create predictions of delivered functionality, s_i, after each iteration.. Taking the median values of the s_i distributions and comparing them to the actual functionality delivered, we can determine the magnitude of relative errors (MRE) for each s_i. The mean values of the MREs give a good overall measure of the accuracy of the model. The mean MRE for s_i before learning was 0.51, an error of over 50%. After learning the mean MRE for s_i reduces to 0.026 - an extraordinary level of accuracy for a software process model.

One of the great advantages of a BN model is

Figure 8. Project Velocity model

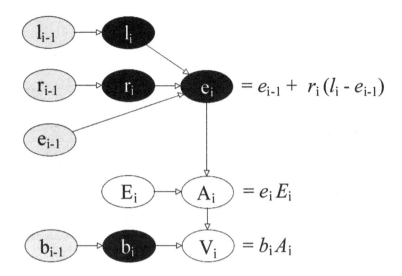

its ability to deliver natural assessments of risk. If we take the cumulative probability distribution of an s_i node, then this allows us to read off the probability that any given amount of functionality will be delivered. An example for s_8 is shown in Figure 10. In this case we are trying to read off the probability of delivering up to 200 Ideal Engineering Days (IEDs) of completed functionality. (An IED is a day spent by a developer doing detailed design, writing code, or testing code and is assumed to be directly proportional to a fixed amount of delivered functionality.) Before learning, the model predicted that there was a 25% chance of delivering 200 IEDs or less. i.e. There was a 75% of delivering more than 200 IEDs. After learning the model reduced this to a 35% chance of delivering 200 IEDs or more - the model was initially too optimistic.

XP is the most common agile development method. Another common methodology is Scrum (Takeuchi & Nonaka 1986; Schwaber & Beedle 2002; Sutherland 2004). This approach uses *burndown charts* to plan a project. A burndown chart starts with a fixed amount of functionality that must be delivered. This reduces with each iteration as more and more functionality is completed.

The slope of the burndown chart gives the project velocity, while its intercept with the horizontal time axis gives the projected completion date. We can model a burndown chart very easily using a modified version of the XP model. Instead of letting s_i represent the cumulative functionality delivered, we define it to be the amount of functionality remaining. We can then set s_i as evidence values, rather than V_i as in XP, and learn how the burndown chart must be altered as each iteration completes. An example is shown in Figure 11.

LEARNING MODEL FOR ITERATIVE TESTING AND FIXING DEFECTS

The models discussed earlier contain fixed relationships between variables. The model discussed here (see Figure 12) is a learning model in the sense that it learns the impact of particular predictors on dependent variables using a set of past data. The aim for this model is to predict the number of defects found and fixed in an iterative testing and fixing process. This iterative process assumes that all functionality has been developed prior to testing. The testing and fixing process is divided

Figure 9. Project velocity predictions before and after learning

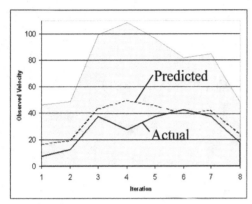

Predicted and actual median velocity values before any actual values have been entered into the model. The solid grey area shows the predicted values +/- 2 sd.

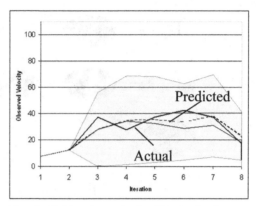

After v1 and v2 have been entered, and improved customer access has been added, the predictions improve significantly. The uncertainty surrounding the model's predictions also decrease. The solid grey line shows the predictions after v1 and v2, but before customer access has been added.

into series of iterations lasting a variable amount of time. More information on earlier versions of this model and its assumptions can be found in (Radliński et al. 2008b).

Links in this model reflect causal relationships. Testing process factors (effort, process and people quality and other factors) impact on *testing effectiveness* which, after utilizing the number of *residual defects* at a given point of time, determine the number of *defects found* during a specific testing iteration. The number of *open defects* from the past iterations plus the number of *defects found* in the current iteration form an upper limit for the number of *defects fixed* in the current iteration. The second limit comes from the values of fixing process factors in a form of *potentially fixed defects* reflecting how many defects can be fixed given specific process data.

In contrast to traditional software reliability growth models this model does not assume that fixes need to be perfect. This means that it explicitly incorporates the number of *defects inserted* as a result of an imperfect fixing process. The model assumes that the number of *defects inserted* depends on the number of *defects fixed* during a specific iteration and on the fixing process qual-

ity. When many defects have been fixed than it is probable that a proportionate number of defects have also been introduced. When the fixing process is poor then the number of *defects inserted* will be relatively high.

The model works in the following way. A user enters data about the past testing and fixing iterations as well as the defects found and fixed in these iterations. The model uses the entered data to estimate its parameters – *multipliers* for each process factor and the number of *residual defects*. The values of these *multipliers* reflect the importance of each process factor in terms of its impact on the number of defects or defects fixed. Then the user enters planned values for process factors in future iterations – e.g. how much effort is planned to be allocated to testing and fixing defects. The model uses these process factors, learnt *multipliers* and learnt *residual defects* to predict the number of *defects found* and the number of *defects fixed* in future iterations. At this point the user can analyze various scenarios which differ in effort, process and people quality, or other known factors possible in future iterations.

We perform model validation using a semi-randomly generated dataset. We set point values

Figure 10. Cumulative probability distribution of functionality delivered in iteration 8

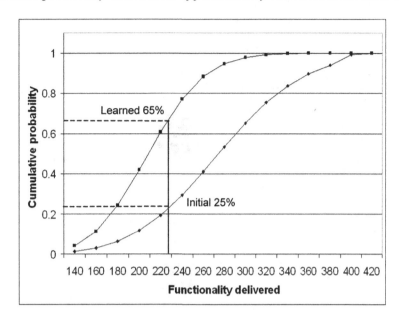

for prior *residual defects* and values of process factor multipliers. Values for process factors were generated randomly and then manually adjusted in some iterations to more realistically reflect the testing and fixing process. The effectiveness of the testing and fixing process increases over time as the process becomes more mature and the software under test becomes better understood. We estimated values for defects found, fixed and inserted using the values of process factors and the relationships as incorporated by the model. We used these generated datasets in the model

Figure 11. Scrum burndown chart, before and after learning

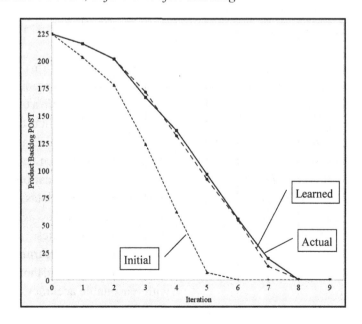

Figure 12. The structure of the LMITFD

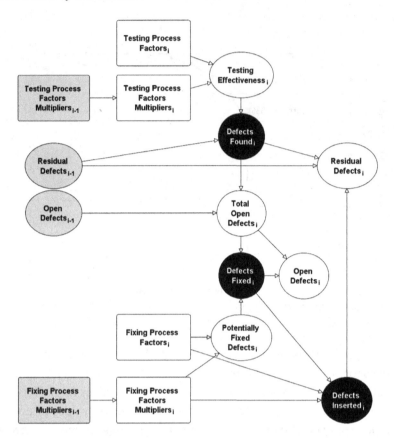

validation stage and treated them as if they were observed values. In the validation stage we tested how fast the model can learn the number of *residual defects* and the values of process factors' *multipliers*.

We tested the model using 30 testing and fixing iterations. First we used a single learning iteration with 29 iterations where values of defects found and fixed were predicted. This was followed by 2 iterations for learning and 28 for prediction, and so on. Figure 13 illustrates the values of relative errors in predicted total number of *defects found* and *defects fixed* as estimated after a different number of learning iterations. This relative error is defined as illustrated on Equation 2.

$$relative\ error = \frac{\left| total\ predicted - total\ actual \right|}{total\ actual}$$

(2)

These results confirm that after only 5 learning iterations, the model predicts the total number of defects found to within a 0.16 relative error of the actual value and predicts total number of defects fixed to within a 0.30 relative error of the actual value. Predictions then become less accurate because of higher fluctuations in actual number of *defects found* in the dataset. But from 8 learning iterations the accuracy again increases (relative error decreases). These results show that the model is capable of learning its parameters after very few iterations and then generates predictions with reasonable accuracy.

Figure 13. Relative errors in predictions for total number of defects found and defects fixed depending on number of iterations used to learn the model

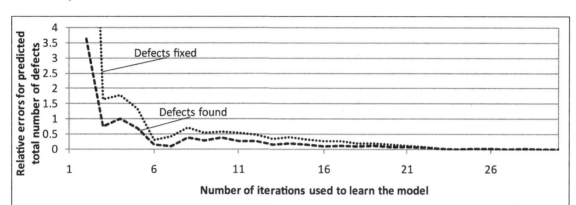

One of the most important advantages of such models is the high potential for performing various types of what-if analyses. After the model learns its parameters, we can set as observations different values for future process factors to see how they influence predicted number of defects found. For example let us analyze model predictions in two scenarios when *fixing process and people quality* is 'very low' or 'very high'. Values of other process factors are the actual values in iterations used for prediction. We use 5 learning iterations and the remaining 25 for prediction. Figure 14 illustrates the model's predictions for this case. We can observe that, as we could expect, with lower *fixing process and people quality*, fewer defects are likely to be fixed in future iterations. These differences are very high, confirming that the model updated its *multipliers* and *residual defects* to reflect the fact that qualitative process factors have a strong influence on *defects found* and *defects fixed*.

We can see that, although we have only modified our observations of *fixing process and people quality*, the predicted values of *defects found* are also different in these two scenarios. The reason is the following. Lower *fixing process and people quality* with *fixing effort* unchanged leads to increased number of *defects inserted* as a result of imperfect fixing. Higher number of

defects inserted causes more *residual defects* in subsequent iterations. Higher number of *residual defects* in turn causes there to be more *defects found* – the more *residual defects* the easier it is to find them.

Another issue which may be surprising in the beginning is the fact that predicted number of *defects fixed* in the late iterations is lower both with 'very low' and 'very high' *fixing process and people quality* compared with the scenario with the original *fixing process and people quality*. But there is also an explanation for such predictions. With 'very low' *fixing process and people quality* it is simply not possible to fix more defects without assigning significantly more *fixing effort*. On the other hand, with 'very high' *fixing process and people quality* defects which were found earlier were also fixed earlier. So in these late iterations there are fewer defects still to be fixed.

REFERENCES

Abdel-Hamid, T. (1989). The dynamics of software projects staffing: A system dynamics based simulation approach. *IEEE Transactions on Software Engineering, 15*(2), 109–119. doi:10.1109/32.21738

Figure 14. Predictions from LMITFD with very high and very low fixing process and people quality after 5 iterations used to learn the model

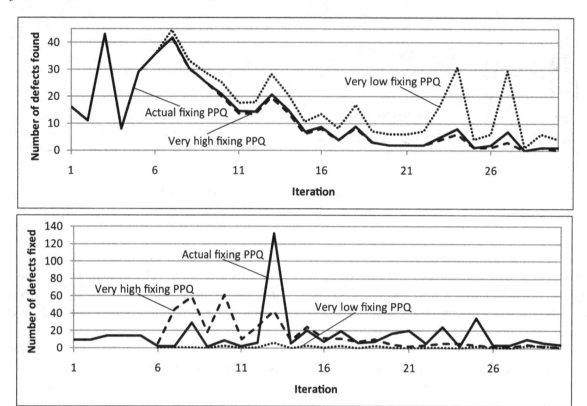

Abrahamsson, P., & Koskela, J. (2004). Extreme programming: A survey of empirical data from a controlled case study. In *Proceedings 2004 International Symposium on Empirical Software Engineering, 2004.* (pp. 73-82). Washington, DC: IEEE Computer Society.

Agena Ltd. (2008). *Bayesian Network and simulation software for risk analysis and decision support.* Retrieved July 9, 2008, from http://www.agena.co.uk/

Agile Manifesto. (2008). *Manifesto for agile software development.* Retrieved July 18, 2008, from http://www.agilemanifesto.org/

Ahmed, A., Fraz, M. M., & Zahid, F. A. (2003). Some results of experimentation with extreme programming paradigm. In *7th International Multi Topic Conference, INMIC 2003,* (pp. 387-390).

Beck, K. (1999). *Extreme programming explained: Embrace change.* Reading, MA: Addison-Wesley Professional.

Bibi, S., & Stamelos, I. (2004). Software process modeling with Bayesian belief networks. In *10th International Software Metrics Symposium Chicago.*

Boehm, B. (1981). *Software engineering economics.* Englewood Cliffs, NJ: Prentice-Hall.

Briand, L. C., El Emam, K., Surmann, D., Wieczorek, I., & Maxwell, K. D. (1999). An assessment and comparison of common software cost estimation modeling techniques. In *21st International Conference on Software Engineering, ICSE* 1999, (pp. 313-322).

Chulani, S., & Boehm, B. (1999). *Modeling software defect introduction and removal: CO-QUALMO (COnstructive QUALity MOdel)*, (Tech. Rep. USC-CSE-99-510). University of Southern California, Center for Software Engineering, Los Angeles, CA.

Fenton, N., Neil, M., Marsh, W., Hearty, P., Marquez, D., Krause, P., & Mishra, R. (2007a, January). Predicting software defects in varying development lifecycles using Bayesian nets. *Information and Software Technology, 49*(1), 32–43. doi:10.1016/j.infsof.2006.09.001

Fenton, N., Neil, M., Marsh, W., Hearty, P., Radlinski, L., & Krause, P. (2007b). Project data incorporating qualitative facts for improved software defect prediction. In *Proceedings of the Third international Workshop on Predictor Models in Software Engineering*, International Conference on Software Engineering (May 20 - 26, 2007). Washington, DC: IEEE Computer Society.

Fenton, N. E., Marsh, W., Neil, M., Cates, P., Forey, S., & Tailor, T. (2004). Making resource decisions for software projects. In *Proceedings of 26th International Conference on Software Engineering* (ICSE 2004), Edinburgh, United Kingdom, May 2004, IEEE Computer Society, (pp. 397-406).

Fenton, N. E., & Neil, M. (1999). A critique of software defect prediction models. *IEEE Transactions on Software Engineering, 25*(5), 675–689. doi:10.1109/32.815326

Fenton, N. E., Neil, M., & Caballero, J. G. (2007). Using ranked nodes to model qualitative judgments in Bayesian Networks. *IEEE Transactions on Knowledge and Data Engineering, 19*(10), 1420–1432. doi:10.1109/TKDE.2007.1073

Finnie, G. R., Wittig, G. E., & Desharnais, J. M. (1997). A comparison of software effort estimation techniques: Using function points with neural networks, case-based reasoning and regression models. *Journal of Systems and Software, 39*(3), 281–289. doi:10.1016/S0164-1212(97)00055-1

Glass, R. L. (2006). The Standish report: Does it really describe a software crisis? *Communications of the ACM, 49*(8), 15–16. doi:10.1145/1145287.1145301

Hearty, P., Fenton, N., Marquez, D., & Neil, M. (in press). Predicting project velocity in XP using a learning dynamic Bayesian Network model. *IEEE Transactions on Software Engineering.*

ISBSG. (2005). *Estimating, Benchmarking & Research Suite Release 9*. Hawthorn, Australia: International Software Benchmarking Standards Group.

Jeffries, R., Anderson, A., & Hendrickson, C. (2000). *Extreme programming installed*. Reading, MA: Addison-Wesley Professional.

Jensen, F. (2001). *Bayesian Networks and decision graphs*, New York: Springer-Verlag.

Jones, C. (1986) *Programmer productivity*. New York: McGraw Hill.

Jones, C. (1999). Software sizing. *IEE Review, 45*(4), 165–167. doi:10.1049/ir:19990406

Jones, C. (2002). *Software quality in 2002: A survey of the state of the art*. Software Productivity Research.

Jones, C. (2003). Variations in software development practices. *IEEE Software, 20*(6), 22–27. doi:10.1109/MS.2003.1241362

Kemerer, C. F. (1987). An empirical validation of software cost estimation models. *Communications of the ACM, 30*(5), 416–429. doi:10.1145/22899.22906

Lauritzen, S. L., & Spiegelhalter, D. J. (1988). Local computations with probabilities on graphical structures and their application to expert systems (with discussion). *Journal of the Royal Statistical Society. Series B. Methodological, 50*(2), 157–224.

Lepar, V., & Shenoy, P. P. (1998). A comparison of Lauritzen-Spiegelhalter, Hugin, and Shenoy-Shafer architectures for computing marginals of probability distributions. In G. Cooper & S. Moral (Ed.), *Proceedings of the 14th Conference on Uncertainty in Artificial Intelligence,* (pp. 328-337). San Francisco: Morgan Kaufmann.

Molokken, K., & Jorgensen, M. (2003). A review of software surveys on software effort estimation. In *2003 International Symposium on Empirical Software Engineering* (pp. 223-230). Washington, DC: IEEE press.

Murphy, K. P. (2002). *Dynamic Bayesian Networks: Representation, inference and learning.* PhD thesis, UC Berkeley, Berkeley, CA.

Neil, M. (1992). *Statistical modelling of software metrics.* Ph.D. dissertation, South Bank University, London.

Neil, M., & Fenton, P. (2005). Improved software defect prediction. In *10th European Software Engineering Process Group Conference*, London.

Neil, M., Krause, P., & Fenton, N. E. (2003). Software quality prediction using Bayesian Networks. In T. M. Khoshgoftaar, (Ed.) *Software Engineering with Computational Intelligence.* Amsterdam: Kluwer.

Radliński, Ł., Fenton, N., & Marquez, D. (in press, 2008a). Estimating productivity and defect rates based on environmental factors. In *Information Systems Architecture and Technology.* Wrocław, Poland: Oficyna Wydawnicza Politechniki Wrocławskiej.

Radliński, Ł., Fenton, N., & Neil, M. (in press, 2008b). A Learning Bayesian Net for Predicting Number of Software Defects Found in a Sequence of Testing. *Polish Journal of Environmental Studies.*

Radliński, Ł., Fenton, N., Neil, M., & Marquez, D. (2007). Improved decision-making for software managers using Bayesian Networks. In *Proceedings of 11th IASTED International Conference Software Engineering and Applications (SEA)*, Cambridge, MA, (pp. 13-19).

Sassenburg, J. A. (2006). *Design of a methodology to support software release decisions (Do the numbers really matter?)*, PhD Thesis, University of Groningen.

Schwaber, K., & Beedle, M. (2002). *Agile software development with SCRUM.* Upper Saddle River, NJ: Prentice Hall.

Shepperd, M., & Schofield, C. (1997). Estimating software project effort using analogies. *IEEE Transactions on Software Engineering, 23*(11), 736–743. doi:10.1109/32.637387

Srinivasan, K., & Fisher, D. (1995). Machine learning approaches to estimating software development effort. *IEEE Transactions on Software Engineering, 21*(2). doi:10.1109/32.345828

Stamelos, I., Angelis, L., Dimou, P., & Sakellaris, E. (2003). On the use of Bayesian Belief Networks for the prediction of software productivity. *Information and Software Technology, 45*(1), 51–60. doi:10.1016/S0950-5849(02)00163-5

Standish Group International. (1995). *The Chaos Report.* Retrieved July 9, 2008, from net.educause. edu/ir/library/pdf/NCP08083B.pdf

Sutherland, J. (2004). *Agile development: Lessons learned from the first scrum.* Retrieved July 9, 2008, from http://jeffsutherland.com/Scrum/FirstScrum2004.pdf.

Takeuchi, H., & Nonaka, I. (1986). The new new product development game. *Harvard Business Review, Jan-Feb.*

Wang, H., Peng, F., Zhang, C., & Pietschker, A. (2006). Software project level estimation model framework based on Bayesian Belief Networks. In *Sixth International Conference on Quality Software.*

Williams, L., Shukla, A., & Anton, A. I. (2004). An initial exploration of the relationship between pair programming and Brooks' law. In *Agile Development Conference, 2004*, (pp. 11-20), Agile Development Conference.

Wooff, D. A., Goldstein, M., & Coolen, F. P. A. (2002). Bayesian graphical models for software testing. *IEEE Transactions on Software Engineering, 28*(5), 510–525. doi:10.1109/TSE.2002.1000453

Chapter 2
Using Bayesian Networks for Web Effort Estimation

Emilia Mendes
The University of Auckland, New Zealand

ABSTRACT

Web effort models and techniques provide the means for Web companies to formalise the way they estimate effort for their projects, and help in obtaining more accurate estimates. Accurate estimates are fundamental to help project managers allocate resources more adequately, thus supporting projects to be finished on time and within budget. The aim of this chapter is to introduce the concepts related to Web effort estimation and effort forecasting techniques, and to discuss effort prediction when the estimation technique used is Bayesian Networks.

INTRODUCTION TO WEB EFFORT ESTIMATION

The Web is used as a delivery platform for numerous types of Web applications and services, ranging from complex e-commerce solutions with back-end databases to on-line personal static Web pages, blogs and wikis. We currently have available a sheer diversity of Web application types, Web technologies and services, and such diversity is likely to continue growing. However, such diversity also entails many challenges to those who develop/propose such applications, technologies and services.

One of these challenges relates to the management of Web projects, where the accurate estimation of effort for new projects is paramount to the proper allocation of resources (Mendes, 2007d).

Complementary to the diversity of Web technologies, application types, and services, there is also the issue associated with the characteristics of the companies that generally develop Web applications. They are mostly small to medium, and generally bid for as many Web projects as they can accommodate, delivering applications in domains often unfamiliar to developers (e.g. social networking applications, aggregation services, data 'mash-ups'), and that use technologies and services with which these companies had no previous experience. This scenario

DOI: 10.4018/978-1-60566-758-4.ch002

Figure 1. Steps used to obtain an effort estimate (Mendes, 2007d)

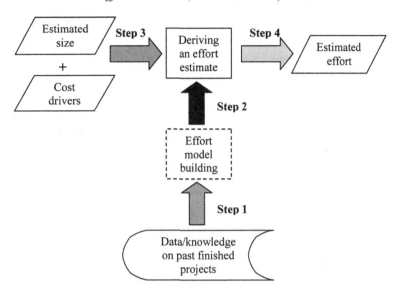

only adds up to the current situation where most Web development projects suffer from unrealistic project schedules, leading to applications that are rarely developed on time and within budget (Reifer, 2000).

In essence, regardless of the existing number of different Web technologies, services and application domains, Web companies need to have sound effort estimation in other to manage projects in a way that enables them to be delivered on time and within budget.

The purpose of estimating effort is to predict the amount of effort (person/time) required to develop an application (and possibly also a service within the Web context), often based on knowledge of 'similar' applications/services previously developed. Figure 1 provides a general overview of an effort estimation process. Estimated characteristics of the new application/service to be developed, and its context (project) are the input, and effort is the output we wish to predict. For example, a given Web company may find that to predict the effort necessary to implement a new e-commerce Web application, it will need to estimate early on in the development project the following characteristics:

Estimated number of new Web pages.
• The number of functions/features (e.g. shopping cart, on-line forum) to be offered by the new Web application.
• Total number of developers who will help develop the new Web application
• Developers' average number of years of experience with the development tools employed.
• The choice of main programming language used.

Of these variables, estimated number of new Web pages and the number of functions/features to be offered by the new Web application characterise the size of the new Web application; the other three, total number of developers who will help develop the new Web application, developers' average number of years of experience with the development tools employed, and main programming language used, characterise the project - the context for the development of the new application, and are also believed to influence the amount of effort necessary to develop this new application. The project-related characteristics are co-jointly named 'cost drivers'.

No matter what the Web development is (application or service), in general the one consistent input found to have the strongest effect on the amount of effort needed to develop an application or service is size (i.e. the total number of server side scripts, the total number of Web pages), with cost drivers also playing an influential role.

In most cases, effort estimation is based on past experience, where knowledge or data from past finished applications & projects are used to estimate effort for new applications & projects not yet initiated. The assumption here is that previous projects are similar to new projects to be developed, and therefore knowledge and/or data from past projects can be useful in estimating effort for future projects.

The steps presented in Figure 1 can be repeated throughout a given Web development cycle, depending on the process model adopted by a Web company. For example, if the process model used by a Web company complies with a waterfall model this means that most probably there will be an initial effort estimate for the project, which will remain unchanged throughout the project. If a Web company's process model complies with the spiral model, this means that for each cycle within the spiral process a new/updated effort estimate is obtained, and used to update the current project's plan and effort estimate. If a Web company uses an agile process model, an effort estimate is obtained for each of the project's iterations. In summary, a company's process model will determine the amount of visibility an effort estimate has, and if the estimate is to be revisited or not at some point during the Web development life cycle.

It should be noted that cost and effort are often used interchangeably within the context of effort estimation since effort is taken as the main component of project costs. However, given that project costs also take into account other factors such as contingency and profit (Kitchenham et al., 2003) we will use the word "effort" and not "cost" throughout this chapter.

The remaining of this chapter is organised as follows: the next Section provides an introduction to Bayesian Networks, and revisits the diagram presented in Figure 1 in order to highlight the sequence of effort prediction steps that characterise this technique. This Section is followed by another two Sections presenting a brief literature review of Web effort estimation studies and discussing in more detail the use of Bayesian Networks for Web effort estimation, respectively. Finally, our last two Sections provide a case study detailing the development of a real Web effort estimation Bayesian Model, and the conclusions to this Chapter, respectively.

WEB EFFORT ESTIMATION LITERATURE REVIEW

There have been numerous attempts to model effort estimation for Web projects, but, except for (Mendes, 2007a; 2007b; 2007c), none have used a probabilistic model beyond the use of a single probability distribution. Table 1 presents a summary of previous studies. Whenever two or more studies compare different effort estimation techniques using the same dataset, we only include the study that uses the greatest number of effort estimation techniques.

Mendes and Counsell (2000) were the first to empirically investigate Web effort prediction. They estimated effort using machine-learning techniques with data from student-based Web projects, and size measures harvested late in the project's life cycle. Mendes and collaborators also carried out a series of consecutive studies (Fewster & Mendes, 2001; Mendes & Kitchenham, 2004; Mendes & Counsell, 2000; Mendes & Mosley, 2002; Mendes et al., 2001; Mendes et al., 2002a; 2002b; 2002c; 2003a; 2003b; 2005a; 2005b) where models were built using multivariate regression and machine-learning techniques using data on student-based and industrial Web projects. Recently Mendes (2007a, 2007b, 2007c, 2008) and Mendes and Mosley (2008) investigated the use

Table 1. Summary Literature Review (adapted from Mendes, 2007a)

Study	Type	# datasets - (# datapoints)	Subjects	Size Measures	Prediction techniques	Measure Prediction Accuracy
1st (Mendes & Counsell, 2000)	Case study	2 - (29 and 41)	2nd year Computer Science students	Page Count, Reused Page Count, Connectivity, Compactness, Stratum, Structure	Case based reasoning, Linear regression, Stepwise regression	MMRE
2nd (Reifer, 2002)	Not detailed	1 - (46)	professionals	Web objects	WEBMO (parameters generated using linear regression)	Pred(n)
3rd (Mendes et al., 2001)	Case study	1 - (37)	Honours and postgraduate Computer Science students	Length size, Reusability, Complexity, Size	Linear regression Stepwise regression	MMRE
4th (Fewster & Mendes, 2001)	Case study	1 - (37)	Honours and postgraduate Computer Science students	Structure metrics, Complexity metrics, Reuse metrics, Size metrics	Generalised Linear Model	Goodness of fit
5th (Mendes et al., 2002a)	Case study	1 - (25)	Honours and postgraduate Computer Science students	Requirements and Design measures, Application measures	Case-based reasoning	MMRE, MdMRE, Pred(25), Boxplots of absolute residuals
6th (Mendes et al., 2002b)	Case study	1 - (37)	Honours and postgraduate Computer Science students	Page Count, Media Count, Program Count, Reused Media Count, Reused Program Count, Connectivity Density, Total Page Complexity	Case-based reasoning, Linear regression, Stepwise regression, Classification and Regression Trees	MMRE, MdMRE, Pred(25), Boxplots of absolute residuals
7th (Ruhe et al., 2003)	Case study	1 - (12)	professionals	Web Objects	COBRA, Expert opinion, Linear regression	MMRE, Pred(25), Boxplots of absolute residuals
8th (Mendes et al., 2003)	Case study	2 - (37 and 25)	Honours and postgraduate CS students	Page Count, Media Count, Program Count, Reused Media Count (only one dataset), Reused Program Count (only one dataset), Connectivity Density, Total Page Complexity	Case-based reasoning	MMRE, Pred(25), Boxplots of absolute residuals

Table 1. (continued)

Study	Type	# datasets - (# datapoints)	Subjects	Size Measures	Prediction techniques	Measure Prediction Accuracy
9th (Baresi et al. 2003)	Formal experiment	1 - (30)	Computer Science students	Information, Navigation and Presentation model measures	Ordinary least squares regression	-
10th (Mangia & Paiano, 2003)	Not detailed	unknown	unknown	Functional, Navigational Structures, Publishing and Multimedia sizing measures	An exponential model named Metrics Model for Web Applications (MMWA)	-
11th (Costagliola et al., 2006)	Case study	1 – (15)	professionals	Web pages, New Web pages, Multimedia elements, New multimedia elements, Client side Scripts and Applications, Server side Scripts and Applications, All the elements that are part of the Web Objects size measure	Linear regression, Stepwise regression, Case-based reasoning, Classification and Regression Trees	MMRE, MdMRE, Pred(25), Boxplots of residuals, boxplots of z
12th (Mendes, 2007a; 2007b; 2007c)	Case study	1 – (150)	professionals	Total Web pages, New Web pages, Total Images, New Images, Features off-the-shelf (Fots), High & Low effort Fots-Adapted, High & Low effort New Features, Total High & Low Effort Features	Bayesian Networks, Stepwise Regression, Mean and Median effort, Case-based reasoning, Classification and regression Trees	MMRE, MdMRE, MEMRE, MdEMRE, Pred(25), Boxplots of residuals, boxplots of z
13th (Mendes, 2008)	Case study	1 – (195)	professionals	Total Web pages, New Web pages, Total Images, New Images, Features off-the-shelf (Fots), High & Low effort Fots-Adapted, High & Low effort New Features, Total High & Low Effort Features	Bayesian Networks, Stepwise Regression, Mean and Median effort,	MMRE, MdMRE, MEMRE, MdEMRE, Pred(25), Boxplots of residuals, boxplots of z
14th (Mendes and Mosley, 2008)	Case study	1 – (195)	professionals	Total Web pages, New Web pages, Total Images, New Images, Features off-the-shelf (Fots), High & Low effort Fots-Adapted, High & Low effort New Features, Total High & Low Effort Features	Bayesian Networks, Stepwise Regression, Mean and Median effort,	MMRE, MdMRE, MEMRE, MdEMRE, Pred(25), Boxplots of residuals, boxplots of z

Figure 2. A small Bayesian Network and three NPTs

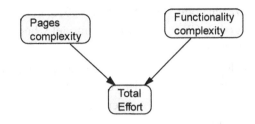

Pages complexity		
Low	*Medium*	*High*
0.2	0.3	0.5

Functionality complexity	
Low	*High*
0.1	0.9

Total Effort (Low, Medium, High)				
Pages complexity	**Functionality complexity**	*Low*	*Medium*	*High*
Low	*Low*	0.7	0.2	0.1
Low	*High*	0.2	0.6	0.2
Medium	*Low*	0.1	0.7	0.2
Medium	*High*	0	0.5	0.5
High	*Low*	0.2	0.6	0.2
High	*High*	0	0.1	0.9

of Bayesian Networks for Web effort estimation, using data on industrial Web projects from the Tukutuku database.

Other researchers have also investigated effort estimation for Web projects: Reifer (2000; 2002) proposed an extension of the COCOMO model, and a single size measure harvested late in the project's life cycle. None were validated empirically. This size measure was later used by Ruhe et al. (2003), who further extended a software engineering hybrid estimation technique, named CoBRA© (Briand et al., 1998), to Web projects, using a small data set of industrial projects, mixing expert judgement and multivariate regression. Later, Baresi et al. (2003), and Mangia and Paiano (2003) investigated effort estimation models and size measures for Web projects based on a specific Web development method, namely the W2000. Finally, Costagliola et al. (2006) compared two sets of existing Web-based size measures for effort estimation.

Table 1 shows that most Web effort estimation studies to date used data on student-based projects; estimates obtained by applying Stepwise regression or Case-based reasoning techniques; accuracy measured using the Mean Magnitude of Relative Error (MMRE), followed by the Median Magnitude of Relative Error (MdMRE) and Prediction at 25% (Pred(25)) (Mendes et al., 2003b).

INTRODUCTION TO BAYESIAN NETWORKS

A Bayesian Network (BN) is a model that supports reasoning with uncertainty due to the way in which it incorporates existing knowledge of a complex domain (Pearl, 1988). This knowledge is represented using two parts. The first, the qualitative part, represents the structure of a BN as depicted by a directed acyclic graph (digraph) (see Figure 2). The digraph's nodes represent the relevant variables (factors) in the domain being modelled, which can be of different types (e.g. observable or latent, categorical). The digraph's arcs represent the causal relationships between variables, where relationships are quantified probabilistically (Pearl, 1988).

The second, the quantitative part, associates a conditional probability table (CPT) to each node, its probability distribution. A parent node's CPT describes the relative probability of each state (value) (Figure 2, nodes 'Pages complexity' and 'Functionality complexity'); a child node's NPT describes the relative probability of each state conditional on every combination of states of its parents (Figure 2, node 'Total Effort'). So, for example, the relative probability of 'Total Effort' being 'Low' conditional on 'Pages complexity' and 'Functionality complexity' being both 'Low' is 0.7. Each row in a CPT represents a conditional probability distribution and therefore its values sum up to 1 (Pearl, 1988). Formally, the posterior distribution of the Bayesian Network is based on Bayes' rule (Pearl, 1988):

$$p(X \mid E) = \frac{p(E \mid X)p(X)}{p(E)} \tag{1}$$

where:

$p(X \mid E)$ is called the posterior distribution and represents the probability of X given evidence E;

$p(X)$ is called the prior distribution and represents the probability of X before evidence E is given;

$p(E \mid X)$ is called the likelihood function and denotes the probability of E assuming X is true.

Once a BN is specified, evidence (e.g. values) can be entered into any node, and probabilities for the remaining nodes automatically calculated using Bayes' rule (Pearl, 1988). Therefore BNs can be used for different types of reasoning, such as predictive, diagnostic, and "what-if" analyses to investigate the impact that changes on some nodes have on others (Stamelos et al., 2003).

Bayesian Networks have only recently been used for Web effort estimation (Mendes, 2007a;

2007b; 2007c; 2008; Mendes and Mosley, 2008). Mendes (2007a, 2007b, 2007c) built a single hybrid BN model where the BN's causal structure was based on feedback (expert opinion) from a Web developer (domain expert) with more than 10 years of Web development and management experience, and the CPTs' probabilities were learnt using data on past Web projects from the Tukutuku database (Mendes et al. 2005a). The expert-based BN structure is shown in Figure 3. Results showed that the predictions obtained using this hybrid BN model were superior to those obtained using other effort estimation techniques such as Stepwise Regression Analysis, Case-based reasoning, Classification and Regression Trees, and mean- and median-based models. However, results have been mixed. Mendes and Mosley (2008) and Mendes (2008) built eight and four different BN models, respectively, and found that their predictions were always significantly worse than predictions obtained using stepwise regression. One reason for these results could be that the BN causal structures were not reduced taking into account the correlations between factors and effort. Another reason could be the relatively small dataset used, which does not provide enough data to account for many of the combinations of parents' states in regard to effort.

The description of the all variables used in the BN model presented in Figure 3 is provided in Table 2.

It is our view that BNs provide more flexibility than any of the techniques used to date for Web effort estimation (regression analysis, case-based reasoning, classification & regression trees), due to the following reasons:

- A BN model, i.e. a BN causal structure and its CPTs, can be automatically built from data (data-driven model). The downside is that this choice requires a reasonable number of project data in order to derive as many of the CPTs' probabilities as possible.

Figure 3. A real Bayesian Network Structure

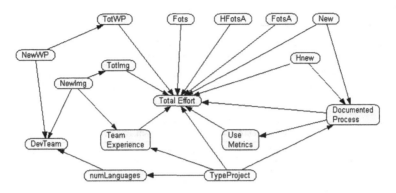

- A BN causal structure and its CPTs can be elicited from a combination of data and feedback from Domain Experts (hybrid model). A Domain Expert within this context can be one or more Web developers, and/or one or more Web project managers who have expertise in effort estimation.
- A BN causal structure and its CPTs can be completely elicited from Domain Experts (expert-driven model).

This means that if a Web company has only a small amount of past data on finished Web proj-

ects, it can either build a hybrid or expert-driven model. The sequence of steps part of an estimation process (see Figure 4) that is followed when applying BNs is as follows:

1. Past data and/or knowledge of past finished projects is used to build a BN model (Step 1).
2. A BN model is built based on the past data and/or expertise obtained in a) (Step 2).
3. Evidence is entered on some of the nodes that are part of the model created in b). Such evidence corresponds to values/categories

Figure 4. Steps used to obtain an effort estimate using a BN model

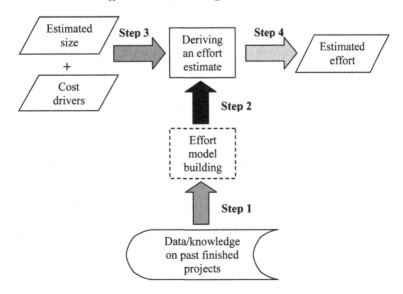

Table 2. Variables used in Figure 3

Variable Name	Scale	Description
Project data		
TypeProject	Categorical	Type of project (new or enhancement).
numLanguages	Ratio	Number of different development languages used
Documented Process	Categorical	If project followed defined and documented process.
Use Metrics	Categorical	If project team part of a software metrics programme.
DevTeam	Ratio	Size of a project's development team.
Team Experience	Ratio	Average team experience with the development language(s) employed.
Total Effort	Ratio	Actual total effort in person hours used to develop a Web application.
Web application		
TotWP	Ratio	Total number of Web pages (new and reused).
NewWP	Ratio	Total number of new Web pages.
TotImg	Ratio	Total number of images (new and reused).
NewImg	Ratio	Total number of new images created.
Fots	Ratio	Number of features reused without any adaptation.
HFotsA	Ratio	Number of reused high-effort features/functions adapted.
Hnew	Ratio	Number of new high-effort features/functions.
FotsA	Ratio	Number of reused low-effort features adapted.
New	Ratio	Number of new low-effort features/functions.

for the estimated size and cost drivers relative to the new project to which effort is to be estimated (Step 3).

4. The model generates a set of probabilities associated with each of the effort states (Step 4).

In the case of BNs, the estimated effort will have an associated probability distribution over a set of states. So assuming that estimated effort was measured using two states – high and low, the BN model will provide the probability that estimated effort will be high, and the probability the estimated effort will be low.

There are techniques that can be used in order to obtain estimated effort as a discrete value; however they are outside the scope of this chapter. Interested readers, please refer to (Mendes, 2007a).

HOW TO BUILD A WEB EFFORT MODEL USING BAYESIAN NETWORKS

Section introduces the process model that we employ to build BNs. This process is an adaptation of the Knowledge Engineering of Bayesian Networks (KEBN) process (Woodberry et al., 2004), and presented in Figure 5.

In Figure 5 arrows represent flows through the different tasks, which are depicted by rectangles. Such tasks are executed either by people – the Knowledge Engineer (KE) and the Domain Experts (DEs) (light colour rectangles), or automatic algorithms (dark grey rectangles). Dark grey cornered rectangles represent tasks that can be done either automatically, manually, or using a combination of both.

The three main steps part of the KEBN process are the Structural Development, Parameter

Figure 5. KEBN, adapted from (Woodberry et al., 2004)

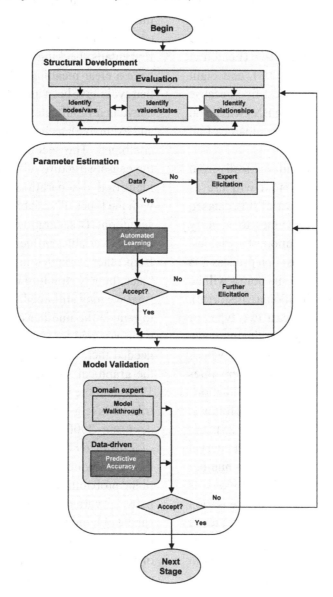

Estimation, and Model Validation. The KEBN process iterates over these steps until a complete BN is built and validated. Each of these steps is described below, and as they are explained we also provide our views on how to apply this process when building BNs solely from data; from data and domain experts; solely from domain experts:

Structural Development: Entails the creation of the BN's graphical structure (causal graph) containing nodes (variables) and causal relation-

ships. These can be identified by DEs, directly from data, or using a combination of both.

In addition to identifying variables, their types (e.g. query variable, evidence variable) and relationships, domain experts in general also choose what states (values) each variable should take, and if they are discrete or continuous. In practice, however, currently available BN tools require that continuous variables be discretised, therefore numerical variables are converted into multinomial variables. There are no strict rules as to how many discrete approximations should be used. Some studies have employed three (Pendharkar et al. 2005), others five (Fenton et al., 2004), seven (Bibi et al. 2003), and eight (Stamelos et al. 2003). We suggest five because anecdotal evidence from eliciting BNs with local Web companies has shown that companies find three to five categories sufficient.

When building a structure automatically from existing data (dataset), a BN tool will use as nodes the variables that are part of this dataset, and will use variables' data values to identify possible causal relationships amongst variables. In addition, during the discretisation process it is also important to specify how data points will be allocated to discrete approximations (categories). In general BN tools offer at least two types of discretisation algorithms – equal-width intervals, whereby all intervals have an equal range of values (e.g. a numerical variable contains integer values ranging from 0 to 25; five discrete approximations being used, thus intervals are organised as follows: 0 to 5, 6 to 10, 11 to 15, 16 to 20, 21 to 25); and equal-frequency intervals, whereby each interval contains n/N data points where n is the number of data points and N is the number of intervals (this is also called maximal entropy discretisation (Wong and Chiu, 1987)). Existing evidence tends to suggest the use of equal-frequency intervals (Knobbe and Ho, 2005). Once the BN causal structure has been learnt from data, the knowledge engineer can at this point also use this structure as basis for discussion with a domain expert, and the modified structure is the one used later for automated learning (see next).

When the BN causal graph is being built solely based on the Domain expert's knowledge, there are techniques available that can help minimise the elicitation process. We point the reader to the following reference for a good overview of such techniques (van der Gaag et al., 1999).

It is also important that throughout the Structural Development step the knowledge engineer evaluates the structure of the BN in two stages. The first entails checking if: variables and their values have a clear meaning; all relevant variables for that cycle have been included; variables are named conveniently; all states are appropriate (exhaustive and exclusive); a check for any states that can be combined. The second stage entails reviewing the causal structure of the BN to make sure any identified d-separation dependencies comply with the types of variables used and causality assumptions. D-separation dependencies are used to identify variables influenced by evidence coming from other variables in the BN (Jensen, 1996). Once the BN structure is assumed to be close to final we may still need to optimise this structure to reduce the number of probabilities that need to be assessed for the network. If optimisation is needed then we employ techniques that change the graphical structure (e.g. divorcing (Jensen, 1996) and the use of parametric probability distributions (e.g. noisy-OR gates (Druzdzel & van der Gaag, 2000).

Parameter Estimation: Represents the quantitative component of a BN, which results in conditional probabilities that quantify the relationships between variables (Jensen, 1996). Probabilities can be obtained via Expert Elicitation, automatically (Automated learning), or using a combination of both. When probabilities are obtained automatically we also encourage readers to ask a domain expert to revisit the priors obtained by automatic means given that the dataset used may not be large enough, or may not represent accurately the current evidence in a domain.

Model Validation: This step validates the BN constructed from the two previous steps, and determines the necessity to re-visit any of those steps. Two different validation methods are generally used - Model Walkthrough and Predictive Accuracy (Woodberry et al., 2004). Both verify

Table 3. Tukutuku Variables (adapted from Mendes et al., 2005a)

	Variable Name	Description
Project Data	*TypeProj*	Type of project (new or enhancement).
	nLang	Number of different development languages used
	DocProc	If project followed defined and documented process.
	ProImpr	If project team involved in a process improvement programme.
	Metrics	If project team part of a software metrics programme.
	DevTeam	Size of a project's development team.
	TeamExp	Average team experience with the development language(s) employed.
Web application	*TotWP*	Total number of Web pages (new and reused).
	NewWP	Total number of new Web pages.
	TotImg	Total number of images (new and reused).
	NewImg	Total number of new images created.
	Fots	Number of features reused without any adaptation.
	HFotsA	Number of reused high-effort features/functions adapted.
	Hnew	Number of new high-effort features/functions.
	TotHigh	Total number of high-effort features/functions
	FotsA	Number of reused low-effort features adapted.
	New	Number of new low-effort features/functions.
	TotNHigh	Total number of low-effort features/functions

if predictions provided by a BN are on average, better than those currently obtained by a DE. Predictive Accuracy is normally carried out using quantitative data, where existing data from the domain being modelled is used.

Model walkthrough represents the use of real case scenarios that are prepared and used by a DE to assess if the predictions provided by a BN correspond to the predictions (s)he would have chosen based on his/her own expertise. In addition, real case scenarios can also be obtained using domain data that is available. Success is measured by the frequency with which the BN's predicted value with the highest probability for a target variable (e.g. total effort) corresponds to the DE's own assessment, or the actual value if using domain data. If there is a mismatch then this means that some of the probabilities need to be revisited.

Model Validation is a very important process since it is used to check to what extent the model

and probabilities provided are capturing the patterns in the domain. Once a BN model has been validated and is in use by a Company it is good practice to regularly contact the company to check whether the model needs further calibration (validation).

Figure 6. Medical example, adapted from Jensen (1996)

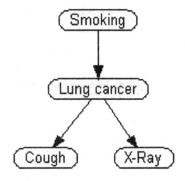

Figure 7. First BN Causal Model for the Web Effort BN model

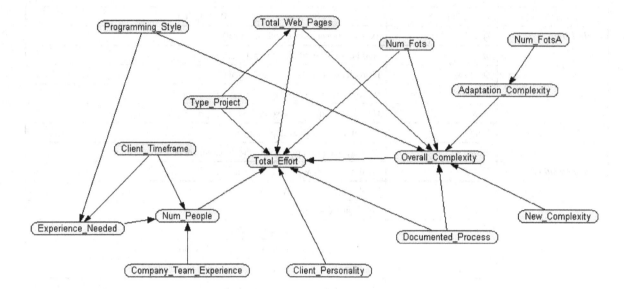

A CASE STUDY BUILDING A REAL WEB EFFORT MODEL USING BAYESIAN NETWORKS

This Section describes a case study where a real Web effort estimation model was built using Bayesian Networks. In order to do so, we revisit the adapted KEBN process (see Figure 5), detailing the tasks carried out for each of the three main steps that form part of that process. Before starting the elicitation of the Web effort BN model, the Domain Expert (DE) participating was presented with an overview of Bayesian Network models, and examples of "what-if" scenarios using a made-up BN. This, we believe, facilitated the entire process as the use of an example, and the brief explanation of each of the steps in the KEBN process, provide a concrete understanding of what to expect. We also made it clear that the knowledge Engineers were facilitators of the process, and that the Web company's commitment was paramount for the success of the process. The entire process took 18 hours to be completed, corresponding to 36 person hours in six 3-hour slots.

The DE who took part in this case study is the project manager (and owner) of a well-established Web company in Auckland (New Zealand). The company has one project manager, two developers employed by the company, and several subcontractors. The project manager has worked in Web development for more than 10 years, and his company develops a wide range of Web applications, from static & multimedia-like to very large e-commerce solutions. They also use a wide range of Web technologies, thus enabling the development of Web 2.0 applications. Previous to using the BN model created, the effort estimates provided to clients would deviate from actual effort within the range of 10% to 40%.

Detailed Structural Development and Parameter Estimation

In order to identify the fundamental factors that the DE took into account when preparing a project quote we used the set of variables from the Tukutuku dataset (Mendes et al., 2005a) as a starting point. We first sketched them out on a white board, each one inside an oval shape, and then explained what each one meant within the

Figure 8. A new version of the BN causal model for the Web Effort BN model

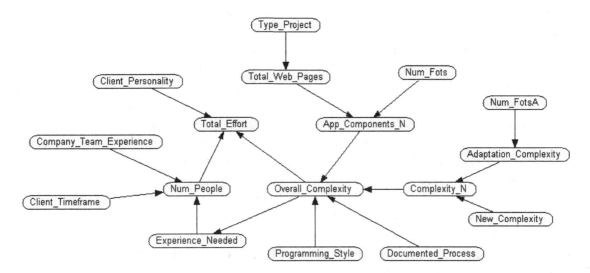

context of the Tukutuku project. Our previous experience eliciting BNs in other domains (e.g. ecology) suggested that it was best to start with a few factors (even if they were not to be reused by the DE), rather than to use a "blank canvas" as a starting point. The set of Tukutuku variables used are detailed in Table 3, below. Table 3 presents a superset of the variables already introduced in

Table 2.

Within the context of the Tukutuku project, a new high-effort feature/function requires at least 15 hours to be developed by one experienced developer, and a high-effort adapted feature/ function requires at least 4 hours to be adapted by one experienced developer. These values are based on collected data.

Figure 9. Final version of the Web Effort BN model

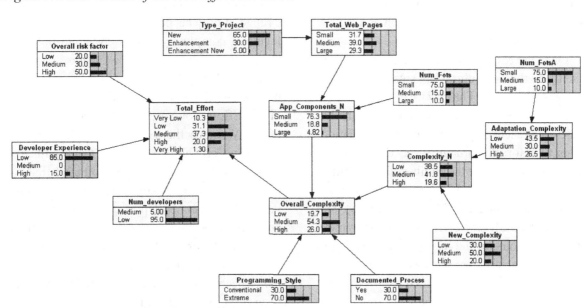

Once the Tukutuku variables had been sketched out and explained, the next step was to remove all variables that were not relevant for the DE, followed by adding to the white board any additional variables (factors) suggested by the DE. We also documented descriptions for each of the factors suggested.

Next, we identified the states that each factor would take. All states were discrete. Whenever a factor represented a measure of effort (e.g. Total effort), we also documented the effort range corresponding to each state, to avoid any future ambiguity. For example, 'very low' Total effort corresponded to 0+ to 8 person hours, etc.

Once all states were identified and documented, it was time to elicit the cause and effect relationships. As a starting point to this task we used a simple medical example from [10], and showed in Figure 6.

This example clearly introduces one of the important points to consider when identifying cause and effect relationships – timeline of events. If smoking is to be a cause of lunch cancer, it is important that the cause precedes the effect. This may sound obvious with regard to the example used; however, it is our view that the use of this simple example significantly helped the DE understand the notion of cause and effect, and how this related to Web effort estimation and the BN being elicited.

Once the cause and effect relationships were identified the Web effort BN's causal structure was as follows (see Figure 7):

Nodes 'Total effort' and 'Overall Complexity' were each reached by a large number of relationships; therefore this structure needed to be simplified in order to reduce the number of probabilities to be elicited. New nodes were suggested by the KE (names ending in '_N', see Figure 8), and validated by the DE. The DE also made a few more changes to some of the relationships, leading to the BN causal structure presented in Figure 8.

At this point the DE seemed happy with the BN's causal structure and the work on eliciting

the probabilities was initiated. All probabilities were created from scratch, a very time consuming task.

While entering the probabilities, the DE decided to re-visit the BN's causal structure; therefore a new iteration of the Structural Development step took place. The final BN causal structure is shown in Figure 9. Here we present the BN using belief bars rather than labelled factors, so readers can see the probabilities that were elicited. Note that this BN corresponds to the current model being used by the Web company, which was also validated, to be detailed next.

Detailed Model Validation

Both Model walkthrough and Predictive accuracy were used to validate the Web Effort BN model, where the former was the first type of validation to be employed. The DE used four different scenarios to check whether the node Total_effort would provide the highest probability to the effort state that corresponded to the DE's own suggestion. All scenarios were run successfully; however it was also necessary to use data from past projects, for which total effort was known, in order to check the model's calibration. A validation set containing data on eight projects was used. The DE selected a range of projects presenting different sizes and levels of complexity: four were small projects; three were medium and one was large.

For each project, evidence was entered in the model, and the highest probability provided for 'Total Effort' compared to that project's actual effort. Whenever there was a mismatch this meant that some probabilities needed to be adjusted. In order to know which nodes to target first we used a Sensitivity Analysis report, which provided the effect of each parent node upon a given query node. Within our context, the query node was 'Total Effort'. Whenever probabilities were adjusted, we re-entered the evidence for each of the projects in the validation set that had already been used in the validation step. This was done to ensure that each calibration would always be an improved upon the previous one. Once all eight projects were used to calibrate the model the Validation step was assumed to be complete, a decision made by the DE.

This BN model has been in production since the second semester 2008 and has been successfully used to estimate effort on four projects, ranging from medium to large. We believe that the successful development of the Web effort BN model was greatly influenced by the commitment of the company, and also by the detailed and the DE's very good knowledge and experience on estimating effort.

CONCLUSION

Effort estimation is the process by which a company estimates early on in the development life cycle the amount of effort needed to complete a Web development project on time and within budget. There are numerous challenges to providing a sound effort estimate, some of which were discussed in this chapter.

In addition, one of the techniques used for Web effort estimation – Bayesian Networks, was introduced, presenting our view on the process to be used when building a Bayesian Network for Web effort estimation and a real industrial case study described. Finally, a literature survey of previous Web effort estimation studies was also presented.

REFERENCES

Angelis, L., & Stamelos, I. (2000). A Simulation Tool for Efficient Analogy Based Cost Estimation. *Empirical Software Engineering, 5*, 35–68. doi:10.1023/A:1009897800559

Baresi, L., Morasca, S., & Paolini, P. (2003). Estimating the design effort of Web applications, In *Proceedings Ninth International Software Measures Symposium*, September 3-5, (pp. 62-72).

Bibi, S., Stamelos, L., & Angelis, L. (2003) Bayesian Belief Networks as a Software Productivity Estimation Tool. In *Proceedings 1st Balkan Conference in Informatics, Thessaloniki.*

Briand, L. C., El Emam, K., & Bomarius, F. (1998). COBRA: A Hybrid Method for Software Cost Estimation, Benchmarking and Risk Assessment. In *Proceedings of the 20th International Conference on Software Engineering*, 1998, (pp. 390-399).

Briand, L. C., El-Emam, K., Surmann, D., Wieczorek, I., & Maxwell, K. D. (1999). An Assessment and Comparison of Common Cost Estimation Modeling Techniques. In *Proceedings of ICSE 1999*, Los Angeles, CA, (pp. 313-322).

Brieman, L., Friedman, J., Olshen, R., & Stone, C. (1984). *Classification and Regression Trees.* Belmont, CA: Wadsworth.

Costagliola, G., Di Martino, S., Ferrucci, F., Gravino, C., Tortora, G., & Vitiello, G. (2006). Effort estimation modeling techniques: a case study for web applications, In *Proceedings of the Intl. Conference on Web Engineering* (ICWE'06), (pp. 9-16).

Druzdzel, M. J., & van der Gaag, L. C. (2000). Building Probabilistic Networks: Where Do the Numbers Come From? *IEEE Transactions on Knowledge and Data Engineering, 12*(4), 481–486. doi:10.1109/TKDE.2000.868901

Fenton, N., Marsh, W., Neil, M., Cates, P., Forey, S., & Tailor, M. (2004). Making Resource Decisions for Software Projects. In Proceedings of ICSE, 04, 397–406.

Fewster, R. M., & Mendes, E. (2001). Measurement, Prediction and Risk Analysis for Web Applications. In *Proceedings of the IEEE METRICS Symposium,* (pp. 338-348).

Jeffery, R., Ruhe, M., & Wieczorek, I. (2001). Using Public Domain Metrics to Estimate Software Development Effort. In *Proceedings of the 7th IEEE Metrics Symposium*, London, (pp. 16-27).

Jensen, F. V. (1996). *An introduction to Bayesian networks*. London: UCL Press.

Kadoda, G., Cartwright, M., Chen, L., & Shepperd, M. J. (2000). Experiences Using Case-Based Reasoning to Predict Software Project Effort. In *Proceedings of the EASE 2000 Conference,* Keele, UK.

Kitchenham, B. A., Pickard, L. M., Linkman, S., & Jones, P. (2003, June). Modelling Software Bidding Risks. *IEEE Transactions on Software Engineering*, *29*(6), 542–554. doi:10.1109/TSE.2003.1205181

Knobbe, A. J., & Ho, Y. E.K. (2005). Numbers in Multi-Relational Data Mining, In: Proceedings of PKDD 2005, Portugal

Mangia, L., & Paiano, R. (2003). MMWA: A Software Sizing Model for Web Applications, In: Proceedings of the Fourth International Conference on Web Information Systems Engineering, (pp. 53-63).

Mendes, E. (2007a). Predicting Web Development Effort Using a Bayesian Network. In Proceedings of EASE, 07, 83–93.

Mendes, E. (2007b). The Use of a Bayesian Network for Web Effort Estimation. In *Proceedings of International Conference on Web Engineering*, (LNCS Vol. 4607, pp. 90-104). Berlin: Springer.

Mendes, E. (2007c). A Comparison of Techniques for Web Effort Estimation. In *Proceedings of the ACM/IEEE International Symposium on Empirical Software Engineering*, (pp. 334-343).

Mendes, E. (2007d). *Cost Estimation Techniques for Web Projects*. Hershey, PA: IGI Global.

Mendes, E. (2008). The Use of Bayesian Networks for Web Effort Estimation: Further Investigation. In *Proceedings of ICWE '08*, (pp. 2-3-216).

Mendes, E., & Counsell, S. (2000). Web Development Effort Estimation using Analogy. In *Proceedings of the 2000 Australian Software Engineering Conference*, (pp. 203-212).

Mendes, E., Counsell, S., & Mosley, N. (2000). Measurement and Effort Prediction of Web Applications. In *Proceedings of 2nd ICSE Workshop on Web Engineering,* June, Limerick, Ireland, (pp. 57-74).

Mendes, E., & Kitchenham, B. A. (2004). Further Comparison of Cross-company and Within-company Effort Estimation Models for Web Applications. In *Proceedings IEEE Metrics Symposium,* (pp. 348-357).

Mendes, E., & Mosley, N. (2002). Further Investigation into the Use of CBR and Stepwise Regression to Predict Development Effort for Web Hypermedia Applications. In *Proceedings ACM/IEEE ISESE*, Nara, Japan, (pp. 79-90).

Mendes, E., & Mosley, N. (2008). Bayesian Network Models for Web Effort Prediction: a Comparative Study. In *Transactions on Software Engineering*, (Accepted for publication).

Mendes, E., Mosley, N., & Counsell, S. (2001). Web Measures – Estimating Design and Authoring Effort. *IEEE Multimedia Special Issue on Web Engineering*, *8*(1), 50–57.

Mendes, E., Mosley, N., & Counsell, S. (2002a). The Application of Case-based Reasoning to Early Web Project Cost Estimation. In *Proceedings of IEEE COMPSAC*, (pp. 393-398).

Mendes, E., Mosley, N., & Counsell, S. (2002c, June). Comparison of Length, complexity and functionality as size measures for predicting Web design and authoring effort. *IEEE Proc. Software, 149*(3), 86–92. doi:10.1049/ip-sen:20020337

Mendes, E., Mosley, N., & Counsell, S. (2003a). Do Adaptation Rules Improve Web Cost Estimation? In *Proceedings of the ACM Hypertext conference 2003*, Nottingham, UK, (pp. 173-183).

Mendes, E., Mosley, N., & Counsell, S. (2003b). A Replicated Assessment of the Use of Adaptation Rules to Improve Web Cost Estimation. In *Proceedings of the ACM and IEEE International Symposium on Empirical Software Engineering*, Rome, Italy, (pp. 100-109).

Mendes, E., Mosley, N., & Counsell, S. (2005a). Investigating Web Size Metrics for Early Web Cost Estimation. *Journal of Systems and Software, 77*(2), 157–172. doi:10.1016/j.jss.2004.08.034

Mendes, E., Mosley, N., & Counsell, S. (2005b) The Need for Web Engineering: an Introduction, Web Engineering. In E. Mendes, & N. Mosley, (Eds.) *Web Engineering: Theory and Practice of Metrics and Measurement for Web Development*, (pp. 1-26). Berlin: Springer-Verlag

Mendes, E., Watson, I., Triggs, C., Mosley, N., & Counsell, S. (2002b). A Comparison of Development Effort Estimation Techniques for Web Hypermedia Applications. In *Proceedings IEEE Metrics Symposium*, June, Ottawa, Canada, (pp. 141-151).

Mendes, E., Watson, I., Triggs, C., Mosley, N., & Counsell, S. (2003c). A Comparative Study of Cost Estimation Models for Web Hypermedia Applications. *Empirical Software Engineering Journal, 8*(2), 163–196. doi:10.1023/A:1023062629183

Pearl, J. (1988). *Probabilistic Reasoning in Intelligent Systems*. San Mateo, CA: Morgan Kaufmann

Pendharkar, P. C., Subramanian, G. H., & Rodger, J. A. (2005). A Probabilistic Model for Predicting Software Development Effort. *IEEE Transactions on Software Engineering, 31*(7), 615–624. doi:10.1109/TSE.2005.75

Reifer, D. J. (2000). Web development: estimating quick-to-market software. *IEEE Software, 17*(6), 57–64. doi:10.1109/52.895169

Reifer, D. J. (2002). Ten deadly risks in Internet and intranet software development. *IEEE Software*, (2): 12–14. doi:10.1109/52.991324

Ruhe, M., Jeffery, R., & Wieczorek, I. (2003) Cost Estimation for Web Applications. In *Proceedings of ICSE 2003*, Portland, OR, (pp. 285-294).

Schofield, C. (1998). An empirical investigation into software estimation by analogy. Unpublished Doctoral Dissertation, Dept. of Computing, Bournemouth University, Bournemouth, UK.

Selby, R. W., & Porter, A. A. (1988). Learning from examples: generation and evaluation of decision trees for software resource analysis. *IEEE Transactions on Software Engineering, 14*(12), 1743–1757. doi:10.1109/32.9061

Shepperd, M. J., & Kadoda, G. (2001). Using Simulation to Evaluate Prediction Techniques. In *Proceedings of the IEEE 7th International Software Metrics Symposium*, London, UK, (pp. 349-358).

Stamelos, I., Angelis, L., Dimou, P., & Sakellaris, E. (2003, January 1). On the use of Bayesian belief networks for the prediction of software productivity. *Information and Software Technology, 45*(1), 51–60. doi:10.1016/S0950-5849(02)00163-5 van der Gaag, L. C., Renooij, S., Witteman, C. L. M., Aleman, B. M. P., & Taal, B. G. (1999) How to Elicit Many Probabilities. In *Proceedings UCAI,* (pp. 647-654). San Francisco: Morgan Kaufmann

Wong, A. K. C., & Chiu, D. K. Y. (1987). Synthesizing Statistical Knowledge from Incomplete Mixed-mode Data. *IEEE Transactions on Pattern Analysis and Machine Intelligence, PAMI-9*(6), 796–805. doi:10.1109/TPAMI.1987.4767986

Woodberry, O., Nicholson, A., Korb, K., & Pollino, C. (2004). Parameterising Bayesian Networks. In *Proceedings of the Australian Conference on Artificial Intelligence*, (pp. 1101-1107).

Chapter 3
Optimizing Software Development Cost Estimates using Multi–Objective Particle Swarm Optimization

Tad Gonsalves
Sophia University, Japan

Kei Yamagishi
Sophia University, Japan

Ryo Kawabata
Sophia University, Japan

Kiyoshi Itoh
Sophia University, Japan

ABSTRACT

Software development projects are notorious for being completed behind schedule and over budget and for often failing to meet user requirements. A myriad of cost estimation models have been proposed to predict development costs early in the lifecycle with the hope of managing the project well within time and budget. However, studies have reported rather high error rates of prediction even in the case of the well-established and widely acknowledged models. This study focuses on the improvement and fine-tuning of the COCOMO 81 model. Although this model is based on software development practices that were prevalent in the 80s, its wide use in industry and academia, the simple form of the parametric equations and the availability of the data in an online repository make it attractive as a test-bed for further research in software development cost estimation. In this study, we show how the recently developed Computational Intelligence techniques can effectively improve the prediction power of existing models. In particular, we focus on the adaptation of the Multi-Objective Particle Swarm Optimization (MOPSO) algorithm in simultaneously minimizing two objective functions – prediction error rate and model complexity. This provides the project manager with an opportunity to choose from a set of optimal solutions represented in a trade-off relationship on the Pareto front. Traditional search algorithms use

DOI: 10.4018/978-1-60566-758-4.ch003

knowledge of the terrain and expert heuristics to guide the search; such uses make them problem-specific and domain-dependent. The MOPSO meta-heuristic approach relies neither on the knowledge of the problem nor on the experts' heuristics, making its application wide and extensive.

INTRODUCTION

Every software development project is expected to meet at least the following three key goals. First, the developed software fulfills customers' needs. Second, the developed software is well engineered so that it allows smooth integration, maintenance, and further development. Third, the software is delivered on time. However, a lot of software is created in a hurry under unrealistic plans. Projects that commit themselves to unrealistic schedules run late and ship unfinished software with bad quality (Jaaksi, 2003). Software development projects are notorious for being completed behind schedule and over budget and for often failing to meet user requirements (Fox & Spence, 2005). According to recent statistics, roughly 50 percent of all IT projects fail to meet chief executives' expectations (Wysocki, 1998). The Standish Group reports that, in the year 2000, only 28 percent of all IT application development projects have succeeded, while 23 percent failed (cancelled before completion or never implemented) and 49 percent were challenged (completed but failed to achieve the project goals like cost, time or specifications) (Johnson, 2001). IT projects that go wildly over budget or drag on long past their scheduled completion have been called 'runaway projects" (Glass, 1998; Keil, Rai, Mann, & Zhang, 2003).

Delivering a software product on time, within budget, and with an agreed level of quality is a critical concern for software organizations. Underestimating software costs can have detrimental effects on the quality of the delivered software and thus on a company's business reputation and competitiveness. Overestimation of software cost, on the other hand, can result in missed opportunities to use funds in other projects (Briand, Langley, & Wieczorek, 2000). In response to the industry demand, software development organizations and project managers need accurate estimates during the early stages in the lifecycle of the project to allocate and manage the project resources properly. Expert judgment and algorithmic models have been the two dominant estimation methods practiced through the years. Although expert judgment is difficult to measure and quantify, it is found to be effective in estimating software development costs (Gray & MacDonell, 1997). Algorithmic (or parametric) models attempt to express the relationship between the project development effort and the project characteristics in the form of equations. Software size (measured as kilo lines of code, KLOC) is the most prominent characteristic in the estimation equations. Function points (Albrecht & Gaffney, 1983), SLIM (Putnam, 1978), PRICE-S (Jensen, 1983), COCOMO 81 (Boehm, 1981) and COCOMO II (Boehm et al., 2001) are some of the well-known cost estimation algorithmic models.

The algorithmic as well as the non-algorithmic (based on expert judgment) cost estimation models, however, are not without errors. In the research conducted by the Standish group in 2001 (Standish Group Report, 2001), it is reported that 53% of the US software projects ran over 189% of the original estimate. COCOMO is a well-established and widely acknowledged software cost estimation model. By plugging in the carefully measured cost drivers, one would expect this handy "off the shelf model" to deliver a fairly accurate cost estimate for a new project. Unfortunately, there is considerable evidence that this off the shelf approach is not always successful. Kemerer (1987),

Kitchanham & Taylor (1984) and Miyazaki & Mori (1985) have reported rather high errors in off the shelf application of the COCOMO model.

In recent years, a number of studies including the application of Artificial Intelligence (AI) have been devoted to the refinement of the cost estimation models. Feature subset selection using machine learning and data mining (Chen, Menzies, Port, & Boehm, 2005b; Kohavi & John, 1997), neural networks (Smith & Mason, 1997) and Genetic Algorithm (Yang & Honavar, 1998) are some of the AI techniques in use. The inventor of the COCOMO model, Boehm, together with co-workers, has suggested a way of refining CO-COMO estimates by using the Wrapper method of data mining (Chen, Menzies, Port, & Boehm, 2005a). Although advanced AI techniques have been successfully applied to diverse engineering fields, very few studies dealing with the application of AI to software cost estimation are found in the literature. As pointed out above, data mining is one of the very few AI research areas applied to software development. Many experts have suggested that it is appropriate to use more than one method when predicting software development effort. We believe the application of AI will not only solve complex problems in software development but will also bring fresh and new insights into the field.

AI itself has undergone dramatic changes in its five-decade history. Traditional AI is witnessing the emergence of a new discipline called "Computational Intelligence", comprising neural networks, fuzzy systems and evolutionary computation (Konar, 2005). Neural networks solve complex problems by emulating the brain's learning process; fuzzy logic can process inexact and ambiguous information and is routinely used in control systems and decision-making tasks; evolutionary computation including swarm intelligence tackles combinatorial optimization problems by iteratively evolving the problem solving strategy. In the words of Zadeh (1994), "the difference between traditional artificial intelligence and computational intelligence is that AI is based on hard computing whereas CI is based on soft computing". Combinations of the new computational intelligence tools among themselves as well as with more traditional approaches, such as statistical analysis, have been used to facilitate solving problems that were previously difficult or impossible to solve. Moreover, the CI tools are capable of yielding results in a relatively short time (Eberhart & Shi, 2007).

Evolutionary computation is inspired by biological processes which are at work in nature. Genetic algorithm (GA) modeled on the Darwinian evolutionary paradigm is the oldest and the best known Evolutionary Algorithm. It mimics the natural processes of selection, cross-over and mutation to search for optimum solutions in massive search spaces. Another very recent algorithm belonging to the class of biologically inspired methods is the Particle Swarm Optimization (PSO) (Kennedy & Eberhart, 1995; 1997; 2001). PSO imitates the social behaviour of insects, birds or fish swarming together to hunt for food. PSO is a population-based approach that maintains a set of candidate solutions, called particles, which move within the search space. During the exploration of the search space, each particle maintains a memory of two pieces of information - the best solution (*pbest*) that it has encountered so far and the best solution (*gbest*) encountered by the swarm as a whole. This information is used to direct the search. Evolutionary Algorithms are primarily used in the optimization of a single objective. They have been further extended and used in the simultaneous optimization of multiple objectives. NSGA-II (an extension of GA) and MOPSO (an extension of PSO) are, for example, two well-known algorithms used in Evolutionary Multi-objective Optimization (EMO). Evolutionary algorithms offer a particularly attractive approach to multicriteria optimization because they are effective in high-dimensional search spaces (Mitchell, 1996).

In this study, we show how to apply MOPSO

in simultaneously optimizing two diverse objective functions in COCOMO 81. This software cost estimation model was proposed by Barry Boehm in 1981. It was based on the software development methods and trends prevalent in the 80s. However, in the 90's the software development process had undergone drastic changes. In 1992, Barry Boehm and his team updated the basic COCOMO in response to the changing software production environment and came up with CO-COMO II. Fairley (2006) presents an overview of the evolution of the COCOMO models for software estimation from COCOMO 81 to Ada COCOMO to COCOMO II and describes the many ways in which COCOMO has influenced, and continues to influence, software engineering education and training. Numerous studies on the variations of COCOMO models and their extensive applications are also reported in the literature (Helm, 1992; Abdel-Hamid, 1993; Schooff & Haimes, 1999; Hale, Parrish, Dixon & Smith, 2000; Yang, et al, 2006; Yahya, Ahmad & Lee, 2008).

It may be objected that COCOMO 81 was developed in 1981 based on software development projects that are quite different from the most recent development projects. The foremost reason for selecting COCOMO 81 for our study is the *availability* of data for experimentation. COCOMO 81 datasets are readily available in the PROMISE online repository. According to the survey published by Jorgensen and Shepperd (2007) on software development studies, in spite of the fact that COCOMO 81 was published in 1981, the data set has been used in as many as 12 journal papers to evaluate estimation methods, calibration of methods, and estimation model size measures since 1995. Jorgensen analyzed the use of historical data sets in the journal papers and found that there are good reasons to claim that the *availability of a data set* is more indicative for its use than its representativeness or other properties.

Rather than optimizing a single objective, we have cast the problem as a Multi-Objective

Optimization problem (MOOP) and adapted the MOPSO meta-heuristic evolutionary algorithm to simultaneously minimize two objective functions – prediction error rate and model complexity. The goal of multi-objective optimization is to find a set of optimal solutions (rather than a single solution) by taking all objectives into consideration, without assigning greater priority to any one objective over other objectives. The ultimate choice as to which solution should be used is left to the project management team, which can use its expertise to select the desired solution from the set of the optimal solutions. The motivations for minimizing these two diverse objectives are: (1) Any cost estimation model is expected to keep the prediction or the estimation error to a minimum. The lower the prediction error, the higher the performance of the model is. (2) Selecting the most relevant features from a large and complex dataset is called feature subset selection. Minimization of the feature subset size (i.e. model complexity) is important because collecting reliable and sufficient data for model training and validation is still a challenging task in cost estimation research (Nguyen, Steece, & Boehm, 2008). (3) Having a set of optimal solutions to choose from is more desirable than having just one optimal solution.

RELATED WORK

Expert judgment, regression analysis and analogy are some of the traditional methods used in cost estimation. Although on a relatively small scale, data mining techniques are also used to learn a model from large datasets. In this section, we briefly describe these methods before introducing the MOPSO meta-heuristic method which is the focus of this study.

Regression Analysis

Regression analysis is the most widely used technique to develop software cost estimation models.

Most software estimation studies use regression as the major or complementary technique in their modeling process. Suppose there are p predictors in a dataset with N observations and the response is effort. In the COCOMO dataset, $p = 16$ and $N = 63$. Let $x_i = (x_{i1}, x_{i2}, ..., x_{ip})$, $i = 1, 2, ..., N$, be the vector of p predictors, and y_i be the response for the ith observation. The multiple linear regression model is expressed as:

$$y_i = \alpha_0 + \alpha_1 x_{i1} + ... + \alpha_p x_{ip} + \varepsilon_i \qquad (1)$$

where α_0, α_1, ..., α_p are regression coefficients, and ε_i is the error term for the ith observation. The prediction equation is:

$$\hat{y} = \bar{a}_0 + \bar{a}_1 x_{i1} + ... + \bar{a}_p x_{ip} \qquad (2)$$

where $\bar{a}_0$, $\bar{a}_1$ and $\bar{a}_p$ are the estimates of coefficients, and $\hat{y}$ is the estimate of response for the ith observation.

The ordinary least squares estimates for the regression coefficients are obtained by minimizing the sum of squared errors. The estimate of the response lies on a regression line from which the sum of squared distance to the corresponding observed response is minimized. Although regression is a standard method for estimating software cost models, it often results in an over-fitted model when unnecessary predictors remain in the model. Some of the predictors in the software cost data are highly correlated. Such collinearity may cause high variances and covariances in coefficients and result in poor predictive performance when dealing with new data. These problems can be mitigated by reducing the number of predictor variables. Other regression techniques are stepwise subset selection (Miller, 2002), Lasso (Tibshirani, 1996) and Ridge (Hoerl & Kennard, 1970).

Analogy

Estimation by analogy is a form of case-based reasoning (CBR). The major steps in estimating by analogy are the identification of a problem as a new case (target), the retrieval of similar cases from a repository (source), the reuse of knowledge derived from previous cases and the suggestion of a solution for the new case (analogue). A similarity function is used to measure how close the target is to the source. Similarity is defined in terms of project features, such as the application domain, the development method, the number of interfaces, and so forth. In most cases, the similarity function is based on the normalized unweighted Euclidean distance in n-dimensional space, where each dimension corresponds to a particular feature (Briand, Langley, & Wieczorek, 2000).

Shepperd and Schofield (1997) note the following advantages of estimating software development cost by analogy:

- It avoids the problems associated both with knowledge elicitation and extracting and codifying the knowledge.
- Analogy-based systems can also handle failed cases (i.e., those cases for which an accurate prediction was not made). This is useful as it enables users to identify potentially high-risk situations.
- Analogy is able to deal with poorly understood domains (such as software projects) since solutions are based upon what has actually happened as opposed to chains of rules in the case of rule based systems.

Data Mining Techniques

Feature subset selection is a widely-used technique in the data mining community. It consists in selecting from a set a subset of relevant features that optimize a given objective. Feature selection not only helps improve performance accuracy, but also results in better understanding and interpretation of the data. Given a set of n features and M samples x = {x_{ij} ; i =1, . . ., M; j = 1, . . ., n}, feature subset selection methods find a subset x_s = {x_{i1}, . . ., x_{is}}, with $s < n$, that optimizes an objective function. Feature subset selection requires a search strategy to select candidate subsets and an objective function to evaluate these candidates. Two different general approaches are commonly considered (Sanchez-Marono, Alonso-Betanzos, & Castillo, 2005):

- Filter algorithms, in which case the selection method is used as a preprocessing step that does not attempt to optimize directly the predictor (machine learning method) performance.
- Wrapper algorithms, in which the selection method optimizes the predictor performance directly.

The Wrapper feature subset selection method has been applied to the COCOMO 81 parametric software cost estimation model. Using datasets from the PROMISE repository, Barry Boehm and co-workers (Chen, Menzies, Port, & Boehm, 2005a) have shown that Wrapper significantly and dramatically improves COCOMO's predictive power. In the wrapper approach to feature subset selection, a search for an optimal set of features is made using the induction algorithm as a black box. The estimated future performance of the algorithm is the heuristic guiding the search. Statistical methods for feature subset selection including forward selection, backward elimination, and their stepwise variants can be viewed as simple hill-climbing techniques in the space of feature subsets (Kohavi & John, 1997). The approach, evidently, has two drawbacks:

1. The hill-climbing techniques soon get trapped in a local minimum.
2. WRAPPER is quite slow, since in the worst case it has to explore all subsets of the available columns.

COCOMO Models

The COst COnstructive MOdel (COCOMO) was introduced by Barry Boehm in 1981 as a model for estimating effort, cost, and schedule for software projects in his classic text, *Software Engineering Economics* (Boehm, 1981). The COCOMO 81 model was defined based on the analysis of 63 completed projects from diverse domains during the 70s and the early 80s. It has been extensively used in industry as well as academia. The model consists of a hierarchy of three increasingly detailed and accurate forms. The first level, Basic COCOMO, is good for quick, early, rough order of magnitude estimates of software costs. Intermediate COCOMO takes 15 different cost drivers or effort multipliers into account. Detailed CO-COMO additionally accounts for the influence of individual project phases.

In 1997, COCOMO 81 was extended to COCOMO II to include the newer paradigms in software development and finally published in a book in 2001 (Boehm et al., 2001). COCOMO II is better suited for estimating modern software development projects. Among the main upgrades are the introduction of new functional forms that use scale factors and new cost drivers and a set of parameter values. However, unlike COCOMO 81, COCOMO II datasets are not publicly available for verification and further research.

In both the COCOMO models, the effort required to develop a project can be written in the following general form:

$$PM = a*(KLOC)^b*(\Pi_j EM_j) \qquad (3)$$

where,

PM = effort estimate in person months
a = productivity coefficient
b = economies (or diseconomies) of scale coefficient
EM = effort multipliers or cost drivers

Figure 1. Values of a & b in COCOMO 81 model

Software Project	a	b
Organic	3.2	1.05
Semi-detached	3	1.12
Embedded	2.8	1.2

In COCOMO 81, the b term is an exponential constant which is usually greater than 1.0, indicating diseconomies of scale. In COCOMO II, b is defined as a function of scale factors, in the form of:

$$b = \beta_0 + \sum_{j=1}^{5} (\beta_j SF) \qquad (4)$$

COCOMO 81 identifies 15 effort multipliers (Figures 1 and 2), while COCOMO II uses 17 in its Post-Architecture model (Figure 3).

COCOMO applies to three classes of software projects:

- Organic projects - are relatively small, simple software projects in which small teams with good application experience work to a set of less than rigid requirements.
- Semi-detached projects - are intermediate (in size and complexity) software projects in which teams with mixed experience levels must meet a mix of rigid and less than rigid requirements.
- Embedded projects - are software projects that must be developed within a set of tight hardware, software, and operational constraints.

Figure 2. COCOMO 81 cost driver values model (Adapted from Boehm, 1981)

Cost Driver	Very Low	Low	Nominal	High	Very High	Extra High
ACAP	1.46	1.19	1	0.86	0.71	
PCAP	1.42	1.17	1	0.86	0.7	
AEXP	1.29	1.13	1	0.91	0.82	
MODP	1.24	1.1	1	0.91	0.82	
TOOL	1.24	1.1	1	0.91	0.83	
VEXP	1.21	1.1	1	0.9		
LEXP	1.14	1.07	1	0.95		
DATA	0.94	1	1.08	1.16		
CPLX	0.7	0.85	1	1.15	1.3	1.65
TURN	0.87	1	1.07	1.15		
VIRT	0.87	1	1.15	1.3		
STOR	1	1.06	1.21	1.56		
TIME	1	1.11	1.3	1.66		
RELY	0.75	0.88	1	1.15	1.4	
SCED	1.23	1.08	1	1.04	1.1	

Figure 3. COCOMO II cost driver values (Adapted from Boehm et al, 2000)

Cost Driver	Very Low	Low	Nominal	High	Very High	Extra High
PREC	6.2	4.96	3.72	2.48	1.24	0
FLEX	5.07	4.05	3.04	2.03	1.01	0
RESL	7.07	5.65	4.24	2.83	1.41	0
TEAM	5.48	4.38	3.29	2.19	1.1	0
PMAT	7.8	6.24	4.68	3.12	1.56	0
RELY	0.82	0.92	1	1.1	1.26	
DATA	0.9	1	1.14	1.28		
CPLX	0.73	0.87	1	1.17	1.34	1.74
RUSE	0.95	1	1.07	1.15	1.24	
DOCU	0.81	0.91	1	1.11	1.23	
TIME	1	1.11	1.29	1.63		
STOR	1	1.05	1.17	1.46		
PVOL	0.87	1	1.15	1.3		
ACAP	1.42	1.19	1	0.85	0.71	
PCAP	1.34	1.15	1	0.88	0.76	
PCON	1.29	1.12	1	0.9	0.81	
AEXP	1.22	1.1	1	0.88	0.81	
PEXP	1.19	1.09	1	0.91	0.85	
LTEX	1.2	1.09	1	0.91	0.84	
TOOL	1.17	1.09	1	0.9	0.78	
SITE	1.22	1.09	1	0.93	0.86	0.8
SCED	1.43	1.14	1	1	1	

The values of the productivity coefficient, 'a' and those of the economies (or diseconomies) of scale coefficient, 'b' for the above three classes of software projects are given in Figure 1.

MULTI OBJECTIVE OPTIMIZATION

Most real-world optimization problems have multiple objectives which are often conflicting. The goal of multi-objective optimization (MOOP) is to optimize the conflicting objectives simultaneously. In this section, we define the general form of a MOOP and Pareto dominance for identifying optimal solutions. Towards the end of the section, we describe the use of Evolutionary Algorithms to solve MOOPs.

MOOP Formulation

In general, a multi-objective minimization problem with M decision variables and N objectives can be stated as:

Minimize $f_i(\mathbf{x})$ $i = 1,..., N$ (5)
where $\mathbf{x} = (x_1, ..., x_m) \in X$
subject to: $g_j(\mathbf{x}) = 0$ $j = 1,..., M$ (6)
$h_k(\mathbf{x}) \leq 0$ $k = 1,..., K$

Here, f_i is the ith objective function, $\mathbf{x}$ is the decision vector that represents a solution and X is the variable or parameter space. The functions g_j and h_k represent the equality and the inequality constraints, respectively. The desired solution is in the form of a "trade-off" or compromise among the parameters that would optimize the given objectives. The optimal trade-off solutions among the objectives constitute the Pareto front. MOOP deals with generating the Pareto front, which is the set of non-dominated solutions for problems having more than one objective. A solution is said to be non-dominated if it is impossible to improve one component of the solution without worsening the value of at least one other component of the solution. The goal of multi-objective optimization is find the true and well-distributed Pareto front consisting of the non-dominated solutions.

Pareto Dominance

Most multi-objective optimization algorithms use the concept of domination. In these algorithms two solutions are compared on the basis of whether one solution dominates the other or not. Assume that there are M objective functions to be optimized and the problem is one of minimization. A solution $x^{(1)}$ is said to dominate the other solutions $x^{(2)}$, if conditions (1) and (2) are both true (Deb, 2001).

1. The solution $x^{(1)}$ is no worse than $x^{(2)}$ in all objectives, or $f_j(x^{(1)}) \not> f_j(x^{(2)})$ for all $j = 1, 2,...M$.
2. The solution $x^{(1)}$ is strictly better than $x^{(2)}$ in at least one objective, or $f_j(x^{(1)}) < f_j(x^{(2)})$ for at least one j belonging to $\{1,2,..M\}$.

Figure 4. Pareto Dominance (min-min problem)

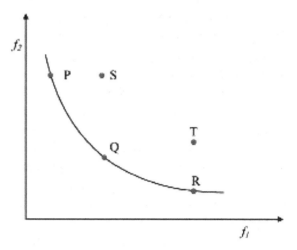

Figure 4. Pareto Dominance (min-min problem)

If any of the above conditions is violated the solution $x^{(1)}$ does not dominate the solution $x^{(2)}$. The non-dominated solutions give rise to a Pareto wavefront. The points on the wavefront are used to select a particular combination of functions that are in a trade-off balance.

Figure 4 illustrates the concept of Pareto dominance for the minimization of two objective functions. Solution S is dominated by solution P in the f_1 objective, while solution T is dominated by solution R in the f_2 objective. The solutions P, Q, R are Pareto-optimal solutions since none of them is dominated by any other solutions.

Evolutionary Algorithms for Multi-Objective Optimization

Evolutionary Algorithms (EA) seem to be especially suited to MOOP problems due to their abilities to search simultaneously for multiple Pareto optimal solutions and to perform better global search of the search space (Mitchell, 1996). Many evolutionary algorithms have been developed for solving MOOP. Examples are: NSGA-II (Deb, Agrawal, Pratab, & Meyarivan, 2000) which is a variant of NSGA (Non-dominated Sorting Genetic Algorithm); SPEA2 (Zitzler, Laumanns, and Thiele, 2000) which is an improved version of SPEA (Strength Pareto Evolutionary Algorithm) and PAES (Pareto Archived Evolution Strategy) (Knowles & Corne, 2000). These EAs are population-based algorithms that possess an in-built mechanism to explore the different parts of the Pareto front simultaneously. The Particle Swarm optimization (PSO) which was originally designed for solving single objective optimization problems is also extended to solve multi-objective optimization problems. Among those algorithms that extend PSO to solve multi-objective optimization problems are Multi-objective Particle Swarm Optimization (MOPSO) (Coelho, Pulido, & Salazar, 2004), Non-dominated Sorting Particle Swarm Optimization (NSPSO) (Li et al., 2003) and the aggregating function for PSO (Parsopoulos & Vrahatis, 2002).

PARETO FRONT FOR COCOMO ESTIMATES

In this study, we consider two objectives to be simultaneously optimized – minimization of the prediction error rate (f_1) of COCOMO 81 and the minimization of the number of attributes or features (cost drivers and LOC) (f_2) used in the model. Minimization of the prediction error rate of the model increases its reliability, while the reduction in the selected features makes data collection easier and less expensive. The min-min optimization problem is solved by MOPSO.

Prediction Error Rate (f_1)

MMRE and PRED are the most widely used metrics for evaluation of the accuracy of cost estimation models (Chen, Menzies, Port, & Boehm, 2005; Briand, El Emam, Surmann, Wieczorek, & Maxwell, 1999). These metrics are calculated based on a number of actuals observed and estimates generated by the model. They are derived from the basic magnitude of the relative error

MRE, which is defined as:

$$MRE_j = \frac{|ActualEffort_j - PredictedEffort_j|}{ActualEffort_j}$$

(7)

The mean of MRE of N estimates is defined as:

$$MRE_j = \frac{|ActualEffort_j - PredictedEffort_j|}{ActualEffort_j}$$

(8)

Yet another metric common among project managers used for model evaluation is PRED. PRED(l) is defined as the percentage of estimates where MRE is not greater than l, that is PRED(l) = k/n, where k is the number of estimates with MRE falling within l, and n is the total number of estimates. For single optimization problems, PRED value is considered as a standard in reporting COCOMO calibration and model improvement in previous studies (Briand, Basili, & Thomas, 1992).

Model Complexity (f_2)

Selecting the most relevant features from a large and complex dataset is called feature subset selection. Minimization of the feature subset size (i.e. model complexity) is important because collecting reliable and sufficient data for model training and validation is still a challenging task in cost estimation research (Nguyen, Steece, & Boehm, 2008). COCOMO 81 has 16 attributes – 15 for effort multipliers (cost drivers) and one for the project size (LOC), while COCOMO II has 17 effort multipliers. In practical situations, it is very difficult to collect data encompassing all the attributes while building a new model. Minimizing the number of attributes while at the same time minimizing the prediction error caused by using those attributes in the model would be beneficial for a practical project.

PARTICLE SWARM OPTIMIZATION

The Particle Swarm Optimization (PSO) is a population-based swarm intelligence evolutionary algorithm, imitating the collective behaviour of bird flocks or fish schools hunting for food. In the following subsection, we describe the basic PSO and its extension to solve multi-objective optimization problems.

Single Objective Particle Swarm Optimization

The population-based PSO conducts a search using a population of individuals. The individual in the population is called the particle and the population is called the swarm. The performance of each particle is measured according to a predefined fitness function. Particles are assumed to "fly" over the search space in order to find promising regions of the landscape. In the minimization case, such regions possess lower functional values than other regions visited previously. Each particle is treated as a point in a d-dimensional space which adjusts its own "flying" according to its flying experience as well as the flying experience of the other companion particles. By making adjustments to the flying based on the local best (*pbest*) and the global best (*gbest*) found so far, the swarm as a whole converges to the optimum point, or at least to a near-optimal point, in the search space.

The notations used in PSO are as follows. The ith particle of the swarm in iteration t is represented by the d-dimensional vector, $x_i(t) = (x_{i1}, x_{i2}, \ldots, x_{id})$. Each particle also has a position change known as velocity, which for the ith particle in iteration t is $v_i(t) = (v_{i1}, v_{i2}, \ldots, v_{id})$. The best previous position (the position with the best fitness value) of the ith particle is $p_i(t-1) = (p_{i1}, p_{i2}, \ldots, p_{id})$. The best particle in the swarm, i.e., the particle with the smallest function value found in all the previous iterations, is denoted by the index g. In a given iteration t, the velocity and position of each particle is updated using the following equations:

$$v_i(t) = wv_i(t-1) + c_1 r_1(p_i(t-1) - x_i(t-1)) + c_2 r_2(p_g(t-1) - x_i(t-1)) \qquad (9)$$

and

$$x_i(t) = x_i(t-1) + v_i(t) \qquad (10)$$

where, $i = 1, 2, \ldots, NP$; $t = 1, 2, \ldots, T$. NP is the size of the swarm, and T is the iteration limit; c_1 and c_2 are positive constants (called "social factors"), and r_1 and r_2 are random numbers between 0 and 1; w is inertia weight that controls the impact of the previous history of the velocities on the current velocity, influencing the trade-off between the global and local experiences. A large inertia weight facilitates global exploration (searching new areas), while a small one tends to facilitate local exploration (fine-tuning the current search area). Equation 9 is used to compute a particle's new velocity, based on its previous velocity and the distances from its current position to its local best and to the global best positions. The new velocity is then used to compute the particle's new position (Equation 10).

Multi Objective Particle Swarm Optimization

The Multi Objective Particle Swarm Optimization (MOPSO) is an extension of the single objective Particle Swarm Optimization (PSO). In PSO, *gbest* and *pbest* act as guides for the swarm of particles to continue the search as the algorithm proceeds. The main difficulty in MOPSO is to find the best way of selecting the guides for each particle in the swarm. This is because there are no clear concepts of *pbest* and *gbest* that can be

Figure 5. Randomly generated particles in MOPSO

Particle Number	A 1	2	3	T 4	T 5	R 6	I 7	B 8	U 9	T 10	E 11	S 12	13	14	15	16	FUNCTIONS f_1	f_2
1	1	0	1	1	0	1	0	1	0	1	1	0	0	0	0	1	8	16.65
2	1	1	0	1	1	1	0	1	1	1	0	1	0	1	0	1	11	14.57
3	1	1	0	0	0	1	0	1	0	1	1	0	0	0	0	1	7	17.96
4	0	0	1	0	1	1	1	0	0	1	0	0	1	0	1	1	8	23.15
5	1	1	0	1	0	1	1	0	0	1	0	1	0	1	0	1	9	19.15
6	1	0	1	0	0	1	0	1	1	1	0	1	0	0	0	1	8	15.90
7	1	0	1	0	1	1	1	0	0	1	0	1	1	0	0	1	9	20.66
8	1	0	0	1	0	1	0	1	0	0	0	0	0	0	0	1	5	20.31
9	0	0	0	0	1	1	0	0	1	0	1	0	0	0	0	1	5	25.12
10	1	1	1	0	0	1	0	1	1	1	1	0	1	1	0	1	11	14.28
11	1	1	1	1	1	1	1	0	1	1	1	0	0	0	1	1	12	20.93
12	1	1	1	0	0	1	0	0	0	1	1	0	0	0	0	1	7	21.15
13	1	0	0	0	0	1	1	1	0	1	0	1	0	0	0	1	7	16.58
14	1	1	0	0	0	1	0	1	0	1	0	0	1	0	0	1	7	18.19
15	0	0	0	1	1	1	0	1	0	1	0	0	1	0	1	1	8	19.56
16	1	0	0	1	0	1	0	0	0	1	0	0	1	0	0	1	6	19.71
17	0	0	0	0	0	1	0	1	0	1	1	1	0	0	0	1	6	19.14
18	1	0	0	0	0	1	0	1	0	0	0	0	0	1	0	1	5	19.39
19	1	1	1	0	0	0	1	0	0	1	1	0	0	0	0	1	7	22.18
20	1	1	1	1	1	1	0	1	0	1	0	1	0	0	0	1	10	19.39

identified when dealing with a set of multiple objective functions. Our algorithm is similar to the ones described in the works of Coelho & Lechunga (2002), Coelho, Pulido, & Salazar (2004) and Alvarez-Benitez, Everson, & Fieldsend (2005). It maintains an external archive A, containing the non-dominated solutions found by the algorithm so far. In our problem, f_1 (number of attributes in the model) consists of uniformly distributed discrete points. Therefore, we do not need a clustering or a gridding mechanism that is the source of substantial computational overhead in most of the MOPSO algorithms.

MOPSO Algorithm

The algorithm begins with the initialization of an empty external archive, A. A population of N particles is randomly generated. The particle positions (x_i) and velocities (v_i) are initialized

randomly. This is done by drawing a random number r in the interval $(0, 1)$ for each COCOMO 81 attribute represented by the particles. If $r < 0.5$, it is reset to 0; else it is reset to 1. Figure 5 shows an initial population of randomly generated 20 particles. The 16 columns represent the 16 attributes in the cost model. The inclusion or exclusion of a particular attribute in the model is represented by 1 or 0 bit, respectively. The values of f_1 and f_2 for each particle are shown on the right. Initially, the velocities of each particle are similarly initialized. The initial position of each particle is considered to be its personal best ($P_i = x_i$) as well as the global best ($G_i = x_i$).

At each iteration t the velocities and the positions of the particles are updated using equations 9 and 10, respectively. The particle positions and velocities are checked for feasibility after each update. If $x_{ij} < 0$, $x_{ij} = 0$; if $x_{ij} > 1$, $x_{ij} = 1$. Similarly, velocities of each particle are forced into the feasible bounds, if they have crossed the bounds. The objective functions f_1 and f_2 are then evaluated for each of the particles.

The crucial parts of the MOPSO algorithm are selecting the personal and the global guides. If the current position of x_i weakly dominates P_i or if x_i and P_i are mutually non-dominating, then P_i is set to the current position. Members of A are mutually non-dominating and no member of the archive is dominated by any x_i. All the members of the archive are, therefore, candidates for the global guide. The algorithm pseudo-code is shown below.

```
A:=  ∅ (Initialize an empty archive)
{ x_i, v_i, G_i, P_i}  i = 1,…,N (Initialize
particle positions & velocities (random))
for t:= 1: G  (G generations)
  for i:= 1: N(N particles (population
size))
    for k:= 1: K      (Update velocities
and positions)
       v_ik:= wv_ik + r_1(P_ik − x_ik) + r_2(G_ik −
x_ik)

       x_ik:= x_ik + v_ik
    end
    x_i := Check for feasibility(x_i)
    y_i:= f (x_i)        (Evaluate objective
functions)
    if x_i  ≼ u ∀u ∈ A       (Add non-dom-
inated x_i to A)
       A:= {u ∈ A | u ≺ x_i } (Remove
points dominated by x)
       A:= A U x_i      (Add x_i to A)
    end
  end
    if x_i  ≤  P_i    (Update personal
best)
       P_i:=  x_i
    end
    G_i:= select Guide(x_i, A)
End
```

COCOMO OPTIMIZATION USING MOPSO

In this section, we describe the various experiments we carried out on the COCOMO 81 datasets using the MOPSO algorithm developed in the previous section.

Datasets

We used the COCOMO I dataset for our experimentation because it is an open model with published data. The details are published in the text *Software Engineering Economics* (Boehm, 1981). Besides, the datasets are publicly available online in the PROMISE repository (Shirabad & Menzies, 2005).

- COCOMO 81: There are 63 projects in this data set. They are collected from a variety of domains including science, engineering and finance.
- NASA: There are 60 projects coming from aerospace applications.
- Projects 02, 03, 04 (p02, p03, p04): These three are subsets of NASA. There are 22 projects in p02, 12 in p03 and 14 in p04.

Each project in the above datasets has 16 attributes – actual size in kilo lines of code and 15 cost drivers or effort multipliers (Figure 1). Each cost driver is a categorical variable which has values of Very Low (VL), Low (L), Nominal (NOM), High (HI), Very High (VH), or Extra High (EH). These symbolic values are stored in the dataset, and they are mapped to numeric scales when the objective function needs to be computed. Incidentally, the details of COCOMO II model are available, but not the datasets. It is reported that the datasets for studies on COCOMO II were supplied by the companies on condition of confidentiality (Chen et al., 2005a).

Model Validation

The most important criterion for rejection or acceptance of a cost estimation model is in its ability to predict using new data. Ideally the prediction error of a new cost model is calculated using data of future projects. This approach, however, is usually impossible in practice because new data are not always available at the time the model is developed. Instead, model developers have to use the data that are available to them for both constructing and validating the model. This strategy is usually referred to as cross validation. Many cross-validation approaches have been proposed, the most common of which are a simple holdout strategy (or data-splitting) and a computer intensive called k-fold cross validation. The holdout approach splits the dataset into to distinctive subsets, training and test sets. The training set is used to fit the model, and the test set is used to obtain estimates of the prediction errors. In our experiments, we have used two-thirds of the projects in the datasets for multi-objective optimization and the remaining one-third for testing.

Feature Subset Selection

Feature subset selection (also known as column-cuts) is frequently used in machine learning algorithms. The 16 attributes in the COCOMO 81 data sets are arranged as columns and the projects as rows. In each iteration, the learning algorithm systematically cuts a group of columns from the data set and subjects it to learning. The learning algorithm returns the optimum model that is learnt by cutting a particular number of columns.

We carried out similar experiments on all the five datasets of COCOMO 81 using MOPSO. However, we minimized not one, but two objective functions simultaneously – the mean relative error in prediction (MMRE) and the number of columns left uncut in the model. The trade-off between the number of columns included in the model and the corresponding MMRE is shown in

Figure 6 and Figure 7. For all the five datasets, number of columns between 3 and 9 produces the true Pareto front. Only in the case of the COCOMO dataset does it extend from 3 to 14 columns. Two important conclusions can be drawn from our experiments:

1. They confirm the results produced by Chen, Menzies, Port, & Boehm (2005a, 2005b). Accurate cost estimates for a new project can be made with *fewer* cost drivers. In other words, the developers need not put in all the 16 attributes prescribed by the classical parametric model. With fewer data points the complexity of the model decreases and the cost involved in collecting data is indirectly reduced.
2. The Pareto front (Figure 7) represents a set of non-dominated (optimal) solutions. It shows a trade-off between MMRE and the number of attributes included in the model. If the number of attributes in the model is increased, MMRE decreases and vice-versa. It is left to the expertise of the development team to make a judicious choice.

Stratification

Stratification is the process of cutting rows (projects) when performing machine learning from a given dataset. Feature subset selection along with stratification is found to produce rather high prediction accuracy (Chen, Menzies, Port, & Boehm, 2005a, 2005b; Shepperd & Schofield, 1997). Sometimes there are irrelevant features or noise present in the data. Feature subset selection and stratification act as filters cutting off the extra noise.

In our second set of experiments, we used MOPSO to minimize the MMRE while simultaneously minimizing the total number of rows and columns to be included in the model. The results are shown in Figures 8 and 9. This time we use only three datasets – COCOMO, NASA and a

Figure 6. Optimized values of number of attributes (f_1) & MMRE (f_2)

Number of Attributes (f_1)	COCOMO MMRE (f_2)	NASA2 MMRE (f_2)	p02 MMRE (f_2)	p03 MMRE (f_2)	p04 MMRE (f_2)
1	91.29	81.28	73.69	95.22	82.98
2	92.00	62.98	35.27	84.46	73.98
3	71.26	54.16	16.09	65.86	38.89
4	63.86	50.98	15.49	51.73	30.64
5	56.41	49.17	15.44	44.94	29.03
6	53.32	47.37	14.90	43.89	25.96
7	51.92	46.76	15.79	42.77	25.30
8	45.67	46.14	15.60	40.79	25.43
9	42.04	46.26	15.58	40.25	23.25
10	38.95	47.61	16.50	43.97	23.99
11	36.86	49.76	16.40	43.08	23.23
12	35.61	51.39	16.28	46.19	24.38
13	34.37	53.89	17.63	49.93	28.25
14	32.61	56.58	16.81	49.92	26.75
15	33.15	58.50	17.40	50.75	30.27
16	32.46	60.33	15.83	55.71	31.30

combination of p02, p03 and p04. Figure 9 shows the total number of columns and rows included in the prediction model (RC), the corresponding average MMRE (AV) and standard deviation (SD). True Pareto fronts are produced for data points roughly between 20 and 55. This implies that fewer than 20 data points are not sufficient to produce a good prediction. It also implies that more than 55 data points are not necessary to produce optimal solutions. The management can choose the trade-off points between 20 and 55 by referring to the Pareto fronts shown in Figure 8.

CONCLUSION AND FUTURE WORK

Very few AI techniques have been applied to research dealing with the estimation of costs in software development. In this study, we have shown how the recently developed Computational Intelligence techniques can effectively improve the prediction power of existing models. In particular, our study has focused on the adaptation of the Multi-Objective Particle Swarm Optimization (MOPSO) algorithm in simultaneously minimizing two objective functions – prediction error rate and model complexity (number of attributes to be included in the model). The motivation for selecting these objectives is that accuracy in prediction is expected from any cost model, while collecting sufficient data for building practical projects is a daunting task. For all the data subsets in the PROMISE repository, except for COCOMO subset, our results have shown that true Pareto fronts are produced when three to ten attributes are included in the parametric model. However, this does not necessarily imply that including fewer than ten attributes will produce excellent results than with all the variables suggested by the COCOMO model. Expert judgment is still indispensible for further intelligent fine-tuning. However, the results give us an important insight

Figure 7. Pareto fronts for five datasets (column-cuts)

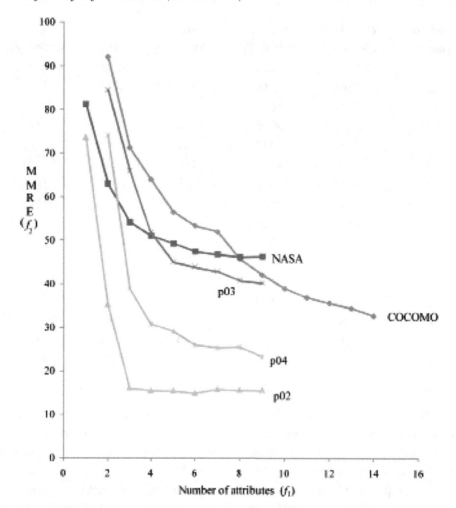

that COCOMO has far too many cost drivers, which means that the model is over-specified. The Pareto front extending between three and ten data points provides the management with a set of optimal trade-off solutions to choose from.

The meta-heuristic approach presented in this study is not problem-specific or domain-specific. It is expected to yield good results when applied to other problems in other domains. As an extension of this work, we would like to experiment on other datasets, especially those with a relatively large search space which is appropriate for a meta-heuristic evolutionary algorithm. Secondly, we would like to compare the results produced by

MOPSO to those obtained by other multi-objective optimization algorithms.

ACKNOWLEDGMENT

This research has been supported by the Open Research Center Project funds from "MEXT" of the Japanese Government (2007-20011).

Figure 8. Pareto fronts for three datasets (row & column cuts)

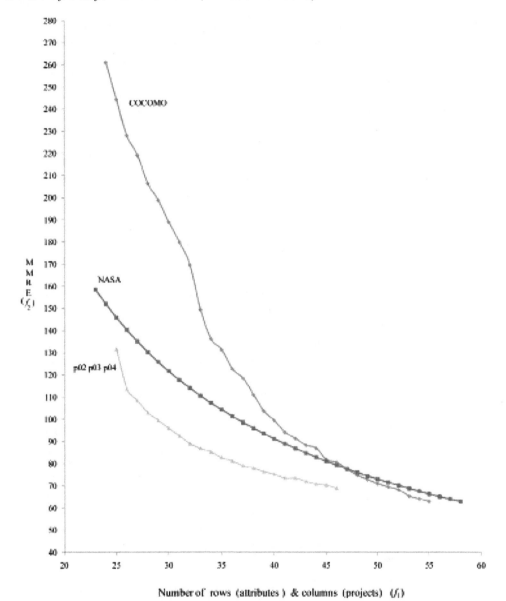

REFERENCES

Abdel-Hamid, T. K. (1993). Adapting, correcting, and perfecting software estimates: a maintenance metaphor. *Computer*, *26*(3), 20–29. doi:10.1109/2.204681

Albrecht, A. J., & Gaffney, J. R. (1983). Software function, source lines of code, and development effort prediction: A software science validation. *IEEE Transactions on Software Engineering*, *SE-9*(6), 639–648. doi:10.1109/TSE.1983.235271

Figure 9. Optimized values of number of rows & columns (f_1) & MMRE (f_2)

RC	COCOMO		NASA 2		p02 p03 p04	
	AV	SD	AV	SD	AV	SD
20	317.88	42.35	221.98	68.61	208.63	59.58
21	287.17	27.24	214.30	62.99	189.32	67.66
22	262.55	1.66	201.80	62.38	182.88	49.82
23	252.28	0.47	158.58	0.00	136.72	11.08
24	261.06	26.94	151.97	0.00	124.33	5.43
25	244.33	28.96	145.89	0.00	131.73	35.42
26	228.02	11.61	140.28	0.00	113.68	5.40
27	219.27	9.99	135.09	0.00	108.35	5.08
28	206.35	2.26	130.26	0.00	102.91	4.50
29	198.86	1.24	125.77	0.00	99.50	2.88
30	188.96	5.60	121.58	0.00	95.85	1.87
31	179.87	7.28	117.65	0.00	92.53	2.49
32	169.55	9.58	113.98	0.00	88.93	1.48
33	149.36	3.89	110.52	0.00	86.85	1.52
34	136.20	6.69	107.27	0.00	85.25	1.59
35	131.28	4.32	104.21	0.00	82.58	1.49
36	122.65	5.43	101.31	0.00	81.13	1.34
37	118.51	4.79	98.58	0.00	79.09	2.30
38	111.07	5.37	95.98	0.00	78.06	1.59
39	103.75	1.32	93.52	0.00	76.44	1.19
40	99.49	3.83	91.18	0.00	75.27	2.82
41	94.26	2.23	88.96	0.00	73.47	2.64
42	91.34	5.21	86.84	0.00	73.42	1.67
43	88.32	4.59	84.82	0.00	72.00	1.90
44	87.04	4.83	82.89	0.00	70.87	0.92
45	81.90	2.70	81.05	0.00	70.33	1.00
46	80.61	1.60	79.29	0.00	69.02	0.87
47	77.47	3.17	77.60	0.00	68.00	0.67
48	74.70	1.10	75.99	0.00	66.89	3.11
49	72.80	2.66	74.43	0.00	66.30	1.15
50	70.94	2.15	72.95	0.00	65.18	2.22
51	69.47	4.01	71.52	0.00	64.95	2.22
52	68.15	1.42	70.14	0.00	73.71	20.17
53	65.40	3.45	68.82	0.00	65.66	2.46
54	64.17	1.99	67.54	0.00	66.32	5.19
55	62.92	1.33	66.31	0.00	75.82	17.62
56	64.09	2.62	65.13	0.00	68.80	7.12
57	62.01	2.28	63.99	0.00	76.87	14.78
58	59.57	2.40	62.88	0.00	67.36	7.56
59	57.23	1.94	84.94	40.05	67.01	7.47
60	57.06	1.16	138.41	68.02	67.32	8.53

Alvarez-Benitez, J. E., Everson, R. M., & Fieldsend, J. E. (2005). A MOPSO algorithm based exclusively on Pareto dominance concepts. *Evolutionary Multi-Criterion Optimization,* (LNCS Vol. 410, pp. 459-473). Berlin: Springer.

Boehm, B. W. (1981). *Software engineering economics*. Upper Saddle River, NJ: Prentice Hall.

Boehm, B. W., Horowitz, E., Madachy, R., Reifer, D., Clark, B. K., Steece, B., et al. (2001). *Software cost estimation with COCOMO II*. Upper Saddle River, NJ: Prentice Hall.

Briand, L. C., Basili, V. R., & Thomas, W. M. (1992). A pattern recognition approach for software engineering data analysis. *IEEE Transactions on Software Engineering, 18*(11), 931–942. doi:10.1109/32.177363

Briand, L. C., El Emam, K., Surmann, D., Wieczorek, I., & Maxwell, K. D. (1999). An assessment and comparison of common software cost estimation modeling techniques. *Proceedings of the 1999 International Conference on Software Engineering,* (pp. 313 – 323).

Briand, L. C., Langley, T., & Wieczorek, I. (2000). A replicated assessment and comparison of common software cost modeling techniques. *Proceedings of the 2000 International Conference on Software Engineering,* Limerick, Ireland, (pp. 377-386).

Chen, Z., Menzies, T., Port, D., & Boehm, B. (2005a). Feature subset selection can improve software cost estimation accuracy. *Proceedings of the 2005 workshop on predictor models in software engineering,* St. Louis, Missouri, (pp. 1 – 6).

Chen, Z., Menzies, T., Port, D., & Boehm, B. (2005b). Finding the right data for software cost modeling. *Software, 22*(6), 38–46. doi:10.1109/MS.2005.151

Coelho, C., & Lechunga, M. (2002). MOPSO: A proposal for multuiple objective particle swarm optimization. *Proceedings of the 2002 Congress on Evolutionary Computation* (pp. 1051-1056). Washington, DC: IEEE Press.

Coelho, C., Pulido, G., & Salazar, M. (2004). Handling multiobjectives with particle swarm optimization. *IEEE Transactions on Evolutionary Computation, 8,* 256–279. doi:10.1109/TEVC.2004.826067

Deb, K. (2001). *Multi-objective optimization using evolutionary algorithms*. New York: John Wiley & Sons.

Deb, K., Agrawal, S., Pratab, A., & Meyarivan, T. (2000). A fast elitist nondominated sorting genetic algorithm for multiobjective optimization: NSGA-II. *Proceedings of Parallel Problem Solving from Nature VI Conference,* 849–858.

Eberhart, R., & Shi, Y. (2007). *Computational intelligence: Concepts to implementations*. San Francisco: Morgan Kaufman.

Fairley, R. E. (2006). The Influence of COCOMO on Software Engineering Education and Training. *Proceedings of the 19th Conference on Software Engineering Education and Training,* (pp. 193 – 200).

Fox, T. L., & Spence, J. W. (2005). The effect of decision style on the use of a project management tool: An empirical laboratory study. *The Data Base for Advances in Information Systems, 32*(2), 28–42.

Glass, R. L. (1998). *Software runaways*. Upper Saddle River, NJ: Prentice-Hall.

Gray, A. R., & MacDonell, S. G. (1997). A comparison of techniques for developing predictive models of software metrics. *Information and Software Technology, 39,* 425–437. doi:10.1016/S0950-5849(96)00006-7

Hale, J., Parrish, A., Dixon, B., & Smith, R. K. (2000). Enhancing the Cocomo estimation models. *IEEE Software, 17*(6), 45–49. doi:10.1109/52.895167

Helm, J. E. (1992). The viability of using COCOMO in the special application software bidding and estimating process. *IEEE Transactions on Engineering Management, 39*(1), 42–58. doi:10.1109/17.119662

Hoerl, A. E., & Kennard, R. W. (1970). Ridge regression: Biased estimation of non-orthogonal problems. *Technometrics.*

Jaaksi, A. (2003). Assessing software projects – tools for business owners. *ACM SIGSOFT Software Engineering Notes, 28*(5), 15–18. doi:10.1145/949952.940074

Jensen, R. (1983). An improved macrolevel software development resource estimation model. *5ᵗʰ ISPA Conference* (pp. 88-92).

Johnson, J. H. (2001). Micro projects cause constant change. *Second International Conference on Extreme Programming and Agile Processes in Software Engineering,* Cagliari, Italy, (pp. 20-23).

Jorgensen, M., & Shepperd, M. (2007). A systematic review of software development cost estimation studies. *IEEE Transactions on Software Engineering, 33*(1), 33–53. doi:10.1109/TSE.2007.256943

Keil, M., Rai, A., Mann, J. E. C., & Zhang, G. P. (2003). Why software projects escalate: The importance of project management constructs. *IEEE Transactions on Engineering Management, 50*(3), 251–261. doi:10.1109/TEM.2003.817312

Kemerer, C. F. (1987). An empirical validation of software cost estimation models. *Communications of the ACM, 30*(5), 416–429. doi:10.1145/22899.22906

Kennedy, J., & Eberhart, R. C. (1995). Particle swarm optimization. *Proceedings of IEEE International Conference on Neural Networks,* Piscataway, NJ, (pp. 1942–1948).

Kennedy, J., & Eberhart, R. C. (1997). A discrete binary version of the particle swarm algorithm. *Proceedings of the 1997 IEEE Conference on Systems, Man, and Cybernetics,* Piscataway, NJ, (pp. 4104-4109).

Kennedy, J., & Eberhart, R. C. (2001). *Swarm intelligence.* San Francisco: Morgan Kaufmann.

Kitchanham, B. A., & Taylor, N. R. (1984). Software cost models. *ICL Technology Journal, 4*(3), 73–102.

Knowles, J., & Corne, D. (2000). Approximating the nondominated front using the Pareto archived evolution strategy. *Evolutionary Computation, 8,* 149–172. doi:10.1162/106365600568167

Kohavi, R., & John, G. (1997). Wrappers for feature subset selection . *Artificial Intelligence, 97,* 273–324. doi:10.1016/S0004-3702(97)00043-X

Konar, A. (2005). *Computational intelligence: Principles, techniques and applications.* Berlin: Springer.

Li, X., et al. (2003). A nondominated sorting particle swarm optimizer for multiobjective optimization. In E. Cantú- Paz et al., (Eds.), *Proceedings of Genetic and Evolutionary Computation,* GECCO 2003, (LNCS Vol. 2723, pp. 37-48). Berlin: Springer.

Miller, A. (2002). *Subset selection in regression,* (2nd Ed.). Boca Raton, FL: Chapman Hall.

Mitchell, M. (1996). *An introduction to Genetic Algorithms.* Cambridge, MA: MIT Press.

Miyazaki, Y., & Mori, K. (1985). COCOMO evaluation and tailoring. *Proceedings of the Eighth International Software Engineering Conference.* London: IEEE CS Press.

Nguyen, V., Steece, B., & Boehm, B. (2008). *A constrained regression technique for COCOMO calibration*. Retrieved January 14, 2009 from http://sunset.usc.edu/csse/TECHRPTS/2008/usc-csse-2008-806/usc-csse-2008-806.pdf

Parsopoulos, K., & Vrahatis, M. (2002). Particle swarm optimization method in multiobjective problems. *Proceedings of 2002 ACM Symposium on Applied Computing (SAC'2002)*, Madrid, Spain, (pp. 603-607).

Putnam, L. H. (1978). General empirical solution to the macro sizing and estimation problem. *IEEE Transactions on Software Engineering, SE-4*(4), 345–361. doi:10.1109/TSE.1978.231521

Sanchez-Marono, N., Alonso-Betanzos, A., & Castillo, E. (2005). A New Wrapper method for feature subset selection. *ESANN 2005 proceedings - European Symposium on Artificial Neural Networks*, Bruges, Belgium.

Schooff, R. M., & Haimes, Y. Y. (1999). Dynamic multistage software estimation. *IEEE Transactions on Man, and Cybernetics, 29*(2), 272–284. doi:10.1109/5326.760571

Shepperd, M., & Schofield, C. (1997). Estimating software project effort using analogies. *IEEE Transactions on Software Engineering, 23*(11), 736–743. doi:10.1109/32.637387

Shirabad, J. S., & Menzies, T. J. (2005). *The PROMISE repository of software engineering databases*. School of Information Technology and Engineering, University of Ottawa, Canada. Retrieved January 14, 2009 from http://promise.site.uottawa.ca/SERepository

Smith, A., & Mason, A. (1997). Cost estimation predictive modeling: Regression versus neural network. *The Engineering Economist, 42*(2), 137–161. doi:10.1080/00137919708903174

Standish Group Report: Extreme Chaos, (2001). Retrieved January 14, 2009 from http://www.vertexlogic.com/processOnline/processData/documents/pdf/extreme_chaos.pdf

Tibshirani, R. (1996). Regression shrinkage and selection via the lasso. *Journal of the Royal Statistical Society. Series A, (Statistics in Society), 58*, 267–288.

Wysocki, B. (1998). Some firms, let down by costly computers opt to 'de-engineer.' *Wall Street Journal*, A1- A6.

Yahya, M.A., Ahmad, R., & Lee, S. P. (2008). Effects of software process maturity on COCOMO II's effort estimation from CMMI perspective. *IEEE International Conference on Research, Innovation and Vision for the Future*, (pp. 255 – 262).

Yang, D., Wan, Y., Tang, Z., Wu, S., He, M., & Li, M. (2006). COCOMO-U: An Extension of COCOMO II for Cost Estimation with Uncertainty. In Q. Wang, D. Pfahl, D.M. Raffo & P. Wernick, (Eds.) *Software Process Change*. (LNCS, 3966, pp. 132–141). Berlin: Springer.

Yang, J., & Honavar, V. (1998). Feature subset selection using a genetic algorithm. *IEEE Intelligent Systems and Their Applications, 13*(2), 44–49.

Zadeh, L. A. (1994). Soft computing and fuzzy logic. *IEEE Software, 11*(6), 48–56. doi:10.1109/52.329401

Zitzler, E., Laumanns, M., & Thiele, L. (2000). SPEA2: Improving the strength Pareto evolutionary algorithm. *Proceedings of EUROGEN 2001*.

Chapter 4
Auto–Associative Neural Networks to Improve the Accuracy of Estimation Models

Salvatore A. Sarcia
Università di Roma Tor Vergata, Italy

Giovanni Cantone
Università di Roma Tor Vergata, Italy

Victor R. Basili
University of Maryland, USA

ABSTRACT

Prediction of software engineering variables with high accuracy is still an open problem. The primary reason for the lack of high accuracy in prediction might be because most models are linear in the parameters and so are not sufficiently flexible and suffer from redundancy. In this chapter, we focus on improving regression models by decreasing their redundancy and increasing their parsimony, i.e., we turn the model into a model with fewer variables than the former. We present an empirical auto-associative neural network-based strategy for model improvement, which implements a reduction technique called Curvilinear component analysis. The contribution of this chapter is to show how multi-layer feedforward neural networks can be a useful and practical mechanism for improving software engineering estimation models.

INTRODUCTION

Prediction of software engineering variables such as project cost, fault proneness, and number of defects is a critical issue for software organizations. It is important to get the best estimate possible when planning a new project, activity, or task. For instance,

we may have to predict the software cost, the effort in carrying out an activity (e.g. coding a module), or the expected number of defects arising from a module or sub-system. Improving the prediction capability of software organizations is one way of improving their competitive advantage. Better predictions can improve the development process in terms of planning resources, setting and achieving quality goals, and making more informed decisions

DOI: 10.4018/978-1-60566-758-4.ch004

about the schedule. The point is that, prediction is a major problem when trying to better manage resources, mitigate project risk, and deliver products on time, on budget and with the required features and functions (quality) (Boehm, 1981).

Despite the fact that prediction of software variables with high accuracy is a very important issue for competing software organizations, it is still an unsolved problem (Shepperd, 2007). A large number of different prediction models have been proposed over the last three decades (Shepperd, 2007). There are predefined mathematical functions (e.g., FP-based functions, COCOMO-I, and COCOMO-II), calibrated functions (e.g., function based on a regression analysis on local data), machines learning (e.g., estimation by analogy, classification and regression trees, artificial neural networks), and human-based judgment models. There exist a large number of empirical studies aimed at predicting some software engineering variable (Myrtveit, 2005). Most often, the variable is software project cost, which we will use as the main exemplar of the approach described in this chapter.

In this chapter, we present a computational intelligence technique to improve the accuracy of parametric estimation models based on regression functions. The improvement technique is defined, tested, and verified through software cost estimation data (Sarcia, Cantone, & Basili, 2008). In particular, this chapter offers a technique that is able to improve the accuracy of log-linear regression models in the context of the COCOMO-81 projects (Boehm, 1981; Shirabad, & Menzies, 2005). From a mathematical point of view, even if we change the model variables, e.g., we predict effort instead of predicting the number of defects, or vice versa, the strategy to improve the estimation model does not change at all. This means that we can apply the improvement strategy to any set of variables in any kind of development context without change. Of course, it does not mean that the improvement technique will succeed in every context.

It is important to note that, even if we were making predictions through human-based judgment, to increase estimation accuracy we would have to build parametric models calibrated to the local data and use them to estimate variables of interest for the specific context of the organization (McConnell, 2006). For instance, productivity (lines of code/time) may change according to the context of the organization (e.g., capability of analysts and developers, complexity of the software system, environment of the development process). The point is that, even experts should use regression functions for gathering suitable information from the context in which they are operating. Therefore, apart from the kind of estimation model used, when improving estimation accuracy, calibrating regression functions is a required activity. We believe that, enhancing accuracy of regression functions is the core of any estimation activity. That is why we focus upon improving regression functions and do not deal with other approaches.

We begin with an introduction that provides the general perspective. Then, we provide some background notes, required terminology, and define the problem. We present, from a practical point of view, the main issues concerning parametric estimation models, multi-layer feed-forward neural networks, and auto-associative neural networks. We illustrate the empirical strategy for dealing with the problem (the solution). We conclude with a discussion of the benefits and drawbacks of the methodology and provide some ideas on future research directions.

PARAMETRIC ESTIMATION MODELS

The estimation models that we refer to are based on parametric models as illustrated in Figure 1.

Mathematically, the estimation model (EM) in Figure 1 can be represented by a regression function f_R such that $y = f_R(x,\beta) + \varepsilon$, where x is a set of independent variables, y is the dependent

Figure 1. Parametric estimation model (regression functions)

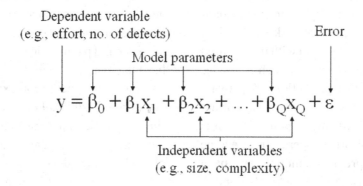

variable, and $\beta = (\beta_0 \ldots \beta_Q)$ is a set of parameters defining f_R. The component ε is the aleatory part of the model (i.e. the unknown part depending on the probability of future events) representing our uncertainty about the relationship between the independent and dependent variables, with $E(\varepsilon) = 0$ and $cov(\varepsilon) = \sigma^2 I$ (Weisberg, 1985). To calculate function f_R, we need to know every point of the population. This almost never happens. Then, since we know only a finite sample from the population, we can only estimate β by finding a set of estimators $B = (b_0 \ldots b_Q)$ such that they minimize an error function, e.g., the least squares error function. To estimate B, we use previous observations of both dependent (Y) and independent (X) variables (Figure 2).

We consider the relationship $Y = f_R(X, B)$, where Y is a set of observations of the dependent variable, X is the observation matrix including N observations of Q independent variables, and B

is the vector of parameters estimating β (Figure 2). Note that, we use a lowercase letter (e.g., x) to refer to the variables and an uppercase letter (e.g., X) to refer to the data. Because of ε, the least squares estimate, i.e. B in Figure 2, are different from parameters β. Thus, f_R fed with X provides $Y_{est} = f_R(X, B)$, not Y. Then, the difference $e = Y - Y_{est}$ is a vector of errors representing ε (called residuals, with $e \neq \varepsilon$). The most important part in modeling is to find the best estimates for β. This activity is called parameter estimation, fitting, or calibration. Note that, the LS estimate in Figure 2 is based on finding the minimum of the sum of squares of the error. From a practical point of view, the minimum of the sum of squares of the error can be found by setting the gradient to zero, where the derivative is made with respect to each parameter. Therefore, minimizing the cost function means solving a system of equations of partial derivatives set to zero (McQuarrie & Tsai, 1998, Pedhazur,

Figure 2. Least squares estimate

$$Y = \begin{pmatrix} y_1 \\ \vdots \\ y_N \end{pmatrix} \quad X = \begin{pmatrix} 1 & x_{11} & \cdots & x_{1Q} \\ \vdots & \vdots & & \vdots \\ 1 & x_{N1} & \cdots & x_{NQ} \end{pmatrix} \quad B = (X^TX)^{-1}X^TY = \begin{pmatrix} b_0 \\ b_1 \\ \vdots \\ b_Q \end{pmatrix}$$

$$\underbrace{\hspace{10cm}}$$

Observations $\qquad\qquad$ Least squares estimate

1997). If the system of equations is composed of a linear combination of the sought parameters, the EM is linear in the parameters, and we have a closed solution (B in Figure 2). If the system of equations is composed of non-linear equations of the sought parameters, the EM is non-linear in the parameters and the solution can be found iteratively (there is no closed solution).

Note that, even a non-linear polynomial such as $y = \beta_0 + \beta_1 x_1 + \beta_2 x_2 + \beta_3 x_1 x_2 + \beta_4 x_1^2 + \beta_5 x_2^2$ is linear in the parameters. This can be obtained by transforming its variables as follows $x_1 x_2 = x_3$, $x_1^2 = x_4$, and $x_2^2 = x_5$. Therefore, $y = \beta_0 + \beta_1 x_1 + \beta_2 x_2 + \beta_3 x_3 + \beta_4 x_4 + \beta_5 x_5$, which is still a linear model where we can apply the least squares estimate in Figure 2. Another important transformation is about turning a geometric model into a linear model through logarithms. The resulting function is called log-linear regression function. For instance, $y = x_1^a \Pi_{i=1..k} c_i$ is a geometric model having a variable x_1, a coefficient "a" as a power of x_1, and k multiplicative coefficients. Taking the logarithm of both sides of $y = x_1^a \Pi_{i=1..k} c_i$, we can break down the product into sums. Based on the logarithm properties, i.e. $\ln(pq) = \ln(p) + \ln(q)$ and $\ln(p^q) = (q)\ln(p)$, we can write $\ln(y) = \beta_1 \ln(x_1) + \beta_2 \ln(c_1) + \ldots + \beta_{k+1} \ln(c_k)$, where we have used the letter β to indicate the model parameters (with a $= \beta_1$). Then, we can set $z = \ln(y)$, $h_1 = \ln(x_1)$, $h_2 = \ln(c_1) \ldots h_{k+1} = \ln(c_k)$ and add an intercept (β_0) so that the log-linear model becomes $z = \beta_0 + \beta_1 h_1 + \beta_2 h_2 + \ldots + \beta_{k+1} h_{k+1}$, which is still a model linear in its parameters where we can use the least squares estimate in Figure 2. Note that, we use an intercept (β_0) because if the remaining monomials (i.e., $\beta_i h_i$, with i = 1 to k+1) vanish (in case of non-correlation), the equation $z = \beta_0 + \beta_1 h_1 + \beta_2 h_2 + \ldots + \beta_{k+1} h_{k+1}$ continues to be satisfied ($z = \beta_0$).

Note that, if we want to get the best linear unbiased estimators (BLUE) of β (Gauss-Markov theorem) and use the model for inference, LS requires some assumptions (Pedhazur, 1997):

- Errors ε are not x correlated.
- The variance of the errors is constant (homoscedasticity), $cov(\varepsilon) = \sigma^2 I$.
- Errors ε are not auto-correlated.
- The probability density of the error is Gaussian, $\varepsilon \sim NID(0, \sigma^2 I)$, i.e. there are no outliers, skewed/kurtotic distributions, and measurement error.

Since the characteristic expressing the relationship between inputs and output is called *model shape*, the equation in Figure 1 has a linear shape and is linear in the parameters. For instance, a third degree polynomial has a cubic shape and is still linear in the parameters. *Complexity* of a model is another characteristic expressing the number of parameters composing the model. The more parameters the model has, the more flexible the model is. Models that are linear in the parameters have as many parameters as variables (i.e., one and only one parameter for each variable). Therefore, to increase the model flexibility (i.e. the number of parameters) of a linear-in-the-parameter model we have to increase its variables (e.g., increasing the polynomial degree). Barron (1993) proves that the number of parameters required to execute an approximation with a fixed accuracy increases exponentially with the number of variables for models that are linear in the parameters, while it increases linearly with the number of variables for models that are non-linear in the parameters. This means that, to take advantage fully of parsimony we should consider non-linear-in-the-parameter models instead of the linear ones. If we use models that are non-linear in their parameters such as multi-layer feed-forward neural networks, we can increase the model flexibility (i.e. increasing the number of parameters) without adding new variables. This is the real essence of the parsimony (Dreyfus, 2005, pp. 13-14).

However, as mentioned above, non-linear models do not have a closed solution for estimating parameters B. Therefore, to overcome this problem, researchers and practitioners often prefer to use models that are linear in the parameters instead of using the non-linear ones. However, if we choose models that are linear in the parameters, finding the model shape that best fits the data is much more difficult than if we used models that are non-linear in the parameters (Dreyfus, 2005, pp. 136-138). Conversely, iterative procedures require a lot of experience to be effectively used in practical problems. For instance, iterative procedures may provide different parameter estimates depending on the initialization values (Bishop, 1995, pp. 140-148; Dreyfus, 2005, pp. 118-119). Therefore, finding the right parameters may require many attempts as well as the use of optimization techniques to reduce the calibration time.

Estimation Model Accuracy

Prediction models may be evaluated in terms of Absolute Error (AE), i.e. AE = Actual − Estimated = $Y - Y_{est}$. However, an absolute error measure makes no sense when dealing with estimation model accuracy for software engineering variables (e.g., effort, defects). In fact, an Absolute Error would increase with the size of what we were predicting. Let AE_1 (= 0.30) and AE_2 (= 0.25) be the absolute errors calculated by feeding the estimation model with data from two different objects (e.g. project 1 and 2). Then, we might argue that the model is less accurate for project 1 than for project 2 because AE_1 expresses a lower accuracy than AE_2, i.e., $AE_1 > AE_2$. However, if Y_1 (the actual value from which AE_1 has been calculated) were much greater than Y_2, i.e., $Y_1 >> Y_2$, and $AE_1 \approx AE_2$ or even $AE_1 > AE_2$, then looking at the absolute error AE_1, we would incorrectly judge that the estimation model accuracy on object 1 is worse than the accuracy on object 2. Actually, we should judge the accuracy on object 1 as better than the accuracy on object 2, i.e. the (absolute) error should be evaluated with respect to the magnitude of the predictions. For

instance, it should be much more severe having a prediction error AE = 0.30 for a project of 100 man/months than a prediction error AE = 0.30 for a project of 10,000 man/months. This means that, an absolute measure should not be used for model comparison. When predicting software engineering variables, the right choice is to consider a relative error measure, i.e. a measure that takes into account the size of what we are predicting (Myrtveit, Stensrud, & Shepperd, 2005). For this reason, Boehm (1981) defined the performance of his software cost model (COnstructive COst MOdel, COCOMO) in terms of *Relative Error* (RE), Eqn. 1.

$$RE = (Actual - Estimated)/Actual = (Y - Y_{est})/Y. \quad (1)$$

Note that, currently the Boehm's model has enhanced into the COCOMO-II (Boehm et al., 2000), but the accuracy evaluation principles have not changed. The evaluation procedure of the model accuracy is shown in Figure 3.

We start with considering a *data set* of size N, which is split up into two subsets, a training set and a test set. The training set size is TR = (2/3)N and the test set size is TE = (1/3)N, thus N = TR + TE. We choose the splitting proportion 2/3-1/3 because it is a usual choice when dealing with hold-out methodologies (Chen, Menzies, Port, & Boehm, 2005; Kohavi & John, 1997). A further valid proportion is 80%-20% (Dreyfus, 2005, pp. 103-106). Based on the training set, we calibrate function f_R, i.e., estimate parameters B by the least squares estimates (Figure 2). Note that, to avoid any confusion between the training set and the test set, we use an apostrophe to point out that the data belongs to the training set (i.e., X' and Y'). Moreover, it is important noting that, differently from X' (Figure 3), the test set X (Figure 3) does not have a vector of 1s in the first column. Once we have calculated the parameters B, we feed X into f_R and obtain the estimated values Y_{est}. Notice that, the size of Y_{est} is TE, i.e. $Y_{est} = (Y_{est}^{(1)} \dots Y_{est}^{(TE)})$. Then, accuracy is evaluated by calculating two

Figure 3. Evaluating estimation models

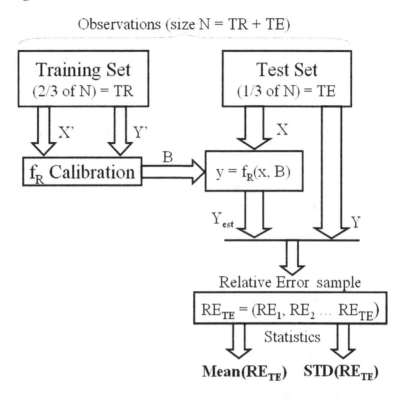

summary statistics over the Relative Error sample as shown in Figure 3. In particular, $Mean(RE_{TE})$ = $(1/TE)\Sigma_{i=1..TE}(RE_i)$ is a measure of the *bias* of f_R and $STD(RE_{TE})$ = $SQRT\{(1/N)\Sigma_{i=1..TE}([RE_i -Mean(RE_{TE})]^2)\}$ is a measure of the *spread* of f_R. Note that, a correct evaluation can be done through both statistics at the same time. For instance, if we find out that a model has a $Mean(RE_{TE})$ closer to zero with respect to another model, we can infer that the former is more accurate than the latter in terms of *correctness*. Moreover, if the former has a narrower $STR(RE_{TE})$ than the latter, we can infer that the former is more accurate in terms of *reliability* (stability).

It is very important to note that, sometimes parametric models are evaluated in terms of *Magnitude of Relative Error* (MRE) (Conte, Dunsmore, & Shen, 1986; Shirabad & Menzies, 2005), where $MRE_i = abs(RE_i)$. The evaluation is performed by two summary statistics, as well. The first one is $MMRE = (1/TE)\Sigma_{i=1..TE}(MRE_i)$

and the second one is PRED(H), Eqn. (2).

$$PRED(K) = (100/TE)\sum_{i=1..TE}\begin{cases}1 \to MRE_i \leq (K/100) \\ 0 \to otherwise\end{cases}$$

(2)

A PRED(25) = 80% means that 80% of the estimates have an error not greater than 0.25. Since when calculating the MMRE, differently from $Mean(RE_{TE})$, positive errors and negative errors do not cancel reciprocally, MMRE would seem a better statistic than $Mean(RE_{TE})$. However, Kitchenham et al. (2001) prove that MMRE and PRED(K) cannot be used for comparing estimation model accuracy because neither MMRE nor PRED(H) express *bias* or *spread* of the model. In particular, they show that MMRE and PRED(N) measure *spread* and *kurtosis* of the random variable Z = Estimated/Actual, respectively. Nevertheless, MMRE may be a useful measure when evaluating the goodness-of-fit of a model.

THE PROBLEM

The problem that we deal with in this chapter is to improve (parametric) models that are linear in the parameters. There are many ways of improving regression model accuracy. For instance, we can (1) choose a better function, e.g. the one that has a more suitable shape or (2) select input variables that are more relevant. In the former, the game is to select a function shape that best fits the data. In the latter, the real problem is that, once we have selected the complete input variable set, we need to remove redundancy that negatively affects the performance of the estimation model (e.g., by taking out irrelevant variables).

As reported in the Section "*Parametric Estimation Models*", however, practitioners and researchers prefer using models that are linear in the parameters because they have a closed solution to the problem of calculating the model parameters (Figure 2), while models that are non-linear in the parameters do not. Then, to support those practitioners and researchers in their practical problems the best that we can do is to improve regression models that they actually use, i.e. the linear-in-the-parameter ones. That is why, we focus on removing the redundancy of linear models, and we do not consider non-linear models as a way of improving estimation accuracy.

Taking out redundancy is about finding a model that is more parsimonious (i.e., the one having fewer input variables). Such a model is preferable because it is able to provide better estimates with the same number of observations. Let N be this number. If we use a function having fewer variables, we can get further degrees of freedom to calibrate its parameters. Vice versa, since N is constant, if we consider functions having additional variables, the degrees of freedom in calibrating the model parameters decrease and the estimates will be less accurate (Barron, 1993; Dreyfus, 2005, p. 14). Therefore, parsimony can be considered as a power multiplier for regression functions. Intuitively, the rationale of this power

enhancement is the same as the example of a plane calculation. We cannot define a plane using only two points because a plane has three parameters, i.e. we need at least three points to determine the equation of a plane. Therefore, since the data set size (N) stays constant, if we reduce the number of input variables (i.e., making the model more parsimonious), we can increase the accuracy of the model.

To increase parsimony of a regression function we have substantially two options. We can (1) shrink the input set into an equivalent pattern or (2) remove irrelevant variables. The former is usually performed by applying Principal Component Analysis (PCA) (Jollife, 1986). The latter is based on methods where the least irrelevant variables are taken out stepwise (Chen, Menzies, Port, & Boehm, 2005; Kohavi & John, 1997). Actually, there would be another option to make the model more parsimonious, but it is generally inapplicable because of its too high computational cost. This technique is the *exhaustive procedure*. It consists of considering all the combinations that we can get with Q elements. For instance, if we have Q variables, we have to consider 2^Q different combinations, i.e. 2^Q models, each having different variables from each other. The basis of the power is 2 because an element can belong to the set or not (binary choice). For each model, the procedure goes on by calculating the error. Then, the model having the highest accuracy is selected.

In this work, we present an empirical strategy to shrink the input set by applying an improved version of PCA called Curvilinear Component Analysis (CCA) or non-linear Principal Component Analysis (Sarcia, Cantone, & Basili, 2008). We apply CCA instead of using PCA because CCA is able to overcome some drawbacks affecting PCA. For instance, PCA can just find linear redundancy, while CCA can find both linear and non-linear redundancy. Note that, to increase the model parsimony we focus on input reduction techniques instead of the stepwise ones because the former can be completely automated while the latter cannot. In fact, stepwise techniques require making a decision as to variables to be removed, i.e. the least relevant variables. If we do not know the relevance of each variable, stepwise techniques may be difficult to be correctly applied.

CURVILINEAR COMPONENT ANALYSIS

CCA is a procedure for feature reduction that consists of turning a training set into a more compact and equivalent representation. CCA is a compression technique that maps a set into another set having fewer variables, where the mapping is non-linear. We implement CCA through auto-associative multi-layer feed-forward neural networks (Bishop, 1995, pp. 314-319). Implementing CCA does not require being an expert in neural network (NN). A CCA implementation can be found in any mathematical application that is able to deal with NNs and/or matrices. CCA requires just a few lines of code. Even if one does not have the opportunity to use a mathematical suite, a CCA algorithm can be easily implemented through the same programming language used for estimating the LS parameters. Before delving into details of auto-associative neural networks, we provide some background on multi-layer feed-forward neural networks.

Multi-Layer Feed-Forward Neural Networks

A neuron is a function $y = \theta (w_0 + \Sigma_{i = 1..Q} w_i X_i)$, where θ can be linear or non-linear (Figure 4). If θ is linear (i.e., is the identity function), the neuron is called linear neuron and is the same as a polynomial of first degree. In other words, a linear polynomial is a particular case of a linear neuron. If θ is non-linear, the neuron is called non-linear, e.g., θ can be a sigmoid function such as the logistic function or the hyperbolic tangent function (Dreyfus, 2005, pp. 2-3).

Figure 4. Representation of a neuron

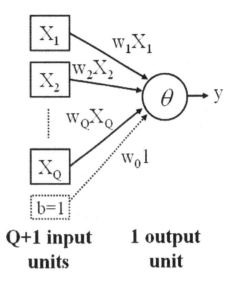

Q+1 input units   **1 output unit**

A neuron (also called unit) calculates an output (y) by summing the products between a weight w_i and an input X_i, with i = 1 to Q. Note that, weights are called parameters, as well. Function θ is called *activation function*. The input labeled "b=1" is called *bias*. It is an input that provides a constant value of 1. The bias unit plays the same role as the intercept in a polynomial.

A Multi-layer Feed-forward Neural Network (MFNN) is generally composed of non-linear neurons arranged on some layers (Figure 5). In a feed-*forward* network, data can only flow from the inputs toward the outputs. In *recurrent networks*, the data can flow backward, as well. In Figure 5, h may be different from θ. For instance, in regression problems, h is non-linear and θ is linear (the identity function). In discrimination problems, both h and θ are non-linear. In Figure 5, units in the middle (labeled h) are called *hidden* because they are hidden from the outside. Note that, the hidden layer expresses the complexity of the model. The more hidden units, the more parameters the model has. For instance, an MFNN having two hidden units is more complex than an MFNN with just one hidden unit, just as a second order polynomial is more complex than a first-order polynomial.

Figure 5. A multi-layer feed-forward neural network

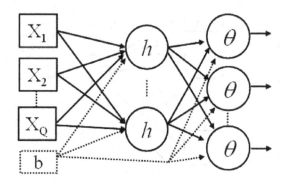

**Q+1 input   H hidden   Θ output
  units   units   units**

The problem is to calculate the model weights (w$_i$) such that the input values are mapped to the output values. The weight calculation is also called model training. Since we force the model to learn the (observed) output values through the training procedure, the network training is called *supervised*. To estimate the model parameters, a cost function has to be minimized just like the LS procedure in Figure 2 (Bishop, 1995, pp.194-201).

The difference is that, the closed solution of B in Figure 2 does not apply to MFNNs. We have to estimate the model parameters iteratively. The most effective iterative training technique is the Backpropagation (Rumelhart, Hilton, & Williams, 1986). This is a method based on calculating the gradient of the cost function step-by-step. For each step, the gradient is used to update the parameters found in the previous step. The algorithm stops when satisfactory conditions have been met. It is important to note that, the hidden neurons play a primary role here. In fact, their output can be considered as a representation of the input in mapping the output (Rumelhart, Hilton, & Williams, 1986). This property will be used for implementing Auto-Associative Neural Networks.

Auto-Associative Multi-Layer Feed-Forward Neural Networks

An Auto-Associative Neural Network (AANN) is a particular kind of MFNN. Figure 6 shows an example of its topology.

The aim of this kind of neural network is to perform an input dimensionality reduction in a

Figure 6. An auto-associative multi-layer feed-forward neural network for non-linear dimensionality reduction

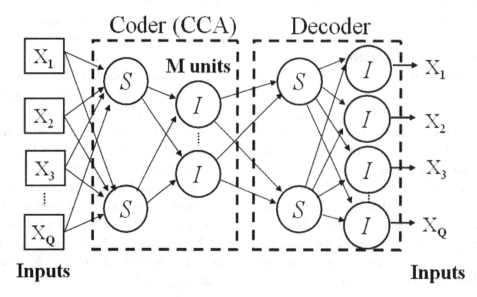

non-linear way. The strategy is based on mapping Q input variables into Q output variables. The observed outputs used to train the network (targets) are just the observed inputs themselves (for this reason this network is called auto-associative). The AANN in Figure 6 maps each observed input into itself (Bishop, 1995, p. 314). This strategy can be effectively used for dimensionality reduction if the number of the neurons in the second hidden layer (i.e., M in Figure 6) is less than Q. So, the sub-network that we call *Coder* performs a compression of the Q inputs implementing the CCA. The sub-network that we call *Decoder* assures that the compression performed by the Coder is consistent with the input data.

To perform a correct non-linear dimensionality reduction, both units in the second hidden layer and the output units must be linear (I = Identity function). Units in the first and third hidden layers must be non-linear (S = Sigmoidal function). The training of this kind of network is based on minimizing a cost function similar to the one used for MFNNs (Bishop, 1995, p. 314).

Note that, the Coder projects the data from a Q-dimensional space into an M-dimensional space, while the Decoder performs the inverse mapping back to the Q-dimensional space. Curvilinear components are encapsulated in the Coder. This means that, once the AANN has been calibrated, the Coder can be used for transforming any input into an equivalent representation with respect to the original one exploiting fewer variables (from Q to M). In other words, the Coder can execute a non-linear dimensionality reduction (CCA). This important result is made possible because of the presence of non-linear functions in the first and third hidden layer (S). This kind of AANN is able to perform also a linear dimensionality reduction as a particular case of the non-linear one.

THE EMPIRICAL STRATEGY FOR MODEL IMPROVEMENT

The aim of the model improvement strategy is to find empirically the most accurate model. Consider two distinct models EM_1 and EM_2 being compared. As discussed in the Section *"Estimation Model Accuracy"*, we can argue that EM_1 is more accurate (correct) than EM_2 if two conditions are satisfied at the same time: (1) the bias of EM_1 is closer to zero than the bias of EM_2 and (2) the spread of EM_1 is not worse than the spread of EM_2. The problem is that, CCA can be applied with different reduction rates, i.e. with respect to Figure 6, the number of the units in the second hidden layer (M) may be set to M = Q through to 1, where M = Q means no reduction and M = 1 means that the shrunken input data is expressed by only one component. But, we do not know the best CCA reduction rate (M), i.e. the one that bears the most accurate estimation model. To find it, we use an empirical strategy reported below (Sarcia, Cantone, & Basili, 2008). The authors show that the strategy together with CCA can significantly improve accuracy of log-linear regression models calibrated on the COCOMO 81 data set (Shirabad & Menzies, 2005). The strategy is the following.

Precondition

- Rely on a data set (DS) of past observations where each of them is expressed by Q independent variables x_1, x_2 ... x_Q and the DS size is N (i.e. DS_{QXN}) with N (= TR + TE) statistically significant
- Independent variables x_1, x_2 ... x_Q are relevant to predict the dependent variable y and constitute the complete input set (Dreyfus, 2005, pp. 95-96).

Procedure

1. Split up DS_{QXN} into two subsets (training and test set) as explained in Figure 3, obtaining

Figure 7. Data management for the empirical strategy

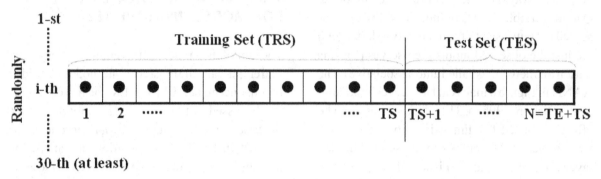

TRS = (X', Y') and TES = (X, Y) (Figure 7)

2. Use TRS (i-th row in Figure 7) to train Q − 1 models (e.g. a log-linear regression function) by applying CCA as many times, where each time TRS is reduced by 1 component through 1 starting from Q − 1 components, i.e. in the first CCA application M = Q − 1, in the second one M = Q − 2 and so on up to M = 1

3. For each of the Q − 1 models in step 2, calculate the $\text{Mean}(RE_{TE})$ and $\text{STD}(RE_{TE})$ as explained in Figure 3, i.e. feed TES into each of the Q − 1 models

4. Based on the Q − 1 models obtained in step 2, select the model having the best $\text{Mean}(RE_{TE})$ i.e., the closest to zero

5. Use TRS to train a model without applying CCA (labeled NO-CCA hereafter), i.e. a model without reduction

6. Calculate the $\text{Mean}(RE_{TE})$ and $\text{STD}(RE_{TE})$ feeding TES into the NO-CCA model (step 5)

7. Repeat Steps 1 through 6 for a statistically sufficient number of times (e.g. 30) changing randomly the composition of TRS and TES (Figure 7) and get two samples (and so two distributions) for each considered summary statistic (Figure 8), i.e., $\text{MnRE}_{CCA} \equiv \{\text{Mean}_{CCA}(RE_{TE}^{(1)}) \dots \text{Mean}_{CCA}(RE_{TE}^{(30)})\}$, $\text{STDRE}_{CCA} \equiv$

$\{\text{STD}_{CCA}(RE_{TE}^{(1)}) \dots \text{STD}_{CCA}(RE_{TE}^{(30)})\}$, and $\text{MnRE}_{NO\text{-}CCA} \equiv \{\text{Mean}_{NO\text{-}CCA}(RE_{TE}^{(1)}) \dots \text{Mean}_{NO\text{-}CCA}(RE_{TE}^{(30)})\}$, $\text{STDRE}_{NO\text{-}CCA} \equiv \{\text{STD}_{NO\text{-}CCA}(RE_{TE}^{(1)}) \dots \text{STD}_{NO\text{-}CCA}(RE_{TE}^{(30)})\}$, respectively

8. Based upon suitable statistical tests (i.e., parametric or non-parametric), evaluate the hypotheses whether (1) MnRE_{CCA} is significantly better than $\text{MnRE}_{NO\text{-}CCA}$ and (2) STDRE_{CCA} is insignificantly different from $\text{STDRE}_{NO\text{-}CCA}$. If the statistical tests significantly confirm hypotheses (1) and (2) at the same time, then execute steps 9 and 10, otherwise stop this procedure because CCA cannot significantly improve the accuracy. In the latter case, we can conclude that the data set DS_{NxQ} has no curvilinear redundancy hence any compression will make worse accuracy of the model

9. Select the model corresponding to the best value in $\text{MnRE}_{CCA} \equiv \{\text{Mean}_{CCA}(RE_{TE}^{(1)}) \dots \text{Mean}_{CCA}(RE_{TE}^{(30)})\}$. If two models have the same bias choose the one having the smallest spread; if two models have both the same bias and spread, choose one of them randomly

10. Use the chosen model for prediction.

Figure 8. Samples of statistics obtained by randomization

$MnRE_{CCA}$	$STDRE_{CCA}$	$MnRE_{NO\text{-}CCA}$	$STDRE_{NO\text{-}CCA}$
$Mean_{CCA}(RE_{TE}^{(1)})$	$STD_{CCA}(RE_{TE}^{(1)})$	$Mean_{NO\text{-}CCA}(RE_{TE}^{(1)})$	$STD_{NO\text{-}CCA}(RE_{TE}^{(1)})$
$Mean_{CCA}(RE_{TE}^{(2)})$	$STD_{CCA}(RE_{TE}^{(2)})$	$Mean_{NO\text{-}CCA}(RE_{TE}^{(2)})$	$STD_{NO\text{-}CCA}(RE_{TE}^{(2)})$
$\vdots$	$\vdots$	$\vdots$	$\vdots$
$Mean_{CCA}(RE_{TE}^{(30)})$	$STD_{CCA}(RE_{TE}^{(30)})$	$Mean_{NO\text{-}CCA}(RE_{TE}^{(30)})$	$STD_{NO\text{-}CCA}(RE_{TE}^{(30)})$

FUTURE RESEARCH DIRECTIONS

The application of this strategy to the COCOMO 81 data set (Sarcia, Cantone, & Basili, 2008) was able to improve the accuracy of log-linear models by randomizing the COCOMO 81 data set and applying two treatments, i.e., CCA and NO-CCA, and checked the results of both distributions using the Mann-Whitney and the Signed rank tests. We believe this successful application of the strategy is an encouraging step for the use of computational intelligence techniques. It offers a new direction for supporting traditional approaches in dealing with estimation problems. To increase the confidence of the software engineering community in the use of such emerging technologies, scholars, researchers, and practitioners should focus on replicating past experiments and performing new investigations based on different settings, e.g., by changing contexts and variables of interest.

An important future area of research is to compare the proposed CCA strategy to stepwise feature selection techniques, as well as exploring the possibility of defining a new strategy that combines both techniques.

CONCLUSION

In this chapter, we have discussed some issues concerning parametric estimation models based on regression functions. We have shown that these functions are relevant for any kind of estimation methodology even for human-based judgment techniques (McConnell, 2006, pp. 105-112). The problem of improving the performance of regression functions is a major issue for any software organization that aims at delivering their products on time, on budget, and with the required quality. To improve the performance of regression functions, we have presented an empirical strategy based on a shrinking technology called CCA and showed its implementation by auto-associative neural networks. We have discussed the reasons why CCA is able to increase accuracy (correctness) without worsening the spread (variability) of the model (Sarcia, Cantone, & Basili, 2008). We have focused on the possibility of CCA to make models more parsimonious.

Let us now consider the implications of the empirical strategy reported above. From a practical point of view, an advantage of applying CCA is that we do not need to know the relevance of each attribute being removed with respect to the considered context. This is an advantage because, if we do not know the relevance of the attributes being removed, as stepwise feature selection techniques do, we cannot improve the model making it more parsimonious (Chen, Menzies, Port, & Boehm, 2005; Kohavi & John, 1997). Moreover, CCA does not suffer from multicollinearity, which affects stepwise methods. Multicollinearity is a statistical effect based on the impossibility of separating the influence of two or more input variables on the output (Weisberg, 1985). CCA overcomes this problem by considering the simultaneous effect of every input variable by finding non-linear redundancy of input variables in predicting the output. A further advantage is that, CCA can be completely automated, i.e. it does not require any human interaction to be carried out.

A real application of the presented strategy, is reported in (Sarcia, Cantone, & Basili, 2008), where the authors provide some suggestions as to experimental setting, data management, and statistical tests. The authors find that, with respect to the COCOMO 81 data set, the proposed strategy increases correctness without worsening the reliability of log-linear regression models. Note that, the authors not only compared the medians, but also the standard deviations of the two distributions (i.e., CCA and NO-CCA). As presented above, they applied two non-parametric tests (Mann-Whitney and Signed rank) because a preliminary normality test on both distributions showed that the distributions could not be considered as coming from a normal population. Further results were that, applying the proposed strategy reduces the occurrence of outliers. In other words, estimates obtained by models treated with CCA show fewer outliers than models treated without applying CCA. This means that, CCA can improve reliability in terms of outlier reduction even though correctness may not be improved. This is a valuable result for researchers and practitioners because they may just use the strategy to build models less prone to outliers.

The strategy has some drawbacks. For instance, it has been built on the assumption of having enough data to split up the data set into two subsets (TRS and TES). Conversely, if we do not

have enough data, CCA would not be applicable. CCA is based on building specific multi-layer neural networks, which require some optimization techniques to reduce the training time (Hagan & Menhaj, 1994).

REFERENCES

Barron, A. (1993). Universal approximation bounds for superposition of a sigmoidal function. *IEEE Transactions on Information Theory, 39*(3), 930–945. doi:10.1109/18.256500

Bishop, C. (1995). *Neural Network for Pattern Recognition*. New York: Oxford University Press.

Boehm, B. (1981). *Software Engineering Economics*. Upper Saddle River, NJ: Prentice-Hall.

Boehm, B., Horowitz, E., Madachy, R., Reifer, D., Clark, B. K., Steece, B., et al. (2000). *Software Cost Estimation with COCOMO II*. Upper Saddle River, NJ: Prentice-Hall.

Chen, Z., Menzies, T., Port, D., & Boehm, B. W. (2005). Feature Subset Selection Can Improve Software Cost Estimation Accuracy. In T. Menzies (Ed.), *PROMISE '05* (pp. 1-6). New York: ACM.

Conte, S. D., Dunsmore, H. E., & Shen, V. Y. (1986). *Software Engineering Metrics and Models*. Menlo Park, CA: The Benjamin/Cummings Publishing Company, Inc.

Dreyfus, G. (2005). *Neural Networks Methodology and Applications*. Berlin, Germany: Springer.

Hagan, M. T., & Menhaj, M. B. (1994). Training Feedforward Networks with the Marquardt Algorithm. *IEEE Transactions on Neural Networks, 5*(6), 989–993. doi:10.1109/72.329697

Jollife, I. T. (1986). *Principal Component Analysis*. Berlin, Germany: Springer.

Kitchenham, B., MacDonell, S., Pickard, L., & Shepperd, M. (2001). What accuracy statistics really measure. *IEE Proceedings: Vol. 148. Software Engineering* (pp. 81-85). Washington, DC: IEE Proceeding.

Kohavi, R., & John, G. H. (1997). Wrappers for feature subset selection. *ACM Artificial Intelligence, 97*(1-2), 273–324. doi:10.1016/S0004-3702(97)00043-X

McConnell, S. (2006). *Software Estimation – Demystifying the Black Art.* Redmond, WA: Microsoft press.

McQuarrie, A. D. R., & Tsai, C. (1998). *Regression and Time Series Model Selection.* Singapore: World Scientific Publishing Co. Pte. Ltd.

Myrtveit, I., Stensrud, E., & Shepperd, M. (2005). Reliability and Validity in Comparative Studies of Software Prediction Models. *IEEE Transactions on Software Engineering, 31*(5), 380–391. doi:10.1109/TSE.2005.58

Pedhazur, E. J. (1997). *Multiple Regression in Behavioral Research.* Orlando, FL: Harcourt Brace.

Rumelhart, D. E., Hilton, G. E., & Williams, R. J. (1986). Learning Internal Representations by Error Propagation. In D. Rumelhart & J. McClelland (Ed.): *Parallel Distributing Computing: Explorations in the Microstructure of Cognition: Vol. 1.* (pp. 318-362). Cambridge, MA: The MIT press.

Sarcia, S. A., Cantone, G., & Basili, V. R. (2008). Adopting Curvilinear Component Analysis to Improve Software Cost Estimation Accuracy. Model, Application Strategy, and an Experimental Verification. In G. Visaggio (Ed.), *12th International Conference on Evaluation and Assessment in Software Engineering.* BCS eWIC.

Shepperd, M. (2007). Software project economics: a roadmap. *International Conference on Software Engineering 2007: Vol. 1. IEEE Future of Software Engineering* (pp. 304-315). New York: IEEE Computer Society

Shirabad, J. S., & Menzies, T. (2005). The PROMISE Repository of Software Engineering Databases. *School of Information Technology and Engineering of the University of Ottawa, Canada.* Retrieved August 31, 2008, from http://promise.site.uottawa.ca/SERepository.

Weisberg, S. (1985). *Applied Linear Regression.* New York: John Wiley and Sons.

ADDITIONAL READING

Aha, D. W., & Bankert, R. L. (1996). *A comparative evaluation of sequential feature selection algorithms. Artificial Intelligence and Statistics.* New York: Springer-Verlag.

Angelis, L., & Stamelos, I. (2000). A Simulation Tool for efficient analogy based cost estimation. *Empirical Software Engineering, 5*(1), 35–68. doi:10.1023/A:1009897800559

Basili, V. R., & Weiss, D. (1984). A Methodology for Collecting Valid Software Engineering Data. *IEEE Transactions on Software Engineering, SE-10*(6), 728–738. doi:10.1109/TSE.1984.5010301

Bishop, C., & Qazaz, C. S. (1995). Bayesian inference of noise levels in regression. *International Conference on Artificial Neural Networks: Vol. 2. EC2 & Cie* (pp. 59-64). ICANN95.

Briand, L. C., Basili, V. R., & Thomas, W. (1992). A pattern recognition approach to software engineering data analysis. *IEEE Transactions on Software Engineering, 18*(11), 931–942. doi:10.1109/32.177363

Briand, L. C., El-Emam, K., Maxwell, K., Surmann, D., & Wieczorek, I. (1999). An Assessment and Comparison of Common Cost Software Project Estimation Methods. *Proceeding of the 1999 International Conference on Software Engineering* (pp. 313-322). Washington, DC: IEEE Computer Society.

Briand, L. C., Langley, T., & Wieczorek, I. (2000). A Replicated Assessment and Comparison of Common Software Cost Modeling Techniques. *Proceeding of the 2000 International Conference on Software Engineering* (pp. 377-386). Washington, DC: IEEE Computer Society.

Cantone, G., & Donzelli, P. (2000). Production and maintenance of goal-oriented measurement models. *World Scientific, 105*(4), 605–626.

Fenton, N. E. (1991). *Software Metrics: A Rigorous Approach*. London: Chapman & Hall.

Finnie, G., Wittig, G., & Desharnais, J.-M. (1997). A comparison of software effort estimation techniques using function points with neural networks, case based reasoning and regression models. *Journal of Systems and Software, 39*(3), 281–289. doi:10.1016/S0164-1212(97)00055-1

Foss, T., Stensrud, E., Kitchenham, B., & Myrtveit, I. (2003). A Simulation Study of the Model Evaluation Criterion MMRE. *IEEE Transactions on Software Engineering, 29*(11), 985–995. doi:10.1109/TSE.2003.1245300

Gulezian, R. (1991). Reformulating and calibrating COCOMO. *Journal of Systems and Software, 16*(3), 235–242. doi:10.1016/0164-1212(91)90018-2

Guyon, I., & Gunn, M. Nikravesh, & Zadeh, L. (2005). *Feature Extraction foundations and applications*. Berlin, Germany: Springer.

Jeffery, R., & Low, G. (1990). Calibrating estimation tools for software development. *Software Engineering Journal, 5*(4), 215–221. doi:10.1016/S0266-9838(05)80014-0

John, G., Kohavi, R., & Pfleger, K. (1994). Irrelevant features and the subset selection problem. *11th Intl. Conference on Machine Learning* (pp. 121-129). San Francisco: Morgan Kaufmann.

Kemerer, C. F. (1987). An Empirical Validation of Software Cost Estimation Models. *ACM Communications, 30*(5), 416–429. doi:10.1145/22899.22906

Khoshgoftaar, T. M., & Lanning, D. L. (1995). A Neural Network Approach for Early Detection of Program Modules Having High Risk in the Maintenance Phase. *Journal of Systems and Software, 29*(1), 85–91. doi:10.1016/0164-1212(94)00130-F

Khoshgoftaar, T. M., Lanning, D. L., & Pandya, A. S. (1994). A comparative-study of pattern-recognition techniques for quality evaluation of telecommunications software. *IEEE Journal on Selected Areas in Communications, 12*(2), 279–291. doi:10.1109/49.272878

Kirsopp, C., & Shepperd, M. (2002). *Case and Feature Subset Selection in Case-Based Software Project Effort Prediction. Research and Development in Intelligent Systems XIX*. New York: Springer-Verlag.

Menzies, T., Port, D., Chen, Z., & Hihn, J. (2005). Validation Methods for Calibrating Software Effort Models. *Proceeding of the 2000 International Conference on Software Engineering* (587- 595). Washington, DC: IEEE Computer Society.

Myrtveit, I., & Stensrud, E. (1999). A controlled experiment to assess the benefits of estimating with analogy and regression models. *IEEE Transactions on Software Engineering, 25*(4), 510–525. doi:10.1109/32.799947

Myrtveit, I., & Stensrud, E. (2004). Do Arbitrary Function Approximators make sense as Software Prediction Models? *12-th International Workshop on Software Technology and Engineering Practice* (pp. 3-9). Washington, DC: IEEE Computer Society.

Neumann, D. E. (2002). An Enhanced Neural Network Technique for Software Risk Analysis. *IEEE Transactions on Software Engineering, 28*(9), 904–912. doi:10.1109/TSE.2002.1033229

Rao, C. R. (1973). *Linear Statistical Inference and its Applications*. New York: Wiley & Sons.

Srinivasan, K., & Fisher, D. (1995). Machine Learning Approaches to Estimating Software Development Effort. *IEEE Transactions on Software Engineering, 21*(2), 126–137. doi:10.1109/32.345828

Stensrud, E., Foss, T., Kitchenham, B., & Myrtveit, I. (2002). An empirical Validation of the Relationship between the Magnitude of Relative Error and Project Size. *Proceeding of the 8-th IEEE Symposium on Software Metrics* (pp. 3-12). Washington, DC: IEEE Computer Society.

Vapnik, V. N. (1995). *The Nature of Statistical Learning Theory*. New York: Springer-Verlag.

Wohlin, C., Runeson, P., Höst, M., Ohlsson, M. C., Regnell, B., & Wesslén, A. (2000). *Experimentation in Software Engineering – An Introduction*. Berlin, Germany: Springer.

Section 2
Requirements Engineering and Specification

Chapter 5
From Textual Scenarios to Message Sequence Charts

Leonid Kof
Technische Universität München, Germany

ABSTRACT

Requirements engineering, the first phase of any software development project, is the Achilles' heel of the whole development process, as requirements documents are often inconsistent and incomplete. In industrial requirements documents natural language is the main presentation means. In such documents, the system behavior is specified in the form of use cases and their scenarios, written as a sequence of sentences in natural language. For the authors of requirements documents some facts are so obvious that they forget to mention them. This surely causes problems for the requirements analyst. By the very nature of omissions, they are difficult to detect by document reviews: Facts that are too obvious to be written down at the time of document writing, mostly remain obvious at the time of review. In such a way, omissions stay undetected. This book chapter presents an approach that analyzes textual scenarios with the means of computational linguistics, identifies where actors or whole actions are missing from the text, completes the missing information, and creates a message sequence chart (MSC) including the information missing from the textual scenario. Finally, this MSC is presented to the requirements analyst for validation. The book chapter presents also a case study where scenarios from a requirement document based on industrial specifications were translated to MSCs. The case study shows feasibility of the approach.

DOI: 10.4018/978-1-60566-758-4.ch005

DOCUMENT AUTHORS ARE NOT AWARE THAT SOME INFORMATION IS MISSING

Some kind of requirements document is usually written at the beginning of every software project. The majority of these documents are written in natural language, as the survey by Mich, Franch, and Novi Inverardi (2004) shows. This results in the fact that the requirements documents are imprecise, incomplete, and inconsistent. The authors of requirements documents are not always aware of these document defects. From the linguistic point of view, document authors introduce three defect types, without perceiving them as defects (Rupp (2002), p. 169:[1])

- **Deletion:** "...is the process of selective focusing of our attention on some dimensions of our experiences while excluding other dimensions. Deletion reduces the world to the extent that we can handle."
- **Generalization:** "...is the process of detachment of the elements of the personal model from the original experience and the transfer of the original exemplary experience to the whole category of objects."
- **Distortion:** "...is the process of reorganization of our sensory experience."

It is one of the goals of requirements analysis, to find and to correct the defects of requirements documents. This book chapter focuses on the "deletion"-defects in scenarios. Deletion manifests itself in scenarios in the form of missing action subjects or objects or even in whole missing actions. One of the reasons for the deletion may be the fact that some information is too obvious for the author of the requirements document, so that she finds it unnecessary to write down this information.

Missing information can affect any part of the requirements document. In the case of scenarios it is especially crucial because in this case some

Figure 1. MSCs: Terminology Definition

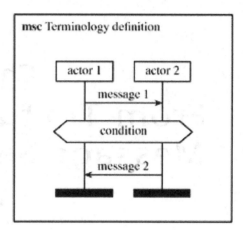

portions of the desired system behavior are just omitted. It is the goal of the approach presented in this book chapter, to identify missing parts of the scenarios written in natural language and to produce message sequence charts (MSCs) containing the reconstructed information. These MSCs must be validated and can then be used in further project run.

- **Terminology:** For the remainder of the book chapter we use the following terminology: A scenario is a sequence of natural language sentences. Every sentence consists of several segments (subordinate phrases). An MSC consists of a set of actors, a sequence of messages sent and received by these actors, and a sequence of conditions interleaved with the message sequence. Figure 1 illustrates the introduced terminology.
- **Outline:** The remainder of the book chapter is organized as follows: Section "Case Study: the Instrument Cluster" introduces the case study used to evaluate the presented approach, and Section "Computational Linguistics Prerequisites" introduces the applied linguistic tools. Section "From Textual Scenarios to Message Sequence Charts" is the core of the whole book

Figure 2. Scenario "Activation of the instrument cluster", manual translation to MSC

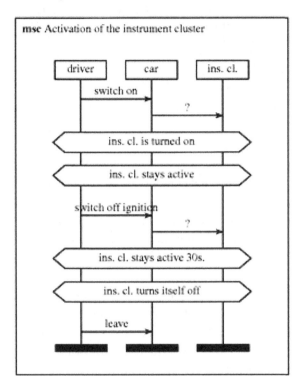

its hardware, and, most importantly, its behavior. The behavior is specified as a set of scenarios, like this (Buhr et al., 2004, p. 3):

1. The driver switches on the car (ignition key in position ignition on).
2. The instrument cluster is turned on and stays active.
3. After the trip the driver switches off the ignition.
4. The instrument cluster stays active for 30 seconds and then turns itself off.
5. The driver leaves the car.

If we translate this scenario to an MSC containing solely messages and conditions, we get the MSC in Figure 2.[2] This translation is surely incomplete, in the sense that timing, ". . . stays active for 30 seconds", is not taken into account. Theoretically, MSCs allow also to set timers and for every timer to perform some actions when the timer expires. Such MSCs can be constructed by a human analyst. However, extraction of MSCs with timers by means of computational linguistics requires semantic analysis, going far beyond the capabilities of state-of-the-art linguistic tools. Thus, in the presented work we focus on MSCs consisting of messages and conditions only.

There are apparent problems if we try to translate the above scenario to an MSC. Firstly, there is no one-to-one correspondence between sentences and messages. For example, sentences number 2 and 4 contain two potential messages or conditions each: Sentence 2 contains actions "The instrument cluster is turned on" and "The instrument cluster stays active" and sentence 4 contains actions "The instrument cluster stays active for 30 seconds" and "The instrument cluster turns itself off". Furthermore, the MSC contains missing messages from the car to the instrument cluster, most probably, something like "turn on" and "turn off in 30 seconds". These messages were simply forgotten by the scenario author. It is the goal of the approach presented in this book

chapter; it presents the approach translating textual scenarios to MSCs. Finally, Sections "Related Work", "Summary", and "Future Work" present an overview of related work, the summary of the book chapter, and possible directions for future work, respectively.

CASE STUDY: THE INSTRUMENT CLUSTER

Authors of requirements documents tend to forget to write down facts that seem obvious to them. Even in a relatively precise requirements document, as for example the instrument cluster specification by Buhr et al. (2004), some missing facts can be identified. The instrument cluster specification describes the optical design of one part of the car dashboard (the instrument cluster),

Figure 3. Parse tree for "The driver switches on the car"

The	driver	switches	on	the	car
DT	NN	VBZ	IN	DT	NN
NP[nb]/N	N	S[dcl]\NP	((S\NP)\(S\NP))/NP	NP[nb]/N	N

```
      The      driver    switches             on                the     car
      DT        NN         VBZ                IN                 DT      NN
    NP[nb]/N     N       S[dcl]\NP   ((S\NP)\(S\NP))/NP       NP[nb]/N    N
   _____                                          _____
        NP[nb]                                                   NP[nb]
                              _____
                                      (S[X]\NP)\(S[X]\NP)
                              _____
                                             S[dcl]\NP
   _____
                                    S[dcl]
```

First line = the parsed sentence itself

Second line = tag sequence provided by the tagger

Horizontal lines = non-leaf parse tree nodes

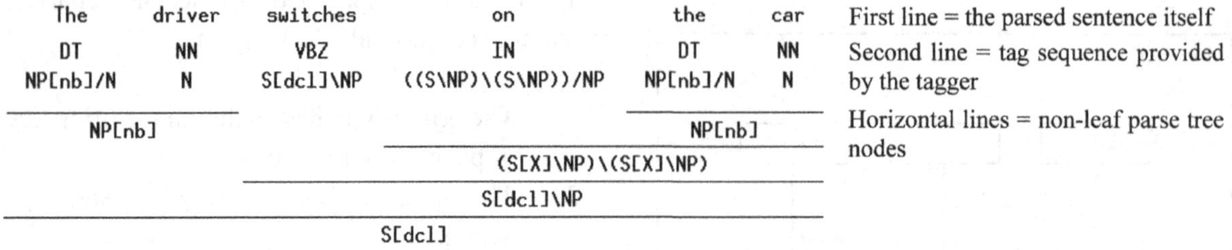

chapter, to resolve such incomplete specifications and present the results to a human analyst for validation.

COMPUTATIONAL LINGUISTICS PREREQUISITES

Two techniques of natural language processing are used to translate scenarios to MSCs: part-of-speech (POS) tagging and parsing. POS tagging marks every word of a given sentence with one of the predefined parts-of-speech (substantive, adjective, ...) by assigning a POS tag. For example, the words of the sentence "The driver switches on the car" are marked in the following way: The|DT driver|NN switches|VBZ on|IN the|DT car|NN. Here, DT means a determiner, NN a noun, VBZ a verb, and IN a preposition. Following tags are the most important ones in the context of the presented work, cf. Section "From Textual Scenarios to Message Sequence Charts": (1) any tag starting with "VB", identifying different verb forms, (2) tag "VBN", identifying past

participle (e.g., "done", "activated"), and (3) tag "CC", identifying conjunction (e.g., "and"). Tagging technology is rather mature, there are taggers available with a precision of about 97%, as for example the tagger from the C&C tool suite (C&C Tools, 2007; Curran, Clark, & Vadas, 2006), used in the presented work.

Parsing, as compared to tagging, provides not only part-of-speech information, but also a parse tree. An example, the parse tree for the sentence "The driver switches on the car", is shown in Figure 3. The parse tree consists of two main subtrees, one of them representing the subject, represented by the noun phrase (NP) "The driver", and the other subtree representing the rest of the sentence. The rest of the sentence, in turn, can be decomposed into finer constituents.

A parse tree can be represented as a set of dependencies as well. A dependency represents a link from a non-leaf node of the parse tree, represented in Figure 3 by a horizontal line, to one of its subtrees. A dependency is a triple consisting of (1) dependency type, (2) the lexical head (the most important word) of the parent node, and

Table 1. Dependency representation for the parse tree from Figure 3

Dependency	Grammatical meaning
(det driver 1 The 0)	"The" is a determiner of "driver" (dependency type "det")
(det car 5 the 4)	"the" is a determiner of "car" (dependency type "det")
(dobj on 3 car 5)	"car" is a direct object of "on" (dependency type "dobj")
(ncmod switches 2 on 3)	"on" is a modifier of "switches" (dependency type "ncmod")
(ncsubj switches 2 driver 1)	"driver" is a subject of "switches" (dependency type "ncsubj")

(3) the lexical head (the most important word) of the child node. For the sentence "The driver switches on the car" the parser provides the set of dependencies presented in Table 1.

The dependency type provides valuable information about the grammatical role of the child subtree. For example, the dependency (ncsubj switches_2 driver_1) states that the word "driver", with its subtree, is a subject (dependency type "ncsubj") of the word "switches". This kind of parse tree representation eases identification of subjects and direct objects: the subject is identified as the child subtree of the "ncsubj"-type dependency, and the direct object as the child subtree of the "dobj"-type dependency. This information will be used to identify actors in Section "Extraction of Actors".

Parsers available at the moment are less precise than taggers. They have the precision of about 80%, as for example the parser from the C&C tool suite (C&C Tools, 2007; Clark & Curran, 2004), used in the presented work. For this reason, the actual translation from scenarios to MSCs uses POS tags as far as possible. Information provided by the parser is used to identify actors and to decide which sentences should be translated to conditions.

FROM TEXTUAL SCENARIOS TO MESSAGE SEQUENCE CHARTS

Message Sequence Charts (MSCs) are a convenient means for concise and precise representation of action sequences. An MSC consists of a set of actors. These actors exchange messages, whereas every message has a well defined sender and receiver. Graphically, actors are represented as rectangles, and messages as arrows; the time line is directed top down, (see Figure 2).

When translating scenarios, written in natural language, to MSCs, it is necessary to deal with typical deficiencies of natural language texts: It can happen that either the message sender or the receiver are not explicitly mentioned, or the whole action is just omitted. For example, if we directly translate the scenario introduced in Section "Case Study: The Instrument Cluster" to an MSC, a possible translation is the MSC in Figure 2. The problems of this translation are apparent: there are definitely missing messages from the car to the instrument cluster, otherwise the instrument cluster cannot know that it should be turned on or off. Furthermore, some sentences, like "The instrument cluster is turned on", do not specify the message receiver and it is problematic to translate them to messages. Even if we rephrase this sentence to active voice ("The instrument cluster turns on"), the message receiver remains unspecified.

The approach presented below tackles the above problems. As the approach is rather complex, it is presented in four sections:

- **Basic algorithm:** The basic algorithm has two major constraints:
    ◦ It assumes that every sentence contains exactly one verb. Thus, it cannot treat compound or passive sentences.
    ◦ It translates every sentence of the scenario to a message, it cannot generate conditions.

The basic algorithm takes a predefined set of actors and a scenario as input and produces an MSC consisting of messages only. This algorithm is presented in Section "Basic Algorithm".

- **Treatment of compound sentences:** To handle compound sentences, the presented approach splits them into segments. Each segment is then treated by the basic algorithm. This part is presented in Section "Treatment of Compound Sentences".
- **Translation of certain sentence types to conditions:** Basic algorithm translates every sentence to a message. However, for certain sentence types, it makes no sense to

translate them to messages. For example, general statements about the environment, like "It is raining", should be translated to conditions. The algorithm to decide which sentences should be translated to conditions is presented in Section "Sentence Types Translated to Conditions".

- **Extraction of actors:** All algorithms introduced above assume that the set of actors is provided as input. To really automate the translation of scenarios to MSCs, it is necessary to automate the extraction of actors too. The algorithm to extract actors is presented in Sections "Extraction of Actors".

Algorithms presented in Sections "Basic Algorithm" and "Treatment of Compound Sentences" are not really suitable for evaluation, as they cannot handle certain sentence types or MSC elements. Sections "Sentence Types Translated to Conditions" and "Extraction of Actors" present evaluation of the whole approach.

Basic Algorithm

The basic algorithm to translate scenarios to MSCs is based on three major assumptions:

1. Every sentence to be translated contains exactly one verb.
2. The set of actors is provided.
3. Every sentence should be translated to a message.

When analyzing scenarios, we want to identify which messages are missing, as in the example in Figure 2. When translating a sentence to an MSC message, first, we identify the message sender and message receiver. For this purpose we consider the sentence parts before and after the main verb: The message sender/receiver is the longest word sequence before/after the verb, contained in the provided set of actors. For example, if the concepts "driver", "drunk driver", and "car" are

all contained in the set of actors, then, then in the sentence "The drunk driver switches on the car", "drunk driver" is identified as the message sender, and "car" as the receiver. This heuristics works under the assumption that the sentence is in active voice and contains exactly one verb.

To find the verb and to verify that the sentence contains exactly one verb, we apply the POS-tagger to every sentence of the scenario. If the tagged sentence contains several words with the "VB" (verb) tag, the sentence contains more than one verb and should be rephrased in order that the basic algorithm becomes applicable. Technically, presence of several verbs can be detected if the tagged sentence contains the regular expression VB.*VB. If the sentence contains exactly one verb, identified by the VB-tag, we can search for the message sender (resp. receiver) in the word sequence before (resp. after) the verb.

The above procedure to identify the message sender/receiver works fine if the sentence contains both of them. Otherwise, the message sender/receiver has to be inferred. The inference procedure and some examples of the application of the basic algorithm are shown in section "From Textual Scenarios to Message Sequence Charts".

Message Stack

Even when every sentence contains exactly one verb, identification of message senders and receivers is not always simple. In order to avoid the identification of wrong objects, e.g. sent messages, as senders/receivers for an MSC, we accept only objects contained in the previously extracted set of actors as message senders and receivers. This leads to the problem that in some sentences we cannot identify the message sender or receiver. The problem arises additionally from the fact that some sentences, like "instrument cluster turns on", do not explicitly mention the sender or the receiver. We solve this problem by introducing a default sender and receiver for every sentence under analysis. Obviously, the default sender and receiver depend on the messages previously sent. Management of this dependency is *the core* of the approach to MSC construction presented in this book chapter.

To identify default senders and receivers, we organize the messages in a stack. The idea of organization of messages in a stack is based on the following analogy: Grosz, Joshi, and Weinstein (1995) introduce a situation stack to explain how the human attention focuses on different objects during a discourse. The focus depends on the sequence of sentence heard so far. By default, a sentence defines some situation and is pushed onto the stack. If a sentence reverts the effect of some previous sentence, the corresponding stack element is popped:

John enters the shop //push "enter"
—Some actions in the shop —
John leaves the shop //pop "enter" and the above
    stack elements

This idea can be transferred to MSCs in the following way: If a new message m represents a reaction to some previously pushed message *m',* *m'* and the messages above it are popped from the stack. Otherwise, the new message m is pushed onto the stack. The subsequent sections describe the transfer of the situation stack idea to MSCs in more detail.

Identifying the Sender and Receiver in Incomplete Sentences

When translating a sentence to an MSC message, we say that the message sender/receiver is the longest word sequence before/after the verb[3] that is contained in the set of actors. The problem arises when we cannot identify the sender or receiver. For example, if we translate the sentence "The instrument cluster turns on" to an MSC message, we know that "instrument cluster" is the message sender, but we do not know the receiver. To iden-tify missing message senders and receivers, we analyze the sender and receiver of the message on the top of the stack. Here we assume that the message stack contains the sent messages, for which no corresponding reaction message is available yet. The exact rules of stack management will be described below.

When identifying missing message receiver, we distinguish three cases, shown in Figure 4:

- The sender of the message under analysis equals to the receiver of the message on the top of the stack, as in Figure 4(a). In this case we assume that the message under analysis is a reaction to the message on the top of the stack. The receiver of the message is then the sender of the message on the top of the stack. In the case of Figure 4(a) it is "Actor 1".

- The sender of the message under analysis equals to the sender of the message on the top of the stack, as in Figure 4(b). In this case we assume that the message under analysis augments the message on the top of the stack and, thus, has the same receiver. In the case of Figure 4(b) it is "Actor 2".

- The sender of the message under analysis does not equal to the sender nor to receiver of the message on the top of the stack, as in Figure 4(c). In this case we assume that some message is missing from the MSC, denoted by the dashed message in Figure 4(c), and that the message under analysis is a reaction to the missing message. The sender of the missing message and the receiver of the message under analysis coincide with the receiver of the message on the top of the stack. In the case of Figure 4(c) it is "Actor 2".

A missing message sender can be identified in a similar way.

Figure 4. Missing message receiver, possible situations

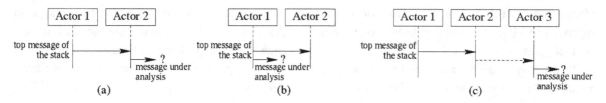

Identifying Missing Messages

When every message has a defined sender and receiver, we can determine the necessary operations on the message stack. Following situations are taken into account:

• The sender of the message under analysis equals to the sender of the first message, starting the whole MSC. In this case we assume that the message under analysis starts a completely new MSC segment. This is the case, for example, for the sentence "After the trip the driver switches off the ignition" in the introductory scenario in Section "Case Study: The Instrument Cluster". Thus, we empty the stack and re-initialize it with the new message.

• The sender and the receiver of the message under analysis are equal to the sender and the receiver of the message on the top of the stack, respectively. In this case we assume that the new message augments the message on the top of the stack. Thus, we just add the new message to the MSC but do not change the stack.

• The sender of the message under analysis equals to the receiver of the message on the top of the stack, as in Figures 5(a) and 5(c). We call an object "active" if it is a sender of some message contained in the stack (for example, "Actor 1" and "Actor 3" in Figure 5(c)) or is the receiver of the top message on the stack.

• If the receiver of the message under analysis is not an active object (Figure 5(a)), we

Figure 5. Identification of missing messages and stack management

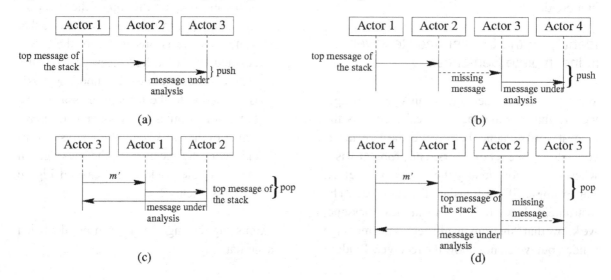

Table 2. Organization of MSC messages in a stack

sentence	extracted sender	extracted receiver	sender assumed for MSC	receiver assumed for MSC	stack action (push/pop)	pushed/popped messages
The driver switches on the car.	driver	car	driver	car	push	driver → car
The instrument cluster turns on	ins. clust.	—	ins. clust.	car	2x push 2x pop	car →ins. clust. ins. clust.→car
The instrument cluster stays active.	ins. clust.	—	ins. clust	car	—	—
After the trip the driver switches off the ignition.	driver	—	driver	car	empty, push	driver → car
The instrument cluster stays active for 30 seconds.	ins. clust.	—	ins. clust.	car	2x push 2x pop	car →ins. clust ins. clust.→car
The instrument cluster turns itself off.	ins. clust	—	ins. clust	car	—	—
The driver leaves the car	driver	—	driver	car	empty, push	driver → car

add the new message to the MSC and push it onto the stack.

- If the receiver of the message under analysis (*m*) is an active object ("Actor 3" in Figure 5(c)), we assume that m is the reaction to some message *m'* sent by this active object. We pop m' and all the messages contained in the stack above *m'*.

- The sender of the message under analysis is not equal to the receiver of the message on the top of the stack, as in Figures 5(b) and 5(d). In this case some message is missing. We add a missing message to the MSC, as shown in Figures 5(b) and 5(d).

- If the receiver of the message under analysis is not an active object (Figure 5(b)), we add a new message to the MSC and push it onto the stack.

- If the receiver of the message under analysis (*m*) is an active object ("Actor 4" in Figure 5(d)), we assume that m is the reaction to some message *m'* sent by this active object. We pop *m'* and all the messages contained in the stack above *m'*.

Application of the procedure described above can be easily exemplified on the scenario presented in Section "Case study". Table 2 shows a slightly changed scenario, so that each sentence contains exactly one verb[4]. For the analysis we assume that the previously extracted set of actors contains "instrument cluster", "driver", and "car", but no other nouns used in the scenario.

We initialize the analysis with an empty stack. In the first sentence the driver is identified as the message sender and the car as the message receiver. The message "driver → car" is pushed onto the stack. In the second sentence the instrument cluster is identified as the message sender, but the sentence does not contain any message receiver. The situation corresponds to Figure 4(c). Thus, "car" is identified as the receiver. Then, the missing message "ins. clust. → car" and the message "car → ins. clust." are added to the MSC, as in Figure 5(d). The next sentence, "The instrument cluster stays active", results in a message that augments the previous message. Thus, the stack remains unchanged. Then, the next sentence causes the emptying of the stack and the same sequence of push and pop operations is performed again. The resulting MSC is shown in Figure 6.

This example shows that the presented idea of message stack works for this simple scenario. More examples of the application of the basic algorithm are presented in the next section.

Application of the Basic Algorithm, Examples

The examples presented below originate from the instrument cluster specification (Buhr et al., 2004). Although not used in an industrial development project, this specification was derived from real industrial documents. This specification was also intended to serve as the contract basis between the car manufacturer and the supplier of the instrument cluster. The set of actors, necessary for the translation of scenarios to MSCs, was extracted in our previous work (Kof, 2005) and then manually corrected.

The original scenarios from (Buhr et al., 2004) have to be rephrased in order to be translated to MSCs by the basic algorithm. The necessity to rewrite the scenarios was caused by the extensive usage of passive in the original version. Furthermore, some sentences contain several actions, like "The instrument cluster stays active for 30 seconds and then turns itself off". Table 3 shows the corrections necessary to make the basic algorithm applicable. Sentences in bold font are the new versions of the corresponding sentences on the left hand side. It is easy to see that the corrections are not so big. The corresponding MSCs are shown in Figures 6, 7 and 8.

Treatment of Compound Sentences

The basic idea for the translation of compound sentences to MSC messages is fairly simple: We split every sentence into *elementary segments* and translate every segment to an MSC message, as in the basic algorithm. An *elementary segment* is defined as a sentence segment that does not

Figure 6. MSC for the scenario "Activation of the instrument cluster" from Table 3

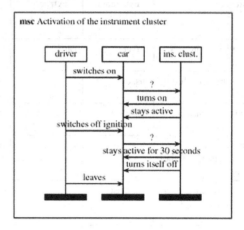

contain any conjunctions or commas/colons. For example, the sentence "The instrument cluster is turned on and stays active" consists of two segments: "The instrument cluster is turned on" and "stays active".

Generally, we want to take following issues into account when splitting sentences to segments:

- If we split the original sentence into elementary segments, it can happen that one of the segments lack the grammatical subject. For example, the sentence "The instrument cluster is turned on and stays active" would be split into "the instrument cluster is turned on" and "stays active". The second segment lacks the subject. However, the subject is necessary to identify the message sender. This problem can be solved by propagation of the grammatical subject from the first segment of the sentence to the second one.

- If the sentence consists of several segments and some segments contain no own verb, the verbs should be accordingly propagated. For example, in the sentence "The driver drives more than 30 km/h and less than 50 km/h" the verb "drives" should be propagated to the segment "less than 50

Table 3. Original scenarios (left) and corrected scenarios (right)

Use Case: activation of the instrument cluster	Use Case: activation of the instrument cluster
The driver switches on the car (ignition key in position ignition on). The instrument cluster is turned on and stays active After the trip the driver switches off the ignition. After the trip the driver switches off the ignition. The instrument cluster stays active for 30 seconds and then turns itself off. The driver leaves the car	The driver switches on the car (ignition key in position ignition on). **The instrument cluster turns on** **The instrument cluster stays active.** **The instrument cluster stays active for 30 seconds.** **The instrument cluster turns itself off.** The driver leaves the car.
Use Case: temporary activation of the instrument cluster	Use Case: temporary activation of the instrument cluster
The driver opens the door. The instrument cluster is activated temporarily. The instrument cluster turns itself off after 30 seconds. The driver leaves the car.	The driver opens the door. **The instrument cluster turns on temporarily.** The instrument cluster turns itself off after 30 seconds. The driver leaves the car.
Use Case: show RPM (revolutions per minute)	Use Case: show RPM (revolutions per minute)
The driver switches on the car by turning the ignition key to the switched on position. The car is switched on and the pointer of the rev meter display goes from the technical initial position to the initial position of the scale (0 min-1), damped as described below. The input signals from the motor are sent regularly. The system determines the engine speed and displays it. The driver switches off the car by turning the ignition key to the switched off position. The car is switched off and the pointer of the rev meter display falls back to its technical initial position, damped as described below. The driver leaves the car.	The driver switches on the car by turning the ignition key to the switched on position. The pointer of the rev meter display goes from the technical initial position to the initial position of the scale (0 min-1), damped as described below. **The motor regularly sends input signals.** **The system determines the engine speed.** **The system displays the engine speed.** The driver switches off the car by turning the ignition key to the switched off position. **The pointer of the rev meter display falls back to its technical initial position, damped as described below.** The driver leaves the car.

km/h".

As the technical means for splitting the sentences into segments and for identification of the verb we use a part-of-speech (POS) tagger. The translation of tagged sentences to sentence segments goes in four steps:

Figure 7. MSC for the scenario "Temporary activation of the instrument cluster" from Table 3

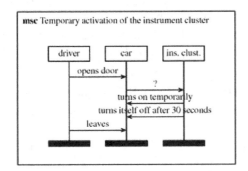

1. Every tagged sentence is split into elementary segments, not containing any conjunctions or commas/colons.

2. Every sentence segment is annotated as either active or passive or sentence segment without any verb.

3. For every sentence segment, the grammatical subjects, objects, and verbs are extracted, if possible.

4. The extracted grammatical subjects and objects are propagated to other sentence segments, if necessary.

Each of these steps is explained below in detail. The obtained sentence segments are then forwarded to the basic algorithm.

Splitting of tagged sentences: The POS tagger appends a tag to every word using the character "|", so that the tagged sentence looks like this:

Figure 8. MSCs for the scenario "Show RPM" from Table 3

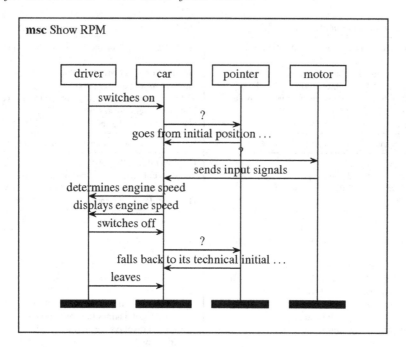

The|DT instrument|NN cluster|NN is|VBZ turned|VBN on|RP and|CC stays|NNS active|JJ .|.

This form allows to split every sentence into elementary segments. As splitting marks we use the regular expression matching conjunctions: " [^]*\|CC " (space, followed by a character sequence without spaces, followed by "|", followed by the conjunction tag, followed by space)[5], and also regular expressions matching tagged punctuation: " [^]*\|, " (matching coma), " [^]*\|\.[ ]*" (matching period), and " [^]*\|:[ ]*" (matching colon). The splitting mark matching conjunctions splits the sentence "The instrument cluster is turned on and stays active" into "The instrument cluster is turned on" and "stays active". The splitting mark matching punctuation would decompose constructions like "X, Y, and Z do something" into "X", "Y", and "Z do something".

Annotation of sentence segments: The annotation of sentence segments as either active or passive or sentence segment without verb is necessary for two reasons:

- For sentence segments without verbs the verbs have to be accordingly adopted from other segments.
- Knowledge whether a particular segment is active or passive is important to generate conditions, cf. Section "Sentence Types Translated to Conditions".

For the annotation of sentence segments it is possible to use regular expressions based on POS-tags, again. A tagged sentence segment is annotated as passive if and only if it matches the regular expression ".* *<be−form>*. *VBN.*" (any character sequence, followed by some form of the verb "to be", followed by a verb participle[6], followed by any character sequence). In this expression hbe−formi can be equal to "be", "am", "are", "is", "was", "were", or "been". For example, the segment "the|DT instrument|NN cluster|NN is|VBZ turned|VBN on|RP" is annotated as passive because the verb "is" is followed by the participle "turned|VBN".

If the tagged segment does not match the

regular expression ".*|VB.*" (i.e., it does not contain any verb tag), it is annotated as "segment without verb". Otherwise, if the segment contains a verb but does not match any of the passive expressions, the segment is annotated as active, as for example the segment "the|DT driver|NN leaves|VBZ the|DT car|NN".

Extraction of subjects and objects: To extract subjects and objects, active sentence segments are spilt on the basis of the POS-tags into three parts: the verb, the word sequence before the verb, and the word sequence after the verb. Passive sentence segments are split into four parts: the auxiliary verb, the word sequence before the auxiliary verb, the participle, the word sequence after the participle. Then, a provided set of actors is used to identify the subject and object, similar to the identification of message sender and receiver in Section "Basic Algorithm". The longest word sequence before the (auxiliary) verb, contained in the provided set of actors, is declared to the subject. In the case of active segments, the object is the longest word sequence after the verb, contained in the provided set of actors. In the case of passive segments, the object is the longest word sequence after the participle, contained in the provided set of actors. Although the obtained word sequences can differ from the real grammatical subject/object, they are sufficient for our purpose to identify the message sender/receiver in every sentence segment.

Propagation of subjects, objects, and verbs: Propagation of subjects, objects and verbs is necessary due to the fact that some sentence segments do not explicitly contain them but share with other segments. The propagation algorithm can be most simply illustrated on the tagged sentence

"The|DT driver|NN accelerates|VBZ and|CC drives|VBZ faster|JJR than|IN 30km/h|CD and|CC less|JJR than|IN 50km/h|CD .|.",

taken from the instrument cluster specification (Buhr et al., 2004, p. 34). This sentence contains three elementary segments:

1. The|DT driver|NN accelerates|VBZ
2. drives|VBZ faster|JJR than|IN 30km/h|CD
3. less|JJR than|IN 50km/h|CD

The first segment contains a subject ("driver") and a verb ("accelerates"). The second segment contains no subject but contains a verb ("drives"). Thus, the second segment inherits the subject ("driver") from the first one and results in the segment "driver drives faster than 30km/h". The third segment, in turn, lacks both subject and verb. Thus, it inherits them from the modified second segment and turns into "driver drives less than 50km/h. In a similar way the objects can be propagated as well.

The segments without verb inherit the active/passive annotation together with the verb. When the verb propagation is completed, there are no segments annotated as "segment without verb" any more. This propagation algorithm can be easily generalized to the case where the first sentence segment lacks a verb and also to passive segments.

Translation of sentence segments to messages: After propagation, it is theoretically possible to translate every segment to an MSC message: We can forward active segments directly to the basic algorithm. As for passive segments, we can forward them to the basic algorithm with a special flag indicating that the message sender and receiver should be swapped: In such a way, the basic algorithm would translate the segment "the instrument cluster is activated by the driver" to a message from the driver to the instrument cluster. Additionally, we would have to augment the basic algorithm, in order that it could cope with passive segments, containing two verbs. This is not a big deal, as it would involve just searching for the message receiver before the auxiliary

Figure 9. Scenario "Activation of the instrument cluster", translation without conditions

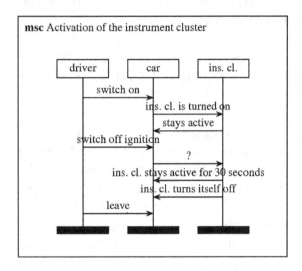

verb (some form of the verb "be" in a passive sentence), and for the message sender after the main verb (verb with the "VBN"-tag in a passive sentence). However, as will be shown in Section "Sentence Types Translated to Conditions", it makes no sense to translate passive segments to messages, anyway.

Sentence Types Translated to Conditions

The algorithm for translation of scenarios to MSCs translates every sentence[7] to a message. This causes problems when translating sentences just stating something about the system or its environment. For example, for the scenario presented in Section "Case Study", the sentences "the instrument cluster is activated" and "the instrument cluster stays active" are interpreted as messages by the basic algorithm, which results in the MSC in Figure 9. This translation is correct under the constraint that every sentence has to be translated to a message. However, the translation in Figure 2 is more appropriate; as it translates statements about system states like "instrument cluster is activated" to conditions saying something about

system states.

The algorithm extension presented below solves this problem by translating some sentences to conditions. The main problem here is to identify sentences that should be translated to conditions by means of computational linguistics. By manual analysis of the available textual scenarios the following candidates were identified:

- passive sentences (e.g., "the instrument cluster is activated")
- sentences without direct object (e.g., "the instrument cluster stays active for 30 seconds")
- sentences where no message sender can be identified (e.g., "it is raining")

These sentence types can be identified on the basis of information provided by the POS tagger or parser. Furthermore, it is possible to combine the heuristics and to translate several different sentence types into conditions as described in the following examples.

Sentence Types Translated to Conditions: Identification Rules

In order to achieve good precision in identification of sentence types, the identification algorithms rely on tagging information as far as possible.

- **Passive sentences:** A sentence is considered as passive if it contains some form of the verb "be" (i.e., "is", "are", "was", "were", "been"), followed by a past participle (e.g., "done", "activated"). A past participle is recognized by means of the special tag ("VBN") assigned by the tagger.
- **Sentences without direct object:** Here, the information provided by the tagger is not sufficient. However, if we parse a sentence and take the representation of the parse tree as a set of dependencies, among the dependencies we also get information

about objects. For example, for the sentence "The driver switches on the car" the parser provides the dependencies listed in Table 1. One of these dependencies has the type "dobj", which indicates direct object. This observation is used to identify sentences without direct object: If none of the dependencies representing the parse tree has the "dobj" type, the sentence has no direct object.

- **Sentences without message sender:** To identify sentences without message sender we use the same basic algorithm to identify message senders: We tag the sentence and consider the word sequence before the verb. If this word sequence does not contain any element from the provided set of actors, the sentence is considered as a sentence without message sender.

It is possible that a concrete sentence falls into several categories. For example, the sentence "Some operation was performed" is passive, it contains no direct object, and it contains no message sender.

Whenever a sentence is translated to a condition, it does not influence the analysis of subsequent sentences. Most importantly, if a sentence is translated to a condition, the message stack, as constructed by the basic algorithm remains unchanged.

Evaluation of Identification Rules

There are three different sentence types that potentially can be translated into conditions. This results in eight possibilities to generate conditions: each of the three sentence types can be translated either into a condition or into a message.

All possibilities to generate conditions were evaluated on the same set of scenarios, taken from the instrument cluster specification (Buhr et al., 2004). This specification contains 10 use cases, with one main scenario and several error handling scenarios for every use case, a total of 42 scenarios. 41 out of 42 scenarios were used for evaluation, due to technical difficulties of batch processing the 42nd scenario. The following rules were applied to evaluate the correctness of the generated MSCs:

- General statements that are actually irrelevant for the MSC (e.g., "There is no difference between rising and falling temperature values") should be translated to conditions.
- General statements about the system state (e.g., "The instrument cluster is activated") can be translated both to messages and to conditions.
- For a statement sequence like "X activates Y", "Y is activated", the first statement should be translated to a message, the second one to a condition.
- If a statement does not have to be translated to a condition due to one of the above rules, it should be translated to a message.
- If, for any particular actor, it is known that this actor cannot receive messages, as for example some sensors used in automobiles, no messages should be sent to this object. Here it is important to emphasize that this rule was used solely to evaluate MSCs, not to generate them. No application domain knowledge was used for MSC generation.

Evaluation was performed with the same set of actors as the examples shown in the "Basic Algorithm" Section. This set of actors was extracted using techniques from our previous work (Kof, 2005) and then manually corrected in order to eliminate definitely irrelevant actors.

Evaluation results are shown in Table 4. These results make clear that, at least, sentences without direct object and sentences where no message sender can be identified should be translated to conditions. Translation of passive sentences to

Table 4. Evaluation: translation of different sentence types to conditions

passive sentences translated to conditions	sentences without direct object translated to conditions	sentences without message sender translated to conditions	correct MSCs	
			absolute number	percentage
no	no	no	6	15%
no	no	yes	22	54%
no	yes	no	22	54%
no	yes	yes	**31**	**76%**
yes	no	no	15	37%
yes	no	yes	29	71%
yes	yes	no	25	61%
yes	yes	yes	**31**	**76%**

conditions is not compulsory: when sentences without direct objects and sentences where no message sender can be identified are already translated to conditions, translation of passive sentences to conditions does not have any effect. However, as the analysis of the table shows, translation of passive sentences to conditions makes the approach more robust. For this reason, further case studies were carried out with the tool configuration translating all three sentence types (passive, without direct object, without message sender) to conditions.

Extraction of Actors

Case studies conducted with the algorithms presented in Section "From Textual Scenarios to Message Sequence Charts" have shown that the correctness of the produced MSCs is highly sensitive to proper definition of the provided set of actors. Furthermore, although existing semiautomatic tools (Kof, 2005) can be used to construct the initial version of the provided set of actors, this set of actors has to be manually post-processed to improve the resulting MSCs.

In order to eliminate manual work necessary to construct the provided set of actors, actors can be extracted directly from scenarios. Previously applied technique to extract actors (Kof, 2005)

considers every word sequence occurring as a grammatical subject or object somewhere in the requirements document as a potential actor. This strategy results in too many potential actors. Unnecessary actors lead to wrong MSCs, as they influence the identification of message senders and receivers. Figure 10 shows an example MSC containing unnecessary actors for the example scenario introduced in Section "Case Study". This MSC contains unnecessary actors "trip" and "seconds" that occur as objects somewhere in the requirements document. These unnecessary actors make no sense from the point of view of human analyst. Furthermore, they cause a rather strange message flow, as from "car" to "trip" and from "instrument cluster" to "seconds". If we restrict the set of actors for this use case to "driver", "car" and "instrument cluster", we get the MSC in Figure 11, which is a definitely better formalization of the scenario.

Manual analysis of the available scenarios showed that several heuristics for the extraction of actors are possible. An actor can be:

1. a subject of an active sentence containing a direct object, like "driver" in "The driver switches on the car"
2. a subject of an active sentence containing no direct object, like "instrument cluster" in

Figure 10. Example: MSC containing unnecessary actors

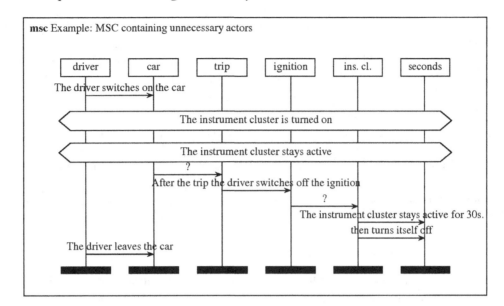

"The instrument cluster stays active"
3. a subject of a passive sentence, like "instrument cluster" in "The instrument cluster is activated"
4. a direct object, like "car" in "The driver switches on the car"

Figure 11. Example: MSC without unnecessary actors

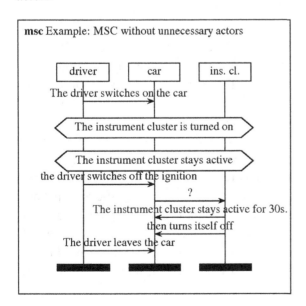

5. the default sender/receiver (manually provided actors that initiate the scenario. For the instrument cluster specification, "driver" is the default sender and "car" the default receiver in every scenario.)

Furthermore, the scope for the extraction of actors can be defined in two different ways:

- **Local:** for a particular scenario, only actors extracted from this scenario are relevant.
- **Global:** for a particular scenario, any actor extracted from any scenario is relevant.

Following rules are used to implement actor identification on the basis of the information provided by the tagger and the parser:

- A sentence is considered as passive if it contains some form of the verb "be" (i.e., "is", "are", "was", "were", "been"), followed by a past participle, marked by the tag "VBN". Otherwise it is considered as active.
- A sentence is considered as containing a

Table 5. Heuristics to identify actors, sequence of comparisons

1st heuristics	2nd heuristics	Difference: 2nd vs. 1st	Winning heuristics
subject of an active sentence containing a direct object, local	subject of an active sentence containing no direct object, local	absence vs. presence of direct object	1st
subject of an active sentence containing a direct object, local	subject of an active sentence containing a direct object + subject of a passive sentence, local	augmentation: subjects of passive sentences, local	1st
subject of an active sentence containing a direct object, local	subject of an active sentence containing a direct object + direct object, local	augmentation: direct objects, local	1st
subject of an active sentence containing a direct object, local	subject of an active sentence containing a direct object + default sender/receiver, local	augmentation: default sender and receiver	2nd
subject of an active sentence containing a direct object + default sender/receiver, local	subject of an active sentence containing a direct object + default sender/receiver, global	global vs. local	draw

direct object, if and only if one of the dependencies produced by the parser has the type "dobj".

- The subject of the sentence is the child subtree of the dependency of the type "ncsubj".
- The direct object of the sentence is the child subtree of the dependency of the type "dobj".

A systematic comparison of all different possibilities to extract actors would result in $2^5 \times 2 = 64$ case studies, which is too laborious. For this reason a greedy search was used to determine the best set of heuristics to extract actors. Heuristics combinations were compared pairwise, and the winning combination was used for further comparisons. This resulted in the sequence of comparisons summarized in Table 5.

The case studies were performed on the same set of 41 scenarios as the case studies on translation of certain sentence types to conditions, presented in Section "Evaluation of Identification Rules". To generate MSCs, the algorithm variant translating all three condition candidates (passive sentences, sentences without direct object, sentences without message sender) to conditions was used. Among the two best performing variants this one was

chosen as the more robust one. To evaluate the generated MSCs, the same rules as in Section "Evaluation of Identification Rules" were used. Table 6 shows the evaluation summary. It shows that the best heuristics to extract actors is one of the simplest: just subjects of active sentences containing a direct object, augmented with the default sender/receiver.

RELATED WORK

The idea to use computational linguistics to analyze requirements documents is surely not new. There was a lot of work in this area in recent years. There are three areas where natural language processing is applied to requirements engineering: assessment of document quality, identification and classification of application specific concepts, and analysis of system behavior.

There are three areas where natural language processing is applied to requirements engineering: assessment of document quality, identification and classification of application specific concepts, and analysis of system behavior. Approaches to the analysis of document quality were introduced, for example, by Rupp (2002), Fabbrini, Fusani, Gnesi, and Lami (2001), Kamsties, Berry, and

Table 6. Evaluation: heuristics to identify actors

Evaluated heuristics	correct MSCs		wrong MSCs		
	absolute number	percentage	wrong, with un-necessary actors	wrong due to missing actors	others
subject of an active sentence containing a direct object, local	31	76%	2	2	6
subject of an active sentence containing no direct object, local	15	37%	7	19	0
subject of an active sentence containing a direct object + subject of a passive sentence, local	28	62%	5	2	6
subject of an active sentence containing a direct object + direct object, local	5	12%	34	2	0
subject of an active sentence containing a direct object + default sender/receiver, local	**33**	**80%**	2	0	6
subject of an active sentence containing a direct object + default sender/receiver, global	**33**	**80%**	4	0	4

Paech (2001), Chantree, Nuseibeh, de Roeck, and Willis (2006). These approaches have in common that they define writing guidelines and measure document quality by measuring the degree to which the document satisfies the guidelines. These approaches have a different focus from the approach presented in this book chapter: their aim is to detect poor phrasing and to improve it, they do not target at behavior analysis.

Another class of approaches, like for example those by Goldin and Berry (1997), Abbott (1983), and Chen (1983) analyze the requirements documents, extract application specific concepts, and provide an initial model of the application domain. These approaches do not perform any behavior analysis, either.

The approaches analyzing system behavior, as for example those by Vadera and Meziane (1994), Gervasi and Zowghi (2005), Rolland and Ben Achour (1998), and Dıaz, Pastor, and Matteo (2005), translate requirements documents to executable models by analyzing linguistic patterns. In this sense, they are similar to the approach presented in this book chapter. Vadera and Meziane (1994) propose a procedure to translate certain linguistic patterns to first order logic and then to the specification language VDM (Jones,

1990), but they do not provide automation for this procedure. Gervasi and Zowghi (2005) introduce a restricted language, a subset of English. They automatically translate textual requirements written in this restricted language to first order logic. In the presented book chapter, to the contrary, the language is not restricted, full expressiveness of English is allowed. Rolland and Ben Achour (1998) state that the behavior can consist of pairs of service request and provision, which is comparable to the stack idea building the core of the approach presented in this book chapter. However, they do not explicitly introduce stack discipline and do not provide automation. Dıaz et al. (2005) introduce a transformation technique producing UML sequence diagrams. However, the input to this transformation technique is semantical representation of the sentences and not plain text as in the presented book chapter.

To summarize, to the best of our knowledge, there is no approach to requirements documents analysis that is able to analyze scenarios written in natural language and to identify missing pieces of behavior, yet.

SUMMARY

The approach to translation of textual scenarios into MSCs solves three important problems of requirements analysis:

- It detects information missing from scenarios.
- It translates textual scenarios to MSCs.
- If applied with a previously constructed set of actors, it validates the set of actors. Validation of the set of actors is achieved by the analysis of wrong MSCs and identifying unnecessary actors that caused errors in the MSCs.

To summarize, the presented approach can translate textual scenarios to MSCs without manual intervention. Surely, this does not mean that the generated MSCs can be directly used to implement the system. A generated MSC gives one possible interpretation of the scenario, not necessarily the same interpretation as intended by the document author. Thus, the generated MSCs have to be validated by a domain expert. When validated, they can be used in further software development. Thus, the presented approach makes a contribution to behavior modeling and validation, as well as to formalization of functional requirements.

FUTURE WORK

The work presented in this book chapter can be further developed in different directions. The technique of translation sentences into MSC messages can be made more intelligent by taking more different sentence types into account. The technique to derive missing model elements (senders, receivers, and messages in the presented approach) can be extended from MSCs to automata. Furthermore, the presented approach can be integrated with approaches to MSC validation

and automata generation. These possibilities are discussed below.

- **Taking different sentence constructions into account:** Rolland and Ben Achour (1998) list several linguistic forms that sentences describing the same action can take. They show where in the sentence the message sender, receiver, and the message content are placed, depending on the linguistic form. Taking these linguistic form explicitly into account could facilitate the process of the sender/receiver identification and increase precision of the text-to-MSC translation.
- **Extension of the technique to automata:** The presented approach implements a kind of discourse context modeling for sentence sequences: The sequence of the analyzed sentences builds the interpretation context for the next sentence. This allows to derive the message sender or receiver if this information is missing from the sentence. The same idea can be applied to translate pieces of text to automata. In this case we could consider every sentence as a state transition and use discourse context to infer the start or the end state of the transition if these states are not explicitly specified.
- **Tool-based validation of the produced MSCs:** Broy, Krüger, and Meisinger (2007) proposed MSCs as the means to formalize partially specified system behavior. To achieve such formalization, the presented approach can be combined with the PlayEngine (Harel & Marelly, 2003) and the tool Smyle (Bollig, Katoen, Kern, & Leucker, 2006). The PlayEngine provides interactive validation of MSCs. It takes a set of MSCs and allows the user to send input signals to the system. Then it picks at random one of the MSCs that suit the user input and shows the user the system output. In the case that the user registers

an undesirable system reaction, she has to correct the MSCs specifying the system.

Smyle takes a set of MSCs and generates other MSCs, corresponding to not yet specified parts of system behavior. The analyst has to decide which of the generated MSCs represent allowed system behavior. When Smyle has gathered enough information, it generates an automaton for each actor.

A solution to these challenges would further improve the presented approach and make it industrially applicable.

ACKNOWLEDGMENT

I am grateful to two anonymous referees who helped to improve the paper.

REFERENCES

Abbott, R. J. (1983). Program design by informal English descriptions. *Communications of the ACM, 26*(11), 882–894. doi:10.1145/182.358441

Bollig, B., Katoen, J.-P., Kern, C., & Leucker, M. (2006, October). *Replaying Play in and Play out: Synthesis of Design Models from Scenarios by Learning* (Tech. Rep. No. AIB-2006-12). RWTH Aachen, Germany. Retrieved August 13, 2008 from http://www.smyle-tool.org/wordpress/wp-content/uploads/2008/02/2006-12.pdf

Broy, M., Krüger, I., & Meisinger, M. (2007). *A formal model of services. ACM Transactions on Software Engineering Methodology (TOSEM), 16*(1). Retrieved August 13, 2008 from http://doi.acm.org/10.1145/1189748.1189753

Buhr, K., Heumesser, N., Houdek, F., Omasreiter, H., Rothermehl, F., Tavakoli, R., et al. (2004). *DaimlerChrysler demonstrator: System specification instrument cluster.* Available August 13, 2008 from http://www.empress-itea.org/deliverables/D5.1_Appendix_B_v1.0_Public_Version.pdf

C&C Tools (2007). Retrieved August 13, 2008 from http://svn.ask.it.usyd.edu.au/trac/candc

Chantree, F., Nuseibeh, B., de Roeck, A., & Willis, A. (2006). Identifying nocuous ambiguities in natural language requirements. In *RE'06: Proceedings of the 14th IEEE International Requirements Engineering Conference (RE'06)*, (pp.56–65). Washington, DC: IEEE Computer Society.

Chen, P. (1983, May). English sentence structure and entity-relationship diagram. *Information Sciences, 29*(2-3), 127–149. doi:10.1016/0020-0255(83)90014-2

Clark, S., & Curran, J. R. (2004). Parsing the WSJ using CCG and log-linear models. In *ACL'04: Proceedings of the 42nd Annual Meeting on Association for Computational Linguistics* (p. 103). Morristown, NJ: Association for Computational Linguistics.

Curran, J. R., Clark, S., & Vadas, D. (2006). Multi-Tagging for Lexicalized-Grammar Parsing. In *21ˢᵗ International Conference on Computational Linguistics and 44th Annual Meeting of the Association for Computational Linguistics*, Sydney, Australia, July 17-21.

Dıaz, I., Pastor, O., & Matteo, A. (2005). Modeling interactions using role-driven patterns. In RE'05: *Proceedings of the 13th IEEE International Conference on Requirements Engineering (RE'05)*, (pp. 209–220). Washington, DC: IEEE Computer Society.

Fabbrini, F., Fusani, M., Gnesi, S., & Lami, G. (2001). The linguistic approach to the natural language requirements quality: benefit of the use of an automatic tool. In *26th Annual NASA Goddard Software Engineering Workshop*, (pp. 97–105). Greenbelt, Maryland: IEEE Computer Society. Retrieved August 13, 2008 from http://fmt.isti.cnr.it/WEBPAPER/fabbrini_nlrquality.pdf

Gervasi, V., & Zowghi, D. (2005). Reasoning about inconsistencies in natural language requirements. *ACM Transactions on Software Engineering and Methodology, 14*(3), 277–330. doi:10.1145/1072997.1072999

Goldin, L., & Berry, D. M. (1997). AbstFinder, A Prototype Natural Language Text Abstraction Finder for Use in Requirements Elicitation. *Automated Software Engineering, 4*(4), 375–412. doi:10.1023/A:1008617922496

Grosz, B. J., Joshi, A. K., & Weinstein, S. (1995). Centering: A Framework for Modeling the Local Coherence of Discourse. *Computational Linguistics, 21*(2), 203-225. Retrieved August 13, 2008 from citeseer.ist.psu.edu/grosz95centering.html

Harel, D., & Marelly, R. (2003). *Come, Let's Play: Scenario-Based Programming Using LSCs and the Play-Engine.* Berlin: Springer–Verlag.

Jones, C. B. (1990). *Systematic software development using VDM.* Upper Saddle River, NJ: Prentice-Hall. Retrieved from citeseer.ist.psu.edu/jones95systematic.html

Kamsties, E., Berry, D. M., & Paech, B. (2001). Detecting Ambiguities in Requirements Documents Using Inspections. In *Workshop on Inspections in Software Engineering*, (pp.68 –80), Paris, France.

Kof, L. (2005). *Text Analysis for Requirements Engineering.* Unpublished doctoral dissertation, Technische Universität München. Retrieved August 13, 2008 from http://www4.in.tum.de/publ/html.php?e=914

Mich, L., Franch, M., & Novi Inverardi, P. (2004). Market research on requirements analysis using linguistic tools. *Requirements Engineering, 9*(1), 40–56. doi:10.1007/s00766-003-0179-8

Rolland, C., & Ben Achour, C. (1998, March). Guiding the construction of textual use case specifications. *Data & Knowledge Engineering Journal, 25*(1–2), 125–160. doi:10.1016/S0169-023X(97)86223-4

Rupp, C. (2002). *Requirements-Engineering und -Management.* Professionelle, iterative Anforderungsanalyse für die Praxis (2nd Ed.). Munich: Hanser–Verlag.

Vadera, S., & Meziane, F. (1994). From English to Formal Specifications. *The Computer Journal, 37*(9), 753–763. doi:10.1093/comjnl/37.9.753

ENDNOTES

[1] The following translations are translations of the definitions by Rupp (2002), in German.

[2] To make the figures compacter, in all figures "instrument cluster" is abbreviated as "ins. cl.".

[3] Please note that here we consider only sentences containing exactly one verb.

[4] To make the table compacter, "instrument cluster" is abbreviated in Table 2 as "ins. clust."

[5] Here the Java syntax for regular expressions is used. For details see http://java.sun.com/j2se/1.5.0/docs/api/java/util/regex/Pattern.html

6   verb participle is denoted by the VBN-tag

7   The precise distinction between complete sentences and sentence segments was important in Section 4.2, it is unimportant in the remainder of the book chapter. To simplify the presentation, every textual unit of analysis used for text-to-MSC translation is called "sentence" from now on.

Chapter 6
A Bayesian Network for Predicting the Need for a Requirements Review

José del Sagrado Martínez
University of Almería, Spain

Isabel María del Águila Cano
University of Almería, Spain

ABSTRACT

One of the major problems when developing complex software systems is that of Requirement Engineering. The methodologies usually propose iterations in which requirements are to be reviewed and re-written until the final version is obtained. This chapter focuses on the construction of "Requisites", a Bayesian network designed to be used as a predictor that tells us whether a requirements specification has enough quality to be considered as a baseline. Requisites have been defined using several information sources, such as standards and reports, and through interaction with experts, in order to structure and quantify the final model. This Bayesian network reflects the knowledge needed when assessing a requirements specification. The authors show how Requisites can be used through the study of some use cases. After the propagation over the network of information collected about the certainty of a subset of variables, the value predicted will determine if the requirements specification has to be revised.

INTRODUCTION

Product software is a worldwide industry providing the software applications found in countless types of systems, such as telecommunications, military, industrial processes, and entertainment. This software must be developed just as any other industrial product, by applying engineering methods to ensure a quality final product. Software Engineering (SE),

appears in this context, and has been defined as: "The application of a systematic, disciplined, and quantifiable approach to the development, operation, and maintenance of software; that is, the application of engineering to software." (IEEE, 1990, p. 67).

SWEBOK (Software Engineering Body of Knowledge) (Abran et al., 2004), one of the major works in SE, gives us an agreed description of scope of SE, defining ten related areas of knowledge: software requirements, software design, software construction, software testing, software maintenance,

DOI: 10.4018/978-1-60566-758-4.ch006

software configuration management, software engineering management, software engineering process, software engineering tools and methods, and software quality.

This chapter deals with how to apply a specific formalism, Bayesian Network (Pearl, 1988; Jensen, 2001), which originated in artificial intelligence and knowledge engineering fields for the purpose of enhancing specific activities related to the one of these SE knowledge areas, namely software requirements. Requirements play a key role in determining the success or failure of software projects and in determining the quality of software to be developed. This knowledge area has been selected for two basic reasons. On the hand, this area is different from the others because requirements reside basically in the problem space whereas other software artefacts reside in the solution space (Cheng & Atlee, 2007), and on the other hand, when requirement-related tasks are poorly defined or executed, the software product is typically unsatisfactory (Sommerville, 2006; Standish Group 1994, 2003), and therefore, any improvement in requirements will favourably affect the whole software lifecycle.

The requirements in any particular software project are usually a complex combination of requirements from stakeholders, and their identification is not a simple single step, but rather a cyclic activity (Sommerville, 2005; Nuseibeh & Easterbrook, 2000; Sawyer, Sommerville, & Viller 1997). Moreover, these requirements evolve and change, but at some point, a contract, called the requirement specification, needs to be agreed upon to generate a starting point for the project. This chapter explores the use of Bayesian networks to represent the relationships between various factors and the quality of requirements specification.

The rest of the chapter is organized in six sections. Section 2 describes how the main tasks involved in defining software requirements have evolved, resulting in the field known as *requirement engineering*. Section 3 outlines how requirement engineering can be improved, specifically

focusing on Bayesian networks. This formalism is described in Section 4. Section 5 describes the development of our Bayesian network model, Requisites. Once it is obtained we show how to use it in order to give advice on the goodness of requirement specifications. Finally, we present the future research directions and the conclusions.

FROM SOFTWARE REQUIREMENT TO REQUIREMENT ENGINEERING

Software requirements express the needs and constraints placed on a software product that contribute to the solution of some real world problem (Kotonya & Sommerville, 2000). The process or set of tasks applied to find out, analyse, document and check these needs and constraints, have nowadays become the category of a subject called Requirement Engineering (RE).

Traditionally, obtaining requirements has been considered a fuzzy step in the software development lifecycle, in which a set of informal ideas must be translated into formal expressions. Nevertheless, tasks related to requirements are regarded as a key stage in software development, because "the primary measure of the success and quality of a software system is the degree to which it meets the purpose for which it was intended" (Nuseibeh & Easterbrook, 2000, p. 37), which is client satisfaction.

Requirements have different characteristics or properties that can be used as classification criteria, so usually, the meaning of "requirement" is narrowed down with adjective labels: system, hardware, software, user, client, functional, non-functional, performance, etc. (Duran & Bernárdez, 2000; Sommerville, 2006). Requirements can be classified according to their scope, leading to system requirements, hardware requirements or software requirements. They can also be classified by the nature of the feature they describe, leading to functional requirements, non-functional requirements or domain requirements. Finally, depending on the audience, they may distinguish between user/client requirements, developer requirements (also called software requirements) or software design specifications. A requirement may also belong to more than one of these classes. In this chapter, we use the last classification, because it shows how requirements evolve. Requirements are originally described in the user world, that is, in the problem domain, and therefore must be translated into the solution domain. In other words, "the requirement problem space is less constrained than the software solution space – in fact, it is the requirement's definition that helps to delimit the solution space" (Cheng & Atlee, 2007, p. 287).

Requirements play a key role in quality software development. This is supported by the information collected and analysed in reports, (Glass, 2002; Standish Group, 1994, 2003) which point out that an unsuccessful requirements study is the cause of 50% of cancelled or troubled software projects (about a 70%). Besides if tasks related to requirements are not correctly performed, 35% of all software development projects will not meet the desired and expected quality. The solution is to transform the software project requirement definition process into an engineering process itself. Thus, Requirement Engineering must be understood as the need to apply controlled systematic processes and skills to the definition, analysis, specification and validation of the user's needs.

Historically developers have assumed that the client was able to provide the requirements, and therefore the software development life cycle has always started with the documentation and analysis of a set of given requirements. However, empirical data have demonstrated that it is a more complex task. Requirements are iterated towards a level of quality and detail which is sufficient to permit design in most cases and typically stakeholders need help to formulate them. Understanding of requirements continues to evolve as design and development proceeds.

It is almost impossible to formulate all the re-

quirements without having to revert back at some point in the process. The possibility that conflicts or new requirements that were hitherto hidden may appear during validation of the requirements must be considered. Under these circumstances, such conflicts must be solved and new requirements agreed. Even when the software has been released to the client, requirements are still alive due to requests for change, when this task is then called change management.

There are several methodologies that set what must be done during tasks related to requirements in any given software development project. Figure 1(a) shows the SWEBOK's RE task proposal. This illustration also shows other RE methodologies which have been proposed (Duran & Bernárdez, 2000; Sommerville, 2006; Loucopoulos & Karakostas, 1995). These proposals are very similar and include iterative tasks. The big difference in these methodologies resides in how the activities are grouped. Sommerville, (2006) groups elicitation and analysis, whereas Duran & Bernárdez (2000) removes specification as a separate task, including it in elicitation for the specification of user requirements, and in analysis for the specification of the software requirements. Moreover, it should be noted that historically, in previous proposals, as in Loucopoulos & Karakostas (1995), analysis work was included in drafting the requirements specification.

In the SWEBOK consensus proposal, the main iteration is elicitation–analysis–specification-validation. These tasks are described below:

- **Requirements Elicitation** tasks are concerned with identifying the sources of information about the project and finding and collecting the requirements from them. The main goals of this activity are firstly, know the problem domain in order to understand clients and users, and secondly, discovering their real needs.

- **requirements analysis** work is concerned with detecting requirement conflicts,

Figure 1. Requirement engineering task proposals

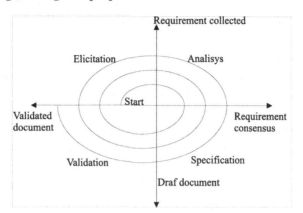

trying to reconcile conflicting views, and generating, and agreeing to, a consistent set of requirements (Boehm et al, 1994). The software boundaries and its interaction with its environment, and user requirements, or what are also called the C-requirements, from which the developer, or D-requirements, will be derived (Braude, 2000), must also be drafted. The development of real-world problem models is a key in software analysis. Several kinds of models can be developed: data and control flows, state models, data models, user interaction models, and many others.

- **Requirements Specification**. In software engineering, the term "specification" refers to the production of a document, or its electronic equivalent, which can be systematically reviewed, evaluated, and approved. Requirements Specification is concerned with what must and what must not be included in a user and software requirement specification in such a way that stakeholders and software developers can both understand it.

- **Requirements Validation**. Requirements are validated to ensure that the software engineer has understood and correctly recorded the requirements. This checking

avoids extending errors to the following software development stages and generating imperfect software products.

The outcome of the RE process is a statement of user requirements and its transformation into software requirements. But, what format should be used for this? A document or report may be in natural language or it can use a modelling language. Models are a good alternative that can be used to represent the whole range of products of the RE process, but often they cannot be understood by stakeholders. In fact, authors who point to the modelling task as a main RE working area (Nuseibeh & Easterbrook, 2000) also include a communications task, which focuses on facilitating effective communication of these requirements to the stakeholders.

Thus, preparing the requirements specification document is a basic RE task, because it establishes a software project commitment. Models can be included as part of this specification too. Moreover, this specification is the contract, or baseline, between the client and the development team, and both must understand it.

There is no standard for this specification document. Projects that are long and complex usually have three documents, but in different organisations they may have different names and different structures. The IEEE Computer Society labels these documents Concept of Operations (ConOps) Document (IEEE 1362-1998), System Requirements Specifications (IEEE 1233-1998), and Software Requirements Specification (IEEE Std 830-1998), which is the best known, and is always necessary, even in small projects, whether as a document or its electronic equivalent, if not in terms of its structure, at least in terms of its content.

The Software Requirements Specifications (SRS), as described in (IEEE Std 830-1998), are for a particular software product, program, or set of programs that performs certain functions in a specific environment.

Following (IEEE Std. 830-1998, p. 3), the basic SRS issues are:

- *Functionality.* What the software is supposed to do.
- *External interfaces.* How the software interacts with people, the system hardware, other hardware, and other software
- *Performance.* The speed, availability, response time, recovery time, etc., of software functions
- *Attributes.* The portability, correctness, maintainability, security, etc.
- *Design constraints imposed on an implementation.* Are there any current standards, implementation language, database integrity policies, resource limits, operating environment(s) etc., required?

This standard also defines the characteristics of good SRS as correct, unambiguous, complete, consistent, ranked for importance and/or stability, verifiable, modifiable, and traceable.

Since requirements remain alive throughout the software lifecycle, including maintenance, the SRS needs to evolve as the development of the software product progresses and not just be a closed report. In fact, the biggest breakthrough in requirement management is when you stop thinking of documents and start thinking about information. (Hood et al., 2008). And to being able to handle this information you have to resort to databases, particularly documental databases that have evolved into what nowadays are called CARE (Computer-Aided Engineering Requirement) tools, which allow complete requirement management, supporting generation of reports, such as the SRS, conducting requirement metrics, and integration with other CASE tools (Computer-aided software engineering) for its unification with the rest of the lifecycle of the software. Among the best known are the IRqA, Telelogic DOORS, Borland Caliber, and the IBM-Rational Requisite Pro. A complete list and description of their functionalities can be found in (INCOSE, 2008)

With SRS, requirements are assessed before designing can begin and reduces later redesign. It should also provide a realistic basis for estimating product cost, risks and schedules. Assuring the quality of the SRS therefore represents a profitable effort within SE work.

REQUIREMENT ENGINEERING ENHANCEMENT USING BAYESIAN NETWORKS

RE, in contrast to other SE activities, is inherently difficult. Descriptions of requirements are supposedly written in terms of the domain, describing how this environment is to be affected by the new software product. In contrast, other software process artefacts are written in terms of the internal software entities and properties (Cheng & Atlee, 2007). Because RE problems have a major impact on the effectiveness of the software development processes, an RE challenge is enhancing it by defining specific techniques or methods. This enhancement can be achieved in two different ways, either by improving the RE process itself, or improving techniques or methods applied in each activity or artefact used in the RE process.

There are two main approaches to RE process improvement (Thomas & McGarry, 1994). The top-down approach compares an organisation's process with some generally accepted standard process. Process improvement is then the elimination of differences between an existing process and a standard, such as the Capability Maturity Model Integrated (CMMI) (Paulk et al., 1993). In RE there are specific improvement models such as the one proposed by Sommerville (Sawyer et al., 1997, Sommerville & Ransom, 2005) that deal with improving what the process involves to determine the level of RE maturity (Niazi et al 2008), and subsequently make concrete improvements. The bottom-up approach assumes that changes are defined by the local domain instead of applying a universal set of accepted practices (Thomas & McGarry, 1994). For example, Method Engineering (Brinkkemper et al, 2008) could be applied or an information model (Hall & Rapanotti, 2003) could be defined.

The second path for improving RE techniques and methods has progressed enormously, from scenarios to model-driven engineering and reuse. The goal of these techniques is to improve how user and software requirements are developed. However, these new methods are not enough (Fenton, 1993). There must be empirical measures to assess their effectiveness. These metrics help managers to make decisions in a specific project in order to select the next step that must be carried out during RE tasks.

One of RE's main characteristics is the lack of certainty about individual requirements. The success of a software process resides in taking decisions about requirements under uncertainty (Maynard-Zhang et al, 2005). RE starts building a requirements specification through iteration. This iterative process culminates in the contract. Here the problem lies in knowing when the requirements specification is good enough to stop the iterative process. So the requirements engineer has to take the uncertain decision about the stability of the requirements specification; and either stops the

process or not. A Bayesian network can model a domain with uncertainty and be used as a tool for managerial decision support in predicting the need for a requirements review. This proposal can be considered a leverage technology, that is, the combination and adaptation of technological advances in computing and related fields to problems in RE. An example of an application of leverage technology is the KARE methodology, which has demonstrated its benefits in terms of accuracy and consistency of SRS improvement, reducing the number of iterations (Ratchev et al. 2003).

Bayesian networks have been successfully applied in SE as models for predicting the resources necessary to accomplish a software project and also for predicting quality in the development of software products. For example, Bayesian network models have been proposed for predicting the software development effort (Pendharkar et al., 2005; Radlinski et al 2007), defects in software (Fenton et al., 2007), the size and quality of the software delivered (Radlinski et al 2007) and as a software maintenance management tool (de Melo & Sánchez, 2008). In RE, Bayesian networks can provide an algorithmic approach to modelling the relationship between user and system requirements, as well as their architectural significance (Barry & Laskey, 1999). From the viewpoint of RE, is interesting to make use of predictors about the quality of the requirements specification given under the form of a contract or baseline. Bayesian networks have demonstrated their utility as an aid in software development projects. Our goal is to build a Bayesian network model that predicts whether it is necessary to redefine the SRS, and run a new iteration, or not.

Bayesian Networks Basics

Bayesians networks (Pearl, 1988; Jensen, 2001; Neapolitan, 2004; Jensen & Nielsen 2007; Kjaerulff & Madsen, 2008) allow us to represent graphically and concisely knowledge about an uncertain domain. The uncertainty is represented in terms of a probability distribution whose relations of independence are codified into a network structure. Bayesian networks also offer an inference mechanism, i.e., propagation algorithms, making possible reasoning under uncertainty.

More formally, a Bayesian network is a pair (G, P), where G = (U, A) is a directed acyclic graph (DAG), in which the set of nodes U = $\{V_1, V_2, ..., V_n\}$ represents the system variables, and the set of directed edges (or arcs) A represents the direct dependence relationships between variables. The second component of the pair, P, is a joint probability distribution over U that can be factorized according to:

$$P(V_1, V_2, \cdots, V_n) = \prod_i P(V_i \mid Pa(V_i))$$

where *i* ranges from 1 to *n* and $P(V_i|Pa(V_i))$ is the conditional probability for each variable V_i in U given its set of parents $Pa(V_i)$ in the DAG. These local conditional probability distributions measure the strength of the direct connections between variables.

The basic steps that have to be performed in order to build a Bayesian network (Korb & Nicholson, 2003; Neapolitan, 2004; Buntine 1996; Heckerman, 1999; Henrion, 1989) are:

0. *Feasibility study.* Decide if a Bayesian network model can handle the domain and the type of application.
1. *Variable identification.* At this stage, some modelling decisions have to be made about how to represent the knowledge domain and what is going to be represented in the Bayesian network.
2. *Structure elicitation.* The topology of the network must capture relationships between variables, i.e., two variables should be connected by an arc if one affects the other. In general, any independence suggested by a lack of an arc must correspond to real independence in the knowledge domain.

3. *Parameter elicitation.* Once the DAG structure has been set up, the strength of the relationships between variables has to be quantified by specifying the conditional probabilities (Cestnik, 1990; Jensen & Nielsen 2007; Kjaerulff & Madsen, 2008).
4. *Validation and testing.* Checks if the model meets the criteria for use.

As stated in the Feasibility Study step, before starting the construction of a Bayesian network model, it is a good idea to ensure whether this is the appropriate model. A Bayesian network would not be appropriate (Korb & Nicholson, 2003) if:

*   The problem is highly complex.
*   The problem has a very limited utility (it is going to be used only a few times).
*   There are no domain experts or useful data for finding knowledge about the domain.
*   The problem can be solved by learning an explicit function from available data (then machine learning techniques can be applied).

Once it has been decided that Bayesian network modelling is plausible, the next step, *Variable Identification*, must be tackled. The expert and the Bayesian network builder must agree on the variables involved in the problem, and their possible values or states. When the Bayesian network model is being organised, it must not be forgotten that its purpose is to estimate certainties for unobservable (or observable at an unacceptable cost) events (Jensen & Nielsen, 2007). These events are called hypothesis events, and once they are detected, they are grouped into sets of mutually exclusive and exhaustive events to form hypothesis variables. Achievable information relevant (in the sense of revealing something) to the hypothesis variables must also be collected. Then these pieces of information are grouped into information variables. The identification of variables can be accomplished not only by means of expert elicitation, but also by applying unsupervised classification (see, for example, (Kaufman & Rousseeuw, 2005)).

The purpose of the *Structure Identification* step is to set up the qualitative part of the model, with directed links connecting the variables in a DAG. The topology of this DAG should represent qualitative relationships between variables. Thus, if one variable influences the other, they should be connected by a directed link, the direction of which indicates the direction of the effect. However, in the real world, such links cannot be expected to be accomplished easily. Causal relations, understood as actions that change the state of the world, are not always obvious. As an aid, when there are data available, we can use structural learning approaches, such as the work of (Spirtes et al., 1991), based on the detection of independences, and that of (Cooper & Herskovitz, 1992), based on applying search plus score techniques, instead of relying completely on the expert's opinion.

The *Parameter Elicitation* step aims to acquire the numbers necessary to estimate the conditional probabilities for the Bayesian network model. Of course, the acquisition of numbers is not exempt from real-world difficulties. Statistical methods for learning parameters in Bayesian networks can be found in (Buntine 1996; Cestnik, 1990). When enough data are available, structure identification and parameter elicitation can also be done automatically by automatic learning methods. These two tasks cannot be totally independent of each other. In order to estimate the conditional probabilities, the graphic structure must be known, and some probabilistic independence test will have to be performed to determine this structure and help establish the direction of links between variables. A detailed description of learning methods is out of the scope of this chapter, but (Buntine, 1996) provides extensive reviews, and (Heckerman, 1999) is an excellent introduction.

Finally, the purpose of the *Validation and Testing* step is to check the suitability of the Bayesian network model for the job it is designed to do,

answering such questions as: Does the structure reflect the fundamental independence relationships of the problem? What is the level of predictive accuracy acquired? And, is the network sensitive to changes? As Korb & Nicholson (2003) point out, these questions can be of assistance in validating the network and understanding how the network can best be used in the field. Also it is important not to forget to measure usability and performance at this point to find out whether the Bayesian network software meets customer use criteria (Korb & Nicholson, 2003).

A Bayesian network can be used as a predictor simply by considering one of the variables as the class and the others as predicting variables (characteristics or features that describe the object that has to be classified). The prediction is found by means of probability propagation over the class variable. The posterior probability of the class is computed given the characteristics observed. The value assigned to the class is that it reaches the highest posterior probability value. A predictor based on a Bayesian network model provides more benefits, in terms of decision support, than traditional predictors, because it can perform powerful what-if problem analyses.

A Bayesian Network Model for Assessment SRS: Requisites

Requirements engineering of complex systems are inherently uncertain (Maynard-Zhang et al, 2005), but decisions about requirements have to be made. Our problem is to decide if a requirement specification is good enough to serve as basis for the rest of the software development project's life cycle. Within the RE world, many of the tools for requirements management offer utilities for the assessment of individual requirements. For example, IRqA Quality Analyzer has been developed as an additional tool for requirement quality assessment, inside the IRqA CARE tool.

In this section we are going to define a Bayesian Network model that enables software developers to assess the quality of SRS. Next, we are going to build this model, that we have called Requisites.

This modelling process relies on having several distinct information sources: experts, standards and reports (technical and research). The experts involved in this modelling process have previously collaborated in the development of a web-CASE tool for the elicitation of requirements (Orellana et al. 2005) and in the development of various complex software systems that combine classical software components with those based on knowledge (Cañadas, 2002; del Águila et al 2003; del Sagrado & del Águila 2007). IEEE Std 830-1998 and Chaos reports (Standish Group, 1994, 2003) are included as other information sources. Thus, from the need for a tool to aid in this area and the fact of having data and experts to rely on during the whole modelling process, it can be conclude that Requisites is feasible.

The variable identification step starts with a study of how to characterize the goodness of a SRS, taking as basis metrics over requirements (i.e. completeness, variability ...) and over the processes realized in order to define these requirements.

The set of preselected variables are shown in Table 1. The variables ranking from a.i to a.viii are obtained from IEEE Standard Std-830-1998, which describes the characteristics of a good specification of the requirements. From the Chaos Reports (Standish Group, 1994, 2003) we have only considered those variables that were defined as the causes of failures of projects concerning requirements, i. e. variables b.i to b.iv. Ebert & Man (2005) describe some factors influencing the uncertainty of the requirements. These factors are the causes of changes in the requirements and functionality missing (variable from c.i to c.vi). Finally, variables d.i to d.vi have been included based on expert opinions. These variables cover aspects related to the experience of those actors involved in software and other projects on emerging trends in reuse requirements.

This list is the starting point to decide, through interaction with experts, which variables are to be included in the Bayesian network model. Some of the variables have been unified since they have the same meaning. Others have been grouped under a single name because they represent nuances within the same concept of a descriptive SRS. Other variables have not been taken into account in the final model because they are not relevant to decide whether there is a need for a review. Table 2 shows the name, an identifier, origin, description and domain of the variables finally included in the Bayesian network model.

The final variables of Requisites are described below:

- **Stakeholders' expertise** represents the degree of familiarity the stakeholders have in the tasks relating to requirements engineering. If stakeholders have already collaborated in other projects, using techniques, skills and processes of RE, it will be clearer what is expected of them and will commit fewer errors such as those that appear in the report Chaos (Standish Group, 1994, 2003).

- **Domain expertise** expresses the level of knowledge about the domain of the project and its environment that the development team has. When developers use the same concepts than other stakeholders, communication will be correct and fewer iterations are needed.

- **Reused requirement** checks if there are requirements reused. Reusing requirements is a new trend in RE, trying to reduce the development cost, to enhance the quality and the productivity of the development team (Toval et al., 2002). There are several reusing strategies: building libraries of reusable requirements or defining product lines. Anyway we need tools that support these reutilization strategies. When one or several requirements have been labelled as reusable, we can conclude that they have been sufficiently validated. Thus, if the number of requirements of a project that came from reusable libraries is big, the overall specification of the requirements does not need new iterations.

Table 1. Preselected variables

Source	ID	Name of candidate variable	Description.
From 830 IEEE	a.i	Correct	A SRS is correct if every requirement stated therein is one that the software shall meet. The customer or user can determine if the SRS reflects their needs.
	a.ii	Unambiguous	A SRS is unambiguous if every requirement has only one interpretation.
	a.iii	Complete	A SRS is complete if it includes all significant requirements and responses of all inputs
	a.iv	Consistent	A SRS is consistent if no subset of requirements describe a conflict
	a.v	Ranked for importance and/or stability	A SRS is ranked for importance if all requirements has a value of its importance and stability
	a.vi	Verifiable	A SRS is verifiable if all requirements are verifiable
	a.vii	Modifiable	Changes can be easily and consistently performed
	a.viii	Traceable	If the origin of each requirement is clear.
From Standish group reports	b.i	Incomplete requirement	Several significant requirements are not elicited and/or specified, a 13% of these projects fail
	b.ii	Lack of user involvement	If users don't collaborate actively during RE process the project can be cancelled around 13%
	b.iii	Unrealistic expectations	Requirements are not properly expressed, no realistic requirements, a 10% of the projects have errors
	b.iv	Changing requirement and specifications	Requirements evolve and change (9%)
From Ebert 2005	c.i	Conflict of interest; commitments not maintained	The requirements are a complex combination of requirements from different stakeholders, at different levels, and some can generate conflict that unbalance the specification.
	c.ii	Unexpected dependencies between requirements	Interactions between requirement, lead to the necessity to perform new iterations in order to adjust the requirements
	c.iii	Cost/benefit of individual requirements unclear	The effort invested in the implementation of a requirement is not justified
	c.iv	Incomplete requirement	Several significant requirement are not elicited and /or specified
	c.v	Requirement changing	Caused by c.i,c.ii, c.ii and c.iv
	c.vi	Insufficient functionality	Caused by c.i and c.iv
Based on specialist's experience	d.i	Domain expertise	Requirement writers are at the interface between the domain of the stakeholders and that of software engineering. If writers know the project domain, the specification will be more accurate
	d.ii	Developer expertise	The developers that have expertise in RE related tasks, usually will obtain more accurate specifications
	d.iii	Other Stakeholder expertise	If stakeholders have earlier participated in a software project, applying requirements engineering skills, its collaboration will more successfully
	d.iv	Degree of Reused requirements	If a high degree of the requirements are reused, have already been tested in other projects
	d.v	Homogeneity of the descriptions	We must demand the same level of detail in all the requirements
	d.vi	Degree of revision	The degree with which the specification should be revised

Table 2. Variables included in Requisites

ID	Variable selected	Come from	Description	Values
1	Stakeholders' expertise	d.iii	Expertise in early RE projects	(High, Medium, Low)
2	Domain expertise	d.i	Requirements engineers domain expertise	(High, Medium, Low)
3	Reused requirements	d.iv	Number of requirements reused	(Many, Few, None)
4	Unexpected dependencies	c.ii	There are unexpected dependencies between requirements that were initially unrelated	(Yes, No)
5	Specificity	a.ii, a.iv a.vi bii	Number of the requirements that are all interpreted in the same way	(High, Medium, Low)
6	Unclear cost benefit	c.iii	Number of requirements that don't have a clear cost/benefit rate	(High, Medium, Low)
7	Degree of commitment	c.i b.iii	Number of the requirements that have need to be agreed	(High, Medium, Low)
8	Homogeneity of the description	d.v	The degree of uniformity in the level of description of the requirements (all should be detailed at a similar level of the description)	(Yes, No)
9	Requirement completeness	a.iii, b.i, c.iv c.vi	The degree of completeness in the specification of the requirements	(High, Medium, Low)
10	Requirement variability	b.iv, c.v	The degree of change in requirements	(High, Medium, Low)
11	Degree of revision	a.i, d.vi	Degree of revision in definition of the requirements	(High, Medium, Low)

- **Unexpected dependencies** reflects situations when, in the active version of the SRS, dependencies have been detected between requirements that initially were not related. Initially individual requirements are usually grouped by subject, by hierarchical classification, by stakeholder responsible of it, or due to other classification criteria, fixed by the specific project. The membership to one of these types or groups, implies the existence of implicit dependencies or relationships between them. But in some cases, unexpected dependencies or relations between requirements or groups of them can appear, that usually involves a new revision of the specification of the requirements.

- **Specificity** represents the number of requirements that have the same meaning for all stakeholders. That is, if stakeholders use the same terminology, we will need less revision and a shorter process of negotiation in order to reach a commitment. The greater the number of requirements unambiguous and consistent is, the greater the specificity will be. The unambiguity and consistency of the requirements needs the involvement of the user. Thus, specificity comes from the unification of a.ii, a.iv, a.vi and b.ii.

- **Unclear cost/benefit** represents that stakeholders or developers include requirements that do not have quantifiable benefits for the business or the organization in where the software to be developed will operate.

- **Degree of commitment** represents the number of the requirements that have needed a negotiation, and result from the unification of b.iii and c.i. The requirements of a project are a complex combination of requirements from different stakeholders, at different levels, and some can generate conflict that unbalance the specification.

- **Homogeneity of the description** has as meaning that a good SRS must to be described at the same level of detail. From specialist opinions, if some requirements can be described in detail, all the requirements of this SRS should be described at the same level. If there is not homogeneity, the SRS will be incomplete and will need to be revised.

- **Requirement completeness** indicates if all significant requirements are elicited and/or specified. This variable is equivalent to the initial variables a.iii, b.i and c.iv. One effect of the lack of completeness in requirements is that the software does not reach the desired functionality, so the variable c.vi has not been taken into account in the model.

- **Requirement variability** represent that changes in requirement have occurred. When a specification of the requirements have changed, it is quite possible that these changes affect the whole specification of the requirements and will need additional revision. This variable is equivalent to the initial variables b.iv and c.v.

- **Degree of revision** is the value that we want to predict with Requisites, and indicates that a SRS is sufficiently accurate as to not require further revisions. It is equivalent to a.i.

The variable d.ii is eliminated because requirements engineers are assumed to be able enough to make a specification of the requirements although they need more effort or training if they lack experience. The initial variables, a.v, a.vii, a.viii were also removed from the Bayesian network as they were not relevant to represent knowledge on the kindness of the SRS. Variable a.v indicates that requirements must be prioritized and is a funda-

mental property in software project planning and execution, but it tells us nothing about the need for requirements review. Variables a.vii and a.viii refer to the format of the document on which SRS is written. This format must be modifiable and traceable.

Once the variables have been selected, the next two steps in the development of a Bayesian network model are structure and parameter elicitation. Due to the lack of data bases in order to build the Bayesian network automatically, we have developed it manually with the help of experts, through a two stages iterative process. The first stage of this process consists of assessing the model during several oral interviews with the experts. During the second stage the model is evaluated. It is obvious that this manual process is difficult, time consuming and prone to errors (Druzdel & van der Gaag, 1995). So, during this process we have used Elvira (Elvira Consortium, 2002), a software package for the creation and evaluation of Bayesian networks, as a help facility for the model developer and the domain experts. Figure 2 shows the structure of the Bayesian network REQUISITES.

In the qualitative structure of Requisites can be seen that *specificity, unexpected dependencies, reused requisites*, the *stakeholder's expertise* and *domain expertise* are not affected by any other variables. In other words, they cannot be determined on the basis of other values. Based on our experience with requirements engineering, we can assume that the a priori value for specificity can be set *high* since the stakeholders must have similar vision system software and unexpected dependencies can be set *no* because we do not expect the existence of unexpected dependences between requirements. Also, before starting a software development process, we do not know, a priori what is the level of expertise of stakeholders and that of the domain, even if will be possible to reuse requirements. This is the reason why the values of these variables are equally likely.

Requisites also shows another interesting set

Figure 2. Structure of the Bayesian network REQUISITES

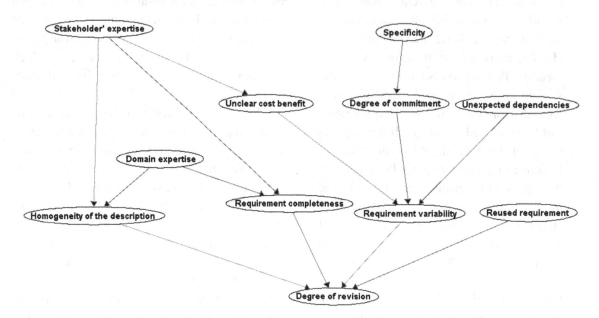

of relationships. Let us begin focusing on *degree of commitment* and *unclear cost benefit*. If the degree of commitment, number of requirements that have to be negotiated, increases, then the level of specificity will be low. In other words, if there are many requirements that every stakeholder understood in different ways, the number of requirements that need to be agreed upon will be higher. The same happens with *unclear cost benefit*, if stakeholders have little experience in the processes of RE, then it is more likely to lead to requirements which are unclear in terms of cost/benefits.

The *homogeneity of the description* and *requirement completeness* are influenced by the experience of software and requirement engineers in the domain of the project and by stakeholders in the processes or tasks of RE. If experience is high on both sides, all the requirements will be discovered and therefore the specification will be complete and homogeneous, because developers will be able to describe the requirements with the same level of detail.

The *requirement variability* node represents the number of changing requirements. A change in the requirements will be more likely to occur if unexpected dependencies are discovered, there are requirements that do not add something to the end software, requirements are missing, or if requirements have to be negotiated.

Finally, *degree of revision* is the main variable in the network. It increases when there are missing functionalities and/or if there have been many changes, and yet decreases if many requirements, belonging to other projects or libraries of reusable requirements, are reused.

After setting the network structure the quantitative parameters have to be fixed. At this point it is worth emphasising that the probability values are given by experts. So, numerical values used to specify the conditional probability distributions of the Bayesian network rely essentially on our experts experience and must reflect the influences previously identified. The elicitation of the quantitative parameters was carried out with the help of two software engineers, whose primary work concerns to the development of some CASE tools and expert systems in agriculture. The process

Figure 3. Initial variable quantification in the Bayesian network REQUISITES

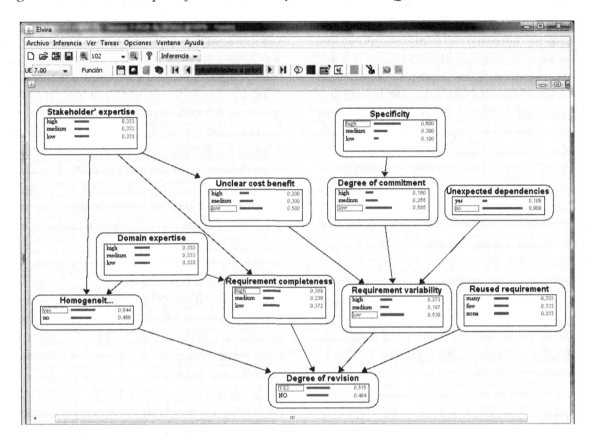

used consists of an interview-evaluation cycle. After each interview to assess the probabilities, the resulting prototype was evaluated. This iterative process was repeated 5 times until the definitive model was reached. In the case of Requisites the number of estimated parameters was 111 of which 36, 27 and 18 correspond to the conditional probability distributions associated with requirement variability, degree of revision and requirement completeness, respectively. Figure 3 shows the initial quantification of each variable in the Requisites network.

The Requisites network was evaluated by studying the influences between variables by setting the certainty value of certain variables (for example, the level of expertise of the stakeholder is high) and observing its impact over the rest of the variables. This process helped us to detect

some incorrect values. Also the model was tested during the development of a software project for a decision support system applied to pest control in olive tree (del Sagrado & del Águila, 2007).

Use of the Model REQUISITES

The use of the Bayesian network Requisites consists on considering information stating with certainty the value of a subset of variables in the network (this is called evidence) and computing the posterior probability of the rest of the variables by propagating the evidence through the network. Then we will observe the value assigned to *degree of revision* that reaches the highest posterior probability value, in order to make a prediction about the need for a requirements review.

Imagine a situation in which the both the

domain expertise and the cost benefits are set at a medium level. This evidence is introduced and propagated into Requisites producing a prediction value of 52% in favour of the need for revising the requirements. Now, if we also confirm that the level of stakeholders' expertise is low, then the situation reinforces the prediction in favour of the reviewing the requirements, increasing to a value 54% (see Figure 4).

Now, suppose that as in the previous situation the development team has a medium degree of domain expertise but it has been necessary to reach a commitment on a large number of requirements. Requisites predicts a need for reviewing the requirements with a value of a 57%. However, all significant requirements have been elicited, that is to say, we have received evidence supporting that a high degree of completeness has been reached. Then the prediction will change and Requisites will indicate that the need for a review is reduced to a value of 39% (see Figure 5).

As it can be seen, as a situation evolves, Requisites changes prediction .In this way, Requisites could be used to predict the quality of the requirement specification in order to translate it to a contract or baseline.

FUTURE RESEARCH DIRECTIONS

In future work, it would be of interest to study how Requisites can be embedded inside InSCo Requisites (DKSE, 2005; Orellana et al, 2005). This CASE tool has been developed by the Data Knowledge and Software Engineering group at the University of Almería. This tool helps in the development of *hybrid software systems*. Uncertainty, incompleteness and inconsistency are inherent in the components based on knowledge, so its requirements are subjective and unstructured. Whereas components not based on knowledge present a valid solution for those parts of the system related to a traditional software application. Nonetheless, requirements of these two kinds of

components need to be studied homogeneously. InSCo Requisites helps us to do that and provides electronic support for the SRS, offering functions for eliciting and structuring requirements. Thus the use of Requisites could give extra functionality to InSCo Requisites, providing an insight of the quality of the SRS in course.

The construction of Requisites could benefit from the availability of a set of data about measures of real software development projects. This database could serve as a basis for learning a Bayesian network model automatically in order to compare it with Requisites and upgrading qualitative and quantitatively the model, and not relying uniquely on the knowledge elicited from the experts. We have therefore established a line of collaboration with Visure Solutions, an enterprise that develops and commercialises a RE tool called IRqA, in order to obtain this set of data directly from measurements that can be defined on individual requirements in IRqA.

Another open research direction consists of permitting the use of other modelling languages, different from the natural language, to specify the SRS. Modelling notations help to raise the level of abstraction in requirements descriptions and allow for the definition of measures different from those used in Requisites and that can be estimated easily over the proper models defined. Between modelling notations, scenario-based, and specifically use cases (Cockburn, 2001; Jacobson, 1992) models have been considered as recent trends in requirement elicitation. It would also be interesting to study how to extend Requisites in order to asses these requirements models. This expansion could be done in two directions: adding new variables and relationships to Requisites that make it possible to handle these requirements models or learning a completely new Bayesian network based on the requirements model selected to be applied.

Figure 4. Requisites' Prediction: a) with a medium level of domain expertise and cost benefits; b) after also confirming that the stakeholders' expertise is low

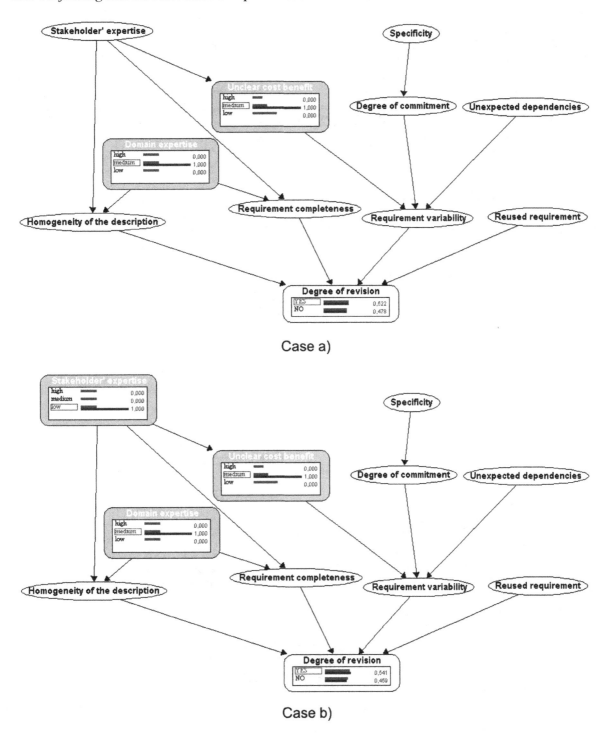

Case a)

Case b)

Figure 5. Requisites' Prediction: a) with a medium level of domain expertise and high degree of commit-ment; b) after confirming that there is a high degree of completeness of the requirement specification

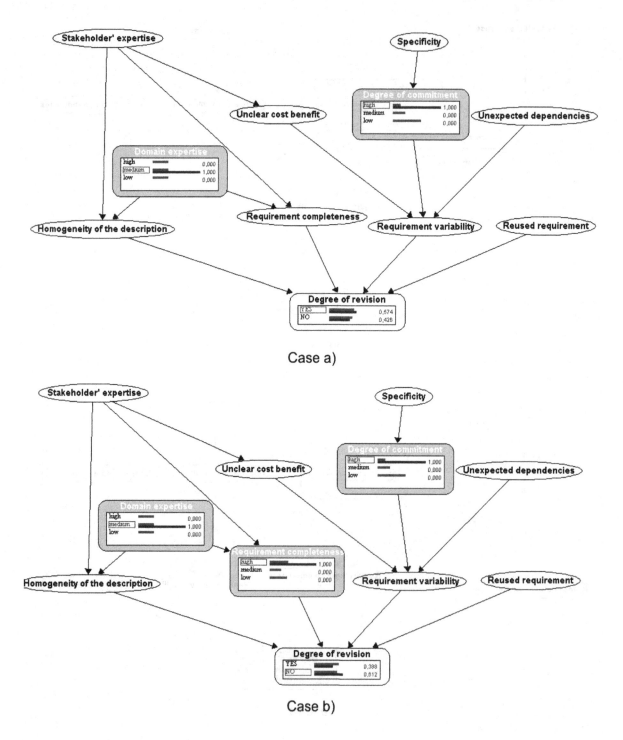

CONCLUSION

The purpose of our work is to transfer methods between two important disciplines, software engineering and knowledge engineering. Developers and managers need to make important decisions and Bayesian networks are a well-known artificial intelligence technique suitable for use in handling decision-making problems involving uncertainty. SE tasks related with requirements are inherently uncertain and iterative in nature; therefore Bayesian networks can be used to improve some RE tasks.

We have presented and described a Bayesian network model, Requisites, designed to be used as a predictor that tells us whether the software requirements specification (SRS) has enough quality, stopping the iterations needed in order to define the SRS. We have also described the set of well defined steps applied in the construction of a Bayesian network. During the construction of Requisites, specifically during variable identification, we have studied how to characterize the goodness of a requirement specification, taking as basis several information sources, such as standards and reports. The relationships between the variables of the model Requisites, as well as their associated probability distributions, have been obtained from the analysis of those previous work and through interaction with experts.

The Requisite model obtained can be used by software engineers and stakeholders as an aid in the requirements definition process for a specific software project. Once some of the previously identified measures have been computed or obtained, their values will be introduced as evidence and the propagation of belief will be used to determine if the requirements specification should or should not to be revised. This process has been exemplified through the description of several use cases.

ACKNOWLEDGMENT

This work was supported by the Spanish Ministry of Education and Science under projects TIN2004-05694 and TIN2007-67418-C03-02.

REFERENCES

Abran, A., Moore, J., Bourque, P., Dupuis, R., & Tripp, L. (2004). *Guide to the Software Engineering Body of Knowledge 2004 Version*. Los Alamitos, CA: IEEE Computer Society.

Barry, P. S., & Laskey, K. B. (1999). An Application of Uncertain Reasoning to Requirements Engineering. In K.B. Laskey and H. Prade (Eds.), *Proceedings of the 15th Conference on Uncertainty in Artificial Intelligence* (pp. 41-48). Stockholm, Sweden: Morgan Kaufmann.

Boehm, B., Bose, P., Horowitz, E., & Ming-June Lee. (1994). Software requirements as negotiated win conditions. In *Proceedings of the First International Conference on Requirements Engineering* (pp.74-83). Colorado Springs, CO: IEEE Computer Society.

Braude, E. J. (2000). *Softwre Engineering: An Object-Oriented Perspective*. New York: John Wiley & Sons.

Brinkkemper, S., van de Weerd, I., Saeki, M., & Versendaal, J. (2008). Process improvement in requirements management: A Method Engineering Approach. In B. Paech & C. Rolland (Eds.), *Requirements Engineering: Foundation For Software Quality,* (LNCS 5025, pp. 6-22). Berlin: Springer-Verlag.

Buntine, W. (1996). A guide to the literature on learning probabilistic networks from data. *IEEE Transactions on Knowledge and Data Engineering, 8*, 195–210. doi:10.1109/69.494161

Cañadas, J. J., del Águila, I. M., Bosch, A., & Túnez, S. (2002). An Intelligent System for Therapy Control in a Distributed Organization. In H. Shafazand & A. Min Tjoa (Eds.), *Proceedings of EurAsia-ICT 2002: Information and Communication Technology, First EurAsian Conference,* (LNCS 2510, pp. 19-26). Berlin: Springer-Verlag.

Cestnik, B. (1990). Estimating probabilities: A crucial task in Machine Learning. In L. Aiello (Ed.), *Proceedings of the 9th European Conference on Artificial Intelligence (ECAI-90)* (pp. 147-149). London/Boston: Pitman.

Cheng, B. H. C., & Atlee, J. M. (2007). Research Directions in Requirements Engineering. In *Future of Software Engineering, 2007. FOSE '07* (pp. 285-303). Minneapolis: IEEE Computer Society.

Cockburn, A. (2001). *Writing Effective Use Cases.* Upper Saddle River, NJ: Addison-Wesley.

Cooper, G., & Herskovitzs, E. (1992). A Bayesian method for the induction of probabilistic networks from data. *Machine Learning, 9,* 309–347.

Data Knowledge and Software Engineering Research Group (DKSE) (2005). InSCo Requisite. Retrieved from http://www.dkse.ual.es/insco/index.do.

de Melo, A. C., & Sanchez, A. J. (2008). Software maintenance project delays prediction using Bayesian Networks. *Expert Systems with Applications, 34*(2), 908–919. doi:10.1016/j.eswa.2006.10.040

del Águila, I. M., Cañadas, J. J., Bosch, A., Túnez, S., & Marín, R. (2003). Knowledge Model of a Therapy Administration Task - Applied to an Agricultural Domain. In V. Palada, R.J. Howlett and L.C. Jain (Eds.), *Knowledge-Based Intelligent Information and Engineering Systems 2003,* (LNAI 2774, pp. 1227-1283). Berlin: Springer-Verlag.

del Sagrado, J., & del Águila, I. M. (2007). Olive Fly Infestation Prediction Using Machine Learning Techniques. In D. Borrajo, L. Castillo, and J. M. Corchado (Eds.), *Current Topics in Artificial intelligence: 12th Conference of the Spanish Association For Artificial intelligence, CAEPIA 2007, Salamanca, Spain, November 12-16, 2007. Selected Papers, LNAI 4788* (pp. 229-238). Berlin: Springer-Verlag.

Druzdel, M. J., & van der Gaag, L. (1995). Elicitation of Probabilities for Belief Networks: Combining Qualitative and Quantitative Information. In P. Besnard & S. Hanks (Eds.), *Proceedings of the 11th Conference on Uncertainty in Artificial Intelligence* (pp. 141-148). San Francisco, CA: Morgan Kaufmann.

Duran Toro, A., & Bernárdez Jiménez, B. (2000). *Metodología de elicitación de requisitos de sistemas software. Versión 2.1,* (Tech. Rep.). Sevilla, Spain: University of Seville, Dpt. of Languages and Informatics Systems.

Ebert, C., & Man, J. D. (2005). Requirements Uncertainty: Influencing Factors and Concrete Improvements. In G-C Roman, W.G. Griswold & B. Nuseibeh (Eds.), *Proceedings of the 27th International Conference on Software Engineering, ICSE 2005* (pp. 553-560). St. Louis, MO: ACM.

Elvira Consortium. (2002). Elvira: An Environment for Probabilistc Graphical Models. In J.A. Gámez & A. Salmerón (Eds.), *Proceedings of the First European Workshop on Probabilistic Graphical Models* (pp. 222-230). Retrieved January 10, 2009, from http://www.informatik. uni-trier.de/~ley/db/conf/pgm/pgm2002.html

Fenton, N. (1993). How effective are software engineering methods? *Journal of Systems and Software, 22*(2), 141–146. doi:10.1016/0164-1212(93)90092-C

Fenton, N., Neil, M., Marsh, W., Hearty, P., Marquez, D., Krause, P., & Mishra, R. (2007). Predicting software defects in varying development lifecycles using Bayesian nets. *Information and Software Technology, 49*(1), 32–43. doi:10.1016/j.infsof.2006.09.001

Glass, A. R. L. (2002). *Facts and Fallacies of Software Engineering*. Boston: Pearson Education, Inc.

Hall, J. G., & Rapanotti, L. (2003). A Reference Model for Requirements Engineering. In *Proceedings of the 11th IEEE international Conference on Requirements Engineering* (pp. 181-187). Washington, DC: IEEE Computer Society.

Heckerman, D. (1999). A tutorial on learning with Bayesian networks. In M. I. Jordan, (Ed.) *Learning in Graphical Models* (pp. 301-354). Cambridge, MA: MIT Press.

Henrion, M. (1989). Some Practical Issues in Constructing Belief Networks. In L. Kanal, T. Levitt, & J. Lemmer (Eds.), *Uncertainty in Artificial Intelligence 3* (pp. 161-173). Amsterdam: Elsevier Science Publishers.

Hood, C., Wiedemann, S., Fichtinger, S., & Pautz, U. (2008). *Requirements Management: The Interface Between Requirements Development and All Other Systems Engineering Processes*. Berlin: Springer-Verlag.

IEEE guide for developing system requirements specifications (1998). *IEEE Std 1233, 1998 Edition*. Retrieved January 9, 2008, from http://ieeexplore.ieee.org/xpls/abs_all.jsp?tp=&isnumber=16016&arnumber=741940& punumber=5982

IEEE guide for information technology - system definition - Concept of Operations (ConOps) document (1998). *IEEE Std 1362-1998*. Retrieved January 9, 2008, from http://ieeexplore.ieee.org/xpls/abs_all.jsp?tp=&isnumber =16486&arnumber=761853&punumber=6166

IEEE recommended practice for software requirements specifications (1998). *IEEE Std 830-1998*. Retrieved January 9, 2008, from http://ieeexplore.ieee.org/xpl/tocresult.jsp?isNumber=15571

IEEE standard glossary of software engineering terminology (1990). Retrieved January 9, 2008, from http://ieeexplore.ieee.org/xpl/tocresult.jsp?isNumber=4148

INCOSE. (2008). International Council on Systems Engineering: Requirements Management Tools Survey. Retrieved January 9, 2008 from http://www.paper-review.com/tools/rms/read.php

Jacobson, I. (1992). *Object-Oriented Software Engineering: A Use Case Driven Approach*. Reading, MA: Addison-Wesley.

Jensen, F. V. (2001). *Bayesian Networks and decision graphs*. New York: Springer-Verlag.

Jensen, F. V., & Nielsen, T. (2007). *Bayesian networks and decision graphs*. New York: Springer-Verlag.

KARE, Knowledge Acquisition and Sharing for Requirement Engineering (KARE), (ESPRIT project No. 28916).

Kaufman, L., & Rousseeuw, P. (2005). *Finding Groups in Data: An Introduction to Cluster Analysis*. Hobokonen, NJ: John Wiley & Sons Inc.

Kjaerulff, U. B., & Madsen, A. (2008). *Bayesian Networks and Influence Diagrams: A Guide to Construction and Analysis*. New York: Springer-Verlag.

Korb, K., & Nicholson, A. (2003). *Bayesian Artificial Intelligence*. Boca Ratón, FL: Chapman & Hall/CRC.

Kotonya, G., & Sommerville, I. (1998). *Requirements Engineering: Processes and Techniques*. Chichester, UK: John Wiley and Sons.

Kristensen, K., & Rasmussen, I. A. (2002). The use of a Bayesian network in the design of a decision support system for growing malting barley without use of pesticides. *Computers and Electronics in Agriculture, 33*(3), 197–217. doi:10.1016/S0168-1699(02)00007-8

Loucopoulos, P., & Karakostas, V. (1995). *System Requirements Engineering.* New York: McGraw-Hill, Inc.

Maynard-Zhang, P., Kiper, J. D., & Feather, M. S. (2005). Modeling Uncertainty in Requirements Engineering Decision Support. In *Workshop on Requirements Engineering Decision Support, Paris, France, August 29, 2005.* Retrieved January 9, 2008 from http://trs-new.jpl.nasa.gov/dspace/handle/2014/37769

Neapolitan, R. E. (2004). *Learning Bayesian Networks.* Upper Saddle River, NJ: Pearson Prentice Hall.

Niazi, M., Cox, K., & Verner, J. (2008). A measurement framework for assessing the maturity of requirements engineering process. *Software Quality Control, 16*(2), 213–235.

Nuseibeh, B., & Easterbrook, S. (2000). Requirements engineering: a roadmap. In *Proceedings of the Conference on the Future of Software Engineering* (Limerick, Ireland, June 04 - 11, 2000). ICSE '00 (pp. 35-46). New York: ACM.

Orellana, F. J., Guil, F., del Águila, I. M., & Túnez, S. (2005). A WEB-CASE Tool Prototype for Hybrid Software Development. In R. Moreno-Díaz, F. Pichler & A. Quesada-Arencibia (Eds.) *Computer Aided Systems Theory – EUROCAST 2005, 10th Internacional Conference on Computer Aided Systems Theory,* (LNCS 3643, pp. 217-222). Berlin: Springer-Verlag.

Paulk, M., Curtis, B., Chrissis, M., & Weber, C. (1993). *Capability Maturity Model for Software (Version 1.1)* (Tech. Rep. CMU/SEI-93-TR-024) Pittsburg, PA: Carnegie Mellon University, Software Engineering Institute. Retrieved January 9, 2008, from http://www.sei.cmu.edu/publications/documents/93.reports/93.tr.024.html

Pearl, J. (1988). *Probabilistic reasoning in intelligent systems: networks of plausible inference.* San Mateo, CA: Morgan Kaufman.

Pendharkar, P., Pendharkar, P., Subramanian, G., & Rodger, J. (2005). A probabilistic model for predicting software development effort. *IEEE Transactions on Software Engineering, 31*(7), 615–624.

Radlinski, L., Fenton, N., & Neil, M. (2007). Improved Decision-Making for Software Managers Using Bayesian Networks. In J. Smith (Ed.), *Proceedings of the 11th IASTED Int. Conf. Software Engineering and Applications (SEA)* (pp. 13-19). Cambridge, MA: Acta Press.

Ratchev, S., Urwin, E., Muller, D., Pawar, K. S., & Moulek, I. (2003). Knowledge based requirement engineering for one-of-a-kind complex systems. *Knowledge-Based Systems, 16*(1), 1–5. doi:10.1016/S0950-7051(02)00027-8

Sawyer, P., Sommerville, I., & Viller, S. (1997). Requirements process improvement through the phased introduction of good practice. *Software Process Improvement and Practice, 3*(1), 19–34. doi:10.1002/(SICI)1099-1670(199703)3:1<19::AID-SPIP66>3.0.CO;2-X

Sommerville, I. (2005). Integrated Requirements Engineering: A Tutorial. *IEEE Software, 22*(1), 16–23. doi:10.1109/MS.2005.13

Sommerville, I. (2006). *Software Engineering: (Update) (8th Edition) (International Computer Science).* Boston: Addison-Wesley Longman Publishing Co., Inc.

Sommerville, I., & Ransom, J. (2005). An empirical study of industrial requirements engineering process assessment and improvement. *ACM Transactions on Software Engineering and Methodology, 14*(1), 85–117. doi:10.1145/1044834.1044837

Spirtes, P., Glamour, C., & Scheines, R. (1991). An algorithm for fast recovery of sparse causal graphs. *Social Science Computer Review, 9*(1), 62–72. doi:10.1177/089443939100900106

Standish Group. (1994). *Chaos Report* (Tech. Rep.). Standish Group International.

Standish Group. (2003). *Chaos Chronicles v3.0.* (Tech. Rep.). Standish Group International.

Thomas, M., & McGarry, F. (1994). Top-Down vs. Bottom-Up Process Improvement. *IEEE Software, 11*(4), 12–13. doi:10.1109/52.300121

Toval, A., Nicolás, J., Moros, B., & García, F. (2002). Requirements Reuse for Improving Information Systems Security: A Practitioner's Approach. *Requirements Engineering, 6*(4), 205–219. doi:10.1007/PL00010360

ADDITIONAL READINGS

Blum, B. I. (1996). *Beyond Programming: To a New Era of Design.* New York: Oxford University Press, Inc.

Borland. (2008). *Caliber.* Retrieved from http://www.borland.com/us/products/caliber/index.html

Castillo, E., Gutiérrez, J. M., & Hadi, A. S. (1997). *Expert systems and probabilistic network models.* New York: Springer-Verlag.

Chang, S. K. (2002a). *Handbook of Software Engineering and Knowledge Engineering, Volume 1 Fundamentals.* River Edge, NJ: World Scientific Publishing Company.

Chang, S. K. (2002b). *Handbook of Software Engineering and Knowledge Engineering, Volume 2 Emerging Technologies.* River Edge, NJ: World Scientific Publishing Company.

Cowell, R. G., Dawid, A., Lauritzen, S. L., & Spiegelhalter, D. J. (1999). *Probabilistic networks and experts systems.* New York: Springer-Verlag.

Darwiche, A. (2008). Bayesian Networks. In F. van Harmelen, V. Lifschitz & B. Porter (Eds.), *Handbook of Knowledge Representation,* (Vol. 3, pp. 467-509). St. Louis, MO: Elsevier.

Davis, A. M. (1989). *Software Requirements: Analysis and Specification.* Upper Saddle River, NJ: Prentice Hall Press.

del Águila, I. M., Cañadas, J., Palma, J., & Túnez, S. (2006). Towards a Methodology for Hybrid Systems Software Development. In K. Zhang, G. Spanoudakis, G. Visaggio (Eds.): *Proceedings of the Eighteenth International Conference on Software Engineering & Knowledge Engineering (SEKE'2006),* San Francisco, CA, July 5-7, (pp. 188-193).

del Sagrado, J., & Moral, S. (2003). Qualitative combination of Bayesian networks. *International Journal of Intelligent Systems, 18*(2), 237–249. doi:10.1002/int.10086

del Sagrado, J., & Salmerón, A. (2004), Representing canonical models as probability trees. In R. Conejo, M. Urretavizcaya, J-L. Pérez-de-la-Cruz (Eds.) *Current Topics in Artificial Intelligence, 10th Conference of the Spanish Association for Artificial Intelligence, CAEPIA 2003, and 5th Conference on Technology Transfer, TTIA 2003, San Sebastian, Spain, November 12-14, 2003. Revised Selected Papers.* (LNCS 3040, pp. 478-487). Berlin: Springer.

Díez, F. J. (1993) Parameter adjustment in Bayes networks. The generalized noisy OR-gate. In D. Heckerman and A. Mamdani (Eds.), *Proceedings of the 9th Conference on Uncertainty in Artificial Intelligence* (pp. 99-105). San Mateo, CA: Morgan Kaufman.

Díez, F. J., & Druzdel, M. J. (2001) Fundamentals of canonical models. In A. Bahamonde and R.P. Otero (Eds.), *Actas de la IX Conferencia de la Asociación Española para la IA (CAEPIA'2001)*, Vol II (pp 1125-1134). Oviedo, Spain: Servicio de Publicaciones de la Universidad de Oviedo.

Fenton, N., Krause, P., & Neil, M. (2002). Software measurement: Uncertainty and Causal Modelling. *IEEE Software, 19*(4), 116–122. doi:10.1109/MS.2002.1020298

Finkelstein, A., & Sommerville, I. (1996). The Viewpoints FAQ: Editorial - Viewpoints in Requirements Engineering. *Software Engineering Journal, 11*(1), 2–4.

Goguen, J., & Linde, C. (1993). Techniques for Requirements Elicitation. In *Proceedings of the First IEEE International Symposium on Requirements Engineering (RE'93), San Diego, CA, 4-6th January 1993* (pp.152-164). New York: IEEE Computer Society.

IBM. (2009). *Telelogic DOORS Analyst.* http://www-01.ibm.com/software/awdtools/doors/analyst/

IBM. (2009). *Rational Requisite Pro.* http://www-01.ibm.com/software/awdtools/reqpro/

Lauría, E. J., & Duchessi, P. J. (2006). A Bayesian belief network for IT implementation decision support. *Decision Support Systems, 42*(3), 1573–1588. doi:10.1016/j.dss.2006.01.003

Neill, C., & Laplante, P. (2003). Requirements Engineering: The State of the Practice. *IEEE Software, 20*(6), 40–45. doi:10.1109/MS.2003.1241365

Rolland, C., & Prakash, N. (2000). From conceptual modelling to requirements engineering. *Annals of Software Engineering, 10*(1/4), 151–176. doi:10.1023/A:1018939700514

Sommerville, I., & Sawyer, P. (1997). *Requirements Engineering: A Good Practice Guide.* Chichester, UK: John Wiley & Sons.

Thayer, R., & Dorfman, M. (Eds.). (1997). *Software Requirements Engineering (2nd Edition).* New York: IEEE Computer Society Press.

Van Koten, C., & Gray, A. (2006). An application of Bayesian network for predicting object-oriented software maintainability. *Information and Software Technology, 48*(1), 59–67. doi:10.1016/j.infsof.2005.03.002

Zhu, J. Y., & Deshmukh, A. (2003). Application of Bayesian decision networks to life cycle engineering in Green design and manufacturing Engineering. *Applied Artificial Intelligence, 16*, 91–103. doi:10.1016/S0952-1976(03)00057-5

Chapter 7
Knowledge Engineering Support for Software Requirements, Architectures and Components

Muthu Ramachandran
Leeds Metropolitan University, UK

ABSTRACT

The demands of SE imply a growing need for using AI to support all aspects of the software development process. This chapter provides insights into the application of knowledge based approaches to the development of agile software development, software product line, software components and architecture. In particular, it presents three research systems that demonstrate the potential benefits of utilising knowledge based approaches to support agile methods. The first system, called SoBA, supports the use of a story card for agile software development; the second system, called .NET designer, provides design rationale for choosing appropriate architectural solutions, and the third system, called RAIS, provides reuse assessment and improvement for designing reusable software components.

INTRODUCTION

The term Artificial Intelligence (AI) was coined at Dartmouth in 1958 and nearly ten years later the term Software Engineering (SE) was coined at the same place in 1968. AI can be defined as "the study of how to make computers do things at which, at the moment, people are better" (AmI, 2008). Knowledge is gained from experience and highly related to all living things and Engineering is a human activity which aims to create, innovate,

and produce a product. Therefore, there are common activities amongst AI, KE & KBS (Knowledge Engineering and Knowledge Based Systems), ES (Expert Systems), KM (Knowledge Management), Neural Networks, Fuzzy Logics, and SE. All these activities aim to solve a complex problem and follow a similar pattern, viz: identify the problem, identify common patterns, look up a similar problem which has been solved in the past, and produce a conclusion, product and result. Widely used AI methods include:

DOI: 10.4018/978-1-60566-758-4.ch007

- Rule-based systems, where knowledge is represented in the form of if-then production rules.
- Case-based systems, where past problem-solution pairs are stored and then subsequently used to help solve new problems by adapting the solution of past similar problems.
- Experience-based systems where the reasoning is by previous experience, however it is difficult to implement a full working system as knowledge is a continuous activity.

Software Engineering has emerged as a discipline that aims to develop and manage software development as a structured and systematic activity. One of its key challenges has been to address the software crisis, which is a situation where software projects are often late and over budget. Today SE is rich in terms of its achievements in modelling tools (UML), technology (CASE), programming languages (Java, C#), education, standardisation, and its impact on the global economy and workforce (world wide impact on establishing offshore software development and its contribution to local economy in places like India, China, and other countries). SE remains a highly skilled human intensive activity and relies on problem solving skills of human knowledge and experiences. Therefore AI, ES, and KE will continue to play a major role in automating numerous software development activities. Rech and Altoff (2008) say "The disciplines of Artificial Intelligence and Software Engineering have many commonalities. Both deal with modeling real world objects from the real world like business processes, expert knowledge, or process models". Therefore, the interplay between these two areas is significant and it makes sense to take advantage of their mutual strengths.

This chapter aims to identify work on knowledge based support for agile based software requirements elicitation techniques, software

architecture design and software components. The chapter is organised as follows. The next section summarises the relationship between intelligent systems and software engineering. This is followed by three sections, each of which describe research systems that explore particular aspects of the relationship: the first system, SoBa, explores how Story Boards can be used to support agile methods, the second system demonstrates how it is possible to support the design of .Net based systems, and the third system, called RAIS, illustrates how it is possible to automatically assess the reusability of a design and provide guidance on developing more reusable components.

INTELLIGENT SYSTEMS AND SOFTWARE ENGINEERING

This section presents a summary of the relationship between various aspects of SE and intelligent systems and then presents some of the main research that aims to develop intelligent tools for supporting software engineering. Figure 1 shows some of the current and futuristic research strategies based on integrating KBS and SE (KBSE). These are the building blocks for an experience based knowledge factory or learning organisation. The other techniques, such as capturing knowledge based best practices, software design guidelines, process improvement techniques, and knowledge based automated tools will continue to grow. The emerging areas, such as Software as a Service (SaaS), require additional domain expertise on service engineering that will make use of existing solutions, and enterprise knowledge management (Ramachandran 2008, Chapter 13).

Problem solving is one of the key skills that humans have acquired and experienced over the centuries. We can assimilate the problem solving process as a generic process as shown in Figure 2.

The generic process shown in Figure 2 is also generic to the SE problem solving strategy

Figure 1. KBSE research directions

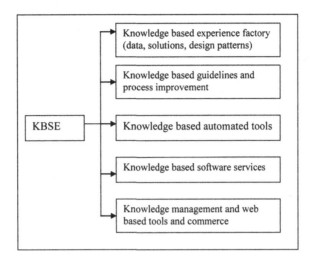

and in particular to CBSE (Component Based Software Engineering) where problem requirements are specified and used to identify existing solutions such as patterns and components which are retrieved. The selected components are then used to compose the required system. Finally the composed system is validated against the initial problem statements. The last step in the SE process is different, since this is based on customer requirements and a business contract. Therefore, the proposed solution should, if necessary, be adapted to match the problem. KBS and agents will play a major role in creating distributed software development environments where distributed requirements, reusing software development knowledge and experiences from previous projects, distributed programming and testing activities will gain access to vast arrays of knowledge and experiences from across software industries. This knowledge based approach will play a major role

Figure 2. Generic problem solving process in AI

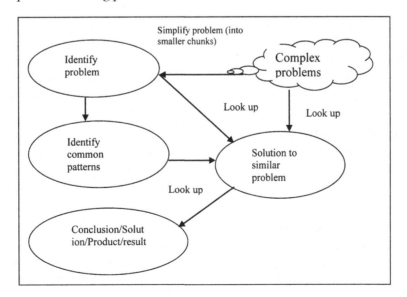

Figure 3. Generic KBS based Software Development Environment

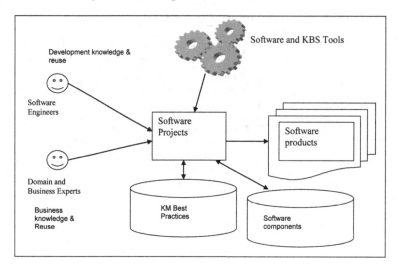

in creating learning software organizations (LSO) and experience based software factories.

Figure 3 shows a generic environment for knowledge based support for software development where the application of KBS and the reuse based SE technologies work together.

Software engineers provide development expertise and knowledge to software projects whereas domain and business experts provide business & reuse knowledge to software projects. Each new project takes advantage of the previous project knowledge and assets (components, patterns, frameworks, test scripts, and architecture) where previous solutions and domain knowledge have been encoded in a knowledge-based repository which can be distributed and retrieved across the globe. This is the way in which software products can be produced with minimum effort and at the same time with improved quality since they have been used and tested in different projects.

There are different types of intelligent systems which can be categorised as follows (Riva 2005):

- Ambient Intelligence: These systems provide a vision for the application of pervasive computing into every day life devices including wearable computing. These provide challenges for all researchers since the nature of multi-disciplinary applications (devices+intelligence+software = AmI). The application of AmI includes mobile systems, healthcare, entertainment, games, wearables, television, ad-hoc and wireless networked systems (see AmI, http://www.ambientintelligence.org/).

- Expert Systems/Decision support systems: These are based on expert rules which represent knowledge and experiences. These types of systems are mainly suitable for a specific domain or application and can be difficult to generalize across applications.

- AI systems and intelligent learning systems: the aim of these systems is to develop a complete human type of reasoning, knowledge acquisition, sensing, actions, decisions, etc.

- Computational Intelligence: These types of systems are useful which makes computations based on current data and conducts intelligent predictions such weather forecasting.

The future research will impact on the following areas: Intelligence and Natural Language understanding that can be used in day to day life for software system will grow as seen in voice recognition systems. The software to understand NL's will also grow rapidly. AI for autonomic robotic cars will evolve which can drive the vehicle with little human intervention. Digital imaging to identify and compare similarities again will grow rapidly to be able to use in various detection systems. Work on neural networks will help to identify various predictions. Most of the intelligence systems will also play a major role in various applications including semantic web. The following sections will provide examples of projects which have successfully used intelligence and knowledge based support for utilizing best practices of software development principles that have evolved over several years.

Our approach to software development is knowledge-based, guideline-based, and support for reuse and best practices. Software guidelines have been collected across major aspects of the software development life cycle artifacts: requirements, design, and components. Software guidelines form the basis for knowledge representation, domain analysis, and best practices. In our work, the emphasis is on reuse and software development best practices supporting developers and software engineers with appropriate skills and experiences or otherwise they have to gain from many years of experiences. Figure 4 shows the software development lifecycle along side our methods and tools which are described in the following section. We believe this approach could set a standard for a new generation of software development technologies in the years to come. This approach also represents a shorter lifecycle which the software industry has been demanding for many years, and supports productivity and automation. In addition, an important aspect in our approach is that new best practices and guidelines can be added to the systems: SoBA, .NET designer, and RAIS which are described, in detail, in the following sections.

STORY BASED AGILE SOFTWARE DEVELOPMENT (SOBA) METHOD AND PROCESS FOR REQUIREMENTS ELICITATION

Story cards (contain user story) are the unit of functionality which are written by the customer to express their business needs (Cohn 2004). Depending on the functionality written on the cards, the developer makes a rough estimate of "how long it will take". Based on that estimate, the customer prioritizes them. In a story writing session, the users have to make sure the Story cards provide the right unit of functionality in one or two sentences, because the story cards work as a reminder, which can be refined at a later stage. User stories on the story cards must not be too long or too short. If it is too long, then the customers have to divide them to fit into a single iteration. If it is too short, then the customers can move it into another story card or merge with a short story to fit into a single iteration.

Stories are written by customers perhaps, with the help of an agile development member. Therefore each user story and story card must be split into a unique and independent requirement. We have developed a model which is based on user stories. Figure 5 shows an outline of the SoBA model, which consists of a number of steps such as capturing user stories, developing story cards, structuring story cards, and prioritizing story cards (Patel and Ramachandran 2008).

Each step in the model is based on a set of guidelines for agile and non-agile practitioners:

- Capturing user stories and refining: The customer, user or stakeholder discusses their business requirements with a pair of developers. We envisage supporting all possible multimedia formats to capture user stories or requirements like audio, video, electronic discussion, sharing knowledge and experiences from similar systems, and face to face communication.

Figure 4. Integrated software development lifecycle

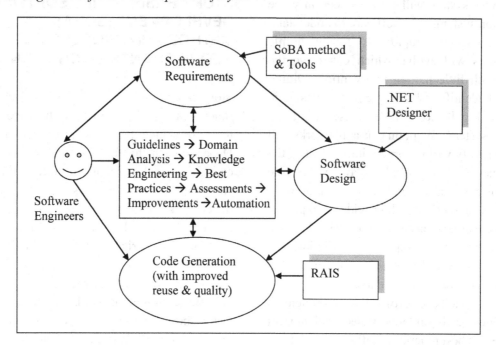

Sometimes, customers are not clear about their requirements and therefore multimedia support is mandatory for supporting agile based development. Our new approach

of refinements of user stories with a customer and a pair of developers helps us to find out the precise set of requirements.

• Developing story cards: Once the precise

Figure 5. Story card based agile requirements method (SoBA)

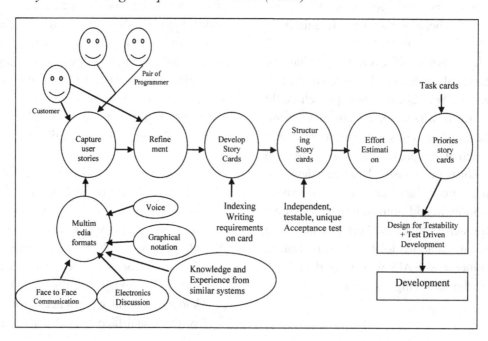

set of requirements is defined, then those requirements take the form of user stories on story cards. Writing the requirements on story cards and indexing the story cards take place here.

- Structuring story cards: The developed story cards are structured according to the guidelines of the story cards. We have to make sure the stories are independent, small enough to fit in the release, testable, estimatable and valuable to the customer. We write the acceptance test to check that the customer is not vague in his requirements. The acceptance tests also helps in effort estimation. There is a direct correlation between acceptance tests and size of the user stories on a story card.

- Effort estimation: Developers provide the estimation based on the structured story cards and their software complexity.

- Prioritising story cards: Based on the developer's estimation, the customer defines which story cards are to be developed first and which later on. We assume that the customers know their business needs better than the developers in helping to identify priorities of story cards.

Creating best practices on agile software engineering requires knowledge on agile software engineering principles which can be encoded as knowledge into a system where analysis and improvement can take place in dialogue with agile software engineers. A scenario for an agile KBS tool is proposed in the following section.

SoBA Tool Support and Architecture

SoBA is easy to use because it provides a graphical notation of the story driven development compared to the traditional XP text based story cards. The SoBA tool bridges the XP practices with best practices of a traditional software development methodology. In the analysis phase of the traditional methods, we do the exploration of the user requirements. The SoBA tool supports them in an extreme way by selecting the new project, followed by adding new story cards or editing existing story cards with acceptance tests. This helps the developer to provide an accurate estimate based on the acceptance test. There is a correlation between the number of acceptance tests and size of the story cards. Too many acceptance tests mean the story card is too big to fit into a single iteration and therefore the estimated effort will also be too long.

We have developed a prototype sub-tool supporting pair wise programming within the SoBA tool for Story card driven development, effort estimation and coding via Test Driven Development (TDD). TDD is the new notion in agile software engineering which deals with developing system from the system testing perspective (Beck 2002). The SoBA tool supports non-functional requirements by bridging design for testability with test driven development. Iteration and refinement of the story cards is supported by a domain analysis and knowledge-driven processes within the SoBA methodology and tool. Unit testing and TDD help to redefine acceptance tests as required.

In our approach, the SoBA tool provides a story card template that automatically generates acceptance, effort estimation and unit test cases. It also provides knowledge based support for acceptance testing and evaluating customer requirements. The SoBA tool has been designed to support:

- Comprehensive story cards driven development.
- An alternative approach to the Adapt Tool of Eclipse.
- Generation of templates for test driven development.
- Architecture-driven development for testability and non-functional requirements.
- Multimedia support for story card driven development.

Figure 6. Knowledge based tool support for SoBA

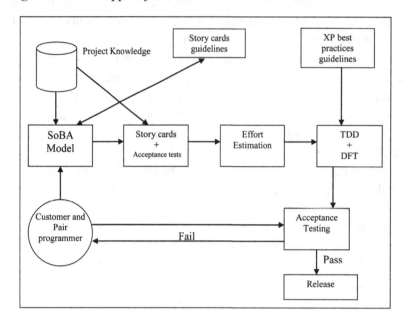

- Knowledge based support for agile best practices.
- Domain analysis for reuse of requirements through story cards.

Traditionally, in XP the planning game is played by a senior developer or QA Manager and a Customer. XP strongly recommends collective code ownership and supports communication with customers. If we do not involve everybody in the planning session then they will not be aware of project progress. Therefore, in SoBA we have considered all the issues. SoBA provides all interfaces and IDE graphically compared to traditional text based tools. Consider Figure 6 which shows a high level architecture diagram of the SoBA tool. This tool provides knowledge based support for eliciting agile requirements. A user starts by defining a story with the help of a domain analysis process and interaction with the project knowledge base so that identical or similar story cards can be retrieved automatically from the existing project knowledge which is encoded into the system. The system also directs structuring story cards based on best practice guidelines built into the

system. SoBA interacts with the user to identify effort estimation, acceptance testing, testability, and code generation from story cards.

SoBA supports graphical notations and a voice based XML system for story card driven development to capture functional and non-functional software requirements by mutual interactions with customers and clients of the system to be built. Figure 7 shows a typical scenario based on SoBA's user interface for requirements negotiation.. The story card template has been generated automatically by the systems with help of built-in domain knowledge and user stories that are captured earlier on a simple user expressions/ user requirements. The SoBA tool also retrieves similar story cards that exist in the knowledge base and recommends relevant user stories in order to save time and effort.

The SoBA tool provides a number of options to gather requirements quickly based on built-in domain analysis for a family of products. The process is generic and allows new domain knowledge to be developed quickly. SoBA supports tools for a complete software lifecycle based on best practice guidelines. The story card best practice

Figure 7. User requirements negotiation using best practice knowledge

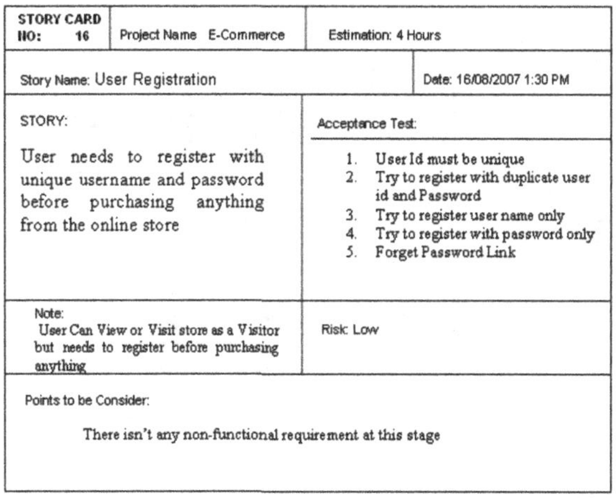
STORY CARD NO: 16 | Project Name E-Commerce | Estimation: 4 Hours

Story Name: User Registration | Date: 16/08/2007 1:30 PM

STORY:

User needs to register with unique username and password before purchasing anything from the online store

Acceptance Test:

1. User Id must be unique
2. Try to register with duplicate user id and Password
3. Try to register user name only
4. Try to register with password only
5. Forget Password Link

Note:
User Can View or Visit store as a Visitor but needs to register before purchasing anything

Risk: Low

Points to be Consider:

There isn't any non-functional requirement at this stage

guidelines are classified into various story card attributes such as structuring, completeness, unambiguous, simplicity of expressing user stories, etc. these guidelines form the knowledge base of the system.

KNOWLEDGE BASED SUPPORT FOR ARCHITECTURAL DESIGN

Architecture is a much-used term in the field of software and systems engineering. Architecture can be associated with many distinct areas in computing such as domain modelling, software frameworks and application composition to name a few. Many definitions can be found that attempt to characterise the precise meaning of 'software architecture'. Common to most of them are the concepts of a number of sub-systems co-operating to create a larger unified system, communication that takes place between subsystems and the notion of interfaces that provide the access point to and from an entity that is external to the sub-system.

Due to its importance in any system's design, there have been a number of architectural solutions for the past two decades (Shaw and Garlan 1996; Bass et al. 1998; Chappell 2002; Kruchten 1995). Therefore it has proved difficult for software engineers to assess and choose an architectural solution that is suitable for their current problem. Our previous work (Ramachandran and Sommerville 1995) has evolved to select an architectural solution automatically during the development of reusable software components. This system has encoded knowledge on reuse.

In this work we have developed a framework and a tool that supports automatic identification and selection of a suitable architectural solution during the design or prior stage of the software development process. This system also allows users to make an assessment of the selected solution using its knowledge based reasoning process. The novel approach to our work includes:

- A framework for the development of software architectures.
- A classification scheme for knowledge retrieval.
- A rule based reasoning system for architectural design.
- A tool to support automated reasoning for selecting a solution.

In the following section we describe our approach to classification of software system's archi-

Figure 8. Knowledge based Reasoning for Architectural Design

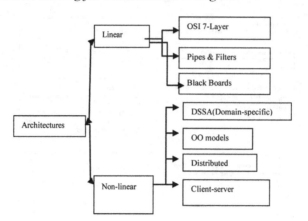

tectures and provide a description of the tool.

KNOWLEDGE-BASED REASONING

There exist a variety of architectural styles invented and used in practice for so many years now (Shaw and Garlan 1996; Bass, Clements, and Kazman 2003). However, this has also introduced issues such as, 'which is a suitable architecture that makes the system more adaptable and flexible?'; 'How do we verify that the chosen architecture can support the desired design quality and the product quality?'. Also one more point to remember is that systems are often designed with a combination of a variety of architectural solution to suit each part and subsystem. This makes it even harder for software engineers to assess the suitability of the architectural solutions. In general we can classify the existing and more popular architectural models into the following categories:

- Linear structures where the system is more hierarchical such as the OSI 7-layer model.
- Non-linear structures where the system is more discrete but tightly coupled such as the object-oriented models.

The classification structure shown in Figure 8 only presents a simple model for different architectural styles that are correlated to each other. There exists a wide variety of architectural styles within each category and sub-category. For each architectural style we have developed a set of design rules which are then encoded as knowledge for reasoning.

In order to develop a knowledge based system, we need to formulate best practice design guidelines and to represent them as rules. Our approach to knowledge representation is based on rules and some of those design rules can be expressed as follows:

- If you choose a window XP platform then choose .NET architecture
- If you design an application for a real-time system then choose event-driven architecture
- If you are designing under .NET architecture then choose .NET Foundation Services which provide building blocks of components and services

These rules are used to guide the users interactively. The system is shown in Figure 9 guides software engineers interactively when making a design solution. The architectural design knowl-

Figure 9. Knowledge based Reasoning for Architectural Design

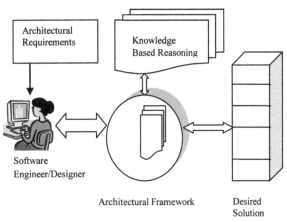

edge are based on a set of best practice guidelines that have been formulated over several years of experience in software development and a wide body of knowledge from the literature.

We have encoded the design knowledge as rules which are known to be effective as a knowledge representation technique. Since we have implemented them using XML scheme, this provides us the flexibility to update the design guidelines in the future when newer architectural design methods are evolved.

KNOWLEDGE REPRESENTATION AND IMPLEMENTATION

In this section we describe how the design guidelines are represented as rules using XML scheme and how a system has been implemented to support novice software engineers and developers to build applications using the .NET architecture. The .Net Framework includes a large number of classes that can be used by developers to create a wide variety of applications including graphical interface based Windows or web applications and service type components that can be packaged as traditional components or XML Web Services.

The .Net Framework library is large and can be daunting to first time users. A tool that can be used to guide novice developers in the use of the framework would be a valuable resource in helping developers to build applications in accordance with best practices. A number of expert system shells were considered for building the tool but were disregarded because of compile problems and runtime errors that were experienced with initial tests. The resources chosen to develop the design assistant application include ASP .Net for the user application and interface and an XML document to contain the knowledge base.

The application presents the user with some option questions and then displays a list of related options or answers. This is an iterative process that continues until it results in some suggestions that will detail the .Net framework classes that may be used to solve the problem. A suggested class constitutes an answer. An XML schema has been developed to enforce a structure on the XML knowledge base. The detailed structure and tool illustration has been described by Ramachandran and Mangano (2003). The .NET designer tool shown in Figure 10 is a snapshot of user dialogue with the system to suggest best design solutions based on the built-in architectural knowledge. The user interface has been designed to be easy to use by any novice developer to .NET architecture. The user application is written in C# and is a basic web form that submits the value of a target

Figure 10. The .NET designer user interface snapshot

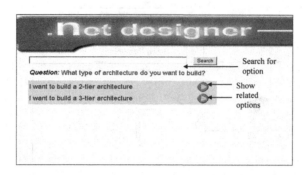

node identifier **<nodeid>** when an appropriate button is pressed.

The associated target node question and options are displayed as a result of the form that was submitted. Our future work includes extending this tool to add most of the well known architectural styles and solutions. The tool uses a simple hierarchical knowledge data set to lead to suggestions on which .Net framework classes may be appropriate for a particular architectural function or requirement. The XML data source is flexible and can be used by many types of application, which gives it an advantage over the use of an expert system shell. The application does not have the in-built intelligence of an expert system shell instead it relies on the **<nodeid>** elements for inter-relating information **<nodesets>** that are not strictly hierarchically related. The use of an XML source also allows the possibility of updating the knowledge base through the use of a text editor or additional application function.

KNOWLEDGE ENGINEERING AND SOFTWARE COMPONENTS

Our work on component generation for reuse is described in detail in Ramachandran (2005) and Ramachandran and Sommerville (1995). More recently, Ramachandran (2008) has extensively studied best practice guidelines and applications for component based systems. A general model

of the tool for systematic reuse assessment and improvement (RAIS) has been developed as shown in Figure 11. The important features of this system are:

- Identifying domain abstractions, attributes and architectures, and language attributes and structures that affect component reusability.
- The integration of language knowledge (supporting language-oriented reusability) and domain knowledge (supporting domain-oriented reusability).
- Providing reusability advice and analysis.
- Assisting the SE in the process of assessing and improving his component for reuse.

RAIS considers a component specification rather than an implementation. However, this system can also generate implementation templates. We believe that reuse of specifications has definite advantages over reuse of implementations. The RAIS system consists of a language analyser which is supported by built-in language knowledge and provides reusability analysis and advice, and a domain analyser which is supported by built-in domain knowledge and provides reusability analysis and advice.

An Ada component is firstly submitted to the language analyser which parses the component and applies the language-oriented guidelines to the code. Some of these guidelines require human

Figure 11. Reuse and Assessor & Approver system

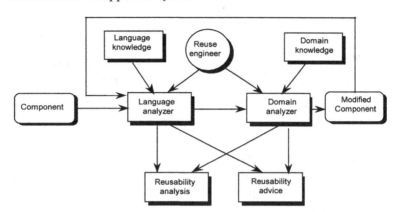

input from the reuse engineer. RAIS predicts and records existing language constructs, and provides reuse advice and analysis. For example, the system can determine if the component processes arrays and if language attributes are used. However, it cannot automatically determine whether a component parameter refers to an array dimension and thus breaches the reuse guideline.

The language analyser assesses for reuse and changes the code after consulting the reuse engineer. The system interacts with the engineer to discover information that can't be determined automatically. The conclusion of this first pass is an estimate of how many guidelines are applicable to the component and how many of these have been breached. The report generator produces a report with all the information that has been extracted about that component and changes that have been made for reuse.

The second pass involves applying domain knowledge to the system. The component templates have been modelled representing static and dynamic structures. Their reusability is assessed by comparing the component against that template. Domain-specific reuse improvement is done by adding methods automatically. Operation classes are identified by interaction with the reuse engineer. If some operations are found to be missing, skeleton implementations of these can be generated from the template for expansion to create a

reusable component. The support provided by the system ensures that the reuse engineer carries out a systematic analysis of the components according to the suggested guidelines. He or she need not be a domain expert. Again, an analysis is produced which allows the engineer to assess how much work is required to improve system reusability.

There are formulated reuse guidelines that emphasise the need for a packaging mechanism just like in Ada. Conceptually, packaging is a powerful mechanism for reuse. Some of these guidelines may only be possible with the Ada packaging mechanism such as private typing, the concept of specification which is independent of its body, and most importantly the concept of generics in order to achieve parameterisation. However, the approach and the methodology that are adopted by this system can easily be applied to any component. In this domain, RAIS uses the classification scheme in which each abstract data structure is classified into linear and non-linear structures and again these are classified into static and dynamic structures.

As well as this analysis, the system can also produce some reusability advice, generated from the guidelines, which is intended to assist the engineer in improving the reusability of the component. The knowledge of language and domain experts can be made available to the reuse engineer. An ultimate

141

Figure 12. Automating reuse guidelines

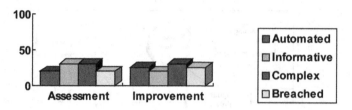

objective is automatic reusability improvement where the system takes its own advice and some human guidance and modifies the component. A report and compilable code are produced. As our work shows, it is possible to use the language-oriented and domain-oriented guidelines to infer some code transformations which will improve reusability.

KNOWLEDGE BASED SUPPORT FOR ASSESSMENT AND IMPROVEMENT

Reuse assessment is a process of assessing the reuse potential of a component. It depends on the number of reuse guidelines that are satisfied by the component. RAIS predicts this and reports to the reuse engineer. RAIS measures the reusability strength of a component based on the percent of guidelines satisfied such as *weakly* (less than 50%), *strongly* (50-70%), *limitedly* (70-90%), *immediately reusable* (more than 90%) and also it takes into account the significance of a guideline (its importance for reuse). For example, let us consider one of our domain guidelines:

• For all complex structures, the components should be implemented as a generic package with the element type as a generic parameter.

For instance, if a component of complex structure doesn't possess a generic package then the significance of this guideline becomes very

important and therefore the system immediately reports to the reuse engineer that the component is weakly *reusable*. The system can make such structural modification automatically if the engineer decides to do so by responding to the dialogue.

In this way reuse assessment is being done by RAIS. The result of the assessment process allows implementations to be compared, reuse improvements to be assessed, and it allows the reuse engineer to re-plan well before reusing components. The report generator produces the complete details of a component submitted to the systems in a tabular form which mainly consists of object name, its class, details of all the subprograms including the details of formal parameters and their class, and details of private types, etc.

Figure 12 illustrates a simple classification reuse guidelines which have been checked for this component by the system as described above. These fall into two main classes such as guidelines for reuse assessment and guidelines for reuse improvement. These are further classified into four categories of guidelines realisation:

a.   Informative, a set of guidelines that provided more knowledge on reuse

b.   Fully automated, a set of guidelines that are completed realised by the system

c.   Complex, a set of guidelines went through a further number of steps of implementation (by invoking more automated guidelines) and also means these types of components are reusable but needed extra effort to modify/re-modify to fit-in with new requirements

d. Partially automated, a set of guidelines that are breached nor met by the component for any reason and also because of their complexity involved in a complete realisation.

As the data shows for this particular input, there are 20% automated, 30% informative, 30% complex, and 20% breached of the assessment guidelines, and are 25% automated, 20% informative, 30% complex, and 25% breached of the improvement guidelines.

RESEARCH TRENDS AND FUTURE DIRECTIONS

The future research will focus mainly on automated tools, gathering experience data which are specific to activities and sub-activities. Also knowledge management strategies will emerge to address the needs of large enterprises and will make use of tools and techniques that are highly knowledge encoded and experience-based. Application of intelligent systems into software development will play a major role in automatically documenting system artefacts and user experiences.

The SoBA tool currently has limited understanding of the natural language expressions. Further work will include incorporating NL and voice expressions and to translating them into user stories is one of our main aim for further work in this area. We also plan to map the generated story cards into architectural design which will then link to our work on .NET designer tools which provides knowledge based support for architectural design and implementation. These tools have a direct link to the RAIS system as this system generates code which is reusable and with improves quality. The future of software components and architectures for semantic web and service oriented computing will make use of some the research directions identified in this section.

CONCLUSION

This chapter has identified the importance of integrating AI and SE research. The demands of SE imply a growing need for knowledge based systems to support novice developers for using advanced technologies more effectively. Also, developing intelligent and ambient systems requires the experience and skills of the best software development practices that have evolved over several years.

This chapter has also described various software research tools that are based on domain knowledge and best practice software guidelines. We have successfully developed a framework for knowledge based support for architectural design and a toolset supporting knowledge based reasoning for identifying and developing software components and architectures. Our future work includes enhancing our framework for architectural design methods, classifying and improving the toolset which incorporates most of the well known methods. We are also currently investigating neural networks and other KB approaches to solve requirements problems and product line engineering.

REFERENCES

AmI. (2008). *Ambient Intelligence*. Retrieved from http://www.ambientintelligence.org/

Arango, G. (1994). A Brief Introduction to Domain Analysis. *Proceedings of the 1994 ACM symposium on Applied Computing, April*, Phoenix, Arizona, United States, March, 1994, (pp. 42-46). New York: ACM Press.

Atkinson, et al (2001, September). *Component-Based Product Line Engineering with the UML*. Reading, MA: Addison Wesley.

Bass, L. Clements, P. Kazman, R (2003). *Software Architecture in Practice*, (2nd Ed.). Reading, MA: Addison Wesley

Beck, K. (2002). *Test Driven Development*. Reading, MA: Addison Wesley.

Boasson, M. (1995). The Artistry of software architecture. *IEEE Software*, *6*(November/December).

Chappell, D. (2002). *Understanding. NET: A Tutorial and Analysis*. Reading, MA: Addison Wesley.

Cohn, M. (2004). *User stories applied for agile software development*. Reading MA: Addison Wesley Press.

Coplien, J., Hoffman, D., & Weiss, D. (1998). Commonality and variability in software engineering. *IEEE Software*, *6*(November/December).

Gomma, E. (2004). *Design Software Product Lines*. Reading, MA: Addison Wesley.

Howe, J. (2007) The Nature of Artificial Intelligence, Artificial Intelligence at Edinburgh University: a Perspective. Retrieved from http://www.inf.ed.ac.uk/about/AIhistory.html

Jacobson., et al. (1992). *Object-Oriented Software Engineering: A use case driven approach*. Reading, MA: Addison Wesley.

Jazayeri, M., Ran, A., & van der Linden, F. (2000). *Software architecture for product families*. Reading, MA: Addison Wesley.

Kruchten, P. (1995). The 4+1 view model of software architecture. *IEEE Software*, *6*(November/December).

Kuusela, J., & Savolainen, J. (2000). Requirements Engineering for Product Families. *ICSE 2000*, Limerick, Ireland.

Mannion, M., & Kaindl, M. (2001). Requirements-Based Product Line Engineering. *Proceedings of the 8th European Software Engineering Conference held jointly with 9th ACM SIGSOFT International Symposium on Foundations of Software Engineering 2001*, Vienna, Austria, September 10-14, 2001.

Mohan, K., & Ramesh, B. (2007). Tracing variations in software product families. *CACM, December, 50*(12).

O'Brien, L. & Smith, D. (2002). MAP and OAR Methods: Techniques for Developing Core Assets for Software Product Lines from Existing Assets. *CMU/SEI*, April.

Patel, C., & Ramachandran, M. (2008). Story card process improvement framework. *Intl. conf. on Software Engineering Research and Practice (SERP-08)*, July, Florida, USA.

Poulin, S. J. (1997). Measuring software reuse. Reading, MA: Addison Wesley.

Press, C. M. Phoenix, Arizona, United Ardis, M. (2000). *Commonality analysis for defining software product lines, Tutorial*, ICSE 2000, Limerick, Ireland. New York: IEEE CS Press.

Prieto-Diaz (1998). Domain Analysis. *ACM SIGSOFT Software Engineering Notes*, May.

Ramachandran, M. (2005). Commonality and Variability Analysis in Industrial Practice for Product Line Improvement. *Journal of Software Process Improvement and Practice, 10*.

Ramachandran, M. (2005). Reuse guidelines. *ACM SIGSOFT Software Engineering Notes, 30*(3), May.

Ramachandran, M. (2008). *Software Components: Guidelines and Applications*. New York: Nova Publishers.

Ramachandran, M. & Mangano, D. (2003). Knowledge Based Reasoning for Software Architectural Design Strategies. *SE Notes*, March.

Ramachandran, M., & Sommerville, I. (1995). A framework for analysing reuse knowledge. *7the Intl. conf. on Software Eng and Knowledge Eng (SEKE'95)*, Washington DC, June 22-24.

Rech, J., & Althoff, K.-D. (2008). *Artificial Intelligence and Software Engineering: Status and Future Trends*. Retrieved from www.iis.uni-hildesheim.de/files/staff/althoff/Publications/KI_AI-SE-Survey.pdf

Ritch, C. & Waters, R. C. (1988). The programmers' apprentice project: research overview. *IEEE Computer*, November.

Riva, G., et al. (Eds.). (2005). *Ambient Intelligence*. Amsterdam: IOS Press. Retrieved from http://www.ambientintelligence.org/

SEI. (2005). *Software Product Lines*. Retrieved from http://www.sei.cmu.edu/productlines/bibliography.html

Shaw, M., & Garlan, D. (1996). Software Architecture -- Perspectives on an Emerging Discipline. Upper Saddle River, NJ: Prentice Hall.

Somerville, (2004). *Software Engineering*, (7th Ed.). Reading, MA: Addison Wesley.

Sommerville, I., & Kotenya, G. (1998). *Requirements Engineering: Processes and Techniques*. New York: Wiley.

Sommerville, I., & Sawyer, P. *Requirements Engineering: A Good Practice Guide*. New York: Wiley.

Weiss, M. D. (1998). Commonality Analysis: A Systematic Process for Defining Families. *Second International Workshop on Development and Evolution of Software Architectures for Product Families*, February.

Weiss, M. D., Lai, R. T. C (1999). *Software Product-Line Engineering: A Family Based Software Development Process*.

Chapter 8
MUSTER
A Situational Tool for Requirements Elicitation

Chad Coulin
University of Technology Sydney, Australia & LAAS CNRS, France

Didar Zowghi
University of Technology Sydney, Australia

Abd-El-Kader Sahraoui
LAAS CNRS, France

ABSTRACT

In this chapter they present a collaborative and situational tool called MUSTER, that has been specifically designed and developed for requirements elicitation workshops, and which utilizes, extends, and demonstrates a successful application of intelligent technologies for Computer Aided Software Engineering and Computer Aided Method Engineering. The primary objective of this tool is to improve the effectiveness and efficiency of the requirements elicitation process for software systems development, whilst addressing some of the common issues often encountered in practice through the integration of intelligent technologies. The tool also offers an example of how a group support system, coupled with artificial intelligence, can be applied to very practical activities and situations within the software development process.

INTRODUCTION

Requirements elicitation is a fundamental part of the software development process, but often considered a major problem area, and widely regarded as one of the more challenging activities within the scope of Requirements Engineering (RE). Heavily dependent on the experience and expertise of the

DOI: 10.4018/978-1-60566-758-4.ch008

participating analyst, the elicitation of requirements is often performed badly in practice, as true experts in this area are few and far between. The subsequent effects of poor software requirements elicitation regularly include costly rework, schedule overruns, poor quality systems, stakeholder dissatisfaction, and project failure (Hickey & Davis, 2002). But despite the obvious need for an appropriate level of structure and rigor, this critical, complex, and potentially expensive activity is more commonly performed in an ad-hoc manner, without a defined process or methodology.

Furthermore, many of the current techniques, approaches, and tools for the elicitation of requirements are either unknown or too complex for novices, and a general unwillingness to adopt them by industry, results in a significant gap between requirements elicitation theory and practice (Hickey, 2003). Just as important is the current gap between expert and novice analysts, which can be attributed to a number of factors, not least of which is the extensive skill set and range of experiences that is often required to successfully conduct this difficult yet vital activity (Hickey & Davis, 2003). A lack of systematic methods with situational process guidance, and supporting tools that can easily be applied to real-world situations, are additional reasons for the current state of requirements elicitation in practice.

Subsequently, in this chapter the MUSTER tool is presented, which embodies and enhances the situational OUTSET approach for requirements elicitation (Coulin, Zowghi & Sahraoui, 2006; Coulin, 2007), and is based on the principles of Computer Aided Software Engineering, Computer Aided Method Engineering, Group Support Systems, and Artificial Intelligence. The purpose of this chapter is therefore to present an intelligent tool for software requirements elicitation workshops, which is both useable and useful to practicing analysts. However, the overriding intention of MUSTER is to improve the overall effectiveness and efficiency of the requirements elicitation process specifically for the development of software systems.

BACKGROUND

Computer Aided Software Engineering (CASE) tools support one or more techniques within a software development method (Jarzabek & Huang, 1998). These tools are attractive to use during activities such as design, coding, testing,

and validation, mainly because of their potential to provide substantial gains in quality, productivity, management, and communication (Hoffer, George & Valacich, 2002). Furthermore, CASE tools have been found to be efficient in both research and practice for recording, retrieving, and manipulating system specifications (Pohl et al., 1994), partly by automating some aspects of the system development.

Computer Aided Method Engineering (CAME) tools support the construction and management of adaptable methods (Saeki, Tsuchida & Nishiue, 2000). These tools are useful in automating part of the process of engineering a method, to conduct one or more of the various system development activities, by reusing parts of existing methods (Saeki, 2003). In addition, CAME tools have shown to be successful in providing the appropriate amount of process guidance, based on the specific needs of software development problems and projects (Dahanayake, 1998).

A common criticism of CASE tools is that they do not provide appropriate supporting guidance for the development process (Pohl et al., 1994), which can be directly addressed by the integration of a CAME tool. This would result in a process-based environment whereby the users can select, create, and modify method components for specific system development activities, in addition to performing the required system development tasks. The Phedias environment (Wang & Loucopoulos, 1995), referred to as a "CASE shell", was an early attempt at producing a combined CASE and CAME tool. This tool enabled a method to be modeled at a Meta-level (i.e. a CAME tool), and corresponding CASE tools designed, developed, and integrated within this model and environment in order to provide support for the various activities (i.e. it was also a Meta-CASE tool (Alderson, 1991)). As a precursor to MUSTER, Phedias is of particular interest because it was specifically targeted towards the development of methods and models of non-functional requirements for software engineering.

Group Support Systems (GSS) (Nunamaker, Briggs & Mittleman, 1996), or groupware, on the other hand, when used within the context of development projects, typically takes the form of a software-based tool focused on supporting communication, coordination, and collaboration within a team working towards common goals, on interconnected workstations, in shared workspaces (Ellis, Gibbs & Rein, 1991). The use of a GSS is particularly appropriate because of the number of key functions often provided by groupware applications that correspond directly to many of the tasks involved in requirements elicitation. These include activities such as information sharing, document authoring, knowledge management, and providing a suitable framework for stakeholder interaction. Furthermore, Group Support Systems have been found to be highly successful in improving group meeting productivity, and outcomes in real world settings (Hickey, Dean & Nunamaker, 1999), as well as enabling larger groups to collaborate faster, particularly when matched with a specific requirements elicitation process (Hannola, Elfvengren & Tuominen, 2005).

Subsequently, the idea of combining a GSS with requirements elicitation has been relatively popular. In fact Hickey et al. state that the challenges of gathering accurate requirements, the inefficiencies of user interviews, and the difficulty of achieving effective group meetings, were early driving forces for GSS research (Hickey, Dean & Nunamaker, 1999). As a result, there has been significant attention in research directed towards integrating groupware and requirements elicitation (den Hengst, van de Kar & Appelman, 2004; Tuunanen, 2003; Venable & Travis, 1999), and of particular note are tools such as GroupSystems (Hickey, Dean & Nunamaker, 1999), which has been used to collaboratively define scenarios, AMORE (Wood, Christel & Stevens, 1994), which utilized advanced multimedia technology, and TeamWave (Herela & Greenberg, 1998), which specifically addressed distributed software development.

In (Liou & Chen, 1993), a GSS, the Joint Application Development (JAD) method, and CASE tools, were integrated to support the requirements specification process. In this work it was identified that support for requirements elicitation, and specifically collaborative requirements elicitation meetings, was a major function missing from CASE research and products. It was also acknowledged that in order for a GSS to be successful in supporting requirements elicitation, it must also be supported with an appropriate methodology for its use, however no such specific process guidance was supplied. Therefore, the additional integration of a CAME tool, would enable not only the development and utilization of a contextual and dynamic method, but also the integration of different techniques to support the overall requirements elicitation process.

As a result, the name 'MUSTER' was chosen for the combined CASE / CAME / GSS tool, because it aims to bring together or 'muster' the different tasks, data types and techniques of requirements elicitation for software development, into an integrated situational process within a workshop environment, in what is referred to in (Pohl et al., 1994) as a "process-aware CASE tool". However, unlike most CASE tools, MUSTER is intended to be used by groups rather than individuals, by applying the additional principles of groupware applications and workshop facilitation, combined with intelligent technologies.

DEVELOPMENT OF THE TOOL

There were a number of important constraints in the development of the MUSTER tool, which had significant impact on its design and construction. Firstly, the system had to be developed by the researchers, and with a timeframe acceptable to the overall schedule of the project. Because there was no budget allocated to the project, it was also necessary for the system to be developed using only available and free technologies. The system needed to implement the OUTSET approach, and support interactive and incremental requirements elicitation workshops. Furthermore, it was decided that the system should be as platform independent as possible, and thereby be able to run on most standard computer hardware platforms and operating systems.

A first prototype of the MUSTER tool was constructed, with a preliminary set of standard features, and a detailed list of requirements elicitation related tasks. This prototype was tested and evaluated at a relatively high-level by numerous people both familiar and unfamiliar with the larger research project, including the research supervisors and fellow researchers. Although the prototype was found to be structured and extensive, it was essentially static with only limited process flexibility. Based on this feedback, a second prototype was developed with considerably more focus on the functionality required to make the tool less constrictive, more dynamic, and offer appropriate situational support. This resulted in several changes to better support the underlying approach, and to provide a suitable foundation for the planned evaluations. The details of this final prototype are described in the following subsections.

High-Level Requirements

The detailed list of requirements used for the development of the tool was based on the results of a literature review, a survey of practice, and the need to support the OUTSET approach, in addition to the "wish list" of 70 requirements for Requirements Engineering techniques proposed in (Macaulay, 1996). At a high-level, and in accordance with the goals of the research, the overall objectives of the tool were identified as; 1) improve the process of requirements elicitation in terms of the time and effort required, and 2) directly address some of the common issues and challenges often encountered in practice, such as an incomplete understanding of needs and ill-defined system

boundaries. It is therefore important to note that the principle focus of the tool is to improve the process of requirements elicitation, rather than improve the quality of the results, although better quality results are expected from improvements to the elicitation process.

The main functional areas required within the tool were established as 1) visualization, navigation, and administration through the elicitation process, 2) externalization, representation and organization of the elicited information, 3) process guidance, 4) cognitive support, 5) task automation, 6) interaction assistance for the participants, and 7) education of the users on requirements elicitation, primarily by osmosis. Although the primary usage of the tool is by an analyst to facilitate group workshops, it was determined that the system should also be usable during a traditional one-on-one interview by the analyst with a stakeholder, as well as offline and independently by both the participating analyst and stakeholders. Although this functionality did not affect the design of the tool in any major way, it did provide the tool with an extra and potentially useful element of flexibility.

Architecture and Technologies

The application of artificial intelligence (AI) during requirements elicitation offers the potential to provide the type of help a novice analyst might receive from being mentored by an expert, and stakeholders with the kind of advice and guidance offered by a specialist workshop facilitator. This idea is supported in (Scott & Cook, 2003), where a classical blackboard system with autonomous agents based on a knowledge repository is suggested in order to achieve such goals. Because Requirements Engineering, and especially elicitation, is essentially a cognitive activity, AI presents an appropriate opportunity to address this activity by providing situational cognitive support to both the analyst and stakeholders (Zeroual, 1991). This is confirmed by (Maiden & Sutcliffe, 1993) which states that "requirements engineering is complex, error-prone, and in need of intelligent tool support to assist the capture, modeling and validation of requirements".

Subsequently, two basic architectural orientations were identified as being potentially suitable for the development of the MUSTER tool and its intelligent components, being 1) a Multi-agent system such as JACK and JADE, or 2) an Expert system using Lisp or Prolog for example. It was also determined however that the concept of 'intelligent plug-ins' was not only similar to that of having multiple agents work cooperatively, but was also consistent with the operation of a partitioned expert system. Furthermore, the use of a plug-in architecture would provide many of the advantages of both Multi-agent and expert systems (e.g. the ability to use artificial intelligence), and at the same time enable a much wider choice in the selection of implementation technologies.

Following a thorough evaluation of available options, it was decided that the tool would be an online browser-based application, and the sever-side components would be based on the LAMP platform (Linux operating system, Apache web server, MySQL database system, PHP scripting language) with HTML (Hyper Text Markup Language), JavaScript, VBScript, and CSS (Cascading Style Sheets) incorporated where necessary. The advantages of the specific technologies chosen include the fact that they are easy to learn, use, and therefore maintain, and are entirely open source and completely free of charge, with extensive Internet based support networks. Furthermore, the amount of time required to produce a working prototype of the basic functionally required using PHP with MySQL was anticipated to be less when compared to the other option of a Java with XML based system. Because of the underlying environment, the tool would also be portable, scalable, and most importantly, flexible with respect to the integration of other technologies, tools, and components, necessary for a successful plug-in architecture.

Data Repository

The foundation of the tool is a central Data Repository (DR), which enables the storage and retrieval of large amounts of requirements, and requirements-related data, elicited from the stakeholders during the workshops, as well as configuration information about the tool, projects, and users.

User Interface

The User Interface (UI) of the tool provides the ability to navigate through the required tasks, whilst interacting with other components of the system. As can be seen in Figure 1 below, the 'Home' screen displayed after a successful login has three major areas, as described in detail later, being 1) the Task List, 2) the Main Window, and 3) the Advice Panel. In developing the UI, a number of recognized Internet resources were used, including (Rolston, 2005), to ensure that the overall look and feel of the tool was both simple and consistent.

The Task List (Figure 1, left hand side) provides a dynamically generated list of tasks for requirements elicitation process navigation and execution, which the workshop participants are recommended to perform during the various sessions. This task list is populated by the support plug-ins in accordance with the underlying approach. Each task may be composed of several subtasks, and each task and subtask may have its own corresponding and specific Main Window.

The content of the Main Window (Figure 1, centre right hand side) is dependent on the task currently selected. There is no restriction on what should be displayed for each task, therefore the screen could be purely informational, or provide an editor for some related part of the Data Repository.

The Advice Panel (Figure 1, bottom right hand side) presents the users with situational advice generated in real-time by the support plug-ins,

Figure 1. The MUSTER tool 'Home' screen

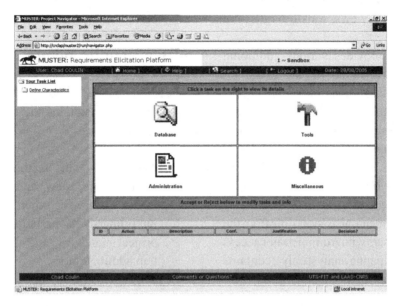

based on the current state of the data in the repository (see the "Plug-ins for the Tool" section below for more details).

Database Menu

The Database menu, accessible from the 'Home' screen, contains links to Data Repository (DR) maintenance screens for the available data types supported by the tool. By using these editors, which are based on the List-Detail-Post paradigm, users can select any data type in order to directly view, add, change, or delete specific entries within the DR for the current project.

Tools Menu

The Tools menu, also accessible from the 'Home' screen, contains the following features and functionalities:

- **Glossary** – enables the user to maintain a project glossary by being able to add, change, delete, and view definitions of terms, acronyms, and abbreviations.
- **Data Dictionary** – enables the user to

maintain a record of data types within the project related to the system under investigation.

- **References** – enables the user to maintain references to other material sources related to the project and/or the target system.
- **Appendixes** – enables the user to maintain a list of the required appendixes to the deliverables that will be generated as a result of the project.
- **Issues** – enables the user to record project related issues that arise during the workshops, as well as their status, who they are assigned to, and their resolution.
- **Actions** – enables the user to record actions that need to be performed during the project, as well as their status, who they are assigned to, and their resolution.
- **Idea Hotpots** – enables all users to record and maintain miscellaneous suggestions and proposals related to the project in order for other users to respond and comment on them anonymously at any time.
- **Reports** – provides a list of onscreen and exportable reports, enabling the user to produce deliverables from the information

stored in the Data Repository (DR), for the purpose of reviews, walkthroughs, and inspections.

- **Resources** – provides various additional resources and material for the users, including templates, examples, and checklists, in order to further support the process of requirements elicitation and the workshop participants.

Administration Menu

The Administration menu, also accessible from the 'Home' screen by users with Administrator access (typically the participating analyst only), contains the following features and functionalities:

- **Projects** – allows the user to maintain projects in the system.
- **Users** – allows the user to maintain user accounts in the system.
- **Sessions** – allows the user to record details of the various requirements elicitation sessions performed during a project, including the start time, end time, participants, and location, for generate reports and performance metrics.
- **Tasks** – enables the user to view, add, change, and delete tasks in the dynamically generated Task List for each project and workshop.
- **Plug-ins** – enables the user to view, add, change, and delete information about the support plug-ins of the system, includes being able to install, enable and disable them.
- **Configuration** – enables the user to view information about the various configuration parameters of the MUSTER system, and change their values.
- **Rules** – enables the user to maintain rules and rule sets used by the Processor (see Processor in the Miscellaneous Menu below for more information). The system has

default sets of rules however these can also be customized.

Miscellaneous Menu

The Miscellaneous menu, also accessible from the 'Home' screen, contains the following features and functionalities:

- **Messages** – This feature enables the users to record, view, and update messages in the system for other project members, but primarily the participating analysts, the project managers, and the MUSTER system administrators.
- **Logs** – This feature captures and records all events and actions performed by the users and the system. These include logins, logouts, as well as Add, Change, and Delete operations on data in the repository.
- **Categorizor** – This feature endeavors to categorize user entered pieces of miscellaneous textual information into their most appropriate Info Type, based on a small Artificial Neutral Network (ANN) that utilizes a number of key and common word lists. The concept behind this feature is that novice analysts are sometimes unsure as to how to categorize elicited information, especially with respect to goals versus requirements, and functional requirements versus non-functional requirements, for example.
- **Processor** – This feature enables the user at any time during the project to run one or more sets of rules over the information in the Data Repository to check for aspects of quality such as completeness, consistency, etc. For example, this feature could be used to completeness by ensuring that at least one actor has been assigned to each Use Case description, or to check that each feature has one or more individual functional requirements associated to it.

- **Technique Selector** – This feature, which utilizes a simple weighted values criteria approach, provides support for the user in selecting which technique to use for a task prescribed by the process guidance. The Technique Selector takes into account several factors, including the skill level of the participating analyst, the current project situation, and the specific characteristics of the task at hand.

- **Ask REG** – REG (Requirements Elicitation Guide) is a web-enabled pedagogic agent based on the famous and competition winning A.L.I.C.E. chat-bot engine (A.L.I.C.E. AI Foundation Inc, 2005), and AIML (Artificial Intelligence Markup Language). The intention is that REG acts as an interactive assistant by providing help for all MUSTER users, by responding to entered questions from a knowledge base of general information about requirements elicitation, and more specific information linked to a set of predefined topics and concepts.

PLUG-INS FOR THE TOOL

MUSTER system plug-ins provide the situational process guidance and intelligent cognitive support for the users during the workshop sessions. The primary role of these plug-ins is to add, change, or delete tasks and subtasks in the project Task List, however they can also provide suggestions to the users dynamically, proactively, and reactively, such as introducing tasks, describing relevant background concepts, offering tips and tricks, as well as being able to directly manipulate data in the repository. As a result, plug-ins can provide the users with process guidance, decision support, and knowledge acquisition assistance. Plug-ins may provide generic support, or be based on a specific process or task, as well as a particular method (e.g. SADT, SSM, UML), technique (e.g. Scenarios, Viewpoints, Goals), or system type

(e.g. Information, Embedded, Critical).

All advice generated by the installed and configured plug-ins appears in the Advice Panel of the screen, together with a justification and a confidence rating, generated internally by the specific plug-in responsible for that particular piece of advice. The advice provided by the plug-ins can be based on the characteristics of the individual project and workshop, as well as the information already elicited and stored in the data repository. Each piece of advice from the plug-ins presented in the Advice Panel may be rejected or accepted by the users, and an upper and lower threshold for the confidence rating is configured as a project characteristic to determine which advice is automatically accepted, and which is automatically rejected.

Plug-in Architecture

Regardless of the technologies used for its actual implementation, the architecture of a plug-in requires the following four components:

1. **Characteristics** – these are additional (non standard) situational characteristics which may be used by the conditions of the plug-in to determine which advice should be offered and when. The user is requested by the system to enter values for each of the new characteristics when the plug-in is run for the first time.

2. **Conditions** – these represent the rules and logic of the plug-in, which is typically based on selected data from the repository, and the values entered for relevant characteristics. The conditions themselves can be implemented in almost any web-based technology, and can range from basic condition statements through to complex intelligent algorithms.

3. **Advice** – these are the specific pieces of situational and intelligent support that may be offered by the plug-in. These are based

on the triggering of or results from the above mentioned conditions, and are presented to the users for action.

4. **Action** – these are the subsequent and prescribed results of accepting the offered advice. Each piece of advice offered by a plug-in will perform one or more action operations in the system if accepted. These typically take the form of modifications to the task list, or manipulation of the data in the repository.

All the plug-ins are run automatically when any major event in the system occurs, which typically involves an Add, Change, or Delete operation on data in the repository. New advice generated by running the plug-ins is added directly to the bottom of the list presented in the Advice Panel with a status of 'Open'. Once a piece of advice in the list has been either rejected or accepted by the users, and the appropriate actions taken by the system, it is marked with a status of 'Closed', and removed from the Advice Panel list.

Advice can be presented, and appropriate actions performed, using the standard functions available in the Plug-in Function Library (PFL). Operations supported by the PFL include adding a Task or Subtask, adding an Info Type, checking if a particular piece of advice has already been given, and checking if a particular piece of advice was previously accepted or rejected. Depending on the configuration of the plug-in, a piece of advice may be presented only once for each session whether it is accepted or not, or it may be presented multiple times if not previously accepted for that particular project.

Creating Plug-ins

The overall plug-in architecture for the MUSTER system provides the ability for the tool to store and use the knowledge of both methodologists and requirements elicitation experts, within a integrate environment.

Plug-ins can be built using any single or combination of technologies, provided they are executable via the web server through a web page, which includes C++, VB, and Java. As a result, a wide audience is able to design and develop plug-ins for the MUSTER system, since no specific or proprietary technology-based expertise is required. The level of support, in terms of scope and complexity, is also not restricted, and at the higher end of the scale, almost any type of soft computing and machine learning method could be used as the basis for a plug-in, such as Bayesian Conditional Probability, Case Based Reasoning, and Artificial Neural Networks.

The process of installing a new plug-in is as simple as copying the relevant executable web page and associated files into the 'Plug-ins' directory of the MUSTER system. Using the Plug-in Maintenance Utility, details of the specific plug-in are then added to the system, including its status, and the name of the executable file in the directory. The final step is to enter values to the plug-in specific characteristics, which are installed the first time it is run. It is important to note that all plug-ins can be enabled or disabled at any time during a project using this same utility.

Plug-in Example

The example 'Select Info Types' plug-in, as summarized in Table 1 below, provides advice for the users on which Info Types should be elicited for each workshop, and to what level of detail they should be investigated. This plug-in uses a small Artificial Neural Network (ANN) (Young, 2004) to determine the advice offered to the users, developed using a corpus of 15 example but real-world requirements documents from successful industrial projects, and several widely accepted and used requirement document templates. The ANN was trained by running 10 examples through 1000 times each, with the appropriate input values and corresponding output values, and the remaining 5 examples were then used to test the results

Table 1. Summary of the 'Select Info Types' plug-in

Name:	Select Info Types
Description:	Determines which Info Types should be elicited during the various requirements workshops
Technology:	Artificial Neural Network (ANN)
Characteristics:	Input Nodes for the ANN - 1) Project Size 2) Project Definition 3) Project Domain 4) Project Deliverable 5) Workshop Type 6) Cut-off Level
Conditions:	Output Nodes for the ANN - 1) Goals 2) Assumptions 3) Constraints 4) Environmental 5) Opportunities 6) Challenges 7) Risks 8) Stakeholders 9) Work Processes 10) Functional Aspects 11) Non-functional Aspects 12) Implementation
Advice:	Elicit each Info Type with a value above the cut-off level
Action:	Add Task for each Info Type suggested and accepted

of the trained ANN.

In this case, the characteristics are used by this plug-in as input nodes for the ANN, and include the Project Size, Project Definition, Project Domain, Project Deliverable, and the Workshop Type. Each output node represents a potential Info Type, and the values generated by the ANN for a particular set of input node value, determines what Info Types are recommended for elicitation during the workshop. For each output node (Info Type) with a value above the cut-off level characteristic, an entry is displayed in the Advice Panel, which if accepted, will add a first-level task to the dynamic Task List stating the need to elicit that particular Info Type. Therefore, this plug-in determines which Info Types should be elicited (via the output node values) based on the specified characteristics (from the input node values).

Developed Plug-ins

This subsection contains descriptions of the initial set of plug-ins developed for the MUSTER tool. These plug-ins were developed both as a proof of concept for the designed and developed architecture, and for planned evaluations of the MUSTER tool.

New Requirements Elicitation Project: The 'New Requirements Elicitation Project' plug-in provides initial and core tasks and characteristics for new requirements elicitation projects. This plug-in primarily uses the '3Ds' characteristics from the OUSTET approach (i.e. Definition, Domain, and Deliverable), to determine which tasks should be performed, and was designed to use a basic rules approach, based on a variety of sources from the literature including (Sommerville & Sawyer, 1997) and (Robertson & Robertson, 1999).

Requirements Elicitation Workshop: The 'Requirements Elicitation Workshop' plug-in provides core tasks and additional characteristics for conducting requirements elicitation workshops. This plug-in also uses the '3Ds' characteristics from the OUSTET approach to determine which tasks should be performed, and was designed to use a rules approach based on a variety of sources from the literature such as (Gottesdiener, 2002).

Select Info Types: The 'Select Info Types' plug-in provides guidance on which Info Types should be elicited for the specific project and workshop, based on both project and workshop level characteristics. As described previously, this plug-in was developed using an Artificial Neural Network (ANN) (Young, 2004). A number of sources were used to design this plug-in including 15 example but real-world requirements documents from successful industrial projects, and several requirements specification templates including (IEEE, 1998a), (Atlantic Systems Guild, 2003), (IEEE, 1998b), and (Wiegers, 2003).

Select Goal Subtasks: The 'Select Goal Subtasks' plug-in provides guidance on which subtasks should be performed during the elicitation of both system and project goals. In addition to presenting information to the workshop participants about what a goal is, and how one should be stated, the plug-in also provides instructions on how to brainstorm and prioritize goals. This plug-in was based on separate sources for goal elicitation (Dardenne, van Lamsweerde & Fickas, 1993), brainstorming, and prioritization (Wiegers, 2007).

Goal Investigation: The 'Goal Investigation' plug-in assists users to both decompose goals (by suggesting AND and OR

relationships), and elaborate on goals (by proposing 'Why' and 'How' questions), in order to refine them in such a way as to elicit precise goals and related requirements. Several goal-based techniques for requirements elicitation were used as the basis for this plug-ins including (Yu, 1997) and (Dardenne, van Lamsweerde & Fickas, 1993).

Example BIS Constraints: The 'Example BIS Constraints' plug-in provides users with general and example constraints that are common or typical in software development projects for Business Information Systems. The intention of this plug-in is for the workshop participants to use the example constraints presented as the basis for the elicitation of similar constraints specific to the project at hand. The plug-in was designed based on the constraints listed in a relevant subset of 15 requirements documents from successful projects, and a variety of other sources, then implemented using a rules approach.

Use Case Questionnaire: The 'Use Case Questionnaire' plug-in proposes questions and provides suggestions to users on Use Cases that the system under investigation should support. This plug-in was implemented using Bayesian Conditional Probability (Meagher, 2004), and uses Use Cases previously elicited and stored in the data repository, with their corresponding characteristic values, as the basis for questioning the workshop participants about the required Use Cases, and suggesting additional Use Cases to include.

IEEE Functional Headers: The 'IEEE Functional Headers' plug-in uses an Artificial Neural Network (ANN) (Young, 2004) to determine the most appropriate way to group functional requirements (i.e. by mode, by user class, by object, by feature, by stimulus, or by functional hierarchy), based on the options presented in the IEEE Recommended Practice for Software Requirements Specifications (IEEE, 1998a). Coded values for project characteristics are used as the input nodes of the ANN, with the weighted value of the output nodes representing the relative appropriateness for each of the available options for grouping the functional requirements.

Features Questionnaire: The 'Features Questionnaire' plug-in proposes questions and provides suggestions to users on features that the system under investigation should include. This plug-in was implemented using Bayesian Conditional Probability (Meagher, 2004), and uses features previously elicited and stored in the data repository, with their corresponding characteristic values, as the basis for questioning the workshop participants about the required features, and suggesting additional features to include.

Feature Investigation Questionnaire: The 'Feature Investigation Questionnaire' plug-in dynamically generates a project specific questionnaire, to be used by the workshop participants for the elicitation of functional requirements. A list of high-level questions is created by the plug-in from a simple rule set developed from the researcher's experience, which can then be used to investigate and decompose each feature that has been elicited into specific functional requirements.

Non-functional Requirements: The 'Non-functional Requirements' plug-in provides users with additional support information for the elicitation of non-functional requirements. This includes a number of definitions and a list of typical non-functional requirements types gathered from a number of sources in the literature including (Sommerville, 2001), with relevant examples.

Example BIS Non-functional Requirements: The 'Example BIS Non-functional Requirements' plug-in provides users with general and example non-functional requirements that are common or typical in software development projects for Business Information Systems. The intention of this plug-in is for the workshop participants to use the example non-functional requirements presented as the basis for the elicitation of similar non-functional requirements specific to the project at hand. The plug-in was designed based on the non-functional requirements listed in a relevant subset of 15 requirements documents from successful projects, and a variety of other sources, then implemented using a rules approach.

MUSTER TOOL IN ACTION

The following section provides a basic walk-through of the functionality and usage of the MUSTER system using a typical but simple project for the custom development of a small business information system. Although not all the features and utilities are demonstrated, this example does provide an overview of the general process of requirements elicitation using MUSTER within a workshop environment. In accordance with the process framework prescribed by the OUTSET approach, the following illustration of the system has been divided into three simple stages being 1) Preparation - setup of the new project in MUSTER, 2) Performance - running the workshops using MUSTER, and 3) Presentation - production of the requirements document from MUSTER, as described below.

Preparation

The first step in the preparation of a new MUSTER project is for the participating analyst to log into the maintenance utility of the system using an

Figure 2. Plug-in maintenance utility of the MUSTER system

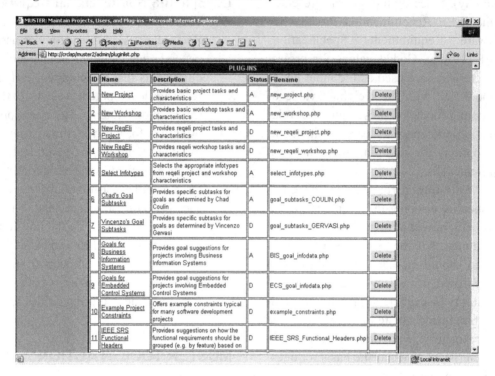

account with Administrator privileges. From the MUSTER Maintenance Utility menu, the analyst can then add a new Project and new Users to the system, as well as selecting the appropriate plug-ins to use. Each plug-in has a default status (either 'Active' or Disabled'), which provides a standard configuration of active and disabled plug-ins for new projects, that can be then modified by the analyst. As can be seen from Figure 2, only some of the installed and available plug-ins within the system have been enabled by the analyst for this particular project.

The analyst can then immediately log out of the MUSTER system, and log back into the newly created project in order to enter values for the situational project characteristics, required by the select plug-ins, as the first task of the new project (see Figure 3 below). The 'Define Characteristics' task has been added to the situational Advice Panel, and subsequently the dynamic Task List, by the 'New Project' plug-in. The characteristics for each of the enabled plug-ins have been added,

and in some cases loaded with default values, automatically the first time they are run, which in this case was triggered by the event which added the 'Define Characteristics' task to the dynamic Task List.

For this example, the current project is small in size, and involves the production of a requirements document for the custom development of a business information system. Furthermore, the analyst's intention is to elicit as much of the information as possible in a simple combined workshop with multiple sessions.

Performance

As values for the characteristics are entered, tasks are added to the list, and data is maintained in the repository, the plug-ins are repeatedly triggered, and are therefore able to start and continue providing situational support to the users via the advice panel. From Figure 4 below, it can be seen that after only some of the characteristics

Figure 3. Situational project characteristics maintenance screen

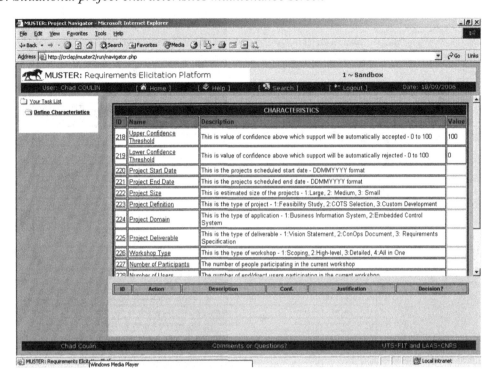

values have been entered, the system has already provided several items of advice via the plug-ins, including the addition of core tasks such as the elicitation of system goals and the elicitation of project constraints.

Both the analyst and the stakeholders participating in the requirements elicitation workshop make their way through the task list, adding data to the repository for the recommended and accepted data types, through task specific instructional and maintenance screens. Task specific advice from the plug-ins, including the addition of subtasks, may in some cases only be offered if the dependent first-level task has been added, and once that particular first-level task has been started.

In a screen shot taken towards the end of the workshop (Figure 5), it can be seen that several more tasks and sub-tasks have been added to the list, such as "Brainstorm Goals" and "Elicit Constraints". Furthermore, the only item remaining in the advice panel relates to the presentation of the data in the repository, by way of quality

check and export, in the format of the required deliverable type. In this case, the 'Presentation' task has been offered by a plug-in and added to the advice panel only after each of the data types has had at least one entry recorded for it in the MUSTER system.

The workshop may come to a conclusion either 1) when the participants have run out of allocated and available time, or 2) when the participants can no longer think of additional relevant data to enter into the MUSTER system, and the plug-ins can no longer offer meaningful advice to them. At this point the project is ready for presentation as described below.

Presentation

Before exporting the results of the workshop out of the MUSTER system, the elicited information can be reviewed collaboratively, or individually, by the participants. In order for the necessary walkthroughs and inspections to take place, the

Figure 4. System screen shot after some characteristic values entered

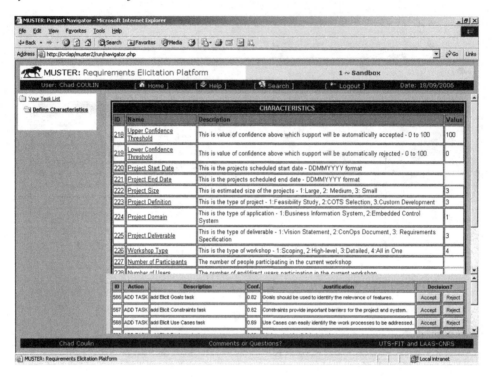

Figure 5. Screen shot of the MUSTER system near the end of the workshop

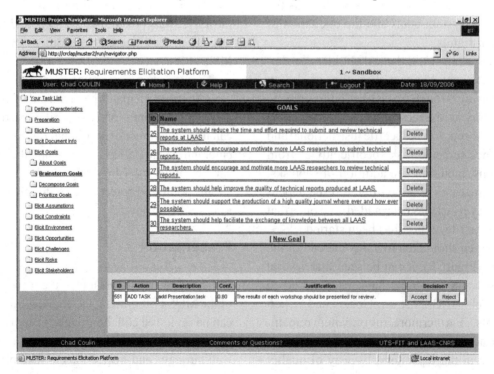

Figure 6. List of available standard reports in the MUSTER system

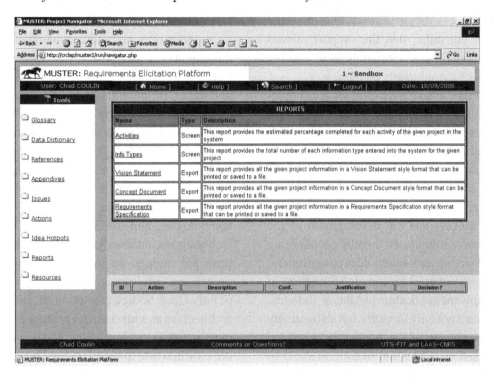

data from the repository is formatted and exported using one of the available standard reports (see Figure 6 below).

The resultant deliverable of this process, as produced by MUSTER, is then ready for feedback and approval by the appropriate workshop participants and other stakeholders.

DISCUSSION

A number of additional features were considered but not implemented for MUSTER, including Instant Messaging, Discussion Boards, Reuse Utility, and a Workflow Engine. The reasons for their exclusion were for the most part related to the potential benefit they would provide, compared to their relevance to the overall goals of the research project. Also considered useful, but somewhat out of scope with respect to the focus and objectives of the tool, were the use of visual effects such as zooming user interfaces, mouse over magnifica-

tion, and wheel or web data representations. In addition, several features such as the Online Help, Categorizor, Technique Selector, and Ask REG, were only partially developed despite their novelty, because of the effort required to implement and evaluate them to a level that would provide substantial enhancement.

The use of a simple and open plug-in architecture has given the tool a number of important advantages, including the ability to utilize different technologies, and offer different types of support to the users. However because these plug-ins can originate from many sources, and may be based on subjective and imprecise reference material (e.g. experience), the potential result of all the advice offered by the combined plug-ins is difficult to predict. Consequently the effectiveness and usefulness of the MUSTER system is heavily dependent on the quality of the advice offered by the plug-ins, and the way in which expert knowledge is presented within the workshop environment. As a result, it is not possible to claim that the tool is as good or better than having a participating requirements elicitation expert facilitate the workshops, but rather that the support offered will be of benefit to novice analysts in guiding the process of requirements elicitation

Furthermore, in addition to providing an implementation of the situational OUTSET approach, MUSTER addresses some of the issues often experienced in requirements elicitation practice. For example, the tool allows end users of the system to communicate openly, access project information, and be actively involved in both the elicitation process and the development of the target system requirements, thereby encouraging project ownership and stakeholder commitment. MUSTER also overcomes a major limitation of many groupware applications (Alho & Sulonen, 1998), in that it not only supports, but also actively encourages, the use of a dynamically generated process based on contextual factors. In order to achieve this, the MUSTER tool has endeavored to be as flexible and configurable as possible, whilst still providing an appropriately structured and rigorous foundation for requirements elicitation, creative thinking, idea crystallization, and constructivist learning.

CONCLUSION

In a retrospective report on lessons learnt from ten years of Group Support Systems (GSS) research (Nunamaker, Briggs & Mittleman, 1996), it was determined that a GSS can significantly reduce time and effort, but does not replace leadership. Likewise, the MUSTER system is intended to provide practical benefits and support for the analyst and stakeholders during requirements elicitation, rather than replace the role of a workshop facilitator completely. In the same report, it was stated that Group Support Systems should include separate special purpose modules to permit flexible process design, which MUSTER has also endeavored to satisfy through the use of an overriding plug-in

architecture for the usage of the tool and generation of intelligent and situational guidance.

In terms of being a virtual workbench for requirements elicitation, and as a special purpose CASE/CAME application, MUSTER provides a number of potential benefits over existing requirements elicitation tools. Through direct interaction with the analyst and stakeholders during the workshops, MUSTER removes the need for costly and time-consuming meeting transcription and report writing, whilst still being collaborative and combinational. The utilization of web-based technologies, and the integration of intelligent technologies, enables contextual support to be provided through an integrated situational approach and environment. Furthermore, the use of only Open Source technologies, and a plug-in architecture as a mechanism to store and transfer expert requirements elicitation knowledge was not only new and innovative, but also allowed the implementation of intelligence into the tool for process guidance and cognitive support.

Three empirical evaluations of the tool have been conducted (Coulin, 2007), showing that MUSTER improved both the overall effectiveness and efficiency of the requirements elicitation process, and provided a system that was both useful and useable to the participating analysts.

REFERENCES

Alderson, A. (1991). Meta-case Technology. *European Symposium on Software Development Environments and CASE Technology,* Konigswinter, Germany, June 17-19.

Alho, K., & Sulonen, R. (1998). Supporting Virtual Software Projects on the Web. *Seventh IEEE International Workshop on Enabling Technologies: Infrastructure for Collaborative Enterprises (WET ICE '98),* Stanford, USA, June 17-19.

A.L.I.C.E. AI Foundation Inc. (2005). *A.L.I.C.E.* Retrieved 2005, from http://www.alicebot.org/

Atlantic Systems Guild (2003). *Volere Requirements Specification Template.*

Coulin, C. (2007). *A Situational Approach and Intelligent Tool for Collaborative Requirements Elicitation.* PhD Thesis, University of Technology Sydney & Paul Sabatier University, Australia.

Coulin, C., Zowghi, D., & Sahraoui, A. E. K. (2006). A Situational Method Engineering Approach to Requirements Elicitation Workshops in the Software Development Process. *Software Process Improvement and Practice, 11,* 451–464. doi:10.1002/spip.288

Dahanayake, A. N. W. (1998). Evaluation of the Strength of Computer Aided Method Engineering for Product Development Process Modeling. *9th International Conference on Database and Expert Systems Applications.* Vienna, Austria, August 24-28.

Dardenne, A., van Lamsweerde, A., & Fickas, S. (1993). Goal-Directed Requirements Acquisition. *Science of Computer Programming, 20*(1-2), 3–50. doi:10.1016/0167-6423(93)90021-G

den Hengst, M., van de Kar, E., & Appelman, J. (2004). Designing Mobile Information Services: User Requirements Elicitation with GSS Design and Application of a Repeatable Process. *37th Hawaii International Conference on System Sciences,* Big Island, Hawaii, January 5-8.

Ellis, C. A., Gibbs, S. J., & Rein, G. L. (1991). Groupware: Some issues and experiences. *Communications of the ACM, 34*(1), 39–58. doi:10.1145/99977.99987

Gottesdiener, E. (2002). *Requirements by Collaboration: Workshops for Defining Needs.* Boston: Addison-Wesley.

Hannola, L., Elfvengren, K., & Tuominen, M. (2005). Improving Requirements Elicitation with GSS in Software Development. *Annual ISPIM Conference, International Society for Professional Innovation Management.* Porto, Portugal, June 19-22.

Herela, D., & Greenberg, S. (1998). Using a Groupware Space for Distributed Requirements Engineering. *Seventh Workshop on Enabling Technologies: Infrastructure for Collaborative Enterprises,* Stanford, USA, June 17-19.

Hickey, A. M. (2003). Requirements Elicitation Techniques: Analyzing the Gap between Technology Availability and Technology Use. *Comparative Technology Transfer and Society, 1*(3), 279–302. doi:10.1353/ctt.2003.0026

Hickey, A.M. & Davis, A.M. (2002). The Role of Requirements Elicitation Techniques in Achieving Software Quality. *Eighth International Workshop of Requirements Engineering: Foundation for Software Quality.* Essen, Germany, September 9-10.

Hickey, A. M., & Davis, A. M. (2003). Elicitation Technique Selection: How Do Experts Do It? *Eleventh IEEE International Requirements Engineering Conference.* Monterey Bay, CA, September 8-12.

Hickey, A. M., Dean, D. L., & Nunamaker, J. F. (1999). Establishing a Foundation for Collaborative Scenario Elicitation. *The Data Base for Advances in Information Systems, 30*(3-4), 92–110.

Hoffer, J. A., George, J. F., & Valacich, J. S. (2002). *Modern Systems Analysis and Design,* (3rd Ed.). Upper Saddle River, NJ: Prentice Hall.

IEEE. (1998a). *IEEE Std 830-1998.* Recommended Practice for Software Requirements Specifications.

IEEE. (1998b). *IEEE Std 1362*. System Definition - Concept of Operations (ConOps) Document.

Jarzabek, S., & Huang, R. (1998). The Case for User-Centered CASE Tools. *Communications of the ACM, 41*(8), 93–99. doi:10.1145/280324.280338

Liou, Y. I., & Chen, M. (1993). Integrating Group Support Systems, Joint Application Development, and Computer-Aided Software Engineering for Requirements Specification. *26th Annual Hawaii International Conference on System Sciences,* Wailea, Hawaii, January 5-8.

Macaulay, L. (1996). Requirements for Requirements Engineering Techniques. *International Conference on Requirements Engineering*, Colorado Springs, CO, April 15-18.

Maiden, N. A. M., & Sutcliffe, A. G. (1993). Requirements Engineering by Example: an Empirical Study. *IEEE International Symposium on Requirements Engineering*. San Diego, CA, January 4-6.

Meagher, P. (2004). *Implement Bayesian inference using PHP, Part 1: Build intelligent Web applications through conditional probability*. Retrieved 2005, from http://www-106.ibm.com/developerworks/web/library/wa-bayes1/

Nunamaker, J. F., Briggs, R. O., & Mittleman, D. D. (1996). Lessons from a Decade of Group Support Systems Research. *29th Annual Hawaii International Conference on System Sciences,* Maui, Hawaii, January 3-6.

Pohl, K., Assenova, P., Doemges, R., Johannesson, P., Maiden, N., Plihon, V., et al. (1994). Applying AI Techniques to Requirements Engineering: The NATURE Prototype. *International Conference on Software Engineering*, Edinburgh, UK, May 23-28.

Robertson, S., & Robertson, J. (1999). *Mastering the Requirements Process*. London: Addison-Wesley.

Rolston, D. (2005). *LAMP, MySQL/PHP Database Driven Websites - Parts I, II, and III*. Retrieved 2005, from http://www.phpfreaks.com/tutorials/

Saeki, M. (2003). CAME: The First Step to Automated Method Engineering. *Workshop on Process Engineering for Object-Oriented and Component-Based Development,* Anaheim, CA, October 26-30.

Saeki, M., Tsuchida, M., & Nishiue, K. (2000). Supporting tool for assembling software specification and design methods. *24th Annual International Computer Software and Applications Conference,* Taipei, Taiwan, October 25-27.

Scott, W., & Cook, S. C. (2003). An Architecture for an Intelligent Requirements Elicitation and Assessment Assistant. *13th Annual International Symposium - INCOSE 2003,* Crystal City, USA, July 1-3.

Sommerville, I. (2001). *Software Engineering* (6th Ed.). Reading, MA: Addison-Wesley.

Sommerville, I., & Sawyer, P. (1997). *Requirements Engineering: A Good Practice Guide*. Chichester, UK: John Wiley & Sons.

Tuunanen, T. (2003). A New Perspective on Requirements Elicitation Methods. *Journal of Information Technology Theory and Application, 5*(3), 45–62.

Venable, J. R., & Travis, J. (1999). Using a Group Support System for the Distributed Application of Soft Systems Methodology. *10th Australasian Conference on Information Systems*, Wellington, New Zealand, December 1-3.

Wang, X., & Loucopoulos, P. (1995). The Development of Phedias: a CASE Shell. *Seventh International Workshop on Computer-Aided Software Engineering,* Toronto, Canada, July 10-14.

Wiegers, K. E. (2003). *Software Requirements* (2nd Ed.). Redmond, WA: Microsoft Press.

Wiegers, K. E. (2007). *Process Impact*. Retrieved 2007, from http://www.processimpact.com/

Wood, D. P., Christel, M. G., & Stevens, S. M. (1994). A Multimedia Approach to Requirements Capture and Modeling. *First International Conference on Requirements Engineering,* Colorado Springs, CO, April 18-22.

Young, E. (2004). *Artificial Neural Network in PHP*. Retrieved 2005, from http://coding.mu/archives/2004/03/19/artificial_neural_network_in_php/

Yu, E. S. K. (1997). Towards Modeling and Reasoning Support for Early-Phase Requirements Engineering. *Third IEEE International Symposium on Requirements Engineering,* Washington, DC, January 5-8.

Zeroual, K. (1991). A Knowledge-based Requirements Acquisition System. *6th Annual Knowledge-Based Software Engineering Conference.* Syracuse, NY, September 22-25.

Section 3
Software Design and Implementation

Chapter 9
An Intelligent Computational Argumentation System for Supporting Collaborative Software Development Decision Making

Xiaoqing (Frank) Liu
Missouri University of Science and Technology, USA

Ekta Khudkhudia
Missouri University of Science and Technology, USA

Lei Wen
Missouri University of Science and Technology, USA

Vamshi Sajja
Missouri University of Science and Technology, USA

Ming C. Leu
Missouri University of Science and Technology, USA

ABSTRACT

Many design decisions need to be made in a software development process. The development process usually involves many participants from multiple perspectives, who may be in geographically dispersed locations. Existing argumentation based software design rationale capturing methods and systems can support software development decision making by documenting design rationale for critical decisions. However, their applications are very limited since their argumentation networks are usually very large and they are hard to comprehend and use for effective decision making. In this chapter, we present a web-based intelligent computational argumentation method for supporting collaborative software development decision making. It provides tools for argumentation reduction, assessment of impact of

DOI: 10.4018/978-1-60566-758-4.ch009

indirect arguments on design alternatives, and detection of self-conflicting arguments using fuzzy logic for supporting decisions in software development processes. A software application case study is provided to demonstrate the effectiveness of the proposed method and system.

INTRODUCTION

Development of software is an evolutionary process which requires intelligent decision making for selecting the best software design or other alternative at every phase of the software development lifecycle. The software development decision making becomes difficult when it involves many stakeholders with conflicting objectives and requirements from multiple perspectives. These stakeholders may be in geographically dispersed locations, which make software development decision making more challenging. In addition, many of the design objectives and requirements are vague and imprecise. In order to resolve conflicts, the participants usually put forward their arguments to justify their respective points of view. Since there are many people involved in the decision making, the number of arguments grows very fast and it becomes very hard to keep track of them. In order to be able to make an efficient and reasonable decision, an effective argumentation based conflict resolution method is needed.

To address the above problems we have developed a web-based system using an intelligent computational argumentation model for collaborative decision making in software development and selection of the most favored development alternative. It provides users with a solid decision making support in software development by allowing stakeholders to capture their development rationale from multiple perspectives and identifying their most favored alternative based on intelligent evaluation of alternatives and assessment of arguments in an argumentation network using fuzzy logic based argumentation inference mechanisms.

The objective of this chapter is to present a

fuzzy logic based intelligent computational argumentation method and the development of a web-based system using this method for supporting collaborative decision making in software development. The chapter is organized as follows. The background section reviews related research work. Next the main section discusses the intelligent computational argumentation for collaborative decision making in software development using fuzzy logic, including the framework, intelligent argumentation network, intelligent argumentation reduction, intelligent priority assessment, and detection of self-conflicting arguments. An application case study is then used to illustrate how the proposed method and system are applied. Future research directions are next discussed. A conclusion is provided in the end.

BACKGROUND

Argumentation based design rationale capture methods and tools have been developed to capture software development rationale for supporting collaborative development decision making. They are built based primarily on a classical model of argumentation developed by philosopher Toulmin (1958). An earlier method gIBIS (graphical IBIS) represents design dialogs as a graph (Conklin & Begeman, 1988). While representing issues, positions, and arguments, gIBIS failed to support representation of goals (requirements) and outcomes. REMAP (REpresentation and MAintenance of Process knowledge) extended gIBIS by providing the representation of goals, decisions, and design artifacts (Ramesh & Dhar, 1992). The REMAP work focused on capturing the process knowledge, i.e., the history about the design decisions in the

Figure 1. A Framework for an Intelligent Argumentation System for Software Development Decision Making

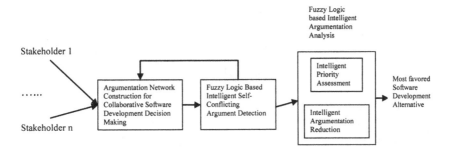

early stages of the lifecycle of a project. Unfortunately, these systems lack intelligent capabilities to reason about argumentation. As opposed to these systems, Sillence (1997) proposed a more general argumentation model. His model is a logic model where dialogs are represented as recursive graphs. Both rhetoric and logic rules are used to manage the dialog and to determine when the dialog has reached closure. Potts and Burns (1988) outlined a generic model for representing design deliberation and the relation between the deliberation and the generation of method-specific artifacts. In their model, design history is regarded as a network consisting of artifacts and deliberation nodes in which artifacts represent specifications or design documents, and deliberation nodes represent issues, alternatives or justifications. They highlighted the importance of recording of design deliberations. A main drawback of this model is that it does not support decision making. HERMES (Karacapilidis & Papadias, 1998) is a system that aids decision makers to reach a decision, not only by efficiently structuring the discussion rationale but also by providing reasoning mechanisms that constantly update the discourse status in order to recommend the most backed-up alternative. It is an active system which not only captures the informal organizational memory embodied in decision making settings but also helps the user during the decision making process. However, a drawback of this system is that the weighting factor is not effective as it does not relate to the position entered.

A common challenge with the above systems is that the sizes of their argumentation networks are often too large to comprehend. It is difficult to use them to help make design decisions because they are qualitative and not computational. In this chapter, we propose a fuzzy logic based intelligent computational argumentation method to address the common problems and challenges with the above methods. It provides a capability of reasoning with argumentation in large argumentation networks, incorporates priority assessment, and supports collaborative decision making in a software development process.

INTELLIGENT COMPUTATIONAL ARGUMENTATION FOR COLLABORATIVE DECISION MAKING IN SOFTWARE DEVELOPMENT

Framework

The overall framework of the proposed web-based intelligent argumentation system for collaborative software development decision making is shown in Figure 1. It allows stakeholders to capture their development rationale by specifying their alternatives for a given critical development issue, their supporting and attacking arguments about the issue and alternatives, and their priorities using

Figure 2. Argumentation Tree

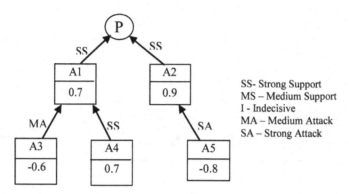

SS- Strong Support
MS – Medium Support
I - Indecisive
MA – Medium Attack
SA – Strong Attack

statements and linguistic terms in a structured manner.

Fuzzy logic based intelligent analysis is used to assess impact of indirect arguments on development alternatives, to detect self-conflicting arguments, and priority assessment, and to identify the most favored alternative (Liu, Raorane, Zheng & Leu, 2006; Liu, Zheng & Leu, 2007; Dubois & Prade, 1984; Yager, 1991; Zadeh, 1986; Zimmermann, 1991). This system is implemented using JAVA and MySQL.

Intelligent Argumentation

A computational argumentation model for collaborative software development decision making is developed to enable achieving consensus among stakeholders. It enables identifying the most favorable development alternative by computing the favorability of each alternative from all arguments in the argumentation network based on fuzzy logic. The model involves stakeholders, requirements, conflicts, development issues, development alternatives, arguments, and decisions. An argumentation dialog for a development issue in the model can be captured as a weighted argumentation tree as shown in Figure 2. The nodes in the argumentation tree are design alternatives and arguments. An arrow represents a relationship (attack or support) from an argument to a development alternative or another argument.

The strength of the relationship is represented as a linguistic label in fuzzy logic with a real number in the range [-1, 1]. Supporting arguments have a positive strength and attacking arguments have a negative strength, with the strength of zero reserved for indecisive arguments.

As stated earlier, the size of the argumentation network for collaborative software development decision making may become too large to be easily comprehensible and dealt with. A method is thus developed for argumentation tree reduction. The basic idea is to assess the impacts of indirect arguments on development alternatives using fuzzy logic. The impact of an argument on a design alternative can be assessed with the following four general heuristic argumentation reduction rules:

Argumentation Reduction Rule 1: If argument B supports argument A and argument A supports position P, then argument B supports position P.

Argumentation Reduction Rule 2: If argument B attacks argument A and argument A supports position P, then argument B attacks position P.

Argumentation Reduction Rule 3: If argument B supports argument A and argument A attacks position P, then argument B attacks position P.

Argumentation Reduction Rule 4: If argument

Figure 3. Fuzzy Association Memory (FAM) Matrix for Argumentation Reduction

X

		SS	MS	I	MA	SA
	SS	SS	MS	I	MA	SA
	MS	MS	MS	I	MA	SA
Y	I	I	I	I	I	I
	MA	MA	MA	I	MS	MS
	SA	SA	MA	I	MS	SS

B attacks argument A and argument A attacks position P, then argument B supports position P.

Twenty-five fuzzy argumentation inference rules are generated based on the above general fuzzy argumentation inference rules. They are specified in a fuzzy association memory matrix using five linguistic variables: Strong Support (SS), Medium Support (MS), Indecisive (I), Medium Attack (MA) and Strong Attack (SA), as shown in Figure 3. The membership functions for the five linguistic variables are shown in Figure 4.

A fuzzy inference engine has been developed using the fuzzy association memory matrix for argumentation reduction. It enables quantitative assessment of impacts of indirect arguments on software development alternatives. Let's consider an example of argumentation tree for a design al-

ternative P shown in Figure 5, where A1, A2, A3, etc. index the arguments. Under each argument is a value specifying the strength of the supporting or attacking argument and under the value is an identification for the owner of the argument. After argumentation reduction using the fuzzy inference engine, all arguments can be directly attached to the design alternative P, and their impacts on the design alternative are derived as shown in Figure 6. The favorability of a software development alternative is then computed using weighted summation of strengths of arguments, which are directly attached to the alternative after argumentation reduction.

Figure 4. Fuzzy Membership Functions for Linguistic Variables

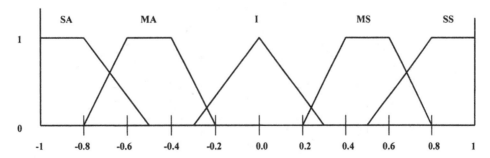

Figure 5. An example of Argumentation Tree

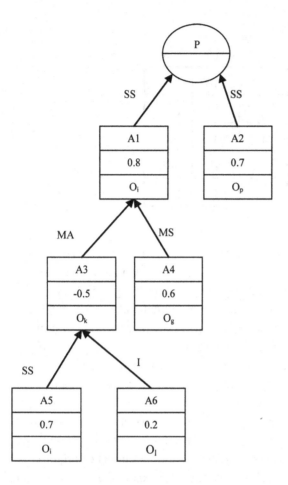

Assessment of Impact of Priorities of Participants

Different stakeholders in an argumentation process may carry different weights. Two methods have been developed and implemented for incorporating priorities of participants into the computational argumentation network for collaborative software development decision making: 1) weighted summation and 2) re-assessment of strengths of arguments by incorporating participants' priorities using fuzzy logic (Liu, Zheng & Leu, 2007). The first method involves straightforward calculation. In the following discussion we focus on the second method.

A set of heuristic rules are developed to re-assess the strength of an argument based on the priority of the owner of the argument. Each participant is assigned a priority, which is a number between 0 and 1. The heuristic priority re-assessment rules are given below:

Priority Re-assessment Rule 1: If the owner of an argument has a high priority, the strength of this argument may become higher.

Priority Re-assessment Rule 2: If the owner of an argument has a low priority, the strength of this argument may become lower.

Figure 6. Argumentation Tree after Argumentation Reduction

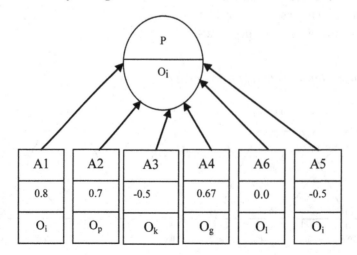

Figure 7. Fuzzy Association Memory (FAM) Matrix for Priority Re-assessment

	Y		
	H	**M**	**L**
SS	SS	SS	MS
MS	SS	MS	I
I	I	I	I
MA	SA	MA	I
SA	SA	SA	MA

X

Figure 8. Fuzzy Membership Functions for Priority

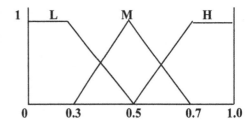

The above two rules are based on to generate fifteen priority fuzzy rules in a Fuzzy Association Memory Matrix as shown in Figure 7.

The assigned priority values are characterized as fuzzy sets in three linguistic variables: High (H), Medium (M) and Low (L). Their fuzzy membership functions are shown in Figure 8. A fuzzy inference engine is developed to re-assess the strengths of arguments based on the priorities of their owners using the fuzzy inference engine. The modified strengths of arguments are used in the argumentation reduction and the computation of favorability for design alternatives (Liu, Zheng & Leu, 2007).

Detection of Self-Conflicting Arguments

The robustness of an argumentation network is fundamental to making a convincible decision over multiple positions. The problem of self-conflicting may hamper the network's robustness and cause negative consequences. Self-conflicting refers to the arguments of a participant which are contradictory among themselves. An algorithm is developed and implemented for detection of

self-conflicting arguments in an argumentation network based on the intelligent argumentation reduction method described above.

During the course of argumentation, if a participant enters an argument which contradicts one or more of his/her own arguments entered previously, then the argument should be removed from the argumentation network. In a complicated collaborative design environment with a large number of participants, there may be many self-conflicting arguments. If a participant has several self-conflicting arguments in a network, then regardless of how powerful the participant is, his arguments would provide unaccountable and confusing information instead of positively contributing to the argumentation process (Liu, Zheng & Leu, 2007). The algorithm for detection of self-conflicting arguments is shown in Figure 9. After conflicting arguments have been detected, they can be removed from the argumentation network using a utility provided in the software system.

APPLICATION EXAMPLE

An application case study is conducted to demonstrate the effectiveness of the proposed intelligent collaborative software development decision making system. This case study is based on a U.S. Air Force sponsored simulation project which is being performed by the Missouri University of Science and Technology in collaboration with an indus-

Figure 9. The Algorithm for Detecting Self-conflicting Argument

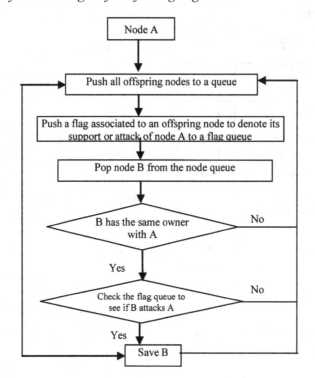

trial partner. A main objective of this project is to develop a CAD model based simulation software system to help train new operators for assembly processes. The development of this system is aimed at simulation of assembly operations using data obtained by a motion capture device in a real assembly process and allows the user to view the simulated assembly process step by step or in an animated form from any desired viewing angles. In this case study, the argumentation system is used to resolve a critical software development issue that arose in the development of the software prototype, i.e., selection of NX5 or OpenGL as the software development platform. The above described argumentation network is coded to capture the rationale based on the arguments provided by six stakeholders from multiple perspectives in order to make an effective collaborative development decision. A final selection is made by the intelligent argumentation system and it is consistent with the stakeholders' expectations.

The software development team consists of six participants. Participant 1 is a manager from the industrial partner with expert knowledge on the assembly processes to be simulated. Participant 2 is an application developer from the company with much experience in programming and manufacturing. Participant 3 is a mechanical Engineering professor, who has done a lot of research on CAD model based simulation. Participant 4 is a mechanical engineering student with knowledge on CAD/CAM. Participant 5 is a computer science professor, who is an expert in software engineering. Participant 6 is a computer science student with capabilities on software programming and algorithm design.

When a design alternative (position) is entered into the intelligent argumentation system, all the participants can enter arguments either supporting or attacking the position or arguments entered by other participants. The lists of arguments from the participants for the two alternative positions are given below.

Design Alternative (Position) 1: Use NX5 as the Software Development Platform

A1.1: Our company is interested in developing the simulation software using NX5 at the bottom layer

A1.2: Our company has several existing NX5 CAD models which can be utilized

A1.3: Student developer does not have experience with NX5

A1.4: The documentation for NX5 contains a large number of API's and it is difficult to go through them in a short period of time

A1.5: Student developer can start by looking at sample programs

A1.6: No sample programs can be found easily by searching on the Internet

A1.7: Examples can be collected from different resources, e.g., Siemens PLM Software website

A1.8: A user license is required in order to get the user-id and password for accessing examples on Siemens PLM Software website

A1.9: Other departments in our company may have example programs that can be looked at

A1.10: Purchase of an additional software license may be needed according to the licensing requirements

A1.11: Academic institutions can obtain NX5 licenses and training materials at very low prices

A1.12: Missouri S&T currently has NX5 licenses

A1.13: NX5 is cost-effective and is also easy to learn

A1.14: Using NX5 requires an understanding of the software framework, which will take time

A1.15: ME student can be of some help to the developer as he is aware of NX5 framework

A1.16: Global technical support for NX5 is available

A1.17: Authorization is required for getting the technical support

A1.18: Even though we are authorized to use the technical support, an NX5 representative might take some time to comprehend our problem

A1.19: Our company has some connection with NX5 technical support team, and is able to allocate someone to help the students

A1.20: A company representative may be assigned to assist the project upon request

Design Alternative (Position) 2: Use OpenGL as the Software Development Platform

A2.1: Student developer has experience in using OpenGL and prefers it

A2.2: Experience is not really necessary, as only predefined functions need to be invoked

A2.3: Expertise is required for customizing predefined functions according to the project requirements

A2.4: A large number of examples and illustrations for OpenGL are available

A2.5: OpenGL's API is very primitive, and it may require a lot of programming effort

A2.6: Boolean operations will require developing an algorithm and software code on our part

A2.7: The complexity of Boolean operations is not very high

After all the arguments and their strengths are entered into the system, the corresponding argumentation trees are shown in Figure 10 and Figure 11, respectively, for Potion 1 and Position 2. Note that under Position 1, two arguments from participant 6 – Argument A1.16 "Global technical support for NX5 is available" and Argument A1.18: "Even though we are authorized to use the technical sup-

Figure 10. Argumentation Tree for Position 1

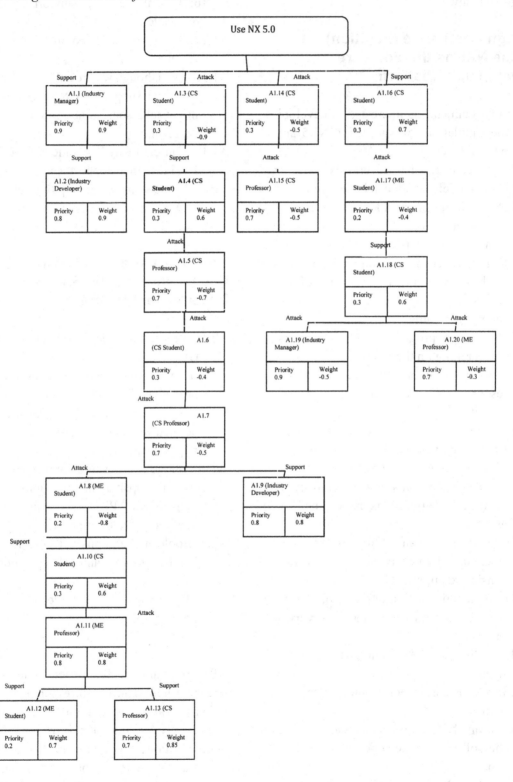

Figure 11. Argumentation Tree for Position 2

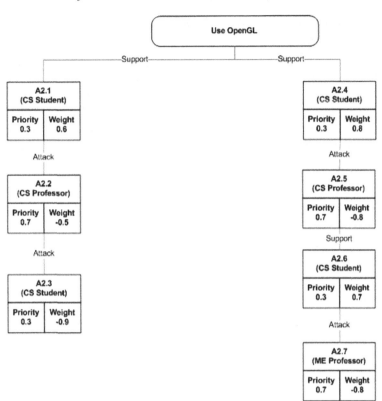

port, an NX5 representative might take some time to comprehend our problem" – are conflicting with each other. The intelligent argumentation system is able to detect these self-conflicting arguments as shown in Figure 12.

We next perform sensitivity analysis with priorities of participants to see how the favorability of each position may change when the participants' priorities change in two scenarios below.

Table 1. Priorities of participants in scenario 1

Participant 1 (Industry Manager)	0.9
Participant 2 (Industry Developer)	0.8
Participant 3 (ME Professor)	0.7
Participant 4 (ME Student)	0.2
Participant 5 (CS Professor)	0.7
Participant 6 (CS Student)	0.2

Scenario 1

The priorities of participants from the industrial company are extremely high and the priorities of the professors are high, while the priorities of the students are low, as showed in Table 1. The favorability factors of two positions are computed using the intelligent argumentation system as shown in Figure 13, which shows that position 1 is the favored alternative.

Scenario 2

The priorities of participants from the industrial company are extremely low, the priorities of the professors are low, and the priorities of the students are extremely high, as shown in Table 2.

After the favorability factors are computed by the intelligent argumentation system, the result in Figure 14 shows that position 2 is the favored

Figure 12. Detection of self-conflicting arguments

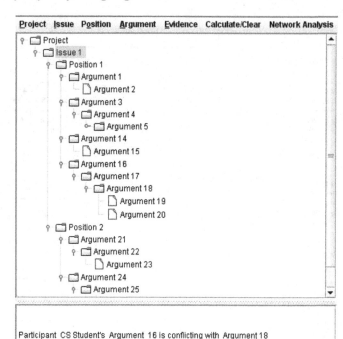

alternative.

From the two scenarios, it can be seen that as the participants' priorities change, the relative favorability of the positions may also change. Since the industrial members and the professors are more experienced than the students, they should have higher priorities. Thus NX5 was selected as the software development platform for the simulation project based on the priorities in Scenario 1. The selection of NX5 as the platform has allowed the simulation project to progress well according to the project requirements with reasonable

Table 2. Priorities of participants in scenario 2

Participant 1 (Industry Manager)	0.1
Participant 2 (Industry Developer)	0.1
Participant 3 (ME Professor)	0.2
Participant 4 (ME Student)	0.9
Participant 5 (CS Professor)	0.2
Participant 6 (CS Student)	0.8

software development effort for the simulation. In the end all the participants are satisfied with this selection.

FUTURE RESEARCH DIRECTIONS

Computational argumentation based decision support has a wide range of applications in software development, especially in collaborative software development involving geographically dispersed team members. Many more issues, such as role-based priority assessment, incorporation of Dempster-Shafer theory (Shafer, 1990) and other intelligent techniques for evidence handling, and validation of the method and system with more practical application examples need to be investigated in future research for the proposed intelligent computational argumentation method. Dempster-Shafer theory is promising because it is very effective in handling evidences in an uncertain environment and can be used to combine

Figure 13. Favorability factors of the two positions for Scenario 1

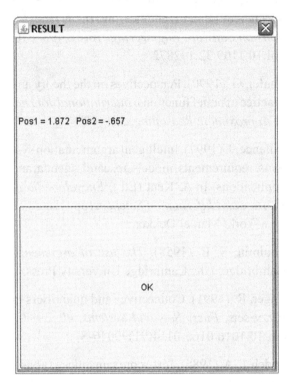

Figure 14. Favorability factors of Positions for Scenario 2

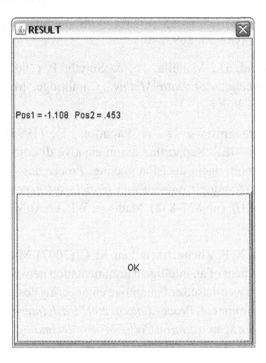

multiple evidences with uncertainty. Data mining techniques (Hand, Mannila & Smyth, 2001) may also be applied to identify patterns of misuse, abuse, and manipulation of participants in the argumentation network.

CONCLUSION

The intelligent argumentation based approach described in this chapter can be a significant methodology for collaborative decision making in software development. It allows many participants from multiple perspectives to contribute collaboratively in a decision making process. The participants' contributions to the decision are explicitly documented and computed through their arguments in an argumentation network. This approach does not require development of complex mathematical models like the multi-

criteria decision making method. This proposed approach has the following unique features: 1) It can capture software development rationale from all members of a development team and identify the most-favored development alternative; 2) It is close to real-world team design because people use arguments to express their views and the rationale behind them in collaborative software development practice; and 3) It is implemented as a web-based system, which is very powerful for collaborative software development involving people in geographically dispersed locations.

REFERENCES

Conklin, J., & Begeman, M. (1988). gIBIS: A hypertext tool for exploratory policy discussion. *Transactions on Office Information Systems*, *6*(4), 303–331. doi:10.1145/58566.59297

Dubois, D., & Prade, H. (1984). Criteria aggregation and ranking of alternatives in the framework of fuzzy set theory. *Studies in the Management Sciences, 20*, 209–240.

Hand, D., Mannila, H., & Smyth, P. (2001). *Principles of Data Mining.*, Cambridge, MA: MIT Press.

Karacapilidis, N., & Papadias, D. (1998). HERMES: Supporting argumentative discourse in multi-agent decision making. *Proceedings of 15th National Conference on Artificial Intelligence (AAAI),* (pp.827-832). Madison, WI: AAAI/MIT Press.

Liu, X. F., Zheng, M., & Leu, M. C. (2007). Management of an intelligent argumentation network for a web-based collaborative engineering design environment. *Proceedings of 2007 IEEE International Symposium on Collaborative Technologies and Systems (CTS 2007),* Orlando, Florida.

Liu, X. F., Raorane, S., Zheng, M., & Leu, M. C. (2006). An internet based intelligent argumentation system for collaborative engineering design. *Proceedings of the 2006 IEEE International Symposium on Collaborative Technologies and Systems (CTS 2006),* Las Vegas, Nevada, (pp. 318-325).

Potts, C., & Burns, G. (1988). Recording the reasons for design decisions. *Proceedings of 10th International Conference on Software Engineering,* Singapore, (pp. 418-427).

Ramesh, B., & Dhar, V. (1992). Supporting systems development by capturing deliberations during requirements engineering. *IEEE Transactions on Software Engineering, 18*(6), 498–510. doi:10.1109/32.142872

Shafer, G. (1990). Perspectives on the theory and practice of belief functions. *International Journal of Approximate Reasoning, 3*, 1–40.

Sillence, J. (1997). Intelligent argumentation systems: requirements, models, research agenda, and applications. In A. Kent (Ed.), *Encyclopedia of Library and Information Science,* (pp. 176-217). New York: Marcel Dekker.

Toulmin, S. E. (1958). *The use of arguments.* Cambridge, UK: Cambridge University Press.

Yager, R. (1991). Connectives and quantifiers in fuzzy sets. *Fuzzy Sets and Systems, 40*, 39–75. doi:10.1016/0165-0114(91)90046-S

Zadeh, L. A. (1986). Test-score semantics as a basis for a computational approach to the representation of meaning. *Literary and Linguistic Computing, 1*(1), 24–35. doi:10.1093/llc/1.1.24

Zimmermann, H. J. (1991). *Fuzzy set theory and its applications.* Amsterdam: Kluwer Academic.

Chapter 10

Supporting Quality–Driven Software Design through Intelligent Assistants

Alvaro Soria
ISISTAN Research Institute and CONICET, Argentina

J. Andres Diaz-Pace
Software Engineering Institute, USA

Len Bass
Software Engineering Institute, USA

Felix Bachmann
Software Engineering Institute, USA

Marcelo Campo
ISISTAN Research Institute and CONICET, Argentina

ABSTRACT

Software design decisions are usually made at early stages but have far-reaching effects regarding system organization, quality, and cost. When doing design, developers apply their technical knowledge to decide among multiple solutions, seeking a reasonable balance between functional and quality-attribute requirements. Due to the complexity of this exploration, the resulting solutions are often more a matter of developer's experience than of systematic reasoning. It is argued that AI-based tools can assist developers to search the design space more effectively. In this chapter, the authors take a software design approach driven by quality attributes, and then present two tools that have been specifically developed to support that approach. The first tool is an assistant for exploring architectural models, while the second tool is an assistant for the refinement of architectural models into object-oriented models. Furthermore, the authors show an example of how these design assistants are combined in a tool chain, in order to ensure that the main quality attributes are preserved across the design process.

DOI: 10.4018/978-1-60566-758-4.ch010

INTRODUCTION

Software design can be seen as the bridge between requirements and implementation. Over the last years, design has become a central practice in software development, mainly due to the growing complexity of today's systems and the impact of *quality attributes* in software products. Quality attributes capture non-functional concerns such as: performance, reliability, security, or modifiability, among others (Bass et al., 2003). Along this line, architecture-centric design approaches are being more and more adopted, since they help to explicitly engineer quality rather than considering it an afterthought. In these approaches, the role of the designer is to plan for a design solution that is "good enough" for the competing interests of the stakeholders. The designer must make decisions for architectural patterns and gross decomposition of functionality as early as possible in the development cycle, in order to reason about the advantages and disadvantages of potential design solutions. There are usually multiple solutions that satisfy the same requirements, and each of these solutions is likely to have tradeoffs regarding quality attributes (Boehm & In, 1996). The notion of *tradeoff* means that the improvement of one quality comes at the cost of degrading another, as it is the case of modifiability versus performance. Therefore, creating a design that meets a set of quality-attribute requirements is a difficult and challenging problem, even for experienced developers. We see here an interesting area for the application of automated design assistance.

According to their granularity, two types of design activities can be identified: *architecture design* and *detailed design*. Architecture design deals with the high-level organization of the system in terms of components, relationships between these components and allocation of functionality. This organization is generally known as the software architecture of the system (Bass et al., 2003). The *software architecture* is the primary carrier of quality attributes for a system because it prescribes how the system should be realized by concrete implementations. Once an architecture exists, detailed design is about the decisions related to the computational implementation of that architecture (e.g., code, existing libraries and components, frameworks, etc.). A common choice for detailed design and implementation is the object-oriented paradigm (Rumbaugh et al., 1991).

Both architecture design and detailed design require designers to apply their technical knowledge and experience to evaluate alternative solutions before making commitments to a definite solution. Normally, a designer starts with a guess of the solution, and then goes back and forth exploring candidate design transformations until arriving to the desired solution (Tekinerdogan, 2000). We conceptualize this exploration of the design space into two main phases: (i) from quality-attribute requirements to (one or more) architectural models - called *QAR-to-AM phase*, and (ii) from an architectural model to (one or more) object-oriented models - called *AM-to-OOM phase*. Making the right design decisions for each phase is a complex, time-consuming and error-prone activity for designers. Although tools for specification and analysis of designs exist, these tools do not support the designer in making informed decisions based on quality-attribute considerations. Along this line, several AI developments have shown the benefits of improving conventional tools with intelligent agents. The metaphor here is that the agent acts like a *personal assistant to the user* (Maes, 1994). This assistant should be able to monitor the designer's work, and offer timely guidance on how to carry out design tasks or even perform routine computations on her behalf. For example, given a modifiability scenario, a design assistant could recommend the use of a Client-Server pattern to satisfy that scenario. If the designer agrees to apply such a pattern, the assistant could also take over the assignment of responsibilities to Client and Server components. Also, the assistant could remind the designer to verify the influences of the pattern instantiation on performance scenarios. In particular, we believe that agent-based tools hold promise for supporting designers in searching for solutions during the QAR-to-AM and AM-to-OOM phases above.

In this context, the objective of this chapter is twofold. First, we introduce a quality-driven design approach, and discuss issues and techniques for its automation. Architecture design and object-oriented design are seen as different types of search, which lead to different automation techniques. Second, we present a tool chain that supports the exploration of the QAR-to-AM and AM-to-OOM spaces. The tool chain consists of two design assistants: ArchE and SAME. *ArchE* (Architecture Expert) is a knowledge-based tool that helps the developer to explore architecture alternatives for quality-attribute scenarios (Bachmann et al., 2004). *SAME* (Software Architecture Materialization Explorer) is a case-based-reasoning tool for deriving object-oriented models, based on previous materialization experiences (Vazquez et al., 2008). The outputs of ArchE serve as inputs for SAME. Throughout the chapter, we use a case study to illustrate how ArchE and SAME complement each other. This integrated tool approach is really beneficial, because it augments the designer's capabilities for navigating the design space and evaluating quality-attribute tradeoffs. Furthermore, our preliminary results have shown that tools like ArchE and SAME can practically enforce quality-attribute requirements across the design process.

BACKGROUND

Software design is "the process of problem-solving and planning for a software solution" (Wikipedia, 2008). Once the stakeholders have determined the business goals and requirements of a system, the developers (or the designers) will design to define a blueprint for developing a software solution. This blueprint gives a plan that, if executed correctly, will derive into an implementation (computer program) that satisfies the requirements specification. In practice, designers have identified recurrent design problems that had been solved by others before. This knowledge is captured in the form of *patterns*. Basically, a pattern is a template describing a solution to a common problem in a given context (Gamma et al., 1994). The use of patterns is very beneficial to improve the quality of design solutions and to speed up the software development process. Several patterns for architectural and object-oriented design have been catalogued (e.g., layers, blackboard, pipes and filters, broker, proxy, observer, among others) (Buschmann et al., 1996; Shaw and Garlan, 1996). Patterns are ruled by general design principles (e.g., abstraction, information hiding, modularization, separation of concerns, coupling, and divide-and-conquer, among others), which have been recently codified under the concept of tactics (Bachmann et al., 2005).

Quality-attribute requirements have a great influence in design, since they drive the main decisions for making a system satisfy its business goals. For example, a web-based system for e-commerce for a new market should have good performance and security in order to be successful. That is, there will be quality-attribute requirements for performance and security that will make the designer apply specific architectural patterns (e.g., Web-based Model-View-Controller, Client-Server, encryption mechanisms, etc.) to the system. Unfortunately, unlike functional requirements, quality-attribute requirements are often underrepresented when defining and implementing a software system. In order to overcome this problem, the Software Engineering Institute (SEI) has proposed a design approach, called the *Attribute-driven Design (ADD) method* (Bass et al., 2003), which starts with the main system's quality-attribute requirements and guides the designer through a series of design steps to the extent necessary to meet those requirements. To do so, the method relies on a vocabulary of architectural concepts such as: quality-attribute scenarios, responsibilities, tactics, patterns and architectural views (Bass et al., 2003).

In parallel to design techniques, the development of tool support for software design has been an active field of research and technology transfer. Many design tools for software architectures and object-oriented systems have been proposed, although not always focused on the analysis of quality attributes. Examples of semi-automated approaches include: rule-based systems, algebraic transformations, model-driven approaches, search-based frameworks, and case-based reasoning, among others. One challenge for the new generation of design tools is how to proactively support developers in a design process that is a mix of opportunistic and prescribed tasks (Robbins et al., 1996).

Many researchers have tried to represent design knowledge using rule-based systems. The first experiments can be traced in the Programmer's Apprentice project at MIT (Waters & Tan, 1991) to build a CASE environment with automated support for requirements, design and implementation. Unfortunately, much of that work failed due to the weak support given by the representation formalism and the inherent complexity associated with the generation of operational programs from requirements. Another relevant effort is a knowledge-based automation of a design method for concurrent systems (Mills & Gomaa, 2002).

From a formal perpective, Tekinerdogan (2000) presents a relational algebra for architecture synthesis. His synthesis process assumes a multi-dimensional design space, where the designer should define every concept in the solution domain. The coordinates in this space represent different types of solutions. The approach also provides heuristics to reduce the number of design alternatives to be evaluated. Both the coordinates and the heuristics may consider some quality-attribute issues. Although basic tool support is provided, a drawback of the approach is that the developer must take care of the construction of

the space (in terms of relevant concepts in the solution domain), as well as of the selection of criteria to prune alternatives.

Recent design tools include ArgoUML and Easel. ArgoUML (Robbins et al., 1996) is one of the first environments proposing "critics" as agents that can work in an autonomous fashion, implementing the "personal assistant" metaphor in the software design domain. These critics are able to check conditions in the object-oriented models being developed, and prompt the designer about the results of her tasks. Easel (Hendrickson et al., 2006) is a tool that focuses on the "designing activity" itself, allowing developers to arrange design versions in layers in such a way they can visualize the design fragments added to or removed from the base architecture.

Other researchers have argued for a view of software engineering as a search framework (Clarke et al., 2003), in which automation is supported by optimization techniques such as hill-climbing, evolutionary algorithms and constraint-based solvers. An important requirement of this view is a well-defined mapping from software concepts to elements supported by an AI search technique. Several early results have been collected by Clarke et al. (2003). Related to this view, Grunske (2006) has applied evolutionary algorithms in the optimization of architectures for satellite domains. Departing from an architectural specification that fulfils its functional requirements as the initial solution, Grunske's tool tries to find solutions with good tradeoffs between reliability and cost requirements. Case-studies have been carried out for limited design spaces. Grunske has also pointed out challenges for the combined use of quality-attribute models and tool support, such as composability, analyzability and complexity issues.

The implementation of software architectures has been mainly approached through object-oriented frameworks (Fayad et al., 1999) and model-driven engineering (MDE) techniques (Ledeczi et al., 2001; Schmidt, 2006). Application frameworks were the first attempts to capture architectural abstractions of related systems, providing reusable object-oriented skeletons for building applications within particular domains. The instantiation of a framework through the standard object-oriented mechanisms (e.g., sub-classing, method overriding, etc.) gives alternative implementations of the underlying software architecture. Along this line, Medvidovic et al. (2006) described a family of frameworks implementing the C2 style, which is an architectural style intended for graphical user interfaces. In Medvidovic's approach, quality-attribute tradeoffs are predefined in each of the alternative frameworks that support the C2 style. Nowadays, the refinement of architectural models is being considered under the general umbrella of MDE. MDE focuses on open standards and supporting tools for system modeling and transformation, usually based on UML profiles. The idea is that MDE tools can generate complete implementations from architectural models. However, despite some positive results in the area of embedded software systems, the use of semi-automated transformation still requires significant efforts. Furthermore, the role of quality attributes along successive model transformations has been little studied.

A number of studies have utilized Case-based Reasoning (CBR) techniques to support reuse of object-oriented models. Fouqué & Matwin (1993) reported an experience with a CBR tool to reuse source code in Smalltalk. This tool is able to locate software components based on the functionality they realize, extending the implementation of the components according to the particular requirements of the problem. The cases include a lexical specification of the component functionality, its implementation idiom and other code properties, which justify the use of the component in a particular context. ReBuilderUML (Gomes & Leitao, 2006) is another CBR tool to reuse fragments of UML class diagrams when addressing functional requirements. This approach is based on domain knowledge to analyze the system requirements

and to search in a repository of class diagrams for a case that is suitable for those requirements. These approaches are targeted only to object-oriented systems and derive object-oriented implementations from functional requirements. Thus, it is not possible to manage the variability imposed by quality-attribute requirements in the object-oriented solutions.

SOFTWARE DESIGN WITH QUALITY ATTRIBUTES

One advantage of ADD is that it helps designers understand quality-attribute tradeoffs early in the design process. According to our experiences, the design process can be planned in two phases called QAR-to-AM and AM-to-OOM. First, the designer identifies and captures those quality-attribute concerns most relevant for the system at the very conception of the software architecture (QAR-to-AM phase). Then, the designer uses the architectural guidance to map the architecture to more concrete object-oriented designs, but ensuring that the quality-attribute characteristics "inherited" from the architecture are preserved (AM-to-OOM phase). This way, it is possible to manage both quality-attribute issues and software complexity at the architectural level, and furthermore, to take advantage of transformational techniques for making the transition from architectural to object-oriented models. We refer to the mapping from architectural elements into object-oriented counterparts as *object-oriented materialization of a software architecture* (Campo et al., 2002).

In order to exemplify how quality attributes can inform both the QAR-to-AM and AM-to-OOM design phases, Figure 1 schematizes the object-oriented materialization of a standard Model-View-Controller (MVC) pattern (Krasner & Pope, 1988; Buschmann et al., 1996). During the QAR-to-AM phase, the MVC pattern permits to easily accommodate changes in the domain, the

Figure 1. Quality attributes as drivers of architecture and object-oriented design

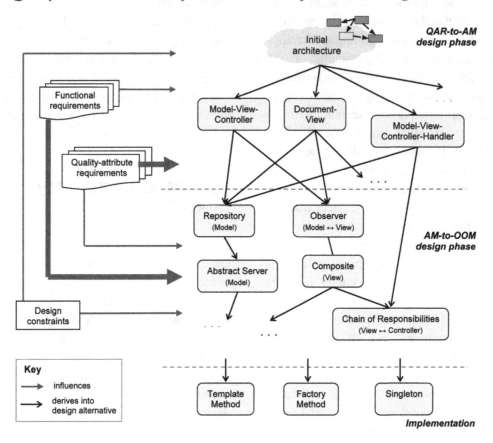

presentation or the user's actions; although this may generate some performance problems when updating views. Given this tradeoff, we can be forced to apply the Document-View variant of MVC that merges the presentation and user's actions into a single component. Other architectural design alternatives may also be explored. As a result of this exploration, we will end up with a coarse-grained MVC structure that balances our modifiability and performance scenarios. From the architecture design perspective, these scenarios will be achieved through an adequate distribution of the system's responsibilities among components and through corresponding interactions among the components. As we move into the AM-to-OOM design phase, we can take a set of use-cases to determine the fine-grained (class-level) details of the architectural components (Sangwan et

al., 2008). Here, we can apply several design patterns such as: Observer, Chain of Responsibility or Composite (Gamma et al., 1994) and further tune performance or modifiability issues. Again, different object-oriented designs may be explored, as long as the designs conform to the quality-attribute requirements and constraints of the MVC architecture.

Even taking a small set of quality-attribute scenarios as drivers for the materialization, the design process can span many alternative paths and require considerable design background and experience. For this reason, the central theme in this chapter is about assistive tools that, making use of existing design knowledge, can point out quality-driven design solutions to the designer. The ArchE and SAME tools are two examples of this trend. Before going into the details of ArchE

Figure 2. CTAS actors and use cases - adapted from (Bachmann et al., 2007)

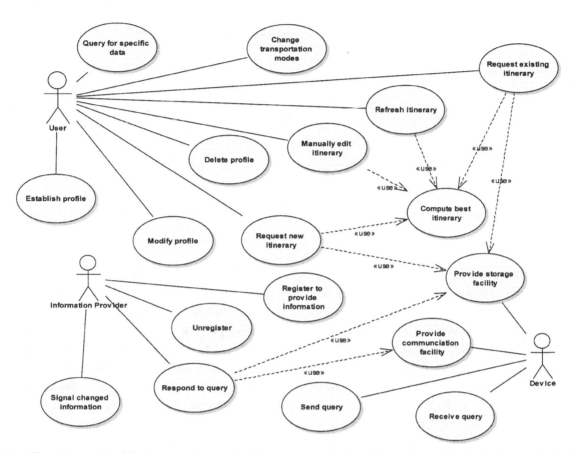

User. The primary actor of the system, who wants to plan, execute and revise a trip to a few routine destinations, in the least expensive, fastest, or shortest manner possible.

Information Provider. A secondary actor that provides for use in computing itineraries. For example: a vehicle in which the CTAS is being transported may provide time-to-destination, a parking lot operation may provide its lot location and availability, etc. An information provider wants to attract business by providing fast response and accurate data. Information providers will change with locale and may change dynamically as they go offline outside their hours of operation.

Device. Any device on which an instance of the CTAS may be hosted. A CTAS device will have a core set of features that may be expandable.

and SAME, we present a case study that will be the basis for articulating the architectural and object-oriented worlds via tool support.

Case Study: The Clemson's Travel Assistant System (CTAS)

The Clemson's Travel Assistant System (CTAS) (McGregor et al., 2007) is a system that allows a traveler to plan an itinerary based on the routes and modes of transportation available for traveling

from one location to another. The system executes on a wireless handheld device, and the travelers can update their information periodically and reconsider their itinerary. Using the CTAS should result in a trip as efficient as possible given the conditions at the time of travel. The stakeholders in the CTAS include: users, developers and business owners. The scope of the CTAS is the software running on the handheld device, and it is assumed that the information services are available. The actors and use cases are depicted in Figure 2.

Figure 3. Responsibilities and functional dependencies in CTAS

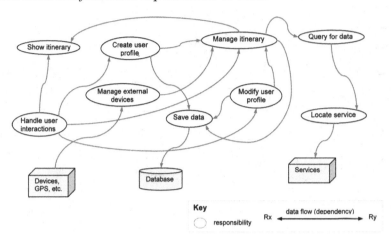

From the use cases, we can identify the main functions of the system and transform them into responsibilities. A responsibility is seen as a function that an architectural component has to deliver (Wirfs-Brock & McKean, 2003). A possible technique is to create a function for each use case, and then derive responsibilities for those functions by analyzing the user-system interactions defined by each use case. As a result of this exercise, we decomposed CTAS into the responsibilities and data flow dependencies shown in Figure 3.

The design of CTAS has to satisfy modifiability and performance requirements. We will use scenarios to capture quality-attribute requirements in a tangible form (Bass et al, 2003). Table 1 lists the CTAS scenarios. One of the purposes of specifying scenarios is that they help designers to "test" quality-attribute requirements. That is, we can elicit the event (called *scenario stimulus*) that will affect the behavior of the system, and also elicit a measure (called *scenario response*) to quantify the results of that event. This stimulus-measure pair is the criterion that determines whether a given architecture fulfills a quality-attribute scenario. For instance, in scenario M2, the response is about a cost constraint for implementing changes in the user profile. If the evaluation of the scenario results in a cost that is below the threshold of 15 person-days, then the scenario is regarded as satis-

fied with the current architecture. If the scenario is not satisfied, we can either negotiate the threshold with the stakeholders or create a new architecture. Another purpose of scenarios is to assess the impact of quality attributes on the architecture. To do so, each scenario is usually mapped to specific responsibilities, which the designer can allocate to design elements (e.g., modules, processes, etc.). Table 2 shows hypothetical mappings of the CTAS scenarios to responsibilities.

From Quality-Attribute Requirements to Software Architectures

The objective of the QAR-to-AM design phase is to move from a set of quality-attribute scenarios to an architectural model that satisfies those scenarios. A premise of architectural design is that the achievement of quality-attribute scenarios comes from applying specific patterns on the architecture. More specifically, the quality-attribute scenarios are goals of attainment that the designer seeks to fulfill by putting tactics and patterns in the architectural model. For instance, the goal of scenario M2 states that profile-related responsibilities should support modifications with reduced change impact. Intuitively, a tactic for that goal in MVC is that of inserting an intermediary between the model and its interacting components, because

Table 1. Modifiability and performance scenarios for CTAS

Scenario	Description
M1	The addition of new features requires changes in the data format. The implementation of the new format has to be done within 3.5 person days of effort.
M2	A new variable to the user profile has to be added within 15 person days of effort.
M3	The driver for a new external device has to be added by a developer within 5.5 person days of effort.
P1	The system has to manage the external devices (under normal load) and handle the operations in less than 15 milliseconds.
P2	A view wishes to attach to the model under normal conditions and do so in less than 9 milliseconds.
P3	The user asks to show the itinerary under normal conditions and the itinerary is shown in less than 16 milliseconds.
P4	The user asks to show the itinerary under normal conditions and the itinerary is shown in less than 16 milliseconds.
P5	The user asks to save the current data on the screen under normal conditions and the data is saved in under 4 milliseconds.

this intermediary breaks the dependencies of the model with other parts of the system. Depending on the dependency type, the designer could apply different patterns to flesh out an architectural alternative, namely: a repository, a naming server, a publisher-subscriber, layers, etc. (Shaw & Garlan, 1996). As sketched in Figure 1, the designer evaluates and combines patterns that make different quality-attribute tradeoffs. We will take advantage of the goal-driven strategy followed in the QAR-to-AM design phase later in the chapter, when presenting the ArchE tool.

Basically, creating an architectural model is about allocating responsibilities to software elements following a design rationale. In CTAS, an initial architecture can be obtained by simply allocating each responsibility to a separate module and linking the components based on the responsibility dependencies. Generally, the designer can provide a guess of the initial architecture, based on previous experiences or personal criterion. Let's consider that the designer attends the interactive characteristics of CTAS and allocates the responsibilities according to a standard MVC pattern (Krasner & Pope, 1988), as depicted in Figure 4. Note that two new "architectural responsibilities" have been added to the design ('Attach to Model' and 'Register Views'), as prescribed by MVC. However, intuition is not enough to say that an MVC-based architecture for CTAS satisfies the modifiability and performance scenarios of Table 1. The designer must perform modifiability and

Table 2. Mapping of quality-attribute scenarios to responsibilities in CTAS

Scenario	Related responsibilities
M1	Save data (R6), Query for data (R2), Show Itinerary (R1)
M2	Create user profile (R3), Modify user profile (R7)
M3	Manage external devices (R8)
P1	Manage itinerary (R4), Manage external devices (R8)
P2	Register views (R10), Attach to model (R9)
P3	Modify user profile (R7), Create user profile (R3), Handle user interactions (R5)
P4	Manage itinerary (R4), Handle user interactions (R5)
P5	Save data (R6), Create user profile (R3)

Figure 4. Top-level module view for CTAS based on MVC

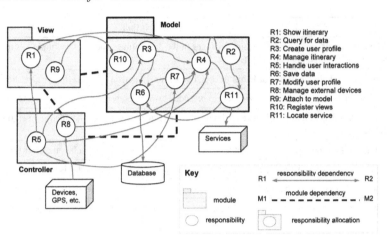

performance analyses on the proposed architecture. These quality-attribute analyses will capture the behavior of the architecture with respect to the scenarios. However, the problem is that designers must have knowledge of many quality attributes and their relationships in order to correctly build analysis models.

Reasoning Frameworks

One useful mechanism for quality-attribute modeling is reasoning frameworks. A *reasoning framework* (Bass et al., 2005) encapsulates the knowledge needed to understand and predict the response of a quality-attribute scenario, in such a way that this knowledge can be applied by non-experts. Internally, reasoning frameworks rely on analytic techniques (e.g., queuing networks for performance, change impact for modifiability, Markov chains for availability, etc.) to determine whether a particular architecture satisfies a set of scenarios. In our case study, the designer would like to have an architecture that optimizes the responses of the modifiability scenarios M1-M3 and the performance scenarios P1-P5, based on the outputs of reasoning frameworks for performance and modifiability.

The scenarios M1-M3 are tackled with a reasoning framework based on a Change Impact

Analysis (CIA) (Bohner, 2002; Bachmann et al., 2004). According to the CIA technique, this reasoning framework transforms the architectural description into a dependency graph, in which the nodes correspond to "units of change" (e.g., responsibilities, modules) while the arcs represent dependencies between the nodes (e.g., functional dependencies, data flows). The dependencies act like "change propagators" between nodes. The transformation from an architecture into a quality-attribute model is known as *interpretation*. To estimate the impact of a change, nodes and arcs are annotated with parameters. A node is annotated with its approximate cost of modification, and an arc is annotated with probabilities of change rippling. Afterwards, the reasoning framework traverses the graph and computes a cost measure as a weighted sum of costs and probabilities. The analysis of the quality-attribute model is known as *evaluation*. For instance, let's assume that the evaluation of the dependency graph for M2 gives a response of 17.5 person days. This prediction would indicate that the scenario is not satisfied with the current MVC architecture. Similar analysis is carried out for the rest of the modifiability scenarios.

The scenarios P1-P5 are concerned with timing requirements for the responsibilities (i.e., latency). Let's consider that the scenarios are analyzed with

Figure 5. Re-design of the initial CTAS architecture by inserting an intermediary

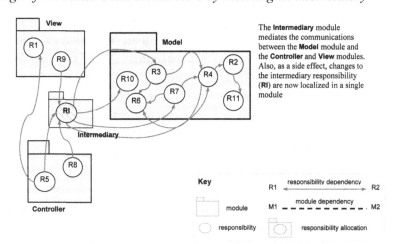

a performance reasoning framework based on Rate Monotonic Analysis (RMA) (Klein et al., 1993). Using the RMA technique, the interpretation procedure transforms the responsibilities into an arrangement of tasks and events linking the tasks. Tasks are annotated with parameters that capture execution time and timing constraints. Then, the evaluation procedure computes the worst-case timing behavior of those tasks, by considering the maximum execution times of the tasks and the worst preemption and blocking effects (Moreno & Merson, 2008). For instance, let's assume that the prediction of the worst-case latency for P3 is 13 milliseconds. This response would indicate that the scenario is effectively satisfied with the current MVC architecture. Nonetheless, an analysis of all the performance scenarios is necessary to determine if the whole system is schedulable.

When the responses for certain scenarios are outside the limits given by the designer, the current architecture must be re-designed by applying one or more tactics. A tactic is a vehicle to control a single quality-attribute through an architectural transformation (Bachmann et al., 2005). Tactics can be also packaged as part of a reasoning framework. For instance, the reason why scenario M2 is not satisfied could be an excessive coupling among modules, which favors the rippling of changes

and increases the total cost (Bachmann et al., 2007). If the modifiability reasoning framework suggests an intermediary to break the involved dependencies, the change is confined to a smaller area of the architecture. A heuristic for finding the place in which the intermediary should be more effective is to seek modules with high coupling. Figure 5 shows the re-design of CTAS with this tactic. After the transformation, the modifiability reasoning framework will re-interpret and re-evaluate the architecture, checking if the cost measure is improved.

In general, design alternatives with different quality-attribute characteristics arise as different tactics are selected and corresponding transformations are executed on the architecture. Since each reasoning framework separately analyzes its own quality-attribute scenarios, the complexity of the design exploration is reduced. Hence, the designer can manage the relationships among multiple quality-attribute techniques without the need of having detailed knowledge about those techniques. The process of interpretation, evaluation, and re-design should continue until the predictions for the scenarios reach values that meet the designer's expectations. This control loop is the core of the architecture design assistance provided by ArchE.

From Software Architectures to Object Structures

Architectural models deliberately defer decisions about specific implementation technologies. Once a given architecture is chosen, the designer is expected to derive a materialization of that architecture using object-oriented technology. Any of the possible materializations should adhere to the design principles dictated by the base architecture. However, there is a well-known mismatch between the abstractions used in architecture design and those used in object-oriented design. For instance, the concept of connector used in architectural models to represent communications between components is not a first-class citizen in object-oriented models. Examples of common connectors include: push/pull procedure call, producer-consumer connectors, event channel and observer connectors, brokers, SOAP connectors, semaphores, or transporters, among others (Shaw, 1996; Fernandez, 1997; Mehta et al., 2000). In object-oriented design, connectors must be necessarily mapped to a set of classes and relationships between objects. The decisions that designers make when doing these mappings affect the properties of the object-oriented model with regard to modifiability, performance, and other quality attributes. In this context, the main objective of the AM-to-OOM design phase is to produce object-oriented models that are faithful to the quality-attribute scenarios addressed by the architecture.

The classical approach to materialization is to define an object-oriented framework for the architecture (Tracz, 1995; Medvidovic et al., 2002). The object-oriented models based on frameworks naturally incorporate a number of features of the object paradigm (e.g., information hiding, encapsulation, and polymorphism), and therefore, the models are mostly focused on modifiability. In previous work (Díaz-Pace & Campo, 2005), we proposed an alternative materialization approach based on the composition of small fragments, called *framelets* (Pree & Koskimies, 1999), in which each framelet reifies a small set of architectural elements into an object-oriented implementation. Unlike the goal-oriented strategy of architectural design, we argue that designers often follow an experience-based strategy to perform object-oriented materializations. That is, designers reuse knowledge from past, proven solutions in order to narrow down the space of "allowed" object-oriented alternatives for an architecture. These solutions can be seen as "patterns" that combine both human experiences with general architectural guidelines. Furthermore, we found out that the framelets used for implementing architectural connectors are very helpful to engineer quality attributes in object-oriented models. Essentially, connectors are the medium through which components realize their responsibilities. For instance, in the MVC pattern, the Model component sends change notifications to the View components, and the View Components may send notifications to the Controller components. The connectors responsible for these interactions convey information that affects the class structure of the implementation alternatives.

Figure 6 shows two framelets for implementing the connectors between Model-View and View-Controller. In the framelet at the top, the connector is materialized by means of an Event-Channel implementation, which promotes modifiability by explicitly decoupling components and notification policies while incurring some performance overheads. The framelet at the bottom presents, instead, an Observer implementation in which the Model and View handle their own event subscribers. The object-oriented structure of this framelet does not allow the possibility of components playing the roles of notifiers or subscribers in different situations. However, the performance is better than the one of the first framelet, due to the lack of intermediary dispatchers in component interactions.

The instantiation and combination of framelets in a meaningful way is not straightforward, and it

Figure 6. Two examples of materialization of a change-notification connector

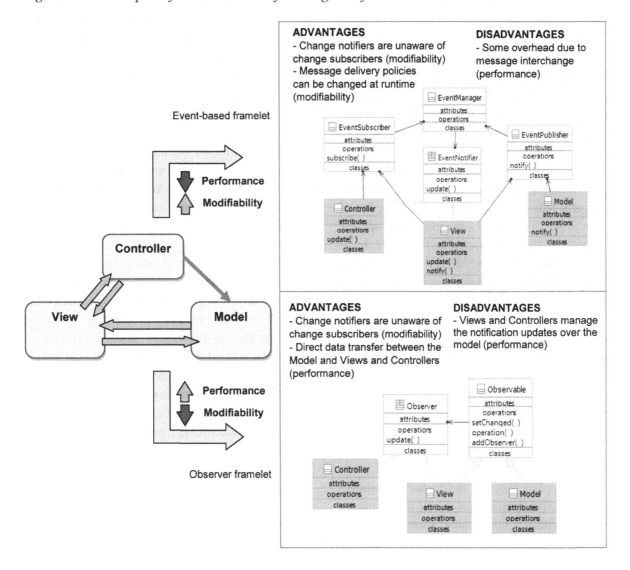

actually requires some kind of tool support. This challenge led to the SAME tool. SAME departs from quality-attribute preferences that the designer attributes to connectors, and is able to instantiate framelets for the connectors that best match the designer's preferences.

ArchE: SUGGESTING TACTICS FOR ARCHITECTURE DESIGN

ArchE is a knowledge-based tool developed by the Software Engineering Institute that aims at helping designers to explore architecture alternatives (Bachmann et al., 2004; Diaz-Pace et al., 2008). In a nutshell, ArchE performs a semi-automated search of the design space, relying on the outputs of reasoning frameworks to direct the search towards solutions that satisfy quality-attribute scenarios. In terms of assistance, ArchE proposes tactics for improving the current architecture and allows the designer to decide on the best alternative.

A typical interaction of ArchE with the CTAS designer is shown in Figure 7. First, the designer inputs the set of responsibilities to be computed by CTAS system (like those responsibilities of Figure 3). In addition, the designer can optionally feed ArchE with the MVC architecture as the initial architecture design. After that, the designer specifies textual scenarios for modifiability and performance (like those of Table 1), and then she proceeds to set the desired response for the scenarios. The scenarios are mapped to specific responsibilities (not shown in Figure 7). In response to these changes, ArchE asks for information for the reasoning frameworks, for example, parameters for dependencies between responsibilities, and execution time or cost of change of the responsibilities. Then, ArchE starts running the reasoning frameworks, which analyze the quality-attribute scenarios and identify which of them are not satisfied by the current architecture design. If some scenarios are not met, ArchE shows a list of questions to the designer. Each question describes a tactic that might improve the current design. The designer can choose one or more tactics. Finally, ArchE applies the selected tactics to produce a new architecture design. In all these interactions, ArchE has no semantic knowledge of the quality-attribute techniques used by its reasoning frameworks; it simply handles basic inputs such as scenarios and responsibilities, then delegates the design work to the reasoning frameworks, and finally assembles their results.

The Expert System

Technically, ArchE is designed as a blackboard (Buschmann et al., 1996) in which different actors collaborate to produce a solution for a problem. Figure 8 shows the main components of the ArchE tool. Each actor is a reasoning framework that can potentially read information that was developed by other actors; and conversely, each actor can introduce new information into the blackboard that could be of interest to anyone else. ArchE is the control component that coordinates the interactions among the actors so as to ensure progress in the architecting process. Both ArchE and the reasoning frameworks have access to a shared repository in which design information is stored.

The ArchE Core is in charge of reasoning about the current architecture and searching for design alternatives for it. The ArchE Core is equipped with a rule-based engine implemented in Jess (Friedman-Hill, 2003) that encodes the main steps of the searching strategy. This strategy determines when the capabilities of each reasoning framework should be activated, and the order in which tactics are generated and evaluated against quality-attribute scenarios.

The Design Repository stores all the items being processed during a design session into a MySQL database. The items include: functions, responsibilities, responsibility dependencies, quality-attribute scenarios, modules, tasks, tactics, etc. Inside the ArchE Core, these items are represented as Jess facts. Control data is also stored for coordination between the ArchE Core and the reasoning frameworks.

ArchE, the reasoning frameworks and the Design Repository work over a network. The communication between the ArchE Core and the reasoning frameworks takes place through a publish-subscribe message-based middleware. A consequence of having this middleware is that reasoning frameworks can be added (or removed) easily without considering others. In order to be recognized by the ArchE Core, a new reasoning framework has to publish a small XML file, called *manifesto*, which states what functionalities are provided by the reasoning framework. After processing the manifesto, ArchE enables the reasoning framework for operation and starts sending it asynchronous commands. Upon the reception of specific commands from ArchE, each reasoning framework can independently evaluate its

Figure 7. Snapshot of ArchE at work

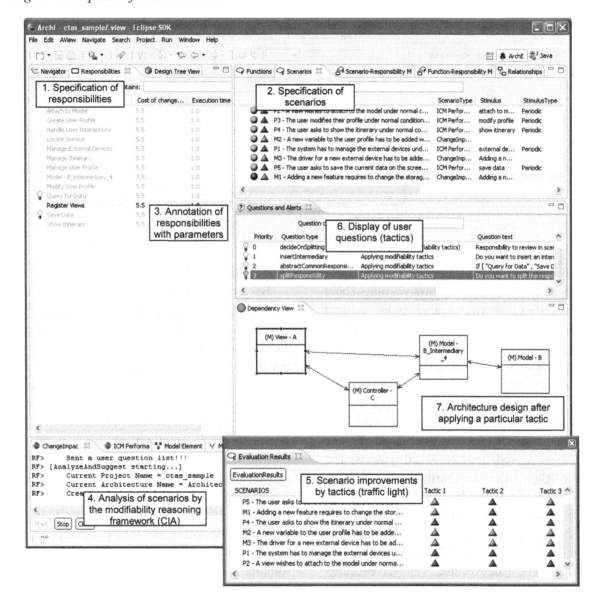

scenarios and propose tactics for them.

Since not all the decisions can be made automatically by ArchE, the user (i.e., designer) becomes an additional actor in the blackboard who makes the final decisions about design proposals. The assignment of parameters to responsibilities and relationships is a joint effort between ArchE and the architect (Bachmann et al., 2004). The architect must set parameters such as cost, execution time, or probability of change rippling for

the relevant responsibilities, based on previous experiences, empirical data or ballpark estimates. ArchE can assign default values to parameters of remaining responsibilities and relationships.

The ArchE GUI is the front-end that allows the designer to enter design information, and displays results and questions. The ArchE GUI implements two mechanisms for interacting with the architect: (i) the so-called "traffic light"; and (ii) the user questions. The user questions are pri-

Figure 8. Main components of the ArchE tool

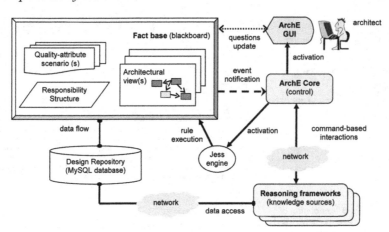

marily intended for showing tactics for the current architecture. Questions also show warnings about the design (e.g., incorrect parameters, inconsistent configurations). The types of questions associated to a reasoning framework must be specified in a special file that supplements the manifesto. This file let ArchE know about the template and parameters of each possible question. The ArchE GUI uses that information to parse questions received from the reasoning frameworks and display the questions in predefined graphical widgets. The traffic light is a decision table that summarizes the available tactics versus the evaluation of quality-attribute scenarios. The payoffs of each alternative are shown using color-coded icons. This way, the designer can analyze the tradeoffs and decide on the right tactic to be executed. A tactic is executed by answering its corresponding question.

Reasoning Framework Implementations

Two reasoning frameworks for modifiability and performance were used to explore alternative solutions for CTAS. The modifiability reasoning framework is a Java implementation of the CIA technique described in (Bohner, 2002; Bachmann et al., 2004), while the performance reasoning framework is a Java wrapper of the Lambda$_{wba}$ analyzer described in (Gonzalez-Harbour et al.,

2001; Hissam et al., 2008).

Basically, the modifiability reasoning framework implements the functionalities of interpretation, evaluation and transformation (via tactics). This reasoning framework uses a module view as the architectural representation. Given a modifiability scenario, the interpretation translates those parts of the module view related to the scenario into a dependency graph suitable for CIA. After the interpretation, the graph will capture the responsibilities, design elements and design relationships that are affected by that scenario. The evaluation computes measures such as cost, cohesion, and coupling, over the elements of the graph. The main measure is the total cost of the change specified by the scenario. This cost is calculated using a formula from (Bachmann et al., 2004). A scenario is satisfied if the actual (predicted) cost is below the cost constraint given for the scenario.

Regarding architectural transformations, we equipped the reasoning framework with three modifiability tactics (Bachmann et al., 2007). The first tactic aims at reducing the cost of modifying a single (costly) responsibility by splitting it into children responsibilities. The second tactic aims at reducing the coupling between modules by inserting an intermediary that breaks module dependencies (an instance of this tactic was shown in Figure 5). The third tactic reduces the cost of two semantically-coherent responsibilities affected by the same change, by moving portions of the two responsibilities to a shared module. All the tactics are materialized through transformations that affect both the module view and the responsibility structure. Each tactic is also associated to a corresponding user question, which is shown by the ArchE GUI when the tactic is selected by the designer. The reasoning framework evaluates candidate tactics by means of screening rules. These rules codify heuristics for identifying problematic areas in the architecture based on the coupling, cohesion and cost of individual modules and responsibilities. In addition, the reasoning framework provides a graphical view that shows the modules and dependencies for the current architecture. This graphical view is useful for tracking the structural changes in the architecture as tactics are being applied.

The performance reasoning framework does not support tactics yet, and it only implements the functionalities of interpretation and evaluation (Bass et al., 2005). The interpretation converts a set of performance scenarios and responsibilities into an architectural format predefined by Lambda$_{WBA}$, which is subsequently translated to a MAST model (Gonzalez-Harbour et al., 2001). The first translation specifies architectural designs in the ICM language (Moreno and Merson, 2008). ICM (Intermediate Constructive Model) is an architectural description language targeted to performance analysis. An ICM design can be seen as a type of component-and-connector (C&C) view with a special focus on the flow of events across the system. The second translation happens inside Lambda$_{WBA}$. The evaluation relies on an implementation of Rate Monotonic Analysis (RMA) with varying priorities provided by MAST. The worst-case latency results are compared against the scenario responses to determine if the whole system is schedulable.

The Search Strategy

The search is divided between the ArchE Core and the reasoning frameworks. On one side, the ArchE Core is in charge of guiding the global search and making an evaluation of the candidate architectures coming from tactics. On the other side, each reasoning framework implements a local search in order to suggest appropriate tactics. Specifically, the search is structured around five commands that govern the interactions with the reasoning frameworks, namely:

- *ApplyTactics:* This asks a reasoning framework to apply a tactic to the current architecture. The tactic must come from a question that was previously shown to the designer and she agreed to apply (see *DescribeTactic* command below). The expected result after the command has been executed is to have a refinement of the current architecture in the repository.

- *AnalyzeAndSuggest:* This asks a reasoning framework to analyze (i.e., interpret and evaluate) the current architecture for scenarios of interest and to suggest new tactics if some scenarios are not fulfilled. The reasoning framework must return the analysis results and any tactics suggested to ArchE.

- *ApplySuggestedTactic:* This asks a reasoning framework to apply a tactic to the current architecture in order to create a new candidate architecture. The tactic must be one of the tactics that the reasoning framework suggested as a result of executing the *AnalyzeAndSuggest* command. The expected result is to have the candidate architecture in the design repository.

- *Analyze:* This asks a reasoning framework to analyze (i.e., interpret and evaluate) a candidate architecture for scenarios of interest. The reasoning framework must return the evaluation results to ArchE. These

Figure 9. Sample tree generated by the interaction of the designer with ArchE

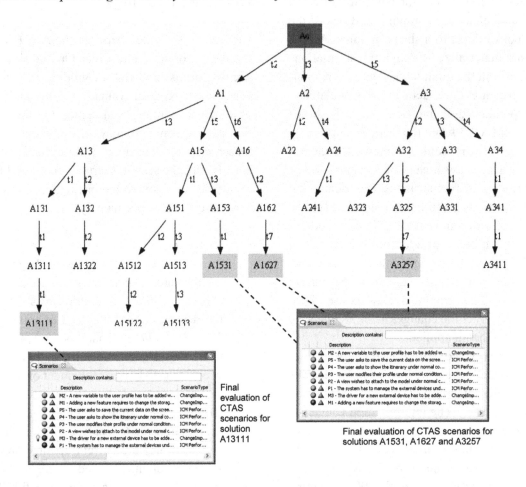

results are used by the ArchE Core to prioritize candidate architectures.

- ***DescribeTactic:*** This asks a reasoning framework to provide ArchE with user-friendly questions that describe tactics or any other recommendations.

The above commands permit to build a tree of alternative solutions that depart from the current architecture as the root of the tree. In this tree, each branch corresponds to a tactic and each node represents the architectural solution derived from that tactic. Figure 9 shows an example of the tree explored for CTAS, in which the architect has selected four candidate architectures (in grey).

Note the tradeoffs of the candidate architectures regarding the satisfaction of the scenarios.

Every time the user makes a change to the design or answers a question, the ArchE Core restarts the search so that the reasoning frameworks can adapt their proposals to the new situation. The search algorithm is a loop of five steps as follows. In step 1, if the change is a tactic to be applied, ArchE Core sends *ApplyTactics* to the reasoning framework that suggested the tactic. For example, our modifiability reasoning framework can insert an intermediary module upon a user's request, and then save this alternative in the repository. In step 2, for every reasoning framework, ArchE Core sends *AnalyzeAndSuggest* sequentially.

Each reasoning framework might modify the current architecture (if needed), in preparation for analysis. For example, our reasoning framework can decorate new responsibilities with costs (if that property is missing). Then, each reasoning framework starts its analysis of the architecture. If some scenarios are not fulfilled, each reasoning framework tries to find suitable tactics. For instance, our reasoning framework may run its change impact analysis, and propose a responsibility splitting as a tactic for certain modifiability scenario. In step 3, ArchE Core iterates over the list of suggested tactics, sending *ApplySuggested-Tactic* to the reasoning framework that generated each tactic. Then, for every reasoning framework, ArchE Core sends *Analyze* in parallel. In step 4, ArchE Core prioritizes all the evaluation results that came from applying suggested tactics. The evaluation results are displayed using the traffic light metaphor. For every reasoning framework, ArchE Core sends DescribeTactic in parallel. Each reasoning framework provides ArchE with questions describing tactics. For example, our reasoning framework would ask the designer to apply the tactic of splitting on a particular responsibility. In step 5, ArchE Core shows all the questions to the designer. The cycle goes back to step 1.

Figure 10 shows the four module views resulting from the search. For instance, solution A3257 shows the application of several tactics. An intermediary was inserted to manage the interactions of controllers with the application's model and the views. Since the responsibility "Query for data" had a high cost, it was split into two parts and assigned to separate modules. A shared portion of the resulting responsibilities dealing with the database was further separated and encapsulated in its own module. Most of the performance and modifiability scenarios were satisfied with this solution, except for scenario M1. There were other alternatives (like solution A1311) that fulfilled scenario M1, but at the cost of leaving M3 and some performance scenarios unsatisfied. Despite the results for M1, let's assume

here that the designer finally preferred solution A3257 as output of ArchE and input to the object-oriented materialization. The designer will then ask the SAME tool to explore object-oriented models that account for M1 when materializing architecture A3257.

Issues, Problems and Lessons Learned

The reliance of ArchE on reasoning frameworks favored integrability and modular reasoning about quality attributes. One of the research questions was the extent to which the interactions (i.e., dependencies) among quality-attribute techniques can be reduced. The current approach of ArchE decouples tradeoffs into two aspects. The first aspect has to do with the "traffic light" metaphor, so that the designer must decide on a tactic making a quality-attribute balance that is good enough for the scenarios. The second aspect comes from the interactions between reasoning framework through the repository. A simple source of tradeoffs is the parameters of responsibilities. For instance, when splitting a responsibility due to modifiability reasons, the modifiability reasoning framework creates child responsibilities that are added to the global responsibility structure. These new responsibilities may have an impact on the schedulability analysis in the performance reasoning framework. ArchE does not have yet mechanisms in place to help the user handle this second aspect of tradeoffs.

The implementations of the two reasoning frameworks, based on the CIA and RMA techniques respectively, allowed us to quickly explore an interesting number of alternatives for CTAS. A caveat regarding the reasoning frameworks mentioned in this section is that they are plausible but have not been fully validated yet. The validation of particular reasoning frameworks with respect to the scope and accuracy of its predictions is the job of the reasoning framework developer but not a portion of ArchE.

Since ArchE has limited searching capabilities, the tactics suggested by the tool were often local optima. In CTAS, we considered tactics as "leads" to alternatives rather than as definite architectural transformations to pursue. In general, a designer can trust the quality-attribute reasoning followed by ArchE when proposing tactics, but she does not have to agree on applying the best tactics found for satisfying the scenarios. The designer can use the architectures produced

Figure 10. Four alternative architectures for CTAS using ArchE

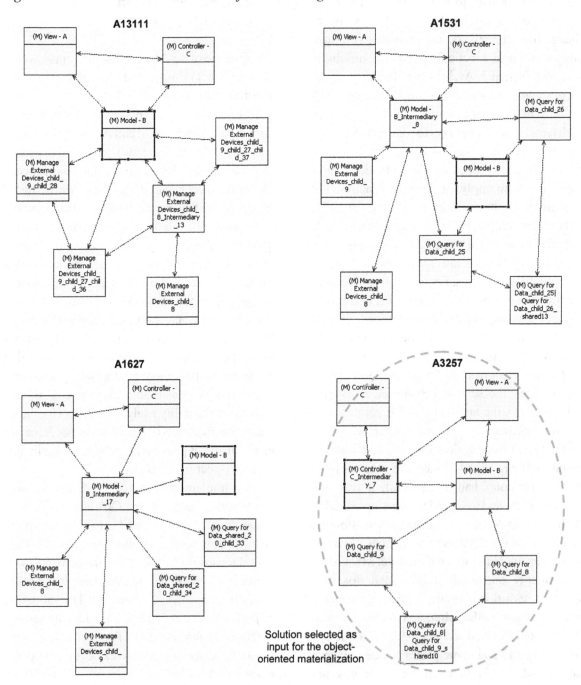

by ArchE as base solutions that, making evident their quality-attribute tradeoffs, can be refined into more realistic architectures.

Each reasoning framework searches for tactics that change the architectural structure. However, these tactics do not always guarantee an improvement of the evaluation function, because it depends on both the architectural configuration and tactic-specific parameters. For instance, when applying the tactic of splitting a responsibility, we must set the costs for the children responsibilities and the rippling probabilities for their dependencies. Different choices for these values lead to different instances of the same tactic, some of which reduce the cost of the change and some others do not. The problem of finding an adequate configuration of values for a given tactic is not trivial, and it needs heuristic search.

The experiments with CTAS exposed some usability drawbacks of the blackboard approach. A first issue is the processing overhead imposed by the centralized search strategy, because ArchE does not know the semantics of the user's actions. A second issue (related also to the search strategy) is that the reasoning framework activities for responding to the interaction commands have limited visibility through the ArchE GUI. Therefore, while ArchE is running, the designer can only handle or inspect reasoning framework features at specific points of the exploration process.

SAME: REUSING EXPERIENCES IN OBJECT-ORIENTED DESIGN

Once the architecture is established, the designer wants to consider object-oriented materializations that preserve the quality attributes prescribed by the architecture. Along this line, SAME is an expert tool developed at the ISISTAN Research Institute that focuses on the role of architectural connectors in the materialization. This relies on the fact that specific types of connectors lead to object-oriented implementation alternatives

embedding quality-attribute information. The assistance provided by SAME is not intended to generate a running implementation of the architecture; rather it supports designers in the construction of a UML skeleton from which they can later produce a final implementation of the system. To do so, the SAME tool mainly supports: (i) the definition and storage of materialization experiences, and (ii) reasoning capabilities for matching materialization experiences. We refer to a *materialization experience* as a pattern that combines three elements, namely: a connector characterization, a set of quality-attribute preferences, and the framelet describing the implementation of the connector using object-oriented constructs. The materialization experiences may come either from available connector-based pattern catalogs or from domain-specific designers' experiences.

SAME relies on the Case-based Reasoning (CBR) paradigm (Kolodner, 1993) in order to operationalize the way in which designers recall and apply connector-based materialization experiences to new architectures. Basically, the CBR technique emphasizes the role of prior experiences during future problem solving, by reusing and (if necessary) adapting the solutions to similar problems that were solved in the past. Consequently, a materialization experience is represented as a case that consists of two sections: the architectural problem and the object-oriented solution.

Figure 11 shows a snapshot of the SAME tool at work. Initially, the designer specifies her architecture and sets her preferences regarding quality attributes for the materialization. In our case study, the input for the materialization is a C&C specification of the CTAS architecture produced by ArchE (solution A3257 in Figure 10). The designer can manipulate the C&C specification using a UML editor offered by SAME. For example, the CTAS architecture is represented by the Model component plus the ItineraryManager and ServiceManager components, which interact with the Model and Profile-Database compo-

Figure 11. Edition of input architecture and retrieval of connector contexts in SAME

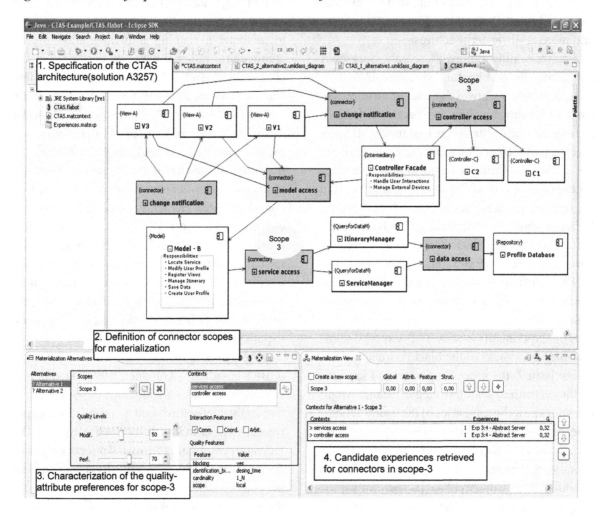

nents though the service-access connector. The interaction between the Controller-Façade and the controllers C1 and C2 is performed by the controller-access connector. Note that connectors are represented by stereotyped components in the diagram. The directed arrows are attachments between components and connectors, and the direction of the arrow indicates a service that a component requires from a connector.

SAME scans the input architecture and, for each connector, gathers information about its neighborhood. This neighborhood (or connector context) includes the target connector and its attached components. For example, we have the service-access and controller-access contexts in the Contexts combo. In the Materialization-Alternatives-View panel, the designer can characterize a connector context in terms of the features of the interaction protocol modeled by the connector. For instance, the 'blocking' feature indicates whether the connector blocks components in their interactions, or the 'identification-binding' feature specifies if the binding among interacting components is established at design-time or at runtime. Connectors sharing similar contexts are grouped into what we call a *scope*. For each scope, the designer can move the sliders of the Materialization-Alternatives-View panel to set the desired quality-attribute levels. Then, the CBR engine performs the retrieval and adaptation tasks. For each connector, the engine retrieves a collection of cases that are relevant to the current context. A case is said to be relevant if: (i) its problem section matches the current architectural context in terms of architectural structure and quality-attribute preferences, and (ii) its solution section describes potentially useful implementations in terms of the connector's interaction services. As we will explain later, both the quality-attribute preferences and feature information are used to compute a similarity measure between problem contexts.

The Materialization-View panel shows the list of cases that SAME proposes for the materialization of each connector context defined in the input architecture. For instance, given the quality-attribute preferences for Scope 3, SAME

has proposed an Abstract-server solution as the case that best matches those preferences. The designer is responsible for assessing the suitability of the materialization experiences, either by accepting or rejecting the proposed case. If the case meets the designer's expectations, the CBR engine will adapt the object-oriented solution of the retrieved case so that it effectively reifies the actual connector context. Conversely, if the proposed solution is inadequate, the designer can adjust the sliders and ask SAME for other cases. Furthermore, the designer may decide to create its own object-oriented solution for the connector context (eventually, based on an existing case) and save it as a new materialization experience.

The interaction between the designer and SAME results in different materialization alternatives. For instance, Figure 12 shows two materializations generated by the adaptation

Figure 12. Two outcomes of the materialization of the CTAS architecture

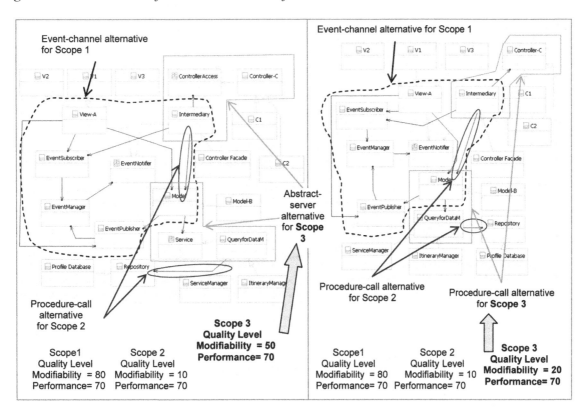

process for the scope of the service-access and controller-access connectors. SAME shows the resulting materializations using UML class diagrams. The first solution (on the right side of Figure 12) shows that the connector in scope 3 has been materialized through a Procedure-Call implementation that makes the Model and the Intermediary know about the type and number of elements that have to be notified. This alternative promotes performance requirements but hinders modifiability. The second solution, in turn, presents an Abstract-server implementation, which fosters modifiability by hiding data representation through an abstract interface. These two examples also show a correspondence with the features of the interaction protocols of both connectors.

The CBR Engine

SAME is designed as a knowledge-based system based on the CBR paradigm. As we mentioned before, a *case* documents a materialization experience in terms of a problem and a solution. The problem is the connector context along with predetermined quality-attribute levels for that context. The solution is a framelet implementing the

interaction services of the connector. The problem serves to the retrieval phase, whereas the solution serves to the adaptation phase. Figure 13 shows the architecture of SAME, which comprises five modules: the Architecture Editor, the UML Editor, the Knowledge Casebase, the CBR Engine and the Experience Manager. Figure 13 also shows two types of users: designer and system maintainer. The designer is in charge of defining the input architecture and interacting with the CBR Engine to derive object-oriented alternatives. The system maintainer is in charge of the administration of the Knowledge Casebase.

The Architecture Editor allows the designer to have C&C architectures as inputs to SAME. Analogously, the UML Editor is used to display the object-oriented alternatives that are outputs of SAME. The CBR Engine is the core component for the retrieval and adaptation of cases. These functionalities are implemented on top of JavaLog (Amandi et al., 2004), a framework integration between Java and Prolog. The CBR Engine interacts with the UML Editor to analyze the input architecture, and after generating a materialization using the cases stored in the Knowledge Casebase, the CBR Engine passes that solution to the UML

Figure 13. Main components of the SAME tool

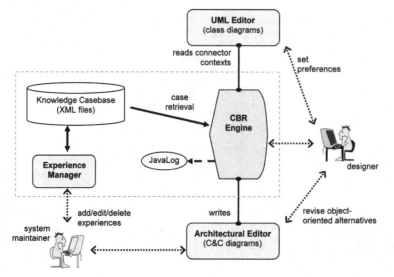

Editor. Before using SAME, the system maintainer needs to feed the Knowledge Casebase with an initial set of experiences. The system maintainer imports experiences into the Knowledge Casebase by means of the Experience Manager.

Similarity of Cases

To retrieve candidate cases, the CBR engine needs to know the degree of similarity between the current connector context and the contexts of the cases stored in the Knowledge Casebase. The comparison of problems is achieved by looking at three dimensions of a connector context: (i) the quality dimension, (ii) the feature dimension, and (iii) the structure dimension.

In the Materialization-Alternative-View depicted in Figure 11, the quality-attribute levels controllable by the sliders represent the *quality dimension* of the current case. The numerical scale ranges from 0 to 1, where 0 means no fulfillment and 1 represents full satisfaction of a quality attribute. The *feature dimension* is about the characteristics of the interaction protocol of the connector. Specifically, the interaction features state how the connector's interaction services are mapped (or need to be mapped) to object-oriented elements. For example, Scope 3 in Figure 11 shows the following features and values: blocking = 'yes', binding = 'design-time', cardinality = '1-to-N'.

The *structure* dimension specifies the configuration of the components attached to the connector in a particular case. Connectors have interfaces (also called roles in C&C languages) that identify components as participants of the interaction represented by the connector. Connector interfaces may have properties constraining the data flow among components and/or the control flow implied by the connector implementation. In order to check whether connectors are compatible or not, we look at the interaction services of the connectors, which are specified by the data/control properties of connector interfaces. Two connectors are compatible if one connector can be replaced by the other, and the original connector's interaction services are still provided after the substitution (probably with different levels of quality, though). The "substitutability" of connectors allows the CBR engine to search the casebase for a variety of compatible connectors that might solve a given materialization context.

Examples of connectors with different values in their dimensions are shown in Figure 14. Note that we can define variants of well-known connectors with subtle differences in their object-oriented materialization. For instance, a variation of the Event-channel connector shown in Figure 14 can be implemented with a blocking event-publication mechanism and/or with a remote access to the publisher and subscriber components.

The similarity metric ranges from 0 (for dissimilar materialization experiences) to 1 (for mostly identical ones). Given two cases, the retrieval algorithm applies a weighted sum of the similarities of their quality-attribute, feature and structure dimensions, according to the following formula:

$$GlobalSim(target, source) = w_1 * QualitySim(target, source) + w_2 * FeatureSim(target, source) + w_3 * StructureSim(target, source)$$

The *QualitySim()* function takes the Euclidean distance across the quality-attribute levels of the two cases. The *FeatureSim()* function iterates through pairs of interaction features from the assessed cases, and determines whether their values match each other. This function computes the feature dimension similarity as the ratio between the number of matching features and the number of evaluated features. The *StructureSim()* function evaluates the compatibility of the graphs of components and connectors given by the cases. This function measures the ratio between the number of matching components from the assessed cases and the average numbers of components in those

Figure 14. Problem specifications for four types of connectors

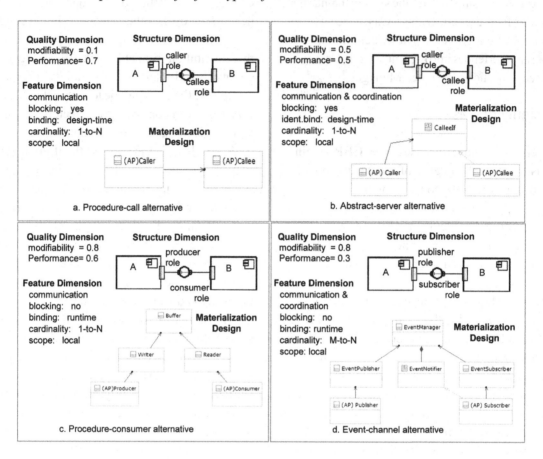

cases. That is, two components match each other when they have the same type and play compatible roles in the connector they are attached to. The weights of the similarity formula were determined through experimentation. Currently, we use the weights $\omega_1 = 0.4$, $\omega_2 = 0.3$ and $\omega_3 = 0.3$. The tool allows the system maintainer to modify the weights, in order to vary the result of the retrieval algorithm and get different rankings of cases. For instance, let's compare both the Event-channel ('modifiability'= 0.8 and 'performance' = 0.3) and Producer-consumer ('modifiability'=0.8 and 'performance'=0.6) experiences with the quality-attribute characterization of Scope 1 ('modifiability'= 0.8 and 'performance'= 0.7). When applying the similarity formula, the first experience ('similarity' = 0.70) scores better than

the second one (similarity = '0.53'). Although the details of the computation are beyond this article, we can say that the Producer-consumer presents more balanced levels of modifiability (0.8) and performance (0.6) than the Event-channel, but the latter favors modifiability, which is important to ensure the quality levels of the connectors in Scope 1. Because of this, SAME (in agreement with the designer) will use the solution part of the Event-channel experience to generate the corresponding materialization for all the connectors in Scope 1.

Adaptation of Cases

For the solution part of a case, SAME uses a specific model of collaboration among objects

Figure 15. Examples of interaction models representing object-oriented solutions (framelets)

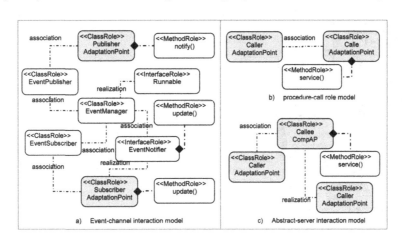

that we call *interaction model.* An interaction model can be seen as a collection of generic roles and relationships between roles, as developed in (Hammouda & Harsu, 2004; Hautamäki, 2005). Furthermore, an interaction model makes it possible to "generalize" the object-oriented solutions of concrete cases to arbitrary configurations of architectural elements (e.g., different number or types of components around a connector). Figure 15 shows three examples of interaction models for the Event-channel, Procedure-call and Abstract-server (we actually used these three cases to derive the two materializations of Figure 12).

Interaction models can be edited with the the UML Editor of SAME. A special type of role, called *adaptation point*, is used to bridge the materialization of a connector and the materializations of the concrete components around it. That is, an adaptation point is a placeholder in which the object-oriented elements that correspond to the components attached to a connector interface are hooked into the object-oriented elements reifying the interaction services provided by the connector. The UML Editor uses a notation extended with stereotypes to deal with roles and adaptation points.

The adaptation algorithm consists of five steps as follows. First, the CBR engine considers the interaction model of the best case produced by the retrieval phase. Second, the engine pulls from the Knowledge Casebase all the roles that are used to reify the components linked to each adaptation point of the new problem being solved. Third, the engine expands the adaptation points of the interaction model into regular roles, which are ready to be instantiated by concrete elements of the new problem. This expansion is dependent upon the concrete configuration of components around a target connector. Fourth, the engine iterates over all the adaptation points in the interaction model and injects their owned roles (e.g., methods or attributes) into the roles used to materialize the associated components. Finally, the engine replicates all the relationships that have an adaptation point as source or as destination, and creates new relationships that connect the materialization of the connector with the materialization of its attached components. This way, we can obtain an object-oriented skeleton that unifies the roles that reify the connector's interaction services and the roles reifying the involved components.

Figure 16 depicts how the adaptation algorithm uses the Event-channel interaction model shown in Figure 15 to derive the object-oriented materialization depicted in Figure 12, which corresponds to the materialization of the connectors of Scope 1. Here, the quality-attribute levels of Scope 1 lead to the retrieval of the Event-channel experience.

Figure 16. Adapting the event-channel interaction model to the change-notification connectors

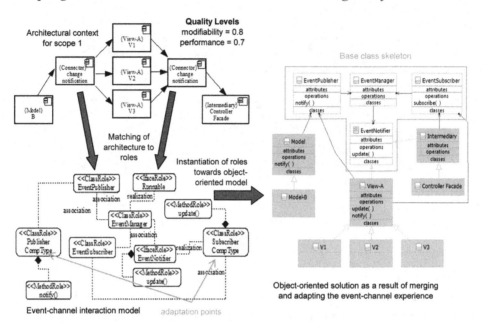

The Model component is then attached to the Publisher role of the first connector and its Subscriber role is played by the View components. These components are attached to the Publisher role of the second connector, in which the Intermediary plays the Subscriber role. During the adaptation of the Event-channel interaction model to the first connector, the Publisher adaptation point is instantiated by the Model class containing both the notify() method and the association to the EventPublisher class. In addition, the Publisher adaptation point is instantiated by the View class, which containing the update() method and the association to the EventSubscriber class. When considering the second connector, the adaptation algorithm injects the notify() method (which plays now the Publisher role) into the View class and creates the association to the EventPublisher class. The adaptation algorithm also creates the Intermediary class containing the update() method and an association to the EventSubscriber class, as a result of adapting the Subscriber role. Since both change-notification connectors share the same roles, only one instantiation of these roles

appears in the concrete object-oriented solution. Note that all the component instances are represented by subclasses that inherit from the component type class, so that the behavior of the components varies for component instances. At last, when the object-oriented skeleton satisfies the constraints captured in the interaction model of the Event-channel experience, we can see that the materializations of the architectural components interact with each other via an event-based mechanism.

Issues, Problems and Lessons Learned

The SAME tool provides a linkage between the architecture and the object-oriented worlds, in which the designer is given a variety of implementation choices for her architecture. In fact, SAME helped us to explore several possible CTAS implementations by mixing and matching the four connection types mentioned in Figure 14. We tried object-oriented materializations departing either from the original MVC architecture or from the transformed architecture produced by ArchE. The resulting materializations were mostly in agreement with the architectural problem they were supposed to solve. Furthermore, having connector-based design experiences helped us to keep a more explicit traceability of connector implementations in the object-oriented design. However, in some cases SAME generated awkward solutions, in which the relationship with quality-attribute characteristics was not apparent. We see three reasons for this problem. First, the similarity function used for case retrieval may have bias. Second, the adaptation procedure is limited to class structure. Third, the repository of cases needs to be periodically maintained.

Regarding case matching, the current similarity function considers a number of important dimensions that we have taken from connector catalogs and related literature. The challenge here is that the quantification of these dimensions in terms of attributes and values is not straightforward, because they depend upon the overall design context, the application domain and even the designer's perspective of the problem. As a consequence of this subjectivity, the results of the similarity function may become unexpected. We assigned a higher value to the weight for the quality dimension than to the weights of the structural and feature dimensions. This simple mechanism makes quality-attribute information prevail in the ranking of cases. However, we observed that an attribute-based Euclidean metric is not always capable of incorporating the whole design structure into the similarity computations.

When it comes to compatibility of components, SAME checks the components by looking at their roles when attached to connectors. This decision has pros and cons. On one side, the adaptation of cases gets simplified, because the interaction models are less complex to write and the adaptation procedure is easy to implement. Actually, although SAME provides an editor to create materialization experiences, the specification of interaction models is a highly manual

task. On the other side, a strong compatibility check would require the components to be also equivalent from a behavioral point of view. For instance, due to the lack of support for modeling architectural behavior, SAME cannot reason about a component that employs the roles of different connectors to realize certain responsibilities. Furthermore, this limitation prevents the generation of UML diagrams, such as sequence diagrams, that would complement the design information of UML class diagrams.

We also noticed that a benefit of SAME is that the repository of cases can be built incrementally. That is, a designer can draw her own materialization experience and add it to the repository, when SAME does not propose satisfactory alternatives. This support for customization helps designers to record the context in which a materialization is made, but it may also lead to a loss of precision in the CBR engine. In order to account for these situations, we had to establish a control policy for the repository of cases. This policy states that all the changes made by designers are subject to approval by the system maintainer. The system maintainer can accept or reject a new case, based on its coherence or overlap with existing cases.

FUTURE RESEARCH DIRECTIONS

Both the ArchE and SAME tools are not designed to perform an exhaustive or optimal search in the design space, but rather to point out good directions to the designer in that space. In our quality-driven approach, a "good direction" is one in which the building blocks used in the design solution are justified by quality-attribute means. Even though the solutions explored with ArchE and SAME are fewer and (sometimes) simpler than those from humans, we did observe that performance and modifiability concerns are really visible in the architectural and object-oriented models. In this context, future research for the two assistants will focus on enhancing the design advice with respect to recording design rationale and quality-attribute tradeoffs.

The two tool infrastructures were designed to provide placeholders for specialized search algorithms. Along this line, efficient search and optimization techniques that can take advantage of a quality-attribute design approach have to be investigated. Furthermore, we envision that the future search capabilities of ArchE and SAME should consider other objectives and constraints besides the optimization of scenario responses (e.g., utility, stability, cost, etc.). Two directions currently under research are the application of SAT solvers and human-guided search (Anderson et al., 2000).

We are also planning to incorporate model-driven techniques into the tools, in order to automate the transformations in reasoning frameworks and the adaptation of materialization experiences in the CBR engine. In this regard, Moreno and Merson (2008) have carried out a development for a performance reasoning framework, which is now being considered for ArchE.

As an extension of the pattern-based approach followed by SAME, we are analyzing the construction of a "design memory" for software organizations implementing architecture-centric practices. We think that SAME can provide a shared repository of pattern-based solutions which amalgamates the knowledge spread among the developers in the organization. A long-term goal of this research is to use this design memory in order to help organizations to standardize the design process.

Two direct opportunities for articulating ArchE and SAME appear in the horizon. The first opportunity has to do with the specification of the screening rules to recommend tactics in a reasoning framework. Currently, this knowledge is provided by expert designers at design time. A way of capturing that knowledge more easily is via CBR techniques. Even if rules for tactics already exist, the cases help to customize those rules to the designer's preferences. The reasoning

frameworks would invoke the CBR system and try to reuse tactics from past design problems to solve new problems. The second opportunity has to do with the designers that can judge the solutions produced by SAME in a subjective way. Because of this limitation, the retrieval and assessment of cases may have variations from one designer to another. A possible solution is to automate the quality-attribute criteria to assess the designs. Here, we conjecture that the reasoning frameworks (of ArchE) can provide automated test suites at the object-oriented level. This approach would ensure some degree of conformance between architecture and implementation.

Another promising line of research is the use of automated negotiation techniques (Fatima et al., 2004) for quality-attribute tradeoffs. A tradeoff resolution problem could be seen as a negotiation between different agents (i.e., reasoning frameworks). These agents could trade different architectural transformations for their design solution (i.e., architecture), reducing or increasing the utility of the quality-attribute scenarios associated to each agent, until an agreement on a design solution that balances the involved quality attributes is reached.

CONCLUSION

During the last decade, there has been much progress in design tools and architecture-centric design techniques. All these efforts have shed light on the constructive principles behind software design that, in our opinion, enable partial automations of the design process. Along this line, we argue that agent-based assistants constitute a promising engineering approach to support designers in making informed decisions during design explorations. In this chapter, we have discussed two assistive tools, ArchE and SAME, to improve software design activities by means of knowledge-based recommendations. These tools share the same quality-attribute design principles, although they work at different levels of abstraction: architecture design and object-oriented design.

In the realm of architecture design, the ArchE tool relies on a collection of reasoning frameworks that are focused on single quality attributes but work together in the creation and analysis of architectural designs. The SAME tool relies on the CBR paradigm as the computational support to derive an object-oriented model from a given architectural design. ArchE is good at exploring high-level design solutions in which the important concerns refer to allocation of functionality to components, externally visible properties of these components, and interaction between components. The added value of an architectural blueprint created with ArchE is its clear quality-attribute design rationale. On the other hand, SAME is good at capitalizing on low-level design experiences for object-oriented systems and producing implementation skeletons for architectural components out of these experiences. In both tools, the designer is still at the driving seat and makes the key design decisions for the system, but she can delegate to intelligent agents a number of routine computations resulting from her decisions.

There is a good synergy between the goal-driven approach of ArchE and the pattern-driven approach of SAME. The ArchE-SAME tool chain is a concept demonstration of how designers can ensure the conceptual integrity of the software architecture in downstream levels of design (and even implementation). Despite limitations and issues that should be addressed in future work, we think that the integration of ArchE and SAME in the context of the CTAS case study provides readers with a practical picture of the links between quality-attribute requirements, architectural and object-oriented solutions. As demonstrated in the development of the case study, the current prototypes have managed to work well in the exploration of architectures based on architectural patterns and the refinement of those architectures in terms of UML class diagrams. Furthermore, the Java-based infrastructures used to support ArchE and SAME have shown that intelligent agent technology pro-

vides good extendibility mechanisms for design tools that need to incorporate, and progressively update, their base of knowledge.

On the other hand, we can say that the implementation of a computational support for a design approach (like the ADD method or the object-oriented materialization method) forces us to re-think the ways in which one creates and reasons about design solutions. In that regard, we had an interesting experience using ArchE to teach software architecture concepts in a graduate design course at Clemson University (McGregor et al., 2007). Among other results, it was reported that the students felt positive about the use of ArchE because it relieved them from the computation aspects of quality-attribute models, fostering instead discussions about granularity of architectural representations or rationale behind particular architectural decisions. The questions and explanations produced by ArchE allowed the students to learn architectural principles more independently. We are planning to replicate the experience using the ArchE-SAME tool chain in a software architecture course at UNICEN University.

Finally, we envision the development of similar tool chains by others in the future, because the combination of tools will be more and more necessary to reduce the complexity of design explorations and make solutions more predictable regarding quality. We hope our work will stimulate researchers and practitioners to apply the design concepts and AI techniques behind ArchE and SAME to other software engineering domains.

REFERENCES

Amandi, A., Campo, M., & Zunino, A. (2004). JavaLog: A framework-based integration of Java and Prolog for agent-oriented programming. *Computer Languages, Systems and Structures (ex Computer Languages - An International Journal)*, *31*(1), 17-33. Elsevier

Anderson, D., Anderson, E., Lesh, N., Marks, J., Mirtich, B., Ratajczack, D., & Ryall, K. (2000). Human-guided simple search. In *Proceedings of National Conference on Artificial Intelligence* (pp. 209-216). Cambridge, MA: AAAI Press/ The MIT Press.

Bachmann, F., Bass, L., Bianco, P., & Klein, M. (2007). *Using ArchE in the classroom: One experience* (Tech. Note CMU/SEI-2007-TN-001). Pittsburgh, PA: Carnegie Mellon University, Software Engineering Institute.

Bachmann, F., Bass, L., & Klein, M. (2004). *Deriving architectural tactics: A step toward nethodical architectural design* (Tech. Rep. CMU/ SEI-2003-TR-004). Pittsburgh, PA: Carnegie Mellon University, Software Engineering Institute.

Bachmann, F., Bass, L., Klein, M., & Shelton, C. (2004). Experience using an expert system to assist an architect in designing for modifiability. In *Proceedings 5th Working IEEE/IFIP Conference on Software Architecture – WICSA'04* (pp. 281-284). Washington, DC: IEEE Computer Society.

Bachmann, F., Bass, L., Klein, M., & Shelton, C. (2005). Designing software architectures to achieve quality attribute requirements. *IEE Proceedings. Software, 152*(4), 153–165. doi:10.1049/ ip-sen:20045037

Bachmann, F., Bass, L., & Nord, R. (2007). *Modifiability tactics* (Tech. Rep. CMU/SEI-2007-TR-002). Pittsburgh, PA: Carnegie Mellon University, Software Engineering Institute.

Bass, L., Clements, P., & Kazman, R. (2003). *Software architecture in practice (2nd edition)*. Boston: Addison-Wesley Professional.

Bass, L., Ivers, I., Klein, M., Merson, P., & Wallnau, K. (2005). Encapsulating quality attribute knowledge. In *Proceedings 5th Working IEEE/ IFIP Conference on Software Architecture – WICSA'05* (pp. 193-194). Washington, DC: IEEE Computer Society.

Boehm, B., & In, H. (1996). Identifying quality-requirement conflicts. *IEEE Software, 13*(2), 25–35. doi:10.1109/52.506460

Bohner, S. A. (2002). Extending software change impact analysis into COTS components. In *Proceedings of 27th Annual NASA Goddard/IEEE Software Engineering Workshop - SEW'02* (pp. 175-182). Washington, DC: IEEE Computer Society.

Bosch, J., & Molin, P. (1999). Software architecture design: Evaluation and transformation. In *Proceedings of the 1999 IEEE Engineering of Computer Based Systems Symposium – ECBS'99* (pp. 4-10). Los Alamitos, CA: IEEE Computer Society.

Buschmann, F., Meunier, R., Rohnert, H., Sommerlad, P., & Stal, M. (1996). *Pattern-oriented software architecture. A system of patterns*. Chichester, UK: John Wiley & Sons Ltd.

Campo, M., Diaz-Pace, A., & Zito, M. (2002). Developing object-oriented enterprise quality frameworks using proto-frameworks. [Wiley]. *Software, Practice & Experience, 32*(8), 837–843. doi:10.1002/spe.462

Clarke, J., Dolado, J., Harman, M., Hierons, R., Jones, R., & Lumkinm, M. (2003). Reformulating software engineering as a search problem. *IEE Proceedings. Software, 150*(3). doi:10.1049/ ip-sen:20030559

Corkill, D. (2003). Collaborating software: Blackboard and multi-agent systems and the future. Invited paper presented at the *International Lisp Conference,* New York.

Díaz-Pace, A., Kim, H., Bass, L., Bianco, P., & Bachmann, F. (2008). Integrating quality-attribute reasoning frameworks in the ArchE design assistant. In Becker, Plasil & Reussner (Eds.), *Proceedings of the 4th International Conference on the Quality of Software Architecture – QoSA'08*, (LNCS 5281, pp. 171-188). Berlin: Springer-Verlag.

Díaz-Pace, J. A., & Campo, M. (2005). ArchMatE: From architectural styles to object-oriented models through exploratory tool support. In *Proceedings of the 20th Annual ACM SIGPLAN Conference on Object Oriented Programming, Systems, Languages, and Applications* (pp. 117-132). San Diego, CA: ACM Press.

Edwards, G., Seo, C., & Medvidovic, N. (2007). Construction of analytic frameworks for component-based architectures. In *Proceedings of the Brazilian Symposium on Software Components, Architectures and Reuse* - SBCARS'07 (pp. 147-160). Campinas, Sao Paulo, Brazil: Institute of Computing UNICAMP.

Fatima, S., Wooldridge, M., & Jennings, N. (2004). Optimal negotiation of multiple issues in incomplete information settings. In *Proceedings of the Third International Conference on Autonomous Agents and Multiagent Systems - AAMAS'04* (pp.1080-1087). New York: ACM Press.

Fayad, M., Schmidt, D., & Johnson, R. (1999). *Building application frameworks: object-oriented foundations of framework design*. Chichester, UK: John Wiley & Sons Ltd.

Fernandez, J. L. (1997). A taxonomy of coordination mechanisms used by real-time processes. In *Ada Letter, 7*(2), 29-54.

Fouqué, G., & Matwin, S. (1993). A Case-based approach to software reuse. [Amsterdam: Kluwer Academic Publishers.]. *Journal of Intelligent Information Systems, 2*(2), 165–197. doi:10.1007/BF00965876

Friedman-Hill, E. (2003). *Jess in action: Java rule-based systems*. Greenwich, CT: Manning Publications Company.

Gamma, E., Helm, R., Johnson, R., & Vlissides, J. (1994). *Design patterns: Elements of reusable object-oriented software*. Boston: Addison-Wesley.

Gero, J. S., & Kannengiesser, U. (2006). A framework for situated design optimization. In *Proceedings of Innovations in Design Decision Support Systems in Architecture and Urban Planning* (pp. 309-324). Dordrecht, the Netherlands: Springer.

Gomes, P., & Leitao, A. (2006). A tool for management and reuse of software design knowledge. In *Proceedings the 15th International Conference on Knowledge Engineering and Knowledge Management*, Podebrady, Czech Republic, (LNAI 4228). Berlin: Springer.

Gonzalez-Harbour, M., Gutierrez García, J. J., Palencia Gutiérrez, J. C., & Drake Moyano, J. M. (2001). MAST: Modeling and analysis suite for real time applications. In *Proceedings 13th Euromicro Conference on Real-Time Systems – ECRTS'01* (pp. 125-134). Washington, DC: IEEE Computer Society.

Grunske, L. (2006). Identifying "good" architectural design alternatives with multi-objective optimization strategies. In *International Conference on Software Engineering (ICSE), Workshop on Emerging Results* (pp. 849-852). New York: ACM Press.

Hammouda, I., & Harsu, M. (2004). Documenting maintenance tasks using maintenance patterns. In *Proceedings of the 8th European Conference on Software Maintenance and Reengineering* - CSMR'04 (pp. 37-47). Washington, DC: IEEE Computer Society.

Hautamäki, J. (2005). *Pattern-based tool support for frameworks: Towards architecture-oriented software development environment*. Ph.D. Thesis, Tampere University of Technology, Publication 521, Finland.

Hendrickson, S., Jett, B., & van der Hoek, A. (2006). A layered class diagrams: Supporting the design process. In *Proceedings of the 9th International Conference on Model Driven Engineering Languages and Systems - MoDELS'06* (pp. 722-736). Berlin: Springer.

Hissam, S. A., Moreno, G. A., Plakosh, D., Savo, I., & Stelmarczyk, M. (2008). Predicting the behavior of a highly configurable component based real-time system. In *Proceedings of 20th Euromicro Conference on Real-Time Systems – ECRTS'08* (pp. 57-68). Washington, DC: IEEE Computer Society.

Klein, M., Ralya, T., Pollak, B., Obenza, R., & Gonzalez-Harbour, M. (1993). *A practitioners' Handbook for real-time analysis: Guide to rate monotonic analysis for real-time systems*. Boston, MA: Kluwer Academic Publishers.

Kolodner, J. (1993). *Case-based reasoning*. San Francisco: Morgan Kaufmann Publishers, Inc.

Krasner, G., & Pope, S. (1988). A description of the model-view-controller user interface paradigm in the Smalltalk-80 system. *Journal of Object Oriented Programming, 1*(3), 26–49.

Ledeczi, A., Maroti, M., Bakay, A., Karsai, G., Garrett, J., Thomason, C., IV, et al. (2001). The generic modeling environment. *Workshop on Intelligent Signal Processing*. Budapest, Hungary. Retrieved from http://www.isis.vanderbilt.edu/projects/gme/

Maes, P. (1994). Agents that reduce work and information overload. *Communications of the ACM, 37*, 30–40. doi:10.1145/176789.176792

McGregor, J., Bachmann, F., Bass, L., Bianco, P., & Klein, M. (2007). Using an architecture reasoning tool to teach software architecture. In *Proceedings 20th Conference on Software Engineering Education & Training - CSEE&T'07* (pp. 275-282). Washington, DC: IEEE Computer Society.

Medvidovic, N., Mehta, N., & Mikic-Rakic, M. (2002). A family of software architecture implementation frameworks. In *Proceedings of the 3rd IEEE/IFIP Conference on Software Architecture: System Design, Development and Maintenance* (pp. 221-235). Washington, DC: IEEE Computer Society.

Mehta, N. R., Medvidovic, N., & Phadke, S. (2000). Towards a taxonomy of software connectors. In *Proceedings of the 22nd international Conference on Software Engineering – ICSE'00* (pp. 178-187). New York: ACM Press.

Mills, K., & Gomaa, H. (2002). Knowledge-based automation of a design method for concurrent systems. [Washington, DC: IEEE Computer Society.]. *IEEE Transactions on Software Engineering, 28*(3), 228–255. doi:10.1109/32.991319

Moreno, G., & Merson, P. (2008). Model-driven performance analysis. In Becker, Plasil & Reussner (Eds.), *Proceedings of the 4th International Conference on the Quality of Software Architecture – QoSA'08,* (LNCS 5281, pp. 171-188). Berlin: Springer-Verlag.

Pree, W., & Koskimies, K. (1999). Framelets - small is beautiful. In Fayad, Schmidth & Johnson (Eds.), *Building application frameworks: Object-oriented foundations of framework design*. Chichester, UK: John Wiley & Sons Ltd.

Robbins, J., Hilbert, D., & Redmiles, D. (1996). Extending design environments to software architecture design. *The International Journal of Automated Software Engineering (Special Issue: The Best of KBSE'96), 5*(3), 261-290.

Rumbaugh, J., Blaha, M., Premerlani, W., Eddy, F., & Lorensen, W. (1991). *Object-oriented modeling and design*. Englewood Cliffs, NJ: Prentice Hall International Inc.

Sangwan, R., Neill, C., El Houda, Z., & Bass, M. (2008). Integrating software architecture-centric methods into object-oriented analysis and design. *Journal of Systems and Software, 81*(5), 727–746. doi:10.1016/j.jss.2007.07.031

Schmidt, E. (2006). Model-driven engineering. *IEEE Computer, 39*(2), 25–31.

Shaw, M. (1996). Procedure calls are the assembly language of software interconnection: Connectors deserve first-class status, In *Proceedings of ICSE'93: Selected papers from the Workshop on Studies of Software Design* (pp. 17-32). Berlin: Springer-Verlag.

Shaw, M., & Garlan, D. (1996). *Software architecture, perspectives on an emerging discipline*. Englewood Cliffs, NJ: Prentice Hall International Inc.

Tekinerdogan, B. (2000). *Synthesis-based software architecture design*. PhD. Dissertation, University of Twente, Enschede, The Netherlands.

Tracz, W. (1995). DSSA (Domain-Specific Software Architecture): a pedagogical example. *SIGSOFT Software Engineering Notes, 20*(3), 49–62. doi:10.1145/219308.219318

Vazquez, G., Campo, M., & Diaz-Pace, A. (2008). A case-based reasoning approach for materializing software architectures onto object-oriented designs. In *Proceedings of the 2008 ACM Symposium on Applied Computing* (pp. 842-843). New York: ACM Press.

Waters, R., & Tan, T. (1991). Toward a design apprentice: Supporting reuse and evolution in software design. *SIGSOFT Software Engineering Notes, 16*(2), 33–44. doi:10.1145/122538.122543

Wikipedia (2008). *Software design*. Retrieved from http://en.wikipedia.org/wiki/Software_design

Wirfs-Brock, R., & McKean, A. (2003). *Object design: Roles, responsibilities and collaborations*. Boston: Addison-Wesley.

Wojcik, R., Bachmann, F., Bass, L., Clements, P., Merson, P., Nord, R., & Wood, B. (2006). *Attribute-Driven Design (ADD), Version 2.0* (Tech. Rep. CMU/SEI-2006-TR-023). Pittsburgh, PA: Carnegie Mellon University, Software Engineering Institute.

APPENDIX: ADDITIONAL READINGS

The Web page of the Software Engineering Institute on software architecture (http://www.sei.cmu. edu/architecture/index.html) provides a wide variety of resources and links, including definitions of software architecture, architecture design and quality attributes. A good book to get started is (Bass et al., 2003).

For more information about the ArchE project, the latest version of the ArchE tool (ArchE 3.0) for download, and documentation on how to develop reasoning frameworks for ArchE 3.0, please refer to http://www.sei.cmu.edu/architecture/arche.html

The use of tactics as basis for analysis of modifiability and performance is discussed in (Bachmann et al., 2004). A set of modifiability tactics and their relationships to Buschmann's catalog of patterns can be found in (Bachmann et al., 2007).

A recent update to the ADD method can be found in (Wojcik et al., 2006). Bosch & Molin (1999) provide an architectural design method that differs from ADD by first considering division to achieve functionality and the transforming this division to achieve other qualities.

In (Swgandan et al., 2008), the authors discuss how to combine ADD ideas with a traditional OO design, and present an interesting case study.

There are many good references to the UML. The work by (Rumbaugh et al., 1991) provides a useful and comprehensive introduction. For more information about UML2, refer to the Object Management Group Web page (http://www.omg.org/uml/).

A good coverage of the MVC pattern and its variants is given in (Krasner & Pope, 1988) and (Buschmann et al., 1996). The Blackboard pattern is also covered in (Buschmann et al., 1996). Corkill (2003) discusses the relationships between blackboard and multi-agent systems. A lot of material about object-oriented frameworks can be found in (Fayad et al., 1999).

Edwards et al. (2007) present an approach to transform component-based models into quality-attribute analysis models by means of model-driven engineering (MDE) techniques.

Gero's work on design theory discusses the issues of design assistants from a general perspective (Gero & Kannengiesser, 2006).

Section 4
Software Testing and Maintenance

Chapter 11
Constraint–Based Techniques for Software Testing

Nikolai Kosmatov
CEA LIST, Software Safety Laboratory, France

ABSTRACT

In this chapter, the authors discuss some innovative applications of artificial intelligence techniques to software engineering, in particular, to automatic test generation. Automatic testing tools translate the program under test, or its model, and the test criterion, or the test objective, into constraints. Constraint solving allows then to find a solution of the constraint solving problem and to obtain test data. The authors focus on two particular applications: model-based testing as an example of black-box testing, and all-paths test generation for C programs as a white-box testing strategy. Each application is illustrated by a running example showing how constraint-based methods allow to automatically generate test data for each strategy. They also give an overview of the main difficulties of constraint-based software testing and outline some directions for future research.

INTRODUCTION

Artificial intelligence (AI) techniques are successfully applied in various phases of software development life cycle. One of the most significant and innovative AI applications is using constraint-based techniques for automation of software testing.

Testing is nowadays the primary way to improve the reliability of software. Software testing accounts for about 50% of the total cost of software development (Ramler & Wolfmaier, 2006). Automated testing is aimed at reducing this cost. The increasing demand has motivated much research on automated software testing. Constraint solving techniques are commonly used in software testing since 1990's. They were applied in the development of several automatic test generation tools.

The underlying idea of constraint-based test generators is to translate the program under test, or its model, and the test criterion, or the test objective, into constraints. Constraint solving allows then to

DOI: 10.4018/978-1-60566-758-4.ch011

find a solution of the constraint solving problem and to obtain test data. The constraint representation of the program, interaction with a constraint solver and the algorithm may be different in each particular tool and depend on its objectives and test coverage criteria.

While learning about constraint-based techniques for the first time, we are often surprised to see that one constraint solver can so efficiently solve so different problems. For example, such as the famous SEND + MORE = MONEY puzzle (Apt, 2003), SUDOKU puzzles, systems of linear equations and many others, where a human would use quite different and sometimes very tricky methods. The intelligence of modern constraint solvers is not only in their ability to solve problems, but also in their ability to solve quite different kinds of problems. Of course, some solvers may be more adapted for specific kinds of problems.

In this chapter, we will discuss some innovative applications of constraint-based techniques to software engineering, in particular, to automatic test generation. We will focus on two particular applications: model-based testing as an example of black-box testing, and all-paths test generation for C programs as a white-box testing strategy. Each application will be illustrated by a running example showing how constraint-based methods allow to automatically generate test data for each strategy. We will also mention the main difficulties of constraint-based software testing and outline some directions for future research.

Organization of the Chapter

The chapter is organized as follows. We start by a short background section on software testing and describe the most popular test coverage criteria. The section on model-based testing contains an overview of the approach, an example of formal model and application of AI techniques to this example. Next, the section on all-paths test generation presents the generation method, its advantages and possible applications. We finish

by a brief description of future research directions and a conclusion.

BACKGROUND

The classical book *The Art of Software Testing* by G. J. Myers defines software testing as "the process of executing a program with the intent of finding errors" (Myers, 1979, p.5). In modern software engineering, various testing strategies may be applied depending on the software development process, software requirements and test objectives. In *black-box testing* strategies, the software under test is considered as a black box, that is, test data are derived without any knowledge of the code or internal structure of the program. On the other hand, in *white-box testing*, the implementation code is examined for designing tests. Different testing strategies may be used together for improved software development. For example, one may first use black-box testing techniques for *functional testing* aimed at finding errors in the functionality of the software. Second, white-box testing may be applied to measure the test coverage of the implementation code by the executed tests, and to improve it by adding more tests for non-covered parts.

Significant progress in software testing was done by applications of artificial intelligence techniques. Manual testing being very laborious and expensive, automation of software testing was the focus of much research since 1970's. Symbolic execution was first used in software testing in 1976 by L. A. Clarke (1976) and J. C. King (1976). Automatic constraint-based testing was proposed by R. A. DeMilli and A. J. Offutt (1991). Since then, constraint-based techniques were applied for development of many automatic test generation tools. Like in manual testing, various *test coverage (test selection) criteria* may be used to control automatic test generation and to evaluate the coverage of a given set of test cases. The possibility to express such criteria in constraints is the key property which allows to apply AI techniques and to automatically generate test cases. Let us briefly discuss coverage criteria used in model-based testing, where the criteria are applied to a formal model of the software under test. They can be classified into several families.

Structural coverage criteria exploit the structure of the model and contain several subfamilies. *Control-flow-oriented coverage criteria* focus on the control-flow aspects, such as the nodes and the edges, the conditional statements or the paths. Some examples for this family include the *all-statements criterion* (every reachable statement must be executed by some test case), the *all-branches criterion* (every reachable edge must be executed) and the *all-paths criterion* (every feasible path must be executed). *transition-based coverage criteria* focus on transitions and include, for example, the *all-transition-pairs* and the *all-loop-free-paths* coverage criteria. *Data-flow-oriented coverage criteria* concentrate on the data-flow information such as *definitions* of variables (where a value is assigned to a variable) and their *uses* (i.e. expressions in which this value is used). So, the *all-definitions criterion* requires to test at least one possible path from each definition of a variable to one of its possible uses. The *all-uses criterion* states that at least one path from each definition of a variable to each of its possible uses must be tested. The *all-def-use-paths criterion* requires to test each possible path from each definition of a variable to each of its possible uses.

The second big family of criteria contains *data coverage criteria* used to choose a few test cases from a large data space. *Statistical data coverage* requires some statistical properties for the chosen test cases (e.g. respecting a given statistical distribution), whereas *boundary coverage* looks for test cases situated on the boundary of the data space. Several boundary coverage criteria were formalized in (Kosmatov, Legeard, Peureux, & Utting, 2004). Some of them may be formulated as optimization problems (e.g. minimization of

a cost function on a given data space), and are suitable for constraint solvers. A data coverage criterion may be applied in combination with a structural coverage criterion as follows: for each test target required by the structural criterion (e.g. statement, branch or path), the choice of test cases covering this target must satisfy the data coverage criterion.

Fault-based coverage criteria are aimed at detecting certain types of frequent faults in the system under test. For example, *mutation coverage* checks if test cases efficiently detect errors in *model mutants,* that is, erroneous versions of the original model obtained from it by introducing *mutations.* Some examples of mutations are confusions between =, >, ≥, <, ≤ and ≠, or between operations + and −, which are considered as frequent faults.

Similar criteria may be used in white-box testing strategies, where they are applied directly to the program code rather than to its model. The reader will find a good general overview of test coverage criteria in (Zhu, Hall, & May, 1997). A. P. Mathur's book (2008) describes modern techniques of software testing. An introduction to constraint programming techniques may be found in K. Apt's book (2003).

MODEL-BASED TESTING

Overview and Benefits of the Approach

Model-based testing is a variant of testing that relies on an explicit model describing the desired behavior of the system under test (SUT). The model is based on the requirements or existing specification documents for the SUT. It is also called *a formal model* or *an abstract model* since it formalizes an informal specification of the SUT and usually focuses on its most important aspects without describing all implementation details.

Various notations may be used to write models. *State-based or Pre/Post notations* (such as B, Z, VDM, JML) model the SUT by a collection of state variables, which define the current state of the system, and some operations, modifying the variables. The operations are usually described by a precondition, which must be verified before executing the operation, and a postcondition, defining the result of its execution.

Transition-based notations include finite-state machines, labeled transition systems, statecharts, UML State Machines, etc. They focus on the transitions between different states of the SUT. They are based on graphical representation, where the nodes represent the states and the edges represent the operations.

Operational notations are used to describe distributed systems and communication protocols. They include process algebras and Petri nets. *Data-flow notations,* such as Lustre, focus on the data rather than on the control flow. A complete classification of model notations can be found in (van Lamsweerde, 2000).

After writing and validating the model and choosing a test coverage criterion, an automatic model-based testing tool is used to generate test cases. A test case includes input data and expected behavior of the system, also called *an oracle.* In model-based testing, as its name suggests, test cases are derived from the model, without any knowledge of the implementation's source code, so this approach is part of *black-box testing.* Next, test cases are transformed into executable tests, executed on the SUT, and the results are analyzed. The reader will find more on automated test execution in the book (Mosley & Posey, 2002).

Although creating an explicit model of the system under test is an additional task unnecessary for manual testing, the effort is recompensed by the benefits of model-based testing. Its main advantage is the possibility of automation. A model-based testing tool uses constraint-based techniques to transform the test generation problem for a given model with a chosen coverage criterion into a number of constraint problems (test targets), and calls a constraint solver to find a solution for each problem. Each solution provides one test input and is completed by a test preamble and an oracle to obtain a test case. Some test targets may be unreachable: their constraints are incompatible and describe a situation that can never occur according to the model. It can happen because the chosen coverage criterion does not take into account the properties of a particular model. For example, the all-transition-pairs coverage criterion requires to activate every pair of adjacent transitions at least once, but the constraint solver will not find a solution for a pair of transitions (t_i, t_j) if t_j can never be executed after t_i in the model (e.g. when the precondition of t_j is incompatible with the postcondition of t_i). The example in the next section will illustrate how constraint-based techniques are used in model-based testing tools for automatic test generation.

To finish our overview of model-based testing, let us cite other benefits of this approach. Systematic and repeatable automated model-based testing reduces testing cost and time. It makes it easier to handle requirements evolution by modifying the model and regenerating test cases. Unlike in manual testing, the quality of generated test cases is not so much dependent on the competence and experience of the test engineer. The engineer may interact with the model-based testing tool to focus the generation on some particular part of the model, specify some special kinds of test cases, control their number and the desired coverage criteria. Writing a model of the SUT also allows to detect possible errors in the requirements and encourages early modeling. We refer the reader to the book (Utting & Legeard, 2006) for a practical guide to the process of model-based testing, its benefits and several applications.

Figure 1. B model of a process scheduler

```
MACHINE
  SCHEDULER
SETS
  PID = {p1, p2, p3, p4}
VARIABLES
  active, waiting, ready
INVARIANT
  active ⊆ PID ∧
  waiting ⊆ PID ∧
  ready ⊆ PID ∧
  card(active) ≤ 1 ∧
  active ∩ waiting = ∅ ∧
  waiting ∩ ready = ∅ ∧
  active ∩ ready = ∅ ∧
  (active = ∅) ⟹ (ready = ∅)

INITIALIZATION
  active, waiting, ready := ∅, ∅, ∅

OPERATIONS
  new(pp)=
    PRE
      pp ∈ PID ∧
      pp ∉ (active ∪ waiting ∪ ready)
    THEN
      waiting := (waiting ∪ {pp})
    END;
```

```
ready(pp)=
  PRE
    pp ∈ waiting
  THEN
    waiting := (waiting \ {pp})  ||
    IF (active = ∅) THEN
      active := {pp}
    ELSE
      ready := ready ∪ {pp}
    END
  END;
swap=
  PRE
    active ≠ ∅
  THEN
    waiting := waiting ∪ active  ||
    IF (ready = ∅) THEN
      active := ∅
    ELSE
      ANY pp
      WHERE pp ∈ ready THEN
        active := {pp}
        ready := ready \ {pp}
      END
    END
  END
END;
```

An Example: Formal Model of a Process Scheduler

To show how constraint-based techniques are used in model-based testing tools we consider an example studied in (Legeard, Peureux, & Utting, 2002). Figure 1 shows a formal model written in B notation, also called *a B abstract machine*. It contains state variables, operations and invariant properties that should be satisfied at each moment. For convenience of the reader, specific B notation for set operations and relations is replaced here by the common mathematical notation.

This model describes a simplified uniprocessor scheduler. At every moment, at most one process may be executed by the processor. When several processes are ready to be executed, they are scheduled in turn one after another. The constant *PID* is the set of all possible process identifiers. The variable *active* represents the set containing the active process, or the empty set when no process is executed (on a real processor, the system idle pro-

cess is executed). The variable *ready* represents the set of processes ready to be scheduled. The variable *waiting* contains the set of processes not ready to be scheduled (e.g. waiting for a disk read request, an input, an authorization to continue or some other event). The sets *active, waiting* and *ready* must be always disjoint and are initially empty. Their union is the set of currently existing processes in the system. The last line in the invariant states that the system may have no active process only if no process is ready to be executed. In this example, the system idle process is not modeled, and only four processes with three operations are considered. The operation **new** adds a process not yet existing in the system into *waiting*. The operation **ready** is executed when some waiting process gets ready, or is allowed, to continue execution: this process is moved into *active* if no process is active at this moment, or into *ready* otherwise. To ensure that all ready processes are executed in turn, the operation **swap** is called regularly to move the active process into *waiting* and, if there

Figure 2. Schema of process moves in the scheduler model

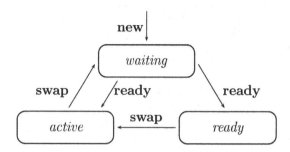

are some ready processes, to move one of them into *active*. A schema of possible process moves and operations is shown in Figure 2. This model was validated using AtelierB, the well-formedness conditions (e.g. respecting the invariant) were generated and proved automatically.

Constraint Solving in Model-Based Testing

Let us now illustrate on the model of Figure 1 how constraint-based techniques are used in model-based testing tools, such as the academic tool BZTT (Ambert et al., 2002) or its industrial version for UML models Test Designer (Smartesting, 2008). First, some test coverage criteria must be selected for test generation. For our example, we choose the all-branches criterion of structural coverage combined with the boundary coverage criterion which requires for each test target to choose two boundary test cases using the min/max heuristic with the cost function f:

$$f = \text{card}(active) + \text{card}(waiting) + \text{card}(ready).$$

In other words, the cost function should achieve its maximum and minimum on some test cases for each target. So, two test cases are in general necessary for a reachable test target (or just one if $\max(f) = \min(f)$ for the target).

The test generation session proceeds as follows.

- (Step 1) First, the model is parsed and the operations are translated into a set of *Before-After predicates* (also called *Pre/Post, or effect predicates*). Each operation may be decomposed into several simpler predicates, for example, using the disjunctive normal form of the model. The degree of decomposition depends on the desired coverage.

Let $\mathfrak{I}$ denote the invariant of the model. Figure 3 shows the generated Before/After predicates. Their Before parts form a partition of the original operations' preconditions. The After part defines the new values of state variables, where the new value of a variable v after the operation is denoted by v'. The operation **new** is expressed by P1, **ready** is decomposed into P2 and P3, and **swap** into P4 and P5.

- (Step 2) Next, each test target that must be covered according to the selected criteria is expressed as a constraint problem. A constraint solver is called to find a solution for the problem.

Test targets and the way the constraint solver is applied to solve them depend on the coverage criteria. The all-branches criterion requires to test each edge in the operations. In our example, we need to cover the test targets $TG_i = Before_i$ ($1 \leq i \leq 5$). Moreover, the combination with the chosen boundary coverage criterion requires to find for each TG_i one solution to minimize f and another one to maximize f, so the five test targets TG_i should be split into ten more specific test targets:

$$TG_i^{min} = Before_i \wedge (f \rightarrow \min) \text{ and } TG_i^{max} = Before_i \wedge (f \rightarrow \max).$$

Figure 4 shows possible solutions that might be generated for these targets by a constraint solver with sets like that of the BZTT tool. The figure contains the system state S_k from which the

Figure 3. Before/After predicates for the scheduler model

P_i	$Before_i$	$After_i$
P_1	$\mathfrak{I} \wedge pp \in PID \wedge$ $pp \notin (active \cup waiting \cup ready)$	$active' := active \wedge$ $waiting' := waiting \cup \{pp\} \wedge$ $ready' := ready$
P_2	$\mathfrak{I} \wedge pp \in waiting \wedge active = \emptyset$	$active' := \{pp\} \wedge$ $waiting' := waiting \setminus \{pp\} \wedge$ $ready' := ready$
P_3	$\mathfrak{I} \wedge pp \in waiting \wedge active \neq \emptyset$	$active' := active \wedge$ $waiting' := waiting \setminus \{pp\} \wedge$ $ready' := ready \cup \{pp\}$
P_4	$\mathfrak{I} \wedge active \neq \emptyset \wedge ready = \emptyset$	$active' := \emptyset \wedge$ $waiting' := waiting \cup active \wedge$ $ready' := ready$
P_5	$\mathfrak{I} \wedge active \neq \emptyset \wedge pp \in ready$	$active' := \{pp\} \wedge$ $waiting' := waiting \cup active \wedge$ $ready' := ready \setminus \{pp\}$

operation B_k (*the test body*) must be executed. The expected result of the execution (*the oracle*) obviously follows from the Before/After predicates of Figure 3 and is not shown here.

- (Step 3) Next, test preambles are generated and final test cases are created.

Notice that Figure 4 does not contain complete test cases. Indeed, to execute the operation B_k on the state S_k, we first have to get the SUT into the correct state. It is done by *a test preamble,* i.e. a sequence of operation calls prior to the test body

execution. Again, constraint-based algorithms may be used to automatically find test preambles for generated test data. For example, the preamble for the state S_1 is empty since S_1 is the initial state of the SUT. A possible preamble for S_2 is **new**(*p1*), **new**(*p2*), **ready**(*p1*), **new**(*p3*). Test preambles for the other S_k are computed similarly.

- (Step 4) Finally, the test cases are executed on the SUT. The results are analyzed.

In practice, a test case of a complete test suite may also contain an observation step (describ-

Figure 4. Solutions for test targets TG_i^{min}, TG_i^{max} generated by constraint solving

k	Target	System state S_k	Test body B_k
1	TG_1^{min}	$active = \emptyset,\ waiting = \emptyset,\ ready = \emptyset$	**new**($p1$)
2	TG_1^{max}	$active = \{p1\},\ waiting = \{p2, p3\},\ ready = \emptyset$	**new**($p4$)
3	TG_2^{min}	$active = \emptyset,\ waiting = \{p1\},\ ready = \emptyset$	**ready**($p1$)
4	TG_2^{max}	$active = \emptyset,\ waiting = \{p1, p2, p3, p4\},\ ready = \emptyset$	**ready**($p1$)
5	TG_3^{min}	$active = \{p1\},\ waiting = \{p2\},\ ready = \emptyset$	**ready**($p2$)
6	TG_3^{max}	$active = \{p1\},\ waiting = \{p2, p3, p4\},\ ready = \emptyset$	**ready**($p2$)
7	TG_4^{min}	$active = \{p1\},\ waiting = \emptyset,\ ready = \emptyset$	**swap**
8	TG_4^{max}	$active = \{p1\},\ waiting = \{p2, p3, p4\},\ ready = \emptyset$	**swap**
9	TG_5^{min}	$active = \{p1\},\ waiting = \emptyset,\ ready = \{p2\}$	**swap**
10	TG_5^{max}	$active = \{p1\},\ waiting = \{p2, p3\},\ ready = \{p4\}$	**swap**

Figure 5. Function min3 returning the minimum in the given array

```
1    //returns minimum in given three-element array a
2    int min3(int a[3]){
3      int min=a[0];
4      if( min > a[1] )
5        min=a[1];
6      if( min > a[2] )
7        min=a[2];
8      return min; }
```

ing how to observe the result on the SUT) and a postamble (resetting the SUT to some state allowing the execution of the following test case). Constraint-based techniques may be also used for postamble computation. We do not model observation and reset operations in our example and do not detail these steps.

ALL-PATHS TEST GENERATION FOR C PROGRAMS

Description of the Method

In the previous section, we have seen how constraint-based techniques are used for test generation in model-based testing, a strategy of black-box testing. This section discusses an advanced technique of white-box testing, where an ingenious combination of constraint logic programming, constraint-based symbolic execution and concrete execution allows to generate test cases for a C function for the all-paths coverage criterion. This technique (with various modifications) was used in several testing tools: PathCrawler developed at CEA LIST (Williams, Marre, & Mouy, 2004; Williams, Marre, Mouy, & Roger, 2005), DART (Godefroid, Klarlund, & Sen, 2005), CUTE (Sen, Marinov, & Agha, 2005), SimC (Xu & Zhang, 2006) and EXE (Cadar, Ganesh, Pawlowski, Dill, & Engler, 2006).

In practice, all-paths coverage can be unrealistic for some programs. For example, if the number of iterations of some loop is determined by an input variable, the all-paths criterion requires exhaustive testing for this input variable. That is why path-oriented testing tools propose weaker versions of this criterion. For instance, given a parameter n, CUTE looks for different paths with a difference in the first n instructions, while PathCrawler can be restricted to paths in which every loop has at most n consecutive iterations. The generation methods for these weaker criteria are easily obtained by slight modifications of the all-paths test generation method.

We will use as a running example the C function shown in Figure 5. The function min3 takes one parameter, an array a of three integers, and returns the minimal value in the array. To simplify the example, we restrict the domain of elements of a to [0, 10].

For test case generation, the user needs to define *a precondition*, i.e. the conditions on the program's input for which the behavior is defined. Here, the precondition contains the definition of the variables' domains. The user can also provide an oracle function to check on-the-fly, during the concrete execution of every generated test case, whether the observed behavior of the program is correct. We assume the oracle is provided, and focus on the generation of test data.

A decision is denoted by the line number of the condition followed by a "+" if the condition is true, and by a "−" otherwise. We can denote an execution path by a sequence of line numbers, e.g. 3, 4⁻, 6⁺, 7, 8. The mark "*" after a condition indicates that the other branch has already been explored (it will be explained in detail below).

Let us now describe a simplified version of the PathCrawler method (following the presentation in (Kosmatov, 2008)). It needs an instrumented version of the program under test to trace the execution path. The main loop in the PathCrawler method is rather simple. Given a partial program path π, also called below *a path prefix,* the main idea is to symbolically execute it in constraints. PathCrawler uses COLIBRI, an efficient constraint solver developed at CEA LIST and shared with two other testing tools: GATeL (Marre & Arnould, 2000) and OSMOSE (Bardin & Herrmann, 2008). A solution of the resulting constraint solving problem will provide a test case exercising a path starting by the prefix π. Then the trick is to use concrete execution of the test case on the instrumented version to obtain the complete path. The path prefixes are explored in a depth-first search.

To symbolically execute a program in constraints, the PathCrawler tool maintains:

- A memory map that represents the program memory state at every moment of symbolic execution. It can be seen as a mapping which associates a value to a symbolic name. The symbolic name may be a variable name or an array element. The value may be a constant or a logical variable.

- Current path prefix π in the program under test. When a test case is successfully generated for the prefix π, the remaining part of the path it activates is denoted σ.

- A constraint store containing the constraints added during the symbolic execution of the current prefix π.

The method contains the following steps:

- Initialization: Create a logical variable for each input and associate it with the input. Set initial values of initialized variables. Add constraints for the precondition. Let the initial prefix π be empty. Continue to (Step 1).

- (Step 1) Let σ be empty. Execute symbolically the path π, that is, add constraints and update the memory according to the instructions in π. If some constraint fails, continue to (Step 4). Otherwise, continue to (Step 2).

- (Step 2) Call the constraint solver to generate a test case, that is, concrete values for the inputs, satisfying the current constraints. If it fails, go to (Step 4). Otherwise, continue to (Step 3).

- (Step 3) Run traced execution of the program on the test case generated in the previous step to obtain the complete execution path. The complete path must start by π. Save the remaining part into σ. Continue to (Step 4).

- (Step 4) Let ρ be the concatenation of π and σ. Try to find in ρ the last unmarked decision, i.e. the last decision without a "*" mark. If ρ contains no unmarked decision, exit. Otherwise, if $x^{\pm}$ is the last unmarked decision in ρ, set π to the subpath of ρ before $x^{\pm}$, followed by the negation of $x^{\pm}$ marked by a "*" as already processed, and continue to (Step 1).

Notice that Step 4 chooses the next path prefix in a depth-first search. It changes the last unmarked decision in ρ to look for differences as deep as possible first, and marks a decision by a "*" when its negation (i.e. the other branch from this node in the tree of all execution paths) has already been fully explored. For example,

if $\rho = a^{-}_{*}, b, c^{+}, d, e^{+}_{*}, f$,

the last unmarked decision is c^{+}, so we take the subpath of ρ before this decision a^{-}_{*}, b, and add c^{-}_{*} to obtain the new prefix $\pi = a^{-}_{*}, b, c^{-}_{*}$.

Figure 6. Depth-first generation of all-paths tests for the function min3 of Figure 5

(1) Memory	Constraints
$a[0] \rightarrow X_0$	$\langle precond \rangle$
$a[1] \mapsto X_1$	
$a[2] \mapsto X_2$	
$\pi = \epsilon$	

$\leadsto$

Test case 1
$X_0 = 3$
$X_1 = 7$
$X_2 = 2$
$\sigma = 3, 4^-, 6^+, 7, 8$

$\rightarrow$

(2) Memory	Constraints
$a[0] \mapsto X_0$	$\langle precond \rangle$
$a[1] \mapsto X_1$	$X_0 \leq X_1$
$a[2] \mapsto X_2$	$X_0 \leq X_2$
$min \mapsto X_0$	
$\pi = 3, 4^-, 6^-_\star$	

$\leadsto$

Test case 2
$X_0 = 2$
$X_1 = 8$
$X_2 = 3$
$\sigma = 8$

$\rightarrow$

(3) Memory	Constraints
$a[0] \mapsto X_0$	$\langle precond \rangle$
$a[1] \mapsto X_1$	$X_0 > X_1$
$a[2] \mapsto X_2$	
$min \mapsto X_0$	
$\pi = 3, 4^+_\star$	

$\leadsto$

Test case 3
$X_0 = 5$
$X_1 = 1$
$X_2 = 10$
$\sigma = 5, 6^-, 8$

$\rightarrow$

(4) Memory	Constraints
$a[0] \mapsto X_0$	$\langle precond \rangle$
$a[1] \mapsto X_1$	$X_0 > X_1$
$a[2] \mapsto X_2$	$X_1 > X_2$
$min \mapsto X_1$	
$\pi = 3, 4^+_\star, 5, 6^+_\star$	

$\leadsto$

Test case 4
$X_0 = 6$
$X_1 = 4$
$X_2 = 3$
$\sigma = 7, 8$

Test Generation for min3

We apply this method to our example and show in Figure 6 how it proceeds. In this figure, the arrows in the column "Memory" indicate the memory mapping, a wavy arrow denotes the application of Step 2 and Step 3, and "$\rightarrow$" denotes the application of Step 4 and Step 1. The empty path is denoted by ε.

In the state (1) in Figure 6, we see that the initialization step associates a logical variable to each input, i.e. to each element of a, and posts the precondition <precond> to the constraint store. Here, <precond> denotes the constraints:

X_0 in [0, 10], X_1 in [0, 10], X_2 in [0, 10].

As the original prefix π is empty, Step 1 is trivial and adds no constraints. Step 2 chooses a first test case. It can be shown that this choice is not important for a complete depth-first search, so we use random generation here. Some solvers may follow deterministic strategies, e.g. minimal values first. In Step 3, we retrieve the complete path traced during the concrete execution of Test case 1, and obtain σ = 3, 4⁻, 6⁺, 7, 8.

Step 4 sets ρ = 3, 4⁻, 6⁺, 7, 8 and, therefore, the new path prefix π = 3, 4⁻, 6⁻ₓ, by negating the last not-yet-negated decision. Now, Step 1 symbolically executes this path prefix in constraints for unknown inputs, and the resulting state is shown in (2). Let us explain this execution in detail. First, the execution of the assignment 3 stores X_0 as the value of min in the memory map since

X_0 is the current value of a[0]. The execution of the decision 4^- adds the constraint $X_0 \leq X_1$ after replacing the variable min by its current value in the memory map X_0. Similarly, the execution of 6^-_* adds the constraint $X_0 \leq X_2$.

During symbolic execution, evaluation routines are called each time when it is necessary to find the current value of an expression (r-value) or the correct symbolic name of the variable being assigned (l-value). The evaluation of complex expressions may introduce additional logical variables and constraints. For instance, if we had an assignment z = a[0] + 5*a[2], its symbolic execution now would create two new logical variables Y and Z, write Z as the value of z in the memory map and post two new constraints: $Y = 5X_2$ and $Z = X_0 + Y$.

Next, Step 2 generates Test case 2, and Step 3 executes it and finds $\sigma = 8$. We are now going from (2) and Test case 2 to (3) in Figure 6. Step 4 computes the complete path $\rho = 3, 4^-, 6^-_*, 8$. As 6^-_* means that its negation has already been explored, the new prefix π is 3, 4^+_*. Step 1 symbolically executes this partial path as shown in (3).

Next, Step 2 generates Test case 3. Step 3 finds $\sigma = 5, 6^-, 8$. We are now moving from (3) and Test case 3 to (4) in Figure 6. Step 4 computes the new prefix $\pi = 3, 4^+_*, 5, 6^+_*$. Step 1 executes π symbolically and updates the memory state and the constraint store as shown in (4). By Step 2 and Step 3, we obtain Test case 4 and the new path end $\sigma = 7, 8$. Finally, Step 4 exits since the whole path $\rho = 3, 4^+_*, 5, 6^+_*, 7, 8$ does not have any unmarked decision. In other words, all the paths have been explored.

Advantages and Applications of All-Paths Testing

The presented method of all-paths test generation mixing symbolic and concrete execution has the following benefits:

- **Soundness**. Concrete execution of the generated test cases on the instrumented code allows to check that each test case really executes the path for which it was generated.

- **Completeness**. If the program has finitely many paths (in particular, all loops are bounded, as it is often required in critical software), depth-first search allows to iterate over all paths of the program. However, this property can be achieved in practice on a program only when symbolic execution of all features of the program is correct and when constraint solving for its paths terminates within a reasonable timeout.

- **Incrementality.** Depth-first search allows us to reuse as much as possible the results of symbolic execution. Each instruction of any given path prefix is executed exactly once, independently of how many paths start by this prefix. This encourages the use of constraint logic programming, which offers backtracking.

- **Fast entry.** Concrete execution of instrumented code permits to quickly deduce a complete feasible path in the program.

All these qualities make this method one of the most scalable test generation methods until now. Moreover, its applications are not limited to software testing of C programs.

PathCrawler has been adapted by N. Williams (2005) to measure the worst-case execution time (WCET). While static analysis is often used to find an upper bound of the WCET, the PathCrawler method with specific heuristics may be used to find and to execute a set of maximal paths with respect to a partial order on paths, and to obtain a close lower bound for the WCET.

A similar technique of all-paths testing is used by the OSMOSE testing tool developed at CEA LIST, which allows to generate test cases based on the binary code only (Bardin & Herrmann,

2008). Binary code testing is very challenging in software engineering. For instance, source code offers syntax to locate jump targets while binary code does not. Because of dynamic jumps, i.e. jumps to a location which must be computed, such tools need to guess possible targets.

Recent research suggested that path-oriented testing can be also used in combination with static analysis techniques (Kröning, Groce, & Clarke, 2004; Yorsh, Ball, & Sagiv, 2006; Gulavani, Henzinger, Kannan, Nori, & Rajamani, 2006). For example, SYNERGY (Gulavani et al., 2006) simultaneously looks for bugs and proofs by combining PathCrawler-like testing and model checking, and takes advantage of information obtained by one technique for the other. Tests give valuable information for refinement of abstractions used in model checking, and therefore contribute to the formal proof.

FUTURE RESEARCH DIRECTIONS

Software testing continues to offer new challenges for artificial intelligence. Possible NP-hardness (respectively, undecidability) of satisfiability for constraint problems with a finite (respectively, infinite) number of potential solutions are inherent difficulties of artificial intelligence problems. They make it impossible to find efficient algorithms in some cases. Nevertheless, specific search heuristics and propagation techniques working well in practice should be identified. We believe that future research in automatic constraint-based testing will be centered along three main axes:

1. improving the representation of programs in constraints,
2. developing more efficient constraint solving techniques,
3. looking for new applications.

Constraint-based symbolic execution is often imperfect. An appropriate representation and efficient algorithms must be found for domains which are not fully supported today by the existing testing tools. For instance, the semantics of operations on *floating-point numbers* often depends on the language, compiler and actual machine architecture, and is difficult to be correctly modeled in constraints (Botella, Gotlieb, & Michel, 2006). Another example is *sequences,* used in models to represent finite lists of elements such as stacks, queues, communication channels, sequences of transitions or any other data with consecutive access to elements. On the borderline of decidability, this data type also requires specific constraint solving techniques and their integration into existing constraint solvers (Kosmatov, 2006). *Aliasing problems* appear during constraint-based symbolic execution with unknown inputs when the actual memory location of a variable value is uncertain. They continue to be a very challenging research area in software testing (Visvanathan & Gupta, 2002; Kosmatov, 2008).

Despite the increasing performances of modern computers, the combinatorial explosion and slowness of constraint solving are still important obstacles to wider application of constraint-based techniques in software engineering. In goal-oriented test generation, (Gotlieb, Botella, & Rueher, 1998) proposes to represent in constraints a whole program, rather than just one path, by modeling conditional and loop instructions by specific constraints. Among the most recent approaches to the path explosion problem in all-paths testing, CUTE (Sen et al., 2005) proposes to approximate function return values and pointer constraints by concrete values, but it makes the search incomplete. Path exploration can be guided by particular heuristics (Cadar et al., 2006), or using a combination of random testing and symbolic execution (Majumdar & Sen, 2007). SMART (Godefroid, 2007) suggests to create on-the-fly function summaries to limit path explosion. (Mouy, Marre, Willams, & Le Gall, 2008) proposes to use a specification of a called function rather than its code while testing the calling function. State-caching, a technique arising from static analysis, is used by (Boonstoppel, Cadar, & Engler, 2008) to prune the paths which are not interesting with respect to given test objectives.

Improved test generation algorithms and larger support of various program features should allow to expand applications of constraint-based methods to new areas of software testing, and more generally, in software engineering. Model-based testing, focused today mostly on functional testing, should spread to other kinds of testing, such as security testing, robustness testing and performance testing. Some new applications of constraint-based path exploration in software engineering were mentioned in the previous section.

Recent techniques are often difficult to objectively evaluate and compare because they are developed for different areas and/or tested on different benchmarks. More comparative studies and testing-tool competitions should be conducted to improve our knowledge of the efficiency of different algorithms, heuristics, solving strategies and modeling paradigms.

CONCLUSION

In this chapter, we gave an overview on the use of artificial intelligence techniques for automation of software testing. We presented two of the most innovative strategies of automatic constraint-based test generation: model-based testing from a formal model written in a state-based notation, and all-paths testing of C programs using symbolic execution. Each method was illustrated by an example showing step-by-step how automatic testing tools use constraint-based techniques to generate tests.

The idea to apply artificial intelligence techniques to software testing was revolutionary in software engineering. It allowed the development of several automatic test generation methods. Extremely expensive and laborious manual testing is more and more often accompanied, or even

replaced, by automatic testing. Constraint-based test generation is used nowadays for testing various types of software with different coverage criteria, and will certainly become more and more popular in the future.

ACKNOWLEDGMENT

The author would like to thank Mickaël Delahaye for many valuable ideas during the preparation of an earlier version of the chapter, as well as Sébastien Bardin, Bernard Botella, Arnaud Gotlieb, Philippe Herrmann, Bruno Legeard, Bruno Marre and Nicky Williams for their comments and/or useful discussions.

REFERENCES

Ambert, F., Bouquet, F., Chemin, S., Guenaud, S., Legeard, B., Peureux, F., et al. (2002). BZ-TT: A tool-set for test generation from Z and B using constraint logic programming. In *Formal Approaches to Testing of Software Workshop (FATES'02) at CONCUR'02*, Brnö, Czech Republic, (pp. 105-120).

Apt, K. (2003). *Principles of constraint programming*. Cambridge, UK: Cambridge University Press.

Bardin, S., & Herrmann, P. (2008). Structural testing of executables. In *the First IEEE International Conference on Software Testing, Verification, and Validation (ICST'08)* (p. 22-31). Lillehammer, Norway: IEEE Computer Society.

Boonstoppel, P., Cadar, C., & Engler, D. R. (2008). RWset: attacking path explosion in constraint-based test generation. In *the 14th International Conference on Tools and Algorithms for the Construction and Analysis of Systems (TACAS'08), Part of the Joint European Conferences on Theory and Practice of Software (ETAPS'08)* (pp. 351-366). Budapest, Hungary: Springer.

Botella, B., Gotlieb, A., & Michel, C. (2006). Symbolic execution of floating-point computations. *Software Testing: Verification and Reliability*, *16*(2), 97–121. doi:10.1002/stvr.333

Cadar, C., Ganesh, V., Pawlowski, P. M., Dill, D. L., & Engler, D. R. (2006). EXE: automatically generating inputs of death. In *the 13th ACM Conference on Computer and Communications Security (CCS'06)* (pp. 322-335). Alexandria, VA: ACM.

Clarke, L. A. (1976). A system to generate test data and symbolically execute programs. *IEEE Transactions on Software Engineering, se-2*(3), 215–222. doi:10.1109/TSE.1976.233817

DeMilli, R. A., & Offutt, A. J. (1991). Constraint-based automatic test data generation. *IEEE Transactions on Software Engineering*, *17*(9), 900–910. doi:10.1109/32.92910

Godefroid, P. (2007). Compositional dynamic test generation. In *the 34th Annual ACM SIGPLAN-SIGACT Symposium on Principles of Programming Languages (POPL'07)* (pp. 47-54). Nice, France: ACM.

Godefroid, P., Klarlund, N., & Sen, K. (2005). DART: Directed automated random testing. In *the ACM SIGPLAN 2005 Conference on Programming Language Design and Implementation (PLDI'05)* (pp. 213-223). Chicago: ACM.

Gotlieb, A., Botella, B., & Rueher, M. (1998). Automatic test data generation using constraint solving techniques. In *the ACM SIGSOFT 1998 International Symposium on Software Testing and Analysis (ISSTA'98)* (pp. 53-62). Clearwater Beach, FL: ACM.

Gulavani, B. S., Henzinger, T. A., Kannan, Y., Nori, A. V., & Rajamani, S. K. (2006). SYNERGY: a new algorithm for property checking. In *the 14th ACM SIGSOFT International Symposium on Foundations of Software Engineering (FSE'05)* (pp. 117-127). Portland, OR: ACM.

King, J. C. (1976). Symbolic execution and program testing. *Communications of the ACM, 19*(7), 385–394. doi:10.1145/360248.360252

Kosmatov, N. (2006). A constraint solver for sequences and its applications. *In the 21st Annual ACM Symposium on Applied Computing (SAC'06)* (pp. 404-408). Dijon, France: ACM.

Kosmatov, N. (2008). All-paths test generation for programs with internal aliases. In *the 19th IEEE International Symposium on Software Reliability Engineering (ISSRE'08)* (pp. 147-156). Redmond, WA: IEEE Computer Society.

Kosmatov, N., Legeard, B., Peureux, F., & Utting, M. (2004). Boundary coverage criteria for test generation from formal models. In *the 15th IEEE International Symposium on Software Reliability Engineering (ISSRE'04)* (pp. 139-150). Saint-Malo, France: IEEE Computer Society.

Kröning, D., Groce, A., & Clarke, E. M. (2004). Counterexample guided abstraction refinement via program execution. In *the 6th International Conference on Formal Engineering Methods (ICFEM'04)* (pp. 224-238). Seattle, WA: Springer.

Legeard, B., Peureux, F., & Utting, M. (2002). Automated boundary testing from Z and B. *In the International Confefence on Formal Methods Europe (FME'02)* (pp. 21-40). Copenhaguen, Denmark: Springer.

Majumdar, R., & Sen, K. (2007). Hybrid concolic testing. In *the 29th International Conference on Software Engineering (ICSE'07)* (pp. 416-426). Minneapolis, MN: IEEE Computer Society.

Marre, B., & Arnould, A. (2000). Test sequences generation from Lustre descriptions: GATeL. In *the 15th IEEE International Conference on Automated Software Engineering (ASE'00)* (pp. 229-237). Grenoble, France: IEEE Computer Society.

Mathur, A. P. (2008). *Foundations of software testing.* Upper Saddle River, NJ: Pearson Editions.

Mosley, D. J., & Posey, B. A. (2002). *Just enough software test automation.* Upper Saddle River, NJ: Prentice Hall PTR.

Mouy, P., Marre, B., Willams, N., & Le Gall, P. (2008). Generation of all-paths unit test with function calls. In *the 2008 IEEE International Conference on Software Testing, Verification, and Validation (ICST'08)* (pp. 32-41). Washington, DC: IEEE Computer Society.

Myers, G. J. (1979). *The art of software testing.* Chichester, UK: John Wiley and Sons.

Ramler, R., & Wolfmaier, K. (2006). Economic perspectives in test automation: balancing automated and manual testing with opportunity cost. In *the 2006 International Workshop on Automation of Software Test (AST'06)* (pp. 85-91). Shanghai, China: ACM.

Sen, K., Marinov, D., & Agha, G. (2005). CUTE: a concolic unit testing engine for C. In *the 5th joint meeting of the European Software Engineering Conference and ACM SIGSOFT Symposium on the Foundations of Software Engineering (ESEC/FSE'05)* (pp. 263-272). Lisbon, Portugal: ACM.

Smartesting. (2008). *The Test Designer tool.* http://www.smartesting.com/.

Utting, M., & Legeard, B. (2006). *Practical model-based testing - a tools approach.* New York: Elsevier Science.

van Lamsweerde, A. (2000). Formal specification: a roadmap. In *the 22nd International Conference on Software Engineering, Future of Software Engineering Track (ICSE'00)* (pp. 147-159). Limerick, Ireland.

Visvanathan, S., & Gupta, N. (2002). Generating test data for functions with pointer inputs. In *the 17th IEEE International Conference on Automated Software Engineering (ASE'02)* (p. 149). Edinburgh, UK: IEEE Computer Society.

Williams, N. (2005). WCET measurement using modified path testing. In *the 5th International Workshop on Worst-Case Execution Time Analysis (WCET'05).* Palma de Mallorca, Spain.

Williams, N., Marre, B., & Mouy, P. (2004). On-the-fly generation of k-paths tests for C functions: towards the automation of grey-box testing. *In the 19th IEEE International Conference on Automated Software Engineering (ASE'04)* (pp. 290-293). Linz, Austria: IEEE Computer Society.

Williams, N., Marre, B., Mouy, P., & Roger, M. (2005). PathCrawler: automatic generation of path tests by combining static and dynamic analysis. In *the 5th European Dependable Computing Conference (EDCC'05)* (pp. 281-292). Budapest, Hungary.

Xu, Z., & Zhang, J. (2006). A test data generation tool for unit testing of C programs. In *the 6th International Conference on Quality Software (QSIC'06)* (pp. 107-116). Beijing, China.

Yorsh, G., Ball, T., & Sagiv, M. (2006). Testing, abstraction, theorem proving: better together! In *the 2006 ACM/SIGSOFT International Symposium on Software Testing and Analysis (ISSTA'06)* (pp. 145-156). Portland, ME: ACM.

Zhu, H., Hall, P. A. V., & May, J. H. R. (1997). Software unit test coverage and adequacy. *ACM Computing Surveys, 29*(4), 366–427. doi:10.1145/267580.267590

Chapter 12
Computational Intelligence for Functional Testing

C. Peng Lam
Edith Cowan University, Australia

ABSTRACT

Software testing is primarily a technique for achieving some degree of software quality and to gain consumer confidence. It accounts for 50% -75% of development cost. Test case design supports effective testing but is still a human centered and labour-intensive task. The Unified Modelling language (UML) is the de-facto industrial standard for specifying software system and techniques for automatic test case generation from UML models are very much needed. While extensive research has explored the use of meta-heuristics in structural testing, few have involved its use in functional testing, particularly with respect to UML. This chapter details an approach that incorporates an anti-Ant Colony Optimisation algorithm for the automatic generation of test scenarios directly from UML Activity Diagrams, thus providing a seamless progression from design to generation of test scenarios. Owing to its anti-ant behaviour, the approach generates non-redundant test scenarios.

INTRODUCTION

Software testing is an important technique for achieving some degree of software quality. It accounts for anything between 50 - 75% of the development cost (Hailpern & Santhanarn, 2002). The three main types of activities associated with software testing are: (1) test case generation, (2) test execution involving the use of test cases with the software under test (SUT) and (3) evaluation of test results. A key task associated with test case generation is obtaining an effective test set. The existence and ease of use of a test oracle is a key issue associated with the evaluation of test results. Owing to the immense input space, exhaustive testing is impossible. Thus, test case generation ensuring their adequacy as well their effectiveness in detecting defects in the software is important.

DOI: 10.4018/978-1-60566-758-4.ch012

This is because testing the SUT with an effective test set will imply its correctness over all possible inputs.

Existing approaches for test case design[1] are categorized as black-box, involving the use of some form of specifications, or white-box, where test cases are derived from the logic of the implemented program. Test case generation in black box testing typically involves exercising a set of rules and procedures found in methods such as equivalence class partitioning and cause-effect graphs on the input domain whereas in white box testing it will typically involved finding test data which will execute a specific, yet to be executed, element of the program such as a statement, branch or path. In order to reduce cost, labour and time as well as to improve the quality of the software, any extensive testing would require the automation of the testing process. However, the current status with test automation is that it primarily deals with the automatic execution of test inputs, code instrumentation and coverage measurements. While there are many available commercial test execution tools, few if any of these specifically address the issue of test case design. A formal specification is required for any significant automation in black-box test case generation. The task of test case design is still largely labour-intensive and hence costly and its automation is still very much in its infancy (McMinn, 2004).

Test cases created and selected on the basis of test adequacy criteria are considered to be more effective in discovering faults in a given SUT. Given a testing criterion (e.g. execution of a specific statement in the program), the task in test case generation is to find an input that will satisfy this criterion. However, it may not be possible to determine whether such an input exists. Given limited resources, the application of meta-heuristic techniques to the problem of automatic test case generation is a promising approach that will provide near-optimal solutions. Lam, Robey, & Li (2003) presented a survey for the application of Artificial Intelligence (AI)/meta-heuristics in

software testing. McMinn (2004) in a comprehensive survey also presented similar findings, showing that the focus of most existing work in search based software testing involved the use of genetic algorithms (GA) and concentrated on structural testing and little has been done to address functional testing. GAs have also been used in temporal behaviour testing and the SEMINAL Network (Harman & Jones, 2001) has stated that in comparisons with purely random test data generation techniques, approaches incorporating GAs have shown substantial improvements. Other AI techniques used for test data generation included Ant Colony Optimisation (ACO) (Li & Lam, 2005a; Lam, Xiao, & Li, 2007), the AI planner approach (Howe, Mayrhauser, & Mraz, 1997) and Simulated Annealing (SA) (Tracey, Clark, Mander, & McDermid, 2002). Some previous work involving the application of meta-heuristics for functional testing involved the work of Jones, Sthamer, & Eyres (1995) using a Z specification and Tracey (2000) who tested the conformance of a Pascal program to its specification using SA and GA.

Modelling is a common approach for specifying the behaviour of a system. The Unified Modelling language (UML) is a visual modelling language that can be used to specify, construct, visualise and document the software artefacts of a system. It is the de-facto industrial standard, and increasingly software developers are using UML and its associated modelling tools for requirements elicitation, design and implementation of software systems. The advantage of UML is that it is powerful enough to specify a software system's models visually and efficiently. However, as diagrams, its disadvantage lies in its lack of a formal semantics and it is difficult to apply meta-heuristic techniques directly on UML models for test case generation. Given that the UML is increasingly used for modelling software systems, it is important that tools are developed to support automatic test case generation directly from these graphical design artefacts. Existing attempts include UMLAUT

(Ho, Jzquel, Guennec, & Pennaneac'h, 1999) and TVG (Jéron & Morel, 1999), tools developed in an academic environment, and integrated together to automatically generate test cases from UML specifications. UMLAUT supports manipulation of UML models and TVG is a test case generation tool for conformance testing of protocols. TOBIAS is another tool that assists a tester in terms of designing test objectives. The TESTOR algorithm (Pelliccione, Muccini, Bucchiarone, & Facchini, 2005) generates test sequences from UML Statecharts and Sequence Diagrams and has been implemented as a plugin component into CHARMY, a validation framework for carrying out architectural analysis. Widespread use of these existing tools is limited owing to (1) the steep learning curve and the need for a strong mathematical background and (2) the format of the languages used in the tools are domain-specific (e.g. SDL in embedded systems, etc).

From the literature it can be seen that a great deal of research has been carried out to develop test case generation techniques that use various UML diagrams (Offutt, Liu, Abdurazik, & Ammann, 2003; Hartmann, Vieira, Foster, & Ruder, 2004; Carniello, Jino, & Chaim, 2005; Briand & Labiche, 2002; Chevalley & Thevenod-Fosse, 2001) but these are often labour intensive and few involve the use of meta-heuristic techniques to automatically generate and select test cases in UML-based testing. Amongst the many possible contributing factors to this situation is the implicit nature of UML specifications that makes the applications of meta-heuristic difficult.

The aim of this chapter is to describe the application of computational intelligence approaches for automatic test case generation, specifically addressing an emerging area in search-based software testing involving the use of UML models and ACO. This chapter introduces an approach that incorporates an ACO-based algorithm for the generation of test threads[2] from UML Activity Diagrams (ADs). The significance of the approach is that the UML ADs exported from UML

tools in the form of XMI are used as input, thus providing a seamless progression from design to the automatic generation of test scenarios.

BACKGROUND

This section presents a brief survey of the work in search-based software testing, followed by a brief description of three meta-heuristic techniques that have been employed in various approaches for test case generation. The area of search-based functional testing has not been investigated to the same extent as work involving structural testing and its focus has been mainly in conformance testing using GAs. As the focus of the chapter involves the use of UMLAD in functional testing, existing approaches in UML-based testing are described, in particular work that generates test scenarios from various UML diagrams.

AI Techniques in Software Testing

AI techniques that have been employed in software testing include GA, SA (Tracey, 2000; Xiao, El-Attar, Reformat, & Miller, 2007), Hill Climbing (Korel & Al-Yami, 1996), ACO, Neural Networks and AI Planner and Multi-objective Evolutionary algorithms (Harman, Lakhotia, & McMinn, 2007). As mentioned previously, GAs have been applied mostly in test case generation involving structural testing and predominantly involving branch coverage (Xanthakis, Ellis, Skourlas, Gall, Katsikas & Karapoulios, 1992; Wegener, Baresel, & Sthamer, 2001; Pargas, Harrold, & Peck, 1999; Bottaci, 2002; Jones, Sthamer, & Eyres, 1996; Michael, McGraw, & Schatz, 2001; Harman et al., 2007). It has also been applied to temporal testing (Wegener, Sthamer, Jones, & Eyres, 1997; Gro, 2003; O'Sullivan, Vssner, & Wegener, 1998), test sequence generation in conformance protocol testing (Derderian, Hierons, Harman, & Guo, 2006; Guo, Hierons & Derderian, 2003), stress testing (Briand, Labiche, & Shousha, 2005) and state-based testing (McMinn & Holcombe, 2003; Li & Lam, 2005a).

In comparison, existing work involving the application of ACO (or other meta-heuristic techniques) in search-based test case generation is preliminary. This is especially the case with functional and UML-based testing. ACO and a Markov Software Usage model were used in the approach by Doerner and Gutjahr (2003) to derive a set of test paths for a software system; McMinn and Holcombe (2003) reported results on the application of ACO to find sequences of transitional statements in generating test data for evolutionary testing and Li & Lam (2005a) described an ACO approach to automatically generate test sequences from UML Statechart diagrams for state-based software testing. Lam, Xiao & Li (2007) described an approach that formulates the test sequence generation problem involving Finite State Machines (FSM) and the W_p method into one of finding the shortest tour in an Asymmetric Travelling Salesman problem (ATSP) using ACO. Their approach excludes redundant test segments, employs the concept of overlap to reduce test sequence length and concatenation. This approach for finding shorter test sequences is applicable to every minimal FSM as each one of them possesses a characterising set. An AI planner technique was used in generating test cases for category-partitioning (Howe *et al.*, 1997), for error recovery testing (Mayrhauser, France, Scheetz, & Dahlman, 2000) and for GUI testing (Memon, Pollack, & Soffa, 2001). For more details on existing work in search-based test case generation, interested readers should refer to McMinn (2004).

Vanmali, Last, & Kandel (2002) employed a Back-propagation Neural Network (NN) as an automated test oracle for evaluation of test results. To determine if the SUT is behaving in an expected manner, a tester manually compares the actual output with the expected output. If an error is uncovered by the test case (i.e. the actual output is different from the expected output),

software modification and retesting will be carried out. Vanmali *et. al.*'s approach used randomly generated test data that conform to the software specification as training data and the trained NN becomes a simulated model of the software system. Subsequently when new versions of the original software system are generated (for example in cases of added system functionalities) the trained NN can be used as an automated testing oracle in regression testing.

The following section briefly describes three meta-heuristic techniques that have been employed in various approaches for test case generation.

Genetic Algorithms

GAs are search algorithms initially developed by Holland (1975) and have their basis in biological evolutionary concepts, with a central theme of '*survival of the fittest*'. Similar to a biological system, individual solutions in the search space are represented by chromosomes with a fixed and uniform length. Originally, Holland used binary strings to encode the chromosomes and individual symbols in a string are known as genes. More recently, other types of encoding included gray code encodings, value encodings and permutation encodings. The different ways in which the chromosomes are encoded have an impact on performance of GAs (Mitchell, 1997). However, there are no specific guidelines to determine a suitable encoding with respect to a particular problem, except to say that the selected encoding should resemble as close as possible to the nature of problem (Mitchell, 1997). Encodings should also be complete and valid. Obviously if the solution cannot be represented via the chosen encoding then it cannot be found via GAs. This implies that the chosen encoding must be able to encode all possible solutions for the problem under consideration. Validity of representation is important for ensuring that all possible encodings should be mapped to corresponding data points in the solution space of the problem. The last consideration involves redundancy in the representation, a scenario where a number of chromosomes represent the same solution. High redundancy may cause problems with convergence since GAs involve searching in the representation space instead of the solution space.

In its most basic form, a GA initially generates a population of chromosomes that corresponds to a random sample of the search space. The following steps are then executed iteratively until the termination conditions are satisfied:

- Evaluate the fitness of all individuals for the current population
- Select parents for reproduction on the basis of the fitness of an individual and a selection mechanism
- Crossover to produce new offspring
- Randomly mutate some individuals

The fitness function is used in the evaluation of the suitability of an individual and ranks all individuals in the current population. Individuals with a higher fitness value are more likely to be selected for reproduction and in this manner, transferring their genetic material to subsequent generations. The choice of the fitness function is important as it drives GAs to evolve to the optimal solution. GAs use selections, crossovers and mutations to iteratively evolve solutions to the corresponding problem.

The selection operator selects individuals with high fitness values for reproduction and can be implemented in a number of ways, namely the Roulette Wheel selection, Tournament selection and Stochastic Universal selection. In the Roulette Wheel selection, the basis of selection is an individual's probability in proportion to their relative fitness. Each segment in the Roulette Wheel is weighted according to the fitness value associated with an individual. By spinning the wheel, an individual from the population may be selected. In this way, an individual possessing a high fitness value has a higher probability to be selected. The Tournament selection approach involves a process that randomly selects the individual with the highest fitness from a pool with a pre-determined number of individuals (commonly 2) from the current population. Lastly, the Stochastic Universal selection approach is a variation of the Roulette Wheel selection. The size of each segment is proportional to the fitness value of the respective individual. A number of pointers representing the number of individuals to be selected in the population are used. The roulette wheel is first spun once initially to set an initial pointer on the roulette wheel. The remaining pointers are then placed over the roulette wheel, with consecutive pointers spaced out at an equal distance apart. The individuals associated with the pointers are then selected. To avoid stagnation in the search, selection pressure can be introduced via Linear Scaling or Power Law scaling of the fitness values (Goldberg, 1989).

The crossover operator is used to recombine the genetic material of one or more of the selected individuals to produce offspring in the next generation. The crossover operator used may be selected from one of the following: One-Point, Two-Point and Uniform crossover. For example in a One-Point crossover, the crossover point is first determined in a random fashion and is followed by the exchange of the tails of the two involved parent strings. The One-point and Two-point crossover will produce two offspring, and Uniform crossover will produce only one.

The *illegal chromosome problem* occurs when invalid solutions are obtained via the crossover operation. The type of crossover operator to be used needs to be chosen carefully and *"custom"* crossover operators may be designed and used to avoid this problem.

The aim of using the mutation operator is to introduce new genetic material for maintaining diversity in a population. In the case of a binary string chromosome, this operation would just involve a toggle of 0 to 1 or vice versa for a randomly selected bit in the string. Similar to the crossover operator, the illegal chromosome problem can occur via this operator. In terms of the termination conditions, there are no definitive rules and commonly, the GA runs for a fixed number of generations or it terminates when convergence of a specified value has been achieved.

Ant Colony Optimisation

ACO is a class of algorithms (Dorigo & Caro, 1999) that simulate the behaviour of some species of ants. These algorithms are based on pheromone trails used by ants to mark out paths of interest (e.g. food trails) which other ants may subsequently follow. Each ant lays down some pheromone as it transverses a path and thus a path used by more ants would have a higher pheromone concentration. Ants in a colony tend to follow paths with higher pheromone concentrations, thus leading to a convergence to the shortest path between the starting point (e.g. nest) and the target (e.g. food). ACO is a probabilistic technique that has been applied to generate solutions for NP-hard problems such as TSP. The artificial ants in the algorithm represent the stochastic solution construction procedures which make use of (1) the dynamic evolution of the pheromone trails that reflect the ants' acquired search experience and (2) the heuristic information related to the problem in hand. Each ant builds an independent solution in parallel and these solutions are evaluated in terms of some criteria (e.g. some form of test adequacy criterion such as branch coverage in structural testing). The first ACO technique is known as Ant System (Dorigo, Maniezzo, & Colorni, 1991) and it was applied to solve the traveling salesman problem (TSP). Since then, many variants of this technique including Elitist Ant System (Dorigo, Maniezzo, & Colorni, 1996; Gambardella & Dorigo, 1995; Stützle & Hoos, 1997; Solnon, 2002) have been produced. ACO has been applied successfully to a wide range of engineering problems such as job scheduling in aluminium foundry (Gravel, Price, & Gagn, 2002), bioreactors optimisation (Jayaraman,

Kulkarni, Gupta, Rajesh, & Kusumaker, 2001) and routing in telecommunication networks (Caro & Dorigo, 1998). Besides its applications in some emerging work in search-based software testing, most recently, it was also used for model-checking (Alba & Chicano, 2007).

In terms of applying ACO to address test case design as an optimization problem, a number of issues have to be considered, namely,

1. Reformulate the test case design problem into a search-based problem;
2. Develop a heuristic measure for evaluating the quality of paths through the search-based representation with respect to a specific testing adequacy criterion;
3. Investigate a mechanism for creating possible solutions efficiently and a suitable criterion to terminate the search;
4. Develop a suitable method for updating the concentration of pheromone; and lastly,
5. Develop a transition rule for determining the probability of an ant traversing from one node in the graph to the next.

Additional considerations would also include the number of ants to be used, balancing exploration and exploitation, and the decision on whether to combine with greedy heuristics or local search.

Simulated Annealing

Simulated Annealing (Kirkpatrick, Gellat, & Vecchi, 1983) is a form of neighbourhood search technique that is based on concepts from thermodynamics, namely the chemical process of annealing. In this process, a material is first heated to a specified temperature until it reaches quasi-equilibrium, and then the material is allowed to cool slowly through phase transitions, thus allowing the material to solidify optimally to the minimum energy state. This state of matter corresponds to the minimum of the cost function in an optimization problem. Simulated Annealing is a variant of a greedy algorithm which can be used to find near-optimal solutions and, like many of its cousins; it also suffers the local minima problem. The concept of temperature is used in Simulated Annealing to overcome this limitation. Initially, at high temperatures, exploration of the parameter space occurs when the algorithm probabilistically accepts solutions that may be inferior. However as the temperature decreases during the duration of the search process, this tendency is also reduced, thus restricting the exploration (i.e. the acceptance of inferior solutions). The temperature in the algorithm is controlled via a cooling schedule and the probability of accepting an inferior solution is controlled via a temperature function which takes an input (time, t) and returns a temperature. The criterion for termination of the algorithm relates to the Boltzmann distribution, characterising thermal equilibrium. From an implementation point of view, this implies that there is no significant improvement in terms of obtaining a new "best" solution from a specified number of consecutive iterations.

There are four key elements to be considered in terms of its implementation, namely determining the representation of the solution space, defining the neighbourhood, defining a quantitative objective function and lastly, defining a cooling schedule and the length of times for which the system is to be evolved. The first three elements are problem specific while the last element is generic and impacts only the search process. The two most common cooling schedules are (1) evaluate several sample solutions at a given temperature, then reduce the temperature by a specified value, and then repeat the steps, or (2) reduce the temperature by a smaller amount between each evaluation of a sample solution. The design of the cooling schedule is still very much an art and often, would require a "trial and error" approach.

Simulated Annealing is computationally expensive, and like many of the other meta-heuristic techniques, it does not guarantee to find the global optimum. The performance of the algorithm may be a function of how its parameters (e.g. initial system temperature, cooling schedule, sufficient number temperature values, etc.) are tuned. Only when the algorithm is run long enough (i.e. given an infinite number of temperature values and time steps), it will return the optimum solution, otherwise it can provide a number of near-optimal solutions.

UML-Based Testing

UML diagrams are categorized as structural or behavioral and can be used to define a specific view of the system. Structural diagrams, incorporating the class, component and deployment diagrams provide a static view of a system and behavioral diagrams, which include activity diagrams, state machines and interaction diagrams specifies the behaviour of a software system. Chandler (2004) completed a survey showing existing research involving the different types of UML diagrams for test case generations in relation to the different phases of software development. Most of the existing work has involved use case diagrams, class diagrams, sequence diagrams, UML statecharts and collaboration diagrams (involving UML 1.x). As the amount of work in the area is quite extensive, this section will only describe a few examples in order to provide an insight into the techniques developed in UML based testing. The UMLTEST tool (Offutt & Abdurazik, 1999) produced test cases from UML statecharts with enabled transitions. This tool was integrated with Rational Rose. Test cases were generated at full predicate and transition pairs level. In addition to various limitations associated with the input file, it also required all variables to be of type Boolean. The approach was then applied to a C implementation of a cruise control module and it detected a number of manually created faults. Other work involving the use of statecharts for test case generation include those of Chevalley and Thevenod-Fosse (2001) in generating statistical test cases and Wu, Chen, & Offut (2003) in deriving context dependent relationships.

Scenarios have mainly been used in the requirements elicitation and analysis phase for the capture and documentation of requirements, thus enhancing communication between the various stakeholders. Weidenhaupt, Pohl, Jarke, & Haumer, (1998) carried out an industry-based survey and two of their many findings are: (1) scenarios have been extensively used for system development and (2) the need for a systematic approach for deriving scenarios for system testing. Leite and Breitman (2003) proposed a model for relating and versioning scenarios as they recognised their use throughout a software life cycle and the need for their management in terms of inter-relationships and traceability. In its simplest form, scenarios are informal text flows written in natural language (as in use cases), making them hard to use and to manage. Other diagrammatic representations may include UML Sequence Diagrams, Use Case Maps, Message Sequence Charts and UML ADs - which are well known for their value in providing a graphical representation for use cases. Systematic development of test scenarios from these artefacts would benefit from the availability of automation tools. However, in many instances, automation will require these representations to be formalized or annotated, thus losing many of the existing advantages associated with their use (e.g. the understand-ability to users).

UML use cases represent the high level system functionality written in natural languages for end-users and thus are good sources for deriving system test artefacts. Examples of existing approaches include Nebut, Fleurey, Traon, & Jzquel (2006) where UML use cases, enhanced with contracts, have been used to generate test cases; Bertolino and Gnesi (2003) annotated use cases, written in Cockburn's template, with category partition method information in order to derive test cases; and Frohlich and Link (2000) transform textual-based use cases into UML Statecharts in order to automatically generate test cases from the

transformed models. It is generally difficult to describe complex dependencies between the use cases (Binder, 1999; Cockburn, 1997). However, UML ADs can be used to describe these inter-dependencies since they capture business workflows, the processing actions, and the use-case flows of execution. In fact, Kosters, Six, & Winters (2001) stated that ADs can specify an entire set of use case scenarios in a single diagram.

A set of ADs can be viewed as the visual "blueprints" of the functionality of a system and Lieberman (2001) has suggested that specific scenarios can be generated by tracing a thread of execution from entry to exit through each AD. Stakeholders can easily understand the system behaviour as well as monitor the development of system functionality by tracing execution paths through the ADs (Lieberman, 2001). Lastly, he also suggested that ADs be used to track the progress of testing where paths are marked to indicate testing priority as well as marking activities covered by each test, thus providing a visual representation of the progress made in testing. However, a point to note is that deriving all possible usage scenarios from a set of *realistic* ADs can be a very time consuming manual process. Examples of testing techniques that use ADs include Briand and Labiche (2002); Bai, Li, & Lam (2004); Liu, Jin, & Liu (2002); Zhang, Liu, & Sun (2001) and Wang and Yuan (2004) but the generation of testing artefacts (in the form of test cases or test scenarios) in most of them have yet to be fully automated.

Test thread derivation, is a frequently used approach for the generation of the test scenarios (Command Control Communications & C3I, 2001; Bai, Tsai, Paul, Feng, & Yu, 2001; Tsai, Bai, Paul, Shao, & Agarwal, 2001; Bai, Lam, & Li, 2004). Thin-threads, in the form of thin-thread trees and associated condition trees, have been derived from scenario-based business models (Command Control Communications & C3I, 2001; Bai et al., 2001) or directly from the UML ADs (Bai et al., 2004) and test scenarios are then subsequently generated from these thin-threads. The generated test scenarios can be prioritised and used to obtain test cases for scenario-based software testing (Bai *et al.*, 2004). One main problem with the generation of thin-threads is that the generation techniques are either completely manual/labor-intensive (Command Control Communications & C3I, 2001; Bai *et al.*, 2001) or not fully automated yet (Bai *et al.*, 2004).

SEARCH BASED UML-BASED TESTING

This section describes a scenario-based testing approach (initially detailed in (Li & Lam, 2005b)) that is provided here in more details and with some modifications made to the original algorithm. The approach takes artefacts (namely UML 2.0 ADs) and uses anti-ant-like agents to automatically generate test scenarios with the aim of ensuring its functional compliance with requirements. Unlike existing ACO-based techniques, ants in this approach always choose to move along paths with the minimum level of pheromone. The ADs used in the approach are exported from commonly used UML modelling tools (e.g. Poseidon) in the form of XMI files. The technique then processes these UML ADs to automatically produce three trees; the thread tree, the condition tree, and the data-object tree, which are subsequently processed for extracting test scenarios and generating test cases. The advantage of the proposed approach is that the ADs, exported from UML tools, are used directly as input (i.e. without any additional annotation), thus providing a seamless progression from requirement and design to testing. This is important as Bertolino, Marchetti, & Muccini (2004) have stated that, any UML-based testing approaches in an industrial context should directly use UML diagrams developed from the analysis and design phase, without the need for modifying these diagrams to include any additional formalism. The use of UML diagrams brings two major benefits for software testers: (1) the availability

of a model for testing and (2) the standardisation arising from the use of UML models will allow testers to share their knowledge and experiences in generating test cases from UML diagrams (Reid, 2005). Lastly, by providing a mechanism for automatic generation of test scenarios from UML ADs, which is a very labour intensive exercise when conducted manually, the approach also supports consistency checking between an AD and its associated use cases from a requirements analysis point of view.

UML 2.0 Activity Diagrams

An UML AD is a flowchart-like diagram that models the control flow between the sequential and/or concurrent activities and is commonly used in requirements analysis and business process modelling. ADs can be used to capture a system's dynamic behavior in terms of its operations, focusing on the end-to-end flows driven by the system's internal processing. They focus on the sequences of actions, guarded alternatives, and concurrency; thus unlike flowcharts, they support parallel activities and their synchronisations. Through the use of vertical swimlanes they also support mapping of behaviour to components and complex activities within ADs can be refined. While UML use cases provide a good representation with regards to the completeness of system functionalities, it does not provide a tester with information about their possible order of occurrence(s); a limitation that can be overcome by using UML ADs as they draw together concepts from a number of other techniques: event diagrams, SDL state modeling techniques and Petri Nets. In earlier versions of UML 1.x, ADs are defined as a type of State Machine Diagrams. However in UML 2.0, ADs have been separated from state machines and their semantics is now based on concepts in Petri Nets.

In general, an AD consists of elements from two categories: Edges and Activity Nodes. The Activity nodes are further differentiated into Action

241

nodes, Control nodes (consisting of Initial node, the Final node, the Fork nodes, the Join nodes, the Branch nodes, the Merge nodes and the Flowfinal nodes) and Object nodes. The edges are used for connecting the nodes and represent transitions involving control flow or data flow between the nodes. In UML 2.0, an AD may have one or more Initial node(s) which indicates a default starting place. Final nodes are used to show where the control flow terminates. Action nodes within the Activity nodes may represent "nested structures"; consisting of a flow of control composed of other activity and action nodes. Condition (or Branch) nodes have one incoming edge and two or more outgoing edges, each with an associated Boolean expression known as a guard condition. Fork/Join nodes indicate situations where a single flow of control is divided into two or more concurrent flows of control.

Various characteristics associated with ADs such as hierarchical (nested) activity diagrams, concurrency (fork-join nodes) and conditional looping make them unsuitable for the applications of techniques such as breadth-first or depth first search techniques. In addition, ADs also contain dynamic edges which may only be accessible based on the evaluation of the associated guard conditions.

The concepts underlying the representation of the thread tree, the condition tree, and the data-object tree, their relationships with UML ADs is briefly described in the next section.

Thread Tree, Condition Tree and Data-Object Tree

Test threads extracted from the system level ADs are categorized into three trees, namely, Thread Tree, Condition Tree and Data-Object Tree. Although test threads and use cases are similar in terms of describing system scenarios, a test thread contains more information and is organized into a tree-like structure. This makes it suitable for various analyses such as dependency analysis, risk

analysis, traceability analysis, coverage analysis, completeness and consistency checking, and test scenario/test case generation (Command Control Communications & C3I, 2001). Test-threads sharing specific commonalities may be assembled into a test-thread group, with the likelihood of such grouping being recursive, i.e., a subset of lower level and *similar* test-thread groups may be subsequently grouped to form a higher level test-thread group. All test-threads and test-thread groups can be arranged hierarchically to form a thread tree (example shown in figure 5). Furthermore, each test thread or each test thread group has associated conditions to identify their activation constraints (Command Control Communications & C3I, 2001). A test thread can only be activated if its associated conditions are satisfied. These associated conditions can also be grouped and organized into a tree-like structure which is subsequently known here as the condition tree.

In addition, UML ADs may contain data storage objects which can be read and/or updated by sub-scenarios. As these data objects can affect or be affected by the associated conditions, Bai, Lam, & Li (2004) proposed the data object tree to capture the important content-dependent coupling relationships between the test-threads. In a similar fashion, these data storage objects can also be classified and organized into a hierarchical tree-like structure and will subsequently be referred to here as the data object tree. However, in terms of the classification of the data objects, its hierarchy closely resembles a normal data storage structure in a relational database. Data objects are placed at the top level of a data object hierarchy and a leaf node only contains part of a data object as different sub-scenarios may be associated with different parts of the same data object. The reading or updating operation attributes are assigned to the leaf nodes to help identify data inter-dependent test-threads. Complex relationships may exist amongst these three trees where a test thread consisting of a group of sequential sub-scenarios, may share common sub-scenarios, conditions and data-objects across its various members.

Generating the Trees using Anti-Ant-Like Agents

The approach for the automatic generation of the three trees involves using a group of anti ant-like agents which cooperatively search a directed graph **G** in order to build the three trees discussed in the previous sub-section. The original ACO algorithm is modified in this approach as the aim was to explore the solution space to find all alternate serialised paths through the concurrent regions and is not just about finding a near optimal solution. The strength of meta-heuristics like ACO is that they can iteratively seek a near optimal solution in an extremely complicated and discontinuous landscape and can be applied to automate manual intensive tasks.

The input, an AD, is first transformed into a directed graph where the activity nodes, the object nodes, the branch nodes, the fork nodes, the join nodes, and the initial nodes are the vertices of the directed graph and the activity edges in the AD are the edges of the graph. Figure 1 shows an extended activity diagram for an ATM machine. This AD contains a data object *Account* which can be accessed by various activity nodes.

Any necessary graph conversion is done on the fly and thus it is different from the approach by Bai *et al.* (2004) where UML ADs were manually transformed into an activity hypergraph before it is processed for generation of the trees. As ADs contain dynamic edges which may only be accessible based on the evaluation of the associated guard conditions, they are not suitable for direct applications of the original ACO algorithms. Two special sets of nodes in an AD are dealt with here in the following manner:

- Final nodes in an AD are classified as poisoned food sources.

- For ease of explanation, a fork node and its associated join node are classified here as being the two opposite banks of a river with every path between the fork-join nodes being considered as a pontoon. Every pair of fork/join nodes and all nodes between the pair will be converted on the fly to execution sequences, called Fork-Join Bridges, by the anti ant-like agents. Details associated with Fork-Join Bridges will be discussed in the *Building Fork-Join Bridge* section.

The behavior of an anti ant-like agent in the modified ACO algorithm is governed by a state machine diagram illustrated in Figure 2. Characteristics associated with this ant include:

- An artificial ant at a node can sense the pheromone trails on the edges emanating from the current vertex, and leave pheromone trails over the edges when it moves between the nodes.

- An artificial ant is killed if it finds the poisoned food.

- To cater for the dynamic nature of the edges in the fork-join node of an AD, an artificial ant must first build a temporary pontoon bridge[3] before it can travel across the two opposite banks.

- An artificial ant is powered by limited energy. It is terminated if it runs out of energy. The main purpose for the introduction of power consumption for the artificial ants is to avoid situations in which an artificial ant runs into a cyclic loop, or in which an ant has stalled in a part of the AD.

- At a node with multiple edges radiating from it, an artificial ant will select to go down the edge with the minimum amount of pheromone. This is different to the original ACO where its ants will select the edge with the highest level of pheromone.

If there are multiple edges with the same amount of pheromone, an artificial ant will choose one of these edges randomly.

Algorithm

The pseudo code below corresponds to the state machine diagram shown in Figure 2 for an artificial ant's possible behavior as it explores an activity graph.

Figure 1. An ATM Activity Diagram. © 2005 Springer Science+Business Media (Used with permission)

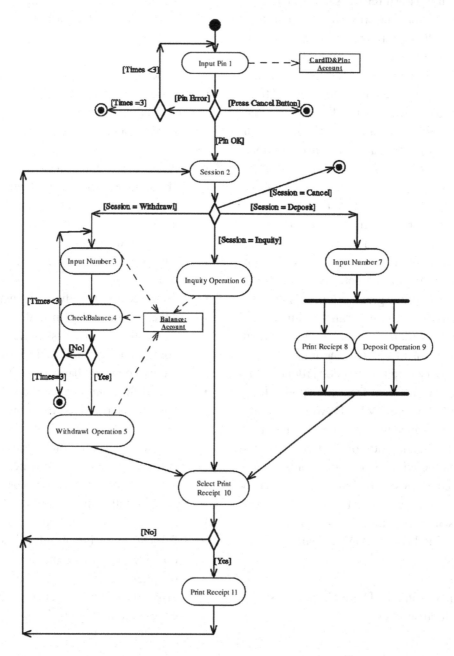

Figure 2. Behavior of an Artificial Ant - The State Machine Diagram. Modified from (Li and Lam, 2005b) (Used with permission- Springer Science+Business Media)

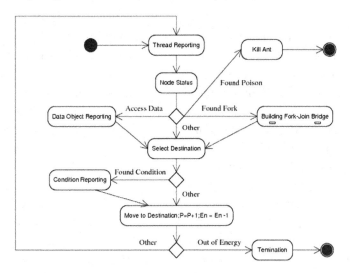

```
/* Initialisation: Set pheromone level to
zero for every edge in the directed graph
*/
   P   = 0;
    ij
 /* Exploration of a group of m ants */
for k = 1 to m do
 EN = Default_Energy; } /* Every ant is
   k
initialised with default energy value */
 i = 0;                      /*Every ant
starts from the initial node*/
 while (EN > 0 do }
         k
    /* Thread reporting */
    Report threads to the thread tree;
    Evaluate status at node i;
    if (Found Poison) do
      Kill ant;
      Break;
    endif;
  /*Data Reporting*/}\\
  if (Access Data) do
    Report data access to the data object
tree;
   endif;
   /* If arrives at a fork node */
   if (Found Fork) do
```

```
   Building Fork-Join Bridge;
   endif;
   Evaluate-pheromone-levels-on-all-ema-
nating-edges;
   /* Find the destination node d which
has the minimum pheromone level */
   /* Do random selection if multiple
nodes have the same minimum value */
   Find min P  ;
             id
   /* Condition reporting */
   if (Found Condition) do
     Report conditions to the condition
tree;
   endif;
   /* Move to the destination node */
   i = d;
   /* Each move consumes energy */
   EN = EN - 1;
     k    k
   /* Update pheromone value over the tra-
versed edge which is not part of the fork
joins */
   P   = P   + 1;
    id    id
   endwhile;
if P   >= 1 for every edge (i,j) do
   ij
 Stop; /*    Every edge has been trans-
versed */
```

```
endif;
endfor;
```

Like ACO, an artificial ant's next move is determined by the concentration of pheromone deposits on the edges. However, unlike ACO, these artificial ants select edges with the minimum concentration of pheromone, thus favouring moves to the unexplored or less-explored edges. This form of repulsive behavior to pheromone concentrations on the edges results in an effective exploration of the ADs as the aim here is to generate the various test scenarios to achieve effective coverage of all activity edges, a problem quite different from obtaining the shortest path required in problems such as the Travelling SalesMan problem involving the original ACO algorithm. The nature of the problem here also does not require a heuristic measure, as stated in dot-point 2 in the Section on ACO, to be developed. In essence, the ants here exhibit an anti-ant behavior in their reaction to the pheromone concentrations.

As the algorithm shown above is relatively straightforward, detailed explanation is provided in the subsequent sections for only two segments, namely Building Fork-Join Bridge and Reporting, both of which requires some further explanations.

Building Fork-Join Bridge

As mentioned in the previous section, a fork node and its associated join node are considered here as two opposite banks of a river and a path (consisting of a number of nodes and edges) between two consecutive nodes being classified as a pontoon. When an artificial ant arrives at a fork river bank, it will build a number of pontoons between the two banks to complete a pontoon bridge over the *fork-join* river in order to cross it. Assuming that there are n pontoons, the procedure involving an ant in building a fork-join (or pontoon) bridge is:

1. Set $k = 1$;
2. Select the pontoon with the minimum pheromone level on its first edge. Otherwise, if there are multiple candidates with same minimum pheromone level on their respective first edges, then randomly select one of these candidates.
3. Take one step forward into the selected pontoon and update the pheromone level of the first edge of the selected pontoon using the formula, $P = P + 1/k$. Then update the pheromone level of the remaining edges of this pontoon using the formula, $P = P + 1/n!$ as the ant continues to move through the selected pontoon;
4. If $k = n$, sequentially connect all pontoons in the respective order to form a pontoon bridge; otherwise set $k = k + 1$ and go to step 2;

As an example, Figure 4 shows two consecutive ant explorations in building bridges for the fork-join nodes found in the ATM example in Figure 1. In Figure 4 the total number of pontoons in the fork join nodes, n, is 2 (one via the node "print reciept" and the other via the node "Deposit Operation"). In the first ant's exploration (Figure 4:A1), the ant arriving at the fork node selects one of the pontoons randomly as there are two candidates with the same minimum pheromone level on their respective first edges. Figure 4:C1 shows the updated pheromone level of the edges after the first ant's exploration has been completed. In the second exploration, the ant arriving at the fork node will select to move into the pontoon with the first edge having a pheromone level of 0.5. Figure 4:C2 shows the updated pheromone level of the edges after the end of the second ant's exploration. The bridge building procedure ensures that every possible combination of execution sequences for the paths between the fork node and the join node will be exercised by the proposed algorithm, and all corresponding traces

Figure 3. Steps involving an Ant in Building a Fork-Join Bridge. Modified from (Li and Lam, 2005b) (Used with permission- Springer Science+Business Media)

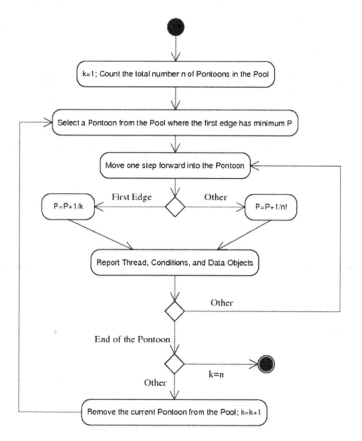

will be recorded in the three trees. However, the bridge building procedure alone can not guarantee that every activity edge in a path between the fork and the join nodes will be visited by at least one ant. Therefore, the deposition of pheromone amounting to *1/n!* is introduced for the remaining edges of the selected pontoon to ensure that if there is an unexplored activity edge between the fork and the join nodes, the proposed ant exploration algorithm will not terminate. Subsequent explorations by other ants over the paths between the fork and join nodes will favor those edges which have not been fully explored. The number of ants, *m*, in the proposed algorithm can be increased to allow for a more exhaustive exploration. When all activity edges between the fork and the join nodes have been visited at least once, one of the

necessary conditions for the termination of the ant exploration algorithm is then satisfied. Figure 3 is an AD that demonstrates the steps involving one ant as it transverses through the Fork-Join region. The idea of using a pontoon bridge, composed of a number of pontoons (direct paths between the fork node and the join node), supports a mechanism for serialisation of paths in the concurrent region by an ant.

Reporting

An ant reports its execution trace to a thread tree as it explores an AD. This completed execution trace is represented as a branch in the thread tree, as illustrated in the Thread tree (Figure 5). When the next ant starts its exploration of the AD, its trace

Figure 4. Building a Fork-Join Bridge using the ATM Example. Modified from (Li and Lam, 2005b) (Used with permission- Springer Science+Business Media)

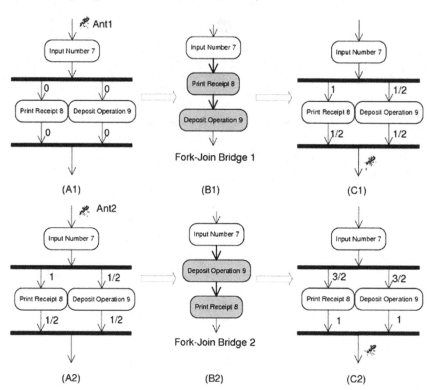

is also reported to the same thread tree. However, for compactness, the part of this ant's trace which is common to an existing branch of the tree is merged into the trunk of the Thread tree, leaving only the part that is different to branch away from the trunk, as shown in the Thread tree.

Note that condition reporting and data reporting are dealt with in similar ways. Exploration of an AD using multiple anti ant-like agents will result in the automatic generation of the three trees which were manually generated in Bai *et al.* (2004). Details associated with the three trees obtained from the application of the proposed approach to the ATM example in Figure 1 can be found in Li and Lam (2005b).

Coverage

In terms of coverage, the approach makes use of a path analysis technique in the generation of the test threads, a strategy commonly used in existing techniques involved in generation of test cases from use cases as indicated in the survey by Denger and Mora (2003). Each ant starts at an initial node of an AD and only finishes at a final or flow final node. With m ants, the algorithm is aimed at listing all possible paths (test scenarios) from the initial node(s) to the final node(s). In terms of the loops and concurrent regions in the ADs, the algorithm is aimed at covering loops atleast once and each combination of serialised paths in the concurrent region is also covered. The use of energy level associated with the ants avoids situations involving infinite loops and its value is chosen to ensure that the AD is covered.

Figure 5. The Thread Tree for the ATM Example. Modified from (Li and Lam, 2005b) (Used with permission- Springer Science+Business Media)

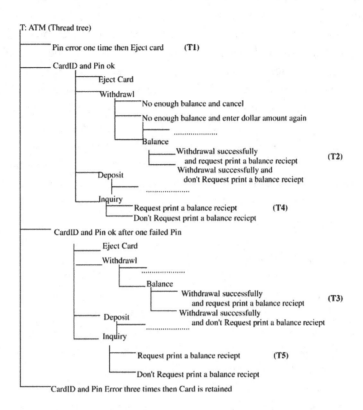

Currently the rule used here is that the default energy value is equal to the number of nodes in the AD multiplied by the number of edges in the AD. It is possible that, with a complex set of ADs, there can potentially be a huge number of paths. Thus it is important that the paths are analysed and prioritised before generating the associated test data as testing resources are not infinite. The prioritisation of test threads will allow the more critical functions to be tested first. In many cases, testers using their experience will select paths that they consider critical to test.

FUTURE RESEARCH DIRECTIONS

One of the issues associated with the application of meta-heuristic techniques in software testing is

recasting the problem into a search-based problem. In most of the existing work involving structural testing, the problem is transformed into a task involving one form or another of a Control Flow Graph (CFG) which is then used in the search for test inputs that satisfies a specified test adequacy criterion. Given the lack of a formal semantics in UML diagrams (and the use of natural language in UML Use cases), it is difficult to use UML models for automatic test case generation. Thus it is only natural that only those diagrams with a certain degree of formalism (e.g. UML Statecharts, AD) have so far been associated with initial work in search-based functional testing. The key challenge in using UML models for search-based functional testing is to work out ways to transform the various UML models into data structures that can support the use of meta-heuristics for automatic test case generation. In the case of UML 2.0 AD, it has Petri Net like semantics (however, it still have many ambiguities and inconsistencies) and future work can investigate how this characteristic may be exploited and incorporated for search-based functional testing. Subsequently, we need to investigate and develop techniques to identify the test objectives from the resulting data structures and transform them into numerical functions which can be maximised (or minimised) via different meta-heuristic techniques.

The advantage of using meta-heuristic techniques such as GA, ACO and simulated annealing is that they usually avoid the problems of being trapped in local minima (unlike most gradient descent methods). The implicit parallelism of GA and ACO also allows them to simultaneously examine many paths -- in contrast to gradient descent techniques which must focus on only one path. However these algorithms have various control parameters (e.g. population size, the number of generations, the rate of reproduction within each generation, cross-over operators, mutation operators and probabilities of crossovers and mutations, termination criterion, neighbourhood size) associated with each of them that impact on their respective performances. While there are various approaches in the literature in terms of selecting the corresponding optimal values, there is no universal recipe and in reality, the values are fine-tuned and tailored to a specific problem and algorithm. This is a hindrance to the uptake of the techniques by industry and thus future research needs to create meta-heuristic based computer aided software engineering (CASE) tools that can facilitate software testers to input their specifications and domain specific knowledge easily as well as strategies that help to tailor the values of the control parameters associated with the approach.

In addition, there is no way in the application of meta-heuristic techniques to test if a solution is near-optimal. There may exist cases where unknowingly (to the user), the algorithms had failed and subsequently resulted in sub-optimal behaviour. There is no guarantee for a near optimal solution and any solution can only be evaluated against the previously obtained solutions. Research needs to be undertaken to examine the association between the characteristics of the problem, the use of a specific meta-heuristic technique and its associated control parameter values with the definition of the near optimal solution for the specific problem. In particular, we also need to examine the suitability, scalability of the meta-heuristic for a specific problem as well as the repeatability and robustness of the results obtained.

CONCLUSION

This chapter has first presented a brief survey of work relating to the application of meta-heuristic approaches in software testing. It can be seen that a great deal of work is in the area of structural testing and temporal testing involving searches for response time extremes. GA is the most commonly used meta-heuristic in both of these two areas and there are a small number of developed strategies involving the use of simulated annealing, AI planner and ACO, with some emerging work that have incorporated Multi-objective Evolutionary algorithms. The area of search-based functional testing has not been investigated to the same extent and its focus has been mainly in conformance testing using GA, seeking input to check whether an implementation conforms to its specification. There is also some emerging work in using ACO for model checking and in UML-based testing.

The chapter has also described an application of an ACO-like approach for automatic generation of test threads, using UML ADs, thus addressing an emerging area in search-based software testing. While the proposed anti-ant algorithm works well for the exploration of UML ADs of complexity level shown here, further experiments need to be performed to verify the efficiency of the proposed algorithm for ADs of higher complexity. In addition, future work to improve the anti-ant algorithm will involve investigating the following:

- Improving and developing new pheromone updating rules as well as to use the idea of evaporating pheromone deposit to improve the exploration of the solution space. In contrast to the original ACO algorithms, the pheromone concentration on the trails in this approach is used to discourage an artificial ant from exploring an edge which has already been well explored. While the simple pheromone updating rules used in the present algorithm serve the purpose, further investigation is required to evaluate how best to improve the exploration strategy of the ants, especially in dealing with a set of more complex ADs.
- The artificial ants used in the current approach are simple memory-less agents and thus they are unable to pre-fetch or look ahead in terms of the future pheromone trails, and are unable to back-track. Further research will explore the possibility of using anti ant-like agents with memory in a goal-oriented approach for improving the generation of test threads.

In conclusion, the anti-ant approach has the following advantages in terms of the generation of the test threads: 1) the developed technique used UML artifacts directly to automatically generate the test-threads and 2) redundant exploration of the test threads is avoided due to the use of the anti-ant-like agents. The approach described here represents initial effort in computational intelligence approaches for automatic test case generation for functional testing using UML models.

ACKNOWLEDGMENT

The author would like to thank Dr. H. Li for his contributions and the many discussions that we had in the development of the anti-ant algorithm.

REFERENCES

Alba, E., & Chicano, F. (2007). Ant Colony Optimization for Model Checking. *Proceedings of the 11th International Conference on Computer Aided Systems Theory (eurocast 2007)*. (Vol. 4739, pp. 523-530). Berlin: Springer.

Bai, X., Lam, C. P., & Li, H. (2004). An approach to generate the thin-threads from the UML diagrams. *Proceedings of Computer Software and Applications Conference (COMPSAC 2004)*, (pp. 546–552).

Bai, X., Li, H., & Lam, C. P. (2004). A risk analysis approach to prioritize UML-based software testing. *5th International Conference on Software Engineering, Artificial Intelligence, Networking, and Parallel/Distributed Computing (SNPD04)*.

Bai, X., Tsai, W., Paul, R., Feng, K., & Yu, L. (2001). Scenario-based business modeling. *IEEE Proc. of APAQS*.

Bertolino, A., & Gnesi, S. (2003). Use case-based testing of product lines. *ESEC/FSE11: Proceedings of the 9th European Software Engineering Conference held jointly with 11th ACM SIGSOFT International Symposium on Foundations of Software Engineering*, (pp. 355–358).

Bertolino, A., Marchetti, E., & Muccini, H. (2004). Introducing a reasonably complete and coherent approach for model-based testing. *Proc. ETAPS 2004 workshop on: Test and Analysis of Component Based Systems (Tacos)*.

Binder, R. (1999). *Testing object-oriented systems: Models, patterns and tools*. Reading, MA: Addison-Wesley Longman.

Bottaci, L. (2002). Instrumenting programs with flag variables for test data search by genetic algorithms. In Gecco 2002: *Proceedings of the Genetic and Evolutionary Computation Conference* (pp. 1337–1342). New York: Morgan Kaufmann Publishers.

Briand, L. C., & Labiche, Y. (2002). A UML-Based Approach to System Testing. *Software and Systems Testing, 1*(1), 10–42.

Briand, L. C., Labiche, Y., & Shousha, M. (2005). Stress testing real-time systems with genetic algorithms. In *Gecco '05: Proceedings of the 2005 Conference on Genetic and Evolutionary Computation* (pp. 1021–1028). New York: ACM.

Carniello, A., Jino, M., & Chaim, M. (2005). Structural testing with use cases. *Journal of Computer Science and Technology, 5*(2), 100–106.

Caro, G. D., & Dorigo, M. (1998). Antnet: Distributed stigmergetic control for communications networks. *Journal of Artificial Intelligence Research, 9*, 317–365.

Chandler, R. (2004). *Test Case Generation From UML Models for Software Integration Testing* (Tech. Rep. No. 1, PhD Proposal). Edith Cowan University, Australia.

Chevalley, P., & Thevenod-Fosse, P. (2001). Automated Generation of Statistical Test Classes from UML State Diagrams. *25th Annual International Computer Software and Applications Conference (COMPSAC'01)*, 205–214.

Cockburn, A. (1997). Structuring Use Cases with Goal. *Journal of Object-Oriented Programming, 9*(6), 56–62.

Command Control Communications. A. S. of Defense for, & C3I, I. A. (2001). *End-to-End Integration Test Guidebook (Tech. Rep. No. Version 1.0)*. Washington, DC: Department of Defense, United States of America.

Denger, C., & Mora, M. M. (2003). *Test case derived from requirement specifications* (Tech. Rep. No. IESE-Report No: 033.03/E). Fraunhofer: Institut Experimentelles, Software Engineering.

Derderian, K., Hierons, R. M., Harman, M., & Guo, Q. (2006). Automated unique input output sequence generation for conformance testing of FSMs. *The Computer Journal, 49*(3), 331–344. doi:10.1093/comjnl/bxl003

Doerner, K., & Gutjahr, W. J. (2003). Extracting test sequences from a markov software usage model by ACO. *Proc. GECCO 2003*, (LNCS, Vol. 2724, pp. 2465-2476).

Dorigo, M., & Caro, G. D. (1999). Ant colony optimization: A new meta-heuristic. In *Proceedings of the Congress on Evolutionary Computation* (pp. 1470–1477). Washington, DC: IEEE Press.

Dorigo, M., Maniezzo, V., & Colorni, A. (1991). *Positive feedback as a search strategy* (Tech. Rep No. 91-016). Politecnico di Milano, Milan, Italy.

Dorigo, M., Maniezzo, V., & Colorni, A. (1996). The Ant System: Optimization by a Colony of Cooperating Agents. *IEEE Transactions on Systems, Man, and Cybernetics-Part B, 26*, 29–41. doi:10.1109/3477.484436

Frohlich, P., & Link, J. (2000). Automated test case generation from dynamic models. *LNCS, 1850*, 472–491.

Gambardella, L. M., & Dorigo, M. (1995). Ant-Q: A Reinforcement Learning Approach to the Travelling Salesman Problem. In A. Prieditis & S. Russell (Eds.), *Proceedings of the Twelfth International Conference on Machine Learning* (pp. 252–260). San Mateo, CA: Morgan Kaufmann.

Goldberg, D. E. (1989). *Genetic Algorithms in Search, Optimization and Machine Learning*. Reading MA: Addition-Wesley.

Gravel, M., Price, W. L., & Gagn, C. (2002). Scheduling continuous casting of aluminum using a multiple-objective ant colony optimization metaheuristic. *European Journal of Operational Research, 143*(1), 218–229. doi:10.1016/S0377-2217(01)00329-0

Gro, H.-G. (2003). An evaluation of dynamic, optimisation-based worst-case execution time analysis. *Proceedings of the International Conference on Information Technology: Prospects and Challenges in the 21st Century*, Kathmandu, Nepal.

Guo, M. H., Hierons, R. M., & Derderian, K. (2003). Computing Unique Input/Output Sequences using Genetic Algorithms. *3rd International Workshop on Formal Approaches to Testing of Software (FATES2003)*, (LNCS Vol. 2931, pp. 164-177).

Hailpern, B., & Santhanarn, P. (2002). Software Debugging, Testing and Verification. *IBM Systems Journal, 41*(1), 4–12.

Harman, M., & Jones, B. (2001). Software Engineering using Metaheuristic INnovative ALgorithms: Workshop Report. *Journal of Information and Software Technology, 43*(14), 905–907. doi:10.1016/S0950-5849(01)00196-3

Harman, M., Lakhotia, K., & McMinn, P. (2007). A multi-objective approach to search-based test data generation. In *Gecco '07: Proceedings of the 9th Annual Conference on Genetic and Evolutionary Computation* (pp. 1098–1105). New York: ACM.

Hartmann, J., Vieira, M., Foster, H., & Ruder, A. (2004). *UML-Based Test Generation and Execution* (Tech. Rep.). Siemens Corporate Research Inc., Princeton, NJ. Retrieved from www.gm.fh-koeln.de/winter/tav/html/tav21/TAV21P6Vieira.pdf

Ho, W., Jzquel, J., Guennec, A., & Pennaneac'h, F. (1999). UMLAUT: an extendible UML transformation framework. *Proc. Automated Software Engineering, ASE'99*.

Holland, J. H. (1975). *Adaptation in Natural and Artificial System*. Ann Arbor, MI: The University of Michigan Press.

Howe, A. E., Mayrhauser, A. v., & Mraz, R. T. (1997). Test Case Generation as an AI Planning Problem. *Automated Software Engineering, 4*(1), 77–106. doi:10.1023/A:1008607721339

Jayaraman, V. K., Kulkarni, B. D., Gupta, K., Rajesh, J., & Kusumaker, H. (2001). Dynamic optimization of fed-batch bioreactors using the ant algorithm. *European Journal of Operational Research, 17*(1), 81–88.

Jéron, T., & Morel, P. (1999). Test generation derived from model-checking. *CAV, 1999*, 108–121.

Jones, B. F., Sthamer, H.-H., & Eyres, D. E. (1995). The Automatic Generation of Software Test Data Sets Using Adaptive Search Techniques. In *Proceedings of 3rd International Conference on Software Quality Management*, (pp. 435–444).

Jones, B. F., Sthamer, H.-H., & Eyres, D. E. (1996). Automatic Structural Testing Using Genetic Algorithms. *Software Engineering Journal, 11*(5), 299–306.

Kirkpatrick, S., Gellat, C. D., & Vecchi, M. P. (1983). Optimization by Simulating Annealing. *Science, 220*(4598), 671–680. doi:10.1126/science.220.4598.671

Korel, B., & Al-Yami, A. M. (1996). Assertion-Oriented Automated Test Data Generation. *Proceedings of 18th. Int'l Conference on Software Engineering*, (pp. 71–80).

Kosters, G., Six, H.-W., & Winters, M. (2001). Coupling use cases and class models as a means for validation and verification of requirements specification. *Requirements Engineering, 6*(1). doi:10.1007/PL00010354

Lam, C. P., Robey, M. C., & Li, H. (2003). Application of AI for Automation of Software Testing. *Proceedings of the ACIS Fourth International Conference on Software Engineering, Artificial Intelligence, Networking and Parallel/Distributed Computing (SNPD '03)*, October 16-18, Lubeck, Germany, (pp. 242–249).

Lam, C. P., Xiao, J., & Li, H. (2007). Ant colony optimisation for generation of conformance testing sequences using a characterising set. *In ACST '07: Proceedings of the Third Conference on IASTED International Conference* (pp. 140–146). Anaheim, CA: ACTA Press.

Leite, J. C. S. P., & Breitman, K. K. (2003). Experiences using scenarios to enhance traceability. *2nd International Workshop on Traceability in Emerging Forms of Software Engineering at the 18th IEEE Conference on Automated Software Engineering.*

Li, H., & Lam, C. P. (2005a). An ant colony optimization approach to test sequence generation for state-based software testing. *Proc. QSIC 2005.* New York: IEEE Computer Society Press.

Li, H., & Lam, C. P. (2005b). Using anti-ant-like agents to generate test threads from the UML diagrams. *Proc. TESTCOM 2005*, (LNCS Vol. 3502).

Lieberman, B. (2001). UML activity diagrams: Versatile roadmaps for understanding system behavior. *The Rational Edge.* Armonk, NY: IBM

Liu, M., Jin, M., & Liu, C. (2002). Design of testing scenario generation based on UML activity diagram. *Computer Engineering and Application*, (pp. 122–124).

Mayrhauser, A. v., France, R., Scheetz, M., & Dahlman, E. (2000). Generating Test-Cases from an Object-Oriented Model wirth an Artificial-Intelligence Planning System. *IEEE Transactions on Reliability, 49*(1), 26–36. doi:10.1109/24.855534

McMinn, P. (2004). Search-based software test data generation: A survey. *Software Testing, Verification and. Reliability, 14*(2), 105–156.

McMinn, P., & Holcombe, M. (2003). The state problem for evolutionary testing. *Proc. GECCO 2003*, (LNCS, Vol. 2724, pp. 2488-2500).

Memon, A. M., Pollack, M. E., & So□a, M. L. (2001). Hierarchical GUI Test Case Generation Using Automated Planning. *IEEE Transactions on Software Engineering, 27*(2), 144–155. doi:10.1109/32.908959

Michael, C. C., McGraw, G., & Schatz, M. A. (2001). Generating software test data by evolution. *IEEE Transactions on Software Engineering, 27*(12), 1085–1110. doi:10.1109/32.988709

Mitchell, M. (1997). *An Introduction to Genetic Algorithms.* Cambridge, MA: The MIT Press.

Nebut, C., Fleurey, F., Traon, Y. L., & Jzquel, J. M. (2006). Automatic test generation: A use case driven approach. *IEEE Transactions on Software Engineering, 32*(3), 140–155. doi:10.1109/TSE.2006.22

O'Sullivan, M., Vssner, S., & Wegener, J. (1998). Testing temporal correctness of real-time systems -a new approach using genetic algorithms and cluster analysis. *Proceedings of the 6th European Conference on Software Testing, Analysis and Review (EuroSTAR 1998)*, Munich, Germany.

O□utt, J., & Abdurazik, A. (1999). Generating test cases from UML specifications. *In 2nd International Conference On The Unified Modelling Language (UML '99).* Colorado, USA.

O□utt, J., Liu, S., Abdurazik, A., & Ammann, P. (2003). Generating Test Data from State-Based Specifications. *Software Testing . Verification and Reliability, 13*(1), 25–53. doi:10.1002/stvr.264

Pargas, R. P., Harrold, M. J., & Peck, R. (1999). Test-data Generation Using Genetic Algorithms. *Software Testing . Verification and Reliability, 9*(4), 263–282. doi:10.1002/(SICI)1099-1689(199912)9:4<263::AID-STVR190>3.0.CO;2-Y

Pelliccione, P., Muccini, H., Bucchiarone, A., & Facchini, F. (2005). Testor: Deriving test sequences from model-based specifications. *Eighth International SIGSOFT Symposium on Component-based Software Engineering (CBSE 2005)*, (LNCS Vol. 3489, pp. 267-282).

Reid, S. (2005). Systematic UML testing. *SQC UK: Conference on Software Testing*, London.

Solnon, C. (2002). Ants can solve constraint satisfaction problems. *IEEE Transactions on Evolutionary Computation, 6*(4), 347–357. doi:10.1109/TEVC.2002.802449

Stützle, T., & Hoos, H. (1997). Improvements on the ant system: Introducing the MAX- MIN ant system. In *Third International Conference on Artificial Neural Networks and Genetic Algorithms*, University of East Anglia, Norwich, UK, Berlin: Springer Verlag.

Tracey, N. (2000). *A Search-based Automatic Test-data Generation Framework for Safety-Critical Software*. Unpublished doctoral dissertation, University of York, UK.

Tracey, N., Clark, J., Mander, K., & McDermid, J. (2002). A search based automated test data generation framework for safety critical systems. *In P. Henderson (Ed.), Systems Engineering for Business Process Change (New Directions)*. Berlin: Springer Verlag.

Tsai, W. T., Bai, X., Paul, R., Shao, W., & Agarwal, V. (2001). End-to-end integration testing design. *Proceedings of 25th Annual International Computer Software and Applications Conference*, 166–171.

Vanmali, M., Last, M., & Kandel, A. (2002). Using a Neural Network in the Software Testing Process. *International Journal of Intelligent Systems, 17*(1), 45–62. doi:10.1002/int.1002

Wang, L., & Yuan, J. (2004). Generating test cases from UML activity diagram based on gray-box method. *Proceedings of the 11th Asia-Pacific Software Engineering Conference*, (pp. 284–291).

Wegener, J., Baresel, A., & Sthamer, H.-H. (2001). Evolutionary Test Environment for Automatic Structural Testing. *Information and Software Technology, 43*, 841–854. doi:10.1016/S0950-5849(01)00190-2

Wegener, J., Sthamer, H.-H., Jones, B. F., & Eyres, D. E. (1997). Testing Real-Time Systems using Genetic Algorithms. *Software Quality Journal, 6*(2), 127–135. doi:10.1023/A:1018551716639

Weidenhaupt, K., Pohl, K., Jarke, M., & Haumer, P. (1998). Scenarios in system development: current practice. *IEEE Software, 15*(2), 34–45. doi:10.1109/52.663783

Wu, Y., Chen, M., & O□ut, J. (2003). UML-based Integration Testing for Component-based Software. *In The 2nd International Conference on COTS-based Software Systems (ICCBSS)*, (pp. 251-260) Ottawa, Canada.

Xanthakis, S., Ellis, C., Skourlas, C., Gall, A. L., Katsikas, S., & Karapoulios, K. (1992). Application of genetic algorithms to software testing. In *Proceedings of the 5th International Conference on Software Engineering* (pp. 625–636). Toulouse, France.

Xiao, M., El-Attar, M., Reformat, M., & Miller, J. (2007). Empirical Evaluation of Optimization Algorithms when used in Goal Oriented Automated Test-data Generation Techniques. *Empirical Software Engineering, 12*, 183–239. doi:10.1007/s10664-006-9026-0

Zhang, M., Liu, C., & Sun, C. (2001). Automated test case generation based on UML activity diagram model. *J. Beijing Uni. Aeronautics and Astronautics, 27*(4), 433–437.

ADDITIONAL READING

Ali, S., Briand, L. C., & Rehman, M. J. ur, Asghar, H., Iqbal, M. Z. Z., & Nadeem, A. (2007). A state-based approach to integration testing based on UML models. *Information and Software Technology, 49*(11-12), 1087–1106. doi:10.1016/j.infsof.2006.11.002

Arcuri, A., & Yao, X. (2008). Search based software testing of object-oriented containers. *Information Sciences, 178*(15), 3075–3095. doi:10.1016/j.ins.2007.11.024

Baldini, A., Benso, A., & Prinetto, P. (2005). System-level functional testing from UML specifications in end-of-production industrial environments. *International Journal on Software Tools for Technology Transfer, 7*(4), 326–340. doi:10.1007/s10009-004-0147-8

Bianchi, L., Gambardella, L. M., & Dorigo, M. (2002). An ant colony optimization approach to the probabilistic traveling salesman problem. In J. J. Guervós, P. Adamidis, H. Beyer, J. L. Martín, & H. Schwefel, (Eds.) *Proceedings of the 7th international Conference on Parallel Problem Solving From Nature,* September 07 – 11, (LNCS Vol. 2439, pp. 883-892). London: Springer-Verlag.

Chen, M., Qiu, X., Xu, W., Wang, L., Zhao, J., & Li, X. (2007). UML Activity Diagram-Based Automatic Test Case Generation For Java Programs. *The Computer Journal.*

Clarke, J., Dolado, J. J., Harman, M., Hierons, R. M., Jones, B., & Lumkin, M. (2003). Reformulating software engineering as a search problem. *IEE Proceedings. Software, 150*(3), 161–175. doi:10.1049/ip-sen:20030559

Colorni, A., Dorigo, M., & Maniezzo, V. (1991). Distributed optimization by ant colonies. In *F. Varela & P. Bourgine (Eds.), Proceedings of the First European Conference on Artificial Life (ECAL)* (pp. 134–142). Cambridge, MA: MIT Press.

Davis, L. D. (1991). *Handbook of genetic algorithm.* Van Nostrand Reinhold Co., New York.

Dorigo, M., Bonabeau, E., & Theraulaz, G. (2000). Ant algorithms and stygmergy. *Future Generation Computer Systems, 16*(8), 851–871. doi:10.1016/S0167-739X(00)00042-X

Dorigo, M., & Sttzle, T. (2002). The ant colony optimization metaheuristic: Algorithms, applications and advances. In F. Glover & G. Kochenberger (Eds.), *Handbook of Metaheuristics.* Kluwer Academic Publishers.

Dorigo, M., & Sttzle, T. (2004). *Ant colony optimization.* Cambridge, MA: MIT Press.

Dorigo, M., Zlochin, M., Meuleau, N., & Birattari, M. (2002). Updating aco pheromones using stochastic gradient ascent and cross-entropy methods. In S. Cagnoni, J. Gottlieb, E. Hart, M. Middendorf, & G. Raidl (Eds.), *Applications of Evolutionary Computing, Proceedings of EVO workshops 2002* (Vol. 2279, pp. 21–30). Berlin: Springer Verlag.

Eiben, A. E., Hinterding, R., & Michalewicz, Z. (1999). Parameter control in evolutionary algorithms. *IEEE Transactions on Evolutionary Computation*, *3*(2), 124–141. doi:10.1109/4235.771166

Groß, H.-G. (2000). *Measuring Evolutionary Testability of Real-Time Software*. Unpublished doctoral dissertation, University of Glamorgan, UK.

Harman, M. (2007). The current state and future of search based software engineering. In *Proceedings of International Conference on Software Engineering/Future of Software Engineering 2007* (ICSE/FOSE 2007) (pp. 342-357). Washington, DC: IEEE Computer Society.

Harman, M., Hu, L., Hierons, R. M., Fox, C., Danicic, S., Wegener, J., et al. (2002). Evolutionary Testing Supported by Slicing and Transformation. *In 18th International Conference on Software Maintenance (ICSM 2002), Maintaining Distributed Heterogeneous Systems*, 3-6 October 2002, Montreal, Canada. Washington, DC: IEEE Computer Society.

Harman, M., & Jones, B. F. (2001). The Seminal Workshop: Reformulating Software Engineering as a Metaheuristic Search Problem. *SIGSOFT Softw. Eng. Notes*, *26*(6), 62–66. doi:10.1145/505532.505548

Hartmann, J., Imoberdorf, C., & Meisinger, M. (2000). Uml-based integration testing. In *ISSTA'00: Proceedings of the 2000 ACM Sigsoft International Symposium on Software Testing and Analysis* (pp. 60–70). New York: ACM.

Li, H., & Lam, C. P. (2004). Optimization of state-based test suites for software systems: An evolutionary approach. *International Journal Computer and Information Science*, *5*(3), 212–223.

Reuys, A., Reis, S., Kamsties, E., & Pohl, K. (2003). Derivation of domain test scenarios from activity diagrams. *International Workshop on Product Line Engineering: The Early Steps: Planning, Modeling, and Managing*.

Samuel, P., Mall, R., & Kanth, P. (2007). Automatic test case generation from UML communication diagrams. *Information and Software Technology*, *49*(2), 158–171. doi:10.1016/j.infsof.2006.04.001

Sthamer, H. H. (1995). *The Automatic Generation of Software Test Data Using Genetic Algorithms*. Unpublished doctoral dissertation, University of Glamorgan, UK.

Whitley, L. D. (2001). An overview of evolutionary algorithms: practical issues and common pitfalls. *Information and Software Technology*, *43*(14), 817–831. doi:10.1016/S0950-5849(01)00188-4

Wu, Q., & Cao, Y. J. (1997). Stochastic optimization of control parameters in genetic algorithms. *IEEE International Conference on Evolutionary Computation*, (pp. 77-80).

Xu, D., Li, H., & Lam, C. P. (2007). A systematic approach to automatically generate test scenarios from UML activity diagrams. *In ACST'07: Proceedings of The Third Conference n IASTED International Conference* (pp. 134–139). Anaheim, CA: ACTA Press.

ENDNOTES

[1]   The terms test case design and test case generation are used interchangeably in this paper.

[2]   Definition of test thread: A complete execution trace (End-to-End (E2E)) of sequence of events resulting from the reaction of a system to a stimulus and ends in a deterministic state. The execution of a test thread demonstrates a method to perform a specified function.

The terms test scenario and test thread are used interchangeably in this paper.

[3] A type of temporary bridge which is quickly built using floating pontoons for the passage of troops. A more detailed explanation of its use in the context of the proposed algorithm can be found in Section *Building Fork-Join Bridge*.

•

Chapter 13
Mining Past–Time Temporal Rules
A Dynamic Analysis Approach*

David Lo
Singapore Management University, Singapore

Siau-Cheng Khoo
National University of Singapore, Singapore

Chao Liu
Microsoft Research – Redmond, USA

ABSTRACT

Specification mining is a process of extracting specifications, often from program execution traces. These specifications can in turn be used to aid program understanding, monitoring and verification. There are a number of dynamic-analysis-based specification mining tools in the literature, however none so far extract past time temporal expressions in the form of rules stating: "whenever a series of events occur, previously another series of events happened before". Rules of this format are commonly found in practice and useful for various purposes. Most rule-based specification mining tools only mine future-time temporal expression. Many past-time temporal rules like "whenever a resource is used, it was allocated before" are asymmetric as the other direction does not holds. Hence, there is a need to mine past-time temporal rules. In this chapter, the authors describe an approach to mine significant rules of the above format occurring above a certain statistical thresholds from program execution traces. The approach start from a set of traces, each being a sequence of events (i.e., method invocations) and resulting in a set of significant rules obeying minimum thresholds of support and confidence. A rule compaction mechanism is employed to reduce the number of reported rules significantly. Experiments on traces of JBoss Application Server and Jeti instant messaging application shows the utility of our approach in inferring interesting past-time temporal rules.

DOI: 10.4018/978-1-60566-758-4.ch013

INTRODUCTION

Different from many engineering products that rarely change, software changes often throughout its lifespan. This phenomenon has been well studied under the umbrella notion of software evolution. Software maintenance effort deals with the management of such changes, ensuring that the software remains correct while additional features are incorporated (Grubb & Takang, 2003). Maintenance cost can contribute up to 90% of software development cost (Erlikh, 2000). *Reducing maintenance cost* and ensuring a program *remains correct during evolution* are certainly two worthwhile goals to pursue.

A substantial portion of maintenance cost is due to the difficulty in understanding an existing code base. Studies show that program comprehension can contribute up to 50% of the maintenance cost (Fjeldstad & Hamlen, 1983; Standish, 1984). A challenge to software comprehension is the maintenance of an accurate and updated specification as program changes. As a study shows, documented specifications often remain unchanged during program evolution (Deelstra et al., 2004). One contributing factor is the short-time-to-market requirement of software products (Capilla & Due-nas, 2003). Multiple cycles of software evolution can render the outdated specification invalid or even misguiding.

To ensure correctness of a software system, model checking (Clarke et al., 1999) has been proposed. It accepts a model and a set of formal properties to check. Unfortunately, difficulty in formulating a set of formal properties has been a barrier to its wide-spread adoption (Ammons et al., 2002). Adding software evolution to the equation, the verification process is further strained. First, ensuring correctness of software as changes are made is not a trivial task: a change in one part of a code might induce unwanted effects resulting in bugs in other parts of the code. Furthermore, as a system changes and features are added, there is a constant need to add new properties or modify

outdated properties to render automated verification techniques effective in detecting bugs and ensuring the correctness of the system.

Addressing the above problems, there is a need for techniques to automatically reverse engineer or mine formal specifications from program. Recently, there has been a surge in software engineering research to adopt machine learning and statistical approaches to address these problems. One active area is specification discovery (Ammons et al., 2002; Cook & Wolf, 1998; Lo & Khoo, 2006; Reiss & Renieris, 2001), where software specification is reverse-engineered from program traces. Employing these techniques ensures specifications remain updated; also it provides a set of properties to verify via formal verification tools like model checking. To re-emphasize, the benefits of specification mining are as follows:

1. Aid program comprehension and maintenance by automatic recovery of program behavioral models, *e.g.*, (Cook & Wolf, 1998; Lo & Khoo, 2006; Reiss & Renieris, 2001).
2. Aid program verification (also runtime monitoring) in automating the process of "formulating specifications", *e.g.*, (Ammons et al., 2002; Yang et al., 2006).

Most specification miners extract specifications in the form of automata (Ammons et al., 2002; Cook & Wolf, 1998; Lo & Khoo, 2006; Reiss & Renieris, 2001) or temporal rules (Lo et al., 2008a; Yang et al., 2006). Usually a mined automaton expresses the whole behaviour of a system under analysis. Mined rules express strongly-observed constraints each expressing a property which holds with certain statistical significance.

Rules mined in (Lo et al., 2008a; Yang et al., 2006) express future-time temporal expressions. Yang et al. mine two event rules of the form: "Whenever an event occurs, eventually another event occurs in the future". Lo et al. mine temporal rules of arbitrary length of the form: "Whenever a series of event occur, eventually another series of event occur in the future". In this work, we extend the above work by mining past-time temporal expressions of this format:

"Whenever a series of events pre occur, previously, another series of events post happened before"

The above rule is denoted as *pre ↪ p post*, where *pre* and *post* correspond to the premise (pre-condition) and consequent (post-condition) of the rule respectively. This set of rules can be expressed in past-time temporal logic (Linear Temporal Logic (LTL) + past time operators (Laroussinie & Schnoebelen, 1995)) and belongs to two of the most frequently used families of temporal logic expressions for verification (i.e., precedence and chain-precedence) according to a survey by Dwyer et al. (1999). Some example specifications of the above format are as follows:

1. Whenever a file is used, it was opened before.
2. Whenever a socket is written, it was initialized before.
3. Whenever SSL read is performed, SSL init was invoked before.
4. Whenever a client requests a resource and the resource is not granted, the resource had been allocated to another client that requested it before.
5. Whenever money is dispensed in an Automated Teller Machine (ATM), previously, card was inserted, pin was entered, user was authenticated and account balance was checked before.

It has been shown that past-time LTL can express temporal properties more succinctly than (pure) future-time LTL (Laroussinie et al., 2002; Lichtenstein et al., 1985). Simple past-time LTL can correspond to more complicated equivalent future-time LTL, many of which are not minable by existing techniques mining future-time LTL

rules from traces. The subset of the past-time LTL mined by the approach presented in this chapter is not minable by previous approaches in (Lo et al., 2008a; Yang et al., 2006). Our work is not meant to replace, rather to complement future-time temporal rule mining.

In static inference of specification, Ramanathan et al. (2007) mine specifications from program source code of the form: 'Whenever an event occurs, previously, another series of events happened before". Different from Ramanathan et al. we analyze program traces and we need to address the issue of repeated behaviors within program traces (due to loops and recursions). Ramanathan et al. use an off-the-shelf data mining algorithm (Agrawal & Srikant, 1995) which ignores repetitions within a sequence. Static analysis has a different set of issues related to the difficulty in analyzing pointers and references (Briand et al., 2006) and the number of infeasible paths (Baskiotis et al., 2007). Also, our target specification format is more general capturing pre-conditions of multiple event length, hence enabling user to mine for more complex temporal properties. Also, as described later, we present a method to compact significant rules by 'early' pruning of redundant rules resulting in a potentially combinatorial speed-up and reduction in the set of mined rules. In (Ramanathan et al., 2007), all significant rules are first generated before redundant ones are removed. The large number of intermediary rules (exponential to the length of the longest rule) might make the algorithm not scalable enough to mine for rules of long length. Also, specification pertaining to behaviour of the system like the 4th specification above is not easily minable from code.

Our mining algorithm models mining as a search space exploration process. The input is a set of sequences of events, where an event corresponds to an interesting method invocation to be analyzed. The output is a set of significant rules that obeys the minimum thresholds of support and confidence – which are commonly used statistics in data mining (Han & Kamber, 2006). We define the support of a rule to be the number of traces where the rule's premise is observed. We define the confidence of a rule to be the likelihood that the rule's premise is preceded by the consequent. Similar to model checking, the algorithm builds the solution in a bottom up fashion. It first constructs rule of shorter length, and utilizes several properties to throw away sub-search space not yet traversed if some short-length rules are not significant. The search space pruning strategy ensures that the runtime is linearly bounded by the number of significant rules rather than the size of the input.

In addition, we observe that some rules are redundant. To address this, we employ additional pruning strategies to throw away redundant rules. We keep the more comprehensive longer rules that capture more information and hence subsume the shorter ones.

We guarantee that all mined rules are significant and non-redundant. Also, all significant and non-redundant rules are mined. In data mining, an algorithm meetings the first and second criteria above is referred to as being correct (sound) and complete respectively, c.f., (Han & Kamber, 2006; Li et al., 2006). In this chapter, we refer to the above criteria as *statistical soundness and completeness*.

To demonstrate our ideas, in this chapter, we experimented with traces from components of JBoss Application Server (JBoss Development Team, 2007) and Jeti instant messaging application (Jeti Development Team, 2006). The experiments show the utility of our approach in mining specifications of an industrial program.

The chapter is organized as follows. First, we describe related work. We then discuss the semantics of mined rules. Next we describe our mining algorithm. We then continue with a description of the experiments performed. We then discuss some future work and trends and finally conclude.

BACKGROUND

One of the most well-known specification mining tool is Daikon (Ernst et al., 2001). It returns value-based invariants (e.g., $x > 5$, etc.) by monitoring a fixed set of templates as a program is run. Different from Daikon, in this work, we consider temporal invariants capturing ordering constraint among events.

Most specification mining tools mine *temporal* specifications in the form of automata (Acharya et al, 2007; Cook & Wolf, 1998; Lo & Khoo, 2006; Lorenzoli et al., 2008; Reiss & Renieris, 2001). An automaton specifies a global behavior of a system. In contrast, mined rules describe *strongly observed* sub-behaviors of a system or properties that occur with statistical significance (i.e., appear with enough support and confidence).

Yang et al. (2006) presented an interesting work on mining two-event temporal logic rules, which are statistically significant with respect to a user-defined 'satisfaction rate'. These rules express: "whenever an event occurs, eventually in the future another event occurs". The algorithm presented, however, does not scale to mine multi-event rules of arbitrary length. To handle longer rules, Yang et al. suggest a partial solution based on concatenation of mined two-event rules. Yet, the method proposed might miss some significant multi-event rules or introduces superfluous rules that are not statistically significant – it is neither statistically sound nor complete.

Lo et al. (2008) extended the work by Yang et al. to mine future-time temporal rules of arbitrary lengths. The algorithm is statistically sound and complete. Rules of *arbitrary lengths* are able to capture more complex temporal properties. Often, simple properties are already known by the programmers while complex properties might be missed or might be an emergent behavior.

Lo et al. (2007b) mined Live Sequence Chart (LSC) from program execution traces. LSC can be viewed as a formal form of a sequence diagram. The LSCs mined are of the format:

"whenever a chart pre is satisfied, eventually another chart main is satisfied". Different from standard temporal rules, LSCs impose specific constraints on the satisfaction of a chart (pre or main). When translated to LTL, LSC corresponds to rather complex temporal expressions (Kugler et al., 2005). Also, different from this work, the work in (Lo et al., 2007b) only mines LSCs that express future time temporal expressions. To the best of our knowledge, LSCs focus on expressing future-time temporal expressions and are usually employed to express liveness properties for reactive systems.

In (Lo et al., 2007a), we proposed iterative patterns to mine frequent patterns of program behavior. Different from rules, patterns do not express any form of entailment constraints. A rule on the other hand expresses a constraint that state when its premise is satisfied, its consequent is satisfied as well. For monitoring and verification purposes, constraints are needed.

There are several studies on extracting specifications from code, e.g., (Alur et al., 2005; Engler et al., 2001; Li and Zhou, 2005; Ramanathan et al., 2007; Weimer & Necula, 2005). The above techniques belong to the *static analysis* family. In contrast, we adopt a *dynamic analysis* approach in extracting specifications from execution traces. Static and dynamic analyses complement each other, *c.f.,* (Ernst, 2003). Their pros and cons have been discussed in the literature (Briand et al., 2006; Ernst, 2003). With dynamic analysis, even with the best algorithms, the quality of specification mined is only as good as the quality of traces. With static analysis, one is faced with the problem of pointers and infeasible paths. Some specifications pertaining to the dynamic behavior of a system can only be mined (or are much easier to mine) via dynamic analysis.

Studies in (Engler et al., 2001; Li and Zhou, 2005; Ramanathan et al., 2007; Weimer & Necula, 2005) mine specifications from code, and present them in the form of rules. The study in (Li and Zhou, 2005) ignores ordering of events and hence mined rules do not describe temporal properties. Past studies on extracting rules expressing temporal properties from code (Engler et al., 2001; Weimer & Necula, 2005) are limited to extract two-event rules. Ramanathan et al. (2007) mine past-time temporal rules from program code. In contrast, in this study, we mine rules from program execution traces, address the issue of repetitions due to loop and recursion in the traces and mine rules with pre-conditions of arbitrary lengths.

CONCEPTS AND DEFINITIONS

This section introduces preliminaries on past-time LTL and formalizes the scope of rules minable by our approach. Also, notations used in this chapter are described.

Past-Time Linear-time Temporal Logic: Our mined rules can be expressed in pastime Linear Temporal Logic (LTL) (Laroussinie & Schnoebelen, 1995). Past-time temporal logic is an extension of (future-time) LTL (Huth & Ryan, 2004). LTL is a logic that works on possible program paths. A possible program path corresponds to a program trace. A path can be considered as a series of events, where an event is a method invocation. For example, (file open, file read, file write, file close), is a 4-event path.

There are a number of LTL operators, among which we are only interested in the operators 'G','F' and 'X' and some of their past-time counterparts 'F^{-1}' and 'X^{-1}'. The operator 'G' specifies that *globally* at every point in time a certain property holds. The operator 'F' specifies that a property holds at that point in time or *at a time in the future*. The operator 'X' specifies that a property holds at the *next* event.

The operator 'F^{-1}' specifies that a property holds at that point in time or *at a time in the past*. The operator 'X^{-1}' specifies that a property holds at the *previous* event.

Let us consider the three examples listed in Table 1.

Table 1. Past-time LTL Expressions and their Meanings

$X^{-1}F^{-1}(file\_open)$ Meaning: *At a time in the past* a file was opened
$G(file\_read \rightarrow X^{-1}F^{-1}(file\_open))$ Meaning: *Globally* whenever a file is read, *at a time in the past* the file was opened
$G((account\_deducted \wedge X\,F(money\_dispensed)) \rightarrow$ $(X^{-1}F^{-1}(balance\_suffice \wedge (X^{-1}F^{-1}(cash\_requested \wedge (X^{-1}F^{-1}(correct\_pin \wedge (X^{-1}F^{-1}(insert\_debit\;card)))))))))$ Meaning: Globally whenever one's bank account is deducted and money is dispensed (from an Automated Teller Machine (ATM)), previously user inserted debit card, entered correct pin, requested for cash to be dispensed and account balance was checked and it sufficed.

Table 2. Rules and their Past-time LTL Equivalences

Notation	LTL Notation
$a \hookrightarrow_p b$	$G(a \rightarrow X^{-1}F^{-1}b)$
$\langle a,b \rangle \hookrightarrow_p c$	$G((a \wedge XFb) \rightarrow (X^{-1}F^{-1}c))$
$a \hookrightarrow_p \langle b,c \rangle$	$G(a \rightarrow X^{-1}F^{-1}(c \wedge X^{-1}F^{-1}b))$
$\langle a,b \rangle \hookrightarrow_p \langle c,d \rangle$	$G((a \wedge XFb) \rightarrow (X^{-1}F^{-1}\,(d \wedge X^{-1}F^{-1}c)))$

Our mined rules state whenever a series of premise events occurs it was preceded by another series of consequent events. A mined rule denoted as $pre \hookrightarrow_p post$, can be mapped to its corresponding LTL expression. Examples of such correspondences are shown in Table 2.

Mapping to common English language sentences and for uniformity purpose, in describing both the premise and consequent of the rule the time goes forward to the future (e.g., $\langle a,b \rangle \hookrightarrow_p \langle c,d \rangle$ is translated to: *a* is *followed* by *b*, is *preceded* by, c is *followed* by *d*). In the corresponding past-time LTL expression we need to reverse the order of *c* and *d*. Also note that although the operator 'X' might seem redundant, it is needed to specify rules such as $a \hookrightarrow_p$ <b,b> where the 'b's *refer to different occurrences of 'b'*. The set of LTL expressions minable by our mining framework is represented in the Backus-Naur Form (BNF) as follows[1]:

Basic Notations: Let *I* be a set of distinct events considered in which an event corresponds to a behavior of interest, e.g. method call. Input to our mining framework is a set of traces. A trace corresponds to a sequence or an ordered list of events from *I*. To formalize, we refer to this set of traces as a sequence database denoted by *SeqDB*. Each trace or sequence is denoted by $<e_1; e_2; ...; e_{end}>$ where $e_i\,t\,I$.

We define a pattern *P* to be a series of events. We use *first(P)* to denote the first event of *P*. A pattern $P_1 + + P_2$ denotes the concatenation of patterns P_1 and P_2. A pattern $P_1(<e_1; e_2; ..., e_n>)$ is considered a subsequence of another pattern $P_2(<f_1; f_2; ...f_m>)$ denoted as $P_1 \sqsubseteq P_2$ if there exist integers $1 \leq i_1 < i2 < ... < i_n \leq m$ such that $e_1 = f_{i1}$, $e_2 = f_{i2}..., e_n = f_{in}$.

$rules := G(pre \rightarrow rpost)$ $pre := (event)\|(event \wedge XF(pre))$ $rpost := (event)\|(event \wedge X^{-1}F^{-1}(rpost))$

Table 3. Example Database – DBX

Identifier	Trace/Sequence
S1	<c, b, a, e, b, a>
S2	<c, b, e, a, e, b, c, a>
S3	<d, a>

MINING PAST TIME TEMPORAL RULES

Each temporal rule of interest has the form $P_1 \hookrightarrow_P P_2$, where P_1 and P_2 are two series of events. P_1 is referred to as the *premise* or *pre-condition* of the rule, while P_2 is referred to as the *consequent* or *post-condition* of the rule. The rules correspond to temporal constraints expressible in past-time LTL notations. Some examples are shown in Table 2.

In this chapter, since a trace is a series of events, where an event corresponds to a software behavior of interest, e.g., method call, *we formalize a trace as a sequence and a set of input traces as a sequence database*. We use the sample trace or sequence database in Table 3 as our running example to illustrate the concepts behind generation of temporal rules.

Concepts & Definitions

Mined rules are formalized as past-time Linear Temporal Logic expressions with the format: $G(... \rightarrow X^{-1}F^{-1}...)$. The semantics of past-time LTL described in Section 3 will dictate the semantics of temporal rules described here. Noting the meaning of the temporal operators illustrated in Table 1, to be precise, a mined past-time temporal rule expresses:

"Whenever a series of events occurred starting at a point in time (i.e. a temporal point), previously, another series of events happened before."

From the above definition, to generate temporal rules, we need to "peek" at interesting temporal points and "see" what series of events are likely to occur *before*. We first formalize the notion of temporal points and the related notion of occurrences.

Definition 1 (Temporal Points): *Consider a sequence S of the form $<a_1, a_2, ..., a_{end}>$. All events in S are indexed by their positions in S, starting at 1 (e.g., a_j is indexed by j). These positions are called temporal points in S. For a temporal point j in $S = <a_1, ..., a_n>$, the suffix $<a_{n-(j-1)}, ..., a_n>$ is called the j-suffix of S.*

Definition 2 (Occurrences & Instances): *Given a pattern P and a sequence S, the occurrences of P in S are defined by a set of temporal points T in S such that for each $j \in T$, the j-suffix of S is a super-sequence of P and first(P) is indexed by j. The set of instances of pattern P in S is defined as the set of j-suffixes of S, for each $j \in T$.*

Example: Consider a pattern $P = <b, a>$ and the sequence S1 in Table 4 (*i.e.,* $<c,b,a,e,b,a>$). The occurrences of P in S1 form the set of temporal points {2,5}, and the corresponding set of instances are {$<b,a>, <b,a,e,b,a>$}.

We define database projection operations to capture events occurring before specified temporal points. The following are two different types of projections and their associated support notions.

Definition 3 (Projected-past & Sup-past): A database projected-past on a pattern P is defined as: $SeqDB_P^{past} = \{(j, px)|$ the jth sequence in SeqDB is s, where s = px++sx, and sx is the minimum suffix of s containing P}. *Given a pattern P, we define $sup^{past}(P, SeqDB)$ to be the size of $SeqDB_P^{past}$ (i.e., the number of sequences in SeqDB containing*

Table 4. (a); $DBX^{past}_{\langle b,a \rangle}$ & (b); $DBX^{past-all}_{\langle b,a \rangle}$

Identifier	Trace/Sequence		Identifier	Trace/Sequence
S1	(1, <c; b; a; e>)		S1$_1$	(1, <c; b; a; e>)
S2	(2, <c; b; e; a; e>)		S1$_2$	(1, <c>)
			S2$_1$	(2, <c; b; e; a; e>)
			S2$_2$	(2, <c>)
	(a)			(b)

P). Reference to the database is omitted, i.e., we write it as sup(P), if the database is clear from the context, e.g., it refers to input sequence database SeqDB.

Definition 4 (Projected-past-all & Sup-past-all): *A database projected-past-all on a pattern P is defined as:* $SeqDB^{past-all}_{\langle b,a \rangle}$ = {(j,px)| the jth sequence in SeqDB is s, where s = px++sx, and sx is an instance of P in s and first(sx) = first(P)}. *For a pattern P, we define* $sup^{past-all}$(P, SeqDB) *to be the size of* $SeqDB^{past-all}_{\langle b,a \rangle}$. Reference to the database is omitted if it is clear from the context.

Definition 3 captures events occurring after the first temporal point. Definition 4 captures events occurring after each *temporal point*.

Example: To illustrate the above concepts, we project and project-all the example database *DBX* with respect to the pattern <b,a>. The results are shown in Table 4 (a) & (b) respectively.

The two projection methods' associated notions of *sup^{past}* and *sup$^{past-all}$* are different. Specifically, sup$^{past-all}$ reflects the number of occurrences of a pattern P in *SeqDB* rather than the number of sequences in *SeqDB* supporting P.

Example: Consider the example database, sup^{past}(<b,a>,DBX) = | $DBX^{past}_{\langle b,a \rangle}$ | = 2.

On the other hand, sup $^{past-all}$ (<b,a>, DBX) = | $DBX^{past-all}_{\langle b,a \rangle}$ | = 4.

From the above notions of temporal points, projected databases and pattern supports, we can define the support and confidence of temporal rules.

Definition 5 (Support & Confidence): Consider a temporal rule R (pre $\hookrightarrow_P$ post). The support of R is defined as the number of sequences in SeqDB where pre occurs, which is equivalent to sup^{past}(pre, SeqDB). The confidence of R is defined as the likelihood of post happening before pre. This is equivalent to the ratio of sup^{past}(post, $SeqDB^{past-all}_{pre_X}$) to the size of $SeqDB^{past-all}_{pre_X}$.

Example: Consider *DBX* and a temporal rule R = <b,a>$\hookrightarrow_P$<c>. From the database, the support of R_X is the number of sequences in *DBX* supporting (or is a super-sequence of) the rule's pre-condition − <b, a>. There are 2 of them − see Table 4 (a). Hence support of *R* is 2. The confidence of the rule *R* (<b, a>$\hookrightarrow_P$<c>) is the likelihood of <c> occurring before each *temporal point* of <b,a>. Referring to Table 4(b), we see that there is a <c> occurring before each temporal point of <b,a>. Hence, the confidence of *R* is 1.

Significant rules to be mined must have their supports greater than the *min-sup* threshold, *and* their confidences greater than the *min_conf* threshold.

In mining program properties, the confidence of a rule (or property), which is a measure of its certainty, matters the most (c.f., (Yang et al., 2006)). Support values are considered to differentiate high confidence rules from one another according to the frequency of their occurrences in the traces.

Rules with confidences less than 100% are also of interest due to the imperfect trace collection and the presence of bugs and anomalies (Yang et al., 2006). Similar to the assumption made by work in bug detection e.g., (Engler et al., 2001), simply put, if a program behaves in one way 99% of the time, and the opposite 1% of the time, the latter likely corresponds to a possible bug. Hence, a high confidence and highly supported rule is a good candidate for bug detection using program verifiers or runtime monitors.

We added the notions of support and confidence to past-time temporal rules. The formal notation of past-time temporal rules is defined below.

Definition 6 (Past-Time Temporal Rules): A temporal rule R is denoted by pre $\hookrightarrow$p post (sup,conf). The series of events pre and post represent the rule's pre- and post- condition and are denoted by R.Pre and R.Post respectively. The notions sup, and conf represent the support, and confidence of R respectively. They are denoted by sup(R) and conf (R) respectively.

Example: Consider *DBX* and the rule R, <b,a>$\hookrightarrow_p$ <c> shown in the previous example. It has support of 2 and confidence of 1. It is denoted by <b,a>$\hookrightarrow_p$ <c> (2,1).

Monotonicity and Non-Redundancy

Our algorithm is a member of the family of pattern mining algorithms, e.g., (Agrawal & Srikant, 1995; Wang & Han, 2004). Monotonicity (a.k.a. apriori) properties have been widely used to ensure efficiency of many pattern mining techniques, e.g., (Agrawal & Srikant, 1995; Wang & Han, 2004). Different mining algorithms often require new or additional apriori property. Fortunately, past-time temporal rules obey the following apriori properties:

Theorem 1 (Monotonicity Property

– Support): If a rule $evs_P \hookrightarrow_P evs_C$ does not satisfy the min_sup threshold, neither will all rules $evs_Q \hookrightarrow_P evs_C$ where evs_Q is a super-sequence of evs_P.

Theorem 2 (Monotonicity Property – Confidence): If a rule $evs_P \hookrightarrow_P evs_C$ does not satisfy the min_conf threshold, neither will all rules $evs_P \hookrightarrow_P evs_D$ where evs_D is a super-sequence of evs_C.

To reduce the number of rules and improve efficiency, we define a notion of rule redundancy defined based on *super-sequence relationship* among rules having the same support and confidence values. This is similar to the notion of *closed* patterns applied to sequential patterns (Wang & Han, 2004).

Definition 7 (Rule Redundancy): *A rule R_X ($pre_X \hookrightarrow_P post_X$) is redundant if there is another rule R_Y ($pre_Y \hookrightarrow_P post_Y$) where:* (1) R_X is a sub-sequence of R_Y (i.e., $post_X{+}{+}pre_X \sqsubseteq post_Y{+}{+}pre_Y$); (2) Both rules' support and confidence are the same. Also, in the case that the concatenations are the same (i.e., $post_X{+}{+}pre_X = post_Y{+}{+}pre_Y$), to break the tie, we call the one with the longer premise as being redundant (i.e., we wish to retain the rule with a shorter premise and longer consequent).

To illustrate redundant rules, consider the following set of rules shown in Table 5, describing an Automated Teller Machine (ATM).

If all of the above rules have the same support and confidence values, rules R2-R5 are redundant since they are represented by rule R1. To keep the number of mined rules manageable, we remove redundant rules. Noting the combinatorial nature of redundant rules, removing redundant rules can drastically reduce the number of reported rules.

A simple approach to reduce the number of rules is to first mine a full-set of rules and then remove redundant ones. However, this "late" re-

Table 5. ATM rules

R1	money_ dispensed $\hookrightarrow_p$ card_inserted, enter_pin, pin_correct, cash_request
R2	money dispensed $\hookrightarrow_p$ card_inserted
R3	money dispensed $\hookrightarrow_p$ enter_ pin
R4	money dispensed $\hookrightarrow_p$ card_inserted, enter_pin
R5	money dispensed $\hookrightarrow_p$ enter_pin, cash_request

moval of redundant rules is inefficient due to the exponential explosion of the number of intermediary rules that need to be checked for redundancy. To improve efficiency, it is therefore necessary to identify and prune a search space containing redundant rules "early" during the mining process. The following two theorems are used for 'early' pruning of redundant rules.

Theorem 3 (Pruning Redundant Pre-Conds):*Given two pre-conditions P_X and P_Y where P_X is a shorter subsequence of P_Y, if $SeqDB_P^{past} = SeqDB_{P_Y}^{past}$ then for all sequences of events post, rules $P_X \hookrightarrow_p post$ is rendered redundant by $P_Y \hookrightarrow_p post$ and can be pruned.*

Proof. Since P_X is a shorter subsequence of P_Y, from Definition 7 of rule redundancy, we only need to prove that the rules $R_X (P_X \hookrightarrow_p post)$ and $R_Y (P_Y \hookrightarrow_p post)$ have the same values of support and confidence.

Since $SeqDB_{P_X}^{past} = SeqDB_{P_Y}^{past}$, the followings are guaranteed: (1) P_X and P_Y must share the same prefix (at least first(P_X) = first(P_Y)) and (2) $\forall s \in SeqDB$, the first instance of P_X corresponds to the first instance of P_Y. From points (1) and (2) above, not only the first instance, but every instance of P_X in SeqDB must also correspond to an instance of P_Y (and vice versa). In other words, $SeqDB_{P_X}^{past} = SeqDB_{P_Y}^{past}$ iff $SeqDB_{P_X}^{past-all} = SeqDB_{P_Y}^{past-all}$.

Since $SeqDB_{P_X}^{past-all} = SeqDB_{P_Y}^{past-all}$, and R_X and R_Y share the same post-condition, R_X and R_Y must have the same support and confidence values.

Hence, R_X is rendered redundant by R_Y and can be pruned. □

Theorem 4 (Pruning Redundant Post-Conds):*Given two rules $R_X = pre \hookrightarrow_p P_X$ and $R_Y pre \hookrightarrow_p P_Y$ if P_X is a shorter subsequence of P_Y and $(SeqDB_{pre}^{past-all})_{P_X}^{past} = (SeqDB_{pre}^{past-all})_{P_Y}^{past}$ then R_X is rendered redundant by R_Y and can be pruned.*

Proof. Since P_X is a shorter subsequence of P_Y, from Definition 7 of rule redundancy, we only need to prove that the rule $R_X = pre \rightarrow P_X$ and $R_Y = pre \rightarrow P_Y$ have the same values of support and confidence. The equality of support values is guaranteed since the two rules have the same pre-condition.

Since $(SeqDB_{pre}^{past-all})_{P_X}^{past} = (SeqDB_{pre}^{past-all})_{P_Y}^{past}$, it implies $sup^{past}(P_X, SeqDB_{pre}^{past-all}) = sup^{past}(P_Y, SeqDB_{pre}^{past-all})$. Hence, the two rules will have the same confidence values. Hence, we have shown that R_X is rendered redundant by R_Y and can be pruned. □

Utilizing Theorems 3 & 4, many redundant rules can be pruned 'early'. However, the theorems only provide sufficient conditions for the identification of redundant rules – there are redundant rules which are not identified by them. To remove remaining redundant rules, we perform a post-mining filtering step based on Definition 7.

Our approach to mining a set of non-redundant rules satisfying the support and confidence thresholds is as follows:

Step 1: Leveraging Theorems 1 & 3, we generate a pruned set of pre-conditions satisfying *min_sup*.

Step 2: For each pre-condition *pre*, we create a *projected-past-all* database $SeqDB_{pre}^{past-all}$ pre

Step 3: Leveraging Theorems 2 & 4, for each $SeqDB_{pre}^{past-all}$, we generate a *pruned* set containing such post-condition *post*, such that the rule $pre \hookrightarrow_P post$ satisfies *min_conf*.

Step 4: Using Definition 7, we filter any remaining redundant rules.

EXPERIMENTS

In this section we discuss our experiments on mining past-time temporal rules from traces of JBoss Application Server (JBoss Development Team, 2007) and Jeti instant messaging application (Jeti Development Team, 2006). They show the utility of our method in recovering specifications of an industrial system.

JBoss AS is one of the most widely used J2EE application server. It contains over 100,000 lines of code and comments. Jeti is an open source instant messaging application that supports many features including file transfer, group chat, picture chat (drawing on shared whiteboard), etc. It contains over 49,000 lines of code and comments[2].The purpose of this study is to show the usefulness of the mined rules to describe the behavior of real software.

Experiments on JBoss AS were performed on a Pentium M 1.6GHz IBM X41 tablet PC with 1.5GB main memory, running Windows XP Tablet PC Edition 2005[3]. Experiments on Jeti were performed on a Core 2 Duo 2GHz Fujitsu E8410 laptop, running Windows Vista Business Edition[4]. The past-time temporal rule mining system is written in C#. The system makes calls to a modified BIDE (Wang & Han, 2004) described in (Lo et al., 2008a) written in C++.

Case 1: JBoss AS Security Component

We instrumented the security component of JBoss-AS using JBoss-AOP and generated traces by running the test suite that comes with the JBoss-AS distribution. In particular, we ran the regression tests on Enterprise Java Bean (EJB) security implementation of JBoss-AS. Twenty-three traces of a total size of 4115 events, with 60 unique events, were generated. Running the algorithm on the traces with the minimum support and confidence thresholds set at 15 and 90% respectively, 4 non-redundant rules were mined. The algorithm completed within 2.5 seconds.

A sample of the mined rules is shown in Table 6 (top). It describes authentication using Java Authentication and Authorization Service (JAAS) for EJB within JBoss-AS. Roughly it describes a rule that states: "Whenever principal and credential information is required (the premise of the rule), previously configuration information is checked to determine authentication service availability (event 1-5 in the consequent), actual authentication events are invoked (event 6-8) and principal information is bound to the subject being authenticated (event 9-12)".

Case 2: JBoss AS Transaction Component

We instrumented the transaction component of JBoss-AS using JBoss-AOP and generated traces by running the test suite that comes with the JBoss-AS distribution. In particular, we ran a set of transaction manager regression tests of JBoss-AS. Each trace is abstracted as a sequence of events, where an event corresponds to a method invocation. Twenty-eight traces with a total size of 2551 events containing 64 unique events, were generated. Running the algorithm on the traces with the minimum support and confidence thresholds set at 25 traces and 90% respectively,

Table 6. A sample rule from JBoss-Security (top) and another from JBoss-Transaction (bottom). Each of the rules are read from top to bottom, left to right.

Premise →ₚ Consequent	
SimplePrincipal.toString() SecAssoc.getPrincipal() SecAssoc.getCredential() SecAssoc.getPrincipal() SecAssoc.getCredential()	XLoginConfImpl.getConfEntry() PolicyConfig.get() XLoginConfImpl$1.run() AuthenticationInfo.copyAppConfEntry() AuthenticationInfo.getName() ClientLoginModule.initialize() ClientLoginModule.login() ClientLoginModule.commit() SecAssocActs.setPrincipalInfo() SetPrincipalInfoAction.run() SecAssocActs.pushSubjectContext() SubjectThreadLocalStack.push()
Premise →ₚ Consequent	
TransactionImpl.isDone()	TransManLocator.getInstance() TransManLocator.locate() TransManLocator.tryJNDI() TransManLocator.usePrivateAPI() TxManager.getInstance() TxManager.begin() XidFactory.newXid() XidFactory.getNextId() XidImpl.getTrulyGlobalId() TransImpl.assocCurrentThread() TransImpl.lock() TransImpl.unlock() TransImpl.getLocalId() XidImpl.getLocalId() LocalId.hashCode() TxManager.getTransaction()

36 non-redundant rules were mined. The algorithm completed within 30 seconds.

A sample of the mined rules is shown in Table 6 (bottom). The rule describes that: "Whenever a check is performed on whether transaction is completed (the premise of the rule), previously connection to a server instance (event 1-4 in the consequent), initialization and utilization of transaction manager and implementation (events 5-6, 10-12), acquiring of ids (event 7-9, 13-15) and obtaining of transaction from the manager (event 16) are performed before."

Case 3: Jeti Instant Messaging Application

We instrumented Jeti instant messaging application and generated traces by running the application and using it to communicate with another Jeti client. Each run of Jeti application produces one trace. We run the Jeti application 25 times corresponding to various usage scenarios of Jeti. Each trace is abstracted as a sequence of events, where an event corresponds to a method invocation. Twenty-five traces with a total size of 2296 events containing 84 unique events were generated. Running the algorithm on the traces with the minimum support and confidence thresholds set at 20 traces and 90% respectively, 31 non-redundant

Table 7. Three sample rules from Jeti Instant Messaging application. Each of the Rules are read from top to bottom, left to right.

Premise → ₚ Consequent	
Jeti.removeFromMenu() Jeti.removeFromMenu()	StatusButton.init() JetiFrame.init() StatusButton.updateLF() ProfileInfo.getProfile() Jeti.close() ChatWindows.askIfClose() Jeti.exit() ChatWindows.exit() Jeti.removeFromRosterMenu() Jeti.removeFromRosterMenu()

Premise → ₚ Consequent	
Jeti.openGroups() Jeti.close() ChatWindows.askIfClose() Jeti.exit() ChatWindows.exit() Jeti.removeFromRosterMenu() Jeti.removeFromRosterMenu() Jeti.removeFromMenu() Jeti.removeFromMenu()	*First 4 evs of first rule's consequent* LoginWindow.btnLogin_actPerformed() ProfileInfo.getProfile() Jeti.preferencesChanged() Jeti.presenceChanged() JetiFrame.initTimer() ChatWindows.presenceChanged()

Premise → ₚ Consequent		
titlescroller.Plugin.unload() Jeti.removeFromRosterMenu() Jeti.removeFromRosterMenu() Jeti.removeFromMenu() Jeti.removeFromMenu()	*First 4 evs of first rule's consequent* LoginWindow.btnLogin_actPerformed() ProfileInfo.getProfile() Jeti.preferencesChanged() Jeti.presenceChanged() Jeti.JetiFrame.initTimer() ChatWindows.presenceChanged() Jeti.openGroups() Jeti.presenceChanged() Jeti.JetiFrame.initTimer() ChatWindows.presenceChanged() ChatWindow.makeMenu() Jeti.getRosterMenuItems() ChatWindow.makeWindow()	ChatSplitPane.init() ChatSplitPane.setParentFrame() titlescroller.Plugin.init() titleflash.Plugin.init() ChatWindow.init() ChatWindow.setLocationOnScreen() titlescroller.Plugin.stop() titleflash.Plugin.Flash.stop() ChatWindows.removeChatWindow() ChatWindow.exit() ChatSplitPane.close() *Evs 5-8 of first rule's consequent* titleflash.Plugin.unload() titleflash.Plugin.Flash.stop()

rules were mined. The algorithm completed within 10 seconds.

Three samples of the mined rules is shown in Table 7. The 3 rules describe a family of requirements or specifications related to one another; each is stricter than the previous one.

The first rule describes that: "Whenever components are removed from the Menu during Jeti termination (the premise of the rule), previously Jeti must have been initialized before (events 1-3 in the consequent), profile must have been loaded when the log-in prompt is presented (event 4 in the consequent), and other termination events must be invoked before (events 5-10 in the consequent)." Note that during Jeti termination, two separate components need to be removed from the menu and another two from roster menu and hence the corresponding methods are invoked more than once.

Compared to the first rule, the second rule describes a stricter temporal requirement when its premise is satisfied. The rule describes that: "Whenever groups are opened and termination events follows (the premise of the rule), previously

Jeti must have been initialized before (events 1-3 in the consequent), profile must have been loaded when the log-in prompt is presented (event 4 in the consequent), login must have been made (event 5 in the consequent), appropriate profile must be obtained (event 6 in the consequent), and detection of change in preferences and other active clients in the roster must have been made (events 7-10 in the consequent)." Different from the first rule, the second rule states the condition that requires user to login to the system (i.e. the 6th event in the consequent of the rule). The support of the second rule is lower than the first rule because not all recorded interactions login to the application. However, if Jeti does invoke openGroups method, the above rule is observed – i.e., the rule has lower support but equal confidence.

Compared to the first 2 rules, the third rule describes a stricter temporal requirement when its premise is satisfied. The rule describes that: "Whenever titlescroller plugin is unloaded and termination events follows (the premise of the rule), previously Jeti must have been initialized before (events 1-3 in the consequent), profile must have been loaded when the log-in prompt is presented (event 4 in the consequent), login must have been made (event 5 in the consequent), appropriate profile must be obtained (event 6 in the consequent), detection of change in preferences and other active clients in the roster must have been made (events 7-10 in the consequent), groups must have been opened (event 11 in the consequent), chat window need to be created and initialized (events 12 -19), titlescroller and titleflasher plugins need to be initialized (event 20-21), other initialization of the chat window need to be made (events 22-23), titlescroller and titleflasher plugins need to be stopped (events 24-25), chat window need to be removed (events 26-28) and a series of other termination events need to be made before (events 29-34)." Different from the first and second rules, the third rule states the condition that requires user to initialize a chat window and the two plugins: titlescroller

and titleflasher. The support of the third rule is lower than the first and second rule because not all recorded interactions start up a chat window. However, again, if Jeti does unload titlescroller plugin, the above rule is observed – i.e., the rule has lower support but equal confidence.

FUTURE TRENDS

In this section, we discuss some related issues and potential future work. Similar to pattern mining algorithms, e.g., (Agrawal & Srikant, 1995), one issue is in the setting of suitable minimum support threshold. It is less straightforward than setting appropriate minimum confidence threshold. In our case studies, we used three different minimum support thresholds: one at 15 (65% of the number of traces), another at 25 (90% of the number of traces) and the last one at 20 (80% of the number of traces). When setting minimum support threshold to 21 (90% of the number of traces) for analyzing traces from the first experiment on JBoss AS, we found no significant rules. In general, the more diverse the trace set is, the lower the minimum support threshold needs to be set. Similar to many data mining processes, we view our mining strategy to be an iterative process; at each step, user provides a set of thresholds, runs the miner and evaluates the mined result to decide whether another refinement, by mining at lower or higher thresholds, is needed. As a future work, we plan to formalize and provide tool support to this iterative process to help users decide on a suitable minimum support threshold.

In this work, we guarantee statistical soundness and completeness. Hypothetically, if the input trace set is sound and complete, we will mine a sound and complete set of specifications. Admittedly, traces generated by running a program are generally not complete. As with other dynamic analysis techniques, the effectiveness of the proposed technique is dependent on the quality and sufficiency of the input traces. For example, the pre-conditions of the rule shown in Table 6 (left) involve multiple occurrences of *SecAssoc.getPrinciple()* and *SecAssoc.getCredential()*. This is the case, as within each trace, in the input trace set, the two methods are called two or more times in tandem. As a future work, we plan to look into employing a synergy of static and dynamic analysis techniques to allow generation of more complete trace set as input to the mining process.

In this study, we use only traces of a few thousand events. In future, we will experiment with traces of longer lengths obtained from a wider variety of software systems. In general, our algorithm will work better with many traces of shorter length, than few very long traces. Employing scenario extraction technique, c.f., (Ammons et al., 2002), will convert trace of long length to sub-traces of shorter lengths. We plan to employ this and use the modified techniques to mine rules from longer traces. The rules will be fewer as a scenario extraction technique usually employs additional constraints to decide on which events are related to another aside from temporal ordering observed in the traces alone. Also, to handle longer traces, user can provide additional constraints to guide the mining process further. We plan to experiment with these options as a future work.

Currently we only consider method calls without consideration of their return and parameter values. Each method call is mapped to a symbol. Often, it is necessary to differentiate a method based on its input parameters or return values. For example, a socket read can return success or failure. Sometimes, the return values can be inferred from a sequence of method call. For example in OpenSSL (OpenSSL Development Team, 2008), if SSL_read() is followed by SSL_get_error(), it is likely to mean that something wrong has happened to the read. In the future, we are looking into incorporation of the return and parameter values to the mining process.

There are alternative definition and other subset of past-time temporal rules to be mined. In this chapter, the occurrence of the rule post-condition occurs before the first event of the rule's premise. Sometimes this condition needs to be modified. For example, consider the specification: "Whenever a function performs a blocking read on the channel and the function exits successfully, a channel write happened before." In the case above, the channel write can occur before the blocking read or between the blocking read and the function exit. A rule capturing the above specification corresponds to a different past-time LTL expression. We leave the modification of the mining algorithm to mine the above variant of our past-time temporal rules as a future work.

In this chapter, only ordering constraint is considered. Often, both ordering and value-based constraints are needed. Consider an embedded software running on a vending machine. A possible specification is: "Whenever a coin is entered but later ejected, it must be the case that the number of drinks to be dispensed == 0". Also, consider the specification: "Whenever a non-blocking resource request is made, but it is not granted, it must be the case that the number of resource left == 0". We plan to follow the approach by Mariani and Pezzè (2005) and Lorenzoli et al. (2008), by merging Daikon (Ernst et al., 2001), that mines value-based invariants, with our tool.

Also similar to the argument made in (Laroussinie et al., 2002), often there is a need to 'forget' past information. Adapting the example in (Laroussinie et al., 2002), consider an automotive system with an alarm notifying problem and a reset button to restore the system to last known good state. A good property is to ensure that the car alarm doesn't sound unless there is a problem before. This corresponds to the past-time property: "whenever an alarm sounds, there must be a problem before". However, this problem must appear after the last reset. One needs to "forget" past information whenever a reset action is taken. In mining software specifications, if these "reset"-like events can be input to the miner, this will improve the mining results and speed up the mining process as well.

In our experiments, we note that some of our mined rules are minor variations of one another. This is the case since we only mine for total order. If there are two events the order between which is irrelevant, the miner might return this partial order as two separate rules. In the future we plan to adopt the approach by Acharya et al. (2007), used for mining automata using static analysis by composing mined partial orders, and adapt it to mine for rules expressing partial order. The partial order miner (Pei et al., 2006) used in (Acharya et al., 2007) ignores repetitions in the input sequence set. A new data mining algorithm might need to be developed to merge our approach with the partial order miner.

Also in the list of our future work is incorporation of negation, disjunction and the remaining LTL/past-time LTL operators not considered so far namely: until and since operators. Integration of the proposed mining technique into automated processes, for example, software verification, runtime monitoring or anomaly detection is also among one of the future work that we are looking into.

CONCLUSION

In this chapter, we propose a technique to mine past-time temporal rules from program execution traces. The rules state: "Whenever a series of events occurs, previously another series of events has happened". These rules capture important properties useful for verification, monitoring and program understanding.

Existing work on mining temporal rules focuses on future-time temporal expressions. Past-time temporal logic is more intuitive and compact to express some classes of important properties. We consider our work as complementing existing techniques mining future-time temporal expressions. To the best of our knowledge, this is the first work on mining past-time temporal rules from program execution traces where repetitions due to

loop and recursion need to be considered. Our rule format is also more general than the precedence rule mined by static-analysis-based approach in (Ramanathan et al., 2007).

Also, the problems of a potentially exponential runtime cost and a huge number of reported rules have been effectively mitigated by employing search space pruning strategies and elimination of redundant rules. Experiments on JBoss Application Server and Jeti instant messaging application show the utility of our technique in recovering specifications of an industrial program.

ACKNOWLEDGMENT

We would like to thank Jianyong Wang and Jiawei Han for allowing us to use BIDE, a closed sequential pattern miner (Wang & Han, 2004). Our proposed algorithm involves making calls to a modified version of BIDE (c.f. (Lo et al., 2008a)).

REFERENCES

Acharya, M., Xie, T., Pei, J., & Xu, J. (2007). Mining API patterns as partial orders from source code: From usage scenarios to specifications. In *Proceedings of SIGSOFT Symposium on Foundations of Software Engineering (FSE)*.

Agrawal, R., & Srikant, R. (1995). Mining sequential patterns. In *Proceedings of IEEE International Conference on Data Engineering (ICDE)*.

Alur, R., Cerny, P., Gupta, G., & Madhusudan, P. (2005). Synthesis of interface specifications for java classes. In *Proceedings of Annual Symposium on Principles of Programming Languages (POPL)*.

Ammons, G., Bodik, R., & Larus, J. R. (2002). Mining specification. In *Proceedings of Annual Symposium on Principles of Programming Lanaguages (POPL)*.

Baskiotis, N., Sebag, M., Gaudel, M. C., & Gouraud, S. (2007). A machine learning approach for statistical software testing. In *Proceedings of International Joint Conference on Artificial Intelligence (IJCAI)*.

Briand, L. C., Labiche, Y., & Leduc, J. (2006). Toward the reverse engineering of UML sequence diagrams for distributed java software. *IEEE Transactions on Software Engineering, 32*(9), 642–663. doi:10.1109/TSE.2006.96

Capilla, R., & Duenas, J. (2003). Light-weight product-lines for evolution and maintenance of web sites. In Proceedings of *European Conference on Software Maintenance and Reengineering (CSMR)*.

Clarke, E., Grumberg, O., & Peled, D. (1999). *Model Checking*. Cambridge, MA: MIT Press.

Cook, J. E., & Wolf, A. L. (1998). Discovering models of software processes from event-based data. *ACM Transactions on Software Engineering and Methodology, 7*(3), 215–249. doi:10.1145/287000.287001

Deelstra, S., Sinnema, M., & Bosch, J. (2004). Experiences in software product families: Problems and issues during product derivation. In *Proceedings of International Software Product Line Conference (SPLC)*.

Dwyer, M., Avrunin, G., & Corbett, J. (1999). Patterns in property specifications for finite-state verification. In *Proceedings of International Conference on Software Engineering (ICSE)*.

Engler, D., Chen, D. Y., Hallem, S., Chou, A., & Chelf, B. (2001). Bugs as deviant behavior: A general approach to inferring errors in systems code. In *Proceedings of Symposium on Operating Systems Principles (SOSP)*.

Erlikh, L. (2000). Leveraging legacy system dollars for e-business. *IEEE IT Pro, May/June,* 17–23.

Ernst, M. (2003). Static and dynamic analysis: Synergy and duality. In *Proceedings of International Workshop on Dynamic Analysis (WODA)*.

Ernst, M., Cockrell, J., Griswold, W., & Notkin, D. (2001). Dynamically discovering likely program invariants to support program evolution. *IEEE Transactions on Software Engineering, 27*(2), 99–123. doi:10.1109/32.908957

Fjeldstad, R., & Hamlen, W. (1983). Application program maintenance-report to our respondents. In Parikh, G. & Zvegintzov, N. (Eds.), *Tutorial on Software Maintenance* (pp. 13–27). Washington, DC: IEEE Computer Soc. Press.

Grubb, P., & Takang, A. (2003). *Software Maintenance: Concepts and Practice*. Singapore: World Scientific.

Han, J., & Kamber, M. (2006). *Data Mining Concepts and Techniques*. San Francisco: Morgan Kaufmann.

Huth, M., & Ryan, M. (2004). *Logic in Computer Science*. Cambridge, UK: Cambridge.

JBoss Development Team. (2007). *JBoss Application Server* (JBoss AS). Retrieved 2007, from http://www.jboss.org.

Jeti Development Team. Jeti, Jabber In Java (version 0.7.6). Retrieved October, 2006, from http://jeti.sourceforge.net/.

Kugler, H., Harel, D., Pnueli, A., Lu, Y., & Bontemps, Y. (2005). Temporal logic for scenario-based specifications. In *Proceedings of International Conference on Tools and Algorithms for the Construction and Analysis of Systems (TACAS)*.

Laroussinie, F., Markey, N., & Schnoebelen, P. (2002). Temporal logic with forgettable past. In *Proceedings of IEEE Symposium on Logic in Computer Science (LICS)*.

Laroussinie, F., & Schnoebelen, P. (1995). A hierarchy of temporal logics with past. *Theoretical Computer Science, 148*(2), 303–324. doi:10.1016/0304-3975(95)00035-U

Li, J., Li, H., Wong, L., Pei, J., & Dong, G. (2006). Minimum description length principle: Generators are preferable to closed patterns. In *Proceedings of AAAI Conference on Artificial Intelligence (AAAI)*.

Li, Z., & Zhou, Y. (2005). PR–miner: Automatically extracting implicit programming rules and detecting violations in large software code. In *Proceedings of SIGSOFT Symposium on Foundations of Software Engineering (FSE)*.

Lichtenstein, O., Pnueli, A., & Zuck, L. D. (1985). The glory of the past. In *Proceedings of Logics of Programs Workshop* (pp. 196–218).

Lo, D., & Khoo, S. C. (2006). SMArTIC: Towards building an accurate, robust and scalable specification miner. In *Proceedings of SIGSOFT Symposium on Foundations of Software Engineering (FSE)*.

Lo, D., Khoo, S. C., & Liu, C. (2007a). Efficient mining of iterative patterns for software specification discovery. In *Proceedings of SIGKDD International Conference on Knowledge Discovery and Data Mining (KDD)*.

Lo, D., Khoo, S. C., & Liu, C. (2008a). Mining temporal rules for software maintenance. *Journal of Software Maintenance and Evolution: Research and Practice, 20*(4), 227–247. doi:10.1002/smr.375

Lo, D., Khoo, S. C., & Liu, C. (2008b). Mining past-time temporal rules from execution traces. In *Proceedings of International Workshop on Dynamic Analysis (WODA)*.

Lo, D., Maoz, S., & Khoo, S. C. (2007b). Mining modal scenario-based specification from execution traces of reactive systems. In *Proceedings of ACM/IEEE International Conference on Automated Software Engineering (ASE)*.

Lorenzoli, D., Mariani, L., & Pezzè, M. (2008). Automatic generation of software behavioral models. In *Proceedings of International Conference on Software Engineering (ICSE)*.

Mariani, L., & Pezzè, M. (2005). Behavior capture and test: Automated analysis for component integration. In *International Conference on Engineering Complex of Complex Computer Systems (ICECCS)*.

Metrics Development Team. (2007). *Eclipse metrics plug-in*. Retrieved 2007, from http://metrics.sourceforge.net/.

OpenSSL Development Team. (2008). *OpenSSL: Documents, SSL_read*(3). Retrieved 2008, from http://www.openssl.org/docs/ssl/SSL_read.html.

Pei, J., Wang, H., Liu, J., Wang, K., Wang, J., & Yu, P. S. (2006). Discovering frequent closed partial orders from strings. *IEEE Transactions on Knowledge and Data Engineering, 18*, 1467–1481. doi:10.1109/TKDE.2006.172

Ramanathan, M., Grama, A., & Jagannathan, S. (2007). Path-sensitive inference of function precedence protocols. In *Proceedings of International Conference on Software Engineering* (ICSE).

Reiss, S. P., & Renieris, M. (2001). Encoding program executions. In *Proceedings of International Conference on Software Engineering (ICSE)*.

Standish, T. (1984). An essay on software reuse. *IEEE Transactions on Software Engineering, se-10*(5), 494–497. doi:10.1109/TSE.1984.5010272

Wang, J., & Han, J. (2004). BIDE: Efficient mining of frequent closed sequences. In *Proceedings of IEEE International Conference on Data Engineering (ICDE)*.

Weimer, W., & Necula, G. (2005). Mining temporal specifications for error detection. In *Proceedings of International Conference on Tools and Algorithms for the Constructions and Analysis of Systems (TACAS)*.

Yang, J., Evans, D., Bhardwaj, D., Bhat, T., & Das, M. (2006). Perracotta: Mining temporal API rules from imperfect traces. In *Proceedings of International Conference on Software Engineering (ICSE)*.

ENDNOTES

[*]   A preliminary version appears in 6th International Workshop on Dynamic Analysis (Lo et al., 2008b).

[1]   *post* in rule *pre* $\hookrightarrow_p$ *post* is in reversed order of *rpost* in the corresponding $G(pre \rightarrow rpost)$.

[2]   Computed using the Eclipse Metrics plug-in (Metrics Development Team, 2007).

[3]   To ensure consistency with results reported in (Lo et al., 2008).

[4]   As the earlier tablet PC is no longer functioning well.

Chapter 14
Artificial Intelligence in Software Engineering
Current Developments and Future Prospects

Farid Meziane
University of Salford, UK

Sunil Vadera
University of Salford, UK

ABSTRACT

Artificial intelligences techniques such as knowledge based systems, neural networks, fuzzy logic and data mining have been advocated by many researchers and developers as the way to improve many of the software development activities. As with many other disciplines, software development quality improves with the experience, knowledge of the developers, past projects and expertise. Software also evolves as it operates in changing and volatile environments. Hence, there is significant potential for using AI for improving all phases of the software development life cycle. This chapter provides a survey on the use of AI for software engineering that covers the main software development phases and AI methods such as natural language processing techniques, neural networks, genetic algorithms, fuzzy logic, ant colony optimization, and planning methods.

INTRODUCTION

The software engineering crisis was diagnosed about a half a century ago. Since then a plethora of methods, methodologies, notations, programming languages and environments have been developed and significant progress has been made. However, the nature and complexity of the software being developed has also changed and this has nearly an-

nulled this progress. High rates of software failure continue to be reported, software is still expensive and over budget and it is still difficult to predict the delivery date of software (Fox & Spence, 2005). Parallel to the development of software engineering, there has been visible growth of related disciplines such as Artificial Intelligence having an impact on software development (Pedrycz & Peters, 1997; Rech & Althoff, 2004). As the preceding chapters of the book show, there is significant potential in

DOI: 10.4018/978-1-60566-758-4.ch014

using AI for supporting and enhancing software engineering. The aim of this chapter is to provide a survey of existing research on using AI methods such as natural language processing techniques, neural networks, genetic algorithms, and planning methods for the full software development life cycle. The chapter is broadly structured in a similar way to the parts of the book. There are sections on AI in Planning and Project Effort Estimation, Requirements Engineering and Software Design and Software Testing. Within each section, there are subsections surveying the use of particular AI techniques. The chapter concludes with a summary of the major issues with using AI for enhancing software development and future directions of research.

USE OF AI IN PLANNING AND PROJECT EFFORT ESTIMATION

Good project planning involves many aspects: staff need to be assigned to tasks in a way that takes account of their experience and ability, the dependencies between tasks need to be determined, times of tasks need to be estimated in a way that meets the project completion date and the project plan will inevitably need revision as it progresses. AI has been proposed for most phases of planning software development projects, including assessing feasibility, estimation of cost and resource requirements, risk assessment and scheduling. This section provides pointers to some of the proposed uses of knowledge based systems, genetic algorithms, neural networks and case based reasoning, in project planning and summarizes their effectiveness.

Knowledge Based Systems

It seems reasonable to assume that as we gain experience with projects, our ability to plan new projects improves. There have been several studies that adopt this assumption and aim to capture this

experience in a Knowledge Based System (KBS) and attempt to utilise it for planning future software development projects. Sathi, Fox & Greenberg (1985) argue that a well defined representation scheme, with clear semantics for the concepts associated with project planning, such as activity, causation, and time, is essential if attempts to utilise KBS for project planning are to succeed. Hence, they develop a representation scheme and theory based on a frame based language, known as SRL (Wright, Fox, & Adam, 1984). Their theory includes a language for representing project goals, milestones, activities, states, and time, and has all the nice properties one expects, such as completeness, clarity and preciseness. Surprisingly, this neat frame based language and the semantic primitives they develop have been overlooked by others and appear not to have been adopted since their development. Similarly, other proposals that aim to utilise a KBS approach for project management, such as the use of production rules and associative networks (Boardman & Marshall, 1990), which seemed promising at the time have not been widely adopted. When considering whether to adopt a KBS approach, the cost of representing the knowledge seems high and unless this can be done at a level of abstraction that allows reuse, one can imagine that it is unattractive to software developers who are keen and under pressure to commence their projects without delay.

Neural Networks

Neural networks (NNs) have been widely and successfully used for problems that require classification given some predictive input features. They therefore seem ideal for situations in software engineering where one needs to predict outcomes, such as the risks associated with modules in software maintenance (Khoshgoftaar & Lanning, 1995), software risk analysis (Neumann, 2002) and for predicting faults using object oriented metrics (Thwin & Quah, 2002). The study by

Hu, Chen, Rong, Mei & Xie (2006) is typical of this line of research. They first identified the key features in risk assessment based on past classifications such as those presented by Wallace and Keil (2004) and further interviews with project managers. They identified a total of 39 risk factors which they grouped into 5 risk categories: project complexity, cooperation, team work, project management, and software engineering. These were reduced to 19 linearly independent factors using principal component analysis (PCA). Projects were considered to have succeeded, partially failed, or failed. In their experiments, they tried both the use of a back propagation algorithm for training and use of GAs to learn networks, using 35 examples for training and 15 examples for testing. The accuracy they obtained using back propagation was 80% and that with a GA trained NN was over 86%, confirming that use of NNs for predicting risk is a worthy approach, though larger scale studies are needed.

Genetic Algorithms

There have been numerous uses of genetic algorithms for project scheduling in various domains (Cheng & Gen, 1994; Hindi, Hongbo, & Fleszar, 2002; Hooshyar, Tahmani, & Shenasa, 2008; Yujia & Chang, 2006; Zhen-Yu, Wei-Yang, & Qian-Lei, 2008). A survey of their application in manufacturing and operations management can be found in (Kobbacy, Vadera, & Rasmy, 2007; Meziane, Vadera, Kobbacy, & Proudlove, 2000). These typically formulate project planning as a constraint satisfaction problem with an objective that needs optimisation and, which is then transformed into a form suitable for optimisation with a GA.

In the area of software development, Shan, McKay, Lokan & Essam (2002) utilise Genetic Programming to evolve functions for estimating software effort. Two target grammars were adopted for the functions that allowed use of a range of mathematical functions (e.g., exp, log, sqrt) as well as a conditional expressions. The approach was

tested on data consisting of 423 software development projects characterised by 32 attributes (e.g. such as intended market, requirements, level of user involvement, application type, etc) from the International Software Benchmarking Standards Group (www.isbsg.org.au) with roughly 50% used for training and 50% used for testing. The results of this study show that the approach performs better than linear and log regression models. An interesting finding of the study was that although the most accurate functions discovered by GP utilised similar parameters to the traditional estimates, a key difference was that it adopted non-linear terms involving team size.

Creating a good assignment of staff to tasks and producing schedules is critical to the success of any software development project. Yujia & Chang (2006) show how it is possible to utilise GAs to produce optimal schedules and task assignments. Their proposal involves a two part chromosome representation. One part includes the assignment of individuals to tasks and another involves representing the topological ordering of the tasks in a way that ensures that the offspring generated using the cross-over operator remain valid schedules. The fitness function is obtained by utilising a systems dynamics simulation to estimate expected task duration given a particular chromosome. The results of their experiments suggest that this is a promising approach, though further work on how to utilise GAs in practice when schedules change is still needed.

An important part of developing an optimal schedule that meets a target completion date is the trade-offs that may occur. For example, attempts at increasing quality can result in increasing cost and possibly compromising completion time but perhaps increasing user satisfaction. Increasing resources on tasks increases the local cost but may result in early completion, higher quality and reduction of overall cost. Hooshyar et al., (2008) propose the use of GAs to optimize schedules to take account of such trade-offs. They represent a schedule by a chromosome consisting of the activity duration and which is ordered based on their dependency. In their experiments, they utilise the standard mutation and two-point cross-over operators and adopt a fitness function that includes the cost and duration. The experimentation is carried out on projects consisting of 10, 20 and 30 activities and conclude that although the well known algorithm due to Siemens (1971) works well for small scale problems, GAs may be more effective for larger scale problems.

Case Based Reasoning

It can be argued that successful project planning and management is heavily based on experience with past cases. It is therefore surprising that there are few studies that propose the use Case Based Reasoning (CBR) for project planning of software development. One of the few exceptions is the study by Heng-Li Yang & Chen-Shu Wang (2008), who explore the combined use of CBR and data mining methods for project planning. They use a structured representation for cases, called Hierarchical Criteria Architecture (HCA), where projects are described in terms of the customer requirements, project resources and keywords describing the domain. The use of HCA enables different weights to be adopted when matching cases, allowing greater flexibility depending on the preferences of the project manager. Given a new project, first similar new cases are retrieved. Then, data mining methods, such as association rule mining, are used to provide further guidance in the form of popular patterns that could aid in project planning. In a trial, based on 43 projects, Yang & Wang (2008), show how the combined use of CBR and data mining can generate useful information, such as "the duration of project implementation was about 26 days and 85% of projects of projects were completed on time", which can be used to provide guidance when planning a similar project.

REQUIREMENTS ENGINEERING AND SOFTWARE DESIGN

Requirements engineering is often seen as the first stage of a software development project. It is the basis of any development project and this is not restricted only to software engineering. It is a broad and multidisciplinary subject (Zave, 1997). Requirements define the needs of many stakeholders. It is widely acknowledged, that because of the different backgrounds of these stakeholders, requirements are first expressed in natural language within a set of documents. These documents usually represent "the unresolved views of a group of individuals and will, in most cases be fragmentary, inconsistent, contradictory, seldom be prioritized and often be overstated, beyond actual needs" (Smith, 1993). The main activities of this phase are requirements elicitation, gathering and analysis and their transformation into a less ambiguous representation. For a detailed list of activities in requirements see Young (2003, pp 3-5). Requirements form the basis of software design. Ideally, all problems encountered during the requirements phase should be resolved before design starts. Unfortunately, in practice some of the problems inherent to requirements are passed into design, making the late discovery of errors occurring during this phase the most expensive to correct. It is therefore not surprising that requirements engineering is seen as the most problematic phase of the software development life cycle.

Problems Associated with Requirements Engineering

There are many problems that have been identified during the requirements engineering phase of the software development process. These can be summarised as follows:

Requirements are ambiguous: It is widely acknowledged, that because of the different backgrounds of the stakeholders, requirements are first expressed in Natural Language (NL). NL is inherently ambiguous and contributes to the incompleteness of requirements as many assumptions are made on some issues. Detecting ambiguities in NL is an old and major research issue in requirements engineering (Presland, 1986). Research in this area will be further discussed later in this chapter.

Requirements are incomplete, vague and imprecise: Requirements are usually incomplete, vague and imprecise in nature. It has been reported that customers do not really know what they want, or have difficulties in articulating their requirements (Yang, Xia, Zhang, Xiao, Li & Li, 2008). It has also been reported that there is a lack of user involvement during requirements (Hull, Jackson & Dick, 2005). In addition, some of these requirements are vague and cannot be easily validated. This includes statements related to system security (what is a secure system?), user interface (what is a user friendly system?) and reliability (what is a reliable system). Yen & Liu (1995) defined an imprecise functional requirement as "a requirement that can be satisfied to a degree". Therefore, there is a need to improve the quality of these requirements before the modelling phase.

Requirements are conflicting: Conflicts in requirements engineering occur when two different requirements compete for the same resources or when the satisfaction of one requirement precludes that of another. Yen & Liu (1995) stated that "Two requirements are conflicting if an increase in the degree to which one requirement is satisfied often decreases the degree to which another requirement is satisfied".

Requirements are volatile: User needs evolve over time. It is not unusual that during the time it takes to develop a system, user requirements have already changed. The causes of these changes may vary from the increasing understanding of the user about the capabilities of a computer system to some unforeseen organisational or environmental pressures. If the changes are not accommodated, the original requirements set will become incomplete and inconsistent with the new situation or in the worst case useless (Meziane, 1994).

There are communication problems between the stakeholders: During the requirements engineering phase, developers have to talk to a wide range of stakeholders with different backgrounds, interests, and personal goals (Zave, 1997). Communication with and understanding all these stakeholders is an extremely difficult and challenging task.

Requirements are difficult to manage: One of the main problems associated with requirements is that of traceability (Hull, Jackson & Dick, 2005). Traceability is the process of following a requirement from its elicitation to implementation and verification and validation. Linking the different phases of requirements validation is often omitted. Other management issues related to software management are: project management, software cost, development time, resources management and managing the changing environment.

The main contribution of AI in the requirements engineering phase are in the following areas:

- Disambiguating natural language requirements by developing tools that attempt to understands the natural language requirements and transform them into less ambiguous representations.
- Developing knowledge based systems and ontologies to manage the requirements and model problem domains.
- The use of computational intelligence to

solve some of the problems associated with requirements such as incompleteness and prioritisation.

In the following sections, we review and discuss some of the systems developed in these areas.

Processing Natural Language Requirements

The idea of transforming NL requirements automatically into specifications and design goes as far back as the early 80s. In his paper, "Program Design by Informal English Description", Abbott (1983), drew an analogy between the noun phrases used in NL descriptions and the data types used in programming languages. It is true that in those days requirements and modelling were not as distinct activities as they are now, but he did nevertheless associate the noun phrases found in NL descriptions to data types and concluded that these data types "divide the word into classes of object". Abbott stated that "associating common nouns with data types, makes the notion of data types more intuitive". He has also highlighted that this is not a straight forward mechanical approach but requires some tacit knowledge related to the problem domain. Booch (1986) further developed this approach when describing his Object-Oriented analysis and design method. It was later noted that verb phrases and to some extent adjectives describe relationships between these entities, operations and functions (Saeki, Horai & Enomoto, 1989; Vadera & Meziane, 1994; Poo & Lee, 1995). Since then and over the last twenty five years, most research in transforming NL requirements into various modelling languages adopted the same approach. Early systems that attempted to transform NL specifications were relatively simple as the NL understanding field was still in its infancy; however most researchers have taken advantage of recent developments in NL processing systems to develop more robust systems. It is not our intension to review all systems that have been developed to transform NL requirements into software models, but we highlight some systems that have attempted to produce formal specification and OO oriented models from NL Requirements.

From NL to Formal Specifications

Saeki, Horai & Enomoto (1989) proposed a framework to translate specifications written in NL (English) into formal specifications (TELL). Their framework suggests the extraction of four tables from the NL requirements that contain verbs, nouns, actions and action relations. However, they noticed that simple extraction of nouns and verbs was not sufficient and deeper semantical analysis is needed. Indeed, nouns can denote objects but also their attributes as verbs can denote relationships and actions. This has been one of the major challenges since in the automatic transformations of NL requirements into other specification languages. Hence, they suggested a human classification of nouns and verbs. They have identified four classes for nouns; class noun, value noun, attribute noun, action noun and 4 verb classes; relational verb, state verb, action verb and action related verb. In the action table, for each action verb, its agent and target object are identified. In the action related table, messages together with their senders and receivers have been identified. A class template is then used to gather the information produced by the four tables and is suggested to be used for the development of the formal specifications. However, their system was not implemented but set the foundations for future systems.

The NL2ACTL system (Fantechi, Gnesi, Ristori, Carenini, Vanocchi, & Moreschini, 1994) aims to translate NL sentences, written to express properties of a reactive system, to statements of an action based temporal logic. It takes each sentence, parses it, and attempts to complete it by identifying any implicit information that is required to produce a well-formed expression in the action based logic called ACTL. First, NL2ACTL shows that it is possible to utilise existing NL processing tools to develop grammars that are useful for analysing English sentences and for producing formal specifications in a given domain. Second, NL2ACTL demonstrates that when there is a specific application domain and target formal specification language in mind, one can develop a system that can help to identify incompleteness at a detailed level.

Vadera & Meziane (1994) developed the FORSEN system which aims to translate NL requirements into the Formal specifications language VDM (Jones, 1990). They used Logic Grammars (LG) to translate the requirements into McCord's logical form language (LFL) (McCord, 1990). This allowed the detection of ambiguities in the NL requirements. If a sentence is ambiguous, the system displays all possible interpretations and the user is then required to select the intended meaning. At the end of the first phase, each sentence has a single associated meaning represented in the LFL. In the second phase, an entity relationship model is developed using nouns and verbs extracted from the LFL. The developed entity relationship model is then translated to a VDM data type. The last phase of the FORSEN system is the generation of VDM specifications. FORSEN generates specifications by filling in pre-defined schemas for a common range of operation specifications such as adding items, deleting items, and listing items that satisfy some conditions. FORSEN was different from previously developed systems as it did not rely on structures or domain specific requirements. The input was a free English text representing the requirements of the system to be developed. However, it was limited in the range of specifications it could generate. A good review of systems that produce formal specifications can be found in Vadera & Meziane (1997).

From NL to OO Specification

Juristo, Moreno & López (2000), defined a general framework for the automatic development of OO models from NL requirements using linguistics instruments. Their framework is composed of the following nine phases: (i) extraction of essential information; (ii) identification of synonyms and polysemies; (iii) separation of static and dynamic information; (iv) static requirements structuring; (v) dynamic requirements structuring; (vi) object model construction; (vii) behaviour model construction; (viii) object model and behaviour model integration; (ix) object model and behaviour model verifications. They argue that these steps will allow the identifications of all the components required by an OO model and will help in the development and validation of these OO models. They stressed, that inputs should be in NL to avoid unnecessary user interaction with the system, a view earlier supported by Mich (1996). The system should also use rules and grammars rather than heuristics to identify entities, attributes and relations (including specialised relation such as generalisations). These steps will also allow the detection of ambiguities in NL requirements, separate the static model from the dynamic model and develop the object model and the behaviour model. As the following reviews show, few of the systems that have been developed exhibit most of these components.

Mich (1996) used the Large –scale Object-based Linguistic Interactor Translator Analyser (LOLITA) NLP system to develop the NL-OOPS which aims to produce OO specifications from NL requirements. In LOLITA knowledge is represented using conceptual graphs SemNet where nodes represent concepts and arcs relationships between concepts. The NL requirements are analysed and corresponding SemNets produced. During this phase, ambiguities are either resolved or flagged to the user. An algorithm is then used to translate the SemNets into an OO model.

Moreno, Juristo & Van de Riet (2000), developed an approach that linked the linguistic world and the conceptual world through a set of linguistic patterns. The patterns have been divided into two categories: static utility language (SUL) that describes the elements of the problem domain, hence seen as the static part of the object model and the dynamic utility language (DUL) that describes the changes to the elements of the static model. Each language has been described using context-free grammars. For example a conceptual patter would be the definition of a relationship between two classes by means of a verb. This allowed this approach to define formal relations between the linguistic world and conceptual world via the mathematical world.

Harmain & Gaizauskas (2003) developed the Class-Model Builder (CM-Builder), a NL based CASE tools that builds class diagrams specified in UML from NL requirements documents. CM Builder is developed using the GATE environment (Gaizauskas,Cunningham, Wilks,Rodgers & Humphreys, 1996). CM-Builder takes as an input a software requirement text in English and produce as an output an OO model in the CASE Data Interchange Format (CDIF) file that is used as an input to a CASE tool that supports UML (Entreprise Modeler in this case). The output file contains the identified classes, their attributes and the relationships among them. The systems used a parser based on feature-based Phrase Structure Grammar that relies on unification. The output from the parser is semantically represented as a predicate-argument structure. They also make use of a simple ontology concept to represent the world knowledge. The strength of GATE as a specialised language engineering tool allowed a deep analysis of the NL requirements and allowed. Further manipulations of the UML are required using Entreprise modeller to complete the model produced by CM-Builder.

Knowledge Based Systems

Requirements engineering is knowledge intensive and include activities such as "Knowledge Elicitation" and "Knowledge Acquisition". It is not surprising that knowledge-based software and requirement engineering received a wide attention since the early 1980. Lubars & Harandi (1987) stated that "The reuse of experts design knowledge can play a significant role in improving the quality and efficiency of the software development process".

The READS tool (Smith, 1993) is developed at the Paramax Systems Corporation, a software contractor to US and foreign government agencies and directly supports the U. S. Government system engineering process. READS supports both the front end activities such as requirement discovery, analysis and decomposition and requirements traceability, allocation, testing, and documentation. READS is composed of many components to achieve its goals. It starts with the windows document where the requirements documents are displayed and requirements are then discovered manually or automatically. It has been reported that the automatic identification of the requirements hits an 80%-90% rate. The identified requirements are saved in the project's database and displayed in the requirements inspection window. During this phase, the requirements are edited, reviewed, allocated and decomposed; "the goal of decomposition is the development of a set of designable requirements: precise, unambiguous, testable statements of a need or condition that can be directly mapped to a physical solution" (Smith, 1993). Children are attached to each requirement denoting the different interpretation if they are ambiguous. The derived requirements are then aggregated into a single non ambiguous requirements document. Requirements are organised into different views using allocation categories (Smith, 1993).

KBS are used in the design phase by storing design patterns or design families. Lubars & Harandi (1987), used a KBS to store design families, upon the development of the requirements, input and outputs of the system's functionality. The Idea system searches the KB and proposes a design schema. This becomes then the top design level of the system. The users need to refine this schema to fully satisfy the user requirements.

Ontologies

An ontology is an explicit specification of a conceptualisation. Ontologies and techniques used for the semantic web have been investigated in the last few years as a way to improve requirements engineering. Ontologies enable the sharing of common information and knowledge within specific domains. "An ontology can be viewed as a special kind of semantic network representing the terminology, concepts, and the relationships among these concepts related to a particular application domain. Semantic web and ontological techniques provide solutions for representing, organizing and reasoning over the complex sets of requirements knowledge and information." (Yang, Xia, Zhang, Xiao, Li & Li, 2008). Ontologies are developed by many organisations to reuse, integrate, merge data and knowledge and to achieve interoperability and communication among their software systems. Reuse has been a hot issue in software design for many years now. It was one of the main strengths of the OO oriented methods and programming languages introduced in the last three decades. Indeed, there are similarities between the classes in an ontology and classes in OO (Vongdoiwang & Batanov, 2005). Ontologies enhance the semantics by providing richer relationships between the terms of concepts/classes (Siricharoen, 2008).

In their research, Yang Yang, Xia, Zhang, Xiao, Li & Li (2008) use semantic web and ontological techniques to elicit, represent, model, analyze and reason about knowledge and information involved in requirements engineering processes. They argue that the use of semantic representation

could improve some of the activities involved in the requirements phase such as filling the communication gap between different stakeholders, effectively support automatic requirements elicitation, detecting incompleteness and inconsistency in requirements, evaluate the quality of requirements, and predict possible requirements changes. Their system uses three ontologies namely: the user ontology provides flexible mechanisms to describe a variety of assumptions about end-users (or customers), and to infer domain-dependent requirements. It is used to support user requirements modelling and elicitation. The enterprise ontology describes business context, structure, rules, goals, tasks, responsibilities, and resources available, for requirements analysts to understand and grasp high-level requirements. The Domain ontology serves as a shared knowledge background among different stakeholders. It is used for consistency and reusability of knowledge accumulated during the project development. The inference rules in the contextual ontologies can be used to elicit implicit requirements, detect incompleteness and inconsistency in requirements description. Automated validation and consistency checking of requirements, to some degree, offer an opportunity for the management of requirement evolution.

Kossmann, Wong, Odeh, Gillies, (2008) developed the OntoREM (Ontology-driven Requirements Engineering Methodology) an ontology-based solution to enable knowledge driven requirements engineering. A metamodel, which is an ontology is designed taking into account the different requirements engineering artifacts, activities, and interrelationships with other domains and disciplines. "The intended application of the OntoREM metamodel ontology is to capture and manage reference knowledge and concepts in the domain of requirements engineering, supported by decision engines that rely on other problem and solution domain ontologies so as to develop high quality requirements for the related domains." (Kossmann, Wong, Odeh, Gillies, 2008). OntoREM supports activities such as 'elicitation', 'analysis and negotiation', 'documentation' and 'validation'. The system produces requirements that are complete and consistent.

Ontologies are also used to develop software Engineering environments. Falbo et al., (2002) have developed the Ontology-based software Development Environment (ODE) based on a software process ontology. Tools for process definition and project tracking were also built based on this ontology. ODE's architectural is composed of two levels: the application level concerns application classes, which model the objects that address some software engineering activity and the meta-level (or knowledge level) that defines classes that describe knowledge about objects in the application base level. The classes in the meta-level are derived directly from the ontology.

In order to capture, represent and structure the domain knowledge about specific model and platform properties Geihs, et al. (2008) use ontologies as a machine-readable formal description technique that supports semantic annotations and reasoning about models and platforms. They developed a systematic support for the automation of model transformations based on domain specific knowledge formally represented by an ontology. "Entities and concepts defined in the ontology are referenced in the platform-independent model (PIM) as well as in a semantic annotation of the target platforms' API. This allows an automatic matching of modelling elements of the PIM to variables, objects and interfaces of the involved target platforms" Geihs et al. (2008). The system ontology links the abstract concepts of the PIM to the concrete platform-specific model (PSM) concepts for objects of the real world. The main benefit of their approach is the reuse of the PIM as well as the reuse of the transformation. Finding the right classes for an object oriented model (often the class diagram) is not an easy task. Siricharoen (2008).proposed the use of ontologies as the inputs of a semi-automatic object model construction program. He attempted to build semi-

automatic object model by using and comparing the concepts in the ontology as objects, slot or properties as attributes, and some properties can act as functions or operation.

Intelligence Computing for Requirements Engineering

Pedrycz & Peters (1997) stated that "The emerging area of Computational Intelligence (CI) provides a system developer with a unique opportunity of taking advantage of the currently developed and highly mature technologies". They argue that each of the techniques developed in CI can play an important role in solving the traditional problems found in software engineering. In these sections we review some of the systems developed using CI techniques to support requirements engineering.

The SPECIFIER system (Miriyala & Harandi, 1991) can best be viewed as a case based system that takes as input an informal specification of an operation where the pre and post-conditions are given as English sentences. The verbs in the sentences are used to identify the concepts. The identified concepts are then used to retrieve associated structure templates (represented as frames). These structure templates have slots that define the expected semantic form of the concepts and have associated rules that can be used to fill in the slots by using the informal specification. A set of rules is used to select specification schemas based on the identified concepts. The specification schemas are then filled by using the rules associated with the slots and the structures of the concepts. Once filled, the specification schemas produce formal specifications in a Larch-like language

When dealing with conflicts in requirements, we often drop one of the requirements or modify it to avoid the conflict. However, Yen & Liu (1995) stated that it is desirable "to achieve an effective trade off among conflicting requirements so that each conflicting requirement can be satisfied to some degrees, while the total satisfaction degree is maximized". Hence they suggested that it is necessary to identify and assess requirements priorities. In their approach they use imprecise conflicting requirements to assess requirements priorities. Users are required to relatively order requirements and to decide how much important a requirement is with regards to other conflicting requirements. They then used fuzzy logic and possibility theory to develop an approximate reasoning schema for inferring relative priority of requirements under uncertainty.

TESTING

Despite the wealth of research in the last two decades, software testing remains an area where, as cases of reported failures and numerous releases of software suggest, we cannot claim to have mastered. Bertolino (2007) presents a useful framework for summarising the challenges that we face in addressing the problems of ensuring that systems are fit for purpose, suggesting further research on: (i) developing a universal theory of testing, (ii) fully automatic testing, (iii) design to facilitate testing and (iv) development of integrated strategies that minimise the cost of repeated testing. This section presents some pointers to attempts at using AI techniques to support particular aspects of the testing process, which has the potential to contribute towards a more integrated dream testing environment of the kind proposed by Bertolino (2007).

Knowledge Based Systems

One of the earliest studies to suggest adoption of a Knowledge Based System (KBS) for testing was by Bering and Crawford (1988) who describe a Prolog based expert system that takes a Cobol program as input, parses the input to identify relevant conditions and then aims to generate test data based on the conditions. DeMasie and Muratore (1991) demonstrated the value of this

approach by developing an expert system to assist in the testing of software for the Space Shuttle. The software testing process for the Space Shuttle had previously involved running it on a simulated environment and use of manual checks to identify errors, which could take more than 40 people over 77 days of testing. Since the criteria for analysing the performance data were well documented, a rule base was developed, enabling automatic identification of potential problems and resulting in a reduction to around 56 days.

Both the above studies are quite application specific. In contrast, Samson (1990, 1993) proposes a generic environment, called REQSPERT, that has, at its heart, a knowledge base that supports the development of test plans from requirements. REQSPERT takes a list of requirements as input, classifies them into particular types of functional and non-functional requirements, identifies suitable test metrics and then proposes a test plan together with the test tools that could be utilized. Although the approach proposed by REQSPERT is interesting, there has been limited adoption of the model in practice, perhaps because of the investment of effort required in instantiating the model for particular applications. Indeed, this might be the reason why progress on the use of KBS for testing appears to have stalled in the late 1990's, since papers that successfully build further on this idea are hard to find in the literature.

AI Planning

A more active area of research since the mid-1990s has been the use of AI planning for testing. von Mayrhauser, Scheetz, Dahlman & Howe (2000) point out that a major disadvantage of white box testing is that we have to wait until the code is developed before commencing the process of producing the tests. An alternative to the use of white-box testing is to model the domain and produce tests from the model. To be able to generate tests, the model should be rich enough to generate a sequence of commands, where each command may include parameters. The primary example of this approach is the Sleuth system (von Mayrhauser, Walls, & Mraz, 1994a, 1994b), which aims to do this by defining three layers, where the top layer aims to define how to sequence commands, the next layer defines individual commands and the bottom layer defines how to instantiate the parameters required by commands. This idea was explored by applying it to generate tests for an interface to a system capable of storing a large number of tape cartridges, known as StorageTek.

The experiences with Sleuth suggest that although it can be effective, considerable effort may be required to develop a model for particular applications. A research group at Colorado State University (Howe, von Mayrhauser, & Mraz, 1995) explored an alternative approach in which they utilize AI planning methods (Ghallab, Nau, & Traverso, 2004). AI planning methods allow the specification of operators, where each operator can be defined by providing a precondition that must hold in order for the operator to be applicable and post-conditions that define the valid states following application of the operator. An AI planner can take an initial state and a goal and then generate a plan that consists of the sequence of operators that transform the initial state to achieve a given goal. Howe et al. (1995) recognized that by representing commands as operators, providing initial states and setting the goal as testing for correct system behaviour, an AI planner could generate test cases, consisting of a sequence of commands (Howe, et al., 1995; Mraz, Howe, von Mayrhauser, & Li, 1995). To evaluate the idea, they modeled the interface to StorageTex, that was used to illustrate Sleuth and conclude that it was easier to represent the domain using the planner based approach, that the test cases generated are provably correct and the different combinations of initial and goal states can result in a wider and more novel range of test cases. However, they acknowledge that test case generation can be slow, though this might have been because of the

particular planner they employed in their study. In a follow up study, they develop their ideas further by showing how it is possible to utilize UML together with constraints on parameters and state transition diagrams to model the domain (Scheetz, von Mayrhauser, & France, 1999; von Mayrhauser, Scheetz, & Dahlman, 1999). The class methods of the UML model are mapped to operators and state transition diagrams together with propositional constraints provide information to define the preconditions and effects of operators. High level test objectives, derived from the UML models, can then be mapped to an initial state and goals for the planner which generates tests based on the objectives (Von Mayrhauser, France, Scheetz, & Dahlman, 2000).

Von Mayrhauser et al. (2000) also shows that the use of AI planning for test generation has the advantage that one can mutate plans to mimic potential errors in the use of a system, for example when a user attempts an incorrect sequence of commands. This mutation of the plans then leads to generation of cases that test the error recovery capabilities of applications.

An important part of testing distributed systems is to check whether it is possible for it to end up in insecure or unsafe states. Gupta, Bastani, Khan & Yen (2004) take advantage of the goal oriented properties of Means-Ends planning by defining potential system actions as operators so that generating tests becomes equivalent to the goal of finding a plan from the current state to specified unsafe or near unsafe states.

Memon, Pollack & Soffa (1999) argue that human generation of test cases for graphical user interfaces requires enumeration of a large number of possible sequences of user actions, making the process inefficient and likely to be incomplete. Instead, as with the above studies, they propose the use AI planning methods, since once the possible actions are specified using operators, a planner can generate tests since it is capable of finding a sequence of actions to achieve a goal from an initial state. There are two interesting aspect of their work: (i) they don't simply specify a single operator for each possible interface action but use abstraction to develop higher level operators, making the search more efficient, (ii) their approach automatically includes verification conditions in the tests that are capable of detecting failure following intermediate actions in a sequence aimed to achieve some goal. They test the feasibility of the approach by applying it to generate test cases for Microsoft Wordpad

Genetic Algorithms

A study by Kobbacy, Vadera and Rasmy (2007) has shown that the use of Genetic Algorithms (GAs) for optimization has grown substantially since the 1980s and this growth has continued while the use of other AI technologies has declined. This trend is also present in their use in testing, with numerous studies aiming to take advantage of their properties in an attempt to generate optimal test cases (Baresel, Binkley, Harman, & Korel, 2004; Baudry, Fleurey, Jezequel, & Le Traon, 2002a, 2002b; Briand, Feng, & Labiche, 2002; Briand, Labiche, & Shousha, 2005; Harman & McMinn, 2007; Liaskos, Roper, & Wood, 2007; Nguyen, Perini, & Tonella, 2008; Ribeiro, 2008; Tonella, 2004; Wappler & Wegener, 2006) .

For example, Kasik and George (1996) utilize GAs for generating tests for user interfaces. They argue that manual testing of interfaces can be inadequate, pointing out that tests are constructed by systems engineers who have a fixed view of how the designed system is meant to be used and hence generate tests that don't really capture the paths that novice users might follow. To overcome this deficiency, they propose a novel system that aims to model novice behavior by use of GAs. The central idea is to represent a sequence of user actions by a gene. A pool of genes then represents potential tests. A tester can then define a fitness function to reflect the extent to which a particular gene resembles a novice and evolution then leads to the best tests. They experiment

with a fitness function that gives greater priority to actions that remain on the same window and attempt three alternative strategies for generating tests. First they give little guidance to the GA and observe that this leads to tests that at "best the resulting scripts seemed more chimpanzee-like than novice-like" (Kasik & George, 1996, p250). Second, they began the tests with a well defined sequence of actions and then allowed the GA to complete the sequence of actions. Although the results were better, they remained unconvinced about the quality of the tests. Thirdly, they provide both the start and end parts of a test and let the GA generate the intermediate actions. Not surprisingly, this approach, which they term pullback mode, results in the most appropriate novice like tests. The most interesting part of their work is that it shows the potential for modeling different types of users which could provide a powerful tool for generating particular types of test suites.

Baudry et al. (2002a, 2002b) present an interesting use of GAs aimed at improving the quality of an initial set of test cases provided by a tester. The central idea is based on mutation testing (Untch, 1992) which involves creation of a set of mutant programs, where each mutant is a version of the original program but with an introduced variation. The introduced variation can be an error or bug or result in behavior that is equivalent to the original program. The effectiveness of a set of test cases can then be measured by calculating the proportion of non-equivalent mutants that can be revealed by the test cases. The task for a tester, then, is to develop a set of tests that maximizes this measure, called a mutation score. Baudry et al. (2002b) explore the use of GAs by taking the fitness function to be the mutation score and each gene to be a test. An initial test set is provided by a tester and evolution using the standard reproduction, mutation, and crossover are utilized where the target application to be tested is a C# parser. Their experience with this approach is not good, and they conclude that the "results are not stable" and that they had to "excessively increase the mutation rate compared to usual application of genetic algorithms" (Baudry, et al. 2002a). Given the target application, the individual genes represent source code and with hindsight, this outcome may not be surprising since the crossover operator may not be particularly suitable on programs. However, they also observe two inherent limitations of using the standard evolution cycle (Baudry, et al., 2002a). First, since GAs focus on the use of the best individuals for reproduction, the mutation operator can lose valuable information and the best new genes may not be as good as those of the previous generation. Second, they point out that a focus on optimizing individual genes doesn't help in minimizing the size of the testing set, which is an important consideration given the time it can take to carry out the tests. To overcome these problems, they propose a model in which new members of the gene pool are obtained by bacterial adaptation, where mutation is used to make gentler improvements to the genes and those genes with a score above a certain threshold are retained. Their experiments on the performance of this revised scheme suggest that it is more stable and it converges more rapidly.

Several authors propose the use of GAs for testing OO programs (Briand, et al., 2002; Ribeiro, 2008; Tonella, 2004; Wappler & Schieferdecker, 2007; Wappler & Wegener, 2006). The main aim of these studies is to construct test cases consisting of a sequence of method calls. Constructing sensible sequences of method calls requires that certain pre-conditions, such as the existence of the target object or parameters required by a method are satisfied. An obvious GA based approach is to code methods as identifiers and to attempt to construct a fitness function. But use of mutation and crossover are bound to result in inappropriate sequences, so how can these be avoided? Wappler and Lammermann (2005) demonstrate that it is possible to devise a fitness function that penalizes erroneous sequences. However, in a subsequent paper, Wappler and Wegener (2006) acknowledge that using a fitness function as the

primary means of avoiding illegal sequences is not efficient. Instead they propose a novel use of Genetic Programming (GP), which aims to learn functions or programs by evolution. The underlying representation with most GP systems is a tree instead of a numeric list. In general, a tree represents a function, where leaf nodes represent arguments and non-terminal nodes denote functions. In context of testing, such trees can represent the dependencies between method calls which can then be linearised to produce tests. Use of mutation and crossover on these trees can result in invalid functions and inappropriate arguments in the context of testing object oriented programs. Hence, Wappler and Wegener(2006), suggest the use of strongly typed GP (Montana, 1995), where the types of nodes are utilized to ensure that only trees with appropriate arguments are evolved. This still leaves the issue of how such trees are obtained in the first place. The approach they adopt is to first obtain a method call dependency graph that has links between class nodes and method nodes. The links specify the methods that can be used to create instances of a class and which instances are needed by a particular method. This graph can then be traversed to generate trees to provide the initial population. The required arguments (objects) for the trees are obtained by a second level process that first involves generating linear method call sequences from the trees and then utilizes a GA to find the instantiations that are the fittest. Once this is achieved, the trees are optimized by use of recombination and mutation operators with respect to goals, such as method coverage.

Ribeiro (2008) also adopt a similar approach in their eCrash tool, utilizing strongly typed GP and a dependency graph to generate the trees. However, a significant refinement of their work in comparison to Wappler and Wegener (2006) is that they reduce the search space by removing methods, known as pure methods, that don't have external side effects. A trial of this pruning process on the Stack class in JDK 1.4.2 resulted in about a two-thirds reduction in the number of generations required to achieve full coverage.

Briand et al. (2002) explore the use of GAs for determining an optimal order for integrating and testing classes. A significant problem when determining a suitable order occurs because class dependency cycles have to be broken resulting in the need to utilize stubs. The complexity of the stubs needed varies, depending on the level of coupling that exists between classes, hence different orderings require different levels of effort for creation of the stubs. Briand et al. (2002) take advantage of previous work on scheduling, for example in the use of GAs for the traveling salesman problem, and utilize a permutation encoding of the classes together with a fitness function that measures the extent of coupling between the classes. The fitness measure is defined so as to reduce the number of attributes, the methods that would need handling if a dependency is cut, and the number of stubs created. In addition, they disallow inheritance and composition dependencies from being cut since they lead to expensive stubs. They experiment with this approach on an ATM case study utilizing the Evolver GA system (Palisade, 1998), compare the results with those obtained using a graph-based approach and conclude that the use of GAs can provide a better approach to producing orderings of class integration and testing.

CONCLUSION

The survey conducted in this chapter has highlighted some trends in the use of AI techniques in the software development process. In software project planning, the use of GAs is by far the most popular proposal. Their ability to easily represent schedules and the flexibility they offer for representing different objectives make them very appropriate for adoption in practice. Neural networks have also been adopted for risk assessment, but as the first chapter of the book describes, the use of Bayesian networks is more transparent and is likely to be more appealing in practice since

project managers, more than most types of users, need to feel they are in control. Likewise, the use of case based reasoning, as proposed by the work of Heng-Li Yang & Chen-Shu Wang (2008) seems to be an attractive approach because it offers transparency and continuous improvement as experience is gained.

In the requirements and design phase, there is a lot of emphasis on identifying errors occurring in the early stages of software development before moving to design. The use of NLP techniques to understand user requirements and attempt to derive high level software models automatically is still and will remain (Chen, Thalheim and Wong, 1999), a hot research topic although there are some issues that are related to these approaches such as the use of ad hoc case studies and difficulties in comparing the developed systems (Harmain and Gaizauskas, 2003). In addition, having a system that can produce full design by automatically analysing NL requirements is not possible as design is a creative activity requiring skills and reasoning that are hard to include in a computer system. KBS have been used to better manage requirements, the requirements process and decisions taken during the design process. In the last few years there has been a lot of interest in the use of ontologies for requirements and design. The development of domain ontologies is making it possible to encapsulate knowledge and rules governing a specific domain in one single resource. Ontologies encompass both the strengths of NLP based systems and KBS in that they allow a better understanding of the problem domain, the detection of ambiguities and incompleteness, and are able to store tacit knowledge, design decisions, and propose metamodels for specific domains.

A number of authors have attempted to utilise GAs and AI planning methods for generating test cases. The current attempts suggest that use of GAs can run into difficulties with generating appropriate valid test cases and a fully automated approach using GAs seems problematic. Hence, a more promising approach is to use strongly typed genetic programming which is capable of reducing the number of ill-defined test sequences. Use of GAs for generating the order of integration of OO classes seems to be more promising with initial trials suggesting it is better than traditional graph based methods. The use of AI planning methods offers an alternative to use of GAs and GP that can offer greater control. The effort required in defining the operators for different applications can be significant, though some progress has been made in defining a framework that could develop into a usable approach in the future.

The survey suggest that there is now good progress in the use of AI techniques in SE but larger scale evaluation studies are needed and further research is required to understand the effectiveness of different approaches. Furthermore, the development of new areas such as intelligent agents and their use in distributed computing, context aware and secure applications will require closer links between SE and AI in the future.

REFERENCES

Abbott, R. J. (1983). Program design by informal English descriptions. *CACM, 26*(11), 882–894.

Baresel, A., Binkley, D., Harman, M., & Korel, B. (2004). Evolutionary testing in the presence of loop-assigned flags: a testability transformation approach. In *Proceedings of the ACM SIGSOFT International Symposium on Software Testing and Analysis* (pp. 108-118). Boston: ACM Press.

Baudry, B., Fleurey, F., Jezequel, J.-M., & Le Traon, Y. (2002a). Automatic test case optimization using a bacteriological adaptation model: application to. NET components. In *Proceedings of the Seventeenth IEEE International Conference on Automated Software Engineering* (pp. 253-256), Edinburgh, UK. Washington DC: IEEE Computer Society.

Baudry, B., Fleurey, F., Jezequel, J. M., & Le Traon, Y. (2002b). Genes and Bacteria for Automatic Test Cases Optimization in the. Net Environment. In *Proceedings of the Thirteenth International Symposium on Software Reliability Engineering (ISSRE'02)* (pp. 195- 206), Annapolis, MD. Washington DC: IEEE Computer Society.

Bering, C. A., & Crawford, M. W. (1988). Using an expert system to test a logistics information system. In *Proceedings of the IEEE National Aerospace and Electronics Conference* (pp. 1363-1368), Dayton, OH. Washington DC: IEEE Computer Society.

Bertolino, A. (2007). Software Testing Research: Achievements, Challenges, Dreams. In *Proceedings of the IEEE International Conference on Software Engineering* (pp. 85-103), Minneapolis, MN. Washington DC: IEEE Computer Society.

Boardman, J. T., & Marshall, G. (1990). A knowledge-based architecture for project planning and control. In *Proceedings of the UK Conference on IT* (pp. 125-132), Southampton, UK. Washington DC: IEEE Computer Society.

Booch, G. (1986). Object-Oriented Development. *IEEE Transactions on Software Engineering, 12*(2), 211–221.

Briand, L. C., Feng, J., & Labiche, Y. (2002). Using genetic algorithms and coupling measures to devise optimal integration test orders. In *Proceedings of the Fourteenth International Conference on Software Engineering and Knowledge Engineering* (pp. 43-50), Ischia, Italy. New York: ACM Press.

Briand, L. C., Labiche, Y., & Shousha, M. (2005). Stress testing real-time systems with genetic algorithms. *In Proceedings of the Conference on Genetic and Evolutionary Computation* (pp. 1021-1028). Washington DC. New York: ACM Press.

Chen, P. P., Thalheim, B., & Wong, L. Y. (1999). Future Directions of Conceptual Modeling. In Chen P. P., Akoka J, Kangassalo H, & Thalheim B. (Eds), *Selected Papers From the Symposium on Conceptual Modeling, Current Issues and Future Directions.* (pp. 287-301), (LNCS vol. 1565). London: Springer-Verlag.

Cheng, R., & Gen, M. (1994). Evolution program for resource constrained project scheduling problem. *In Proceedings of the Proceedings of the 1st First IEEE Conference on Evolutionary Computation* (pp. 736-741), Orlando, FL, USA.

DeMasie, M. P., & Muratore, J. F. (1991). Artificial intelligence and expert systems in-flight software testing. In *Proceedings of the Tenth IEEE Conference on Digital Avionics Systems Conference* (pp. 416-419), Los Angeles, CA. Washington DC: IEEE Computer Society.

Falbo, R. A., Guizzardi, G., Natali, A. C., Bertollo, G., Ruy, F. F., & Mian, P. G. (2002), Towards semantic software engineering environments. *Proceedings of the 14th international Conference on Software Engineering and Knowledge Engineering SEKE '02, vol. 27* (pp. 477-478), Ischia, Italy. New York: ACM.

Fantechi, A., Gnesi, S., Ristori, G., Carenini, M., Vanocchi, M., & Moreschini, P. (1994). Assisting requirement formalization by means of natural language translation. *Formal Methods in System Design, 4*(3), 243–263. doi:10.1007/BF01384048

Fox, T. L., & Spence, J. W. (2005). The effect of decision style on the use of a project management tool: An empirical laboratory study. *The Data Base for Advances in Information Systems, 32*(2), 28–42.

Gaizauskas, R., Cunningham, H., Wilks, Y., Rodgers, P., & Humphreys, K. (1996). GATE: an environment to support research and development in natural language engineering. In *Proceedings of the 8th IEEE International Conference on Tools with Artificial Intelligence.* (pp.58-66). Washington DC: IEEE Computer Society.

Geihs, K., Baer, P., Reichle, R., & Wollenhaupt, J. (2008). Ontology-Based Automatic Model Transformations. In *Proceedings of the 6th IEEE International Conference on Software Engineering and Formal Methods* (pp.387-391), Cape Town, South Africa. Washington DC: IEEE Computer Society.

Ghallab, M., Nau, D., & Traverso, P. (2004). *Automated Planning: Theory and Practice.* San Francisco: Morgan Kaufmann.

Gupta, M., Bastani, F., Khan, L., & Yen, I.-L. (2004). Automated test data generation using MEA-graph planning. In *Proceedings of the Sixteenth IEEE Conference on Tools with Artificial Intelligence* (pp. 174-182). Washington, DC: IEEE Computer Society.

Harmain, H. M., & Gaizauskas, R. (2003). CM-Builder: A natural language-based CASE tool for object-oriented analysis. *Automated Software Engineering Journal, 10*(2), 157–181. doi:10.1023/A:1022916028950

Harman, M., & McMinn, P. (2007). A theoretical & empirical analysis of evolutionary testing and hill climbing for structural test data generation. In *Proceedings of the International Symposium on Software Testing and Analysis* (pp. 73-83). London: ACM.

Hindi, K. S., Hongbo, Y., & Fleszar, K. (2002). An evolutionary algorithm for resource-constrained project scheduling. *IEEE Transactions on Evolutionary Computation, 6*(5), 512–518. doi:10.1109/TEVC.2002.804914

Hooshyar, B., Tahmani, A., & Shenasa, M. (2008). A Genetic Algorithm to Time-Cost Trade off in project scheduling. In *Proceedings of the IEEE World Congress on Computational Intelligence* (pp. 3081-3086), Hong Kong. Washington DC: IEEE Computer Society.

Howe, A. E., von Mayrhauser, A., & Mraz, R. T. (1995). Test sequences as plans: an experiment in using an AI planner to generate system tests. In *Proceedings of the Tenth Conference on Knowledge-Based Software Engineering* (pp. 184-191), Boston, MA. Washington DC: IEEE Computer Society.

Hu, Y., Chen, J., Rong, Z., Mei, L., & Xie, K. (2006). A Neural Networks Approach for Software Risk Analysis. *In Proceedings of the Sixth IEEE International Conference on Data Mining Workshops* (pp. 722-725), Hong Kong. Washington DC: IEEE Computer Society.

Hull, E., Jackson, K., & Dick, J. (2005). *Requirements Engineering.* Berlin: Springer.

Jones, C. B. (1990). *Systematic Software Development Using VDM.* Upper Saddle River, NJ: Prentice Hall International.

Juristo, N., Moreno, A. M., & López, M. (2000). How to use linguistics instruments for Object-Oriented Analysis. *IEEE Software*, (May/June): 80–89.

Kasik, D. J., & George, H. G. (1996). Towards Automatic Generation of Novice User Test Scripts. In *Proceedings of the Conference on Human Factors in Computing Systems* (pp. 244-251), Vancouver, Canada. New York: ACM Press.

Khoshgoftaar, T. M., & Lanning, D. L. (1995). A Neural Network Approach for Early Detection of Program Modules Having High Risk in the Maintenance Phase. *Journal of Systems and Software, 29*, 85–91. doi:10.1016/0164-1212(94)00130-F

Kobbacy, K. A., Vadera, S., & Rasmy, M. H. (2007). AI and OR in management of operations: history and trends. *The Journal of the Operational Research Society, 58*, 10–28. doi:10.1057/palgrave.jors.2602132

Kossmann, M., Wong, R., Odeh, M., & Gillies, A. (2008). Ontology-driven Requirements Engineering: Building the OntoREM Meta Model. *Proceedings of the 3rd International Conference on Information and Communication Technologies: From Theory to Applications, ICTTA 2008,* (pp. 1-6), Damascus, Syria. Washington DC: IEEE Computer Society.

Liaskos, K., Roper, M., & Wood, M. (2007). Investigating data-flow coverage of classes using evolutionary algorithms. In *Proceedings of the Ninth Annual Conference on Genetic and Evolutionary Computation* (pp. 1140-1140), London, England. New York: ACM Press.

Lubars, M. D., & Harandi, M. T. (1987). Knowledge-based software design using design schemas. *In Proceedings of the 9th international Conference on Software Engineering,* (pp. 253-262), Los Alamitos, CA. Washington DC: IEEE Computer Society Press.

McCord, M. (1990). Natural language processing in Prolog. In A. Walker (ed.), *A logical approach to expert systems and natural language processing Knowledge systems and Prolog,* (pp. 391–402). Reading, MA: Addison-Wesley Publishing Company.

Memon, A. M., Pollack, M. E., & Soffa, M. L. (1999). Using a Goal Driven Approach to Generate Test Cases for GUIs. In *Proceedings of the Twenty-first International Conference on Software Engineering* (pp. 257-266), Los Angeles, CA. New York: ACM Press.

Meziane, F. (1994). *From English to Formal Specifications.* PhD Thesis, University of Salford, UK.

Meziane, F., Vadera, S., Kobbacy, K., & Proudlove, N. (2000). Intelligent Systems in Manufacturing: Current Developments and Future Prospects. *The International Journal of Manufacturing Technology Management, 11*(4), 218–238.

Mich, L. (1996). NL-OOPS: from natural language to object, oriented requirements using the natural language processing system LOLITA. *Natural Language Engineering, 2*(2), 161–187. doi:10.1017/S1351324996001337

Miriyala, K., & Harandi, M. T. (1991). Automatic derivation of formal software specifications from informal descriptions. *IEEE Transactions on Software Engineering, 17*(10), 1126–1142. doi:10.1109/32.99198

Montana, D. J. (1995). Strongly Typed Genetic Programming. *Evolutionary Computation, 3*(2), 199–230. doi:10.1162/evco.1995.3.2.199

Moreno, C. A., Juristo, N., & Van de Riet, R. P. (2000). Formal justification in object-oriented modelling: A linguistic approach. *Data & Knowledge Engineering, 33*, 25–47. doi:10.1016/S0169-023X(99)00046-4

Mraz, R. T., Howe, A. E., von Mayrhauser, A., & Li, L. (1995). System testing with an AI planner. In *Proceedings of the Sixth International Symposium on Software Reliability Engineering* (pp. 96-105), Toulouse, France. Washington DC: IEEE Computer Society.

Neumann, D. (2002). An Enhanced Neural Network Technique for Software Risk Analysis. *IEEE Transactions on Software Engineering, 28*(9), 904–912. doi:10.1109/TSE.2002.1033229

Nguyen, C. D., Perini, A., & Tonella, P. (2008). eCAT: a tool for automating test cases generation and execution in testing multi-agent systems. *In Proceedings of the Seventh International Joint Conference on Autonomous Agents and Multiagent Systems* (pp. 1669-1670), Estoril, Portugal. New York: ACM Press.

Palisade. (1998). Evolver, The Genetic Algorithm Super Solver, http://www.palisade.com/evolver/. Newfield, NY: Palisade Corporation

Pedrycz, W., & Peters, J. F. (1997). Computational intelligence in software engineering. *Canadian Conference on Electrical and Computer Engineering,* (pp. 253-256), St. Johns, Nfld., Canada. Washington DC: IEEE Press.

Poo, D. C. C., & Lee, S. Y. (1995). Domain object identification through events and functions. *Information and Software Technology, 37*(11), 609–621. doi:10.1016/0950-5849(95)98298-T

Presland, S. G. (1986). *The analysis of natural language requirements documents.* PhD Thesis, University of Liverpool, UK.

Rech, J. & Althoff, K.D., (2004). Artificial Intelligence and Software Engineering – Status and Future Trends. *Special Issue on Artificial Intelligence and Software Engineering, KI* (3), 5-11.

Ribeiro, J. C. B. (2008). Search-based test case generation for object-oriented java software using strongly-typed genetic programming. In *Proceedings of the GECCO Conference Companion on Genetic and Evolutionary Computation* (pp. 1819-1822), Atlanta, GA. New York: ACM Press.

Saeki, M., Horai, H., & Enomoto, H. (1989). Software development process from natural language specification. In *Proceedings of the 11th international Conference on Software Engineering.* (pp. 64-73), Pittsburgh, PA. New York: ACM Press.

Samson, D. (1990). REQSPERT: automated test planning from requirements. *In Proceedings of the First International Systems Integration Conference* (pp. 702-708), Morristown, NJ. Piscataway, NJ: IEEE Press.

Samson, D. (1993). Knowledge-based test planning: Framework for a knowledge-based system to prepare a system test plan from system requirements. *Journal of Systems and Software, 20*(2), 115–124. doi:10.1016/0164-1212(93)90003-G

Sathi, A., Fox, M. S., & Greenberg, M. (1985). Representation of Activity Knowledge for Project Management. *IEEE Transactions on Pattern Analysis and Machine Intelligence, PAMI-7*(5), 531–552. doi:10.1109/TPAMI.1985.4767701

Scheetz, M., von Mayrhauser, A., & France, R. (1999). Generating test cases from an OO model with an AI planning system. *In Proceedings of the Tenth International Symposium on Software Reliability Engineering* (pp. 250-259), Boca Raton, Florida. Washington DC: IEEE Computer Society.

Shan, Y., McKay, R. I., Lokan, C. J., & Essam, D. L. (2002). Software project effort estimation using genetic programming. *In Proceedings of the IEEE International Conference on Communications, Circuits and Systems* (pp. 1108-1112), Arizona. Washington DC: IEEE Computer Society.

Siemens, N. (1971). A Simple CPM Time-Cost Tradeoff Algorithm. *Management Science, 17*(6), 354–363. doi:10.1287/mnsc.17.6.B354

Siricharoen, W. V. (2008). Merging Ontologies for Object Oriented Software Engineering. *International Conference on Networked Computing and Advanced Information Management,* (Volume 2, pp. 525 – 530).

Smith, T. J. (1993). READS: a requirements engineering tool. *Proceedings of IEEE International Symposium on Requirements Engineering,* (pp. 94–97), San Diego. Washington DC: IEEE Computer Society.

Thwin, M. M. T., & Quah, T.-S. (2002). Application of neural network for predicting software development faults using object-oriented design metrics. In *Proceedings of the Ninth International Conference on Neural Information Processing* (pp. 2312-2316), Singapore. Washington DC: IEEE Computer Society.

Tonella, P. (2004). Evolutionary testing of classes. In *Proceedings of the ACM SIGSOFT International Symposium on Software testing and Analysis* (pp. 119-128), Boston, MA. New York: ACM Press.

Untch, R. H. (1992). Mutation-based software testing using program schemata. *In Proceedings of the Thirtieth ACM South Regional Conference* (pp. 285-291), Raleigh, North Carolina. New York: ACM Press.

Vadera, S., & Meziane, F. (1994). From English to Formal Specifications. *The Computer Journal, 37*(9), 753–763. doi:10.1093/comjnl/37.9.753

Vadera, S., & Meziane, F. (1997). Tools for Producing Formal Specifications: A view of Current Architecture and Future Directions. *Annals of Software Engineering, 3,* 273–290. doi:10.1023/A:1018950324254

van Lamsweerde, R. Darimont, & Massonet P. (1995). Goal-directed elaboration of requirements for a meeting scheduler: Problems and lessons learnt. In *Proceedings of the 2ⁿᵈ IEEE International Symposium on Requirements Engineering.* (pp. 194-203), York, UK. Washington DC: IEEE Computer Society.

von Mayrhauser, A., France, R., Scheetz, M., & Dahlman, E. (2000). Generating test-cases from an object-oriented model with an artifical-intelligence planning system. *IEEE Transactions on Reliability, 49*(1), 26–36. doi:10.1109/24.855534 von Mayrhauser, A., Scheetz, M., & Dahlman, E. (1999). Generating goal-oriented test cases. In *Proceedings of the Twenty-Third Annual International Conference on Computer Software and Applications* (pp. 110-115), Phoenix, AZ. Washington DC: IEEE Computer Society.

von Mayrhauser, A., Scheetz, M., Dahlman, E., & Howe, A. E. (2000). Planner based error recovery testing. In *Proceedings of the Eleventh International Symposium on Software Reliability Engineering* (pp. 186-195), San Jose, CA. Washington DC: IEEE Computer Society.

von Mayrhauser, A., Walls, J., & Mraz, R. T. (1994a). Sleuth: A Domain Based Testing Tool. In *Proceedings of the International Test Conference* (pp. 840-849). Washington, DC: IEEE Computer Society.

von Mayrhauser, A., Walls, J., & Mraz, R. T. (1994b, November). Testing Applications Using Domain Based Testing and Sleuth. In *Proceedings of the Fifth International Symposium on Software Reliability Engineering* (pp. 206-215), Monterey, CA. Washington DC: IEEE Computer Society.

Vongdoiwang, W., & Batanov, D. N. (2005). Similarities and Differences between Ontologies and Object Model. In *Proceedings of The 3th International Conference on Computing, Communications and Control Technologies: CCCT 2005*, Austin, TX.

Wallace, L., & Keil, M. (2004). Software project risks and their effect on outcomes. *Communications of the ACM, 47*(4), 68–73. doi:10.1145/975817.975819

Wappler, S., & Lammermann, F. (2005). Using evolutionary algorithms for the unit testing of object-oriented software. In *Proceedings of the Conference on Genetic and Evolutionary Computation* (pp. 1053-1060), Washington DC. New York: ACM Press.

Wappler, S., & Schieferdecker, I. (2007). Improving evolutionary class testing in the presence of non-public methods. In *Proceedings of the Twenty-second IEEE/ACM International Conference on Automated Software Engineering* (pp. 381-384), Atlanta, Georgia. New York: ACM Press.

Wappler, S., & Wegener, J. (2006). Evolutionary unit testing of object-oriented software using strongly-typed genetic programming. *In Proceedings of the Eighth Annual Conference on Genetic and Evolutionary Computation* (pp. 1925-1932), Seattle, WA. New York: ACM Press.

Wright, J. M., Fox, M. S., & Adam, D. (1984). *SRL/2 User Manual*: Robotic Institute, Carnegie-Mellon University, Pittsburgh, PA.

Yang, H.-L., & Wang, C.-S. (2009). Recommender system for software project planning one application of revised CBR algorithm. *Expert Systems with Applications, 36*(5), 8938–8945. doi:doi:10.1016/j.eswa.2008.11.050

Yang, Y., Xia, F., Zhang, W., Xiao, X., Li, Y., & Li, X. (2008). Towards Semantic Requirement Engineering. *IEEE International Workshop on Semantic Computing and Systems* (pp. 67-71). Washington, DC: IEEE Computer Society.

Yen, J., & Liu, F. X. (1995). A Formal Approach to the Analysis of Priorities of Imprecise Conflicting Requirements. In *Proceedings of the 7ᵗʰ international Conference on Tools with Artificial intelligence.* Washington DC: IEEE Computer Society.

Young, R. R. (2003). *The requirements Engineering Handbook*. Norwood, MA: Artech House Inc.

Yu, Y., Wang, Y., Mylopoulos, J., Liaskos, S., Lapouchnian, A., & do Prado Leite, J. C. S. (2005). Reverse engineering goal models from legacy code. In *Proceedings of the 2nd IEEE International Symposium on Requirements Engineering*, (pp. 363-372), York, UK. Washington DC: IEEE Computer Society.

Yujia, G., & Chang, C. (2006). Capability-based Project Scheduling with Genetic Algorithms. In *Proceedings of the International Conference on Intelligent Agents, Web Technologies and Internet Commerce* (pp. 161-161), Sydney, Australia. Washington DC: IEEE Computer Society.

Zave, P. (1997). Classification of Research Efforts in Requirements Engineering. *ACM Computing Surveys*, *29*(4), 315–321. doi:10.1145/267580.267581

Zhen-Yu, Z., Wei-Yang, Y., & Qian-Lei, L. (2008). Applications of Fuzzy Critical Chain Method in Project Scheduling. In *Proceedings of the Fourth International Conference on Natural Computation* (pp. 473-477), Jinan, China. Washington DC: IEEE Computer Society.

Compilation of References

A.L.I.C.E. AI Foundation Inc. (2005). *A.L.I.C.E.* Retrieved 2005, from http://www.alicebot.org/

Abbott, R. J. (1983). Program design by informal English descriptions. *Communications of the ACM, 26*(11), 882–894. doi:10.1145/182.358441

Abdel-Hamid, T. (1989). The dynamics of software projects staffing: A system dynamics based simulation approach. *IEEE Transactions on Software Engineering, 15*(2), 109–119. doi:10.1109/32.21738

Abdel-Hamid, T. K. (1993). Adapting, correcting, and perfecting software estimates: a maintenance metaphor. *Computer, 26*(3), 20–29. doi:10.1109/2.204681

Abrahamsson, P., & Koskela, J. (2004). Extreme programming: A survey of empirical data from a controlled case study. In *Proceedings 2004 International Symposium on Empirical Software Engineering, 2004.* (pp. 73-82). Washington, DC: IEEE Computer Society.

Abran, A., Moore, J., Bourque, P., Dupuis, R., & Tripp, L. (2004). *Guide to the Software Engineering Body of Knowledge 2004 Version.* Los Alamitos, CA: IEEE Computer Society.

Acharya, M., Xie, T., Pei, J., & Xu, J. (2007). Mining API patterns as partial orders from source code: From usage scenarios to specifications. In *Proceedings of SIGSOFT Symposium on Foundations of Software Engineering (FSE).*

Agena Ltd. (2008). *Bayesian Network and simulation software for risk analysis and decision support.* Retrieved July 9, 2008, from http://www.agena.co.uk/

Agile Manifesto. (2008). *Manifesto for agile software development.* Retrieved July 18, 2008, from http://www.agilemanifesto.org/

Agrawal, R., & Srikant, R. (1995). Mining sequential patterns. In *Proceedings of IEEE International Conference on Data Engineering (ICDE).*

Aha, D. W., & Bankert, R. L. (1996). *A comparative evaluation of sequential feature selection algorithms. Artificial Intelligence and Statistics.* New York: Springer-Verlag.

Ahmed, A., Fraz, M. M., & Zahid, F. A. (2003). Some results of experimentation with extreme programming paradigm. In *7th International Multi Topic Conference, INMIC 2003,* (pp. 387-390).

Alba, E., & Chicano, F. (2007). Ant Colony Optimization for Model Checking. *Proceedings of the 11th International Conference on Computer Aided Systems Theory (eurocast 2007).* (Vol. 4739, pp. 523-530). Berlin: Springer.

Albrecht, A. J., & Gaffney, J. R. (1983). Software function, source lines of code, and development effort prediction: A software science validation. *IEEE Transactions on Software Engineering, SE-9*(6), 639–648. doi:10.1109/TSE.1983.235271

Alderson, A. (1991). Meta-case Technology. *European Symposium on Software Development Environments and CASE Technology,* Konigswinter, Germany, June 17-19.

Alho, K., & Sulonen, R. (1998). Supporting Virtual Software Projects on the Web. *Seventh IEEE International Workshop on Enabling Technologies: Infrastructure for*

Collaborative Enterprises (WET ICE '98), Stanford, USA, June 17-19.

Ali, S., Briand, L. C., & Rehman, M. J. ur, Asghar, H., Iqbal, M. Z. Z., & Nadeem, A. (2007). A state-based approach to integration testing based on UML models. *Information and Software Technology, 49*(11-12), 1087–1106. doi:10.1016/j.infsof.2006.11.002

Alur, R., Cerny, P., Gupta, G., & Madhusudan, P. (2005). Synthesis of interface specifications for java classes. In *Proceedings of Annual Symposium on Principles of Programming Languages (POPL).*

Alvarez-Benitez, J. E., Everson, R. M., & Fieldsend, J. E. (2005). A MOPSO algorithm based exclusively on Pareto dominance concepts. *Evolutionary Multi-Criterion Optimization,* (LNCS Vol. 410, pp. 459-473). Berlin: Springer.

Amandi, A., Campo, M., & Zunino, A. (2004). JavaLog: A framework-based integration of Java and Prolog for agent-oriented programming. *Computer Languages, Systems and Structures (ex Computer Languages - An International Journal), 31*(1), 17-33. Elsevier

Ambert, F., Bouquet, F., Chemin, S., Guenaud, S., Legeard, B., Peureux, F., et al. (2002). BZ-TT: A toolset for test generation from Z and B using constraint logic programming. In *Formal Approaches to Testing of Software Workshop (FATES'02) at CONCUR'02*, Brnö, Czech Republic, (pp. 105-120).

AmI. (2008). *Ambient Intelligence*. Retrieved from http://www.ambientintelligence.org/

Ammons, G., Bodik, R., & Larus, J. R. (2002). Mining specification. In *Proceedings of Annual Symposium on Principles of Programming Lanaguages (POPL).*

Anderson, D., Anderson, E., Lesh, N., Marks, J., Mirtich, B., Ratajczack, D., & Ryall, K. (2000). Human-guided simple search. In *Proceedings of National Conference on Artificial Intelligence* (pp. 209-216). Cambridge, MA: AAAI Press/The MIT Press.

Angelis, L., & Stamelos, I. (2000). A Simulation Tool for efficient analogy based cost estima-

tion. *Empirical Software Engineering, 5*(1), 35–68. doi:10.1023/A:1009897800559

Apt, K. (2003). *Principles of constraint programming.* Cambridge, UK: Cambridge University Press.

Arango, G. (1994). A Brief Introduction to Domain Analysis. *Proceedings of the 1994 ACM symposium on Applied Computing, April*, Phoenix, Arizona, United States, March, 1994, (pp. 42-46). New York: ACM Press.

Arcuri, A., & Yao, X. (2008). Search based software testing of object-oriented containers. *Information Sciences, 178*(15), 3075–3095. doi:10.1016/j.ins.2007.11.024

Atkinson, et al (2001, September). *Component-Based Product Line Engineering with the UML.* Reading, MA: Addison Wesley.

Atlantic Systems Guild (2003). *Volere Requirements Specification Template.*

Bachmann, F., Bass, L., & Klein, M. (2004). *Deriving architectural tactics: A step toward nethodical architectural design* (Tech. Rep. CMU/SEI-2003-TR-004). Pittsburgh, PA: Carnegie Mellon University, Software Engineering Institute.

Bachmann, F., Bass, L., & Nord, R. (2007). *Modifiability tactics* (Tech. Rep. CMU/SEI-2007-TR-002). Pittsburgh, PA: Carnegie Mellon University, Software Engineering Institute.

Bachmann, F., Bass, L., Bianco, P., & Klein, M. (2007). *Using ArchE in the classroom: One experience* (Tech. Note CMU/SEI-2007-TN-001). Pittsburgh, PA: Carnegie Mellon University, Software Engineering Institute.

Bachmann, F., Bass, L., Klein, M., & Shelton, C. (2004). Experience using an expert system to assist an architect in designing for modifiability. In *Proceedings 5th Working IEEE/IFIP Conference on Software Architecture – WICSA'04* (pp. 281-284). Washington, DC: IEEE Computer Society.

Bachmann, F., Bass, L., Klein, M., & Shelton, C. (2005). Designing software architectures to achieve quality attribute requirements. *IEE Proceedings. Software, 152*(4), 153–165. doi:10.1049/ip-sen:20045037

Bai, X., Lam, C. P., & Li, H. (2004). An approach to generate the thin-threads from the UML diagrams. *Proceedings of Computer Software and Applications Conference (COMPSAC 2004)*, (pp. 546–552).

Bai, X., Li, H., & Lam, C. P. (2004). A risk analysis approach to prioritize UML-based software testing. *5th International Conference on Software Engineering, Artificial Intelligence, Networking, and Parallel/Distributed Computing (SNPD04)*.

Bai, X., Tsai, W., Paul, R., Feng, K., & Yu, L. (2001). Scenario-based business modeling. *IEEE Proc. of APAQS*.

Baldini, A., Benso, A., & Prinetto, P. (2005). System-level functional testing from UML specifications in end-of-production industrial environments. *International Journal on Software Tools for Technology Transfer, 7*(4), 326–340. doi:10.1007/s10009-004-0147-8

Bardin, S., & Herrmann, P. (2008). Structural testing of executables. In *the First IEEE International Conference on Software Testing, Verification, and Validation (ICST'08)* (p. 22-31). Lillehammer, Norway: IEEE Computer Society.

Baresel, A., Binkley, D., Harman, M., & Korel, B. (2004). Evolutionary testing in the presence of loop-assigned flags: a testability transformation approach. In *Proceedings of the ACM SIGSOFT International Symposium on Software Testing and Analysis* (pp. 108-118). Boston: ACM Press.

Baresi, L., Morasca, S., & Paolini, P. (2003). Estimating the design effort of Web applications, In *Proceedings Ninth International Software Measures Symposium*, September 3-5, (pp. 62-72).

Barron, A. (1993). Universal approximation bounds for superposition of a sigmoidal function. *IEEE Transactions on Information Theory, 39*(3), 930–945. doi:10.1109/18.256500

Barry, P. S., & Laskey, K. B. (1999). An Application of Uncertain Reasoning to Requirements Engineering. In K.B. Laskey and H. Prade (Eds.), *Proceedings of the 15th*

Conference on Uncertainty in Artificial Intelligence (pp. 41-48). Stockholm, Sweden: Morgan Kaufmann.

Basili, V. R., & Weiss, D. (1984). A Methodology for Collecting Valid Software Engineering Data. *IEEE Transactions on Software Engineering, SE-10*(6), 728–738. doi:10.1109/TSE.1984.5010301

Baskiotis, N., Sebag, M., Gaudel, M. C., & Gouraud, S. (2007). A machine learning approach for statistical software testing. In *Proceedings of International Joint Conference on Artificial Intelligence (IJCAI)*.

Bass, L., Clements, P., & Kazman, R. (2003). *Software architecture in practice (2nd edition)*. Boston: Addison-Wesley Professional.

Bass, L., Ivers, I., Klein, M., Merson, P., & Wallnau, K. (2005). Encapsulating quality attribute knowledge. In *Proceedings 5th Working IEEE/IFIP Conference on Software Architecture – WICSA'05* (pp. 193-194). Washington, DC: IEEE Computer Society.

Baudry, B., Fleurey, F., Jezequel, J. M., & Le Traon, Y. (2002). Genes and Bacteria for Automatic Test Cases Optimization in the.Net Environment. In *Proceedings of the Thirteenth International Symposium on Software Reliability Engineering (ISSRE'02)* (pp. 195-206), Annapolis, MD. Washington DC: IEEE Computer Society.

Baudry, B., Fleurey, F., Jezequel, J.-M., & Le Traon, Y. (2002). Automatic test case optimization using a bacteriological adaptation model: application to. NET components. In *Proceedings of the Seventeenth IEEE International Conference on Automated Software Engineering* (pp. 253-256), Edinburgh, UK. Washington DC: IEEE Computer Society.

Beck, K. (1999). *Extreme programming explained: Embrace change*. Reading, MA: Addison-Wesley Professional.

Beck, K. (2002). *Test Driven Development*. Reading, MA: Addison Wesley.

Bering, C. A., & Crawford, M. W. (1988). Using an expert system to test a logistics information system. In *Proceedings of the IEEE National Aerospace and*

Electronics Conference (pp. 1363-1368), Dayton, OH. Washington DC: IEEE Computer Society.

Bertolino, A. (2007). Software Testing Research: Achievements, Challenges, Dreams. In *Proceedings of the IEEE International Conference on Software Engineering* (pp. 85-103), Minneapolis, MN. Washington DC: IEEE Computer Society.

Bertolino, A., & Gnesi, S. (2003). Use case-based testing of product lines. *ESEC/FSE11: Proceedings of the 9th European Software Engineering Conference held jointly with 11th ACM SIGSOFT International Symposium on Foundations of Software Engineering*, (pp. 355–358).

Bertolino, A., Marchetti, E., & Muccini, H. (2004). Introducing a reasonably complete and coherent approach for model-based testing. *Proc. ETAPS 2004 workshop on: Test and Analysis of Component Based Systems (Tacos)*.

Bianchi, L., Gambardella, L. M., & Dorigo, M. (2002). An ant colony optimization approach to the probabilistic traveling salesman problem. In J. J. Guervós, P. Adamidis, H. Beyer, J. L. Martín, & H. Schwefel, (Eds.) *Proceedings of the 7th international Conference on Parallel Problem Solving From Nature,* September 07 – 11, (LNCS Vol. 2439, pp. 883-892). London: Springer-Verlag.

Bibi, S., & Stamelos, I. (2004). Software process modeling with Bayesian belief networks. In *10th International Software Metrics Symposium Chicago*.

Bibi, S., Stamelos, L., & Angelis, L. (2003) Bayesian Belief Networks as a Software Productivity Estimation Tool. In *Proceedings 1st Balkan Conference in Informatics, Thessaloniki.*

Binder, R. (1999). *Testing object-oriented systems: Models, patterns and tools*. Reading, MA: Addison-Wesley Longman.

Bishop, C. (1995). *Neural Network for Pattern Recognition*. New York: Oxford University Press.

Bishop, C., & Qazaz, C. S. (1995). Bayesian inference of noise levels in regression. *International Conference on Artificial Neural Networks: Vol. 2. EC2 & Cie* (pp. 59-64). ICANN95.

Blum, B. I. (1996). *Beyond Programming: To a New Era of Design*. New York: Oxford University Press, Inc.

Boardman, J. T., & Marshall, G. (1990). A knowledge-based architecture for project planning and control. In *Proceedings of the UK Conference on IT* (pp. 125-132), Southampton, UK. Washington DC: IEEE Computer Society.

Boasson, M. (1995). The Artistry of software architecture. *IEEE Software, 6*(November/December).

Boehm, B. W. (1981). *Software engineering economics*. Upper Saddle River, NJ: Prentice Hall.

Boehm, B. W., Horowitz, E., Madachy, R., Reifer, D., Clark, B. K., Steece, B., et al. (2001). *Software cost estimation with COCOMO II*. Upper Saddle River, NJ: Prentice Hall.

Boehm, B., & In, H. (1996). Identifying quality-requirement conflicts. *IEEE Software, 13*(2), 25–35. doi:10.1109/52.506460

Boehm, B., Bose, P., Horowitz, E., & Ming-June Lee. (1994). Software requirements as negotiated win conditions. In *Proceedings of the First International Conference on Requirements Engineering* (pp.74-83). Colorado Springs, CO: IEEE Computer Society.

Boehm, B., Horowitz, E., Madachy, R., Reifer, D., Clark, B. K., Steece, B., et al. (2000). *Software Cost Estimation with COCOMO II*. Upper Saddle River, NJ: Prentice-Hall.

Bohner, S. A. (2002). Extending software change impact analysis into COTS components. In *Proceedings of 27th Annual NASA Goddard/IEEE Software Engineering Workshop - SEW'02* (pp. 175-182). Washington, DC: IEEE Computer Society.

Bollig, B., Katoen, J.-P., Kern, C., & Leucker, M. (2006, October). *Replaying Play in and Play out: Synthesis of Design Models from Scenarios by Learning* (Tech. Rep. No. AIB-2006-12). RWTH Aachen, Germany. Retrieved August 13, 2008 from http://www.smyle-tool.org/wordpress/wp-content/uploads/2008/02/2006-12.pdf

Booch, G. (1986). Object-Oriented Development. *IEEE Transactions on Software Engineering, 12*(2), 211–221.

Boonstoppel, P., Cadar, C., & Engler, D. R. (2008). RWset: attacking path explosion in constraint-based test generation. In *the 14th International Conference on Tools and Algorithms for the Construction and Analysis of Systems (TACAS'08), Part of the Joint European Conferences on Theory and Practice of Software (ETAPS'08)* (pp. 351-366). Budapest, Hungary: Springer.

Borland. (2008). *Caliber*. Retrieved from http://www.borland.com/us/products/caliber/index.html

Bosch, J., & Molin, P. (1999). Software architecture design: Evaluation and transformation. In *Proceedings of the 1999 IEEE Engineering of Computer Based Systems Symposium – ECBS'99* (pp. 4-10). Los Alamitos, CA: IEEE Computer Society.

Botella, B., Gotlieb, A., & Michel, C. (2006). Symbolic execution of floating-point computations. *Software Testing: Verification and Reliability, 16*(2), 97–121. doi:10.1002/stvr.333

Bottaci, L. (2002). Instrumenting programs with flag variables for test data search by genetic algorithms. In Gecco 2002: *Proceedings of the Genetic and Evolutionary Computation Conference* (pp. 1337–1342). New York: Morgan Kaufmann Publishers.

Braude, E. J. (2000). *Softwre Engineering: An Object-Oriented Perspective*. New York: John Wiley & Sons.

Briand, L. C., & Labiche, Y. (2002). A UML-Based Approach to System Testing. *Software and Systems Testing, 1*(1), 10–42.

Briand, L. C., Basili, V. R., & Thomas, W. M. (1992). A pattern recognition approach for software engineering data analysis. *IEEE Transactions on Software Engineering, 18*(11), 931–942. doi:10.1109/32.177363

Briand, L. C., El Emam, K., & Bomarius, F. (1998). CO-BRA: A Hybrid Method for Software Cost Estimation, Benchmarking and Risk Assessment. In *Proceedings of the 20th International Conference on Software Engineering, 1998*, (pp. 390-399).

Briand, L. C., El Emam, K., Surmann, D., Wieczorek, I., & Maxwell, K. D. (1999). An assessment and comparison of common software cost estimation modeling techniques. *Proceedings of the 1999 International Conference on Software Engineering*, (pp. 313 – 323).

Briand, L. C., Feng, J., & Labiche, Y. (2002). Using genetic algorithms and coupling measures to devise optimal integration test orders. In *Proceedings of the Fourteenth International Conference on Software Engineering and Knowledge Engineering* (pp. 43-50), Ischia, Italy. New York: ACM Press.

Briand, L. C., Labiche, Y., & Leduc, J. (2006). Toward the reverse engineering of UML sequence diagrams for distributed java software. *IEEE Transactions on Software Engineering, 32*(9), 642–663. doi:10.1109/TSE.2006.96

Briand, L. C., Labiche, Y., & Shousha, M. (2005). Stress testing real-time systems with genetic algorithms. *In Proceedings of the Conference on Genetic and Evolutionary Computation* (pp. 1021-1028). Washington DC. New York: ACM Press.

Briand, L. C., Langley, T., & Wieczorek, I. (2000). A replicated assessment and comparison of common software cost modeling techniques. *Proceedings of the 2000 International Conference on Software Engineering*, Limerick, Ireland, (pp. 377-386).

Brieman, L., Friedman, J., Olshen, R., & Stone, C. (1984). *Classification and Regression Trees*. Belmont, CA: Wadsworth.

Brinkkemper, S., van de Weerd, I., Saeki, M., & Versendaal, J. (2008). Process improvement in requirements management: A Method Engineering Approach. In B. Paech & C. Rolland (Eds.), *Requirements Engineering: Foundation For Software Quality,* (LNCS 5025, pp. 6-22). Berlin: Springer-Verlag.

Broy, M., Krüger, I., & Meisinger, M. (2007). *A formal model of services. ACMTransactions on Software Engineering Methodology (TOSEM), 16*(1). Retrieved August 13, 2008 from http://doi.acm.org/10.1145/1189748.1189753

Buhr, K., Heumesser, N., Houdek, F., Omasreiter, H., Rothermehl, F., Tavakoli, R., et al. (2004). *DaimlerChrysler demonstrator: System specification instrument cluster.* Available August 13, 2008 from http://www.empress-itea.org/deliverables/D5.1_Appendix_B_v1.0_Public_Version.pdf

Buntine, W. (1996). A guide to the literature on learning probabilistic networks from data. *IEEE Transactions on Knowledge and Data Engineering, 8*, 195–210. doi:10.1109/69.494161

Buschmann, F., Meunier, R., Rohnert, H., Sommerlad, P., & Stal, M. (1996). *Pattern-oriented software architecture. A system of patterns.* Chichester, UK: John Wiley & Sons Ltd.

C&C Tools (2007). Retrieved August 13, 2008 from http://svn.ask.it.usyd.edu.au/trac/candc

Cadar, C., Ganesh, V., Pawlowski, P. M., Dill, D. L., & Engler, D. R. (2006). EXE: automatically generating inputs of death. In *the 13th ACM Conference on Computer and Communications Security (CCS'06)* (pp. 322-335). Alexandria, VA: ACM.

Campo, M., Diaz-Pace, A., & Zito, M. (2002). Developing object-oriented enterprise quality frameworks using proto-frameworks. [Wiley]. *Software, Practice & Experience, 32*(8), 837–843. doi:10.1002/spe.462

Cañadas, J. J., del Águila, I. M., Bosch, A., & Túnez, S. (2002). An Intelligent System for Therapy Control in a Distributed Organization. In H. Shafazand & A. Min Tjoa (Eds.), *Proceedings of EurAsia-ICT 2002: Information and Communication Technology, First EurAsian Conference,* (LNCS 2510, pp. 19-26). Berlin: Springer-Verlag.

Cantone, G., & Donzelli, P. (2000). Production and maintenance of goal-oriented measurement models. *World Scientific, 105*(4), 605–626.

Capilla, R., & Duenas, J. (2003). Light-weight product-lines for evolution and maintenance of web sites. In Proceedings of *European Conference on Software Maintenance and Reengineering (CSMR).*

Carniello, A., Jino, M., & Chaim, M. (2005). Structural testing with use cases. *Journal of Computer Science and Technology, 5*(2), 100–106.

Caro, G. D., & Dorigo, M. (1998). Antnet: Distributed stigmergetic control for communications networks. *Journal of Artificial Intelligence Research, 9*, 317–365.

Castillo, E., Gutiérrez, J. M., & Hadi, A. S. (1997). *Expert systems and probabilistic network models.* New York: Springer-Verlag.

Cestnik, B. (1990). Estimating probabilities: A crucial task in Machine Learning. In L. Aiello (Ed.), *Proceedings of the 9th European Conference on Artificial Intelligence (ECAI-90)* (pp. 147-149). London/Boston: Pitman.

Chandler, R. (2004). *Test Case Generation From UML Models for Software Integration Testing* (Tech. Rep. No. 1, PhD Proposal). Edith Cowan University, Australia.

Chang, S. K. (2002). *Handbook of Software Engineering and Knowledge Engineering, Volume 1 Fundamentals.* River Edge, NJ: World Scientific Publishing Company.

Chang, S. K. (2002). *Handbook of Software Engineering and Knowledge Engineering, Volume 2 Emerging Technologies.* River Edge, NJ: World Scientific Publishing Company.

Chantree, F., Nuseibeh, B., de Roeck, A., & Willis, A. (2006). Identifying nocuous ambiguities in natural language requirements. In *RE'06: Proceedings of the 14th IEEE International Requirements Engineering Conference (RE'06),* (pp.56–65). Washington, DC: IEEE Computer Society.

Chappell, D. (2002). *Understanding. NET: A Tutorial and Analysis.* Reading, MA: Addison Wesley.

Chen, M., Qiu, X., Xu, W., Wang, L., Zhao, J., & Li, X. (2007). UML Activity Diagram-Based Automatic Test Case Generation For Java Programs. *The Computer Journal.*

Chen, P. (1983, May). English sentence structure and entity-relationship diagram. *Information Sciences, 29*(2-3), 127–149. doi:10.1016/0020-0255(83)90014-2

Chen, P. P., Thalheim, B., & Wong, L. Y. (1999). Future Directions of Conceptual Modeling. In Chen P. P., Akoka J, Kangassalo H, & Thalheim B. (Eds), *Selected Papers From the Symposium on Conceptual Modeling, Current Issues and Future Directions.* (pp. 287-301), (LNCS vol. 1565). London: Springer-Verlag.

Chen, Z., Menzies, T., Port, D., & Boehm, B. (2005). Feature subset selection can improve software cost estimation accuracy. *Proceedings of the 2005 workshop on predictor models in software engineering*, St. Louis, Missouri, (pp. 1 – 6).

Chen, Z., Menzies, T., Port, D., & Boehm, B. (2005). Finding the right data for software cost modeling. *Software*, *22*(6), 38–46. doi:10.1109/MS.2005.151

Chen, Z., Menzies, T., Port, D., & Boehm, B. W. (2005). Feature Subset Selection Can Improve Software Cost Estimation Accuracy. In T. Menzies (Ed.), *PROMISE '05* (pp. 1-6). New York: ACM.

Cheng, B. H. C., & Atlee, J. M. (2007). Research Directions in Requirements Engineering. In *Future of Software Engineering, 2007. FOSE '07* (pp. 285-303). Minneapolis: IEEE Computer Society.

Cheng, R., & Gen, M. (1994). Evolution program for resource constrained project scheduling problem. *In Proceedings of the Proceedings of the 1st First IEEE Conference on Evolutionary Computation* (pp. 736-741), Orlando, FL, USA.

Chevalley, P., & Thevenod-Fosse, P. (2001). Automated Generation of Statistical Test Classes from UML State Diagrams. *25th Annual International Computer Software and Applications Conference (COMPSAC'01)*, 205–214.

Chulani, S., & Boehm, B. (1999). *Modeling software defect introduction and removal: COQUALMO (COnstructive QUALity MOdel)*, (Tech. Rep. USC-CSE-99-510). University of Southern California, Center for Software Engineering, Los Angeles, CA.

Clark, S., & Curran, J. R. (2004). Parsing the WSJ using CCG and log-linear models. In *ACL'04: Proceedings of the 42nd Annual Meeting on Association for Computa-*

tional Linguistics (p. 103). Morristown, NJ: Association for Computational Linguistics.

Clarke, E., Grumberg, O., & Peled, D. (1999). *Model Checking*. Cambridge, MA: MIT Press.

Clarke, J., Dolado, J. J., Harman, M., Hierons, R. M., Jones, B., & Lumkin, M. (2003). Reformulating software engineering as a search problem. *IEE Proceedings. Software*, *150*(3), 161–175. doi:10.1049/ip-sen:20030559

Clarke, L. A. (1976). A system to generate test data and symbolically execute programs. *IEEE Transactions on Software Engineering*, *se-2*(3), 215–222. doi:10.1109/TSE.1976.233817

Cockburn, A. (1997). Structuring Use Cases with Goal. *Journal of Object-Oriented Programming*, *9*(6), 56–62.

Cockburn, A. (2001). *Writing Effective Use Cases.* Upper Saddle River, NJ: Addison-Wesley.

Coelho, C., & Lechunga, M. (2002). MOPSO: A proposal for multuiple objective particle swarm optimization. *Proceedings of the 2002 Congress on Evolutionary Computation* (pp. 1051-1056). Washington, DC: IEEE Press.

Coelho, C., Pulido, G., & Salazar, M. (2004). Handling multiobjectives with particle swarm optimization. *IEEE Transactions on Evolutionary Computation*, *8*, 256–279. doi:10.1109/TEVC.2004.826067

Cohn, M. (2004). *User stories applied for agile software development*. Reading MA: Addison Wesley Press.

Colorni, A., Dorigo, M., & Maniezzo, V. (1991). Distributed optimization by ant colonies. In *F. Varela & P. Bourgine (Eds.), Proceedings of the First European Conference on Artificial Life (ECAL)* (pp. 134–142). Cambridge, MA: MIT Press.

Command Control Communications. A. S. of Defense for, & C3I, I. A. (2001). *End-to-End Integration Test Guidebook (Tech. Rep. No. Version 1.0)*. Washington, DC: Department of Defense, United States of America.

Conklin, J., & Begeman, M. (1988). gIBIS: A hypertext tool for exploratory policy discussion. *Transactions on Office Information Systems, 6*(4), 303–331. doi:10.1145/58566.59297

Conte, S. D., Dunsmore, H. E., & Shen, V. Y. (1986). *Software Engineering Metrics and Models.* Menlo Park, CA: The Benjamin/Cummings Publishing Company, Inc.

Cook, J. E., & Wolf, A. L. (1998). Discovering models of software processes from event-based data. *ACM Transactions on Software Engineering and Methodology, 7*(3), 215–249. doi:10.1145/287000.287001

Cooper, G., & Herskovitzs, E. (1992). A Bayesian method for the induction of probabilistic networks from data. *Machine Learning, 9*, 309–347.

Coplien, J., Hoffman, D., & Weiss, D. (1998). Commonality and variability in software engineering. *IEEE Software, 6*(November/December).

Corkill, D. (2003). Collaborating software: Blackboard and multi-agent systems and the future. Invited paper presented at the *International Lisp Conference,* New York.

Costagliola, G., Di Martino, S., Ferrucci, F., Gravino, C., Tortora, G., & Vitiello, G. (2006). Effort estimation modeling techniques: a case study for web applications, In *Proceedings of the Intl. Conference on Web Engineering* (ICWE'06), (pp. 9-16).

Coulin, C. (2007). *A Situational Approach and Intelligent Tool for Collaborative Requirements Elicitation.* PhD Thesis, University of Technology Sydney & Paul Sabatier University, Australia.

Coulin, C., Zowghi, D., & Sahraoui, A. E. K. (2006). A Situational Method Engineering Approach to Requirements Elicitation Workshops in the Software Development Process. *Software Process Improvement and Practice, 11*, 451–464. doi:10.1002/spip.288

Cowell, R. G., Dawid, A., Lauritzen, S. L., & Spiegelhalter, D. J. (1999). *Probabilistic networks and experts systems.* New York: Springer-Verlag.

Curran, J. R., Clark, S., & Vadas, D. (2006). Multi-Tagging for Lexicalized-Grammar Parsing. In *21st International Conference on Computational Linguistics and 44th Annual Meeting of the Association for Computational Linguistics*, Sydney, Australia, July 17-21.

Dahanayake, A. N. W. (1998). Evaluation of the Strength of Computer Aided Method Engineering for Product Development Process Modeling. *9th International Conference on Database and Expert Systems Applications.* Vienna, Austria, August 24-28.

Dardenne, A., van Lamsweerde, A., & Fickas, S. (1993). Goal-Directed Requirements Acquisition. *Science of Computer Programming, 20*(1-2), 3–50. doi:10.1016/0167-6423(93)90021-G

Darwiche, A. (2008). Bayesian Networks. In F. van Harmelen, V. Lifschitz & B. Porter (Eds.), *Handbook of Knowledge Representation,* (Vol. 3, pp. 467-509). St. Louis, MO: Elsevier.

Data Knowledge and Software Engineering Research Group (DKSE) (2005). InSCo Requisite. Retrieved from http://www.dkse.ual.es/insco/index.do.

Davis, A. M. (1989). *Software Requirements: Analysis and Specification.* Upper Saddle River, NJ: Prentice Hall Press.

Davis, L. D. (1991). *Handbook of genetic algorithm.* Van Nostrand Reinhold Co., New York.

de Melo, A. C., & Sanchez, A. J. (2008). Software maintenance project delays prediction using Bayesian Networks. *Expert Systems with Applications, 34*(2), 908–919. doi:10.1016/j.eswa.2006.10.040

Deb, K. (2001). *Multi-objective optimization using evolutionary algorithms.* New York: John Wiley & Sons.

Deb, K., Agrawal, S., Pratab, A., & Meyarivan, T. (2000). A fast elitist nondominated sorting genetic algorithm for multiobjective optimization: NSGA-II. *Proceedings of Parallel Problem Solving from Nature VI Conference,* 849–858.

Deelstra, S., Sinnema, M., & Bosch, J. (2004). Experiences in software product families: Problems and issues during product derivation. In *Proceedings of International Software Product Line Conference (SPLC)*.

del Águila, I. M., Cañadas, J. J., Bosch, A., Túnez, S., & Marín, R. (2003). Knowledge Model of a Therapy Administration Task - Applied to an Agricultural Domain. In V. Palada, R.J. Howlett and L.C. Jain (Eds.), *Knowledge-Based Intelligent Information and Engineering Systems 2003*, (LNAI 2774, pp.1227-1283). Berlin: Springer-Verlag.

del Águila, I. M., Cañadas, J., Palma, J., & Túnez, S. (2006). Towards a Methodology for Hybrid Systems Software Development. In K. Zhang, G. Spanoudakis, G. Visaggio (Eds.): *Proceedings of the Eighteenth International Conference on Software Engineering & Knowledge Engineering (SEKE'2006)*, San Francisco, CA, July 5-7, (pp. 188-193).

del Sagrado, J., & del Águila, I. M. (2007). Olive Fly Infestation Prediction Using Machine Learning Techniques. In D. Borrajo, L. Castillo, and J. M. Corchado (Eds.), *Current Topics in Artificial intelligence: 12th Conference of the Spanish Association For Artificial intelligence, CAEPIA 2007, Salamanca, Spain, November 12-16, 2007. Selected Papers, LNAI 4788* (pp. 229-238). Berlin: Springer-Verlag.

del Sagrado, J., & Moral, S. (2003). Qualitative combination of Bayesian networks. *International Journal of Intelligent Systems, 18*(2), 237–249. doi:10.1002/int.10086

del Sagrado, J., & Salmerón, A. (2004), Representing canonical models as probability trees. In R. Conejo, M. Urretavizcaya, J-L. Pérez-de-la-Cruz (Eds.) *Current Topics in Artificial Intelligence, 10th Conference of the Spanish Association for Artificial Intelligence, CAEPIA 2003, and 5th Conference on Technology Transfer, TTIA 2003, San Sebastian, Spain, November 12-14, 2003. Revised Selected Papers.* (LNCS 3040, pp. 478-487). Berlin: Springer.

DeMasie, M. P., & Muratore, J. F. (1991). Artificial intelligence and expert systems in-flight software testing. In *Proceedings of the Tenth IEEE Conference on Digital Avionics Systems Conference* (pp. 416-419), Los Angeles, CA. Washington DC: IEEE Computer Society.

DeMilli, R. A., & Offutt, A. J. (1991). Constraint-based automatic test data generation. *IEEE Transactions on Software Engineering, 17*(9), 900–910. doi:10.1109/32.92910

den Hengst, M., van de Kar, E., & Appelman, J. (2004). Designing Mobile Information Services: User Requirements Elicitation with GSS Design and Application of a Repeatable Process. *37th Hawaii International Conference on System Sciences*, Big Island, Hawaii, January 5-8.

Denger, C., & Mora, M. M. (2003). *Test case derived from requirement specifications* (Tech. Rep. No. IESE-Report No: 033.03/E). Fraunhofer: Institut Experimentelles, Software Engineering.

Derderian, K., Hierons, R. M., Harman, M., & Guo, Q. (2006). Automated unique input output sequence generation for conformance testing of FSMs. *The Computer Journal, 49*(3), 331–344. doi:10.1093/comjnl/bxl003

Diaz, I., Pastor, O., & Matteo, A. (2005). Modeling interactions using role-driven patterns. In RE'05: *Proceedings of the 13th IEEE International Conference on Requirements Engineering (RE'05)*, (pp. 209–220). Washington, DC: IEEE Computer Society.

Díaz-Pace, A., Kim, H., Bass, L., Bianco, P., & Bachmann, F. (2008). Integrating quality-attribute reasoning frameworks in the ArchE design assistant. In Becker, Plasil & Reussner (Eds.), *Proceedings of the 4th International Conference on the Quality of Software Architecture – QoSA'08*, (LNCS 5281, pp. 171-188). Berlin: Springer-Verlag.

Díaz-Pace, J. A., & Campo, M. (2005). ArchMatE: From architectural styles to object-oriented models through exploratory tool support. In *Proceedings of the 20th Annual ACM SIGPLAN Conference on Object Oriented Programming, Systems, Languages, and Applications* (pp. 117-132). San Diego, CA: ACM Press.

Díez, F. J. (1993) Parameter adjustment in Bayes networks. The generalized noisy OR-gate. In D. Heckerman and A. Mamdani (Eds.), *Proceedings of the 9th Conference on Uncertainty in Artificial Intelligence* (pp. 99-105). San Mateo, CA: Morgan Kaufman.

Díez, F. J., & Druzdel, M. J. (2001) Fundamentals of canonical models. In A. Bahamonde and R.P. Otero (Eds.), *Actas de la IX Conferencia de la Asociación Española para la IA (CAEPIA 2001)*, Vol II (pp 1125-1134). Oviedo, Spain: Servicio de Publicaciones de la Universidad de Oviedo.

Doerner, K., & Gutjahr, W. J. (2003). Extracting test sequences from a markov software usage model by ACO. *Proc. GECCO 2003*, (LNCS, Vol. 2724, pp. 2465-2476).

Dorigo, M., & Caro, G. D. (1999). Ant colony optimization: A new meta-heuristic. In *Proceedings of the Congress on Evolutionary Computation* (pp. 1470–1477). Washington, DC: IEEE Press.

Dorigo, M., & Stutzle, T. (2002). The ant colony optimization metaheuristic: Algorithms, applications and advances. In F. Glover & G. Kochenberger (Eds.), *Handbook of Metaheuristics*. Kluwer Academic Publishers.

Dorigo, M., & Stutzle, T. (2004). *Ant colony optimization*. Cambridge, MA: MIT Press.

Dorigo, M., Bonabeau, E., & Theraulaz, G. (2000). Ant algorithms and stygmergy. *Future Generation Computer Systems*, *16*(8), 851–871. doi:10.1016/S0167-739X(00)00042-X

Dorigo, M., Maniezzo, V., & Colorni, A. (1991). *Positive feedback as a search strategy* (Tech. Rep No. 91-016). Politecnico di Milano, Milan, Italy.

Dorigo, M., Maniezzo, V., & Colorni, A. (1996). The Ant System: Optimization by a Colony of Cooperating Agents. *IEEE Transactions on Systems, Man, and Cybernetics-Part B*, *26*, 29–41. doi:10.1109/3477.484436

Dorigo, M., Zlochin, M., Meuleau, N., & Birattari, M. (2002). Updating aco pheromones using stochastic gradient ascent and cross-entropy methods. In S. Cagnoni, J. Gottlieb, E. Hart, M. Middendorf, & G. Raidl (Eds.), *Applications of Evolutionary Computing, Proceedings of EVO workshops 2002* (Vol. 2279, pp. 21–30). Berlin: Springer Verlag.

Dreyfus, G. (2005). *Neural Networks Methodology and Applications*. Berlin, Germany: Springer.

Druzdel, M. J., & van der Gaag, L. (1995). Elicitation of Probabilities for Belief Networks: Combining Qualitative and Quantitative Information. In P. Besnard & S. Hanks (Eds.), *Proceedings of the 11th Conference on Uncertainty in Artificial Intelligence* (pp. 141-148). San Francisco, CA: Morgan Kaufmann.

Druzdzel, M. J., & van der Gaag, L. C. (2000). Building Probabilistic Networks: Where Do the Numbers Come From? *IEEE Transactions on Knowledge and Data Engineering*, *12*(4), 481–486. doi:10.1109/TKDE.2000.868901

Dubois, D., & Prade, H. (1984). Criteria aggregation and ranking of alternatives in the framework of fuzzy set theory. *Studies in the Management Sciences*, *20*, 209–240.

Duran Toro, A., & Bernárdez Jiménez, B. (2000). *Metodología de elicitación de requisitos de sistemas software. Versión 2.1*, (Tech. Rep.). Sevilla, Spain: University of Seville, Dpt. of Languages and Informatics Systems.

Dwyer, M., Avrunin, G., & Corbett, J. (1999). Patterns in property specifications for finite-state verification. In *Proceedings of International Conference on Software Engineering (ICSE)*.

Eberhart, R., & Shi, Y. (2007). *Computational intelligence: Concepts to implementations*. San Francisco: Morgan Kaufman.

Ebert, C., & Man, J. D. (2005). Requirements Uncertainty: Influencing Factors and Concrete Improvements. In G-C Roman, W.G. Griswold & B. Nuseibeh (Eds.), *Proceedings of the 27th International Conference on Software Engineering, ICSE 2005* (pp. 553-560). St. Louis, MO: ACM.

Edwards, G., Seo, C., & Medvidovic, N. (2007). Construction of analytic frameworks for component-based architectures. In *Proceedings of the Brazilian Symposium on Software Components, Architectures and Reuse* - SB-CARS'07 (pp. 147-160). Campinas, Sao Paulo, Brazil: Institute of Computing UNICAMP.

Eiben, A. E., Hinterding, R., & Michalewicz, Z. (1999). Parameter control in evolutionary algorithms. *IEEE*

Transactions on Evolutionary Computation, 3(2), 124–141. doi:10.1109/4235.771166

Ellis, C. A., Gibbs, S. J., & Rein, G. L. (1991). Groupware: Some issues and experiences. *Communications of the ACM, 34*(1), 39–58. doi:10.1145/99977.99987

Elvira Consortium. (2002). Elvira: An Environment for Probabilistc Graphical Models. In J.A. Gámez & A. Salmerón (Eds.), *Proceedings of the First European Workshop on Probabilistic Graphical Models* (pp. 222-230). Retrieved January 10, 2009, from http://www.informatik.uni-trier.de/~ley/db/conf/pgm/pgm2002.html

Engler, D., Chen, D. Y., Hallem, S., Chou, A., & Chelf, B. (2001). Bugs as deviant behavior: A general approach to inferring errors in systems code. In *Proceedings of Symposium on Operating Systems Principles (SOSP)*.

Erlikh, L. (2000). Leveraging legacy system dollars for e-business. *IEEE IT Pro, May/June*, 17–23.

Ernst, M. (2003). Static and dynamic analysis: Synergy and duality. In *Proceedings of International Workshop on Dynamic Analysis (WODA)*.

Ernst, M., Cockrell, J., Griswold, W., & Notkin, D. (2001). Dynamically discovering likely program invariants to support program evolution. *IEEE Transactions on Software Engineering, 27*(2), 99–123. doi:10.1109/32.908957

Fabbrini, F., Fusani, M., Gnesi, S., & Lami, G. (2001). The linguistic approach to the natural language requirements quality: benefit of the use of an automatic tool. In *26th Annual NASA Goddard Software Engineering Workshop*, (pp. 97–105). Greenbelt, Maryland: IEEE Computer Society. Retrieved August 13, 2008 from http://fmt.isti.cnr.it/WEBPAPER/fabbrini_nlrquality.pdf

Fairley, R. E. (2006). The Influence of COCOMO on Software Engineering Education and Training. *Proceedings of the 19th Conference on Software Engineering Education and Training*, (pp. 193 – 200).

Falbo, R. A., Guizzardi, G., Natali, A. C., Bertollo, G., Ruy, F. F., & Mian, P. G. (2002), Towards semantic software engineering environments. *Proceedings of the 14th*

international Conference on Software Engineering and Knowledge Engineering SEKE '02, vol. 27 (pp. 477-478), Ischia, Italy. New York: ACM.

Fantechi, A., Gnesi, S., Ristori, G., Carenini, M., Vanocchi, M., & Moreschini, P. (1994). Assisting requirement formalization by means of natural language translation. *Formal Methods in System Design, 4*(3), 243–263. doi:10.1007/BF01384048

Fatima, S., Wooldridge, M., & Jennings, N. (2004). Optimal negotiation of multiple issues in incomplete information settings. In *Proceedings of the Third International Conference on Autonomous Agents and Multiagent Systems - AAMAS'04* (pp.1080-1087). New York: ACM Press.

Fayad, M., Schmidt, D., & Johnson, R. (1999). *Building application frameworks: object-oriented foundations of framework design.* Chichester, UK: John Wiley & Sons Ltd.

Fenton, N. (1993). How effective are software engineering methods? *Journal of Systems and Software, 22*(2), 141–146. doi:10.1016/0164-1212(93)90092-C

Fenton, N. E. (1991). *Software Metrics: A Rigorous Approach*. London: Chapman & Hall.

Fenton, N. E., & Neil, M. (1999). A critique of software defect prediction models. *IEEE Transactions on Software Engineering, 25*(5), 675–689. doi:10.1109/32.815326

Fenton, N. E., Marsh, W., Neil, M., Cates, P., Forey, S., & Tailor, T. (2004). Making resource decisions for software projects. In *Proceedings of 26th International Conference on Software Engineering* (ICSE 2004), Edinburgh, United Kingdom, May 2004, IEEE Computer Society, (pp. 397-406).

Fenton, N. E., Neil, M., & Caballero, J. G. (2007). Using ranked nodes to model qualitative judgments in Bayesian Networks. *IEEE Transactions on Knowledge and Data Engineering, 19*(10), 1420–1432. doi:10.1109/TKDE.2007.1073

Fenton, N., Krause, P., & Neil, M. (2002). Software measurement: Uncertainty and Causal Modelling. *IEEE Software, 19*(4), 116–122. doi:10.1109/MS.2002.1020298

Fenton, N., Marsh, W., Neil, M., Cates, P., Forey, S., & Tailor, M. (2004). Making Resource Decisions for Software Projects. In Proceedings of ICSE, 04, 397–406.

Fenton, N., Neil, M., Marsh, W., Hearty, P., Marquez, D., Krause, P., & Mishra, R. (2007, January). Predicting software defects in varying development lifecycles using Bayesian nets. *Information and Software Technology, 49*(1), 32–43. doi:10.1016/j.infsof.2006.09.001

Fenton, N., Neil, M., Marsh, W., Hearty, P., Radlinski, L., & Krause, P. (2007). Project data incorporating qualitative facts for improved software defect prediction. In *Proceedings of the Third international Workshop on Predictor Models in Software Engineering*, International Conference on Software Engineering (May 20 - 26, 2007). Washington, DC: IEEE Computer Society.

Fernandez, J. L. (1997). A taxonomy of coordination mechanisms used by real-time processes. In *Ada Letter, 7*(2), 29-54.

Fewster, R. M., & Mendes, E. (2001). Measurement, Prediction and Risk Analysis for Web Applications. In *Proceedings of the IEEE METRICS Symposium,* (pp. 338-348).

Finkelstein, A., & Sommerville, I. (1996). The Viewpoints FAQ: Editorial - Viewpoints in Requirements Engineering. *Software Engineering Journal, 11*(1), 2–4.

Finnie, G. R., Wittig, G. E., & Desharnais, J. M. (1997). A comparison of software effort estimation techniques: Using function points with neural networks, case-based reasoning and regression models. *Journal of Systems and Software, 39*(3), 281–289. doi:10.1016/S0164-1212(97)00055-1

Fjeldstad, R., & Hamlen, W. (1983). Application program maintenance-report to our respondents. In Parikh, G. & Zvegintzov, N. (Eds.), *Tutorial on Software Maintenance* (pp. 13–27). Washington, DC: IEEE Computer Soc. Press.

Foss, T., Stensrud, E., Kitchenham, B., & Myrtveit, I. (2003). A Simulation Study of the Model Evaluation Criterion MMRE. *IEEE Transactions on Software Engineering, 29*(11), 985–995. doi:10.1109/TSE.2003.1245300

Fouqué, G., & Matwin, S. (1993). A Case-based approach to software reuse. [Amsterdam: Kluwer Academic Publishers.]. *Journal of Intelligent Information Systems, 2*(2), 165–197. doi:10.1007/BF00965876

Fox, T. L., & Spence, J. W. (2005). The effect of decision style on the use of a project management tool: An empirical laboratory study. *The Data Base for Advances in Information Systems, 32*(2), 28–42.

Fox, T. L., & Spence, J. W. (2005). The effect of decision style on the use of a project management tool: An empirical laboratory study. *The Data Base for Advances in Information Systems, 32*(2), 28–42.

Friedman-Hill, E. (2003). *Jess in action: Java rule-based systems.* Greenwich, CT: Manning Publications Company.

Frohlich, P., & Link, J. (2000). Automated test case generation from dynamic models. *LNCS, 1850,* 472–491.

Gaizauskas, R., Cunningham, H., Wilks, Y., Rodgers, P., & Humphreys, K. (1996). GATE: an environment to support research and development in natural language engineering. In *Proceedings of the 8th IEEE International Conference on Tools with Artificial Intelligence.* (pp.58-66). Washington DC: IEEE Computer Society.

Gambardella, L. M., & Dorigo, M. (1995). Ant-Q: A Reinforcement Learning Approach to the Travelling Salesman Problem. In A. Prieditis & S. Russell (Eds.), *Proceedings of the Twelfth International Conference on Machine Learning* (pp. 252–260). San Mateo, CA: Morgan Kaufmann.

Gamma, E., Helm, R., Johnson, R., & Vlissides, J. (1994). *Design patterns: Elements of reusable object-oriented software.* Boston: Addison-Wesley.

Geihs, K., Baer, P., Reichle, R., & Wollenhaupt, J. (2008). Ontology-Based Automatic Model Transformations. In *Proceedings of the 6th IEEE International Conference on Software Engineering and Formal Methods* (pp.387-391), Cape Town, South Africa. Washington DC: IEEE Computer Society.

Gero, J. S., & Kannengiesser, U. (2006). A framework for situated design optimization. In *Proceedings of Innovations in Design Decision Support Systems in Architecture and Urban Planning* (pp. 309-324). Dordrecht, the Netherlands: Springer.

Gervasi, V., & Zowghi, D. (2005). Reasoning about inconsistencies in natural language requirements. *ACM Transactions on Software Engineering and Methodology*, *14*(3), 277–330. doi:10.1145/1072997.1072999

Ghallab, M., Nau, D., & Traverso, P. (2004). *Automated Planning: Theory and Practice*. San Francisco: Morgan Kaufmann.

Glass, A. R. L. (2002). *Facts and Fallacies of Software Engineering*. Boston: Pearson Education, Inc.

Glass, R. L. (1998). *Software runaways*. Upper Saddle River, NJ: Prentice-Hall.

Glass, R. L. (2006). The Standish report: Does it really describe a software crisis? *Communications of the ACM*, *49*(8), 15–16. doi:10.1145/1145287.1145301

Godefroid, P. (2007). Compositional dynamic test generation. In *the 34th Annual ACM SIGPLAN-SIGACT Symposium on Principles of Programming Languages (POPL'07)* (pp. 47-54). Nice, France: ACM.

Godefroid, P., Klarlund, N., & Sen, K. (2005). DART: Directed automated random testing. In *the ACM SIGPLAN 2005 Conference on Programming Language Design and Implementation (PLDI'05)* (pp. 213-223). Chicago: ACM.

Goguen, J., & Linde, C. (1993). Techniques for Requirements Elicitation. In *Proceedings of the First IEEE International Symposium on Requirements Engineering (RE'93), San Diego, CA, 4-6th January 1993* (pp.152-164). New York: IEEE Computer Society.

Goldberg, D. E. (1989). *Genetic Algorithms in Search, Optimization and Machine Learning*. Reading MA: Addition-Wesley.

Goldin, L., & Berry, D. M. (1997). AbstFinder, A Prototype Natural Language Text Abstraction Finder for Use in Requirements Elicitation. *Automated Software Engineering*, *4*(4), 375–412. doi:10.1023/A:1008617922496

Gomes, P., & Leitao, A. (2006). A tool for management and reuse of software design knowledge. In *Proceedings the 15th International Conference on Knowledge Engineering and Knowledge Management*, Podebrady, Czech Republic, (LNAI 4228). Berlin: Springer.

Gomma, E. (2004). *Design Software Product Lines*. Reading, MA: Addison Wesley.

Gonzalez-Harbour, M., Gutierrez García, J. J., Palencia Gutiérrez, J. C., & Drake Moyano, J. M. (2001). MAST: Modeling and analysis suite for real time applications. In *Proceedings 13th Euromicro Conference on Real-Time Systems – ECRTS'01* (pp. 125-134). Washington, DC: IEEE Computer Society.

Gotlieb, A., Botella, B., & Rueher, M. (1998). Automatic test data generation using constraint solving techniques. In *the ACM SIGSOFT 1998 International Symposium on Software Testing and Analysis (ISSTA'98)* (pp. 53-62). Clearwater Beach, FL: ACM.

Gottesdiener, E. (2002). *Requirements by Collaboration: Workshops for Defining Needs*. Boston: Addison-Wesley.

Gravel, M., Price, W. L., & Gagn, C. (2002). Scheduling continuous casting of aluminum using a multiple-objective ant colony optimization metaheuristic. *European Journal of Operational Research*, *143*(1), 218–229. doi:10.1016/S0377-2217(01)00329-0

Gray, A. R., & MacDonell, S. G. (1997). A comparison of techniques for developing predictive models of software metrics. *Information and Software Technology*, *39*, 425–437. doi:10.1016/S0950-5849(96)00006-7

Gro, H.-G. (2003). An evaluation of dynamic, optimisation-based worst-case execution time analysis. *Proceedings of the International Conference on Information Technology: Prospects and Challenges in the 21st Century*, Kathmandu, Nepal.

Groß, H.-G. (2000). *Measuring Evolutionary Testability of Real-Time Software*. Unpublished doctoral dissertation, University of Glamorgan, UK.

Grosz, B. J., Joshi, A. K., & Weinstein, S. (1995). Centering: A Framework for Modeling the Local Coherence of Discourse. *Computational Linguistics, 21*(2), 203-225. Retrieved August 13, 2008 from citeseer.ist.psu.edu/grosz95centering.html

Grubb, P., & Takang, A. (2003). *Software Maintenance: Concepts and Practice.* Singapore: World Scientific.

Grunske, L. (2006). Identifying "good" architectural design alternatives with multi-objective optimization strategies. In *International Conference on Software Engineering (ICSE), Workshop on Emerging Results* (pp. 849-852). New York: ACM Press.

Gulavani, B. S., Henzinger, T. A., Kannan, Y., Nori, A. V., & Rajamani, S. K. (2006). SYNERGY: a new algorithm for property checking. In *the 14th ACM SIGSOFT International Symposium on Foundations of Software Engineering (FSE'05)* (pp. 117-127). Portland, OR: ACM.

Gulezian, R. (1991). Reformulating and calibrating COCOMO. *Journal of Systems and Software, 16*(3), 235–242. doi:10.1016/0164-1212(91)90018-2

Guo, M. H., Hierons, R. M., & Derderian, K. (2003). Computing Unique Input/Output Sequences using Genetic Algorithms. *3rd International Workshop on Formal Approaches to Testing of Software (FATES2003)*, (LNCS Vol. 2931, pp. 164-177).

Gupta, M., Bastani, F., Khan, L., & Yen, I.-L. (2004). Automated test data generation using MEA-graph planning. In *Proceedings of the Sixteenth IEEE Conference on Tools with Artificial Intelligence* (pp. 174-182). Washington, DC: IEEE Computer Society.

Guyon, I., & Gunn, M. Nikravesh, & Zadeh, L. (2005). *Feature Extraction foundations and applications.* Berlin, Germany: Springer.

Hagan, M. T., & Menhaj, M. B. (1994). Training Feedforward Networks with the Marquardt Algorithm. *IEEE Transactions on Neural Networks, 5*(6), 989–993. doi:10.1109/72.329697

Hailpern, B., & Santhanarn, P. (2002). Software Debugging, Testing and Verification. *IBM Systems Journal, 41*(1), 4–12.

Hale, J., Parrish, A., Dixon, B., & Smith, R. K. (2000). Enhancing the Cocomo estimation models. *IEEE Software, 17*(6), 45–49. doi:10.1109/52.895167

Hall, J. G., & Rapanotti, L. (2003). A Reference Model for Requirements Engineering. In *Proceedings of the 11th IEEE international Conference on Requirements Engineering* (pp. 181-187). Washington, DC: IEEE Computer Society.

Hammouda, I., & Harsu, M. (2004). Documenting maintenance tasks using maintenance patterns. In *Proceedings of the 8th European Conference on Software Maintenance and Reengineering* - CSMR'04 (pp. 37-47). Washington, DC: IEEE Computer Society.

Han, J., & Kamber, M. (2006). *Data Mining Concepts and Techniques.* San Francisco: Morgan Kaufmann.

Hand, D., Mannila, H., & Smyth, P. (2001). *Principles of Data Mining.*, Cambridge, MA: MIT Press.

Hannola, L., Elfvengren, K., & Tuominen, M. (2005). Improving Requirements Elicitation with GSS in Software Development. *Annual ISPIM Conference, International Society for Professional Innovation Management.* Porto, Portugal, June 19-22.

Harel, D., & Marelly, R. (2003). *Come, Let's Play: Scenario-Based Programming Using LSCs and the Play-Engine.* Berlin: Springer–Verlag.

Harmain, H. M., & Gaizauskas, R. (2003). CM-Builder: A natural language-based CASE tool for object-oriented analysis. *Automated Software Engineering Journal, 10*(2), 157–181. doi:10.1023/A:1022916028950

Harman, M. (2007). The current state and future of search based software engineering. In *Proceedings of International Conference on Software Engineering/Future of Software Engineering 2007* (ICSE/FOSE 2007) (pp. 342-357). Washington, DC: IEEE Computer Society.

Harman, M., & Jones, B. (2001). Software Engineering using Metaheuristic INnovative ALgorithms: Workshop

Report. *Journal of Information and Software Technology*, *43*(14), 905–907. doi:10.1016/S0950-5849(01)00196-3

Harman, M., & Jones, B. F. (2001). The Seminal Workshop: Reformulating Software Engineering as a Meta-heuristic Search Problem. *SIGSOFT Softw. Eng. Notes*, *26*(6), 62–66. doi:10.1145/505532.505548

Harman, M., & McMinn, P. (2007). A theoretical & empirical analysis of evolutionary testing and hill climbing for structural test data generation. In *Proceedings of the International Symposium on Software Testing and Analysis* (pp. 73-83). London: ACM.

Harman, M., Hu, L., Hierons, R. M., Fox, C., Danicic, S., Wegener, J., et al. (2002). Evolutionary Testing Supported by Slicing and Transformation. *In 18th International Conference on Software Maintenance (ICSM 2002), Maintaining Distributed Heterogeneous Systems*, 3-6 October 2002, Montreal, Canada. Washington, DC: IEEE Computer Society.

Harman, M., Lakhotia, K., & McMinn, P. (2007). A multi-objective approach to search-based test data generation. In *Gecco '07: Proceedings of the 9th Annual Conference on Genetic and Evolutionary Computation* (pp. 1098–1105). New York: ACM.

Hartmann, J., Imoberdorf, C., & Meisinger, M. (2000). Uml-based integration testing. In *ISSTA'00: Proceedings of the 2000 ACM Sigsoft International Symposium on Software Testing and Analysis* (pp. 60–70). New York: ACM.

Hartmann, J., Vieira, M., Foster, H., & Ruder, A. (2004). *UML-Based Test Generation and Execution* (Tech. Rep.). Siemens Corporate Research Inc., Princeton, NJ. Retrieved from www.gm.fh-koeln.de/winter/ tav/html/ tav21/TAV21P6Vieira.pdf

Hautamäki, J. (2005). *Pattern-based tool support for frameworks: Towards architecture-oriented software development environment*. Ph.D. Thesis, Tampere University of Technology, Publication 521, Finland.

Hearty, P., Fenton, N., Marquez, D., & Neil, M. (in press). Predicting project velocity in XP using a learning dynamic Bayesian Network model. *IEEE Transactions on Software Engineering*.

Heckerman, D. (1999). A tutorial on learning with Bayesian networks. In M. I. Jordan, (Ed.) *Learning in Graphical Models* (pp. 301-354). Cambridge, MA: MIT Press.

Helm, J. E. (1992). The viability of using COCOMO in the special application software bidding and estimating process. *IEEE Transactions on Engineering Management*, *39*(1), 42–58. doi:10.1109/17.119662

Hendrickson, S., Jett, B., & van der Hoek, A. (2006). A layered class diagrams: Supporting the design process. In *Proceedings of the 9th International Conference on Model Driven Engineering Languages and Systems - MoDELS'06* (pp. 722-736). Berlin: Springer.

Henrion, M. (1989). Some Practical Issues in Constructing Belief Networks. In L. Kanal, T. Levitt, & J. Lemmer (Eds.), *Uncertainty in Artificial Intelligence 3* (pp. 161-173). Amsterdam: Elsevier Science Publishers.

Herela, D., & Greenberg, S. (1998). Using a Groupware Space for Distributed Requirements Engineering. *Seventh Workshop on Enabling Technologies: Infrastructure for Collaborative Enterprises,* Stanford, USA, June 17-19.

Hickey, A. M. (2003). Requirements Elicitation Techniques: Analyzing the Gap between Technology Availability and Technology Use. *Comparative Technology Transfer and Society, 1*(3), 279–302. doi:10.1353/ctt.2003.0026

Hickey, A. M., & Davis, A. M. (2003). Elicitation Technique Selection: How Do Experts Do It? *Eleventh IEEE International Requirements Engineering Conference.* Monterey Bay, CA, September 8-12.

Hickey, A. M., Dean, D. L., & Nunamaker, J. F. (1999). Establishing a Foundation for Collaborative Scenario Elicitation. *The Data Base for Advances in Information Systems, 30*(3-4), 92–110.

Hickey, A.M. & Davis, A.M. (2002). The Role of Requirements Elicitation Techniques in Achieving Software Quality. *Eighth International Workshop of Requirements*

Engineering: Foundation for Software Quality. Essen, Germany, September 9-10.

Hindi, K. S., Hongbo, Y., & Fleszar, K. (2002). An evolutionary algorithm for resource-constrained project scheduling. *IEEE Transactions on Evolutionary Computation, 6*(5), 512–518. doi:10.1109/TEVC.2002.804914

Hissam, S. A., Moreno, G. A., Plakosh, D., Savo, I., & Stelmarczyk, M. (2008). Predicting the behavior of a highly configurable component based real-time system. In *Proceedings of 20th Euromicro Conference on Real-Time Systems – ECRTS'08* (pp. 57-68). Washington, DC: IEEE Computer Society.

Ho, W., Jzquel, J., Guennec, A., & Pennaneac'h, F. (1999). UMLAUT: an extendible UML transformation framework. *Proc. Automated Software Engineering, ASE'99.*

Hoerl, A. E., & Kennard, R. W. (1970). Ridge regression: Biased estimation of non-orthogonal problems. *Technometrics.*

Hoffer, J. A., George, J. F., & Valacich, J. S. (2002). *Modern Systems Analysis and Design,* (3rd Ed.). Upper Saddle River, NJ: Prentice Hall.

Holland, J. H. (1975). *Adaptation in Natural and Artificial System.* Ann Arbor, MI: The University of Michigan Press.

Hood, C., Wiedemann, S., Fichtinger, S., & Pautz, U. (2008). *Requirements Management: The Interface Between Requirements Development and All Other Systems Engineering Processes.* Berlin: Springer-Verlag.

Hooshyar, B., Tahmani, A., & Shenasa, M. (2008). A Genetic Algorithm to Time-Cost Trade off in project scheduling. In *Proceedings of the IEEE World Congress on Computational Intelligence* (pp. 3081-3086), Hong Kong. Washington DC: IEEE Computer Society.

Howe, A. E., Mayrhauser, A. v., & Mraz, R. T. (1997). Test Case Generation as an AI Planning Problem. *Automated Software Engineering, 4*(1), 77–106. doi:10.1023/A:1008607721339

Howe, A. E., von Mayrhauser, A., & Mraz, R. T. (1995). Test sequences as plans: an experiment in using an AI planner to generate system tests. In *Proceedings of the Tenth Conference on Knowledge-Based Software Engineering* (pp. 184-191), Boston, MA. Washington DC: IEEE Computer Society.

Howe, J. (2007) The Nature of Artificial Intelligence, Artificial Intelligence at Edinburgh University: a Perspective. Retrieved from http://www.inf.ed.ac.uk/about/AIhistory.html

Hu, Y., Chen, J., Rong, Z., Mei, L., & Xie, K. (2006). A Neural Networks Approach for Software Risk Analysis. *In Proceedings of the Sixth IEEE International Conference on Data Mining Workshops* (pp. 722-725), Hong Kong. Washington DC: IEEE Computer Society.

Hull, E., Jackson, K., & Dick, J. (2005). *Requirements Engineering.* Berlin: Springer.

Huth, M., & Ryan, M. (2004). *Logic in Computer Science.* Cambridge, UK: Cambridge.

IBM. (2009). *Rational Requisite Pro.* http://www-01.ibm.com/software/awdtools/reqpro/

IBM. (2009). *Telelogic DOORS Analyst.* http://www-01.ibm.com/software/awdtools/doors/analyst/

IEEE guide for developing system requirements specifications (1998). *IEEE Std 1233, 1998 Edition.* Retrieved January 9, 2008, from http://ieeexplore.ieee.org/xpls/abs_all.jsp?tp=&isnumber=16016&arnumber=741940&punumber=5982

IEEE guide for information technology - system definition - Concept of Operations (ConOps) document (1998). *IEEE Std 1362-1998.* Retrieved January 9, 2008, from http://ieeexplore.ieee.org/xpls/abs_all.jsp?tp=&isnumber=16486&arnumber=761853&punumber=6166

IEEE recommended practice for software requirements specifications (1998). *IEEE Std 830-1998.* Retrieved January 9, 2008, from http://ieeexplore.ieee.org/xpl/tocresult.jsp?isNumber=15571

IEEE standard glossary of software engineering terminology (1990). Retrieved January 9, 2008, from http://ieeexplore.ieee.org/xpl/tocresult.jsp?isNumber=4148

IEEE. (1998). *IEEE Std 830-1998*. Recommended Practice for Software Requirements Specifications.

IEEE. (1998). *IEEE Std 1362*. System Definition - Concept of Operations (ConOps) Document.

INCOSE. (2008). International Council on Systems Engineering: Requirements Management Tools Survey. Retrieved January 9, 2008 from http://www.paper-review.com/tools/rms/read.php

ISBSG. (2005). *Estimating, Benchmarking & Research Suite Release 9*. Hawthorn, Australia: International Software Benchmarking Standards Group.

Jaaksi, A. (2003). Assessing software projects – tools for business owners. *ACM SIGSOFT Software Engineering Notes, 28*(5), 15–18. doi:10.1145/949952.940074

Jacobson, I. (1992). *Object-Oriented Software Engineering: A Use Case Driven Approach*. Reading, MA: Addison-Wesley.

Jarzabek, S., & Huang, R. (1998). The Case for User-Centered CASE Tools. *Communications of the ACM, 41*(8), 93–99. doi:10.1145/280324.280338

Jayaraman, V. K., Kulkarni, B. D., Gupta, K., Rajesh, J., & Kusumaker, H. (2001). Dynamic optimization of fed-batch bioreactors using the ant algorithm. *European Journal of Operational Research, 17*(1), 81–88.

Jazayeri, M., Ran, A., & van der Linden, F. (2000). *Software architecture for product families*. Reading, MA: Addison Wesley.

JBoss Development Team. (2007). *JBoss Application Server* (JBoss AS). Retrieved 2007, from http://www.jboss.org.

Jeffery, R., & Low, G. (1990). Calibrating estimation tools for software development. *Software Engineering Journal, 5*(4), 215–221. doi:10.1016/S0266-9838(05)80014-0

Jeffery, R., Ruhe, M., & Wieczorek, I. (2001). Using Public Domain Metrics to Estimate Software Development Effort. In *Proceedings of the 7th IEEE Metrics Symposium*, London, (pp. 16-27).

Jeffries, R., Anderson, A., & Hendrickson, C. (2000). *Extreme programming installed*. Reading, MA: Addison-Wesley Professional.

Jensen, F. V. (1996). *An introduction to Bayesian networks*. London: UCL Press.

Jensen, F. V., & Nielsen, T. (2007). *Bayesian networks and decision graphs*. New York: Springer-Verlag.

Jensen, R. (1983). An improved macrolevel software development resource estimation model. *5th ISPA Conference* (pp. 88-92).

Jéron, T., & Morel, P. (1999). Test generation derived from model-checking. *CAV, 1999*, 108–121.

Jeti Development Team. Jeti, Jabber In Java (version 0.7.6). Retrieved October, 2006, from http://jeti.sourceforge.net/.

John, G., Kohavi, R., & Pfleger, K. (1994). Irrelevant features and the subset selection problem. *11th Intl. Conference on Machine Learning* (pp. 121-129). San Francisco: Morgan Kaufmann.

Johnson, J. H. (2001). Micro projects cause constant change. *Second International Conference on Extreme Programming and Agile Processes in Software Engineering*, Cagliari, Italy, (pp. 20-23).

Jollife, I. T. (1986). *Principal Component Analysis*. Berlin, Germany: Springer.

Jones, B. F., Sthamer, H.-H., & Eyres, D. E. (1995). The Automatic Generation of Software Test Data Sets Using Adaptive Search Techniques. In *Proceedings of 3rd International Conference on Software Quality Management*, (pp. 435–444).

Jones, B. F., Sthamer, H.-H., & Eyres, D. E. (1996). Automatic Structural Testing Using Genetic Algorithms. *Software Engineering Journal, 11*(5), 299–306.

Jones, C. (1986) *Programmer productivity*. New York: McGraw Hill.

Jones, C. (1999). Software sizing. *IEE Review, 45*(4), 165–167. doi:10.1049/ir:19990406

Jones, C. (2002). *Software quality in 2002: A survey of the state of the art*. Software Productivity Research.

Jones, C. (2003). Variations in software development practices. *IEEE Software, 20*(6), 22–27. doi:10.1109/MS.2003.1241362

Jones, C. B. (1990). *Systematic software development using VDM*. Upper Saddle River, NJ: Prentice-Hall. Retrieved from citeseer.ist.psu.edu/jones95systematic.html

Jorgensen, M., & Shepperd, M. (2007). A systematic review of software development cost estimation studies. *IEEE Transactions on Software Engineering, 33*(1), 33–53. doi:10.1109/TSE.2007.256943

Juristo, N., Moreno, A. M., & López, M. (2000). How to use linguistics instruments for Object-Oriented Analysis. *IEEE Software*, (May/June): 80–89.

Kadoda, G., Cartwright, M., Chen, L., & Shepperd, M. J. (2000). Experiences Using Case-Based Reasoning to Predict Software Project Effort. In *Proceedings of the EASE 2000 Conference*, Keele, UK.

Kamsties, E., Berry, D. M., & Paech, B. (2001). Detecting Ambiguities in Requirements Documents Using Inspections. In *Workshop on Inspections in Software Engineering*, (pp.68 –80), Paris, France.

Karacapilidis, N., & Papadias, D. (1998). HERMES: Supporting argumentative discourse in multi-agent decision making. *Proceedings of 15th National Conference on Artificial Intelligence (AAAI)*, (pp.827-832). Madison, WI: AAAI/MIT Press.

KARE, Knowledge Acquisition and Sharing for Requirement Engineering (KARE), (ESPRIT project No. 28916).

Kasik, D. J., & George, H. G. (1996). Towards Automatic Generation of Novice User Test Scripts. In *Proceedings of the Conference on Human Factors in Computing Systems* (pp. 244-251), Vancouver, Canada. New York: ACM Press.

Kaufman, L., & Rousseeuw, P. (2005). *Finding Groups in Data: An Introduction to Cluster Analysis*. Hobokonen, NJ: John Wiley & Sons Inc.

Keil, M., Rai, A., Mann, J. E. C., & Zhang, G. P. (2003). Why software projects escalate: The importance of project management constructs. *IEEE Transactions on Engineering Management, 50*(3), 251–261. doi:10.1109/TEM.2003.817312

Kemerer, C. F. (1987). An empirical validation of software cost estimation models. *Communications of the ACM, 30*(5), 416–429. doi:10.1145/22899.22906

Kennedy, J., & Eberhart, R. C. (1995). Particle swarm optimization. *Proceedings of IEEE International Conference on Neural Networks*, Piscataway, NJ, (pp. 1942–1948).

Kennedy, J., & Eberhart, R. C. (1997). A discrete binary version of the particle swarm algorithm. *Proceedings of the 1997 IEEE Conference on Systems, Man, and Cybernetics*, Piscataway, NJ, (pp. 4104-4109).

Kennedy, J., & Eberhart, R. C. (2001). *Swarm intelligence*. San Francisco: Morgan Kaufmann.

Khoshgoftaar, T. M., & Lanning, D. L. (1995). A Neural Network Approach for Early Detection of Program Modules Having High Risk in the Maintenance Phase. *Journal of Systems and Software, 29*(1), 85–91. doi:10.1016/0164-1212(94)00130-F

Khoshgoftaar, T. M., Lanning, D. L., & Pandya, A. S. (1994). A comparative-study of pattern-recognition techniques for quality evaluation of telecommunications software. *IEEE Journal on Selected Areas in Communications, 12*(2), 279–291. doi:10.1109/49.272878

King, J. C. (1976). Symbolic execution and program testing. *Communications of the ACM, 19*(7), 385–394. doi:10.1145/360248.360252

Kirkpatrick, S., Gellat, C. D., & Vecchi, M. P. (1983). Optimization by Simulating Annealing. *Science, 220*(4598), 671–680. doi:10.1126/science.220.4598.671

Kirsopp, C., & Shepperd, M. (2002). *Case and Feature Subset Selection in Case-Based Software Project Effort Prediction. Research and Development in Intelligent Systems XIX*. New York: Springer-Verlag.

Kitchanham, B. A., & Taylor, N. R. (1984). Software cost models. *ICL Technology Journal, 4*(3), 73–102.

Kitchenham, B. A., Pickard, L. M., Linkman, S., & Jones, P. (2003, June). Modelling Software Bidding Risks. *IEEE Transactions on Software Engineering, 29*(6), 542–554. doi:10.1109/TSE.2003.1205181

Kitchenham, B., MacDonell, S., Pickard, L., & Shepperd, M. (2001). What accuracy statistics really measure. *IEE Proceedings: Vol. 148. Software Engineering* (pp. 81-85). Washington, DC: IEE Proceeding.

Kjaerulff, U. B., & Madsen, A. (2008). *Bayesian Networks and Influence Diagrams: A Guide to Construction and Analysis*. New York: Springer-Verlag.

Klein, M., Ralya, T., Pollak, B., Obenza, R., & Gonzalez-Harbour, M. (1993). *A practitioners' Handbook for real-time analysis: Guide to rate monotonic analysis for real-time systems*. Boston, MA: Kluwer Academic Publishers.

Knobbe, A. J., & Ho, Y. E.K. (2005). Numbers in Multi-Relational Data Mining, In: Proceedings of PKDD 2005, Portugal

Knowles, J., & Corne, D. (2000). Approximating the nondominated front using the Pareto archived evolution strategy. *Evolutionary Computation, 8*, 149–172. doi:10.1162/106365600568167

Kobbacy, K. A., Vadera, S., & Rasmy, M. H. (2007). AI and OR in management of operations: history and trends. *The Journal of the Operational Research Society, 58*, 10–28. doi:10.1057/palgrave.jors.2602132

Kof, L. (2005). *Text Analysis for Requirements Engineering*. Unpublished doctoral dissertation, Technische Universität München. Retrieved August 13, 2008 from http://www4.in.tum.de/publ/html.php?e=914

Kohavi, R., & John, G. H. (1997). Wrappers for feature subset selection. *ACM Artificial Intelligence, 97*(1-2), 273–324. doi:10.1016/S0004-3702(97)00043-X

Kolodner, J. (1993). *Case-based reasoning*. San Francisco: Morgan Kaufmann Publishers, Inc.

Konar, A. (2005). *Computational intelligence: Principles, techniques and applications*. Berlin: Springer.

Korb, K., & Nicholson, A. (2003). *Bayesian Artificial Intelligence*. Boca Ratón, FL: Chapman & Hall/CRC.

Korel, B., & Al-Yami, A. M. (1996). Assertion-Oriented Automated Test Data Generation. *Proceedings of 18th. Int'l Conference on Software Engineering*, (pp. 71–80).

Kosmatov, N. (2006). A constraint solver for sequences and its applications. *In the 21st Annual ACM Symposium on Applied Computing (SAC'06)* (pp. 404-408). Dijon, France: ACM.

Kosmatov, N. (2008). All-paths test generation for programs with internal aliases. In *the 19th IEEE International Symposium on Software Reliability Engineering (ISSRE'08)* (pp. 147-156). Redmond, WA: IEEE Computer Society.

Kosmatov, N., Legeard, B., Peureux, F., & Utting, M. (2004). Boundary coverage criteria for test generation from formal models. In *the 15th IEEE International Symposium on Software Reliability Engineering (ISSRE'04)* (pp. 139-150). Saint-Malo, France: IEEE Computer Society.

Kossmann, M., Wong, R., Odeh, M., & Gillies, A. (2008). Ontology-driven Requirements Engineering: Building the OntoREM Meta Model. *Proceedings of the 3rd International Conference on Information and Communication Technologies: From Theory to Applications, ICTTA 2008*, (pp. 1-6), Damascus, Syria. Washington DC: IEEE Computer Society.

Kosters, G., Six, H.-W., & Winters, M. (2001). Coupling use cases and class models as a means for validation and verification of requirements specification. *Requirements Engineering, 6*(1). doi:10.1007/PL00010354

Kotonya, G., & Sommerville, I. (1998). *Requirements Engineering: Processes and Techniques*. Chichester, UK: John Wiley and Sons.

Krasner, G., & Pope, S. (1988). A description of the model-view-controller user interface paradigm in the

Smalltalk-80 system. *Journal of Object Oriented Programming, 1*(3), 26–49.

Kristensen, K., & Rasmussen, I. A. (2002). The use of a Bayesian network in the design of a decision support system for growing malting barley without use of pesticides. *Computers and Electronics in Agriculture, 33*(3), 197–217. doi:10.1016/S0168-1699(02)00007-8

Kröning, D., Groce, A., & Clarke, E. M. (2004). Counterexample guided abstraction refinement via program execution. In *the 6th International Conference on Formal Engineering Methods (ICFEM'04)* (pp. 224-238). Seattle, WA: Springer.

Kruchten, P. (1995). The 4+1 view model of software architecture. *IEEE Software, 6*(November/December).

Kugler, H., Harel, D., Pnueli, A., Lu, Y., & Bontemps, Y. (2005). Temporal logic for scenario-based specifications. In *Proceedings of International Conference on Tools and Algorithms for the Construction and Analysis of Systems (TACAS).*

Kuusela, J., & Savolainen, J. (2000). Requirements Engineering for Product Families. *ICSE 2000*, Limerick, Ireland.

Lam, C. P., Robey, M. C., & Li, H. (2003). Application of AI for Automation of Software Testing. *Proceedings of the ACIS Fourth International Conference on Software Engineering, Artificial Intelligence, Networking and Parallel/Distributed Computing (SNPD'03)*, October 16-18, Lubeck, Germany, (pp. 242–249).

Lam, C. P., Xiao, J., & Li, H. (2007). Ant colony optimisation for generation of conformance testing sequences using a characterising set. *In ACST'07: Proceedings of the Third Conference on IASTED International Conference* (pp. 140–146). Anaheim, CA: ACTA Press.

Laroussinie, F., & Schnoebelen, P. (1995). A hierarchy of temporal logics with past. *Theoretical Computer Science, 148*(2), 303–324. doi:10.1016/0304-3975(95)00035-U

Laroussinie, F., Markey, N., & Schnoebelen, P. (2002). Temporal logic with forgettable past. In *Proceedings of IEEE Symposium on Logic in Computer Science (LICS).*

Lauría, E. J., & Duchessi, P. J. (2006). A Bayesian belief network for IT implementation decision support. *Decision Support Systems, 42*(3), 1573–1588. doi:10.1016/j.dss.2006.01.003

Lauritzen, S. L., & Spiegelhalter, D. J. (1988). Local computations with probabilities on graphical structures and their application to expert systems (with discussion). *Journal of the Royal Statistical Society. Series B. Methodological, 50*(2), 157–224.

Ledeczi, A., Maroti, M., Bakay, A., Karsai, G., Garrett, J., Thomason, C., IV, et al. (2001). The generic modeling environment. *Workshop on Intelligent Signal Processing.* Budapest, Hungary. Retrieved from http://www.isis.vanderbilt.edu/projects/gme/

Legeard, B., Peureux, F., & Utting, M. (2002). Automated boundary testing from Z and B. *In the International Confefence on Formal Methods Europe (FME'02)* (pp. 21-40). Copenhaguen, Denmark: Springer.

Leite, J. C. S. P., & Breitman, K. K. (2003). Experiences using scenarios to enhance traceability. *2nd International Workshop on Traceability in Emerging Forms of Software Engineering at the 18th IEEE Conference on Automated Software Engineering.*

Lepar, V., & Shenoy, P. P. (1998). A comparison of Lauritzen-Spiegelhalter, Hugin, and Shenoy-Shafer architectures for computing marginals of probability distributions. In G. Cooper & S. Moral (Ed.), *Proceedings of the 14th Conference on Uncertainty in Artificial Intelligence,* (pp. 328-337). San Francisco: Morgan Kaufmann.

Li, H., & Lam, C. P. (2004). Optimization of state-based test suites for software systems: An evolutionary approach. *International Journal Computer and Information Science, 5*(3), 212–223.

Li, H., & Lam, C. P. (2005). An ant colony optimization approach to test sequence generation for state-based software testing. *Proc. QSIC 2005.* New York: IEEE Computer Society Press.

Li, H., & Lam, C. P. (2005). Using anti-ant-like agents to generate test threads from the UML diagrams. *Proc. TESTCOM 2005*, (LNCS Vol. 3502).

Li, J., Li, H., Wong, L., Pei, J., & Dong, G. (2006). Minimum description length principle: Generators are preferable to closed patterns. In *Proceedings of AAAI Conference on Artificial Intelligence (AAAI)*.

Li, X., et al. (2003). A nondominated sorting particle swarm optimizer for multiobjective optimization. In E. Cantú- Paz et al., (Eds.), *Proceedings of Genetic and Evolutionary Computation, GECCO 2003*, (LNCS Vol. 2723, pp. 37-48). Berlin: Springer.

Li, Z., & Zhou, Y. (2005). PR–miner: Automatically extracting implicit programming rules and detecting violations in large software code. In *Proceedings of SIGSOFT Symposium on Foundations of Software Engineering (FSE)*.

Liaskos, K., Roper, M., & Wood, M. (2007). Investigating data-flow coverage of classes using evolutionary algorithms. In *Proceedings of the Ninth Annual Conference on Genetic and Evolutionary Computation* (pp. 1140-1140), London, England. New York: ACM Press.

Lichtenstein, O., Pnueli, A., & Zuck, L. D. (1985). The glory of the past. In *Proceedings of Logics of Programs Workshop* (pp. 196–218).

Lieberman, B. (2001). UML activity diagrams: Versatile roadmaps for understanding system behavior. *The Rational Edge*. Armonk, NY: IBM

Liou, Y. I., & Chen, M. (1993). Integrating Group Support Systems, Joint Application Development, and Computer-Aided Software Engineering for Requirements Specification. *26th Annual Hawaii International Conference on System Sciences,* Wailea, Hawaii, January 5-8.

Liu, M., Jin, M., & Liu, C. (2002). Design of testing scenario generation based on UML activity diagram. *Computer Engineering and Application*, (pp. 122–124).

Liu, X. F., Raorane, S., Zheng, M., & Leu, M. C. (2006). An internet based intelligent argumentation system for collaborative engineering design. *Proceedings of the 2006 IEEE International Symposium on Collaborative Technologies and Systems (CTS 2006),* Las Vegas, Nevada, (pp. 318-325).

Liu, X. F., Zheng, M., & Leu, M. C. (2007). Management of an intelligent argumentation network for a web-based collaborative engineering design environment. *Proceedings of 2007 IEEE International Symposium on Collaborative Technologies and Systems (CTS 2007),* Orlando, Florida.

Lo, D., & Khoo, S. C. (2006). SMArTIC: Towards building an accurate, robust and scalable specification miner. In *Proceedings of SIGSOFT Symposium on Foundations of Software Engineering (FSE)*.

Lo, D., Khoo, S. C., & Liu, C. (2007). Efficient mining of iterative patterns for software specification discovery. In *Proceedings of SIGKDD International Conference on Knowledge Discovery and Data Mining (KDD)*.

Lo, D., Khoo, S. C., & Liu, C. (2008). Mining temporal rules for software maintenance. *Journal of Software Maintenance and Evolution: Research and Practice, 20*(4), 227–247. doi:10.1002/smr.375

Lo, D., Khoo, S. C., & Liu, C. (2008). Mining past-time temporal rules from execution traces. In *Proceedings of International Workshop on Dynamic Analysis (WODA)*.

Lo, D., Maoz, S., & Khoo, S. C. (2007). Mining modal scenario-based specification from execution traces of reactive systems. In *Proceedings of ACM/IEEE International Conference on Automated Software Engineering (ASE)*.

Lorenzoli, D., Mariani, L., & Pezzè, M. (2008). Automatic generation of software behavioral models. In *Proceedings of International Conference on Software Engineering (ICSE)*.

Loucopoulos, P., & Karakostas, V. (1995). *System Requirements Engineering*. New York: McGraw-Hill, Inc.

Lubars, M. D., & Harandi, M. T. (1987). Knowledge-based software design using design schemas. *In Proceedings of* the 9*th* international Conference on Software Engineering, (pp. 253-262), Los Alamitos, CA. Washington DC: IEEE Computer Society Press.

Macaulay, L. (1996). Requirements for Requirements Engineering Techniques. *International Conference on Requirements Engineering*, Colorado Springs, CO, April 15-18.

Maes, P. (1994). Agents that reduce work and information overload. *Communications of the ACM, 37*, 30–40. doi:10.1145/176789.176792

Maiden, N. A. M., & Sutcliffe, A. G. (1993). Requirements Engineering by Example: an Empirical Study. *IEEE International Symposium on Requirements Engineering*. San Diego, CA, January 4-6.

Majumdar, R., & Sen, K. (2007). Hybrid concolic testing. In *the 29th International Conference on Software Engineering (ICSE'07)* (pp. 416-426). Minneapolis, MN: IEEE Computer Society.

Mangia, L., & Paiano, R. (2003). MMWA: A Software Sizing Model for Web Applications, In: Proceedings of the Fourth International Conference on Web Information Systems Engineering, (pp. 53-63).

Mannion, M., & Kaindl, M. (2001). Requirements-Based Product Line Engineering. *Proceedings of the 8th European Software Engineering Conference held jointly with 9th ACM SIGSOFT International Symposium on Foundations of Software Engineering 2001*, Vienna, Austria, September 10-14, 2001.

Mariani, L., & Pezzè, M. (2005). Behavior capture and test: Automated analysis for component integration. In *International Conference on Engineering Complex of Complex Computer Systems (ICECCS)*.

Marre, B., & Arnould, A. (2000). Test sequences generation from Lustre descriptions: GATeL. In *the 15th IEEE International Conference on Automated Software Engineering (ASE'00)* (pp. 229-237). Grenoble, France: IEEE Computer Society.

Mathur, A. P. (2008). *Foundations of software testing.* Upper Saddle River, NJ: Pearson Editions.

Maynard-Zhang, P., Kiper, J. D., & Feather, M. S. (2005). Modeling Uncertainty in Requirements Engineering Decision Support. In *Workshop on Requirements Engineering Decision Support, Paris, France, August 29, 2005.* Retrieved January 9, 2008 from http://trs-new.jpl. nasa.gov/dspace/handle/2014/37769

Mayrhauser, A. v., France, R., Scheetz, M., & Dahlman, E. (2000). Generating Test-Cases from an Object-Oriented Model wirth an Artificial-Intelligence Planning System. *IEEE Transactions on Reliability, 49*(1), 26–36. doi:10.1109/24.855534

McConnell, S. (2006). *Software Estimation – Demystifying the Black Art.* Redmond, WA: Microsoft press.

McCord, M. (1990). Natural language processing in Prolog. In A. Walker (ed.), *A logical approach to expert systems and natural language processing Knowledge systems and Prolog*, (pp. 391–402). Reading, MA: Addison-Wesley Publishing Company.

McGregor, J., Bachmann, F., Bass, L., Bianco, P., & Klein, M. (2007). Using an architecture reasoning tool to teach software architecture. In *Proceedings 20th Conference on Software Engineering Education & Training - CSEE&T'07* (pp. 275-282). Washington, DC: IEEE Computer Society.

McMinn, P. (2004). Search-based software test data generation: A survey. *Software Testing, Verification and. Reliability, 14*(2), 105–156.

McMinn, P., & Holcombe, M. (2003). The state problem for evolutionary testing. *Proc. GECCO 2003*, (LNCS, Vol. 2724, pp. 2488-2500).

McQuarrie, A. D. R., & Tsai, C. (1998). *Regression and Time Series Model Selection.* Singapore: World Scientific Publishing Co. Pte. Ltd.

Meagher, P. (2004). *Implement Bayesian inference using PHP, Part 1: Build intelligent Web applications through conditional probability.* Retrieved 2005, from http://www-106.ibm.com/developerworks/web/library/wa-bayes1/

Medvidovic, N., Mehta, N., & Mikic-Rakic, M. (2002). A family of software architecture implementation frameworks. In *Proceedings of the 3rd IEEE/IFIP Conference on Software Architecture: System Design, Development and Maintenance* (pp. 221-235). Washington, DC: IEEE Computer Society.

Mehta, N. R., Medvidovic, N., & Phadke, S. (2000). Towards a taxonomy of software connectors. In *Proceedings of the 22nd international Conference on Software Engineering – ICSE'00* (pp. 178-187). New York: ACM Press.

Memon, A. M., Pollack, M. E., & Soffa, M. L. (1999). Using a Goal Driven Approach to Generate Test Cases for GUIs. In *Proceedings of the Twenty-first International Conference on Software Engineering* (pp. 257-266), Los Angeles, CA. New York: ACM Press.

Memon, A. M., Pollack, M. E., & Soffa, M. L. (2001). Hierarchical GUI Test Case Generation Using Automated Planning. *IEEE Transactions on Software Engineering*, 27(2), 144–155. doi:10.1109/32.908959

Mendes, E. (2007). Predicting Web Development Effort Using a Bayesian Network. In Proceedings of EASE, 07, 83–93.

Mendes, E. (2007). The Use of a Bayesian Network for Web Effort Estimation. In *Proceedings of International Conference on Web Engineering*, (LNCS Vol. 4607, pp. 90-104). Berlin: Springer.

Mendes, E. (2007). A Comparison of Techniques for Web Effort Estimation. In *Proceedings of the ACM/IEEE International Symposium on Empirical Software Engineering*, (pp. 334-343).

Mendes, E. (2007). *Cost Estimation Techniques for Web Projects.* Hershey, PA: IGI Global.

Mendes, E. (2008). The Use of Bayesian Networks for Web Effort Estimation: Further Investigation. In *Proceedings of ICWE'08*, (pp. 2-3-216).

Mendes, E., & Counsell, S. (2000). Web Development Effort Estimation using Analogy. In *Proceedings of the 2000 Australian Software Engineering Conference*, (pp. 203-212).

Mendes, E., & Kitchenham, B. A. (2004). Further Comparison of Cross-company and Within-company Effort Estimation Models for Web Applications. In *Proceedings IEEE Metrics Symposium,* (pp. 348-357).

Mendes, E., & Mosley, N. (2002). Further Investigation into the Use of CBR and Stepwise Regression to Predict Development Effort for Web Hypermedia Applications. In *Proceedings ACM/IEEE ISESE*, Nara, Japan, (pp. 79-90).

Mendes, E., & Mosley, N. (2008). Bayesian Network Models for Web Effort Prediction: a Comparative Study. In *Transactions on Software Engineering*, (Accepted for publication).

Mendes, E., Counsell, S., & Mosley, N. (2000). Measurement and Effort Prediction of Web Applications. In *Proceedings of 2nd ICSE Workshop on Web Engineering*, June, Limerick, Ireland, (pp. 57-74).

Mendes, E., Mosley, N., & Counsell, S. (2001). Web Measures – Estimating Design and Authoring Effort. *IEEE Multimedia Special Issue on Web Engineering*, 8(1), 50–57.

Mendes, E., Mosley, N., & Counsell, S. (2002). The Application of Case-based Reasoning to Early Web Project Cost Estimation. In *Proceedings of IEEE COMPSAC*, (pp. 393-398).

Mendes, E., Mosley, N., & Counsell, S. (2002, June). Comparison of Length, complexity and functionality as size measures for predicting Web design and authoring effort. *IEEE Proc. Software*, 149(3), 86–92. doi:10.1049/ip-sen:20020337

Mendes, E., Mosley, N., & Counsell, S. (2003). Do Adaptation Rules Improve Web Cost Estimation? In *Proceedings of the ACM Hypertext conference 2003*, Nottingham, UK, (pp. 173-183).

Mendes, E., Mosley, N., & Counsell, S. (2003). A Replicated Assessment of the Use of Adaptation Rules to Improve Web Cost Estimation. In *Proceedings of the ACM and IEEE International Symposium on Empirical Software Engineering*, Rome, Italy, (pp. 100-109).

Mendes, E., Mosley, N., & Counsell, S. (2005). Investigating Web Size Metrics for Early Web Cost Estimation. *Journal of Systems and Software, 77*(2), 157–172. doi:10.1016/j.jss.2004.08.034

Mendes, E., Mosley, N., & Counsell, S. (2005) The Need for Web Engineering: an Introduction, Web Engineering. In E. Mendes, & N. Mosley, (Eds.) *Web Engineering: Theory and Practice of Metrics and Measurement for Web Development*, (pp. 1-26). Berlin: Springer-Verlag

Mendes, E., Watson, I., Triggs, C., Mosley, N., & Counsell, S. (2002). A Comparison of Development Effort Estimation Techniques for Web Hypermedia Applications. In *Proceedings IEEE Metrics Symposium*, June, Ottawa, Canada, (pp. 141-151).

Mendes, E., Watson, I., Triggs, C., Mosley, N., & Counsell, S. (2003). A Comparative Study of Cost Estimation Models for Web Hypermedia Applications. *Empirical Software Engineering Journal, 8*(2), 163–196. doi:10.1023/A:1023062629183

Menzies, T., Port, D., Chen, Z., & Hihn, J. (2005). Validation Methods for Calibrating Software Effort Models. *Proceeding of the 2000 International Conference on Software Engineering* (587- 595). Washington, DC: IEEE Computer Society.

Metrics Development Team. (2007). *Eclipse metrics plug-in*. Retrieved 2007, from http://metrics.sourceforge.net/.

Meziane, F. (1994). *From English to Formal Specifications*. PhD Thesis, University of Salford, UK.

Meziane, F., Vadera, S., Kobbacy, K., & Proudlove, N. (2000). Intelligent Systems in Manufacturing: Current Developments and Future Prospects. *The International Journal of Manufacturing Technology Management, 11*(4), 218–238.

Mich, L. (1996). NL-OOPS: from natural language to object, oriented requirements using the natural language processing system LOLITA. *Natural Language Engineering, 2*(2), 161–187. doi:10.1017/S1351324996001337

Mich, L., Franch, M., & Novi Inverardi, P. (2004). Market research on requirements analysis using linguistic tools. *Requirements Engineering, 9*(1), 40–56. doi:10.1007/s00766-003-0179-8

Michael, C. C., McGraw, G., & Schatz, M. A. (2001). Generating software test data by evolution. *IEEE Transactions on Software Engineering, 27*(12), 1085–1110. doi:10.1109/32.988709

Miller, A. (2002). *Subset selection in regression*, (2nd Ed.). Boca Raton, FL: Chapman Hall.

Mills, K., & Gomaa, H. (2002). Knowledge-based automation of a design method for concurrent systems. [Washington, DC: IEEE Computer Society.]. *IEEE Transactions on Software Engineering, 28*(3), 228–255. doi:10.1109/32.991319

Miriyala, K., & Harandi, M. T. (1991). Automatic derivation of formal software specifications from informal descriptions. *IEEE Transactions on Software Engineering, 17*(10), 1126–1142. doi:10.1109/32.99198

Mitchell, M. (1996). *An introduction to Genetic Algorithms*. Cambridge, MA: MIT Press.

Miyazaki, Y., & Mori, K. (1985). COCOMO evaluation and tailoring. *Proceedings of the Eighth International Software Engineering Conference*. London: IEEE CS Press.

Mohan, K., & Ramesh, B. (2007). Tracing variations in software product families. *CACM, December, 50*(12).

Molokken, K., & Jorgensen, M. (2003). A review of software surveys on software effort estimation. In *2003 International Symposium on Empirical Software Engineering* (pp. 223-230). Washington, DC: IEEE press.

Montana, D. J. (1995). Strongly Typed Genetic Programming. *Evolutionary Computation, 3*(2), 199–230. doi:10.1162/evco.1995.3.2.199

Moreno, C. A., Juristo, N., & Van de Riet, R. P. (2000). Formal justification in object-oriented modelling: A linguistic approach. *Data & Knowledge Engineering, 33*, 25–47. doi:10.1016/S0169-023X(99)00046-4

Moreno, G., & Merson, P. (2008). Model-driven performance analysis. In Becker, Plasil & Reussner (Eds.), *Proceedings of the 4th International Conference on the Quality of Software Architecture – QoSA'08,* (LNCS 5281, pp. 171-188). Berlin: Springer-Verlag.

Mosley, D. J., & Posey, B. A. (2002). *Just enough software test automation.* Upper Saddle River, NJ: Prentice Hall PTR.

Mouy, P., Marre, B., Willams, N., & Le Gall, P. (2008). Generation of all-paths unit test with function calls. In *the 2008 IEEE International Conference on Software Testing, Verification, and Validation (ICST'08)* (pp. 32-41). Washington, DC: IEEE Computer Society.

Mraz, R. T., Howe, A. E., von Mayrhauser, A., & Li, L. (1995). System testing with an AI planner. In *Proceedings of the Sixth International Symposium on Software Reliability Engineering* (pp. 96-105), Toulouse, France. Washington DC: IEEE Computer Society.

Murphy, K. P. (2002). *Dynamic Bayesian Networks: Representation, inference and learning.* PhD thesis, UC Berkeley, Berkeley, CA.

Myers, G. J. (1979). *The art of software testing.* Chichester, UK: John Wiley and Sons.

Myrtveit, I., & Stensrud, E. (1999). A controlled experiment to assess the benefits of estimating with analogy and regression models. *IEEE Transactions on Software Engineering, 25*(4), 510–525. doi:10.1109/32.799947

Myrtveit, I., & Stensrud, E. (2004). Do Arbitrary Function Approximators make sense as Software Prediction Models? *12-th International Workshop on Software Technology and Engineering Practice* (pp. 3-9). Washington, DC: IEEE Computer Society.

Myrtveit, I., Stensrud, E., & Shepperd, M. (2005). Reliability and Validity in Comparative Studies of Software Prediction Models. *IEEE Transactions on Software Engineering, 31*(5), 380–391. doi:10.1109/TSE.2005.58

Neapolitan, R. E. (2004). *Learning Bayesian Networks.* Upper Saddle River, NJ: Pearson Prentice Hall.

Nebut, C., Fleurey, F., Traon, Y. L., & Jzquel, J. M. (2006). Automatic test generation: A use case driven approach. *IEEE Transactions on Software Engineering, 32*(3), 140–155. doi:10.1109/TSE.2006.22

Neil, M. (1992). *Statistical modelling of software metrics.* Ph.D. dissertation, South Bank University, London.

Neil, M., & Fenton, P. (2005). Improved software defect prediction. In *10th European Software Engineering Process Group Conference*, London.

Neil, M., Krause, P., & Fenton, N. E. (2003). Software quality prediction using Bayesian Networks. In T. M. Khoshgoftaar, (Ed.) *Software Engineering with Computational Intelligence.* Amsterdam: Kluwer.

Neill, C., & Laplante, P. (2003). Requirements Engineering: The State of the Practice. *IEEE Software, 20*(6), 40–45. doi:10.1109/MS.2003.1241365

Neumann, D. E. (2002). An Enhanced Neural Network Technique for Software Risk Analysis. *IEEE Transactions on Software Engineering, 28*(9), 904–912. doi:10.1109/TSE.2002.1033229

Nguyen, C. D., Perini, A., & Tonella, P. (2008). eCAT: a tool for automating test cases generation and execution in testing multi-agent systems. *In Proceedings of the Seventh International Joint Conference on Autonomous Agents and Multiagent Systems* (pp. 1669-1670), Estoril, Portugal. New York: ACM Press.

Nguyen, V., Steece, B., & Boehm, B. (2008). *A constrained regression technique for COCOMO calibration.* Retrieved January 14, 2009 from http://sunset.usc.edu/csse/TECHRPTS/2008/usc-csse-2008-806/usc-csse-2008-806.pdf

Niazi, M., Cox, K., & Verner, J. (2008). A measurement framework for assessing the maturity of requirements engineering process. *Software Quality Control, 16*(2), 213–235.

Nunamaker, J. F., Briggs, R. O., & Mittleman, D. D. (1996). Lessons from a Decade of Group Support Systems Research. *29th Annual Hawaii International Conference on System Sciences,* Maui, Hawaii, January 3-6.

Nuseibeh, B., & Easterbrook, S. (2000). Requirements engineering: a roadmap. In *Proceedings of the Conference on the Future of Software Engineering* (Limerick, Ireland, June 04 - 11, 2000). ICSE '00 (pp. 35-46). New York: ACM.

O'Brien, L. & Smith, D. (2002). MAP and OAR Methods: Techniques for Developing Core Assets for Software Product Lines from Existing Assets. *CMU/SEI*, April.

O'Sullivan, M., Vssner, S., & Wegener, J. (1998). Testing temporal correctness of real-time systems -a new approach using genetic algorithms and cluster analysis. *Proceedings of the 6th European Conference on Software Testing, Analysis and Review (EuroSTAR 1998)*, Munich, Germany.

Offutt, J., Liu, S., Abdurazik, A., & Ammann, P. (2003). Generating Test Data from State-Based Specifications. *Software Testing . Verification and Reliability, 13*(1), 25–53. doi:10.1002/stvr.264

OpenSSL Development Team. (2008). *OpenSSL: Documents, SSL_read*(3). Retrieved 2008, from http://www.openssl.org/docs/ssl/SSL_read.html.

Orellana, F. J., Guil, F., del Águila, I. M., & Túnez, S. (2005). A WEB-CASE Tool Prototype for Hybrid Software Development. In R. Moreno-Díaz, F. Pichler & A. Quesada-Arencibia (Eds.) *Computer Aided Systems Theory – EUROCAST 2005, 10th Internacional Conference on Computer Aided Systems Theory*, (LNCS 3643, pp. 217-222). Berlin: Springer-Verlag.

Palisade. (1998). Evolver, The Genetic Algorithm Super Solver, http://www.palisade.com/evolver/. Newfield, NY: Palisade Corporation

Pargas, R. P., Harrold, M. J., & Peck, R. (1999). Test-data Generation Using Genetic Algorithms. *Software Testing . Verification and Reliability, 9*(4), 263–282. doi:10.1002/(SICI)1099-1689(199912)9:4<263::AID-STVR190>3.0.CO;2-Y

Parsopoulos, K., & Vrahatis, M. (2002). Particle swarm optimization method in multiobjective problems. *Proceedings of 2002 ACM Symposium on Applied Computing (SAC'2002)*, Madrid, Spain, (pp. 603-607).

Patel, C., & Ramachandran, M. (2008). Story card process improvement framework. *Intl. conf. on Software Engineering Research and Practice (SERP-08)*, July, Florida, USA.

Paulk, M., Curtis, B., Chrissis, M., & Weber, C. (1993). *Capability Maturity Model for Software (Version 1.1)* (Tech. Rep. CMU/SEI-93-TR-024) Pittsburg, PA: Carnegie Mellon University, Software Engineering Institute. Retrieved January 9, 2008, from http://www.sei.cmu.edu/publications/documents/93.reports/93.tr.024.html

Pearl, J. (1988). *Probabilistic reasoning in intelligent systems: networks of plausible inference.* San Mateo, CA: Morgan Kaufman.

Pedhazur, E. J. (1997). *Multiple Regression in Behavioral Research.* Orlando, FL: Harcourt Brace.

Pedrycz, W., & Peters, J. F. (1997). Computational intelligence in software engineering. *Canadian Conference on Electrical and Computer Engineering*, (pp. 253-256), St. Johns, Nfld., Canada. Washington DC: IEEE Press.

Pei, J., Wang, H., Liu, J., Wang, K., Wang, J., & Yu, P. S. (2006). Discovering frequent closed partial orders from strings. *IEEE Transactions on Knowledge and Data Engineering, 18*, 1467–1481. doi:10.1109/TKDE.2006.172

Pelliccione, P., Muccini, H., Bucchiarone, A., & Facchini, F. (2005). Testor: Deriving test sequences from model-based specifications. *Eighth International SIGSOFT Symposium on Component-based Software Engineering (CBSE 2005)*, (LNCS Vol. 3489, pp. 267-282).

Pendharkar, P. C., Subramanian, G. H., & Rodger, J. A. (2005). A Probabilistic Model for Predicting Software Development Effort. *IEEE Transactions on Software Engineering, 31*(7), 615–624. doi:10.1109/TSE.2005.75

Pohl, K., Assenova, P., Doemges, R., Johannesson, P., Maiden, N., Plihon, V., et al. (1994). Applying AI Techniques to Requirements Engineering: The NATURE Prototype. *International Conference on Software Engineering*, Edinburgh, UK, May 23-28.

Poo, D. C. C., & Lee, S. Y. (1995). Domain object identification through events and functions. *Information and*

Software Technology, 37(11), 609–621. doi:10.1016/0950-5849(95)98298-T

Potts, C., & Burns, G. (1988). Recording the reasons for design decisions. *Proceedings of 10th International Conference on Software Engineering,* Singapore, (pp. 418-427).

Poulin, S. J. (1997). Measuring software reuse. Reading, MA: Addison Wesley.

Pree, W., & Koskimies, K. (1999). Framelets - small is beautiful. In Fayad, Schmidth & Johnson (Eds.), *Building application frameworks: Object-oriented foundations of framework design.* Chichester, UK: John Wiley & Sons Ltd.

Presland, S. G. (1986). *The analysis of natural language requirements documents.* PhD Thesis, University of Liverpool, UK.

Press, C. M. Phoenix, Arizona, United Ardis, M. (2000). *Commonality analysis for defining software product lines, Tutorial,* ICSE 2000, Limerick, Ireland. New York: IEEE CS Press.

Prieto-Diaz (1998). Domain Analysis. *ACM SIGSOFT Software Engineering Notes,* May.

Putnam, L. H. (1978). General empirical solution to the macro sizing and estimation problem. *IEEE Transactions on Software Engineering, SE-4*(4), 345–361. doi:10.1109/TSE.1978.231521

Radliński, Ł., Fenton, N., & Marquez, D. (in press, 2008). Estimating productivity and defect rates based on environmental factors. In *Information Systems Architecture and Technology.* Wrocław, Poland: Oficyna Wydawnicza Politechniki Wrocławskiej.

Radlinski, L., Fenton, N., & Neil, M. (2007). Improved Decision-Making for Software Managers Using Bayesian Networks. In J. Smith (Ed.), *Proceedings of the 11th IASTED Int. Conf. Software Engineering and Applications (SEA)* (pp. 13-19). Cambridge, MA: Acta Press.

Radliński, Ł., Fenton, N., & Neil, M. (in press, 2008). A Learning Bayesian Net for Predicting Number of Software

Defects Found in a Sequence of Testing. *Polish Journal of Environmental Studies.*

Radliński, Ł., Fenton, N., Neil, M., & Marquez, D. (2007). Improved decision-making for software managers using Bayesian Networks. In *Proceedings of 11ᵗʰ IASTED International Conference Software Engineering and Applications (SEA),* Cambridge, MA, (pp. 13-19).

Ramachandran, M. & Mangano, D. (2003). Knowledge Based Reasoning for Software Architectural Design Strategies. *SE Notes,* March.

Ramachandran, M. (2005). Commonality and Variability Analysis in Industrial Practice for Product Line Improvement. *Journal of Software Process Improvement and Practice, 10.*

Ramachandran, M. (2005). Reuse guidelines. *ACM SIGSOFT Software Engineering Notes, 30*(3), May.

Ramachandran, M. (2008). *Software Components: Guidelines and Applications.* New York: Nova Publishers.

Ramachandran, M., & Sommerville, I. (1995). A framework for analysing reuse knowledge. *7the Intl. conf. on Software Eng and Knowledge Eng (SEKE'95),* Washington DC, June 22-24.

Ramanathan, M., Grama, A., & Jagannathan, S. (2007). Path-sensitive inference of function precedence protocols. In *Proceedings of International Conference on Software Engineering* (ICSE).

Ramesh, B., & Dhar, V. (1992). Supporting systems development by capturing deliberations during requirements engineering. *IEEE Transactions on Software Engineering, 18*(6), 498–510. doi:10.1109/32.142872

Ramler, R., & Wolfmaier, K. (2006). Economic perspectives in test automation: balancing automated and manual testing with opportunity cost. In *the 2006 International Workshop on Automation of Software Test (AST'06)* (pp. 85-91). Shanghai, China: ACM.

Rao, C. R. (1973). *Linear Statistical Inference and its Applications.* New York: Wiley & Sons.

Ratchev, S., Urwin, E., Muller, D., Pawar, K. S., & Moulek, I. (2003). Knowledge based requirement engineering for one-of-a-kind complex systems. *Knowledge-Based Systems*, *16*(1), 1–5. doi:10.1016/S0950-7051(02)00027-8

Rech, J. & Althoff, K.D., (2004). Artificial Intelligence and Software Engineering – Status and Future Trends. *Special Issue on Artificial Intelligence and Software Engineering, KI* (3), 5-11.

Reid, S. (2005). Systematic UML testing. *SQC UK: Conference on Software Testing*, London.

Reifer, D. J. (2000). Web development: estimating quick-to-market software. *IEEE Software*, *17*(6), 57–64. doi:10.1109/52.895169

Reifer, D. J. (2002). Ten deadly risks in Internet and intranet software development. *IEEE Software*, (2): 12–14. doi:10.1109/52.991324

Reiss, S. P., & Renieris, M. (2001). Encoding program executions. In *Proceedings of International Conference on Software Engineering (ICSE)*.

Reuys, A., Reis, S., Kamsties, E., & Pohl, K. (2003). Derivation of domain test scenarios from activity diagrams. *International Workshop on Product Line Engineering: The Early Steps: Planning, Modeling, and Managing.*

Ribeiro, J. C. B. (2008). Search-based test case generation for object-oriented java software using strongly-typed genetic programming. In *Proceedings of the GECCO Conference Companion on Genetic and Evolutionary Computation* (pp. 1819-1822), Atlanta, GA. New York: ACM Press.

Ritch, C. & Waters, R. C. (1988). The programmers' apprentice project: research overview. *IEEE Computer*, November.

Riva, G., et al. (Eds.). (2005). *Ambient Intelligence*. Amsterdam: IOS Press. Retrieved from http://www.ambientintelligence.org/

Robbins, J., Hilbert, D., & Redmiles, D. (1996). Extending design environments to software architecture design. *The International Journal of Automated Software Engineering (Special Issue: The Best of KBSE'96), 5*(3), 261-290.

Robertson, S., & Robertson, J. (1999). *Mastering the Requirements Process*. London: Addison-Wesley.

Rolland, C., & Ben Achour, C. (1998, March). Guiding the construction of textual use case specifications. *Data & Knowledge Engineering Journal*, *25*(1–2), 125–160. doi:10.1016/S0169-023X(97)86223-4

Rolland, C., & Prakash, N. (2000). From conceptual modelling to requirements engineering. *Annals of Software Engineering*, *10*(1/4), 151–176. doi:10.1023/A:1018939700514

Rolston, D. (2005). *LAMP, MySQL/PHP Database Driven Websites - Parts I, II, and III*. Retrieved 2005, from http://www.phpfreaks.com/tutorials/

Ruhe, M., Jeffery, R., & Wieczorek, I. (2003) Cost Estimation for Web Applications. In *Proceedings of ICSE 2003*, Portland, OR, (pp. 285-294).

Rumbaugh, J., Blaha, M., Premerlani, W., Eddy, F., & Lorensen, W. (1991). *Object-oriented modeling and design*. Englewood Cliffs, NJ: Prentice Hall International Inc.

Rumelhart, D. E., Hilton, G. E., & Williams, R. J. (1986). Learning Internal Representations by Error Propagation. In D. Rumelhart & J. McClelland (Ed.): *Parallel Distributing Computing: Explorations in the Microstructure of Cognition: Vol. 1.* (pp. 318-362). Cambridge, MA: The MIT press.

Rupp, C. (2002). *Requirements-Engineering und -Management.* Professionelle, iterative Anforderungsanalyse für die Praxis (2nd Ed.). Munich: Hanser–Verlag.

Saeki, M. (2003). CAME: The First Step to Automated Method Engineering. *Workshop on Process Engineering for Object-Oriented and Component-Based Development,* Anaheim, CA, October 26-30.

Saeki, M., Horai, H., & Enomoto, H. (1989). Software development process from natural language specification. In *Proceedings of the 11th international Conference on Software Engineering.* (pp. 64-73), Pittsburgh, PA. New York: ACM Press.

Saeki, M., Tsuchida, M., & Nishiue, K. (2000). Supporting tool for assembling software specification and design methods. *24th Annual International Computer Software and Applications Conference,* Taipei, Taiwan, October 25-27.

Samson, D. (1990). REQSPERT: automated test planning from requirements. *In Proceedings of the First International Systems Integration Conference* (pp. 702-708), Morristown, NJ. Piscataway, NJ: IEEE Press.

Samson, D. (1993). Knowledge-based test planning: Framework for a knowledge-based system to prepare a system test plan from system requirements. *Journal of Systems and Software, 20*(2), 115–124. doi:10.1016/0164-1212(93)90003-G

Samuel, P., Mall, R., & Kanth, P. (2007). Automatic test case generation from UML communication diagrams. *Information and Software Technology, 49*(2), 158–171. doi:10.1016/j.infsof.2006.04.001

Sanchez-Marono, N., Alonso-Betanzos, A., & Castillo, E. (2005). A New Wrapper method for feature subset selection. *ESANN 2005 proceedings - European Symposium on Artificial Neural Networks,* Bruges, Belgium.

Sangwan, R., Neill, C., El Houda, Z., & Bass, M. (2008). Integrating software architecture-centric methods into object-oriented analysis and design. *Journal of Systems and Software, 81*(5), 727–746. doi:10.1016/j.jss.2007.07.031

Sarcia, S. A., Cantone, G., & Basili, V. R. (2008). Adopting Curvilinear Component Analysis to Improve Software Cost Estimation Accuracy. Model, Application Strategy, and an Experimental Verification. In G. Visaggio (Ed.), *12ᵗʰ International Conference on Evaluation and Assessment in Software Engineering.* BCS eWIC.

Sassenburg, J. A. (2006). *Design of a methodology to support software release decisions (Do the numbers really matter?),* PhD Thesis, University of Groningen.

Sathi, A., Fox, M. S., & Greenberg, M. (1985). Representation of Activity Knowledge for Project Management. *IEEE Transactions on Pattern Analysis and Machine Intelligence, PAMI-7*(5), 531–552. doi:10.1109/TPAMI.1985.4767701

Sawyer, P., Sommerville, I., & Viller, S. (1997). Requirements process improvement through the phased introduction of good practice. *Software Process Improvement and Practice, 3*(1), 19–34. doi:10.1002/(SICI)1099-1670(199703)3:1<19::AID-SPIP66>3.0.CO;2-X

Scheetz, M., von Mayrhauser, A., & France, R. (1999). Generating test cases from an OO model with an AI planning system. *In Proceedings of the Tenth International Symposium on Software Reliability Engineering* (pp. 250-259), Boca Raton, Florida. Washington DC: IEEE Computer Society.

Schmidt, E. (2006). Model-driven engineering. *IEEE Computer, 39*(2), 25–31.

Schofield, C. (1998). An empirical investigation into software estimation by analogy. Unpublished Doctoral Dissertation, Dept. of Computing, Bournemouth University, Bournemouth, UK.

Schooff, R. M., & Haimes, Y. Y. (1999). Dynamic multistage software estimation. *IEEE Transactions on Man, and Cybernetics, 29*(2), 272–284. doi:10.1109/5326.760571

Schwaber, K., & Beedle, M. (2002). *Agile software development with SCRUM.* Upper Saddle River, NJ: Prentice Hall.

Scott, W., & Cook, S. C. (2003). An Architecture for an Intelligent Requirements Elicitation and Assessment Assistant. *13th Annual International Symposium - INCOSE 2003,* Crystal City, USA, July 1-3.

SEI. (2005). *Software Product Lines.* Retrieved from http://www.sei.cmu.edu/productlines/bibliography.html

Selby, R. W., & Porter, A. A. (1988). Learning from examples: generation and evaluation of decision trees for software resource analysis. *IEEE Transactions on Software Engineering, 14*(12), 1743–1757. doi:10.1109/32.9061

Sen, K., Marinov, D., & Agha, G. (2005). CUTE: a concolic unit testing engine for C. In *the 5th joint meeting of the European Software Engineering Conference and ACM SIGSOFT Symposium on the Foundations of Software Engineering (ESEC/FSE'05)* (pp. 263-272). Lisbon, Portugal: ACM.

Shafer, G. (1990). Perspectives on the theory and practice of belief functions. *International Journal of Approximate Reasoning, 3*, 1–40.

Shan, Y., McKay, R. I., Lokan, C. J., & Essam, D. L. (2002). Software project effort estimation using genetic programming. *In Proceedings of the IEEE International Conference on Communications, Circuits and Systems* (pp. 1108-1112), Arizona. Washington DC: IEEE Computer Society.

Shaw, M. (1996). Procedure calls are the assembly language of software interconnection: Connectors deserve first-class status, In *Proceedings of ICSE'93: Selected papers from the Workshop on Studies of Software Design* (pp. 17-32). Berlin: Springer-Verlag.

Shaw, M., & Garlan, D. (1996). *Software architecture, perspectives on an emerging discipline.* Englewood Cliffs, NJ: Prentice Hall International Inc.

Shepperd, M. (2007). Software project economics: a roadmap. *International Conference on Software Engineering 2007: Vol. 1. IEEE Future of Software Engineering* (pp. 304-315). New York: IEEE Computer Society

Shepperd, M. J., & Kadoda, G. (2001). Using Simulation to Evaluate Prediction Techniques. In *Proceedings of the IEEE 7th International Software Metrics Symposium*, London, UK, (pp. 349-358).

Shepperd, M., & Schofield, C. (1997). Estimating software project effort using analogies. *IEEE Transactions on Software Engineering, 23*(11), 736–743. doi:10.1109/32.637387

Shirabad, J. S., & Menzies, T. J. (2005). *The PROMISE repository of software engineering databases.* School of Information Technology and Engineering, University of Ottawa, Canada. Retrieved January 14, 2009 from http://promise.site.uottawa.ca/SERepository

Siemens, N. (1971). A Simple CPM Time-Cost Tradeoff Algorithm. *Management Science, 17*(6), 354–363. doi:10.1287/mnsc.17.6.B354

Sillence, J. (1997). Intelligent argumentation systems: requirements, models, research agenda, and applications. In A. Kent (Ed.), *Encyclopedia of Library and Information Science,* (pp. 176-217). New York: Marcel Dekker.

Siricharoen, W. V. (2008). Merging Ontologies for Object Oriented Software Engineering. *International Conference on Networked Computing and Advanced Information Management,* (Volume 2, pp. 525 – 530).

Smartesting. (2008). *The Test Designer tool.* http://www.smartesting.com/.

Smith, A., & Mason, A. (1997). Cost estimation predictive modeling: Regression versus neural network. *The Engineering Economist, 42*(2), 137–161. doi:10.1080/00137919708903174

Smith, T. J. (1993). READS: a requirements engineering tool. *Proceedings of IEEE International Symposium on Requirements Engineering,* (pp. 94–97), San Diego. Washington DC: IEEE Computer Society.

Solnon, C. (2002). Ants can solve constraint satisfaction problems. *IEEE Transactions on Evolutionary Computation, 6*(4), 347–357. doi:10.1109/TEVC.2002.802449

Sommerville, I. (2001). *Software Engineering* (6th Ed.). Reading, MA: Addison-Wesley.

Sommerville, I. (2005). Integrated Requirements Engineering: A Tutorial. *IEEE Software, 22*(1), 16–23. doi:10.1109/MS.2005.13

Sommerville, I. (2006). *Software Engineering: (Update) (8th Edition) (International Computer Science).* Boston: Addison-Wesley Longman Publishing Co., Inc.

Sommerville, I., & Kotenya, G. (1998). *Requirements Engineering: Processes and Techniques.* New York: Wiley.

Sommerville, I., & Ransom, J. (2005). An empirical study of industrial requirements engineering process assessment and improvement. *ACM Transactions on Software Engineering and Methodology, 14*(1), 85–117. doi:10.1145/1044834.1044837

Sommerville, I., & Sawyer, P. (1997). *Requirements Engineering: A Good Practice Guide*. Chichester, UK: John Wiley & Sons.

Sommerville, I., & Sawyer, P. *Requirements Engineering: A Good Practice Guide*. New York: Wiley.

Spirtes, P., Glamour, C., & Scheines, R. (1991). An algorithm for fast recovery of sparse causal graphs. *Social Science Computer Review, 9*(1), 62–72. doi:10.1177/089443939100900106

Srinivasan, K., & Fisher, D. (1995). Machine Learning Approaches to Estimating Software Development Effort. *IEEE Transactions on Software Engineering, 21*(2), 126–137. doi:10.1109/32.345828

Stamelos, I., Angelis, L., Dimou, P., & Sakellaris, E. (2003). On the use of Bayesian Belief Networks for the prediction of software productivity. *Information and Software Technology, 45*(1), 51–60. doi:10.1016/S0950-5849(02)00163-5

Standish Group International. (1995). *The Chaos Report*. Retrieved July 9, 2008, from net.educause.edu/ir/library/pdf/NCP08083B.pdf

Standish Group Report: Extreme Chaos, (2001). Retrieved January 14, 2009 from http://www.vertexlogic.com/processOnline/processData/documents/pdf/extreme_chaos.pdf

Standish Group. (1994). *Chaos Report* (Tech. Rep.). Standish Group International.

Standish Group. (2003). *Chaos Chronicles v3.0*. (Tech. Rep.). Standish Group International.

Standish, T. (1984). An essay on software reuse. *IEEE Transactions on Software Engineering, se-10*(5), 494–497. doi:10.1109/TSE.1984.5010272

Stensrud, E., Foss, T., Kitchenham, B., & Myrtveit, I. (2002). An empirical Validation of the Relationship between the Magnitude of Relative Error and Project Size. *Proceeding of the 8-th IEEE Symposium on Software Metrics* (pp. 3-12). Washington, DC: IEEE Computer Society.

Sthamer, H. H. (1995). *The Automatic Generation of Software Test Data Using Genetic Algorithms*. Unpublished doctoral dissertation, University of Glamorgan, UK.

Stützle, T., & Hoos, H. (1997). Improvements on the ant system: Introducing the MAX- MIN ant system. In *Third International Conference on Artificial Neural Networks and Genetic Algorithms*, University of East Anglia, Norwich, UK, Berlin: Springer Verlag.

Sutherland, J. (2004). *Agile development: Lessons learned from the first scrum*. Retrieved July 9, 2008, from http://jeffsutherland.com/Scrum/FirstScrum2004.pdf.

Takeuchi, H., & Nonaka, I. (1986). The new new product development game. *Harvard Business Review, Jan-Feb.*

Tekinerdogan, B. (2000). *Synthesis-based software architecture design*. PhD. Dissertation, University of Twente, Enschede, The Netherlands.

Thayer, R., & Dorfman, M. (Eds.). (1997). *Software Requirements Engineering (2nd Edition)*. New York: IEEE Computer Society Press.

Thomas, M., & McGarry, F. (1994). Top-Down vs. Bottom-Up Process Improvement. *IEEE Software, 11*(4), 12–13. doi:10.1109/52.300121

Thwin, M. M. T., & Quah, T.-S. (2002). Application of neural network for predicting software development faults using object-oriented design metrics. In *Proceedings of the Ninth International Conference on Neural Information Processing* (pp. 2312-2316), Singapore. Washington DC: IEEE Computer Society.

Tibshirani, R. (1996). Regression shrinkage and selection via the lasso. *Journal of the Royal Statistical Society. Series A, (Statistics in Society), 58*, 267–288.

Tonella, P. (2004). Evolutionary testing of classes. In *Proceedings of the ACM SIGSOFT International Symposium on Software testing and Analysis* (pp. 119-128), Boston, MA. New York: ACM Press.

Toulmin, S. E. (1958). *The use of arguments*. Cambridge, UK: Cambridge University Press.

Toval, A., Nicolás, J., Moros, B., & García, F. (2002). Requirements Reuse for Improving Information Systems Security: A Practitioner's Approach. *Requirements Engineering, 6*(4), 205–219. doi:10.1007/PL00010360

Tracey, N. (2000). *A Search-based Automatic Test-data Generation Framework for Safety-Critical Software.* Unpublished doctoral dissertation, University of York, UK.

Tracey, N., Clark, J., Mander, K., & McDermid, J. (2002). A search based automated test data generation framework for safety critical systems. *In P. Henderson (Ed.), Systems Engineering for Business Process Change (New Directions).* Berlin: Springer Verlag.

Tracz, W. (1995). DSSA (Domain-Specific Software Architecture): a pedagogical example. *SIGSOFT Software Engineering Notes, 20*(3), 49–62. doi:10.1145/219308.219318

Tsai, W. T., Bai, X., Paul, R., Shao, W., & Agarwal, V. (2001). End-to-end integration testing design. *Proceedings of 25th Annual International Computer Software and Applications Conference,* 166–171.

Tuunanen, T. (2003). A New Perspective on Requirements Elicitation Methods. *Journal of Information Technology Theory and Application, 5*(3), 45–62.

Untch, R. H. (1992). Mutation-based software testing using program schemata. *In Proceedings of the Thirtieth ACM South Regional Conference* (pp. 285-291), Raleigh, North Carolina. New York: ACM Press.

Utting, M., & Legeard, B. (2006). *Practical model-based testing - a tools approach.* New York: Elsevier Science.

Vadera, S., & Meziane, F. (1994). From English to Formal Specifications. *The Computer Journal, 37*(9), 753–763. doi:10.1093/comjnl/37.9.753

Vadera, S., & Meziane, F. (1997). Tools for Producing Formal Specifications: A view of Current Architecture and Future Directions. *Annals of Software Engineering, 3,* 273–290. doi:10.1023/A:1018950324254

van der Gaag, L. C., Renooij, S., Witteman, C. L. M., Aleman, B. M. P., & Taal, B. G. (1999) How to Elicit Many Probabilities. In *Proceedings UCAI,* (pp. 647-654). San Francisco: Morgan Kaufmann

Van Koten, C., & Gray, A. (2006). An application of Bayesian network for predicting object-oriented software maintainability. *Information and Software Technology, 48*(1), 59–67. doi:10.1016/j.infsof.2005.03.002

van Lamsweerde, A. (2000). Formal specification: a roadmap. In *the 22nd International Conference on Software Engineering, Future of Software Engineering Track (ICSE'00)* (pp. 147-159). Limerick, Ireland.

van Lamsweerde, R. Darimont, & Massonet P. (1995). Goal-directed elaboration of requirements for a meeting scheduler: Problems and lessons learnt. In *Proceedings of the 2ⁿᵈ IEEE International Symposium on Requirements Engineering.* (pp. 194-203), York, UK. Washington DC: IEEE Computer Society.

Vanmali, M., Last, M., & Kandel, A. (2002). Using a Neural Network in the Software Testing Process. *International Journal of Intelligent Systems, 17*(1), 45–62. doi:10.1002/int.1002

Vapnik, V. N. (1995). *The Nature of Statistical Learning Theory.* New York: Springer-Verlag.

Vazquez, G., Campo, M., & Diaz-Pace, A. (2008). A case-based reasoning approach for materializing software architectures onto object-oriented designs. In *Proceedings of the 2008 ACM Symposium on Applied Computing* (pp. 842-843). New York: ACM Press.

Venable, J. R., & Travis, J. (1999). Using a Group Support System for the Distributed Application of Soft Systems Methodology. *10th Australasian Conference on Information Systems,* Wellington, New Zealand, December 1-3.

Visvanathan, S., & Gupta, N. (2002). Generating test data for functions with pointer inputs. In *the 17th IEEE International Conference on Automated Software Engineering (ASE'02)* (p. 149). Edinburgh, UK: IEEE Computer Society.

von Mayrhauser, A., France, R., Scheetz, M., & Dahlman, E. (2000). Generating test-cases from an object-oriented model with an artifical-intelligence planning system. *IEEE Transactions on Reliability, 49*(1), 26–36. doi:10.1109/24.855534

von Mayrhauser, A., Scheetz, M., & Dahlman, E. (1999). Generating goal-oriented test cases. In *Proceedings of the Twenty-Third Annual International Conference on Computer Software and Applications* (pp. 110-115), Phoenix, AZ. Washington DC: IEEE Computer Society.

von Mayrhauser, A., Scheetz, M., Dahlman, E., & Howe, A. E. (2000). Planner based error recovery testing. In *Proceedings of the Eleventh International Symposium on Software Reliability Engineering* (pp. 186-195), San Jose, CA. Washington DC: IEEE Computer Society.

von Mayrhauser, A., Walls, J., & Mraz, R. T. (1994). Sleuth: A Domain Based Testing Tool. In *Proceedings of the International Test Conference* (pp. 840-849). Washington, DC: IEEE Computer Society.

von Mayrhauser, A., Walls, J., & Mraz, R. T. (1994, November). Testing Applications Using Domain Based Testing and Sleuth. In *Proceedings of the Fifth International Symposium on Software Reliability Engineering* (pp. 206-215), Monterey, CA. Washington DC: IEEE Computer Society.

Vongdoiwang, W., & Batanov, D. N. (2005). Similarities and Differences between Ontologies and Object Model. In *Proceedings of The 3th International Conference on Computing, Communications and Control Technologies: CCCT 2005*, Austin, TX.

Wallace, L., & Keil, M. (2004). Software project risks and their effect on outcomes. *Communications of the ACM, 47*(4), 68–73. doi:10.1145/975817.975819

Wang, H., Peng, F., Zhang, C., & Pietschker, A. (2006). Software project level estimation model framework based on Bayesian Belief Networks. In *Sixth International Conference on Quality Software*.

Wang, J., & Han, J. (2004). BIDE: Efficient mining of frequent closed sequences. In *Proceedings of IEEE International Conference on Data Engineering (ICDE)*.

Wang, L., & Yuan, J. (2004). Generating test cases from UML activity diagram based on gray-box method. *Proceedings of the 11th Asia-Pacific Software Engineering Conference*, (pp. 284–291).

Wang, X., & Loucopoulos, P. (1995). The Development of Phedias: a CASE Shell. *Seventh International Workshop on Computer-Aided Software Engineering*, Toronto, Canada, July 10-14.

Wappler, S., & Lammermann, F. (2005). Using evolutionary algorithms for the unit testing of object-oriented software. In *Proceedings of the Conference on Genetic and Evolutionary Computation* (pp. 1053-1060), Washington DC. New York: ACM Press.

Wappler, S., & Schieferdecker, I. (2007). Improving evolutionary class testing in the presence of non-public methods. In *Proceedings of the Twenty-second IEEE/ACM International Conference on Automated Software Engineering* (pp. 381-384), Atlanta, Georgia. New York: ACM Press.

Wappler, S., & Wegener, J. (2006). Evolutionary unit testing of object-oriented software using strongly-typed genetic programming. *In Proceedings of the Eighth Annual Conference on Genetic and Evolutionary Computation* (pp. 1925-1932), Seattle, WA. New York: ACM Press.

Waters, R., & Tan, T. (1991). Toward a design apprentice: Supporting reuse and evolution in software design. *SIGSOFT Software Engineering Notes, 16*(2), 33–44. doi:10.1145/122538.122543

Wegener, J., Baresel, A., & Sthamer, H.-H. (2001). Evolutionary Test Environment for Automatic Structural Testing. *Information and Software Technology, 43*, 841–854. doi:10.1016/S0950-5849(01)00190-2

Wegener, J., Sthamer, H.-H., Jones, B. F., & Eyres, D. E. (1997). Testing Real-Time Systems using Genetic Algorithms. *Software Quality Journal, 6*(2), 127–135. doi:10.1023/A:1018551716639

Weidenhaupt, K., Pohl, K., Jarke, M., & Haumer, P. (1998). Scenarios in system development: current practice. *IEEE Software, 15*(2), 34–45. doi:10.1109/52.663783

Weimer, W., & Necula, G. (2005). Mining temporal specifications for error detection. In *Proceedings of International Conference on Tools and Algorithms for the Constructions and Analysis of Systems (TACAS)*.

Weisberg, S. (1985). *Applied Linear Regression*. New York: John Wiley and Sons.

Weiss, M. D. (1998). Commonality Analysis: A Systematic Process for Defining Families. *Second International Workshop on Development and Evolution of Software Architectures for Product Families,* February.

Weiss, M. D., Lai, R. T. C (1999). *Software Product-Line Engineering: A Family Based Software Development Process*.

Whitley, L. D. (2001). An overview of evolutionary algorithms: practical issues and common pitfalls. *Information and Software Technology, 43*(14), 817–831. doi:10.1016/S0950-5849(01)00188-4

Wiegers, K. E. (2003). *Software Requirements* (2nd Ed.). Redmond, WA: Microsoft Press.

Wiegers, K. E. (2007). *Process Impact*. Retrieved 2007, from http://www.processimpact.com/

Wikipedia (2008). *Software design*. Retrieved from http://en.wikipedia.org/wiki/Software_design

Williams, L., Shukla, A., & Anton, A. I. (2004). An initial exploration of the relationship between pair programming and Brooks' law. In *Agile Development Conference, 2004,* (pp. 11-20), Agile Development Conference.

Williams, N. (2005). WCET measurement using modified path testing. In *the 5th International Workshop on Worst-Case Execution Time Analysis (WCET'05)*. Palma de Mallorca, Spain.

Williams, N., Marre, B., & Mouy, P. (2004). On-the-fly generation of k-paths tests for C functions: towards the automation of grey-box testing. *In the 19th IEEE International Conference on Automated Software Engineering (ASE'04)* (pp. 290-293). Linz, Austria: IEEE Computer Society.

Williams, N., Marre, B., Mouy, P., & Roger, M. (2005). PathCrawler: automatic generation of path tests by combining static and dynamic analysis. In *the 5th European Dependable Computing Conference (EDCC'05)* (pp. 281-292). Budapest, Hungary.

Wirfs-Brock, R., & McKean, A. (2003). *Object design: Roles, responsibilities and collaborations*. Boston: Addison-Wesley.

Wohlin, C., Runeson, P., Höst, M., Ohlsson, M. C., Regnell, B., & Wesslén, A. (2000). *Experimentation in Software Engineering – An Introduction*. Berlin, Germany: Springer.

Wojcik, R., Bachmann, F., Bass, L., Clements, P., Merson, P., Nord, R., & Wood, B. (2006). *Attribute-Driven Design (ADD), Version 2.0* (Tech. Rep. CMU/SEI-2006-TR-023). Pittsburgh, PA: Carnegie Mellon University, Software Engineering Institute.

Wong, A. K. C., & Chiu, D. K. Y. (1987). Synthesizing Statistical Knowledge from Incomplete Mixed-mode Data. *IEEE Transactions on Pattern Analysis and Machine Intelligence, PAMI-9*(6), 796–805. doi:10.1109/TPAMI.1987.4767986

Wood, D. P., Christel, M. G., & Stevens, S. M. (1994). A Multimedia Approach to Requirements Capture and Modeling. *First International Conference on Requirements Engineering,* Colorado Springs, CO, April 18-22.

Woodberry, O., Nicholson, A., Korb, K., & Pollino, C. (2004). Parameterising Bayesian Networks. In *Proceedings of the Australian Conference on Artificial Intelligence,* (pp. 1101-1107).

Wooff, D. A., Goldstein, M., & Coolen, F. P. A. (2002). Bayesian graphical models for software testing. *IEEE Transactions on Software Engineering, 28*(5), 510–525. doi:10.1109/TSE.2002.1000453

Wright, J. M., Fox, M. S., & Adam, D. (1984). *SRL/2 User Manual*: Robotic Institute, Carnegie-Mellon University, Pittsburgh, PA.

Wu, Q., & Cao, Y. J. (1997). Stochastic optimization of control parameters in genetic algorithms. *IEEE In-*

ternational Conference on Evolutionary Computation, (pp. 77-80).

Wu, Y., Chen, M., & Offut, J. (2003). UML-based Integration Testing for Component-based Software. *In The 2nd International Conference on COTS-based Software Systems (ICCBSS),* (pp. 251-260) Ottawa, Canada.

Wysocki, B. (1998). Some firms, let down by costly computers opt to 'de-engineer.' *Wall Street Journal,* A1- A6.

Xanthakis, S., Ellis, C., Skourlas, C., Gall, A. L., Katsikas, S., & Karapoulios, K. (1992). Application of genetic algorithms to software testing. In *Proceedings of the 5th International Conference on Software Engineering* (pp. 625–636). Toulouse, France.

Xiao, M., El-Attar, M., Reformat, M., & Miller, J. (2007). Empirical Evaluation of Optimization Algorithms when used in Goal Oriented Automated Test-data Generation Techniques. *Empirical Software Engineering, 12,* 183–239. doi:10.1007/s10664-006-9026-0

Xu, D., Li, H., & Lam, C. P. (2007). A systematic approach to automatically generate test scenarios from UML activity diagrams. *In ACST '07: Proceedings of The Third Conference n IASTED International Conference* (pp. 134–139). Anaheim, CA: ACTA Press.

Xu, Z., & Zhang, J. (2006). A test data generation tool for unit testing of C programs. In *the 6th International Conference on Quality Software (QSIC '06)* (pp. 107-116). Beijing, China.

Yager, R. (1991). Connectives and quantifiers in fuzzy sets. *Fuzzy Sets and Systems, 40,* 39–75. doi:10.1016/0165-0114(91)90046-S

Yahya, M.A., Ahmad, R., & Lee, S. P. (2008). Effects of software process maturity on COCOMO II's effort estimation from CMMI perspective. *IEEE International Conference on Research, Innovation and Vision for the Future,* (pp. 255 – 262).

Yang, D., Wan, Y., Tang, Z., Wu, S., He, M., & Li, M. (2006). COCOMO-U: An Extension of COCOMO II for Cost Estimation with Uncertainty. In Q. Wang, D.

Pfahl, D.M. Raffo & P. Wernick, (Eds.) *Software Process Change.* (LNCS, 3966, pp. 132–141). Berlin: Springer.

Yang, H.-L., & Wang, C.-S. (2009). Recommender system for software project planning one application of revised CBR algorithm. *Expert Systems with Applications, 36*(5), 8938–8945.doi:doi:10.1016/j.eswa.2008.11.050

Yang, J., & Honavar, V. (1998). Feature subset selection using a genetic algorithm. *IEEE Intelligent Systems and Their Applications, 13*(2), 44–49.

Yang, J., Evans, D., Bhardwaj, D., Bhat, T., & Das, M. (2006). Perracotta: Mining temporal API rules from imperfect traces. In *Proceedings of International Conference on Software Engineering (ICSE).*

Yang, Y., Xia, F., Zhang, W., Xiao, X., Li, Y., & Li, X. (2008). Towards Semantic Requirement Engineering. *IEEE International Workshop on Semantic Computing and Systems* (pp. 67-71). Washington, DC: IEEE Computer Society.

Yen, J., & Liu, F. X. (1995). A Formal Approach to the Analysis of Priorities of Imprecise Conflicting Requirements. In *Proceedings of the 7th international Conference on Tools with Artificial intelligence.* Washington DC: IEEE Computer Society.

Yorsh, G., Ball, T., & Sagiv, M. (2006). Testing, abstraction, theorem proving: better together! In *the 2006 ACM/SIGSOFT International Symposium on Software Testing and Analysis (ISSTA '06)* (pp. 145-156). Portland, ME: ACM.

Young, E. (2004). *Artificial Neural Network in PHP.* Retrieved 2005, from http://coding.mu/archives/2004/03/19/artificial_neural_network_in_php/

Young, R. R. (2003). *The requirements Engineering Handbook.* Norwood, MA: Artech House Inc.

Yu, E. S. K. (1997). Towards Modeling and Reasoning Support for Early-Phase Requirements Engineering. *Third IEEE International Symposium on Requirements Engineering,* Washington, DC, January 5-8.

Yu, Y., Wang, Y., Mylopoulos, J., Liaskos, S., Lapouchnian, A., & do Prado Leite, J. C. S. (2005). Reverse engineering goal models from legacy code. In *Proceedings of the 2nd IEEE International Symposium on Requirements Engineering*, (pp. 363-372), York, UK. Washington DC: IEEE Computer Society.

Yujia, G., & Chang, C. (2006). Capability-based Project Scheduling with Genetic Algorithms. In *Proceedings of the International Conference on Intelligent Agents, Web Technologies and Internet Commerce* (pp. 161-161), Sydney, Australia. Washington DC: IEEE Computer Society.

Zadeh, L. A. (1986). Test-score semantics as a basis for a computational approach to the representation of meaning. *Literary and Linguistic Computing*, *1*(1), 24–35. doi:10.1093/llc/1.1.24

Zadeh, L. A. (1994). Soft computing and fuzzy logic. *IEEE Software*, *11*(6), 48–56. doi:10.1109/52.329401

Zave, P. (1997). Classification of Research Efforts in Requirements Engineering. *ACM Computing Surveys*, *29*(4), 315–321. doi:10.1145/267580.267581

Zeroual, K. (1991). A Knowledge-based Requirements Acquisition System. *6th Annual Knowledge-Based Software Engineering Conference*. Syracuse, NY, September 22-25.

Zhang, M., Liu, C., & Sun, C. (2001). Automated test case generation based on UML activity diagram model. *J. Beijing Uni. Aeronautics and Astronautics*, *27*(4), 433–437.

Zhen-Yu, Z., Wei-Yang, Y., & Qian-Lei, L. (2008). Applications of Fuzzy Critical Chain Method in Project Scheduling. In *Proceedings of the Fourth International Conference on Natural Computation* (pp. 473-477), Jinan, China. Washington DC: IEEE Computer Society.

Zhu, H., Hall, P. A. V., & May, J. H. R. (1997). Software unit test coverage and adequacy. *ACM Computing Surveys*, *29*(4), 366–427. doi:10.1145/267580.267590

Zhu, J. Y., & Deshmukh, A. (2003). Application of Bayesian decision networks to life cycle engineering in Green design and manufacturing Engineering. *Applied Artificial Intelligence*, *16*, 91–103. doi:10.1016/S0952-1976(03)00057-5

Zimmermann, H. J. (1991). *Fuzzy set theory and its applications.* Amsterdam: Kluwer Academic.

Zitzler, E., Laumanns, M., & Thiele, L. (2000). SPEA2: Improving the strength Pareto evolutionary algorithm. *Proceedings of EUROGEN 2001.*

About the Contributors

Farid Meziane is a Reader in Software Engineering in the school of computing, Science and Engineering at the University of Salford, United Kingdom. He received the Ingénieur d'état degree in computer science from the National Institute for Computer Science and a PhD in Computer Science from the University of Salford in 1994. His research interests are in the area of software engineering with particular emphasis on the integration of formal methods in the software development process and electronic commerce. His research is published in journals that include the Annals of Software Engineering, the Computer Journal and the Journal of the Operational Research Society. He was awarded the highly commended award from the literati club in 2001 for a paper published in the Integrated Manufacturing Systems Journal. He is in the programme committee of many international conferences, a reviewer for the data and knowledge engineering journal and in the editorial board of the International Journal of Information Technology and Web Engineering. He was the programme chair and the organiser of the 9th International Conference on the Application of Natural Language to Information Systems (NLDB04). He is a chartered member of the British Computer Society.

Sunil Vadera is a Professor of Computer Science and the current Director of the Informatics Research Institute at the University of Salford. He holds a PhD from the University of Manchester in the area of Formal Methods of Software Development and is a Fellow of the British Computer Society. His research is driven by the desire to close the gap between theory and practice in Artificial Intelligence. This has included work on sensor validation with the Mexican Instituto de Electricas, research on the development a system that advises on the relief venting of explosions in chemical processes for the Health and Safety Executive in the UK and research on machine learning for credit rating of sub-prime loans. His research has been published in journals such as the Software Engineering Journal, Computer Journal, Formal Aspects of Computing, Foundations of Science, Expert Systems and IEEE Transactions of Power Systems. He is co-founder of the European Conference on Intelligent Management Systems in Operations, held at Salford since 1997 and has co-edited several special issues of the Journal of Operational Research Society.

* * *

Felix H. Bachmann is a senior member of the technical staff at the Software Engineering Institute (SEI) working in the Research, Technology, and System Solutions Program. There he is a co-author of the Attribute-Driven Design Method, a SEI-certified ATAM Lead Evaluator as well as a contributor to and instructor for the ATAMSM Evaluator Training, a co-author of Documenting Software Architectures:

Views and Beyond, and leading research on variability management for product lines. Before joining the SEI, Mr. Bachmann was a software engineer at the Robert Bosch GmbH in Corporate Research, where he worked with software development departments to address the issues of increased features and higher quality in the call-control software. Contact him at fb@sei.cmu.edu.

Victor R. Basili is Professor Emeritus at the University of Maryland. He holds a PH.D. in Computer Science from the University of Texas and two honorary degrees. He was Director of the Fraunhofer Center - Maryland and a director of the Software Engineering Laboratory at NASA/GSFC. He has worked on measuring, evaluating, and improving the software development process and product for over 35 years with numerous companies and government agencies. Methods include Iterative Enhancement, the Goal Question Metric Approach (GQM), the Quality Improvement paradigm (QIP), and the Experience Factory (EF). Dr. Basili has authored over 250 peer reviewed publications and is a recipient of several awards including the NASA Group Achievement Awards, ACM SIGSOFT Outstanding Research Award, IEEE Computer Society Harlan Mills Award, and the Fraunhofer Medal. He is Co-EIC of the Springer Empirical software Engineering Journal and an IEEE and ACM Fellow.

Len Bass is a senior member of the technical staff at the Software Engineering Institute (SEI) who participates in the Research, Technology, and System Solutions Program. He has written two award-winning books on software architecture as well as several other books and numerous papers in a wide variety of areas of computer science and software engineering. Mr. Bass is currently working on techniques for the methodical design of software architectures and to understand how to support usability through software architecture. He has been involved in the development of numerous production or research software systems ranging from operating systems to database management systems to automotive systems. Contact him at ljb@sei.cmu.edu.

Marcelo R. Campo is a professor with the Computer Science Department and head of the ISISTAN Research Institute, both at UNICEN University (Tandil, Argentina). He received his Ph.D degree in Computer Science from Universidade Federal de Rio Grande do Sul (Porto Alegre, Brazil) in 1997. His research interests include: intelligent tools for software engineering, software architectures and frameworks, agent technology, and software visualization. Mr. Campo has several papers published in conferences and journals about software engineering topics. He is also a research fellow of the National Council for Scientific and Technical Research of Argentina (CONICET). Contact him at mcampo@exa.unicen.edu.ar.

Isabel María del Águila Cano is currently a Professor of Computer Science in the Department of Languages and Computation at Almería University. He received his B.S., M.S. degrees in Computer Science from the University of Granada. His research interests include Knowledge engineering and Software engineering methods, particularly the unification of these engineering approaches.

Giovanni Cantone is Professor at the University of Rome "Tor Vergata" teaching Software Analysis, Design, and Architectures.

Chad Coulin holds a BEng (Honors) in Microelectronics, a PhD in Computer Science from the University of Technology Sydney, and a PhD in Industrial Systems Engineering from UPS (Toulouse III).

He has worked as a product manager for international software companies in both the US and Europe, and is currently the Information Technology & Communications Manager for a large global mining company. His research interests include requirements elicitation, method engineering, and artificial intelligence.

J. Andres Diaz-Pace is a member of the technical staff at the Software Engineering Institute (SEI), where he works in the Research, Technology, and System Solutions Program. His primary research interests are: quality-driven architecture design, AI techniques in design, architecture-based evolution and architecture conformance. Currently, he works in the development of tool support for the exploration of architectural design alternatives. He has authored several publications on the topic of tools for design assistance. Prior to joining the SEI, Mr. Diaz-Pace was a professor and researcher at UNICEN University (Tandil, Argentina) for more than ten years. He also participated as architect in several technology transfer projects at UNICEN University. Mr. Diaz-Pace received a Ph.D. in computer science from UNICEN University in 2004. Contact him at adiaz@sei.cmu.edu.

Norman Fenton is Professor of Computer Science at Queen Mary (London University) and is also Chief Executive Officer of Agena, a company that specialises in risk management for critical systems. At Queen Mary he is the Director of the Risk Assessment and Decision Analysis Research Group (RADAR). Norman's experience in risk assessment covers a wide range of application domains such as legal reasoning (he has been an expert witness in major criminal and civil cases), medical trials, vehicle reliability, embedded software, transport systems, and financial services. Norman has a special interest in raising public awareness of the importance of probability theory and Bayesian reasoning in everyday life. In addition to his research on risk assessment, Norman is renowned for his work in software engineering, notably software metrics.

Tad Gonsalves received the B.Sc degree in Physics and the M.Sc degree in Astrophysics from the Poona University, Pune, India. He received the Ph.D. in Information Systems Engineering in 2004 from Sophia University, Tokyo, Japan. Currently he is a lecturer in the Department of Information and Communication Sciences, Faculty of Science and Technology, Sophia University. His research interests include Computational Intelligence, Knowledge Engineering, Ontology and Semantic Web

Peter Hearty has a B.Sc. in Mathematics and Physics from the University of Stirling and a Ph.D. in Computer Science from Queen Mary University of London. He worked as a modeller, analyst and designer at Marconi Space and Defence, Reuters, Enhydra Software and SpiritSoft. He has been a consultant to NatWest Bank and Bankers Trust. In 1997 he started his own database company to market and sell the Java relational database InstantDB.

Kiyoshi Itoh received B.Eng, M.Eng, and Dr.Eng in computer science from the Department of Information Science of Kyoto University in 1974, 1976 and 1980, respectively. He has been working in Sophia University since 1979. Currently, he is a Professor and Chair in the Department of Information and Communication Sciences. His research interests include domain engineering, software engineering, collaboration and concurrent engineering, knowledge engineering, and simulation engineering. He is a member of IEEE, ACM, IPSJ, SDPS.

Ryo Kawabata received his Master's degree in Mechanical Engineering from the Sophia University in 1998. He joined the Department of Mechanical Engineering at Sophia University in 1998 as an associate professor. He received the Ph.D in Information Systems Engineering from the same University in 2004. Currently he is an assistant professor in the Department of Information and Communication Sciences. His interests in software engineering have led to research in reusing models, collaboration in systems analysis and Ontology.

Siau-Cheng Khoo is an Associate Professor in the Department of Computer Science at the National University of Singapore. He holds a Ph.D. in Computer Science from Yale University. Siau-Cheng's main research interest lies in the area of program analysis and program transformation. His recent works include development of compilation model for aspect-oriented functional programming languages, and design of mining techniques for software reliability.

Ekta Khudkhudia is a graduate student in the department of computer science at the Missouri University of Science and Technology. Her research interests are in collaborative systems and software engineering.

Leonid Kof studied computer science at the Technische Universitaet Muenchen. Since 2002, he worked as a teaching and research assistant at the same university, where he was a project leader of the research project Verisoft Automotive (www.verisoft.de) in 2003-2007. In 2005, he received his PhD from the Technische Universitaet Muenchen. Since 2007, he is a habilitation candidate. "Habilitation", a further degree after a PhD, is a prerequisite for a professorship in Germany. For the winter term 2008-2009 he was assigned a temporary professorship at the University of Passau (Germany).

Nikolai Kosmatov works as a research engineer at the Software Safety Lab of CEA LIST, one of the biggest research centers in France. Nikolai obtained M.Sc. degree in Mathematics at Saint-Petersburg State University (Russia) in 1997 and a Ph.D. in Mathematics jointly at Saint-Petersburg State University and the University of Besançon (France) in 2001. After receiving M.Sc. degree in Computer Science at the University of Besançon in 2003, Nikolai's research interests have focused on constraint solving, software verification and automatic test generation. Nikolai has taught various courses in Mathematics and Computer Science at Saint-Petersburg State University, the University of Besançon, the University Pierre and Marie Curie in Paris and the RWTH Aachen University in Germany.

Peng Lam is an associate professor at the School of Computer and Information Science, Edith Cowan University, Australia. Her current research interests are focused on two main research areas. The first area involves machine learning, pattern recognition, data mining and image analysis as applied to multimedia, process control, heath and games. The second area is in software engineering and is focused on software testing, component-based software engineering, search-based software engineering and computational intelligence in software engineering. Specific projects include Component Testing and Software Testing, Computational Intelligence and Search Based Software Engineering and Software Engineering in Process Design. She is the co-leader for the Artificial Intelligence and Software Engineering Research Cluster. <http://www.scis.ecu.edu.au/research/Groups/se/>

Ming Leu is the Keith and Pat Bailey Distinguished Professor in integrated product development and manufacturing in the department of mechanical & aerospace engineering at the Missouri University of Science and Technology. His research interests are in CAD/CAM, robotics, rapid prototyping, and intelligent manufacturing. He has over 200 publications in refereed scientific and engineering journals and conference proceedings, and three U.S. patents.

Chao Liu is a researcher in Microsoft Research at Redmond, doing inter-disciplinary research on data mining, software engineering and internet services. He received his Ph.D. in Computer Science from the University of Illinois at Urbana-Champaign in 2007.

Xiaoqing (Frank) Liu is currently a professor and a director of the McDonnel Douglass Foundation software engineering laboratory in the department of computer science at the Missouri University of Science and Technology. He has been working on requirements engineering, software quality management, knowledge based software engineering, collaborative systems, and software engineering applications since 1992. He has published more than 60 papers in peer-reviewed journals and conferences in the above areas. He participates in many research projects, sponsored by the National Science Foundation, Sandia National Laboratory, U.S. Air Force, University of Missouri Research Board, Boeing Corporation, and Toshiba Corporation, as a principal investigator or co-principal investigator. He has served as a program committee member for many conferences. He is a co-chair of program committee for the 2008 IEEE International Conference on Computer Software and Applications.

David Lo is an Assistant Professor in the School of Information Systems, Singapore Management University. He is working in the inter-disciplinary area of data mining and software engineering. In particular he is currently interested in frequent pattern mining, software specification mining and software reliability. He received his PhD in Computer Science from the National University of Singapore in 2008.

José del Sagrado Martinez is currently a Professor of Computer Science in the Department of Languages and Computation at Almería University. He received his B.S., M.S. degrees and Ph.D. in Computer Science from the University of Granada. He is a member of the Spanish Association for Artificial Intelligence (AEPIA). His research interests include probabilistic graphical models, particularly in the field of models combination and construction.

Emilia Mendes is Associate Professor in Computer Science at the University of Auckland (New Zealand). She has active research interests in the areas of Empirical Web & Software Engineering, Evidence-based research, Hypermedia, Computer Science & Software Engineering education, in which areas she has published widely and over 100 refereed publications, which include two books (one edited (2005) and one authored (2007)). A/Prof. Mendes is on the editorial board of the International Journal of Web Engineering and Technology, the Journal of Web Engineering, the Journal of Software Measurement, the International Journal of Software Engineering and Its Applications, the Empirical Software Engineering Journal, Software Quality Journal, and the Advances in Software Engineering Journal. She worked in the software industry for ten years before obtaining in 1999 her PhD in Computer Science from the University of Southampton (UK), and moving to Auckland (NZ).

Neil Martin is Professor in Computer Science and Statistics at the Department of Computer Science, Queen Mary, University of London, where he teaches decision and risk analysis and software engineering. Martin is also a joint founder and Chief Technology Officer of Agena Ltd, who develops and distribute AgenaRisk, a software product for modeling risk and uncertainty and a Visiting Professor in the Faculty of Engineering and Physical Sciences, University of Surrey. Martin has over twenty years experience in academic research, teaching, consulting, systems development and project management and has published or presented over 40 papers in refereed journals and at major conferences . His interests cover Bayesian modeling and/or risk quantification in diverse areas: operational risk in finance, systems and design reliability (including software), software project risk, decision support, simulation (using dynamic discretisation as an alternative to Monte Carlo) cost benefit analysis, AI and personalization, and statistical learning. Martin earned a BSc in Mathematics, a PhD in Statistics and Software Metrics and is a Chartered Engineer.

Łukasz Radliński is working in the Institute of Information Technology in Management, University of Szczecin, Poland. His primary research activities are focused on software project risk management, quality assurance, requirements engineering, applications of Bayesian nets and other AI methods. He has worked as consultant for Bosch and as software developer for local companies. He earned a M.A. degree in computer science and econometrics and a Ph.D. in computer science.

Muthu Ramachandran is currently a Principal Lecturer in the Faculty of Innovation North: Information and Technology, Leeds Metropolitan University, Leeds, UK. Previously he spent nearly eight years in industrial research (Philips Research Labs and Volantis Systems Ltd, Surrey, UK) where he worked on software architecture, reuse, and testing. Prior to that he was teaching at Liverpool John Moores University and received his PhD from Lancaster University. His first career started as a research scientist from India Space Research Labs where he worked on real time systems development projects. Muthu is an author of a book on Software Components: Guidelines and Applications, Nova Publishers, NY, USA, 2008. He has also widely published articles on journals, chapters, and conferences on various advanced topics on software engineering and education. He did his master's degrees from Indian Institute of Technology, Madras and from Madurai Kamaraj University, Madurai, India. Muthu is also a member of various professional organisations and computer societies: IEEE, ACM, BCS, HEA.

Abd-El-Kader Sahraoui obtained his BSc and MSc from the University of Manchester (UMIST) in 1977 and 1979 respectively. He held different positions in industry from 1979 to 1984, and then obtained his PhD and DSc from the University of Toulouse in 1987 and 1994. He has been a lecturer, assistant and associate professor at UPS (Toulouse III) and Tarbes Engineering Institute (ENIT). He is currently Professor at IUT-B (Toulouse II), and research associate at LAAS-CNRS since 1984. He has been an associate researcher at the University of California, Berkeley, and a guest professor and chair of Requirements Engineering at the Hasso Plattner Institute for Software Systems Engineering in Potsdam, Germany.

Vamshi Sajja is a graduate student in the department of computer science at the Missouri University of Science and Technology. Her research interests are in collaborative systems and software engineering.

Salvatore Alessandro Sarcia' received his laurea degree in Computer Science (1994) and master degree with honors in Strategy and Project Management (2001) from the University of Torino (Italy). He received his second laurea degree in Politics (2004) from the University of Trieste (Italy). In December 2008, he received his Ph.D. degree in Informatics and Automation Engineering from the University of Rome "Tor Vergata" (Italy). In 2006-08, he was with the Department of Computer Science of the University of Maryland (College Park, MD, USA) as a Faculty Research Assistant. Mr. Sarcia' is an untenured Professor of Object-Oriented Programming at the DISP - University of Rome "Tor Vergata". His research interests lay in the area of Computational Intelligence (Artificial Neural Networks), Predictive Models, and Statistics. He applies empirical techniques to conduct experiments on Software Engineering, Software Quality, and Risk Analysis.

Alvaro Soria is a PhD student at the ISISTAN Research Institute, UNICEN University (Tandil, Argentina). His main research interests are: object-oriented frameworks, multi-agent systems, quality-driven materialization of software architectures, and fault localization. Mr. Soria has several years of industrial experience in software development, and participated as architect in technology transfer projects at UNICEN University. Contact him at asoria@exa.unicen.edu.ar.

Lei Wen is a graduate student in the department of computer science at the Missouri University of Science and Technology. His research interests are in collaborative systems and software engineering.

Kei Yamagishi received the Bachelor's degree in Mechanical Engineering from Sophia University in 2008. He is currently in the graduate program of the Department of Information and Communication Sciences. His research is mainly in the area of evolutionary multi-objective optimization.

Didar Zowghi is Professor of Software Engineering and the co-director of the research centre for Human-Centred Technology Design in the Faculty of Engineering and Information Technology at the University of Technology, Sydney. She holds a BSc (Honors) and MSc in Computer Science, and a PhD in Software Engineering. She is on the program committee of many conferences including the IEEE International Conference on Requirements Engineering (1998 to 2010), International Working Conference on RE, Foundation for Software Quality, APSEC, and CAiSE. She is the regional editor of the International Requirements Engineering Journal, and associate editor of the Journal of Research and Practice in Information Technology.

Index

Symbols

.NET architecture 138, 139
.Net framework 139, 140

A

absolute error 70
active voice 87, 88
activity diagram (AD) 235, 240, 241, 242, 243, 247, 248, 249, 250
adaptation algorithm 207, 208
adaptation point 207, 208
agile development 14, 15, 17
algorithmic models 46
ambient intelligence (AmI) 129, 132, 143
ant colony optimisation (ACO) 234, 235, 236, 238, 241, 243, 246, 250, 251, 252
anti ant-like agents 243, 248, 251
arbitrary lengths 262, 263
architecture design 182, 186, 191, 192, 193, 194, 211, 212, 214, 215, 216
Architecture Expert (ArchE) 183–216
artificial ant 243, 244, 246, 251
artificial intelligence (AI) 129, 130, 131, 132, 133, 143, 145, 149, 153, 162, 164, 218, 219, 220, 234, 235, 236, 250, 252, 253, 254, 275, 276, 278, 279, 282, 288, 289, 290, 292, 293, 294, 295, 296, 297
artificial neutral network (ANN) 152, 154, 155, 156, 157
attribute-driven design (ADD) method 183, 185, 211, 215, 216

B

auto-associative neural network (AANN) 74, 75
automata 102, 260, 262, 274

Backus-Naur form (BNF) 264
base model 2
Bayesian network (BN) 1, 2, 3, 4, 5, 6, 15, 16, 31, 32, 33, 34, 35, 36, 37, 38, 39, 40, 41, 106, 107, 111, 112, 113, 114, 117, 118, 119, 120, 123, 126, 128
Bayesian network models 1, 2, 4, 5, 6, 15
Bayes' rule 32
Bayes theorem 5
black-box testing 218, 219, 221, 225
burndown chart 17, 19

C

case-based reasoning (CBR) 23, 32, 42, 49, 185, 201, 203, 204, 205, 207, 209, 210, 211, 281, 298
case-based systems 130
causal model 39
change impact analysis (CIA) 190, 196, 199
Clemson's Travel Assistant System (CTAS) 187, 188, 189, 190, 191, 194, 196, 198, 199, 200, 201, 203, 208, 211
computational intelligence 24, 45, 47, 59, 132
computational linguistics 83, 85, 96, 100
computer-aided engineering requirement (CARE) tools 110, 113
computer aided method engineering (CAME) 146, 147, 148, 162, 163, 164